New Concise Bible Dictionary

New Concise Bible Dictionary

Editor: Derek Williams

Inter-Varsity Press, Leicester, England
Lion Publishing, Oxford, England
Tyndale House Publishers, Inc., Wheaton, Illinois, USA

INTER-VARSITY PRESS
38 De Montfort Street, Leicester LE1 7GP, England

LION PUBLISHING PLC
Sandy Lane West, Littlemore, Oxford, England

Published and sold in the USA and Canada by
TYNDALE HOUSE PUBLISHERS, INC.
336 Gundersen Drive, Box 80, Wheaton, Illinois, 60187, USA

First published 1989

British Library Cataloguing in Publication Data

New concise Bible dictionary.
1. Bible
I. Title
220

UK IVP ISBN 0-85110-641-2
IVP ELT edition ISBN 0-85110-943-8
UK Lion ISBN 0-7459-1819-0
USA ISBN 0-8423-4697-X

Set in Palacio
Typeset by Emset, London NW10 4EH
Printed in Great Britain by Richard Clay Ltd, Bungay, Suffolk

Inter-Varsity Press is the book-publishing division of the Universities and Colleges Christian Fellowship.

Contents

A word from the publisher

If you read the Bible at all seriously, sooner or later you will need a Bible dictionary. There are long, specialized dictionaries and there are brief, superficial ones, but we believe that the *New Concise Bible Dictionary* strikes the right balance, accessible to a wide range of readers, serious and reliable but handy and easy to use.

The Bible translation we have used is the Revised Standard Version. This is both reliable and easily understood. It will also act as a bridge for those who prefer the Authorized (King James) Version and others who read the more modern translations. References to other versions are given where appropriate.

Any Bible dictionary will contain its fair share of articles on archaeology. To avoid including too many we have listed among the main articles only those sites mentioned in the RSV. Other important sites not referred to in the Bible are described in the general article ARCHAEOLOGY.

Dictionaries do not appear out of thin air. In compiling this one, editor Derek Williams has made use of material already available in the *New Bible Dictionary* and elsewhere. Our concern is to provide reliable information about the Bible to a wide circle of readers, rather than to make original contributions to scholarship. The result is a book very much shorter but no less authoritative than its predecessor. The *New Bible Dictionary* remains unmatched as a comprehensive, full-scale, one-volume dictionary of the Bible.

We are grateful to everyone else who has contributed to this Dictionary, particularly to Dr John Bimson of Trinity College, Bristol, and Miss Mary Evans of London Bible College, who both commented in detail on the text and made many helpful suggestions.

Our hope is that the *New Concise Bible Dictionary* will bring deeper understanding to a new generation of Bible readers.

How to get the best from this Dictionary

Articles are to be found in alphabetical order.

Cross references to other related articles are printed in capital letters.
It is possible to study a subject from a number of angles by following up the cross references.

Bible references are abbreviated (see list of abbreviations on pages xi and xii).

Chapter and verse numbers are separated by a colon.
Thus James 3:1 = James chapter 3, verse 1.

Further verse references are separated by a comma.

Further chapter references are separated by a semi-colon. Thus James 3:1, 4; 4:5-6 = James chapter 3, verses 1 and 4, and James chapter 4, verses 5 and 6.

f. indicates the verse following.

ff. indicates the verses following, not always limited to two.

The illustrated centre section gives depth and focus. To get full value from the pictures, the articles they refer to should be read. These are given in capitals at the end of the captions.

Abbreviations

General abbreviations

AD	Anno Domini, after Christ	lit.	literally
AV	Authorized Version of the Bible (King James Version)	LXX	Septuagint (Greek version of the OT)
		m	metre(s)
		mg.	margin
BC	Before Christ	mm	millimetre(s)
c.	*circa* (Latin), about, approximately	mod.	modern
		MS (MSS)	manuscript(s)
°C	degrees Centigrade	Mt (Mts)	Mount (mountains)
cc	cubic centimetres	NASB	New American Standard Bible
cent. (cents.)	century (centuries)		
cf.	*confer* (Latin), compare	NEB	New English Bible
ch. (chs.)	chapter(s)	NIV	New International Version of the Bible
cm	centimetre(s)		
cu	cubic	NT	New Testament
e.g.	for example	OT	Old Testament
EVV	English versions (of the Bible)	par.	and parallel(s)
		R.	River
f.	and the following verse	RAV	Revised Authorized Version of the Bible or 'New King James'
ff.	and (an indefinite number of) following verses		
		RSV	Revised Standard Version of the Bible
g	gram(s)		
GNB	Good News Bible (Today's English Version)	RV	Revised Version of the Bible
		sq.	square
HQ	Headquarters	v. (vv.)	verse(s)
JB	Jerusalem Bible		
kg	kilogram(s)	Note:	N, S, E, W, *etc.* indicate north, south, east, west and northern, southern *etc.*
Kh.	Khirbet		
km	kilometre(s)		

Books of the Bible and Apocrypha

A

AARON. The older brother of Moses (Ex. 6:20; 7:7) and younger brother of Miriam. He became Moses' spokesman to the Israelites and the Egyptian king (Ex. 4:14ff.), performing some of the miracles before the king (Ex. 7:8ff., 19; 8:5f., 16f.). He was with Moses on Mt Sinai and shared in the vision of God given there (Ex. 19:24; 24:9ff.). Later, during Moses' prolonged absence he was persuaded to do wrong by making a golden bull-calf which was worshipped as an idol (Ex. 32:1ff.), and like Miriam he became envious of Moses' status (Nu. 12:1ff.).

He was made high priest, with his sons as priests, to minister in the tabernacle (Ex. 28:1ff.; Lv. 8:1ff.). He thus became the first person to enter the inner sanctuary (the holy of holies) on the Day of Atonement, to present the blood of a sacrifice for the people's sin. Later, the Israelite priesthood became known collectively as 'the sons of Aaron'. In the NT, his priesthood is contrasted with the perfect and eternal ministry of Jesus (Heb. 5:4; 7:11).

He married Elisheba. Their sons Nadab and Abihu died after disobeying God (Lv. 10:1ff.). He was barred from entering Canaan, and was buried on Mt Hor. His son Eleazar then became high priest (Nu. 20:22ff.).

AARON'S ROD. After Korah's rebellion (Nu. 16:1ff.), each tribe placed a rod in the tabernacle to establish the priestly status of Aaron's family. The next day, Aaron's rod had budded, a sign that he was God's chosen priest.

ABADDON (lit. 'destroyer'). Satanic angel of the bottomless pit (Rev. 9:11); OT synonym for death and Sheol. See HELL, SHEOL.

ABANA. Syrian river mentioned by Naaman (2 Ki. 5:12). Called 'Golden River' by Greeks. Probably modern R. Barada.

ABARIM (lit. 'regions beyond'). Mountains rising from E shore of the Dead Sea. Site of Israel's last camp before reaching the Jordan (Nu. 33:47f.). Moses viewed Canaan from Mt Nebo at N end of the range (Dt. 32:49).

ABBA. Aramaic word for 'father', conveying both warm intimacy and respect; never used by Jews for God. Jesus applied it to God (Mk. 14:36); Paul saw it as a symbol of a Christian's adoption as a child of God (Rom. 8:15; Gal. 4:6).

ABDON. *Person:* Several, including last of the minor judges (Jdg. 12:13ff.). *Place:* Levitical town in Asher, 6 km inland from Achzib (Jos. 21:30).

ABEDNEGO. Name given to Azariah, Daniel's companion (Dn. 1:7), who escaped the furnace (Dn. 3:26). May mean 'servant of the shining one'.

1

ABEL. *Person:* Second son of Adam and Eve and brother of Cain. A shepherd who brought an acceptable offering to God and was murdered by his brother (Gn. 4:2-8). *Place:* An element of some place-names, chiefly in Transjordan. May mean meadow, or brook, watercourse.

ABEL-BETH-MAACAH. Town in N. Naphtali; identified with Tell Abil 20 km N of Lake Huleh. Captured by Syrians (*c.* 879 BC, 1 Ki. 15:20) and Assyrians (*c.* 733 BC, 2 Ki. 15:29).

ABEL-MEHOLAH. Town in Jordan valley S of Bethshean. Elisha's birthplace (1 Ki. 19:16).

ABIATHAR (lit. 'father of excellence'). He was a priest at Nob who escaped the massacre of his family by Saul to join David (1 Sa. 22:20-22). One of David's counsellors (1 Ch. 27:34), he was sent back to Jerusalem to guard the king's interests when David fled from Absalom (2 Sa. 15:25ff.).

ABIEL (lit. 'God is my father'). 1. Saul's grandfather (1 Sa. 9:1). 2. One of David's heroes (1 Ch. 11:32).

ABIEZER (lit. 'my father is help'). 1. A clan of Manasseh (Jos. 17:2). Gideon belonged to it when it was centred at Ophrah (Jdg. 6:11). 2. One of David's heroes (1 Ch. 11:28).

ABIGAIL (probably 'my father is joy'). 1. The wife of Nabal. She brought gifts to David after her husband had refused rudely. When Nabal died, David married her (1 Sa. 25:1ff.), and she bore his second son Chileab (2 Sa. 3:3; Daniel in 1 Ch. 3:1). 2. The wife of Ithra (2 Sa. 17:25) or Jether (1 Ch. 2:17); the Hebrew names are easily confused.

ABIHAIL (lit. 'my father is might'). Name of several OT men and women.

ABIHU (lit. 'my father is he [God]'). Son of Aaron who died after disobeying God (Lv. 10:1f.).

ABIJAH (lit. 'my father is Yahweh'). Name of several OT men and women. The most notable was the son of Rehoboam, who ruled Judah for three years (2 Ch. 12:16;13:1). In 1 Ki. 15:3 he is censured for corrupt religious practice; in 2 Ch. 13 he defeats Jeroboam I with God's help.

ABILENE. A region of Anti-Lebanon, attached to the city of Abila on the banks of the Abana (modern Barada), 29 km NW of Damascus (Lk. 3:1).

ABIMELECH (lit. 'The [divine] king is my father'). 1. Name of Philistine kings living near Gerah (Gn. 20:2ff; 26:1ff.). 2. A son of Gideon (Jerubbaal) who murdered all but one of his brothers and proclaimed himself king. He was killed when a woman dropped a millstone on his head at Thebez (Jdg. 9).

ABIRAM (lit. 'my father is exalted'). 1. One who rebelled against Moses (Nu. 16). 2. Son of Hiel, who died during the rebuilding of Jericho (1 Ki. 16:34).

ABISHAG (possibly 'father has wandered'). A beautiful Shunnamite girl brought to nurse David in his old age (1 Ki. 1:1ff.).

ABISHAI (lit. 'father of gift'). A high officer in David's army and one of his heroes (2 Sa. 2:18; 23:18).

ABNER. Saul's cousin and commander in chief of his army (1 Sa. 14:50). He was murdered by David's commander Joab through revenge and lack of trust in his friendship after Saul's death (2 Sa. 3:27).

ABOMINATION (*Detestable*, NIV). Anything which offends a person's religious feelings. For example, eating with foreigners (Gn. 43:32); idolatrous practices (2 Ki. 16:3); offerings to God made in the wrong spirit (Is. 1:13); sexual sin (Lv. 18:22); and commercial corruption (Pr. 20:23).

ABOMINATION OF DESOLATION; ABOMINABLE DESOLATION: See DESOLATING SACRILEGE.

ABRAHAM. 'Father of a multitude'; originally called Abram, 'the father is exalted'. Born in Ur, he moved with Terah his father, Sarah (Sarai) his wife, Nahor and Haran his brothers and Lot his nephew, to Haran. After Terah's death he moved into Canaan, aged 75 (Gn. 11:26-12:6). He was respected by leaders of other groups in Canaan, and became wealthy (13:2).

He and Sarah were then childless; at first he made Eliezer of Damascus (his chief servant) his heir (15:2), but God had promised they would have a child. Aged 86, he had a son Ishmael by an Egyptian servant Hagar whom Sarah had given him (16:1ff.), but when he was 100 Isaac was born to Sarah (21:1ff.).

Abraham had a clear faith in one God, unlike his ancestors (Jos. 24:2). He revered God as almighty (Gn. 17:1), eternal (21:33), Lord of heaven and earth (24:3) and judge of all mankind (18:25). He had a close relationship with God (*e.g.* 18:33) and received visions (15:1) and angelic visitors (18:1). He was always willing to obey God's call, even when he was told to sacrifice Isaac at Moriah. He was stopped at the last moment when a ram was provided as a substitute (22:1-14). The incident is an early condemnation of child sacrifice which was itself rare in the ancient Near East. His deception of two leaders by passing off Sarah as his sister (12:11-13; 20:2-11) reveals an apparent weakness in his otherwise strong, generous and just character.

Abraham entered into a covenant-treaty with God, through which he was promised a family and nations as successors (13:16), and the land of Canaan for them (15:17ff.). He himself never owned land and had to buy a burial plot for Sarah (23:4). The covenant was confirmed when Abraham was 99, with the covenant-sign of male circumcision (17:1ff.), and again before Isaac was conceived (18:1ff.) and after the near-sacrifice (22:17f.).

3

Israel was considered 'Abraham's seed', and throughout Scripture God is called 'the God of Abraham'. He was an ancestor of the Messiah (Mt. 1:1). The belief that physical descent from him brought divine blessing was refuted in the NT (Mt. 3:9; Rom. 9:7). Paul sees Abraham's faith as like that which leads to justification by God (Rom. 4:3ff.). He also plays a unique role in both Jewish and Muslim traditions.

See COVENANT; PATRIARCHAL AGE.

ABRAHAM'S BOSOM. In Jesus' parable, the dead beggar Lazarus is pictured reclining against Abraham at the feast in Paradise (Lk. 16:22-23), the position of an honoured guest (Jn. 13:23).

ABSALOM (lit. 'father is/of peace'). The third son of David, by a foreign mother Maacah. An attractive man, he murdered his half-brother Amnon who had raped his sister Tamar (2 Sa. 13:19ff.). He fled from David, and when received back began plotting against him (2 Sa. 15:1ff.). He was killed in battle (2 Sa. 18:9ff.), his life fulfilling Nathan's prophecy (2 Sa. 12:10f.).

ABYSS. 'Bottomless pit.' The abode of demons (Lk. 8:31); the place of the dead (Rom. 10:7); a place of torment (Rev. 9:1f.). See HELL.

ACCAD, AKKAD. A major city founded by Nimrod (Gn. 10:10). The dynasty founded there by Sargon I (c. 2350 BC) was looked back on as a 'golden age'. 'Akkad' was designated N Babylonia until the late Persian period; 'Akkadian' describes Semitic, Assyrian and Babylonian languages.

ACCEPTANCE. Throughout the Bible, God does not accept people on the grounds of social status (Gal. 2:6) or correctly-offered ritual. Offerings were only acceptable when the person offering them was acceptable (e.g. Gn. 4:4-7; Mal. 1:10,13). The encounter between Peter and Cornelius showed the early church that God accepts anyone regardless of nationality or ritual sign (Acts 10:34f.). He does require perfection, which only Jesus has achieved, but those who are united to Jesus by faith are made acceptable to God (Rom. 3:9-25; 5:17).

ACCESS. A sinner has no right of access to God, and is introduced only by Jesus (Rom. 5:2), whose death has removed the barriers (Eph. 2:16).

ACHAIA. A small region of Greece on the S coast of the Gulf of Corinth. In Homer's writings, and in the Hellenistic age (330-37 BC) it was the name for Greece. In Roman times it was governed from Corinth by a pro-consul. In the NT, the name always occurs in relation to Corinth and 'converts in Achaia' (1 Cor. 16:15) refers to Corinth, not the wider province.

ACHAICUS. A Corinthian Christian (1 Cor. 16:17). The name suggests a slave (or ex-slave) from Achaia. See FORTUNATUS.

ACHAN. Contrary to God's instructions, he stole goods from Jericho after Israel had defeated it. Israel was then defeated at Ai; Achan and his family were stoned and their bodies burned (Jos. 7).

ACHISH. Philistine King of Gath during Saul's, David's and Solomon's reigns. David pretended to be mad when first seeking refuge with him (1 Sa. 21:10-15); Achish later made David his bodyguard (1 Sa. 28:1f.).

ACHOR. The valley where Achan was executed (Jos. 7:24), traditionally placed N of Jericho.

ACHSAH (lit. 'anklet'). The daughter of Caleb who married Othniel, Caleb's nephew, and asked for extra land for him (Jdg. 1:12-15).

ACHSHAPH. An important Canaanite city E or SE of Acco, occupied by the tribe of Asher (Jos. 19:25).

ACHZIB. 1. A Canaanite harbour assigned to Asher, taken by Sennacherib in 701 BC; modern ez-Zib 14 km N of Acre. 2. A town of Judah in the Shephelah, also conquered by Sennacherib.

ACTS, BOOK OF THE. *Contents.* It takes up the story where Luke's Gospel left off, with the resurrection of Jesus, recording his ascension, the coming of the Holy Spirit, and the early progress of the Jerusalem church (1-5). Then it describes the dispersal of Christians after Stephen's execution, the evangelization of more distant regions, Paul's conversion and the first Gentile conversions (6-12). From then on, the ministry of Paul and his journeys dominate the narrative. See PAUL.

Origin, date and purpose. It is a companion volume to Luke's Gospel dedicated to Theophilus who may be a representative of Roman society. It concludes with Paul's imprisonment in Rome, probably AD 60-61, but the date of writing cannot be determined precisely. It might have been in a period such as Domitian's rule (AD 81-96) when Christianity had penetrated the imperial family, or in the later sixties when Christians may have wished to dissociate from the Jewish revolt in Palestine. The optimistic end could indicate a date before persecution broke out in AD 64. It could then be an account of Christianity for imperial officials investigating Paul's case. If it is felt that Luke as we have it must be dated after AD 70, then 'the first book' of Acts 1:1 could be 'proto-Luke'. See LUKE, GOSPEL OF; THEOPHILUS.

Author. Generally considered to be Luke, a physician and Paul's fellow-traveller. Three sections indicate his personal presence at some events: 16:10-17; 20:5-21:18; 27:1-28:16. Among his other sources would have been many personal contacts including Philip in Caesarea (21:8) and Mnason, originally from Jerusalem (21:16). See LUKE.

Historical integrity. The narrative is set in a framework of contemporary history which has been amply confirmed by archaeological discovery. His account of Paul's voyage to Rome (27) remains an important document on ancient seamanship.

Apologetic emphasis. Luke is concerned to show that Christianity is not a menace to imperial law and order. He cites the verdicts of officials (*e.g.* 16:19-39), and the decision by Gallio implying that Christianity shares the protection given to Judaism by Roman law (18:12ff.). Luke shows that the riots which accompanied the apostles' preaching were usually caused by Jewish opponents.

Theological interest. The dominating theme is the activity of the Holy Spirit. The Spirit is given to Jews (2) and Gentiles (10); guides the preachers (8:29; 16:6); directs the church (13:2); leads the apostles in difficult decisions (15:28); speaks through prophets (11:28); and initially appoints church leaders (20:28). Supernatural signs revealed the Spirit's power as the apostles discharged their calling.

Acts in the early church. It was not primarily associated with specific churches, and may have been circulated through the Gentile book trade. Marcion (*c.* AD 140) refused to include it in his Bible, because it denied his insistence that the original apostles had been unfaithful to Jesus' teaching. For others, however, it confirmed Paul's status and safeguarded that of other apostles whose writings were included with Paul's in the collection of Scripture.

Abiding value. It provides both a sequel to the gospels and a background to NT letters. In Harnack's

words, it is the pivot-book of the NT. It provides valuable information about a significant phase of world history.

ADAH. 1. A wife of Lamech (Gn. 4:19ff.). 2. A wife of Esau (Gn. 36:2ff.).

ADAM (*place*). A town 28 km N of Jericho where the Jordan was blocked when the Israelites crossed at Jericho (Jos. 3:16). Modern Tell ed-Damiyeh.

ADAM (*person*). The first man, created by God in his image on the sixth day. By contrast to the biblical story, Sumerian and Babylonian creation myths are crude and polytheistic.

Old Testament. As well as being a proper name, 'Adam' is also used some 500 times to mean 'mankind' (the meaning being usually distinguished in Hebrew). He was distinguished from the animals by being made in God's image (Gn. 1:26f.) and was put in a garden, Eden, to care for it (2:8ff.). One of his tasks was to name the animals; his food was apparently fruits, berries, nuts and cereals. Recognizing that 'it was not good that the man should be alone' (2:18), God made Eve to be a help to him (2:22).

Induced by the serpent, she persuaded Adam to eat fruit which God had forbidden him, and the couple were banished from the garden (3:23f.). Up to this moment, they evidently had direct communion with God. Now, conscious of their nakedness, they made loin cloths and faced a more difficult and painful life outside Eden since the ground was cursed and produced thorns and thistles (3:17-19,23). God gave them leather tunics (3:21), implying that they needed protection from uncontrolled vegetation or climate. Three children of the couple are mentioned: Cain, who killed his brother Abel, and Seth. Adam lived 930 years (5:2-5); the precise date and area of his existence is at present disputed. See EDEN, GARDEN OF; FALL.

New Testament. There are occasional references to him in the gospels. He begins Jesus' family tree (Lk. 3:38), and Jesus referred to the union of Adam and Eve as evidence of God's purpose for marriage (Mt. 19:4-6). Paul also refers to the couple as the basis for teaching about sexual relationships, citing Gn. 2:24 in 1 Cor. 6:16 and Eph. 5:31. He alludes to the order in which they were created in his discussions about man/woman relationships (1 Cor. 11:3ff.) and conduct in Christian meetings (1 Tim. 2:11ff.).

Paul's chief use of Adam is as a contrast to Jesus. In 1 Cor. 15 he says that like Adam we all have a physical body which shall die, and like Jesus all shall be raised and receive a new 'spiritual' body. Paul's interchange of 'Adam' and 'man' indicates that he is well aware that 'Adam' means 'mankind'. In Rom. 5:12ff. he alludes to Adam who by sinning set in motion a chain-reaction of sin and its consequence, death. Death did not spread automatically because Adam sinned, but because all sinned (v.12). By contrast, Jesus has inaugurated a saving process in which people receive God's righteousness and 'reign in life'.

Whatever views of human nature are held, it remains true that the human race has a history and a beginning. Paul's point is that all history from the beginning is marked by sin, that mankind is responsible for it and that one person's sin affects others and the world around. See FALL.

ADAMAH. A town in Naphtali, possibly at Qarn Hattin.

ADAMI-NEKEB. A pass on the Naphtali border (Jos. 19:33); modern Kh. ed-Damiyeh.

ADDER: See SNAKE.

ADMAH. A City of the Plain, linked with Zeboiim (Ho. 11:8), now submerged beneath the Dead Sea.

ADONI-BEZEK (lit. 'lord of Bezek'). A Canaanite king who, after the tribes of Judah and Simeon had defeated 10,000 Canaanites at Bezek (probably modern Kh. Ibziq 21 km NE of Shechem) was captured and brought to Jerusalem (Jdg. 1:4ff.).

ADONIJAH (lit. 'my lord is Yahweh'). Several OT people, the chief being the fourth son of David, by his wife Haggith. After the three eldest died, he regarded himself as heir, but David had promised Bathsheba that their son Solomon should succeed him (1 Ki. 1:17). Supported by Joab the army commander and Abiathar the priest he attempted to gain the throne before David died, but was thwarted. He promised loyalty to Solomon but tried vainly to oust him, and was executed (1 Ki. 2:13ff.).

ADONIRAM (lit. 'my lord is exalted'). Solomon's official in charge of forced labour (1 Ki. 4:6; 5:14) who was stoned to death in the revolt under Jeroboam *c.* 922 BC.

ADONI-ZEDEK (lit. 'my lord is righteous'). An Amorite king of Jerusalem who led four other Canaanite kings against Israel. They were defeated by divine intervention then executed by Joshua (Jos. 10).

ADOPTION. It occurs rarely in the OT, probably because there were several other remedies for childless marriage, including polygamy. Records from Mesopotamia and Syria show that in the ancient Near East it was a legal act which brought a person into a new family relationship, with the full privileges and responsibilities of a child by birth. Abraham probably had to adopt his servant Eliezer as his heir (Gn. 15:3). Moses (Ex. 2:10) and Esther (Est. 2:7,15) were almost certainly adopted according to non-Israelite law. The nation Israel was regarded as God's (adopted) son (Je. 3:19).

In the NT, adoption occurs only in Paul, and is a relationship conferred by God's free grace which results in a change of status from slave (to the law) to son (Gal. 4:1ff.). The cry 'Abba! Father!' used in the context of adoption in Rom. 8:15 and Gal. 4:6 may be the traditional cry of an adopted slave. God's adopted son has the right of access to the Father and a share in the divine inheritance (Rom. 8:15ff.). The idea is implied in Jesus' title of God as Father and his parable of the lost son (Lk. 15:19ff.). See FAMILY, HOUSEHOLD.

ADORAIM. City of SW Judah fortified by Rehoboam (2 Ch. 11:9); modern Dura, 8 km SW of Hebron.

ADRAMMELECH. *Pagan god:* A god brought from Sepharvaim to Samaria where children were sacrificed to him (2 Ki. 17:31). *Person:* A son of Sennacherib who with his brother Sharezer murdered their father in 681 BC (2 Ki. 19:37).

ADRAMYTTIUM. Seaport in Mysia, in Roman Asia; modern Karatash. A ship based here took Julius and Paul from Caesarea to the Asian coast (Acts 27:2).

ADRIA, SEA OF. The central Mediterranean across which Paul drifted for 14 days (Acts 27:27); not to be confused with the Gulf of Adria (modern Adriatic Sea).

ADULLAM. A Canaanite city in Judah, where David hid from Saul in a cave (1 Sa. 22:1); modern Tell esh-Sheikh Madhkur, between Jerusalem and Lachish.

ADUMMIM. A steep pass on the road from Jericho to Jerusalem. The traditional scene of the good Samaritan parable (Lk. 10:34).

AENON. 'Fountain.' A place W of Jordan where John baptized (Jn. 3:23); possibly modern Ainun, NE of Nablus.

AFRICA. The knowledge of Africa in the records of ancient peoples was restricted largely to the areas accessible to Mediterranean nations, although Herodotus (5th cent. BC) did believe it was almost entirely surrounded by sea.

Israel's main concern with Africa related to Egypt. Despite the cruel past, Israel felt tenderly towards Egypt (Dt. 23:7) and believed it would eventually share in the worship of the Lord (Is. 19:16ff.). There were Jewish settlements in Ethiopia, which is sometimes coupled with Egypt as representative nations which God will judge (Ezk. 30:4ff.). Despite a long tradition, there is nothing to connect the curse of Ham (Gn. 9:25) with a permanent hatred by God of negroid peoples; the curse is explicitly applied to Canaanites.

Jesus lived on African soil in infancy (Mt. 2:13ff.). Simon, who bore Jesus' cross, came from the African port of Cyrene and his children seem well known in the early church (Mk. 15:21). African Jews were present at Pentecost (Acts 2:10); Philip led an Ethiopian to Christ (Acts 8:26ff.); and the mighty Apollos came from Alexandria (Acts 18:24). But nothing is known of how the church spread in the S Mediterranean lands, even though the Egyptian and N African churches were among the most prominent of the 2nd cent.; a fairly late tradition links Mark and Peter with it.

See EGYPT; ETHIOPA; LIBYA.

AGABUS. A prophet whose predicted famine occurred in the reign of Claudius (Acts 11:27f.) and who then foretold Paul's fate in Jerusalem (Acts 21:10f.).

AGAG. A common title of the kings of Amalek. Used especially of the king spared by Saul but killed by Samuel (1 Sa. 15).

AGAGITE. A description of Haman in Est. 3:1 *etc.* Josephus regarded him as an Amalekite.

AGRICULTURE. Excavations at Jericho have revealed that Palestine was one of the earliest agricultural centres yet discovered. Good irrigation farming can be dated here about 7500 BC. By Abraham's time, irrigation farming was becoming less important in Palestine, although it remained important in Egypt and Babylonia. Farmers depended on rain; the 6 months' summer drought ended with the 'early rains' and in late November or December seed was sown. Heavy winter rains gave crops their main moisture but 'late rains' of March-April were needed to bring the grain to head. The failure of any of these rains was serious, if not disastrous. Other enemies of the farmer included locust invasions, plant disease (*e.g.* mildew), hot sirocco winds, and war which brought invaders at harvest time when they could live off the land.

The main grain crops were wheat and barley, with lentils, peas and beans as secondary crops. Olives provided oil and grapes provided wine and raisins. Cucumbers and melons used heavy summer dew and became an extra source of liquid when streams dried up. Vegetable crops added variety, and herbs flavour, to the diet.

Among the farmer's tools were the sickle with flint teeth set into a bone or wooden haft. Wooden ploughs were better for rocky soil, but by the time of David iron ploughs were common. Large stones marked the boundaries of fields; no fences were used.

See CATTLE; FOOD; FRUIT; GRAIN CROPS; HARROW; HERBS; OLIVE; PLANTS; PLOUGHMAN; SHEEP; VEGETABLES; VINE.

AHAB (lit. 'the [divine] brother is father'). He succeeded his father Omri to become seventh king of Israel for 22 years, c. 874-852 BC (1 Ki. 16:28ff.). He fortified Israelite cities (1 Ki. 16:34), and built a palace decorated with ivory at Samaria (1 Ki. 22:39). He frequently fought Syria, and defeated but spared its king Ben-hadad (1 Ki. 20:26ff.). In 853 BC he sided with Ben-hadad against the Assyrian Shalmaneser III, a cause of later Assyrian attacks on Israel. He died in battle against Syria at Ramoth-gilead (1 Ki. 22:28ff.).

He allowed his wife Jezebel to build a temple to Baal in Samaria, and she sponsored false prophets, killed true ones, and destroyed altars of the Lord. Elijah opposed the idolatry and injustice and his stand was vindicated by God at a contest with the false prophets on Mt Carmel (1 Ki. 18:16ff.).

AHASUERUS (XERXES). In Ezr. 4:6 and probably in Esther, Xerxes I, king of Persia (485-465 BC) is meant. In Dn. 9:1 it is the name of the father of Darius the Mede.

AHAVA. A Babylonian town and canal where Ezra assembled exiles (Ezr. 8:15-31); probably the classical Scenae.

AHAZ (lit. 'he has grasped', an abbreviation of Jehoahaz). King of Judah 735-715 BC, son of Jotham. When Israel and Syria invaded, he appealed for help to Assyria against the advice of Isaiah (Is. 7:1ff.), which began a century of subjection to Assyria. He encouraged pagan worship, closed the temple sanctuary, and burned his son as a religious offering (2 Ki. 16:1ff; 2 Ch. 28:22-25).

AHAZIAH (lit. 'Yahweh has grasped'). 1. He was son and successor of Ahab, king of Israel, whose corrupt religious policy he continued unchanged (1 Ki. 22:51—2 Ki. 1:18). He died prematurely after a fall. 2. Also called Jehoahaz, the youngest son of Jehoram, king of Judah. He reigned for less than a year before being murdered (2 Ki. 8:25ff; 9:16-29; 2 Ch. 22:1-9).

AHIJAH, AHIAH. Name of several OT people, chief of whom was a prophet from Shiloh who protested against Solomon's idolatry by cutting his robe to symbolize the division of the kingdom (1 Ki. 11:29ff.). His prophecy was fulfilled when 10 tribes rebelled against Solomon's son Rehoboam, and made Jeroboam their king.

AHIKAM (lit. 'my brother has arisen'). One sent by Josiah to enquire of the prophetess Huldah (2 Ki. 22:11ff.); he saved Jeremiah's life (Je. 26:24).

AHIMAAZ (lit. 'my brother is wrath'). Among others: a messenger from David's secret allies in Jerusalem during Absalom's rebellion (2 Sa. 15:27; 18:19-32). Famed for his fast running.

AHIMELECH (lit. 'my brother is king'). Among others: priest at Nob who gave David the sacred bread and Goliath's sword (1 Sa. 21-22).

AHIRAM. A son of Benjamin (Nu. 26:38).

AHITHOPHEL (possibly 'brother of foolish talk'). David's respected counsellor, who later conspired with Absalom. As David had prayed, his advice to Absalom proved wrong, and he hanged himself (2 Sa. 15-17).

AHITUB (lit. 'my brother is good'). 1. Son of Phineas (1 Sa. 14:3). 2. 'Chief officer of the house of God' (1 Ch. 9:11).

AHLAB. Town in Asher (Jdg. 1:31), probably modern Kh. el-Mahalib, 8 km NE of Tyre.

AI (lit. 'the heap, ruin'). A city E of Bethel and N of Michmash. The Israelite attack under Joshua was repulsed at first, but after Achan's sin was dealt with, the city was destroyed (Jos. 7-8). Modern Et-Tell, 3 km SE of Bethel, is usually identified as Ai. Excavations revealed a prosperous city which was destroyed *c.* 2400 BC. No further evidence of occupation was found except for a small settlement in the ruins about 1200-1050 BC, thus creating a discrepancy between archaeological and biblical evidence. Perhaps Ai's massive old walls were used as a temporary stronghold by the surrounding population, or Joshua's Ai may be elsewhere.

AIJALON. 1. A hill town commanding from the S the entrance to the Aijalon valley; earliest traces (2000 BC) are at Tell el-Qoqa near Yalo. It was fortified by Rehoboam to guard the NW approach to Jerusalem. 2. A town in Zebulun (Jdg. 12:12).

AKELDAMA. 'Field of blood', Acts 1:19. Formerly the potter's field, usually equated with the potter's house on the S of the Hinnom Valley (Je. 18:2); associated with Judas.

AKRABBIM (lit. 'scorpions'). Mountain pass at S end of the Dead Sea (Nu. 34:4); modern Naqb es-safa.

ALCOHOL: See WINE AND STRONG DRINK.

ALEXANDER. A common Greek name, found frequently in the NT. Among the more significant are:

1. The would-be spokesman for Jewish interests at the riot in Ephesus (Acts 19:33ff.). 2. A bitter enemy of Paul, apparently also from Ephesus (2 Tim. 4:14f.). 3. A false teacher (1 Tim. 1:20), for whom see HYMENAEUS. It is possible that 1 and 2, or 2 and 3, are the same person, but 1 and 3 cannot be because 3 would claim to be a Christian.

ALEXANDER THE GREAT. The youthful king of Macedon whose expedition to liberate the Greeks of Asia Minor in 336 BC unexpectedly demolished the Persian Empire. Thereafter Greek civilization became the international norm, creating agonies for separatist Jews in the Maccabean age (152-37 BC). He is presumably referred to in Dn. 8:21; 11:3.

ALEXANDRIA. A seaport on the NW coast of the Egyptian Delta founded in 332 BC by Alexander the Great on the site of a small settlement, Rakotis. It was apparently laid out on a grid plan, but its remains are now buried beyond reach. In the time of Ptolemy II (c. 285-246 BC) it became an architectural masterpiece; a 1,300 m causeway linked shore and Pharos island, dividing the harbour into two. It became Egypt's capital and banking centre; the greatest Hellenistic (Greek culture) city of its day; a manufacturing centre for cloths, glass and papyrus; a thriving port; and a centre of learning with a massive library. It remained Egypt's administrative capital down to the Byzantine period (AD 324-636).

Besides Greek citizens and native Egyptians, there was a considerable Jewish community there, concentrated in the E sector; one synagogue was so large that flags were used to signal the Amen. The Greek OT (Septuagint) and the apocryphal book Wisdom of Solomon were produced there; the Jewish philosopher Philo lived there. The Christian preacher Apollos was an Alexandrian Jew 'well versed in the Scriptures' (Acts 18:24). The letter to the Hebrews, quoting the OT and using terms familiar in Alexandria, is often associated with the city; Luther speculated that Apollos wrote it. The origins of the Alexandrian church are unknown, apart from an unreliable tradition that Mark evangelized there. But missionary zeal, philosophical apologetics, allegorizing of Scripture, concern for biblical commentary and a passion for synthesizing biblical with other thought characterized the church, making it the heir to Alexandrian Judaism.

ALMIGHTY. Used of God 48 times in the OT (31 of them in Job). Interpreted by early Jewish commentators as 'the all-sufficient'. It carries ideas of power to injure and protect (e.g. Pss. 68:14; 91:1). In the NT a similar term 'all powerful' occurs, mostly in Rev. (e.g. 1:8).

ALMS, ALMSGIVING: See CHARITY.

ALPHA AND OMEGA. The first and last letters of the Greek alphabet; used in Rev. 1:8; 21:6 by God and in Rev. 22:13 by Jesus as a self-description. It refers to the eternal activity of God or Christ in creation and salvation.

ALPHAEUS. 1. The father of the apostle James, the name being used to distinguish him from James the son of Zebedee (Mt. 10:2f.). 2. The father of Levi (*i.e.* Matthew; Mk. 2:14).

ALTAR. An object upon which religious offerings were made. The Patriarchs built their own and offered sacrifices on them without the assistance of a priest, evidently to commemorate some encounter with God (*e.g.* Abraham at Shechem and Bethel, Gn. 12:6-8). Altars were in use in Palestine before the Israelites entered it. One at Ai, dating from the Early Bronze Age (3150-2200 BC) was made of plastered stones and used for animal and food offerings. Temples in Middle Bronze Age Megiddo (2200-1550 BC) had mud-brick and plastered-stone altars.

In Ex. 20:24-26 God instructed Moses to tell the people to make altars for their sacrifices. As this comes in the context of the Ten Commandments, applicable to each Israelite, it may be that individuals were allowed to offer sacrifices, as the altars built by Joshua (Jos. 8:30f.) and Gideon (Jdg. 6:24) would imply. Solomon provided an altar of burnt offering in the Temple (1 Ki. 8:22); from this period archaeologists have found a burnt-offering altar measuring 2.5 m sq. at Arad, and incense altars at Beersheba.

In Ezekiel's vision of the rebuilt Temple (Ezk. 40-44) no incense altar is mentioned but there is a detailed description of the three-tiered burnt-offering altar (43:13ff.). In 169 BC Antiochus Epiphanes took the 'golden altar' from the Temple (1 Macc. 1:21) and two years later erected 'a desolating sacrilege' (probably an image of Zeus) on the burnt-offering altar (1 Macc. 1:54). The Maccabees later built a new altar and restored the incense altar (1 Macc. 4:44ff.). These must have continued in use when Herod enlarged the Temple later in the 1st cent. BC; in his time the burnt-offering altar was a pile of uncut stones approached by a ramp. Various altars are referred to in the NT, and John's vision in Revelation has one in the heavenly 'Temple' (Rev. 8:5).

See HIGH PLACE.

AMALEK, AMALEKITES. The son of Eliphaz and grandson of Esau (Gn. 36:12). Israel was attacked by his descendants at Rephidim in the Sinai desert (Ex. 17:8ff.) when Aaron and Hur supported Moses' praying hands until Israel won. Because of this attack, the Amalekites were to be destroyed (Dt. 25:19). They remained a force to be reckoned with, however; Balaam described them as 'the first of the nations' (Nu. 24:20). Gideon drove them out (Jdg. 7:12ff.); Saul defeated them but wrongly spared their king Agag (1 Sa. 15); David also fought them (1 Sa. 30:1ff.). They later declined in power. See NOMADS.

AMASA. 1. Commander of Absalom's rebel army (2 Sa. 17:25), he was defeated by Joab, pardoned by David, and appointed in place of Joab who then killed him (2 Sa. 18-20). 2. An Ephraimite who obeyed the prophet Oded (2 Ch. 28:9-15).

AMAZIAH (lit. 'Yahweh is mighty'). Several OT people, including son and successor of Joash, king of Judah. Elated with success after defeating Edom, he challenged Israel to battle and was heavily beaten. He was eventually assassinated (2 Ki. 14:1ff.).

AMBASSADOR (*Envoy, messenger,* in some *EVV*). People sent to other nations to congratulate (1 Ki. 5:1), solicit favours (Nu. 20:14), and protest against wrongs (Jdg. 11:12). It is used in the NT for Christ's representative carrying the message of reconciliation (2 Cor. 5:20; Eph. 6:20).

AMBER. Used in AV in Ezk 1:4,27; 8:2 for something shining; perhaps a bright metallic alloy.

AMEN. 'Surely', from a root meaning 'to be firm, steady, trustworthy'. Used in the OT when accepting an oath and its consequences (*e.g.* Dt. 27:15ff.), and as a response in worship (*e.g.* Ps. 41:13). By NT times it was used regularly at the end of prayers (1 Cor. 14:16). Jesus' statement 'Amen (truly) I say to you' gave his words a distinctive authority, and he is called 'the Amen' in Rev. 3:14.

AMMON, AMMONITES. The descendants of Ben-ammi, Lot's younger son, regarded as relatives of the Israelites who were commanded to treat them kindly (Dt. 2:19). Their territory was E of the Jabbok river, and their chief town was Rabbah. Like others, they surrounded their territories by small circular fortresses; archaeology reveals a vigorous Ammonite occupation of the area in the period 840-580 BC. In the 7th cent. BC it flourished under Assyrian control, and the pottery, coffins, seals and statues found in Ammonite tombs of the time point to advanced material culture.

Despite the friendliness of Israel, Ammonites were forbidden to enter into Israel's religious life because they had joined the Moabites in hiring Balaam (Dt. 23:3-6), and intermarriage with them was forbidden after the exile (Ezr. 9:1ff.; Ne. 13:1, 23ff.). They attacked Israel in Saul's reign (1 Sa. 11:1ff.); Solomon included Ammonite women in his harem (1 Ki. 11:1), but hostilities continued in the reigns of Jehoshaphat (2 Ch. 20:1ff.), Joash (2 Ch. 24:26), Jehoiakim (2 Ki. 24:2) and after the fall of Jerusalem (Je. 40:11ff.). The prophets denounced them as enemies (*e.g.* Je. 49:1ff.; Am. 1:13ff.). They survived at least until the 2nd cent. BC, since Judas Maccabaeus fought them (1 Macc. 5:6).

See NOMADS; RABBAH.

AMON. *Pagan god:* 'The hidden'. An Egyptian god often associated with the wind, he was first prominent as a local god of Thebes, later becoming chief god by union with the sun god Re, then state god in the Egyptian Empire (from 1552 BC). The prosperity of Amon and Thebes was doomed according to Jeremiah (46:25). See EGYPT; THEBES.

Person: Son of Manasseh, he reigned for two years over Judah (2 Ki. 21:19ff.) before being murdered. He continued his father's idolatry.

AMORITES. A people of Canaan who were among the opponents of Israel. Sumerian and Akkadian inscriptions from 2500-2000 BC describe them as a desert people unacquainted with civilized life, grain, houses, cities and government. About 2000 BC they moved into Babylon and were partly responsible for the collapse of the powerful 3rd dynasty of Ur. An 'Amorite' dynasty ruled at Babylon, its most powerful king being Hammurapi. Another group settled in the Lebanon, with its capital at Sumur (modern Tell Kazel) S of Arvad; it is mentioned in Jos. 13:4. There was increased Amorite movement in Palestine *c.* 2100-1800 BC, creating general unrest.

Abraham allied with Amorites at Hebron (Gn. 14). When Israel invaded Palestine, Amorite kings ruled E of the Jordan; conquering them was seen as an important milestone (Am. 2:9). Gad, Reuben and half of Manasseh took over their territory; Joshua overcame Amorite strongholds in Palestine itself (Jos. 10:5ff.). After the conquest, the Amorites became slaves, and gradually lost their distinctiveness. See ARCHAEOLOGY (*Hammurapi; Mari*).

AMOS, BOOK OF. *Contents.* It divides into four parts. (1) 1:1-2:16, in which Amos introduces himself and announces judgment on surrounding peoples for offences against humanity, on his native Judah and on Israel (the northern kingdom, sometimes denoted Samaria) for turning away from God's revelation. (2) 3:1-6:14, which contains four addresses showing how Israel has abused its privileges. (3) 7:1-9:10, a series of five visions of judgment. (4) 9:11-15, an epilogue describing the restoration of the Davidic kingdom.

Author and date. Nothing is known about Amos outside of his writings. He came from Tekoa (1:1), 16 km S of Jerusalem, where as a shepherd and sycomore-fig farmer he had not previously considered himself a prophet (1:1; 7:14). He lived during the reigns of Uzziah king of Judah and Jeroboam II king of Israel (779-743 BC) and the level of prosperity reflected in the book indicates a date of composition about 760 BC.

Historical background. Over 40 years before Amos, Assyria had crushed Syria to the N of Israel, which opened up lucrative trade and created a powerful merchant class in Samaria. But the wealth was unevenly distributed, and the peasant class was neglected. The poor were oppressed by the rich (2:6ff.); the rich were self-centred (6:3-6); justice went to the highest bidder (2:6; 8:6). Religion was perverted; the rituals continued but were accompanied by godlessness and immorality (4:4f.), and were offered at the expense of the poor (2:8).

15

Message. Amos strongly condemned the way the religious system was abused. God could not accept such corrupt worship (5:21-23), because making sacrifices was not the sum total of his requirements (5:24f.). God, therefore, was standing at the altar ready to destroy it (9:1ff.). For Amos, God is both creator (4:13) and sustainer (5:8; 9:6) of the world. He also controls the destinies of nations: restraining (1:5), destroying (2:9), raising up (6:14), judging (1:3-2:3). He is righteous, and demands righteousness from his people (5:24). He chose Israel to be his people (3:1f.), made his will known to it through prophets (3:7), and so severely judges it when it disobeys him (4:12). But there is also hope for a brighter future (9:11-15).

AMPHIPOLIS. A commercial centre on the Roman road Via Egnatia 5 km inland from Eion at the N of the Aegean Sea; the capital of Macedonia. Paul passed through it when travelling to Thessalonica (Acts 17:1).

AMPLIATUS. A Latin slave name; Paul's friend (Rom. 16:8). A 1st-cent. tomb inscribed 'Ampliati' in Ephesus, unusually ornate for a slave thus indicating honour in the church, may be connected with him or his family.

AMRAM (lit. 'people exalted'). The husband of Jochebed and ancestor of Moses, Aaron and Miriam (Nu. 26:59).

AMRAPHEL. A king of Shinar who attacked Sodom and its neighbours but was later defeated by Abraham (Gn. 14:1ff.).

ANAH. Son of Zibeon, father of Oholibamah one of Esau's Canaanite wives (Gn. 36:2). He found hot springs in the desert (Gn. 36:24).

ANAK, ANAKIM. The descendants of Anak were among the pre-Israelite inhabitants of Palestine. Their size and strength was proverbial (Dt. 9:2); the spies sent into Canaan by Moses felt like grasshoppers compared with them (Dt. 1:28). They were settled in the hill country, particularly Hebron, from where Caleb eventually drove them out. Nothing is known of them outside the Bible, although some scholars consider them mentioned in 18th-cent. BC Egyptian texts, or class them as early 'Philistines'. See GIANT.

ANAMMELECH. A god worshipped by the colonists put into Samaria by the Assyrians (2 Ki. 17:31). Probably to be identified with An, male counterpart of Anat, in Ugaritic and Phoenician.

ANANIAS (lit. 'Yahweh has dealt graciously'). 1. A dishonest member of the Jerusalem church (Acts 5:1ff.). 2. A Christian in Damascus who befriended Paul (Acts 9:10ff.). 3. High priest AD 47-58 who tried Paul; notorious for greed; murdered by Zealots for his pro-Roman sympathies (Acts 23:2; 24:1).

ANATHEMA. A Greek word used in LXX to denote a curse or something banned and hence to be destroyed. It was known as a cursing formula outside Judaism. No Christian inspired by the Holy Spirit could say 'Jesus anathema' (cursed) (1 Cor. 12:3), although Paul could wish himself 'anathema' (*i.e.* separated from Christ) for the sake of unconverted Jews (Rom. 9:3). He called preachers of any other gospel 'anathema' (Gal. 1:8f.), that is, banned from official recognition. In 1 Cor. 16:22 he puts haters of Christ under anathema (the ban). In Acts 23:14 Paul's would-be assassins put themselves under anathema (a curse) if they should fail. See also BAN; CURSE.

ANATHOTH. A town in the territory of Benjamin assigned to the Levites (Jos. 21:18); modern Ras el-Harrubeh, 5 km N of Jerusalem.

ANCESTOR WORSHIP. Most ancient pagan peoples believed in the existence of good and bad spirits. These included the spirits of dead people which they sought to placate or provide for with burial ceremonies and food and furniture in tombs. Overt worship of the dead is however rare; Confucian China is the best-known example.

In the ancient Near East there were widespread cult practices associated with the dead. The Egyptians made elaborate provisions for the comfort of the dead in an enjoyable future life. Mesopotamians, however, regarded the future life more gloomily and were concerned to prevent the dissatisfied spirits returning to molest them. The cult of the dead is well attested in Syria; at Ras Shamra tombs with pipes through which offerings could be poured have been found.

The cult of the dead played no part in Israel's true religion, although the customs of its neighbours were sometimes adopted. Dt. 26:14 suggests it was necessary to prohibit offerings to the dead; 2 Ch. 16:14 and Je. 34:5 imply that incense was burned for two kings at their burials; and Ezk. 43:7-9 implies that dead kings were worshipped. The practice of calling up the dead was known (1 Sa. 28:7) and condemned (Is. 8:19). However, such actions as Jacob's, in setting up a pillar at Rachel's grave (Gn. 35:20), probably indicate no more than a genuine memorial.

See BURIAL AND MOURNING; DIVINATION.

ANDREW (lit. 'manly'). One of the 12 apostles, from Bethsaida in Galilee (Jn. 1:44); brother of Simon Peter. He was a disciple of John the Baptist who pointed him to Jesus, and he then took Peter to Jesus (Jn. 1:35ff.). The first 3 gospels say little about him, but John reveals him as a home and foreign missionary (1:42; 12:21ff.). He was probably crucified in Achaia.

ANDRONICUS AND JUNIAS. Greeted by Paul in Rom. 16:7 as 'kinsmen' (probably fellow-Jews); 'fellow-prisoners' (though when the imprisonment took place is unknown); and the 'men of note among the apostles' who were Christians before him. There is good reason for believing that Junias (Junia) was a woman.

ANGEL. A messenger of God; an order of being different from mankind, of undoubted integrity and obedience to God, but also endowed with free will so not immune to temptation and even sin. Both Testaments imply that some angels fell from their original holiness under the leadership of Satan (*e.g.* Is. 14:12-15; Mt. 25:41; Rev. 12:9). Both Testaments also use the same word to indicate human messengers.

Old Testament. In Israel's early history, angels were seen bringing God's specific commands (Jdg. 6:11ff.); supporting the needy (1 Ki. 19:5-7); assisting in battle (2 Ki. 19:35); even punishing Israel (2 Sa. 24:16). Man's early thinking associated angels with the stars, prompting the poetic thought of Jb. 38:7 where angels ('sons of God') witness creation. Individual guardian angels are probably reflected in Ps. 91:11, and fallen angels are portrayed mingling with women in Gn. 6:4.

After Israel's exile in Babylon, angels are given more of an independent personality; the 'man' who guides Ezekiel (Ezk. 40:3; *etc.*) is a midway concept. In Daniel, angels are for the first time given names: Gabriel discusses things with Daniel (Dn. 8:16ff.), and Michael guards Israel (Dn. 10:13). Around God's throne are countless angels (Dn. 7:10). Jewish rabbinic writings developed this angelology extensively.

New Testament. As a whole, it suggests a deepening bond of sympathy and service between angels and people (*e.g.* Lk. 15:10). The concept of guardian angel has sharpened (Mt. 18:10); they make special visits (Lk. 1:11, 26); they actively support God's people (Acts 12:7ff.); and they surround God's throne (Rev. 5:11). They are associated with the giving of the law (Gal. 3:19) and the final judgment (Mk. 13:27). Jesus received their help on several occasions (Mt. 4:11; Lk. 22:43).

There is little attempt to describe them, apart from hints about their lustre and other-worldly beauty (Mt. 28:2f.), which Stephen apparently reflected (Acts 6:15). There is also an undertone of hostility towards angels in some passages. Rom. 8:38 refers to fallen angels, as may 1 Cor. 11:10 (*cf.* Gn. 6:4); Heb. 1:4ff. asserts that Jesus is greater than the angels, probably to counter doctrinal error. Jude 9 (and 2 Pet. 2:10f.) implies that even fallen angels retain such status and dignity that God alone can finally judge them.

See CHERUBIM; DEMON; GABRIEL; MICHAEL; SERAPHIM; and next two articles.

ANGEL OF THE LORD. A heavenly being sent by God as his personal agent and spokesman. In many OT passages he is virtually identified with God and speaks as God (*e.g.* Gn. 31:11ff.), but there is no possibility of him being confused with God in the NT. Among his functions are judgment (Acts 12:23); protection (Is. 63:9); and guidance (2 Ki. 1:3). See ANGEL.

ANGELS OF THE CHURCHES.
Those to whom the seven letters of
Rev. 2-3 are addressed. They cannot
be guardian angels because they par-
ticipate in the churches' sins; the common interpretation 'bishop' (or
'leader') has no parallel use to support
it. Perhaps it is a personification of the
church, though this still fails to do full
justice to the now obscured connotations of the original concept.

ANIMAL: See BEAST and articles
about individual animals.

ANNA (lit. 'grace'). An elderly widow
with prophetic insight who commended Jesus as the Messiah when he
was presented at the Temple (Lk.
2:36ff.).

ANNAS. Appointed high priest in AD
6 and deposed by the Romans in AD
15, but still given the title later perhaps
because Jews regarded the office as
life-long; or because members of high
priestly families were sometimes so
described; or because of his influence.
Five of his sons and Caiaphas his son-
in-law became high priests. He conducted the preliminary investigation
at Jesus' trial (Jn. 18:13-24).

ANNUNCIATION. The visit of the
angel to Mary in which the conception
of the Messiah is announced (Lk.
1:26ff.), who is described as human
and divine (v.32ff.). See INCARNA-
TION; VIRGIN BIRTH.

ANOINTING. Persons or objects in
the OT were anointed with oil to
signify their separation to God; *e.g.*
kings (2 Sa. 2:4); priests (Ex. 28:41);
furniture in the tabernacle (Ex. 30:22).
The anointing was regarded as an act
of God (1 Sa. 10:1). The word was also
used to mean the bestowal of divine
favour (Ps. 23:5), and is associated
with the outpouring of the Holy Spirit
(1 Sa. 16:13; Is. 61:1), a usage continued in the NT where in 1 Jn. 2:20, 27
the anointing of the Spirit gives
believers insight into the dangers facing the church. Jas. 5:14 envisages
anointing the sick with oil, pointing to
the Spirit as life-giver. See MESSIAH.

ANT. Mentioned only in Pr. 6:6;
30:25, where it is the harvester (or
agricultural) ant which collects seeds
in spring and summer to store in
underground galleries.

ANTICHRIST. Probably an opponent of Christ, rather than a false
claimant to be Christ, mentioned only
in John's letters although the idea is
more widespread. John does not deny
that such an evil being will come at the
end of this age but also insists that an
attitude characteristic of antichrist
already exists (1 Jn. 2:18). He is defined
as 'denying the Father and the Son' (1
Jn. 2:22; 2 Jn. 7), thus undermining the
foundations of Christian belief. Paul
uses the term 'man of lawlessness' in
2 Thes. 2:3ff. to refer to the same
being; he opposes religion, claims to
be God, owes his power to Satan, but
will be defeated by Jesus. A similar
meaning may be given to the beasts of
Rev. 11:7 and 13:11. The precise identification of such a figure has been and

still is hotly debated.

ANTIOCH (PISIDIAN). A city in Asia Minor (ruined site near Yalvac in modern Turkey), one of 16 Antiochs founded by Seleucus I Nicator (312-280 BC). Some of its Jewish colonists received Paul kindly (Acts 13:14ff.) but some women (who enjoyed prestige there) and leading men had him expelled (vv. 50ff.). The cult of the god Mên was prominent there.

ANTIOCH (SYRIAN). A city on the Orontes river (now Antakya in SE Turkey); founded *c*. 300 BC by Seleucus I Nicator (312-280 BC). The most famous of his 16 Antiochs, it had a fine seaport, Seleucia Pieria. The Seleucids gave immigrant Jews full rights of citizenship. In 64 BC it fell to Pompey who made it a free city. It became the capital of the Roman province of Syria and the third largest city of the empire, with magnificent temples and other buildings. The inhabitants gained a reputation for political activism and they rebelled against Rome several times. Close by were groves of Daphne and a sanctuary of Apollo, where orgiastic rites took place.

It was closely connected with the beginnings of Christianity. Nicolas, one of the seven deacons, came from Antioch (Acts 6:5), and some disciples went there after Stephen's martyrdom (11:19). When numerous conversions occurred, the Jerusalem church sent Barnabas there, and he called in Paul (11:22ff.). The name 'Christian' was first used there (11:26). The church sent a gift to famine-stricken Jerusalem (11:27-30) and became the initiator of foreign mission (13:1-3). However, some Jewish believers felt that Gentile converts should adopt Jewish customs, and the church sent Paul and Barnabas to Jerusalem for a ruling (ch. 15). It is possible that Paul wrote Galatians from Antioch just before the Jerusalem council meeting, and Gal. 2:11f. mentions a visit by Peter to the city during the controversy.

ANTIOCHUS. The name of 13 kings of the Seleucid dynasty which in the 40 years following the death of Alexander the Great in 323 BC had become master of Asia Minor and Syria. They sought to maintain power by founding or resettling a chain of cities where Greek culture predominated.

For Bible readers, Antiochus IV (175-164 BC) is the most significant; rivalry and intrigue at his court is recorded in 2 Macc. 4:32-38. Because of the misbehaviour of Jason and Menelaus, contenders for the Jewish high priesthood, Antiochus visited Jerusalem in 169 BC, entered the holy of holies, and took away some gold and silver. He stopped the sacrifices, and in 167 BC erected a Greek altar on the old one. After a revolt led by Mattathiah, the temple was reconsecrated in 164 BC. Antiochus IV called himself 'Epiphanes', 'God manifest'. See DESOLATING SACRILEGE; MACCABEES, THE.

More friendly to the Jews was Antiochus VII (139-130 BC) who permitted them to coin their own money (1 Macc. 15:1ff.), and in 134 BC he granted religious freedom. The dynasty ended after the reign of Antiochus XIII (69-65 BC); in 64 Pompey annexed Syria to Rome.

ANTIPAS. A martyr at Pergamum (Rev. 2:13), traditionally believed roasted in a brass bowl during Domitian's reign. See also HEROD (TETRARCH or ANTIPAS).

ANTIPATRIS. A city 42 km S of Caesarea (modern Ras el-Ain), rebuilt by Herod the Great in memory of his father Antipater. Paul was taken there en route to Caesarea (Acts 23:31).

APELLES. Greeted by Paul (Rom. 16:10). The name has been found in Imperial households; it was often adopted by Jews.

APHEK, APHEKAH. 'Fortress.' Several places. 1. Area NE of Beirut (Jos. 13:4). 2. A town in Asher (Jos. 19:30; Jdg. 1:31). 3. A town E of Sea of Galilee (1 Ki. 20:26ff.; 2 Ki. 13:17). 4. A town SW of Hebron (Jos. 15:53). 5. A town S of Caesarea (Jos. 12:18; 1 Sa. 4:1; 29:1), for which see ANTIPATRIS.

APOCALYPTIC. Both a kind of literature and its characteristic ideas; the Greek word means 'to reveal'. It is a literature of dreams and visions, often centred on the heavenly throne-room, portraying a future salvation which transcends ordinary experience. It often make use of symbolic images and draws on OT prophecies. Although there is great variety within apocalyptic writings, they generally stress that God is in control of history, that pagan empires survive only for as long as he permits, and that the 'end' will come at a time he has appointed. This final great event amounts to a new creation in which there will be no evil or suffering; even death itself will be conquered. The kingdom of God will replace all earthly empires for ever; the nations may share in this salvation but the oppressors of Israel, and the unfaithful within Israel, will be judged.

Apocalyptic flourished in times of national crisis, when people saw no hope in the present and so looked for God's action in the future. This was especially so in the period between the Testaments when prophecy had ceased, and after the fall of Jerusalem in AD 70. It reasserted the prophetic promises, relating them to the writer's own time. Writers often took the names of OT saints, not to deceive but to express their role as interpreters. They also reviewed history in the form of predictions, again not to deceive but rather to interpret past prophecies to show what had been fulfilled, and what still had to happen.

Among the main apocalyptic books outside the Bible are *1 Enoch* (writings from 5th cent. BC to 1st cent. AD); *The Testament* (or *Assumption*) *of Moses* (2nd or 1st cent. BC); *2 Baruch* and the *Apocalypse of Abraham* come from AD 70-140, as does *2 Esdras* in the Apocrypha. Other works such as *Jubilees* and *The Testaments of the Twelve Patriarchs* contain apocalyptic passages.

In the OT, Dn.; Is. 24-27; 56-66; Joel;

and Zc. 9-14 are apocalyptic in at least some respects. God's future intervention, universal judgment, a new age of salvation and a transformed cosmos are all envisaged. The literary forms of apocalyptic are present in Ezekiel's visions and Zc. 1-6.

Some NT passages resemble Jewish apocalypses (e.g. Mt. 24; Mk. 13; Lk. 21; 1 Thes. 4:16f.; 2 Thes. 2; Rev.). However, the purely future interest of apocalyptic is modified in the NT by the conviction that the new age has already invaded this one, even though it is not yet fulfilled. NT apocalyptic is also Christ-centred, is not written under pseudonyms and does not take a fictional standpoint in the past. See APOCRYPHA; ENOCH; ESCHATOLOGY; JUBILEES.

APOCRYPHA. From a Greek word, 'hidden'. A collection of 12 books which are not recognized as Scripture in Protestant churches, but which are valued for private study. Christian opinion about their status was ambiguous until the 16th cent. when the Roman Catholic Council of Trent included them in the authoritative Scriptures, but Luther and the Church of England allowed them only for private edification. Ancient copies have been preserved mainly in Greek, although many are believed to have been written originally in Hebrew or Aramaic. They are outlined below in the order in which they appear in printed Protestant versions.

1 Esdras. A parallel account of some events recorded in Chronicles, Ezra and Nehemiah, with the addition of the 'Debate of the three youths' (3:1-5:6). This latter is an adaptation of a Persian tale in which a guardsman gains the opportunity to remind the Persian king of his duty to rebuild the Jerusalem temple by winning an argument about the strongest of three powers: wine, women or truth. Originally written in Hebrew or Aramaic, it was probably translated into Greek before Ezra.

2 Esdras. Also known as *4 Ezra*, it is an expansion by Christian writers of a Jewish apocalyptic book. It contains seven visions: 3:1-5:20; 5:21-6:34; 6:35-9:25; 9:26-10:59; 11:1-12:51; 13; 14. They deal with the suffering of Israel and look forward to the new age, and were originally written in Hebrew or Aramaic. See APOCALYPTIC.

Tobit. A short story about Tobit, a righteous Hebrew, and his son Tobias during the captivity of the northern kingdom (Israel). Tobit was persecuted, accidentally blinded, and later healed by a fish-gall applied to his eyes by Tobias, who had long been missing, presumed dead. Probably written originally in Aramaic.

Judith. The story of a courageous Jewish widow who beguiled Holofernes, Nebuchadrezzar's foremost general, and beheaded him; his army then retreated from besieging her city. Completely fictitious, it dates from the 2nd century BC and was originally written in Hebrew.

Additions to Esther. This has 6 passages which embellish the biblical book. Scholars are divided as to whether it is of Hebrew or Greek origin. It claims to have been translated before 114 BC.

The Wisdom of Solomon is perhaps the highlight of Jewish Wisdom writing, which achieves greater formality and precision under the influence of Greek thought. It is an exhortation to seek wisdom, personifying it as a feminine celestial being. It is an encouragement to Jews not to forsake their ancestral faith. It was probably composed in Greek and originated in Alexandria. See WISDOM; WISDOM LITER-ATURE.

Ecclesiasticus. The Greek name for *The Wisdom of Joshua ben-Sira* (or Jesus ben-Sirach). He was a Palestinian living in Jerusalem, *c.* 180 BC. It contains advice for successful living, combining the fear of the Lord and observance of his law with practical 'wisdom'. It represents the beginning of the ideal of the scribe, devoted to God and the law, sober in living. It became a favourite Christian book, and was written originally in Hebrew. See WISDOM; WISDOM LITERATURE.

Baruch is allegedly the work of Jeremiah's friend and scribe. Scholars generally attribute it to several authors who probably composed it in Hebrew. It addresses the exiles in Babylon, praises wisdom, and laments over Jerusalem.

The Letter of Jeremiah is an attack on idolatry in the guise of a letter to the exiles in Babylon similar to that mentioned in Je. 29. It is written in good Greek but may have had an Aramaic original.

The Prayer of Azariah and *Song of the Three Holy Children* were uttered in the furnace in the story of Daniel. The latter is the Benedicite of Christian worship. *Susanna*, another addition to Daniel, is the story of a virtuous Jewess falsely accused of adultery but vindicated by Daniel. *Bel and the Dragon*, also attached to Daniel, contains stories which ridicule idolatry; Daniel destroys a dragon and is preserved alive in the lion's den. These additions probably date from about 100 BC, devived from Hebrew sources.

The Prayer of Manasseh claims to be that referred to in 2 Ch. 33:11ff. It is first attested only in the 3rd cent. AD.

1 and 2 Maccabees are historical books covering the period 175-134 BC, which saw the wars of the Hasmonaeans and the rule of John Hyrcanus. There are discrepancies between the two books, and the first is generally believed to be more reliable. The second contains long excerpts from the otherwise unknown writer Jason of Cyrene. See MACCABEES, THE.

See also NEW TESTAMENT APOCRYPHA; PSEUDEPIGRAPHA.

APOLLONIA. A town 43 km WSW of Amphipolis, through which Paul and Silas passed en route to Thessalonica (Acts 17:1).

APOLLOS. An eloquent Alexandrian Jew who knew the OT and the story of Jesus well but who knew nothing of the outpouring of the Holy Spirit and Christian baptism. This gap in his knowledge was filled by Priscilla and Aquila in Ephesus (Acts 18:24-28). He preached in Corinth, where a faction claimed to follow him (1 Cor. 1:11f.; 3:4-6), and Tit. 3:13 shows he embarked on another journey. He has been suggested as the author of Hebrews, but it is not proven.

APOSTASY. In classical Greek, a technical term for political revolt or defection. 2 Thes. 2:3 uses the word to describe the great rebellion against God which is a sign of the end of the world. It is falling from faith or from God (1 Tim. 4:1; Heb. 3:12), which may be encouraged by false teachers (Mt. 24:11). Restoration after deliberate apostasy is said to be impossible (Heb. 6:4-6; 10:26f.).

APOSTLE. The word derives from a common Greek verb 'to send', but there are few occurrences outside the NT where it means 'a person sent'. In the NT, however, it occurs over 80 times, and is applied to Jesus as the 'sent one' from God (Heb. 3:1); to those sent in the past by God to preach to Israel (Lk. 11:49); and to those sent on missions by the churches (2 Cor. 8:23).

Primarily, however, it refers to the 12 men whom Jesus commissioned to be with him, to preach, heal and encourage (Mk. 3:13-19). Their main function was to witness to Jesus, and their witness was rooted in years of intimate knowledge, hard experience and intensive training (Mk. 8:27ff.). They also witnessed his resurrection (Acts 1:22), which made them effective witnesses to his Person; he himself commissioned them for a world-wide witness empowered by the Holy Spirit

(Acts 1:8). In Jn. 14-17, this witness is said to be the Spirit's own witness (15:26f.); he will remind them of Jesus' words (14:26), guide them into all truth and reveal to them the glory of Jesus (16:13-15). Their witness is thus not left to their memories but to the Holy Spirit.

For this reason they were regarded as the pillars (Gal. 2:9) or foundation (Eph. 2:20) of the church, its doctrine and fellowship. They are to be assessors at the final judgment (Mt. 19:28), their names carved into the structure of the heavenly city (Rev. 21:14). Their ministry was accompanied by spectacular signs (Acts 8:14ff.). Peter betrayed a fundamental principle he had previously accepted, and was rebuked by a colleague (Gal. 2:11f.).

The NT has little to say about them ruling the church. They investigate churches which encounter problems (Acts 11:20-22), but the crucial Jerusalem Council consisted of elders as well as apostles (Acts 15:6), and church government was a distinct gift exercised by local elders (1 Cor. 12:28f.). The identity of function which some see between the apostles and 2nd-cent. bishops is by no means obvious.

The qualifications for the 12 were a call by God and witness to the resurrection, hence Matthias can replace Judas (Acts 1:21-26). Although additional to the 12, Paul can rightly claim the title by virtue of his Damascus road call and vision of the risen Jesus (1 Cor. 9:1).

There are other people in the NT

who are also given the title: James the Lord's brother (Gal. 1:19); Barnabas (Acts 14:14); Andronicus and Junias (Rom. 16:7); it is implied for Silas in 1 Thes. 2:6, and Epaphroditus is called 'messenger' (apostle) in Phil. 2:25. Some have suggested that those who are later called apostles were among the 70 sent out by Jesus (Lk. 10:1ff.).

1 Cor. 15:5,7 implies a distinction between the 12 and 'all the apostles', and the special significance of the 12 is unquestioned. The NT does not envisage the transmission of their apostolic functions because the foundations they laid were recorded in the NT for future generations.

See BISHOP; CHURCH GOVERNMENT; TRADITION.

APPHIA. Possibly Philemon's wife and hostess to the Colossian church (Phm. 2); the name was common in W Asia. See PHILEMON, LETTER TO.

AQUILA AND PRISCILLA (PRISCA). A Jewish tentmaker and his wife who were close friends of Paul. They were expelled with all Jews from Rome by Claudius *c.* AD 49, and were probably already Christians when they met Paul in Corinth (Acts 18:1-3), where they risked their lives for him (Rom. 16:3). They went with Paul to Ephesus where they helped the influential Apollos to fuller faith (Acts 18:24-26). Rom. 16:3 implies they returned to Rome after Claudius' death. The fact that Prisca (the proper form of the name; Priscilla is a familiar form) is usually mentioned first has led some to suggest that she was of higher social rank, or more prominent in the church, than her husband.

AR. The chief city of Moab, E of the Dead Sea; site unknown. The Hebrews were forbidden to settle there (Dt. 2:9,18).

ARABAH. The name of the rift valley which runs from the Sea of Tiberias (Galilee) to the Gulf of Aqabah (Red Sea); today it is applied to the area S of the Dead Sea to the Gulf of Aqabah. The Dead Sea is sometimes called the Sea of Arabah (*e.g.* Jos. 3:16). It comes from a root word meaning 'dry' or 'burnt up', hence 'waste land' or 'desert'. See JORDAN.

ARABIA. *Geography.* The Arabian peninsular is a mass of old crystalline rock forming a range of mountains on the W rising above 3,000 m in places, with younger strata tilted against its E side. In the mountains, and especially in the SW corner (the modern Yemen Arab Republic and the People's Democratic Republic of Yemen), where rainfall exceeds 500 mm, settled life based on irrigation is possible; this is where the ancient kingdoms flourished. Settled life is also possible N along the mountains and E along the Arabian Sea coast, where rainfall averages 100-250 mm, but elsewhere life depends on oases and wells. Inland, apart from sandy and rocky desert, the land is largely steppe supporting a poor nomadic population.

History. In the 2nd cent. BC Semitic-speaking tribes from the N settled in the area of modern Yemen and W

Aden, later to become the kingdoms of Sheba and the Minaeans, among others. They prospered on the trade routes bringing spices to northern countries. Sheba was well organized in the 8th cent. under a ruler who combined priestly functions with his duties. The Minaeans became prominent c. 400 BC, superseded later by the Himyarites.

In the N, the area E of the Jordan was settled 2200-1900 BC, followed by a barren period until the 13th cent. BC. The name 'Arab' first appears in the records of the Assyrian Shalmaneser III in 853 BC. The Nabataeans emerged in the 4th cent. BC, centred on the red-rock city of Petra, and dominated an area from Damascus in the N to Gaza in the S, and far E into the desert, by the 1st cent. BC.

Biblical references. The names of the smaller groups which came from the area occur more often than the general name; among them are descendants of Abraham (Gn. 25) and Esau (Gn. 36). The Ishmaelites and Midianites were nomadic merchants in Jacob's time (Gn. 37:25ff.), but contacts became more prominent in Solomon's time because of his extensive trading from his Red Sea port of Ezion-geber. 'The kings of Arabia' (2 Ch. 9:14) refers to people from the semi-desert areas E and S of Palestine. Most of Israel's contacts were with N Arabians, who were very familiar by Hezekiah's time (Is. 21:13). Some even served as mercenaries defending Jerusalem against Sennacherib. In the closing years of the kingdom of Judah, they were well known as traders (Je.

25:23f.).

Arabia is mentioned only twice in the NT. Paul went there after his conversion (Gal. 1:17), probably to part of the Nabataean kingdom, even Petra itself, possibly to be alone with God. In Gal. 4:25 he refers to Mt Sinai 'in Arabia', meaning the Sinai Peninsular or land just to the E of the Gulf of Aqaba.

See MINAEANS; NABATAEANS; NOMADS; SHEBA; TEMA.

ARAD. A Canaanite town in the desert of Judah whose king attacked Israel after the Exodus; it was destroyed as a result (Nu. 21:1-3). Probably modern Tell Arad, 30 km NE of Beersheba, where excavations have unearthed a large fortified city c. 2500 BC, deserted then reoccupied before the monarchy, c. 1200 BC; among Hebrew inscriptions was one mentioning a 'house of Yahweh'.

ARAM, ARAMAEANS (ARAM-EAN). ('Syria' in OT in AV, RSV, GNB; a misleading title when applied to the period before King Saul, c. 1000 BC.)

Origins. Western Semitic-speaking semi-nomads infiltrated Syria and Mesopotamia from the Arabian desert-fringe, penetrating as far E as the Iranian mountains. A settlement called Aram is known c. 2400-2000 BC N of Elam and ENE of Assyria, an area linked with Aram the son of Shem in Gn. 10:22f.; 1 Ch. 1:17; the tradition is continued by Am. 9:7. Aramu is known as a personal name in the 3rd Dynasty of Ur (c. 2000 BC) and at Mari

(18th cent. BC). 'Aram' may have been a tribal name applied to all Semitic-speaking settlers by the Hurrians who spread across Mesopotamia and into Syria by 2000 BC.

Early history. Abraham and his family, after leaving Ur, settled in upper Mesopotamia at Haran (Gn. 11:28-32), which was in 'Aram-naharaim', 'Aram of the two rivers', within a great bend of the Euphrates river bounded by Carchemish in the W and the river Habur in the E. One part of Abraham's family remained here as 'Aramaeans', named after the place; the wives of Isaac and Jacob came from this branch of the family (Gn. 24:28ff.), thus justifying the later Israelite claim that, 'a wandering Aramaean (Jacob) was my father' (Dt. 26:5). Differences in dialect similar to those indicated in Gn. 31:47 have been noted in Egyptian texts from the 16th cent. BC. Balaam came from Aram-naharaim to curse Israel (Nu. 22:5); its opportunist king oppressed Israel in the time of the Judges (Jdg. 3:7ff.); and the gods of Syria proper are called the gods of Aram (Jdg. 10:6 in Hebrew), indicating the growing influx of Aramaeans in the 12th and 11th cents.

Israel and Aramaean states. The Israelite kings were in regular conflict with Aramaeans. David, for example, defeated Hadadezer king of Aram-zobah N of Damascus (2 Sa. 8:3ff.), whose rule had already extended across to the Euphrates; later Assyrian texts report a 'king of Aram' gaining control of cities on either side of the Euphrates. In Solomon's reign, a bandit Rezon gained control of Damascus

and ruled there *c.* 955-925 BC (1 Ki. 11:23ff.), and when he died Hezion seized the throne. He founded a dynasty that lasted 100 years (1 Ki. 15:18), and Damascus became the chief kingdom in Syria.

Later, Ben-hadad (probably Ben-hadad II) clashed with Ahab (1 Ki. 20), and Hazael with Joram (*c.* 842 BC; 2 Ki. 8:28f.). Joash later recovered the lands lost to Hazael (2 Ki. 13:14ff.). The Aramaean king then was Ben-hadad III (*c.* 796-770 BC), who headed a powerful coalition against Zakur of Hamath. This was defeated by Zakur and the dominance of the Aramaean kingdom of Damascus in Syria ended. Tiglath-pileser III of Assyria finally defeated Damascus in 732 BC (2 Ki. 16:9), and ironically deported the Aramaeans to Qir (Kir), their ancient homeland (Am. 1:4f.).

Culture. Their main contribution was their language, Aramaic, which was employed for commerce and diplomacy, and also as a literary medium. The chief gods of the Aramaeans were Baal-shamain, Hadad the storm god, Canaanite gods such as Ashtar and Mesopotamian gods such as Marduk and Nebo.

See DAMASCUS; NOMADS.

ARAMAIC: See OLD TESTAMENT LANGUAGES.

ARARAT. The name occurs four times in the OT: the mountainous area where Noah's ark grounded (Gn. 8:4); the land the murderers of Sennacherib fled to (2 Ki. 19:37; Is. 37:38); a kingdom mentioned by Jeremiah as summoned to destroy Babylon (Je. 51:27). It was the Urartu of Assyrian inscriptions, a kingdom which flourished near Lake Van in Armenia during the time of the Assyrian empire. It grew in power as Assyria declined; Assyrian attacks into its northern neighbour increased in the 9th cent. BC. It was subdued by Assyria at the end of the 8th cent. (see GOMER), and briefly revived in the mid-7th cent. It probably disappeared as a state early in the 6th cent. BC, about the time of Jeremiah's summons.

ARAUNAH (lit. 'freeman, noble'). A Jebusite whose threshing-floor was bought by David, who had seen an angel there (2 Sa. 24:16ff.). In 1 Ch. 21:18ff. (where Araunah is called Ornan in AV, RSV and NEB) David also bought the surrounding area to be the site of the future Temple (1 Ch. 22:1; 2 Ch. 3:1).

ARCHAEOLOGY (OLD TESTAMENT PERIOD).

I. Purpose, value and development.
Biblical archaeology selects for study the material remains of Palestine (modern Israel and Jordan) and its neighbouring countries which relate to the biblical periods and narratives. Remains of buildings, pottery and art, and carved inscriptions, help us to understand the life and customs of the Hebrews and the nations with which they came into contact. Archaeology has done much to explain, illustrate and sometimes confirm biblical statements, and also to counter false theories. The vast span of time and

geographical area limits the possible scope of excavation, however, and objects made from leather, wood or cloth rarely survive. Many excavations have unearthed documents, and those from Egypt, Assyria and Babylonia are especially valuable when compared with the OT to illustrate the widespread nature of literary styles. Written material has been preserved on papyri and clay tablets (ostraca), as well as on coins and seals.

Interest in the traditional biblical sites revived after the 16th cent. AD Reformation, but the first planned surface exploration was carried out in 1838 by the Americans Edward Robinson and Eli Smith. The first excavation was by the Frenchman De Saulcy near Jerusalem in 1863, followed by a series of surveys by the Palestine Exploration Fund 1865-1914. In 1890, during excavation of Tell el-Hesi, Sir Flinders Petrie realized that different levels of occupation of a site could be recognized by the pottery found in them. Dating of sites based on pottery was established in the 1920s, and the classification scheme developed in Palestine is now applied throughout the world. As more accurate methods of dating and more detailed knowledge have developed, some early conclusions have been revised; for example Kenyon showed that the walls of Jericho, which Garstang had associated with Joshua's time, were in fact of a much earlier period.

Sections II and III below illustrate some of the archaeological evidence relating to the OT period; section IV gives more detail from specific sites mostly relating to the Patriarchal Age and the Exodus.

II. From earliest times to Israel's invasion.
It was in the Near East that man first emerged as a food-gatherer in the Old Stone Age (pre-10,000 BC), and remains of this period have been found in the Carmel caves and elsewhere. From *c*. 9000 BC there are open settlements with huts at Jericho and Beidha near Petra. Also at Jericho, massive defences and unusual plastered skulls and figurines have been found dating *c*. 7500 BC. Invaders (probably from the N) who brought a new type of pottery and who buried their dead in mass graves cut into the rocks are attested in the Early Bronze Age (*c*. 3000 BC). Towns in N Palestine were apparently flourishing *c*. 2900 BC, and texts from Ebla (see IV below) name places such as Lachish, Hazor, Megiddo and Gaza *c*. 2300 BC which are known later in biblical records.

The arrival of the Amorites *c*. 2200 BC is attested by their distinctive burial customs, weapons and pottery. Soon, Canaanite city-states appeared, with a citadel and a lower town surrounded by high ramparts, as at Hazor and Carchemish. There are signs of the invasion of semi-nomads into the scrub-land between the fortified cities *c*. 1950-1550 BC; among them may have been the biblical Patriarchs. Major cities were evidently destroyed violently *c*. 1450 BC, probably by the Egyptians. Over two centuries later they were sacked and burned again, about the time of Joshua's invasion, although the OT implies he did not set fire to many places. Most scholars now date Joshua *c*. 1220 BC but archaeology reveals no town at Jericho at that time: the site seems to have been abandoned *c*. 1300 BC.

III. Israel's occupation of Palestine.
The Philistine settlement of SW Canaan is attested by decorated pottery and iron weapons from 1200 BC onwards. Israel's early settlements dating from about the same time were poor by comparison with the earlier Canaanite strongholds. Saul's citadel at Gibeah had casemate walls (two walls with rubble between them) characteristic of the period. Few building projects can be identified with David's time, but by Solomon's reign Israel's building technique had improved and iron tools and weapons were in wider use. He built residences for district governors at Megiddo and Hazor, with massive granaries at Lachish and Beth-shemesh. His temple in Jerusalem followed a Syro-Phoenician style already adopted at Hazor. Its decoration can be paralleled from contemporary ivories found at Samaria and Nimrud (Iraq); altars, stands, tongs and other utensils have been found during excavations at various sites which illustrate those used in Solomon's temple.

The period of the divided monarchy has been illuminated by several excavations. At Samaria, for example, a royal quarter was built on the hill summit, and many ivories from the palace may have come from Ahab's 'ivory house' (1 Ki. 22:39; Am. 6:4). In the courtyard was an open pool (1 Ki. 22:38), and 63 inscriptions which are accounts of wine and oil brought into the royal stores testify to the administrative organization, probably of Jeroboam II. Ahab appears to have strengthened Hazor with walls which stood until *c.* 150 BC; a piece of pottery (potsherd) inscribed 'belonging to Pekah' from Hazor *c.* 734 BC recalls that at the time of the Assyrian invasion Pekah ruled Israel (2 Ki. 15:29).

The removal by Sargon II of prisoners and their goods from Samaria in 722 BC (2 Ki. 17:23f.) is seen archaeologically by the poorer and partial habitation of the site and foreign pottery found there. The fall of Lachish, also recorded on reliefs (carvings) in Sennacherib's palace at Nineveh, has been confirmed by armour, weapons and helmets of fallen attackers near the ramp leading to the city gate. Carchemish has been shown to have been destroyed in 605 BC, when Nebuchadrezzar II captured it. Many Judaean towns show the ravages of Babylonian attacks in the period of Zedekiah's revolt (589-587 BC). Surveys show that the country was impoverished during the exile of Judah in Babylon, and that not until the 3rd cent. BC were there as many people there as in former times. Locally minted coins are found abundantly by this time, some with Hebrew or Aramaic inscriptions. Silver containers from Persia have been unearthed at Gezer, and carved limestone incense burners from Babylon at Lachish.

IV. Specific excavations.

None of these sites is named in the Bible, but each throws important light on biblical narratives. They are listed in alphabetical order.

Alalah. Capital of a city-state on the R. Orontes in N Syria from which 468 texts dating from 1900 to 1470 BC provide details which may be compared with the Patriarchal period in Gn. Of main interest are the marriage contracts in which the future father-in-law was asked for the bride, to whom betrothal gifts were made; some contracts state that failing the birth of a son within 7 years the husband could marry a concubine (*cf.* Gn. 29:15ff.). However, if the first wife bore a son later, he would be regarded as the first-born (*cf.* Gn. 21:10). An early covenant-treaty text, in common with later covenants, includes divine witnesses and curses. When a king, Idrimi, was enthroned, he made treaties with neighbouring states concerning runaway slaves, a practice possibly followed between Solomon and Gath in 1 Ki. 2:39f., which would also throw light on the extradition ban on Hebrew fugitives in Dt. 23:15f. Other customs referred to include the exchange of villages to preserve inter-state boundaries along natural and defensible features (*cf.* 1 Ki. 9:10ff.).

Amarna. Tell el-Amarna is the modern site of Akhetaten the capital of Egypt *c.* 1375-1360 BC, some 320 km S of Cairo on the E bank of the Nile. The impressive remains include temples, administrative buildings, tombs with wall paintings, and houses on once prosperous estates. But more important for Bible readers are the 380 documents found there. Most are letters from Asiatic rulers to Pharaohs

Amenophis III and IV *c.* 1385-1365 BC; half come from Palestine and Syria. They show that Egyptian influence in Palestine was weakening before Israel entered it under Joshua; they present a picture of intrigues and inter-city strife. An Egyptian official named Yanhamu (a Semitic name) is reminiscent of Joseph because he supervised the grain supply for the pharaoh's Syrian subjects during a shortage, but they cannot be the same person. There are also numerous references to the armed bands of Habiru who inhabited the hills of Palestine. Some have argued that these were the Hebrews under Joshua, rather than people already there before the Israelite conquest, but the letters show that unlike the Israelites they did not operate around larger towns; they worked in small groups rather than en masse; they did not besiege cities; they used chariots; and they were supported by such places as Lachish and Gezer which Joshua destroyed (Jos. 10). The letters were written in Akkadian script (see ACCAD), the international language of the period.

Ebla. The capital of a city-state 70 km S of Aleppo in Syria. An archive of 18,000 documents from *c.* 2300 BC includes accounts of creation and a flood, mythologies, incantations, hymns and proverbs, as well as historical, legal and commercial texts, royal edicts, letters, laws and educational lists of animals, professions and objects. Ebla was at the time a thriving commercial centre with a population of 250,000, trading with Cyprus, Palestine and other major areas in grain, wood, textiles and wine. Written in Sumerian, the documents will be of importance to our understanding of the Patriarchal Age when they have been fully published.

Hammurapi. A governor of Babylon who extended his influence across Mesopotamia, seeking to unite it under one ruler. A selection of his legal judgments survives on an inscribed slab ('stele') found at Susa. A few are worded similarly to OT cases; for example false witness (Ex. 23:1ff.) and kidnapping (Ex. 21:16). Many specific cases have a similar approach including those dealing with sexual offences (*e.g.* the death penalty for adulterers, Dt. 22:22), although in others the Hebrew penalties seem consistently more directed to preserving community and family life than class structure and property. These laws represent a local Babylonian example of the attitude to law common in much of the ancient Near East.

Mari. The modern Tell Hariri, 12 km NNW of Abu Kemal in SE Syria by the Euphrates, Mari was the capital of a major Amorite city-state *c.* 1800 BC. Over 22,000 inscribed clay tablets, a quarter of them state letters, have been found there, and they provide important background information for the Patriarchal Age. Tribal chiefs were described as 'father' and local administration of law and taxation was handled by sub-governors. Relations between neighbours were regulated by written treaties or covenants ratified by the ritual killing of an ass (*cf.* 'sons of Hamor' (ass), Jos. 24:32 with Gn. 34:1-3). Prophets and 'speakers' were attached to each god or temple, their words depending largely on magic techniques, dreams, reading the entrails of sacrificial animals and some astronomical observations. This is in marked contrast to the clarity, range, content and purpose of prophecies in Israel. Among the gods worshipped were Ishtar, Dagon and Baal. Some of the personal names mentioned are similar to OT people but are not to be identified with them. The texts provide detailed insight into the daily life of the 300-room (15-acre) royal palace.

Nuzi. A place near Kirkuk, Iraq, which in the 15th-14th cents. BC was under Hurrian influence. In the palace and private homes over 4,000 clay tablets were found, written in a Hurrian dialect of Akkadian. They cover five generations and so give a detailed picture of an ancient Mesopotamian community in a comparatively short period of time, and provide several points of contact with the biblical narratives about the Patriarchs. Many documents deal with inheritance matters. The elder son received a double share of the family estate (closely paralleled in Dt. 21:17), although the Patriarchs themselves seem to have acted differently (Gn. 25:5f.). An heir could be disinherited for offences against the family, and references to 'disobedience' and 'disrespect' provide useful background to Reuben's demotion in Gn. 49:3f. Adoption occupies an important place in the texts. A man with no heir could adopt an outsider who would provide food and clothing for his aging 'parents' and ensure a proper burial, in return for an inheritance. It is possible that Abraham adopted his servant Eliezer in this manner before Isaac was born (Gn. 15:2ff.). Three further solutions for childless marriage are proposed by the Nuzi texts: to remarry; to take a concubine; or for the wife to give her slave-girl to her husband (Gn. 16:1ff.; 30:1ff.). Daughters are allowed to inherit property, usually in the absence of sons (Nu. 27:8), and there was a periodic release from debt (Dt. 15). Sale of land was sometimes confirmed by the seller lifting his foot and placing the buyer's on the soil, and shoes functioned as legal symbols in some deals (Ru. 4:7f.; *cf.* Am. 8:6). The complaint of Laban's daughters that their father held back their dowry is paralleled by an identical phrase in 5 Nuzi texts.

Ugarit, Ras Shamra. An important trade centre and capital of a city-state in N Syria *c.* 2000-1000 BC, 1 km from the Mediterranean coast and 15 km N of Latakia. Many written documents have been recovered from the palace and houses, most commonly in Babylonian script but also in Egyptian, Cypriot and Hittite systems. To write their own language, scribes devised an alphabet in cuneiform script with 29 letters each representing one consonant, and these were learnt in the same order as Hebrew letters, with additions. Over 1,300 inscriptions in this alphabet, dating from 1400 BC onwards, have been found there. The language itself is closely related to Hebrew, and there are many similar terms used for the sacrifices detailed in

Lv. (although the use of the sacrifices differs from both the spirit and practice of the OT), and in some OT poems. The literature contains an account of the flood, a story about the Babylonian hero Gilgamesh, and a unique version of the 'Babylonian Job'. Some religious epics are several hundred lines long, telling of rivalry among the gods. The texts reveal the degrading results of pagan worship, with an emphasis on war, sacred prostitution, and consequent social degradation. Over 250 gods are named, although only some 15-28 were included in the main pantheon, and these included Baal and Dagon named in the OT; Asherah is also mentioned.

See further ARCHITECTURE; LACHISH; MOABITE STONE; PATRIARCHAL AGE; POTTERY; WRITING; many articles on specific items and places mentioned in the OT also contain relevant archaeological information.

ARCHAEOLOGY (NEW TESTAMENT PERIOD).

For a brief general introduction to the archaeology of Bible lands, see the previous article.

I. Jerusalem.

The massive walls built around the Temple Mount by Herod the Great (37-4 BC) have been found, and rise above the present ground level. Excavations nearby have located a complex of streets and terraces, and in the Upper City have unearthed wall paintings and mosaics from luxurious houses. The 'Tower of David', one of Herod's defensive structures, is known from excavations. The sites of Golgotha and the tomb at the traditional Holy Sepulchre have strong claims to be the sites of the crucifixion and burial of Jesus outside the city walls. A tomb inscribed 'Alexander, son of Simon, of Cyrene' may be that of the son of the man who carried Jesus' cross (Mk. 15:21). An inscription from the Temple enclosure, dating from the same period, prohibits non-Jews from proceeding beyond the barrier which surrounds the Sacred Place on pain of death. The incidents of Acts 21:26-29 must be connected with the prohibition.

II. Other places associated with the gospels.

At Jericho the Herodian palace has a sunken garden and a pool between the two wings, and even the flowerpots remain intact; Herod used the Italian method of building with dried bricks and concrete here, but nowhere else as far as is known. In several of Herod's buildings throughout Palestine underfloor heating, baths and a steam room have been found. At Caesarea the great Herodian harbour, now submerged, is clearly visible from the air. A stone from the Herodian remains in the city itself describes Pontius Pilate as 'prefect of Judaea'. At Capernaum an ancient synagogue has been excavated, dating from the 2nd or 3rd cents. AD; 1st cent. synagogues have been found at the fortresses of Masada and Herodium.

III. Places associated with the early church.

A decree of Claudius found at Delphi

in Greece describes Gallio as proconsul of Achaia (*Corinth*) in AD 51 (Acts 18:12). In Corinth a doorway inscribed 'synagogue of the Hebrews' may indicate where Paul preached (Acts 18:4); a text naming Erastus may refer to the city treasurer of Rom. 16:23; and one naming 'Lucius the butcher' probably marks the site of the meat market of 1 Cor. 10:25. At *Ephesus* parts of the temple of Artemis (Diana) have been found, and at an open-air theatre seating 25,000 people an inscription shows that the assembly of citizens described in Acts 19:28-41 did indeed meet there. A number of inscriptions have vindicated Luke's historical accuracy; the 'politarchs' of Thessalonica (Acts 17:6,8), and the 'chief man' or Governor of Malta (Acts 28:7), once doubted as true titles, are now known to have existed at the time. Luke's references to Quirinius as governor of Syria (Lk. 2:2) and Lysanias as tetrarch of Abilene (Lk. 3:1) are also supported by inscriptions.

See also articles on individual sites.

ARCHIPPUS. A 'fellow soldier' with Paul (Phm. 2), who may have been the son of Philemon and Apphia. He is told to 'remain faithful' in Col. 4:17.

ARCHITECTURE: See BUILDING.

AREOPAGUS. 'The hill of Ares', the Greek god of war corresponding to the Roman Mars; it was a little hill NW of the Acropolis in Athens, on which the Council of the Areopagus originally met and from which it took its name. In NT times it met in the Royal Porch in the Athens market place, except when investigating cases of homicide, and it is probably here that Paul was brought before the Areopagus (Acts 17:19ff.). It was an ancient institution and despite considerable reduction in its powers it still retained great prestige and had special jurisdiction in religious matters. Paul's speech to the Council concluded with the resurrection of Jesus; on hearing that the Council dismissed him as unworthy of consideration.

ARETAS. Aretas IV Philopatris, the last and most famous Nabataean king of that name (*c.* 9 BC-AD 40), is mentioned in 2 Cor. 11:32. His daughter married Herod Antipas who divorced her when he wanted to marry Herodias (Mk. 6:17). He defeated Herod in war in AD 36. From the 2 Cor. reference it seems probable that he held the old Syrian capital of Damascus for a while.

ARGOB. A district E of the Jordan which was ruled by Og king of Bashan before the Israelite conquest under Moses (Dt. 3:3-5). It contained 60 fortified cities and many unwalled towns. Its precise location is uncertain.

ARIEL (lit. 'hearth of God'). *Place:* A cryptic name given to Jerusalem (Is. 29:1-2,7) as the centre of worship of God. *Person:* A delegate sent by Ezra to Casiphia (Ezr. 8:16).

ARIMATHEA. Home town of Joseph in whose tomb the body of Jesus was laid (Mt. 27:57, *etc.*). Also identified by

Eusebius and Jerome with Ramah, the birthplace of Samuel (1 Sa. 1:19). Possibly modern Rentis, 15 km NE of Lydda.

ARIOCH. 1. A king who was defeated by Abraham (Gn. 14:1, 9); the name *Arriwak* is mentioned in the Mari letters (*c.* 1770 BC), and *Ariukki* in the Nuzi texts (15th cent. BC). 2. A bodyguard who introduced Daniel to Nebuchadrezzar II (Dn. 2:14f.).

ARISTARCHUS. A fellow-traveller with Paul who was: seized by the Ephesian mob (Acts 19:29); a delegate to Jerusalem (Acts 20:4); on board ship to Rome (Acts 27:2). Also a 'fellow-prisoner' with Paul in Col. 4:10, a text which implies he was a Jew; the other texts give his home as Thessalonica.

ARK. ('Boat', GNB.) Probably from an Egyptian word meaning coffin or chest, it was evidently intended to be no more than a floating container for Noah's family and animals (Gn. 6-7). The measurements given are about 150 x 25 x 15 m, the construction as gopher wood bound with reeds and covered with bitumen. A word in Gn. 6:16 usually translated 'roof' probably means a window (opening) just below the roof. It came to rest on Mt ARARAT.

ARK OF THE COVENANT. ('Covenant box', GNB.) A rectangular box made of acacia wood, about 122 x 76 x 76 cm, covered with gold and carried on poles. The lid, or 'mercy seat', was a gold plate topped with two cherubs with outspread wings. It contained the two stone tablets inscribed with the Ten Commandments (Dt. 10:1ff.), a pot of manna and Aaron's rod (Heb. 9:4f.). It served as the meeting point in the inner sanctuary where God revealed his will (*e.g.* Ex. 25:22). It was temporarily confiscated by the Philistines (1 Sa. 4), and installed by Solomon in the temple (1 Ki. 8:1ff.). It was presumably lost when Jerusalem was destroyed in 587 BC. Gold-overlaid portable boxes or shrines are known from the ancient Near East before Moses' time.

ARKITE. A descendant of Ham (Gn. 10:17; 1 Ch. 1:15), and ancestor of inhabitants of a Phoenician city 20 km NE of Tripolis, modern Tell Arqa.

ARM. An outstretched or bared arm symbolizes God's mighty acts of judgment or salvation (*e.g.* Ex. 6:6); his protection is symbolized by supporting arms (Dt. 33:27). By contrast, human arms are seen as weak (2 Ch. 32:8), strengthened by God (Ps. 18:34), but broken by him if they act wickedly (Ps. 37:17). See also BODY.

ARMAGEDDON. The assembly-point for battle in John's vision of 'the great day of God' (Rev. 16:16); he may have used the name symbolically. Most scholars identify it with the mountain or hill of Megiddo, in the vicinity of the Carmel range. Important battles, from one fought by Tuthmosis III in 1468 BC to that of Lord Allenby in 1917, have taken place nearby. The 'mountains of Israel' (Ezk. 39: 1-4) probably means Armageddon.

ARMOUR. *Shield.* The earliest battle scenes from Egypt and Mesopotamia depict shields. Shapes and sizes varied with the country and period. Small circular shields were introduced by the Sea Peoples (Philistines) *c.* 1250 BC, and were later common among the Hebrews (*e.g.* the Benjaminites in 2 Ch. 14:8). Shields generally consisted of a wooden frame covered with animal skin and oiled before battle. Metal shields gave better protection but impeded movement.

Helmet. Metal helmets were worn by Sumerian and Akkadian soldiers before 2000 BC. In 2 Ch. 26:14 they were standard issue to Uzziah's army, but may have been made of leather. Bronze helmets were issued to Persian soldiers in the last two centuries BC (1 Macc. 6:35).

Coat of mail. It was worn first by charioteers (Je. 46:4) and archers (Je. 51:3) who could not protect themselves with shields. Coats fitted with metal scales were in widespread use in the Near East by 1500 BC: one ancient text from Nuzi (see ARCHAEOLOGY) mentions a coat with 680 scales and another with 1,035 scales. Nehemiah's builders wore them for protection against sudden attack (Ne. 4:16).

Paul uses armour as a picture of God's protection in Eph. 6:13ff.

See also BOW AND ARROW; CHARIOT; SLING; SPEAR; SWORD; WAR; and next article.

ARMY. The Israelite army began as a tribal militia assembled at a time of crisis. Saul first provided Israel with a small regular army (1 Sa. 13:2). Duels between representatives of armies were occasionally held to avoid unnecessary bloodshed (1 Sa. 17; 2 Sa. 2:12ff.). David's militia was divided into twelve battalions each serving for a month (1 Ch. 27:1ff.). Solomon used chariots (1 Ki. 4:26; 10:26), but Israel probably never had a sizeable cavalry force. The army camped in a circle or square with the senior officers at the centre (1 Sa. 26:5); civilians could visit soldiers with news and food (1 Sa. 17:17ff.).

The Roman army was organized in legions of 4,000-6,000 men, each divided into 10 cohorts, and each cohort divided into 6 centuries. An inscription evidences the Italian Cohort in Syria *c.* AD 69, composed of Roman freedmen (Acts 10:1).

The Bible also refers to spiritual armies under God's command (*e.g.* Jos. 5:13f.; 2 Ki. 6:17). In the final battle between good and evil, Christ appears as the victorious leader of heaven's armies (Rev. 19:11ff.).

See also ARMOUR; BOW AND ARROW; CAPTAIN; CHARIOT; SLING; SPEAR; SWORD; WAR.

ARNON. An important wadi running into the E side of the Dead Sea opposite En-gedi; many forts and fords (Is. 16:2) are found there. The Hebrews gained their first territory after crossing it (Dt. 2:24).

AROER. 1. A town on the N bank of the river Arnon, 22 km E of the Dead

Sea. According to the Moabite Stone, it was extended by Mesha king of Moab, about the time Jehu was king of Israel (*c.* 842-815 BC), and it remained a Moabite town until Jeremiah's time. Earlier, when it was a Reubenite town, David's census began there (2 Sa. 24:5). 2. A town of Judah, 19 km SE of Beersheba, modern Kh. Arareh; David sent gifts there in 1 Sa. 30:26-28.

ARPACHSHAD, ARPHAXAD. The son of Shem, born two years after the flood, who lived for 438 years (Gn. 11:10ff.). An Arphaxad is mentioned in the Apocrypha (Judith 1:1) but this work is largely fiction and there is no guarantee that the name is the same. The name is unknown outside the Bible.

ARPAD. A city and Aramaean province in N Syria, now Tell Rifat, 30 km NW of Aleppo. It opposed Assyria which annexed it in 740 BC; it rebelled in 720 BC and was re-conquered by Sargon II. Its fall represented the overwhelming power of Assyria (Is. 10:9).

ART. Palestine and Syria were occupied by mixed peoples and it is therefore not easy to distinguish Hebrew or Jewish art from that of contemporary nations. Even in the Canaanite period (3000-1200 BC) before Israel's invasion, a sculpture of Baal is a mixture of Egyptian, Anatolian and also Syrian styles. Archaeologists have recovered gold-covered bronze idols from Megiddo, ivory carvings from Megiddo and Lachish, and a good deal of painted pottery, dating from the later part of this period. The Hebrews do not appear to have imported their own art forms. They adorned the tabernacle under the direction of Bezalel, a man skilled in woodwork, metalwork and embroidery (Ex. 35:30ff.). As prosperity increased under David and Solomon, Phoenician artists trained the Hebrews, and from the plans of David's palace and Solomon's temple it seems Hebrew tastes were similar to their neighbours'. The second commandment, forbidding any 'graven image' did not condemn art itself but the idolatry to which it might lead (Ex. 20:4f.), and in practice it seems to have prevented representations of only the human form, for none which are undoubtedly Hebrew have been found. But the temple was highly decorated with winged human-headed lions, winged griffins, and floral and leaf patterns. In later times, the homes of the rich were expensively decorated whereas God's house was neglected, something condemned by the prophets (*e.g.* Hg. 1:4). The Hebrews also encouraged artistic expression through music and literature, which profoundly influenced later art.

Artistic media. Only a few examples of wall-painting are so far known (Je. 22:14; Ezk. 23:14). Wood-carving and panelling in the tabernacle and temple is described in the Bible (*e.g.* Ex. 36:38; 1 Ki. 6:15ff.), and elaborately carved furniture and other wooden objects have been recovered from tombs at Jericho. Ivory and bone have been carved in Palestine since 3300 BC;

carved panels from Megiddo in the 12th to 10th cents. depict lively scenes in one of which a king sits on a throne. Lotus patterns and cherubim are common designs, as well as animals lying down or suckling. Little stone sculpture has survived, although a boulder in the Lachish water-shaft (9th cent. BC), worked into the likeness of a bearded man, shows that Palestinian peoples were never without an inventive spirit. In the Maccabean period (152-37 BC) sculptors carved fruits in stone. There is every indication that the Hebrews were expert metal workers, but little has survived; the 8 cm thick bronze 'sea' of Solomon's Temple, which probably weighed about 23,000 kg and held about 50,000 litres of water, must have been a remarkable achievement of metal working skill.

See also under CARPENTER; EMBROIDERY; IVORY; JEWELS AND PRECIOUS STONES; METALWORK; MUSIC AND MUSICAL INSTRUMENTS; POTTERY; WRITING.

ARTAXERXES. Artaxerxes I ruled over Babylonia 464-424 BC, during which time Ezra and Nehemiah came back to Jerusalem (Ezr. 7:1; Ne. 2:1). It has been argued that in Ezra the Chronicler confused him with Artaxerxes II (404-359 BC), but there is no strong reason to doubt the biblical record.

ARTEMIS. The Greek name of the goddess Diana. She was worshipped as the goddess of the moon and hunting, daughter of Zeus and Leto, and twin sister of Apollo. Her temple at Ephesus, supported on 100 massive columns, was one of the seven wonders of the world, where worship of this 'virgin goddess' seems to have been fused with a fertility cult. Tradition claims that her image fell from the sky, and this is thought to refer to a meteorite. Silversmiths producing small Artemis shrines or souvenir models of the temple caused a riot when Paul visited Ephesus (Acts 19:23ff.). See also DEMETRIUS.

ARVAD. The most N of the four great Phoenician cities; modern Ruad, an island 3 km off the coast of Syria and 80 km N of Byblos (Ezk. 27:8).

ASA. The third king over the independent state of Judah, he reigned 41 years (c. 911-870 BC). He abolished pagan cults and even removed his grandmother Maacah from her official position because of her paganism (1 Ki. 15:13). His zeal was said to be a reason for peace (2 Ch. 15:15ff.), but warfare and illness later in his reign were blamed on his failure to continue in dependence on God (2 Ch. 16:7ff.).

ASAHEL (lit. 'God has made'). Name of several OT people, chief of whom was brother of Joab, one of David's thirty heroes, famous for his amazing speed. His death led to a blood feud (2 Sa. 2:18ff.; 3:27ff.).

ASAPH. A descendant of Levi, nominated as a leading singer when the ark of the covenant was brought to

Jerusalem (1 Ch. 15:17ff.). Several psalms are attributed to him (*e.g.* Pss. 73-83). The 'sons of Asaph' remained the senior family of musicians until the second Temple.

ASCENSION. The final resurrection appearance of Jesus in which the disciples saw him leave the earth (Acts 1:4-11). The story is objected to because it implies an out-dated view of 'heaven above', but it could have been an acted parable for those who did view heaven spatially. Besides, heaven is away from this earth, whatever its nature may be, and so Jesus was observed 'going away' just as he will be seen 'coming again'. The ascension shows that Jesus has gone ahead to prepare a place for his followers (Jn. 14:2); that he has completed his atoning work (Heb. 10:11ff.); that he prays for his people (*i.e.* looks after their interests, Rom 8:34; Heb. 7:25); and that he is waiting to return to establish God's kingdom (1 Cor. 15:24ff.).

ASENATH. An Egyptian priest's daughter given in marriage to Joseph by Pharaoh (Gn. 41:45), mother of Manasseh and Ephraim. Similar names are well attested in Egypt *c.* 2100-1600 BC.

ASHDOD. A major Philistine city, 6 km SE of the modern village. It had a port, and a temple of Dagon (1 Sa. 5:1ff.). It was sacked after it rebelled against Assyria in 711 BC (Is. 20:1), but was partially repopulated. As Azotus, it was attacked for idolatry by the Maccabees (1 Macc. 5:68; 10:84), but flourished (Acts 8:40) until it surrendered to the Emperor Titus.

ASHER (lit. 'happy, blessed'). Name of the eighth son of Jacob, and of an Israelite tribe descended from him. His mother was Leah's maid, Zilpah (Gn. 30:12f.). The name is known from an Egyptian papyrus to have been used at this period. The tribe had five clans (Nu. 26:44ff.), and occupied the Plain of Acre, the W slopes of the Galilean hills behind it, and the coast from Carmel to Tyre and Sidon (Jos. 19:24ff.). In New Testament times the prophetess Anna, who rejoiced to see the infant Jesus, came from the tribe.

ASHERAH. A Canaanite mother-goddess, mentioned in texts from Ras Shamra (see ARCHAEOLOGY) as a goddess of the sea, but associated in the OT with Baal (*e.g.* Jdg. 3:7). The name was also given to images representing her, which were apparently wooden (Dt. 16:21), and which Israel was commanded to destroy (Dt. 12:3).

ASHES. Alone or with sackcloth, ashes were used as a symbol of mourning (*e.g.* Je. 6:26; Mt. 11:21), of worthless objects or ideas (*e.g.* Is. 44:20), and of purification when related to the remains of sacrifices (Heb. 9:13).

ASHIMA. The god or idol of the people of Hamath (2 Ki. 17:30), unknown outside the OT.

ASHKELON. A town on the S Palestinian coast between Jaffa and Gaza, occupied from New Stone Age times to the 13th cent. AD. Captured by Judah (Jdg. 1:18), it re-established independence as a Philistine city (Jos. 13:3). It was attacked by Babylon in 604 BC (Je. 47:5f.), and became a free city in 104 BC. Herod the Great was born there, and embellished it.

ASHKENAZ. A descendant of Noah and ancestor of inhabitants of an area between the Black and Caspian Seas (Gn. 10:3); Herodotus identified them with the Scythians. See NOMADS; SCYTHIANS.

ASHTAROTH, ASHTORETH. *Pagan goddess:* A mother-goddess associated with fertility, love and war. The name was common among many ancient Semitic-speaking peoples; it was transcribed Astarte in Greek scripts. The Israelites began worshipping it soon after arriving in Canaan (Jdg. 2:13). Solomon gave the cult royal sanction (1 Ki. 11:5; 2 Ki. 23:13). Numerous clay plaques depicting naked female images found at Palestinian sites may be representations of the goddess. *Place:* A city 30 km E of the Sea of Galilee, presumably a centre of worship of the goddess. It was the captial of Bashan (Dt. 1:4), captured by Joshua (Jos. 12:4) but not occupied at once (Jos. 13:2,12); it later became a city of the Levites (1 Ch. 6:71), and is mentioned in texts found at Ebla (for which see under ARCHAEOLOGY). It is also referred to as Ashteroth-Karnaim (Gn. 14:5).

ASHURBANIPAL (lit. 'Ashur has made a son'). He became king of Assyria in 669 BC; captured Thebes in Egypt in 663 BC (*cf.* Na. 3:8); probably freed Manasseh from Nineveh (2 Ch. 33:13); and is probably the 'noble Osnappar' (Ezr. 4:10 NEB, RSV) who resettled Samaria. He collected a library of Akkadian (see ACCAD) literature at Nineveh, and died *c.* 627 BC.

ASHURITES, ASHURI. Probably to be translated in 2 Sa. 2:9 as Asherites (NEB) or Asher (GNB, NIV mg.) and linked to Jdg. 1:12 and Jos. 17:7.

ASIA. To the Greeks, Asia was the name commonly given to the region of Asia Minor based on Ephesus, which was handed over to the Romans in 133 BC. Roman control was exercised through nine or more assizes ('courts', Acts 19:38). The region extended inland to the Anatolian plateau and included the whole W coast of Asia Minor. All three metropolitan centres, Pergamum, Smyrna and Ephesus had churches in apostolic times.

ASIARCH. A term used in Acts 19:31 (RSV only) to describe wealthy aristocrats who administered the cities of Asia, and from whose ranks were drawn the honorary high priests of the Emperor cult.

ASS: See DONKEY.

ASSASSINS. A term used in Acts 21:38 (RAV, RSV) to describe armed terrorists; it was usually applied to militant Jewish nationalists. See EGYPTIAN, THE.

ASSEMBLY: See CONGREGATION.

ASSOS. A seaport of NW Asia Minor, modern Berham Koy, built on a cone of rock 230 m high, with an artificial harbour. Paul passed through it (Acts 20:13f.).

ASSURANCE. A pledge or proof giving ground for certainty, as in Acts 17:31 where Paul says that Jesus' resurrection gives 'assurance' (NEB, RSV) or 'proof' (GNB, NIV) that he will judge the world. More often in the NT, however, it means the state of being certain about salvation, based on God-given assurances. Believers may thus enjoy 'the riches of assured understanding' (Col. 2:2); approach God in assured faith (Heb. 10:22); and recall that the gospel was preached with full 'assurance' in the sense of Spirit-induced conviction in both preacher and convert (1 Thes. 1:5). Assured faith has two objects: through it God testifies that the gospel is his truth (e.g. 1 Thes. 2:13), and that believers are his children (e.g. Rom. 8:15f.); in both cases it is the Holy Spirit who provides such assurance (Eph. 1:14; 1 Jn. 3:24). A sense of assurance can be a delusion, and must be checked by external moral and spiritual tests; a believer who has accurate beliefs, is obedient to God and displays love can be confident of salvation (Tit. 1:16; 1 Jn. 2:3ff.; 3:9f.).

ASSYRIA. An ancient country in the upper Mesopotamian plain, roughly bounded on the W by the Syrian desert, on the S by Babylonia, and on the N and E by the Armenian and Persian hills. The most fertile and densely populated area lay E of the river Tigris. There are frequent references to it in the OT, where it is seen as a world power which God permitted to invade Israel and Judah but which was later destroyed for its godlessness.

Early history. Assyria was inhabited from prehistoric times; pottery from the period 5000-3000 BC has been found at Nineveh, Assur and Calah which according to Gn. 10:11f. were founded by immigrants from Babylonia. Sumerians were present at Assur by 2900 BC and Assyrian culture and language owes much to them. The country grew and prospered in the 19th cent. BC, then declined before recovering its former greatness in the 14th cent. BC. It often faced conflict with Babylon, and conflict with Aramaean tribes *c.* 1100-940 BC left David and Solomon free to strike N into Syria.

The Neo-Assyrian period (900-612 BC). Ashurnasirpal II (883-859 BC) subdued tribes and reached the Lebanon and Philistia where coastal cities paid him 'tribute' (taxes). His reign marked the start of a period of Assyrian pressure against the W which was to bring it into conflict with Israel. He used 50,000 prisoners of war to build a citadel palace and temples at Calah, which also had a zoo and a park. Shalmaneser III (858-824 BC) extended the frontiers further, and came into conflict with Hadadezer (probably Benhadad) of Damascus whom King Ahab of Israel supported in the struggle, supplying him with 2,000 chariots and 10,000 men for one battle in 853 BC, according to Assyrian annals. Shalmaneser's 'black obelisk' at Calah (Nimrud) depicts him receiving gifts from Jehu of Israel in 841 BC. Assyrian action against Syria (Aram) gave Israel a respite from attacks from that quarter, and Joash was able to recover N border towns previously lost to Syria (2 Ki. 13:25).

After a century of weakness from internal strife, Assyria under Tiglath-pileser III (744-727 BC) captured Damascus and invaded Israel, taking many prisoners into exile (2 Ki. 15:29f.). Under King Menahem the wealthy Israelites paid Tiglath-pileser 50 shekels of silver, shown by contemporary Assyrian documents to be the price of a slave, probably as a ransom to avoid deportation (2 Ki. 15:20). Judah also suffered in this campaign; Ahaz had to erect a pagan altar as part of his submission (2 Ki. 16:10ff.). When Hoshea king of Israel did not produce his annual payment to Assyria, Shalmaneser V (726-722 BC) besieged Samaria (2 Ki. 17:3ff.). His successor, Sargon II (721-705 BC), removed over 27,000 people from Samaria, breaking Israel as an independent nation.

During Sennacherib's reign (704-681 BC) Assyria moved S against the Egyptians, and Hezekiah of Judah was forced to pay them tribute (2 Ki. 18:14ff.), an act also recorded in Assyrian annals. He incurred Isaiah's disapproval by appealing to Babylon for help (2 Ki. 20:12ff.). Sennacherib besieged Jerusalem but suddenly withdrew and was later assassinated by his sons (2 Ki. 18:17-19:37). He too had used prisoners, including Jews, to rebuild Nineveh and provide it with aqueducts and parks. Esarhaddon (680-669 BC) hoped to avoid revolts by subject states by drawing up covenant-treaties with them requiring their rulers to swear eternal allegiance to Ashur, the national god; among them was Manasseh of Judah (2 Ki. 21:1-9).

After this, Assyria fell quickly. Ashurbanipal (668-c.627 BC) had to deal with the Medes who threatened Assyrian homelands, and the W city-states slowly loosened their ties to Assyria; in Judah this freedom was expressed by Josiah's reforms. The Chaldeans drove Assyria out of Babylonia in 625 BC, and with the Medes captured Assur in 614 BC and Nineveh in 612 BC as foretold by the biblical prophets Nahum and Zephaniah. Assyria was taken over completely by the Babylonians although the name was later used for its former homelands (Ezk. 23:5ff.).

Religion and culture. The Assyrian king acted as regent on earth for the national god Ashur. The Assyrian campaigns were seen at least partly to be holy wars against those who did not recognize his sovereignty. Ashur's main temple was at the capital Assur, and other deities guarded the interests of other cities; Ishtar, for example, was worshipped at Nineveh as the goddess of love and war. Divine consorts and minor deities had shrines in the main temples. Assyrian religion differed little from that of Babylonia, from which it had been derived.

Many ancient documents have been recovered from excavations, especially at Mari and Nuzi (see ARCHAEOLOGY, OLD TESTAMENT), describing military conquests, building operations, oracles, and legal matters. At Ashurbanipal's palace in Nineveh, and in the Nabu temple there, a library of some 10,000 texts has been found. Among them is a Babylonian account of the flood, part of the twelve tablets now called the 'Epic of Gilgamesh' describing its hero's quest for eternal life. An old Babylonian epic of man's creation found there is closer to the OT account than the Gilgamesh Epic, and legends such as that of Sargon who was saved at birth by being placed in a reed basket, rescued by a gardener and brought up to be king, have been compared with OT incidents. Wisdom literature includes a poem about a righteous sufferer (the 'Babylonian Job'), and advice to a prince of the same type, but not in the same spirit, as OT wisdom books. Carefully recorded observations which formed the basis of Akkadian (see ACCAD) science, medicine, and law are closely allied to texts of omens derived from inspection of men, animals, objects and plants.

Many examples of Assyrian art have been recovered. They include wall-paintings, painted glazed panels, sculptured bas-reliefs, statues, ornaments, cylinder seals, ivory carvings and bronze and metal work. The palace sculptures at Nineveh depict the siege of Lachish and the use of Judaean captives to work on building projects (2 Ki. 18:13f.).

Government. The king exercised direct authority over the country, but delegated local jurisdiction to provincial and district governors who collected and forwarded taxes. The Assyrian army was a highly-trained and well-equipped regular force of chariots, siege-engineers, bowmen, spearmen and slingers. Conquered nations were made vassals of the god Ashur, and those which rebelled were punished by invasion, looting and destruction of their cities, death of their leaders, and exile and slavery of their skilled workers; the rest were guarded by pro-Assyrian deputies. This helps to explain the attitude of the Hebrew prophets and the fear of this 'cauldron' boiling over from the north (Je. 1:13).

ATAROTH (lit. 'crowns'). 1. A city on the E of Jordan, modern Kh. Attarus. 2. A city in Ephraim, possibly the same as Ataroth-Addar (Jos. 16:2,5,7).

ATHALIAH. Several OT people, chief of whom was the daughter of Ahab, whose marriage with Jehoram king of Judah marked an alliance between N and S. To retain power, she destroyed the royal family and began to reign *c.* 842 BC (2 Ki. 11:1ff.). Her grandson Joash was hidden and later put on her throne.

ATHENS. Famous for its culture, after

the Roman conquest of Greece it became a city linked to Rome by treaty but with independent government. Apollonius, a contemporary of Paul, rebuked the Athenians for their immoral celebrations at the festival of Dionysus and for their love of human slaughter in the gladiatorial games. Paul discovered their religious interest on his visit (Acts 17:15ff.).

ATONEMENT. God's great purity, his holiness, is such that it is impossible for him to tolerate evil. He created people in order that they might be in relationship with him, but all human beings are sinful (1 Ki. 8:46; Mk. 10:18; Rom. 3:23), and cannot be close to God unless their sin is somehow removed (Is. 59:2; Col. 1:21). Atonement is the process or the means that God uses to take away sin and bring people back into a right relationship with himself. Nobody is capable of dealing with their own sin, which is why God himself has to take action. Atonement is one of the few theological terms which has its roots in Anglo-Saxon (making 'at one') rather than in Greek or Latin, which perhaps serves as a reminder that we are dealing with the everyday reality of relationship and not just an abstract concept.

Old Testament. Atonement is presented as a privilege, a concession God makes because he is gracious and merciful. Not all sin can be atoned for. 'Anyone who sins defiantly, . . . has despised the LORD'S word' and must bear the consequences himself (Nu. 15:30-31); the assumption is that such

a person would not in any case want to be in relationship with God. But for the repentant person who really wants to keep the covenant, God provided a means by which sin could be forgiven and fellowship renewed (Lv. 4:1ff.; 5:14ff.).

Leviticus gives details of a complex system of rituals including animal sacrifices which are to be carried out in order that atonement might be made (Lv. 1-7). Though it is clear, however, that atonement is necessary and that sacrifice effects atonement, it is never really explained how the system works. It appears that it was a picture, with the death of the animal symbolizing the death of the sinner, but it was always clear that the atonement was God's gift and that the sacrifice should never be seen as some kind of magic formula (Lv. 17:11; Je. 7:21-23). Obedience and a life reflecting God's justice were also required (Mi. 6:6-8). In Ps. 51:16 David even seems to indicate that as long as the sinner had a 'contrite heart' then atonement could be possible without sacrifice.

New Testament. The NT explains that although animal sacrifice was useful as a preliminary picture, atonement could be fully effected only by the death of Christ (Heb. 9:15; 10:3-4), and sins committed before this, could be forgiven only because the death of Jesus was already foreseen (Rom. 3:25-26). 'The atonement' has come to be used as a comprehensive term for the life and death of Jesus and for all that was achieved by them. The NT writers concentrate on different aspects, but all agree that the atonement reveals the love of God the Father as well as of the Son (Jn. 3:16; Rom. 5:8; Heb. 2:9 *etc*); that the death of Jesus does bring forgiveness of sins (Mt. 26:28; Rom. 4:25; 1 Pet. 2:24) and that his death was the only way to make such forgiveness possible (Mk. 8:31). The cross vindicates God's justice, showing that he does not overlook sin (Rom. 3:21-26).

Jesus is viewed as dying on our behalf (2 Cor. 5:14; 1 Jn. 2:2), his death was as our substitute so that the penalty of sin could be removed from us (2 Cor. 5:21; Gal. 3:13-14). He is described as a ransom paid for us (Mk. 10:45; 1 Tim. 2:6), and as a sacrificial lamb offered on our behalf (Jn. 1:29; 1 Cor. 5:7; 1 Pet. 1:19). But he is also our great High Priest, the one who brings the sacrifice (Heb. 5 and 8). We are told that the atonement brings freedom from slavery to sin, from God's wrath, from the curse of the law and from death itself (Rom. 6:17ff.; 5:9; Gal. 3:10ff., 1 Cor. 15:55ff.).

The variety of images used shows how complex is the NT picture of the atonement. We must ensure that our understanding of what was involved in the death of Christ does leave room for all these different pictures.

See BLOOD; EXPIATION; FORGIVENESS; PROPITIATION; RECONCILIATION; REDEEMER; SACRIFICE.

ATONEMENT, DAY OF (Yom Kippur). Lv. 16 describes this very solemn special day, the 10th day of the 7th month, just 5 days before the Feast of Tabernacles began. All work was for-bidden and a strict fast held; it was a 'plus' to the regular sacrificial system and was the one day in the year when someone, and then only the high priest, was permitted to enter behind the curtain into the holiest place. It involved a complicated series of rituals for the purification of the high priest himself, the temple and the people. These rituals included sacrifices, sprinkling of sacrificial blood about the temple and one 'scapegoat' being sent out into the desert, symbolizing the carrying away of the people's sins.

The provision for this day further emphasizes the seriousness of sin. The daily animal sacrifices were insuf-ficient for full atonement, and even the Day of Atonement had to be repeated every year. Modern Jews keep the Day of Atonement as a solemn fast, even though there is no longer a temple where they can offer sacrifices.

The Letter to the Hebrews sees these ceremonies as pointing to the atoning work of Christ. Unlike the temporary, inadequate, old system, Jesus' sacrifice was perfect, providing eternal salvation and free access for all believers into the presence of God himself (Heb. 9-10).

ATTALIA. Modern Antalya, near the mouth of the R. Cataractes (modern Aksu); the chief port of Pamphylia. Paul and Barnabas passed through it (Acts 14:25).

AUGUSTUS. An additional name adopted by Caesar Octavianus in 27 BC, to signify his moral authority. It passed to his successors as a title ('His

Imperial Majesty', NEB; 'Emperor', other EVV, in Acts 25:21,25). His long rule (43 BC to AD 14) founded a new era of peace under the Roman Empire.

AUTHORITIES, CITY. The 5 senior magistrates (later 6) at Thessalonica, controlling the republic under Roman supervision (Acts 17:6ff.); the name is also known from other states.

AUTHORITY. Scripture makes clear that all power and authority is ultimately God's, and an aspect of his unchangeable, universal and eternal kingship over his creation (*e.g.* Ps. 29:10), by which he may deal with people as he pleases (Rom. 9:21f.) and claim that all should be subject to him. Throughout the Bible, his authority is demonstrated by the reality of his judgment on those who ignore or challenge his claim. In the OT, he exercised authority through prophets, priests and kings, and through the written Scriptures (*e.g.* 2 Ki. 22-23).

As man and Messiah Jesus was given delegated authority which the centurion recognized (Mt. 8:8ff.); as Son of God he had his own authority. It is expressed through judgment (Jn. 5:22f.,27); the finality of his teaching (Mt. 7:28f.); his power to exorcize (Mk. 1:27) and to forgive sins (Mk. 2:5ff.). After his resurrection he declared he had been given kingship over the world (Mt. 28:18) and was proclaimed the divine ruler in Acts 2:36.

The apostles were Christ's commissioned representatives and were given authority by him to found and regulate his church (2 Cor. 13:10).

They prescribed discipline in his name (1 Cor. 5:4); presented their teaching as God's truth (1 Cor. 2:9ff.); and expected their decisions to be received as the Lord's command (1 Cor. 14:37). Each generation of Christians is to subject its faith and life to the norms these delegates put on record in the NT documents, thus making their authority a permanent reality. Church leaders may also claim obedience as they tend the church under Christ's authority (Heb. 13:17).

Christians should observe the authority of the state so far as it is compatible with God's direct commands (Rom. 13:1-6; Acts 4:19); and authority in the family is given to husbands and parents (Eph. 5:22f.; 6:1ff.). Jesus taught his followers to serve, not lord it over, one another (Mt. 20:25ff.).

AVEN. In Am. 1:5, probably the Beqa valley in the Aramaean kingdom of Damascus. Also used elsewhere as an abbreviation for BETH-AVEN.

AVENGER OF BLOOD. A murder victim's next-of-kin had responsibility for avenging his death; he was allowed to execute the murderer but no-one else (Dt. 24:16). The law of Moses provided safety for accidental killers. See CITIES OF REFUGE; KIN.

AWFUL HORROR: See DESOLATING SACRILEGE.

AZARIAH (lit. 'Yahweh has helped'). A common OT name for 25 different individuals. On two occasions it is used as an alternative name for people better known by other names: as an official 'throne name' for King Uzziah (*e.g.* 2 Ki. 14:21), and the Hebrew name for Daniel's companion Abednego (Dn. 1:6f.).

AZEKAH. A Judaean city in the low agricultural plains along the W coast, perhaps modern Tell ez-Zahariyeh; it was one of few points to resist the Babylonian invasion (Je. 34:7).

B

BAAL. The OT name of Hadad, a pagan storm-god; local Baals may have been distinguished from him, and the Baal Elijah confronted on Mt Carmel was probably Melqart, the god of Tyre (1 Ki. 18). In texts found at Ras Shamra (see ARCHAEOLOGY, OLD TESTAMENT) Baal is said to be son of Dagon, with Ashtaroth and Ashera as consorts. Israelites called God 'Baal' (meaning 'master', 'husband') in innocence, but this naturally caused confusion; Ho. 2:16 suggests an alternative (Hebrew) word for God as 'my husband'.

BAAL-BERITH (lit. 'Lord of the covenant'). A Canaanite god worshipped at Shechem (probably the same as Elberith in Jdg. 9:46).

BAAL-GAD. The N limit of Israel's conquest, at the W foot of Mt Hermon (Jos. 11:17).

BAAL-HAZOR. A mountain 1,016 m high 9 km NNE of Bethel, where Absalom killed Amnon his brother (2 Sa. 13:23ff.).

BAAL-MEON. One of several towns built by the Reubenites in the territory of Sihon the Amorite (Nu. 32:38). Also called Beth-baal-meon, Beth-meon, and Beon.

BAAL-ZEBUB, BEELZEBUB, BEEL-ZEBUL (lit. 'Lord of flies'). In the OT, the god of Ekron (2 Ki. 1:1ff.). In the NT, the prince of demons identified with Satan (*e.g.* Mt. 12:24ff.).

BAAL-ZEPHON (lit. 'Lord of the north'). A place in the Egyptian E Delta near which the Israelites camped; the name comes from a Canaanite god, worshipped at several places in Lower Egypt.

BAASHA. The founder of the second brief dynasty of N Israel (*c.* 900-880 BC). He exterminated Jeroboam's entire family but continued to promote pagan religion (1 Ki. 16:1ff.).

BABEL (lit. 'Gate of god'); Babylon. A city founded by Nimrod in ancient Babylonia (Gn. 10:10); Babylonian tradition says it was founded by the god Marduk. It became a synonym for the confusion of languages which was part of God's punishment for people's pride in its buildings (Gn. 11:1ff.). The tower in Gn. 11:5 was probably a multi-storied ziggurat, first developed in Babylonia *c.* 2800 BC. A Babylonian text of the king of Agade (Accad), *c.* 2250 BC, mentions his restoration of a temple-tower (ziggurat) at Babylon. The only other early reference to such a building in Babylon is by Esarhaddon who restored one in 681-665 BC, named 'The building of the foundation-platform of heaven and earth' whose 'top reaches to heaven'. Its base was 90 x 90 m and 33 m high, with 5 platforms each 6-18 m high, but of smaller area, crowned with a temple. It was demolished by Xerxes in 472 BC. Babel is linked theologically with the broken fellowship between man and God, and between nations.

BABYLON. The city on the river Euphrates, 80 km S of modern Baghdad, Iraq, which became the political and religious capital of Babylonia and its empire. According to Gn. 10:10, it was founded by Nimrod; Babylonian tradition credits its foundation to the god Marduk. Sargon I of Agade (Accad; *c.* 2400 BC) built temples there, possibly on the ruins of an earlier Babylon. About 2000 BC it was attacked by people from Ur and ruled by them. The city flourished under the Amorite 1st dynasty of Babylon until its overthrow by the Hittites *c.* 1595 BC. From then on, it struggled for independence and once petitioned Judah for help (2 Ki. 20:12ff.). Isaiah's account of its destruction (Is. 13) is worded similarly to the account of its attacker, the Assyrian Sargon II. Some of its leading citizens were deported to Samaria where they introduced Babylonian religion (2 Ki. 17:24ff.). The city was again sacked in 689 BC by Sennacherib of Assyria.

As Assyria declined, a new dynasty was founded in Babylon in 626 BC by King Nabopolassar, whose son Nebuchadrezzar II (2 Ki. 24:1) continued to restore the city. He boasted of his great city (Dn. 4:30), to which the Jewish captives were brought (2 Ki. 25:6ff.). Excavations show that at the time the city was protected by double walls large enough for chariots to drive on. The massive Ishtar Gate was at the start of the paved processional road leading to the temple of Marduk; the walls along the route were decorated with enamelled bricks showing lions, dragons and bulls (symbols of the gods). Among the palace remains are vaults believed to have been the supports for the 'hanging gardens' built by Nebuchadrezzar for Amytis, his wife, as a reminder of her homeland.

As both Isaiah and Jeremiah predicted (*e.g.* Is. 47:1ff.; Je. 50-51) Babylon was attacked by the Persians in 539 BC and its king Belshazzar killed (Dn. 5:30); the Jewish exiles were allowed to return to Jerusalem. Xerxes destroyed the city in 478 BC to suppress a rebellion, and it was only partially restored. Texts suggest a temple of Bel survived there until at least AD 75. In the NT, Babylon is used as a symbol of Rome as a world power (*e.g.* Rev. 14:8).

See also both the previous article and the next article.

BABYLONIA. The territory in SW Asia, now S Iraq, which derived its name from its capital city Babylon. It is also called Shinar (*e.g.* Gn. 10:10), and later 'the land of the Chaldeans' (Je. 24:5); in earlier times the N part was called Akkad (Accad), and the S part Sumer. The principal cities (including Babylon, Nippur and Ur) were all located on or near the R. Euphrates.

Early history. It is likely that Semites and Sumerians were among the earliest settlers. The great cities were founded in the period 2800-2400 BC; according to a Sumerian list, 8 or 10 kings ruled before the flood at several cities, including Shuruppak from which came the hero of the Sumerian flood story. Often more than one city-king tried to rule the whole area at the same time, and clashes were frequent. A strong Semitic family under Sargon founded a new city at Agade and the Akkadian dynasty, and may have restored Babylon, *c.* 2400-2200 BC. Sargon developed new methods of war with bows and arrows and gained control of Sumer too. Then the Gutians overran the N (2230-2120 BC), and in Sumer there followed a 'Golden Age' of economic and artistic wealth. Ur became the centre of power 2113-2006 BC, its rulers being given divine honours and its trade contacts extending as far as India. Severe famine and nomadic invasions ended the prosperity; it is possible that the migration of Terah and Abraham took place at this time (Gn. 11:31). Later a series of vigorous rulers in the 1st Amorite dynasty of Babylon (1894-1595 BC) held sway, but its power did not extend into Assyria. Relations between Babylon, Elam and the W at this time made possible such

a coalition as is described in Gn. 14. About 1595 BC Babylon suddenly fell to the Kassites from the E hills, and the country remained weak for some time.

Later history. A long struggle for independence from Assyria began in the 8th cent. BC after the Assyrian Tiglath-pileser III claimed the throne of Babylon in 745 BC. When Sargon II of Assyria died in 705 BC, Merodach-baladan of Babylon proposed an alliance with Hezekiah of Judah to oppose Assyria, which Isaiah denounced (2 Ki. 20:12ff.; Is. 39). Sennacherib of Assyria quelled the rebellion, and his son Esarhaddon took the throne of Babylon and did much to restore the city's fortunes. In May 672 Esarhaddon made all his vassals swear allegiance to Assyria, but rebellions continued after his death and this diverted Assyrian attention from the W and enabled Josiah to gain a measure of independence for Judah.

Nabopolassar took the throne of Babylon in 626 BC and defeated the Assyrians the following year at Sallat. In 614 BC the Medes joined the Babylonians to attack Assur, and the allies captured Nineveh in 612 BC. Then the Babylonians campaigned in Syria, and in 605 BC the crown prince Nebuchadrezzar sacked Carchemish and overran all Syria to Egypt but did not enter the hill country of Judah (2 Ki. 24:7). However, he took some hostages, including Daniel, to Babylon. In 604 BC he claimed tribute-taxes from all Syro-Palestine; Ashkelon refused and was destroyed,

which had a profound effect on Judah
(Je. 47:5ff.). In prolonged fighting between Babylon and Egypt, Jehoiakim
of Judah transferred allegiance to
Egypt, contrary to Jeremiah's advice (2
Ki. 24:1; Je. 27:9-11). In 598 BC
Nebuchadrezzar besieged Jerusalem
and captured Jehoiachin on 16 March
597 (2 Ki. 24:10ff.). Jerusalem was
destroyed in 587 BC and more captives
were taken to Babylon; Jehoiachin is
mentioned in Babylon ration-tablets
dated 595-570 BC.

A later king, Nabonidus, campaigned in Syria and N Arabia while
his son Belshazzar acted as co-regent
in Babylon, but by his return in 544 BC
the country was weak and divided.
Cyrus of Persia entered Babylon on 16
October 539 BC, the invaders having
diverted the Euphrates river in order
to penetrate the defences along the
dry river-bed. His rule in Babylon
(539-530 BC) enabled the Jews to return
home (Ezr. 1:1ff.); in the reign of
Darius (522-486 BC) the Jews completed the rebuilding of the Jerusalem
temple (Ezr. 6:15). After Persian rule,
Alexander the Great ruled Babylon
(331-323 BC), and later the country
passed into the hands of the Seleucids
(312-64 BC), the Parthians and Sassa-
nians, until conquered by the Arabs in
AD 641.

Religion and culture. The chief gods
were Anu the heaven-god, with his
temple at Erech; Enlil, the air-god, and
Ea the god of wisdom who was
especially favourable to mankind.
Ishtar became the goddess of love and
heroine of war, reckoned to be the
daughter of Sin the moon-god. Adad

was god of storms; Nergal ruled the
underworld and was god of plagues.
Marduk (Merodach) became paramount in Babylon itself after the rise of
the Amorites; the creation epic tells of
how Marduk restored order to the
universe. Nabu (Nebo) was god of
science and writing with temples at
Nineveh, Calah and elsewhere. The
spiritual and material realms were
regulated by divine laws, of which
over 100 are known. The gods were
immortal but had limited power;
myths were primarily concerned with
such things as man's search for
immortality and his relationship to the
spiritual world. There were many
classes of temple servants: chief
priests, priests, liturgists, chanters,
and musicians were among them, as
well as cult prostitutes. Exorcism was
practised, and medicine was closely
associated with religion as was the
astrology of the later Chaldean
dynasty. Sacrifices of food and drink
were offered to the gods at regular services. Special festival days were
associated with the gods, the most
outstanding being the New Year
Festival held in Spring; at Babylon this
lasted for 2 weeks, and included processions and a sacred marriage between the king and a priestess
representing the god. Personal
festivals included celebrations of birth
and marriage and the installation of
girls as priestesses.

Babylonian literature was well
developed by *c.* 2800-2500 BC, and was
influential throughout the ancient
Near East down to AD 100. It included
some 50 epics about ancient heroes

and myths; wisdom literature including a 'Babylonian Job'; parables, folk tales, miniature essays and love-songs. Works have been found of medicine, chemistry, geology, alchemy, botany, zoology, mathematics and law. From the 4th cent. BC developments included horoscopes and the zodiac.

See ACCAD; ARCHAEOLOGY, OLD TESTAMENT (*Hammurapi; Mari*); CHALDEA; MERODACH; SUMER; and the two previous articles.

BACA, VALLEY OF. A place mentioned in Ps. 84:6, rendered 'Valley of the Weeper' (JB) because it may have been lined with tombs, and 'thirsty valley' (NEB) because of an association with mulberry trees which grow in arid areas.

BAHURIM. Modern Ras et-Tmim, E of Mt Scopus, Jerusalem, where Shimei cursed David (2 Sa. 16:5).

BALAAM. Probably meaning 'to swallow down', the name occurs 50 times in Nu. 22-24. Balaam was summoned by Balak, king of Moab, to curse Israel. God first opposes Balaam, then lets him continue, then confronts his donkey with an angel before allowing him to complete the journey. Belief in the magical working of curses was widespread, but in this case they were turned into a blessing (*cf.* Ps. 109:28), illuminating that under God's protection no human curse or other magic is to be feared. The oracles of Balaam predict Israel's future greatness under David. He was later found advising the Midianites to lure Israel into the cult of Baal, for which he was killed (Nu. 31:8,16). In the NT he is a symbol of greed (2 Pet. 2:15) and immorality (Rev. 2:14). A text dating from 700 BC from the Jordan Valley tells of his involvement with other gods and reveals his wider fame.

BALAK. The king of Moab who employed Balaam to curse Israel (Nu. 22-24); see previous article.

BALM: See HERBS AND SPICES.

BAMOTH, BAMOTH-BAAL (lit. 'heights'). A stage in Israel's journey to Palestine (Nu. 21:19f.), later given to Reuben, near the river Arnon.

BAN. In the OT, the practice of consecrating to God by destruction or by total separation from common use. Idolatrous people or places were to be destroyed (*e.g.* Jos. 6:17ff.); objects were 'devoted' to the Lord's service (Nu. 18:14). The practice seems to have been neglected after the monarchy. In the NT, Christians were banned from synagogues (*e.g.* Acts 28:16ff.) and they banned immoral people from the fellowship of the church for their own ultimate welfare (1 Cor. 15:1ff.). See ANATHEMA; CURSE.

BANK, BANKER. There was no establishment in Israel for keeping private money or granting credit; valuables were either buried (Jos. 7:21) or deposited with a neighbour (Ex.

51

22:7). Later temples acted as safe-deposits (2 Macc. 3:6,10ff.). There was a banking system in Babylonia *c.* 2000 BC. A money-lender is referred to in Mt. 25:27. See DEBT; MONEY; MONEY-CHANGERS.

BANNER, ENSIGN, STANDARD. A flag which served as a rallying point, as for the Israelite tribes in the desert (Nu. 2:2f.); used symbolically of the Messiah in Is. 11:10 (*cf.* Ex. 17:15).

BANQUET. Sometimes used to represent the happiness of the coming Kingdom of the Messiah (*e.g.* Is. 25:6; Lk. 14:15ff.); Jesus said his Last Supper was a foretaste of the glory to come (Mt. 26:27ff.; Rev. 19:9).

BAPTISM. *John the Baptist.* His was probably the direct forerunner of Christian baptism, and an adaptation of Jewish ritual washings. Some of Jesus' disciples were almost certainly baptized by John (Jn. 1:35ff.), and they appeared to continue the practice early in Jesus' ministry (Jn. 3:22ff.; 4:1f.). John's baptism was primarily an expression of repentance, but also an act of preparation for the coming Messiah, symbolizing the judgment he would bring which itself would be like an immersion in the stream of God's fiery Spirit (Mt. 3:11f.).

Jesus' own baptism. This expressed his dedication to God's will and to ministry, and perhaps also was an expression of his wholehearted identification with his people. After his baptism, the Spirit came upon him (Mt. 3:13ff.), an event some have seen as a model for Christian baptism in water and Spirit, but the Gospel writers do not tie the two events under the single term 'baptism'.

Baptism in Acts. The first converts were baptized as an expression of repentance and faith (Acts 2:38,41). It was administered 'in the name of Jesus' (Acts 2:38; *cf.* Mt. 28:19), and was sometimes accompanied by the laying-on of hands as a sign of acceptance by the church (Acts 8:14ff.). The relation between water baptism and the gift of the Spirit is disputed. For the first Christians the crucial factor was the evident presence of the Spirit, and baptism played an important role in this, but it is difficult to maintain that there was a consistent single view on the subject.

Baptism in Paul's letters. In 1 Cor. 1:13-17 he takes it for granted that baptism is administered in Jesus' name; in Eph. 4:5 he sees baptism as one of the foundations of the Christian community. In Rom. 6:5 and Col. 2:12 he evokes the powerful symbolism of baptism as a burying of the old life with Christ, something he regards as a life-long process (Gal. 2:20; Phil. 3:10). He may well have understood the washing in spiritual rather than sacramental terms; against those who insisted that Christians be circumcised he set faith, not baptism, as a more effective Christian alternative and the reality of the Spirit received through faith (Gal. 3:1-4:7).

Baptism in John's writings. The rich symbolism is open to different interpretations. In Jn. 3:5 the beginning of new life in Christ is thought of perhaps as emerging from water baptism and the gift of the Spirit; as emerging from the cleansing, renewing power of the Spirit; or as requiring spiritual birth as well as natural (water) birth. The dominant thought in John is of the Spirit; 'water' in some places probably refers to the Holy Spirit (as Jn. 4:10ff.) or the old age contrasted to the new (5:2ff.).

Infant baptism. There are no direct references to it in the NT, but the possibility of there being children in the household baptisms (Acts 16:15, 33; 18:8; 1 Cor. 1:16) cannot be excluded. 1 Cor. 7:14 and Mk. 10:13ff. can support the assertion that infants of believers are part of the household of faith, although in Gal. 3 Paul argues that membership of Christ comes through faith not physical descent. The more baptism is seen as the expression of a person's faith, the less easy it is to hold infant baptism; the more baptism is seen as the expression of divine grace, the easier it is to argue for infant baptism. Either way, Christians should beware of overvaluing baptism in the way the Judaizers overvalued circumcision.

See also CIRCUMCISION; JOHN THE BAPTIST; FAITH; LAYING-ON OF HANDS; REPENTANCE; SACRAMENT; SPIRIT; WATER.

BARABBAS. A bandit arrested for murder in political terrorism (Mk. 15:7; Jn. 18:40), who was released instead of Jesus by Pilate, thus becoming an example of the effect of substitutionary atonement. The custom of such a release at Passover time has been associated with a Jewish text allowing a lamb to be offered 'for one whom they have promised to bring out of prison'.

BARAK (lit. 'lightning'). He was called by Deborah to lead Israel to victory over Canaanites under Sisera (Jdg. 4-5); he is numbered among the people of faith in Heb. 11:32.

BARBARIAN. A term applied by the Greeks to all non-Greek-speaking peoples; it was not necessarily abusive. They are included with all others in Christ (Col. 3:11).

BAR-JESUS (lit. 'son of Joshua'). A magician and false prophet also called Elymas, who attempted to persuade proconsul Sergius Paulus not to listen to Paul (Acts 13:6ff.).

BARN. Often a dry cistern in the ground, covered with earth, where grain could be stored for many years.

BARNABAS. Called 'Son of encouragement' by Luke, he was from a Jewish-Cypriot family and a cousin of John Mark (Col. 4:10), who sold his property for the common good (Acts 4:36ff.). He was regarded as an apostle (Acts 14:4,14; 1 Cor. 9:5f.). His warm-heartedness, spiritual insight and the great respect others had for him, sometimes had momentous results. He convinced the chief apostles of the genuineness of Paul's conversion (see Acts 9:27). He represented the apostles at Antioch when the number of Gentile converts caused controversy, and recognized the situation as God's work (Acts 11:19ff.), but he did temporarily withdraw from them with Peter (Gal. 2:13). He journeyed with Paul, and until they left Cyprus it was he who was apparently leader, but then Paul took over (Acts 13-14). However at the Jerusalem Council his pre-eminence in the Gentile question is recognized at the hearing and in the letter (Acts 15:1ff.). He then insisted on taking Mark on a second missionary journey, which Paul resisted (Acts 15:36ff.), breaking their working partnership but not their friendship. He was still alive when 1 Corinthians was written, but little is known about his later life.

BARRENNESS. To be a wife without bearing children was regarded as something to be condemned as well as a matter of regret, as in the case of Hannah (1 Sa. 1:10ff.). See FAMILY.

BARTHOLOMEW. One of the 12 apostles but otherwise unmentioned in the NT; being often associated with Philip, he is sometimes identified with Nathanael (Jn. 1:45ff.; *cf.* 21:2).

BARTIMAEUS. A blind beggar healed by Jesus (Mk. 10:46ff.). The story is remarkable for the persistence of his faith. The accounts in Mt. 20:29ff. and Lk. 18:35ff. contain several differences.

BARUCH (lit. 'blessed'). Jeremiah's attendant who wrote down his prophecies and read them to the people (Je. 36:4ff.). He was taken with him to Egypt (Je. 43:1ff.) where according to one tradition both died, although the Jewish historian Josephus says both were later taken to Babylon. Several apocryphal books have been ascribed to him, and Jewish tradition speaks of him as Ezra's teacher.

BARUCH, BOOK OF: See APOCRYPHA.

BARZILLAI (lit. 'man of iron'). 1. A follower of David (2 Sa. 17:27). 2. Father of Adriel who married Saul's daughter (2 Sa. 21:8).

BASEMATH (probably 'fragrant'). 1. Esau's wife (Gn. 36:3). 2. Solomon's daughter (1 Ki. 4:15).

BASHAN. A region E of Jordan and N of Gilead, famous for its fertility (*e.g.* Ps. 27:12). When Israel conquered Palestine it was ruled by Og with his capital at Ashtaroth. He was defeated at Edrei (Dt. 3:1ff.) and it was given to Manasseh. After its conquest by Tiglath-pileser III (2 Ki. 15:29) it formed part of Assyrian, Babylonian and Persian empires.

BASIC PRINCIPLES: See ELEMENTS, ELEMENTAL SPIRITS.

BASKET. The word describes containers of varying shapes and sizes, including a round basket for figs (Je. 24:1f.); a flat basket for bread (Nu. 6:15); a hamper (Mt. 14:20); and a larger container (Acts 9:25).

BATH, BATHING. The heat and dust

of E lands made constant washing essential for both health and refreshment; according to Herodotus Egyptian priests bathed four times daily (*cf.* Ex. 2:5). Bathing as it is known today is rarely mentioned in the Bible; there is no evidence of public baths in Palestine before the NT period. Bodily cleanliness was bound up with ceremonial occasions, and there are many allusions to ritual washings.

BATHSHEBA. The woman David took while her husband Uriah was an officer in the Israelite army besieging Rabbah, the Ammonite capital. David arranged for Uriah's murder and Bathsheba's entry into the royal harem, earning a rebuke from Nathan the prophet (2 Sa. 11-12).

BDELLIUM. A fragrant, transparent yellowish gum-resin, the sap of a tree, valued as a perfume. The hardened gum resembled a precious stone to which it gave its name. See COSMETICS AND PERFUMES; JEWELS AND PRECIOUS STONES.

BEAR. The last brown bear in Palestine was killed in the 1930s. Referred to proverbially in 2 Sa. 17:8 and Am. 5:19, the bear was more feared than the lion because of its greater strength and less predictable actions. In winter it might attack livestock when wild fruits were scarce.

BEARD. Israelites and their neighbours generally wore full round beards, regarding them as signs of manly vitality. To shave or cover it was a sign of grief (Is. 15:2). See HAIR.

BEAST. Used in some EVV (especially AV and RV) as a general term for animals, often replaced by 'animal' in RSV, NIV and other EVV. It refers to any living creature with sensation and voluntary movement, but more often to four-footed animals. For the beast of Revelation, see next article. See also separate articles about specific animals.

BEAST (OF REVELATION). Two beasts are mentioned. One comes from the bottomless pit (Rev. 11:7), a symbol of the last anti-Christian empire (*cf.* Dn. 7:3ff.). It is destroyed by Jesus (Rev. 20:10). The second (also called 'the false prophet') is 'from the earth' and is the public relations officer of the first (Rev. 13:11ff.). It is likewise destroyed.

BEE. From earliest times, bees were encouraged to occupy simple basket or earthenware hives, although much honey was gathered from wild bees nesting in hollow trees or rocks. Is. 7:18 reflects a tradition that people called their bees by whistling. See also HONEY.

BEELZEBUB, BEELZEBUL: See BAAL-ZEBUB.

BEER (lit. 'well or cistern'). 1. An unknown desert site on the Hebrews' journey where they received water (Nu. 21:16). 2. An unknown site to which Jotham fled (Jdg. 9:21).

BEER-LAHAI-ROI (possibly 'the well of the living one who sees me'). A place where God appeared to Hagar (Gn. 16:7ff.), and where Isaac lived (Gn. 24:62; 25:11).

BEERSHEBA (lit. 'the well of seven (lambs)'). An important well, and also the local town and district; the present town is 77 km SW of Jerusalem and about midway between the Mediterranean and S Dead Sea. Several wells are in the area, the largest 3.75 m in diameter cut through 5 m of solid rock. Abraham spent much time there (Gn. 22:19); it probably had no urban population as the seasonal nature of the pasture land would not have supported one. Isaac also lived there (Gn. 28:10), and Jacob offered sacrifices there (Gn. 46:1). It was the southernmost place of the land (Jdg. 20:1).

BEHAVIOUR: See ETHICS.

BEHEMOTH. Used in several EVV for the Hebrew plural of a general word, 'beast', and is generally reckoned to mean this everywhere except in Jb. 40:15, where it seems to be the hippopotamus, an animal which received its English name after the AV was published. It was known in the lower Nile until the 12th cent. AD and in the Orontes R. in Syria until after the time of Joseph. It is aquatic but also able to climb steep slopes in search of food (Jb. 40:20).

BEL. The name of the chief Babylonian god Marduk. It was one of the original triad of Sumerian gods, with Anu and Enki. Daniel and his friends were commanded to worship it (Bel and the dragon 3ff.). See also MERODACH.

BEL AND THE DRAGON: See APOCRYPHA.

BELIAL. Occasionally used in EVV (*e.g.* 2 Cor. 6:15) as a synonym for Satan. The derivation is obscure; it may mean 'worthless' or 'the engulfer'.

BELL. Bells for religious purposes are known from Assyria; for personal adornment from Egypt (*cf.* Ex. 28:33f.); and as part of the trappings for horses (Zc. 14:20). Early bells were openwork metal containers with a metal ball inside; clapper bells appeared after 1000 BC.

BELSHAZZAR (lit. 'Bel has protected his kingship'). The ruler of Babylon who was killed when Persians captured it in 539 BC (Dn. 5); son of Nabonidus and probably grandson of Nebuchadrezzar II. He was co-regent for 10 years while Nabonidus fought in Arabia; Daniel (7:1; 8:1) may date events by the co-regency whereas contemporary texts continued to refer to Nabonidus.

BELTESHAZZAR (possibly 'may the lady (wife of Bel) protect the king'). The Babylonian name given to Daniel (Dn. 1:7).

BENAIAH (lit. 'Yahweh has built up'). Name of several OT people including the captain of David's foreign bodyguard (2 Sa. 8:18) who was among David's 30 heroes (2 Sa. 23:20-23). Another Benaiah was in the second group of 30 (2 Sa. 23:30).

BEN-AMMI (lit. 'son of my kinship'). The child born to Lot through his incestuous union with his daughter. The Ammonites were descended from him (Gn. 19:38).

BENE-BERAK. A town in Dan (Jos. 19:45), modern el-Kheiriyeh, 6 km E of Jaffa.

BENEDICTUS. The name given to the prophecy of Zechariah from the first word in its Latin version (Lk. 1:68-79). Like other Hebrew prophecies, it reflects on previous revelations, especially in the Psalms and Isaiah. It sees the role of the Christ in spiritual terms, in keeping with the thoughts of a pious priest filled with the Holy Spirit; the concept of a religious or priestly redeemer was already known in Judaism.

BENEFACTOR. A title used in the 1st cent. to commemorate services rendered; also a title of Egyptian and Syrian kings (see Lk. 22:25).

BENE-JAAKAN. A camping ground of the Israelites W of the Wadi Arabah (Nu. 33:31f.), and a clan name (1 Ch. 1:42).

BEN-HADAD. The name of three rulers of the Aramaean Kingdom of Damascus. 1. Ben-hadad I was ruling in *c.* 900-860 BC. Asa king of Judah enlisted his aid against Baasha king of Israel (1 Ki. 15:18ff.). 2. Ben-hadad II probably ruled *c.* 860-843 BC, and was an opponent of Ahab king of Israel (1 Ki. 20). It has been suggested that he is the same person as 1 above but 1 Ki. 20:34 implies that Omri had been defeated by Ben-hadad I. 3. Ben-hadad III ruled *c.* 796-770 BC, and continued to oppress Israel, but was repelled by Jehoash (2 Ki. 13:14ff., 25). See also ARAM; DAMASCUS.

BENJAMIN (lit. 'son of the right hand'; *i.e.* 'lucky'). *Person:* The youngest son of Jacob born to the dying Rachel, who also named him 'son of my sorrow' (Gn. 35:18). After Joseph's disappearance, he became his father's favourite son. *Tribe:* The descendants of Benjamin. The name is known from 18th-cent. BC texts found at Mari in Syria, but cannot conclusively be equated with the biblical tribe. The Benjaminites occupied a strip of land in the passes between Mt Ephraim and the hills of Judah. Benjamin himself was dubbed 'a ravenous wolf' (Gn. 49:27), and the tribe was reputed for courage and skill in war, especially for its left-handed slingers (Jdg. 20:15f.). It remained largely loyal to Saul, but when Jerusalem became the capital Benjamin was drawn closer to Judah; from the restoration under Nehemiah the distinction between them was preserved only in personal genealogies.

BERACAH (lit. 'blessing'). *Person:* A

warrior who joined David (1 Ch. 12:1ff.). *Place:* A valley between Jerusalem and Hebron, W of Tekoa (2 Ch. 20:26).

BERNICE. The eldest daughter of Herod Agrippa I, born AD 28. She married her uncle Herod of Chalcis; when he died she lived with her brother Herod Agrippa II (Acts 25:13) before becoming mistress of the future emperor Titus.

BEROEA, BEREA. Modern Verria, a city of S Macedonia, a prosperous Jewish colony in NT times. Paul visited it from Thessalonica (Acts 17:5-11).

BETEN. A town of Asher (Jos. 19:25); possibly modern Abtun, E of Mt Carmel.

BETHABARA (probably 'house of the ford'). Used in AV in Jn. 1:28, for which see BETHANY.

BETH-ANATH (lit. 'temple of Anat'). A city allotted to Naphtali (Jos. 19:38), possibly Safed el-Battikh NW of Galilee.

BETH-ANOTH (probably 'temple of Anat'). A city allotted to Judah (Jos. 15:59); modern Beit Anun NNE of Hebron.

BETHANY. 1. A village 3 km from Jerusalem on the road to Jericho; the home of Jesus' friends Mary, Martha and Lazarus. 2. The place E of the Jordan where John the Baptist baptized

(Jn. 1:28). Origen used the name 'Bethabara' because it was known in his day, but the otherwise unknown 'Bethany' is more probably correct.

BETH-ARBEL. A city known only from Ho. 10:14, possibly Arbela, 30 km SE of the Sea of Galilee.

BETH-AVEN (lit. 'house of iniquity'). W of Michmash (1 Sa. 13:5), possibly different to that E of Bethel (Jos. 7:2); probably a synonym for Bethel in Hosea.

BETH-DAGON. Several places, including one in Judah (Jos. 15:41) and one in Asher (Jos. 19:27).

BETHEL (lit. 'house of God'). Tell Beitin 19 km N of Jerusalem, probably established in the Middle Bronze Age (2200-1550 BC). During that time it was prosperous and Abraham built an altar to the Lord near it (Gn. 12:8). Jacob had a vision of God there (Gn. 28:11ff.). It was allotted to the Joseph tribes which captured it (Jdg. 1:22ff.), and became a sanctuary for the ark of the covenant (Jdg. 20:18ff.). It prospered under Saul and David, and was destroyed by fire in the 6th cent. BC. Returning exiles settled there (Ne. 11:31), and it was fortified by the Syrian Bacchides *c.* 160 BC (1 Macc. 9:50). Captured by Vespasian in AD 69, it became a Roman township and flourished until the Arab conquest.

BETHESDA, BETHZATHA. A pool in Jerusalem near the Sheep Gate; there is textual uncertainty about the name. Bethesda means 'house of mercy' or 'place of outpouring'. A twin pool with porticos N of the temple area was discovered at St Anne's Church in 1856; some have identified it with that mentioned in Jn. 5:2.

BETH-HARAN. A fortified settlement of the Gadites E of the Jordan (Nu. 32:36); modern Tell-Iktanu 12 km NE of the river's mouth.

BETH-HORON (lit. 'house of Hauron', a Canaanite god of the underworld). Two towns ('upper' and 'lower') in Ephraim, about 16 km NW of Jerusalem, controlling an important route between the coastal plain and the hill country. Rebuilt by Solomon (2 Ch. 8:5), they were fortified by the Jews after the exile (Judith 4:4f.) and by the Syrian Bacchides (1 Macc. 9:50).

BETH-JESHIMOTH (lit. 'house of the deserts'). A place near the NE shore of the Dead Sea allotted to Reuben by Moses.

BETHLEHEM (lit. 'house of bread', *i.e.* 'food'). The city of David 9 km S of Jerusalem, previously called Ephrath (Gn. 35:19). Jesus was born there; it was prophesied as the Messiah's birthplace (Mi. 5:2). A second Bethlehem lay 11 km NW of Nazareth.

BETH-MARCABOTH (lit. 'house of the chariots'). A place allotted to Simeon (Jos. 19:5), probably a strongpoint on the Judaean-Philistine border.

BETH-NIMRAH (lit. 'house of pure water' or 'house of leopard'). Possibly 24 km E of Jericho (Nu. 32:36).

BETH-PEOR (lit. 'Temple of Peor'). A place in the hill country E of the Jordan, near which the Israelites received their final exhortation before entering Palestine and near where Moses was buried (Dt. 4:45f.; 34:6).

BETHPHAGE (lit. 'place of young figs'). A village near Bethany (Mt. 21:1); the site is unknown.

BETH-SAIDA (lit. 'house of fishing'). A town on the N shores of Galilee, E of the Jordan, built by Philip the Tetrarch, who called it Julius; Mk. 6:45 may refer to a suburb of Julius on Jordan's W bank.

BETHSHEAN, BETHSHAN. A city at the important junction of the Jezreel and Jordan valleys; modern Tell el-Hosn near the village of Beisan. In the 15th cent. BC Tuthmosis III of Egypt claimed to control it, and remains of the time include an extensive temple dedicated to Mekal, 'the Lord (Baal) of Bethshan'. Later Egyptian remains have also been recovered, and Philistine coffins from the 12th cent. suggest these people occupied a mercenary garrison for Rameses II, whose statue was found there. Temples dedicated to Resheph and Antit may have been those of Dagon and Ashteroth in which Saul's head and armour were displayed (1 Sa. 31:10; 1 Ch. 10:10). The city must have finally fallen to Israel under David;

there are few remains from then until the Hellenistic period (330-37 BC).

BETH-SHEMESH (lit. 'house of the sun'). An important city of Judah on the N border with Dan in a valley 24 km W of Jerusalem, commanding a route from the hill country to the coastal plains; probably modern Tell er-Rumeileh. It was first settled before 2000 BC, and became a strongly-fortified Canaanite city later inhabited by the Philistines. The Israelites must have taken it because it was given to the Levites (Jos. 21:16); by Samuel's time it was certainly under their control because the ark of the covenant was returned there (1 Sa. 6). It was destroyed in the 10th cent., probably by the Egyptian king Shishak (1 Ki. 14:25ff.), but a century later was the scene of Israel's victory over Judah (2 Ki. 14:11ff.). It was finally destroyed by Nebuchadrezzar in the 6th cent. BC.

BETH-SHITTAH (lit. 'house of the acacia'). An otherwise unknown town near Abel-meholah (Jdg. 7:22).

BETHZATHA: See BETHESDA.

BETH-ZUR. A city in Judah (Jos. 15:58), modern Kh. et-Tubeiqah, 6 km N of Hebron. The Hyksos built massive defensive walls there in the 17th cent. BC but it was largely abandoned during the late Bronze Age (1550-1200 BC), so offered no defence to Joshua. It was occupied throughout the monarchy, abandoned during the exile and resettled in the Persian period (587-330 BC), but came to greatest importance in the Hellenistic period (330-37 BC). It was then a garrison guarding the Jerusalem-Hebron road on the Judah-Idumaea border, and it figured prominently in the Maccabean wars.

BEULAH. 'Married.' A symbolic name for Israel's land in Is. 62:4 (AV), expressing its relationship to God and its people.

BEZALEL, BEZALEEL (lit. 'in the shadow (protection) of God'). A skilled craftsman (Ex. 31:1ff.; 35:30ff.).

BIBLE. The name is from a Greek word for 'books'; the Bible contains the books which are acknowledged by the Christian church as authoritative. The earliest use of the name is in 2 Clement 14:2 (c. AD 150). In the NT, the term 'the writings' or 'the scriptures' is used for all or part of the OT (e.g. Mt. 21:42; 2 Tim. 3:15f.). In churches of the Reformation, the Bible is the final court of appeal in matters of faith and doctrine, while in Roman, Greek and other ancient communions it is placed alongside the living tradition of the church as the ultimate authority.

Content. There is not complete agreement among Christians. Some branches of the Syrian church do not include 2 Peter, 2 and 3 John, Jude and Revelation in the NT. The Roman and Greek churches include some books which are regarded as useful but not authoritative by Anglicans and Lutherans and so included in the 'Apocrypha', but which other

Reformed churches have excluded altogether.

The two 'testaments' are so called from a word which is more usually translated 'covenant'. The OT books are associated with the old covenant between God and man (Ex. 24:7f.), and look forward to a new one (Je. 31:31ff.) which the NT sees as inaugurated by Christ (1 Cor. 11:25; Heb. 8:13).

The Old Testament. The 39 books are arranged in three divisions: the Law (Genesis—Deuteronomy); the Prophets (the 'Former Prophets', Joshua, Judges, Samuel, Kings; the 'Latter Prophets', Isaiah, Jeremiah, Ezekiel and the twelve 'minor prophets'); and the Writings (the rest). The origin of this arrangement of the books cannot be traced. The divine revelation is conveyed in two ways—through mighty works and prophetic words. The events of the Exodus, for example, would not have acquired their abiding significance if Moses had not explained them to the people as God's acts of deliverance—and his words would have been fruitless without the event. This explains why history and prophecy are intermingled in the OT. It also records people's response to God's revelation for warning and encouraging future generations (1 Cor. 10:11). In it the apostles found a clear witness to Jesus Christ (Jn. 5:39) and to the way of salvation (Rom. 3:21).

The New Testament. This records the final word which God spoke in his Son, summing up, confirming and transcending the earlier revelation (Heb. 1:1f.). Most Christians for the past 1,600 years have accepted all 27 books which divide naturally into four divisions: the Gospels; the Acts of the Apostles; 21 letters written by apostles and 'apostolic men'; Revelation. This order is also roughly chronological as far as subject matter is concerned. The first to be written, however, were some of Paul's letters between AD 48 and 60. The Gospels and other writings were produced between 60 and 100. The Gospels were brought together by the early 2nd cent. By the end of the 1st cent. Paul's letters had begun to be circulated as a collection rather than individually, arranged not chronologically but in descending order of length. By the mid-2nd cent. Justin Martyr could report that 'the memoirs of the apostles or the writings of the prophets' were read at Christian meetings, setting the NT material alongside the OT.

Message. Its central message is the story of salvation, with three strands: the bringer of salvation, Jesus; the way of salvation, God's grace calling for a response of faith and obedience; and the heirs of salvation, the covenant people of Israel and the church. The Greek Bible had used the word 'church' to denote Israel as the 'assembly' of God, so the continuity between the message of the two testaments was clearer then than it may be at first to English readers. The Bible's authority stems from the fact that it is God's message to man conveyed in many ways (Heb. 1:1f.).

See also the next three articles; APOCRYPHA; INSPIRATION; OLD

TESTAMENT CANON; NEW TESTAMENT CANON; REVELATION; SCRIPTURE; TEXTS AND VERSIONS.

BIBLE, ENGLISH VERSIONS.

Anglo-Saxon and medieval versions. There was no complete English Bible until the time of John Wyclif (*c.* 1320-84). Before him, the Venerable Bede referred to poetry by a herdsman Caedmon who sang the substance and themes of Scripture in the late 7th cent., and Bede himself has been credited with at least a translation of John's Gospel, although his work has not survived. Aldhelm (640-709) may also have translated much of the Bible; a Latin Psalter with Anglo-Saxon inter-linear translation dates from his time. The Lindisfarne Gospels have an inter-linear translation dating from *c.* 950. About 1300, a metrical version of the Psalms appeared. Nicholas Hereford translated the OT soon after, and his work was completed and circulated by Wyclif and his followers. It was made from a Latin base.

Sixteenth-century developments. William Tyndale was the first to translate the NT directly from Greek into English, making use of the 1519 and 1522 editions of Erasmus' Greek NT. He was forced by English opposition to work from Germany. Two editions of 3,000 copies each were printed in 1525/6, and revised editions in 1535/6. Many copies were destroyed by opponents of the project, but it opened a new chapter of the history of the Bible and its simplicity, freshness, and vitality had a profound influence on later translations. Tyndale also published portions of the OT in 1534, based on the Hebrew text with Luther's German version and the Latin Vulgate to assist him.

Miles Coverdale also worked on the European mainland, producing the first complete Bible to be printed in English (1535), made from German and Latin versions and aided by Tyndale's. It was dedicated to Henry VIII and was licensed by the king, marking a change in royal and ecclesiastical attitudes. His capacity for beautiful rhythm and phrasing made an enduring contribution to the tradition of English Bible translation. In 1537 the so-called Matthew Bible, probably the work of John Rogers, one of Tyndale's followers, was authorized by the king to be bought and read; it was largely a compilation of Tyndale's and Coverdale's work.

Matthew's Bible was revised by Coverdale at the request of Thomas Cromwell, and appeared as the 'Great Bible' in 1539. Later editions had a preface by Archbishop Cranmer, and it was authorized for use in every church. The Psalter of this Bible is still contained in the Church of England's Book of Common Prayer.

Protestants in exile on the European continent produced the Geneva NT in 1557, which was largely the work of William Whittingham, based on the Tyndale Bible. The complete Geneva Bible was published in 1560, and dedicated to the new Queen of England, Elizabeth I. It introduced the verse divisions and used italics to identify words inserted by the translator to clarify the meaning. Because it used the word 'breeches' for the loin-cloths made by Adam and Eve (Gn. 3:7), it became known as the 'Breeches Bible'. It was more accurate than the Great Bible, but was not officially endorsed. Instead, Matthew Parker, then Archbishop of Canterbury, promoted a revision of the Great Bible which was published in 1568 and became known as the Bishops' Bible.

Meanwhile English Roman Catholics, including Gregory Martin and William Allen, themselves exiled to Europe during Elizabeth's reign, produced a NT in Rheims in 1582. It was largely based on the Latin Vulgate text, but they did refer to the Greek and to previous English versions. The OT was published in 1609-10 at Douai which gave its name to the version.

The Authorized (King James) version. At a conference at Hampton Court in 1604, John Reynolds, president of Corpus Christi College, Oxford, proposed a new translation. A majority were not in favour, but the idea appealed to King James I who wanted a uniform translation made by the finest scholars at Oxford and Cambridge, reviewed by the bishops and finally ratified by him. He appointed 54 translators who were divided into 6 teams. Their aim, stated in the preface, was 'to make a good translation better, or out of many good ones, one principal good one', which could be understood 'even of the very vulgar'. They worked from the Hebrew (OT) and Greek (NT), consulted translators and commentators in various languages, and did not slavishly stick to uniform phrasing but allowed themselves to vary it with synonyms; it is reckoned that about 60% of its text came from previous translations. On publication in 1611 it immediately displaced the Bishops' Bible in churches and slowly replaced the Geneva Bible in popularity.

Eighteenth- and nineteenth-century versions. Many revisions of the AV or new translations were made in the next 200 years. William Mace published a Greek and English NT in 1729. William Whiston (1745) and John Wesley (1755) published revisions of the AV. The Unitarian Samuel Sharpe produced a new OT from the Greek text in 1840, and many AV revisions were made using new textual information which was continually being discovered. Two versions are often credited with being the forerunners of 'modern speech' versions, Andrew Norton's translation of the Gospels (1855) and Leicester Ambrose Sawyer's NT (1858). Efforts were also made to improve the Roman Catholic English version by Cornelius Nery (NT, 1718) and Robert Witham (NT, 1730). Richard Challoner published two revisions of the Douai OT and five of the NT (1749-72), providing a simpler, more idiomatic, type of text which continued to be used into the mid-twentieth cent.; he sometimes followed the AV when he approved of its renderings.

The Revised Version. In 1870 a formal revision of the AV was undertaken by scholars belonging to the Church of England. It was agreed to make as few changes as possible to the AV, and that the changes introduced should be expressed in the language of the AV. They worked for 10 years, enlisting help from Americans, and published the NT in 1881 and the OT in 1885. They aimed at consistent translation of original words with given English words, but lost some of the rhythm and music of the AV. In 1901 American preferences were incorporated into the American Standard Edition of the RV.

Twentieth-century developments. Since the RV, there has been an unceasing flow of translations, revisions and paraphrases—in the case of the NT, at the average rate of more than one a year. They have often been inspired to make 'everyday' translations by the view that the NT Greek was the popular dialect and not the scholarly language. Notable were Weymouth's NT (1903), and Moffatt's attempt to arrange the NT in a conjectured order of literary growth and date of composition (1901); his translation of the OT was first published in 1924. Goodspeed's American NT was published in 1921, and an OT counterpart by A.R. Gordon and others in 1927.

One of the most influential versions was the Revised Standard Version, a revision of the American RV, which allows itself more freedom than both AV and RV (NT, 1946; OT, 1952; Catholic edition, 1965). J.B. Phillips' paraphrase appeared steadily from 1947 to 1957; the *Amplified NT* in 1958; and William Barclay's NT in 1968-9. Other major or influential versions include the *New American Standard Bible* (1963), prepared by evangelical scholars and admirable for study purposes; the *New International Version* (NT, 1974; OT, 1978), a freer translation than the NASB; the *New English Bible* (1961-70), an even freer rendering; and the highly popular *Today's English Version* (or *Good News Bible*; NT, 1966; OT, 1976) and the *Living Bible*, a free paraphrase (1962-71).

Roman Catholic translations include the *Westminster Version* (1913-35), with a solemn style; and R.A. Knox's NT which was authorized by the church in 1945. The *Jerusalem Bible* (1966) is related to a modern French version although not a simple translation of it. The *New American Bible* (1970) was sponsored by the Bishops' Doctrine Committee and represented a major translation effort.

See also the previous article and the next two articles.

BIBLE, INTERPRETATION OF. The Bible is given to us not just as a book to be read, but as God's word to be understood and acted upon. In general, the meaning of the text is clear but if we are to grasp its full significance it is vital that we take it seriously within its own context and this means asking several preliminary questions. A great variety of literary forms is used in different books and even within each book. So we must ask whether the passage we are reading is history, poetry, prediction, parable, teaching or anything else.

Similarly we need to think about the intention of the passage. Is a command or promise given to a specific individual, to a group within Israel, to the whole nation, to Christians or to all human beings? And if given to one group are there any indications that it is meant to apply to others? Remembering that God deals with real people in real situations, does the historical setting, or the geography of the region, or the human circumstances of the people involved throw any light on what is being said? It would be a mistake, for example, to treat Jesus' instruction to the disciples to throw the net on the boat's right side (Jn. 21:6) as a command applying at all times to all fishermen, or to assume that Is. 40:31 means that all believers will sprout wings of the same size and shape as an eagle's.

But biblical interpretation involves more than placing the texts into their appropriate literary, historical, geographical and human settings. All the books of the Bible come together to form a unity and each part must be interpreted in the light of the whole. For example, Judaeans of Jeremiah's time were wrong in taking God's promise that he would live permanently in the temple, without also heeding his warning that this depended on their obedience (1 Ki. 6:12-13; Je. 7:4). The NT sees the OT scriptures as a unity with the fact that they point forward to the work of Christ as their main unifying factor. Christians have a standard and pattern of interpretation in Jesus' use of the OT and the Holy Spirit's help is available to aid their understanding.

See also next article; BIBLE; INSPIRATION; SCRIPTURE.

BIBLICAL CRITICISM. The application to biblical writings of certain techniques to establish as far as possible their original wording, date and manner of composition, authorship and sources. There are four main types.

Textual criticism. The attempt to restore the original wording of a document which has been altered by error during the course of copying. Copies are compared and questions are asked about the scribal habits of each copyist, and the remoteness or nearness of the copy to the original. No original biblical documents or copies signed by the author exist, so textual criticism is important in establishing a reliable text for Bible study.

Literary criticism. Part of its activity is also called 'source criticism'. Source criticism can be more certain when the original source for a biblical document still exists; for example, Chronicles draws on Samuel and Kings, and Mark is generally believed to have been a principal source for Matthew and Luke. But if we only had the 2nd cent. compilation of the Gospels woven into a single narrative, known as Tatian's *Diatessaron*, it would be impossible to reconstruct the four separate Gospels. This is the kind of situation faced in the Pentateuch (Genesis to Deuteronomy). It is to now generally agreed that several sources underlie it, but what they are, what their relationship to each other is, and when they were written and incorporated into the Pentateuch, are questions on which scholars disagree.

Documents can be dated by references in them to events known from other sources, although the predictive element in prophecy requires some caution; for example, Nahum's prophecy should be dated before the fall of Nineveh (612 BC) which it foretells, but after the fall of Thebes (663 BC) which it reports.

Form and tradition criticism. Some scholars have insisted on the importance of determining the oral background of written documents and classifying them into 'forms' of narrative, utterance, poetry and so on. The Psalms have been thus classified and each type related to a characteristic setting in life, which has greatly helped our understanding of the Psalter. Form criticism applied to the Gospels in an attempt to get behind the supposed written sources to the pre-literary tradition is commonly associated with scepticism about the historical trustworthiness of the Gospels, but this is due more to the theological perspective of some scholars than to form criticism itself. To establish the life-setting of the early church in the Gospel tradition does not exclude an original life-setting in the ministry of Jesus. A major task today is to establish the continuity between the earliest form of the tradition and the historical Jesus.

Redaction criticism. Biblical authors may have received material handed down by tradition, but they shaped their material according to their own points of view. For example, much of the material in the Gospels is common to all four, but each author produced

a distinctive work. If 'tradition criticism' of the Gospels is concerned with rediscovering the teaching of Jesus, then redaction criticism is concerned with rediscovering the teaching of the Gospel writers.

See also previous article and BIBLE; GOSPELS; PENTATEUCH; TEXTS AND VERSIONS.

BILHAH. A servant given to Rachel when she married Jacob and who bore Dan and Naphtali to Jacob in her mistress' place (Gn. 29:29ff.).

BINDING AND LOOSING. Rabbinic terms used in Mt. 16:19 for Peter's authority to declare what is permitted in doctrine, and in Mt. 18:18 for the apostles' authority to condemn or absolve in disciplinary matters. See also POWER OF THE KEYS.

BIRTHDAY. The anniversary of birth was usually a day of rejoicing and often feasting. Only two are recorded in Scripture: Joseph's king (Gn. 40:20) and Herod Antipas (Mt. 14:6). Birthday celebrations are mentioned in Egyptian texts in the 13th cent. BC.

BISHOP, OVERSEER. ('Presiding elder', JB; 'church leader', GNB.) The Greek word (*episkopos*) was used of magistrates, the Roman emperor, and philosophers who acted as spiritual directors. In the NT it is applied to Christ ('Guardian', 1 Pet. 2:25, RSV); to the apostolic office (Acts 1:20); and to (several) leaders of a local congregation (Phil. 1:1). It is virtually certain that it refers to the same person and function as the word 'presbyter', usually translated 'elder', as in Acts 20:17,28 where Paul uses both words to describe the same group. The moral and spiritual qualifications for bishops are listed in 1 Tim. 3:1ff. and Tit. 1:7ff. There is no trace in the NT of church government by a single bishop; the position of James at Jerusalem was unique (Acts 15:13). Jerome, commenting on Tit. 1:5, remarks that in the early church the supremacy of a single bishop arose 'by custom rather than by the Lord's actual appointment'. See also CHURCH GOVERNMENT; ELDERS; MINISTRY.

BITHYNIA. A territory on the Asiatic side of the Bosporus administered with Pontus by the Romans as a single province. There was a well-established church there by AD 111 (cf. 1 Pet. 1:1).

BITUMEN. A natural derivative of crude petroleum found ready to hand in Mesopotamia and Palestine; it would have been the 'pitch' used to smear over Noah's ark and Moses' basket (Gn. 6:14; Ex. 2:3).

BLASPHEMY. *Old Testament.* An insult to the honour of God, which carried the death penalty (Lv. 24:10ff.). Generally it was committed by pagans (2 Ki. 19:22), and Israel's idolatry was seen as committing the blasphemy of pagans (Is. 65:7). *New Testament.* Here the meaning is also extended to God's representatives; an insulting word spoken against them is really directed against God in whose name they speak (Lk. 10:16). In Mk. 3:28 and elsewhere it is also used of slanderous language addressed to people, and is better rendered 'slander' or 'abuse', a serious thing because people are made in God's image (Jas. 3:9). Mk. 3:29 speaks of 'blasphemy against the Spirit' which can never be forgiven, a persistent and deliberate rejection of the Spirit's call to salvation through Christ. Repentance is no longer possible to a person so hardened that they cannot recognize their sin.

BLEACHING (FULLING). The process of cleansing cloth of its natural oils before dyeing or clothes-making. The cloth was trodden on a stone submerged in water (cf. 2 Ki. 18:17, 'Fuller's Field', RSV, NEB; 'Washerman's Field', NIV). Nitre imported from Egypt and mixed with white clay was sometimes used for soap; alkali for bleaching was made from the ash of the soda plant. See also DYEING; EMBROIDERY; SPINNING AND WEAVING.

BLESSED. When applied to God in the OT it has the sense of praise (*e.g.* Ps. 28:6); when applied to people it denotes a state of happiness (1 Sa. 26:25). In the NT it has a strong spiritual connotation, as in the Beatitudes (Mt. 5:3ff.), used of people to be envied or congratulated even when outwardly they may be pitied.

BLESSING. In the OT, it generally means a bestowal of (often material) good; sometimes it describes a formula of words (Gn. 27:36). In the NT it often means the spiritual good bestowed by the gospel (Eph. 1:3).

BLOOD. In both OT and NT, blood represents the violent death of a victim for the purpose of atonement. 'The blood of Christ' is often used in this sense (e.g. Rom. 5:9f.; Col. 1:20), and even in contexts where his death is seen as a sacrifice, the focus is on his blood shed in death, which makes the 'sacrifice' effective. Although it has been held that blood represents 'life', as in Lv. 17:11, 'the life of the flesh is in the blood', it can still be interpreted as life yielded up in death. See also ATONEMENT.

BOANERGES. The name given to James and John (Mk. 3:17), probably meaning 'sons of thunder', perhaps appropriate to their fiery temper (Lk. 9:54f.).

BOAT: See ARK; SHIPS AND BOATS.

BOAZ. A wealthy farmer in Bethlehem who married Ruth, who was the widow of a distant relative, and became great-grandfather of David. See RUTH, BOOK OF.

BODY. In Hebrew (OT) thought, there were no clear unifying concepts of the physical body such as the nervous or circulatory systems, and sometimes various organs are spoken of almost as if they had independent action. However, the body was not generally regarded as distinct from the soul or spirit as it was in later Greek thought. The NT avoids the Greek view that the body is evil, although Paul does use 'body of sin' indicating the sphere in which sin operates. Although there are hints at a distinction between body and spirit (e.g. 1 Thes. 5:23), even after death people are viewed as having a body as a form of expression. This may not involve a regrouping of the same material atoms, but is a 'spiritual body' like Jesus' resurrection body (1 Cor. 15:35ff.). See also articles on specific parts of the body, and FLESH; SOUL; SPIRIT.

BODY OF CHRIST. This phrase has three uses in the NT. 1. The human body of Jesus (1 Jn. 4:2f.), its transformation at the resurrection being a guarantee of the believer's resurrection body (1 Cor. 15:35ff.). 2. The bread at the Last Supper which Jesus called 'my body' (Mt. 26:26), interpreted historically as both 'This represents my sacrifice' and 'This is myself'. (See LORD'S SUPPER.) 3. Paul's description of a group of Christians (e.g. Rom. 12:5). In Romans and 1 Corinthians it refers to the unity between local church members, and in Colossians and Ephesians it signifies the universal church. It reminds Christians that their unity depends on Christ and that each individual can promote or imperil that unity.

BONES. The most durable part of the human body, and used to describe deep feelings or afflictions (e.g. Gn. 29:14). Contact with bones of a dead person caused ritual uncleanness (Nu. 19:16).

BOOK OF LIFE, BOOK OF THE LIVING. Used in the OT to describe natural life, as in Ps. 69:28. In Dn. 12:1 and in the NT it is the roster of believers (Phil. 4:3; Rev. 3:5 *etc.*). Everyone not enrolled in it will be consigned to the fiery lake (Rev. 20:12ff.).

BOOTH. Sometimes used to describe a temporary shelter made of woven boughs, used as a shelter by farmers and soldiers, and at the Feast of Tabernacles. See TABERNACLES, FEAST OF; TENT.

BOTTOMLESS PIT: See ABYSS.

BOW AND ARROW. The composite bow was usually made from strips of wood bonded with animal horn and sinews or bronze (Ps. 18:34). Arrows were made from reeds tipped with metal, and sometimes carried in a leather quiver holding 30 arrows. The Israelite tribes of Benjamin, Reuben, Gad and Manasseh were famed for their bowmen.

BOWELS. In modern EVV, used only for 'intestines' (*e.g.* 2 Sa. 20:10, RSV). In AV, used of various internal organs and as a synonym for compassion, *e.g.* 2 Cor. 6:12.

BOX. Used in AV for 'vial' (2 Ki. 9:1) and 'bottle' (Mt. 26:7).

BOZEZ and SENEH. 'Slippery' and 'pointed rock', where Jonathan entered the Philistine garrison (1 Sa. 14:4ff.); the location is unknown.

BOZRAH. A city of Edom, usually identified with modern Buseirah, 60 km N of Petra and 40 km SSE of the Dead Sea, controlling the King's Highway from Elath. Its overthrow was predicted by Amos (1:12).

BRANCH. Literally used as the bough of a tree, it is also used symbolically of the shoot from David's 'family tree' who would later rule Israel in righteousness—the Messiah (Je. 23:5; 33:15; *cf.* Is. 11:1). Zc. 3:8; 6:12 show it was a recognized Messianic term after the exile.

BREAD. The all-important commodity of the ancient Near East. In Babylonia, cereal was used as money; Hosea also partly paid for his wife in grain. Barley bread was the most widely used, but wheat bread was quite common. Ezk. 4:9 shows that even lentil and bean meal could be used for bread.

The grain was crushed in a mortar with a pestle, or ground in a mill between two stones, usually by women. The flour was mixed with water, seasoned with salt, and kneaded into dough. A small quantity of old fermented dough was added as 'leaven' to make it rise (but unleavened bread, like thin cakes, was also baked on occasions). The round flat loaves were baked over fire on heated stones or a griddle, or in an oven. Bread was early used in sacred meals (Gn. 14:18). Jesus called himself 'the bread of life' (Jn. 6:33, 35). See also FOOD; GRAIN CROPS; MEALS.

BREAD OF THE PRESENCE, SACRED BREAD, SHOWBREAD. Placed in two rows on the table in the holy place of the tabernacle (Ex. 25:30), it consisted of 12 baked cakes made from fine flour, upon which frankincense was burned, and was changed each sabbath day; the priests ate the old bread in the holy place (Lv. 24:5ff.). It was this bread which David requested (1 Sa. 21:1ff.; *cf.* Mt. 12:4). It probably signified that God is man's provider and sustainer.

BREAD, UNLEAVENED: See FEASTS; PASSOVER.

BREAST. The breast of an animal was often used as a 'wave offering' (*e.g.* Ex. 29:26). In some EVV in Jn. 13:23, it refers to Jesus' chest and John's closeness to him.

BREASTPIECE OF THE HIGH PRIEST. A square pouch with gold rings at the corners, set with 12 gems engraved with the names of Israel's tribes and containing the Urim and Thummim (Ex. 28:15ff.). It symbolized the nation resting on a high-priestly person and work; the nation being carried lovingly into God's presence; and the priest as announcer of God's will. See also DRESS; URIM AND THUMMIM.

BRICK. The commonest building material in the ancient biblical world; usually a rectangular lump of mud or clay strengthened with sand or chopped straw and usually dried in the sun; kiln-baked bricks were rare in Palestine until Roman times. The straw released an acid as it decayed which made the clay more workable. Bricks in Egypt and Babylonia were often stamped with the names of kings or of the building they were used for. In Palestine city and house walls were often built of bricks on a stone foundation. See next article; BUILDING.

BRICK-KILN. Burnt bricks were almost indestructible, and were used in Mesopotamia for facing and paving in important buildings, but were largely unknown in Palestine until Roman times; the reference to brick-kilns in 2 Sa. 12:31 (AV, RSV, NEB) is incorrect, the word being that for a mould for sun-dried bricks. The furnace into which Daniel and friends were thrown was probably a brick-kiln; a Babylonian letter (*c.* 1800 BC) and an Assyrian court regulation (*c.* 1130 BC) refer to such punishments. See also previous article.

BRIDE, BRIDEGROOM. Is. 62:5 extends the rich biblical concept of marriage and the joy of the newlyweds to God's joy in his people who are regarded as his 'bride'. This prepares the way for NT references to the church as the 'bride of Christ' (*e.g.* Eph. 5:25ff.; Rev. 19:7), in which the Lord is the divine Bridegroom lovingly seeking his bride and entering into a covenant relationship with her. Jesus used the idea himself in Mk. 2:19f., and John the Baptist in Jn. 3:29. See also MARRIAGE.

BRIMSTONE. A Middle-English word meaning 'burning stone', retained in AV, RSV and sometimes by NEB (*e.g.* Gn. 19:24); translated in GNB, NIV and occasionally in NEB as 'burning sulphur'. It is a yellow crystalline solid which burns easily in air and is found in regions of volcanic activity such as the Dead Sea valley.

BROOK. Sometimes used in EVV for a perenniel stream, the flow of water itself, and a dry river-bed.

BROTHERLY LOVE: See LOVE.

BROTHERS OF JESUS. Four men are thus described in the Gospels: James, Joses, Simon and Judas (Mk. 6:3). Three views about them have been expressed. First, they were younger children of Joseph and Mary, a natural assumption because Jesus is described as 'first-born' (Lk. 2:7) and Mt. 1:25 implies normal marital relations between Joseph and Mary after Jesus' birth. This is the common Protestant view. Secondly, they were the children of Joseph by a former wife, the doctrine of the Eastern Orthodox Church, which is without direct NT support. Thirdly, they were cousins of Jesus, the official Roman Catholic view which defends the doctrine of Mary's perpetual virginity. It is based on arbitrary assumptions about the relations between people mentioned in the Gospels. See also JESUS CHRIST, LIFE AND TEACHING.

BUILDING(S). The remains of buildings in Palestine are generally unimpressive, partly because there were few periods in its history when it was prosperous enough to sponsor monumental projects. Some of the most imposing remains from biblical times are to be found in Egypt, Mesopotamia and Greece.

Building materials. In the Roman period marble was transported up to 1,500 km, but this was unusual and transport problems usually restricted building materials to what was relatively close at hand. In the hill country of Palestine local limestone was used; on the coastlands, sandstone; in Syria, basalt. Squared masonry, as opposed to rough-hewn stones, was not used in Palestine until *c.* 1400 BC, because it was expensive and labour-intensive. Marble was used in the classical period in Greece and Asia Minor.

Timber was plentiful in Palestine; Solomon imported cedar and cypress from Lebanon for the temple (1 Ki. 5:6ff.), and excavations at Gibeah uncovered a fortress from *c.* 1000 BC which appears to have had a predominantly wooden superstructure. Wood was important for roof support, wall stresses, door and window frames even in stone buildings. Reeds were often laid across wooden rafters to form a secure base for a plaster covering to make the roof—which could easily be removed (Mk. 2:4).

Mud bricks were used from 4000 BC in Mesopotamia, later in Palestine, and were mortared to each other with mud and then coated with mud plaster; the plaster would have to be renewed each year to keep the building waterproof.

Building methods. Sites were surveyed with a measuring line (*e.g.* Ezk. 40:3), and alignment was checked with a plumb-line (Am. 7:7f.). A master builder supervised the work (*cf.* 1 Cor. 3:10) of skilled and unskilled labourers. The site was levelled if necessary, sometimes by building a stone retaining wall and filling the space behind it with rubble; the building was then erected using the wall as a foundation. Foundation-laying was sometimes accompanied by religious ritual. Foundations were prepared carefully—those of Solomon's temple were built from expensively-trimmed stone blocks (1 Ki. 5:17)—and are often all that remains of ancient buildings today. Brick houses usually had stone foundations and wooden baulks in the walls to prevent them warping as the mud bricks dried out. Some buildings had wooden beams laid on the foundation, with the bricks built on to the wood; Solomon's temple apparently employed this technique (1 Ki. 6:36). Large city walls consisted of a stone footing and a sloping rampart, which was plastered over; inside the rampart were brick walls sometimes containing rooms. Roofs, upper floors and balconies were supported by the walls and in large buildings also by rectangular pillars: rows of pillars have been found which supported the storehouses at Megiddo. Cylindrical pillars have also been found at Lachish, from the Persian period (587-330 BC). Pillars were made from wood, stone or mud bricks, and carved capitals (tops) have been recovered at some sites, the most elaborate at the Persian palaces at Persepolis and Susa.

Types of buildings. Settlements were often fortified with thick walls and fortresses. Temples and shrines are often hard to distinguish from large houses or palaces except by the objects found inside them. Temples were built to many designs and there is little uniformity; at Bethshan two have been uncovered which used Egyptian designs but were dedicated to Canaanite gods. An Israelite temple at Arad had a broad room sanctuary and a courtyard with an altar in it. A Philistine temple at Tell Qasile (*c.* 1000 BC) had wooden pillars to support the roof (*cf.* Jdg. 16:29). A palace at Megiddo, dating *c.* 1500-1200 BC, had several upper storeys arranged around a courtyard. Normal houses in Palestine were also built round courtyards with rooms on three sides.

Biblical allusions. Buildings and builders are sometimes used by Bible writers to illustrate spiritual truths. God the builder established Israel (Ps. 69:35), and the NT church is his 'building' (1 Pet. 2:4ff.). Christ is its foundation or cornerstone (1 Cor. 3:11; Eph. 2:20), on whom believers are urged to build their lives (Lk. 6:48; *cf.* 1 Tim. 6:19), and the church is like a pillar upholding God's truth (1 Tim. 3:15).

See also BRICK; CARPENTER; CORNERSTONE; FORTIFICATION;

HOUSE; PALACE; PILLAR (MO-NUMENTAL); STONEMASON; TEMPLE; TREES (for types of wood used in building).

BURDEN. Something which makes body or mind uneasy; as much as someone can bear. Used also of responsibility (Nu. 11:17); Christ's laws (Mt. 11:30); the ceremonial law and human tradition (Mt. 23:4); human infirmity (Gal. 6:2).

BURIAL AND MOURNING. *Old Testament.* In patriarchal times, successive generations were buried in cave or rock-cut family tombs: Sarah, Abraham, Isaac, Rebekah, Leah and Jacob were all buried in a cave at Machpelah. Mourning might last 7 days and included weeping, tearing clothes and wearing sackcloth (Gn. 37:34f.). The embalming of Jacob and Joseph and the use of a coffin was Egyptian practice (Gn. 50:2f.; 26). The laws of the Pentateuch (Gn.—Dt.) required prompt burial, even for executed criminals (Dt. 21:22f.). They allowed mourning by weeping and tearing clothes, but forbad cutting the flesh or beard because this was a pagan practice.

When Israel was in Palestine, the practice of burial in ancestral tombs was continued when possible. Tombs were usually outside the town; land was set aside outside Jerusalem for 'the graves of the common people' (2 Ki. 23:6). The kings of Israel were buried in a special area near Jerusalem, close to the King's Garden and the pool of Shelah (*cf.* Ne. 3:15f.); the loca-

tion was plundered by John Hyrcanus in the 2nd cent. BC, and also by Herod according to the Jewish historian Josephus. David's tomb was remembered in NT times (Acts 2:29). The most likely location is the spur which juts S between the Tyropoean and Kedron valleys overlooking the gardens and pool of Siloam. Long horizontal tunnels cut into the rock here may have been the burial places of the Davidic kings.

Graves of criminals or enemies were sometimes marked with a heap of stones (Jos. 7:26); cremation was not a normal Hebrew practice. Pottery and other objects left in tombs was a pure formality in the Israelite period compared with the elaborate Canaanite provisions for the dead. Typical mourning rites are described in 2 Sa. 1:11f., although some of the forbidden practices were also sometimes included (*e.g.* the references to shaving the head in Is. 22:12). After the funeral, a meal was usually served to mourners. Mourning is also associated with repentance (*e.g.* Ezr. 9:3). See also PILLAR (MONUMENTAL).

New Testament. The corpse of Tabitha was washed and displayed in an upstairs room (Acts 9:37). In the cases of Lazarus and Jesus, the arms and legs were bound in linen bandages impregnated with perfumes, and a linen scarf was wound round their hands (Jn. 11:44; 20:6f.). The body presumably was clothed; the 'shroud' of Mk. 15:46 (RSV; 'linen sheet', NEB) may refer to a simple robe. The Turin Shroud, which was displayed in France in the 14th cent.

and which aroused more recent debate, is a piece of linen 3 m x 1 m with the impression of a human corpse on it, which was said to be Jesus. NT and other early texts do not indicate the use of this kind of shroud in the 1st cent., and scientific evidence points to a medieval origin.

Mourning included weeping and wailing (Mk. 5:38) which a large crowd and hired musicians might join in (Mt. 9:23), and people probably beat their breasts in grief (Lk. 23:48). Many rabbinic texts encouraged burial on the same day as death occurred (*cf*. Jn. 19:31). When Jesus met a funeral procession at Nain, the body was being carried on a bier (Lk. 7:12ff.); King Herod's body in 4 BC was displayed on a golden couch studded with precious stones, and his son Archelaus threw a sumptuous funeral banquet. Mourning usually continued after the funeral for several days (*cf.* Ecclus. 22:12).

Ancient rock-cut tombs *c*. 40 BC-AD 135 surrounded three sides of the walls of Jerusalem, the most magnificent being that of Queen Helena of Adiabene. Tombs for poorer people had one or more chambers with a low square entry, with ledges for the bodies. The stone to close the entrance was either like a cork fitting into a slot round the entrance, or a rough boulder. The Gospel descriptions indicate that this was the kind of tomb Jesus was buried in. Undisturbed tombs have been found to contain ossuaries, small limestone chests in which the bones were gathered up and reburied. It is likely that the Holy Sepulchre site in Jerusalem is, or is close to, the actual burial place of Jesus; tombs in the vicinity are of the regular 1st-cent. type. The 'Garden Tomb', an attractive garden site with a simple rock-cut tomb, was first suggested as Jesus' tomb only in the 19th cent. It is not of the NT period, probably dating from the 2nd cent., but it does give the visitor an impression of what the earlier tombs were like.

BURNING BUSH. The call of Moses to be Israel's deliverer from Egypt came when he saw a bush which was in flame but was not being burnt up (Ex. 3:2). It revealed to him a living, self-sufficient, holy God who promised to be with Moses and to fulfil his past promises.

BURNING SULPHUR: See BRIMSTONE.

BUZI. The father of Ezekiel, probably from an important priestly family because Ezekiel was among the valued hostages taken to Babylon.

CABUL. A border city in Asher, 16 km NE of Carmel.

CAESAR. The name of a branch of the aristocratic Roman family Julii which controlled the republic from Augustus (31 BC) to Nero's death (AD 68). Their control was exercised through a novel compound of legal and social powers, producing such a thorough change in government that when the family was eliminated the position of 'Caesar' was institutionalized and the name taken by its holders. For Caesars mentioned in the NT, see AUGUSTUS; CLAUDIUS; NERO; TIBERIUS; see also ROMAN EMPIRE; ROME.

CAESAREA. A city built by Herod the Great on the Mediterranean shore 37 km S of Mt Carmel and named in honour of the Roman emperor Caesar Augustus. It was the official residence of the Herodian kings and Roman procurators. Standing on an overland trade route from Tyre to Egypt and with an artificial harbour, it was an important commercial centre. It had magnificent palaces and public buildings, a huge amphitheatre, and a large temple dedicated to Caesar and Rome. The population was mixed Jew and Gentile. Philip the evangelist came from it and brought Christianity to it (Acts 8:40; 21:8); Peter saw his vision of Gentile equality fulfilled there (Acts 10:1ff.); and Paul, who visited it several times, was sent there for trial (Acts 23:23ff.).

CAESAREA PHILIPPI. A city at the foot of Mt Hermon on the main source of the river Jordan, where Peter made his 'confession' of faith (Mt. 16:13ff.). Possibly the OT Baal-gad, it became Paneas under the Greeks who worshipped Pan there. Herod the Great built a temple to Caesar Augustus there, and Philip the tetrarch named it after the emperor; the title 'Philippi' distinguished it from the port.

CAESAR'S HOUSEHOLD. The equivalent of a modern civil service providing experts in most aspects of state life, a development of the Roman aristocrat's household of domestic and professional assistants. Some Roman Christians belonged to it (Phil. 4:22).

CAIAPHAS. High Priest AD 18-36, son-in-law of Annas with whom he worked closely. He was high priest at Jesus' trial.

CAIN. The eldest son of Adam and Eve, an agriculturalist. His offering to God was rejected (Gn. 4:3ff.) because he was 'of the evil one' (1 Jn. 3:12), and he killed his brother Abel. He became a nomad, but was marked in some way by God to protect him from being killed himself (Gn. 4:15).

CALAH. A city 40 km S of Nineveh on the E bank of the river Tigris (Gn. 10:11). The main citadel was rebuilt by Ashurnasirpal II of Assyria in 879 BC, when the city covered an area of 40 sq km and had a population of 60,000.

CALEB. Several OT people, chief among whom was one of the spies sent by Moses into Canaan and who believed it could be conquered; for his faith he was allowed to enter it (Nu. 13:30; 14:24). He directed the invasion of Judaea and settled at Hebron.

CALENDAR. *Old Testament.* The Hebrew year consisted of 12 lunar months (cf. 1 Ki. 4:7), beginning in the spring with the month Abib (March-April, known as Nisan after the exile). There is some evidence to suggest that the civil year began with the autumn month of Tishri (September-October). As the lunar year is some 11 days shorter than the solar year, the Hebrews must have inserted periodically a thirteenth month so that the new year was not celebrated before the spring; 1 Ki. 12:33 refers to 'the month which [Jeroboam] had devised of his own heart'. Months began when the thin crescent of the new moon was first visible at sunset. The autumn and spring equinoxes controlled the calendar, and the new year began with the new moon nearest to the spring equinox, when the sun was in Aries. Early month names were probably local Palestinian references to the seasons, but months are often referred to only by their numbers. After the exile, the Jews followed Babylonian month names. They also indicated the time of year by referring to the agricultural season: the dry season, the rainy season, the first rains, the later rains, the summer fruit, harvest and so on.

New Testament. Dates given in the NT are sometimes reckoned according to Gentile rulers, *e.g.* Lk. 3:1f., which dates John the Baptist's ministry by referring to Tiberius Caesar, Pilate, Herod, Philip, Lysanias, and the high priests Annas and Caiaphas. More usually, however, the writers measure time according to the current Jewish calendars, in which the religious feasts are used as significant markers (*e.g.* Jn.

2:13, the Passover). The calendar generally followed the Sadducees' reckoning, which regulated the temple services, reckoning Pentecost as the fiftieth day from the first Sunday after Passover. The Pharisees had minor differences in their calendar, but there was also a third (sectarian) calendar, known from the book *Jubilees* and from the Qumran community. If Jesus and his disciples followed this one, it might explain why they ate the Passover before his arrest while the chief priests and their associates ate it after his crucifixion (Jn. 18:28). See also FEASTS; SABBATH; TIME.

CALF, GOLDEN. The image set up by Aaron and the Israelites after the Exodus which they worshipped during Moses' absence; Moses destroyed it (Ex. 32:1ff.). There were bull-cults in Egypt's E Delta close to Goshen where the Israelites had lived, linked with worship of Horus. The bull was a symbol of fertility in nature, and of strength. In Canaan, the bull or calf represented Baal (Hadad), god of storm, fertility, vegetation and strength. There were other Semites in the Delta beside the Israelites, so the action in the desert may have blended contemporary beliefs.

Later, when the kingdom of Israel was split, the first king of the N kingdom, Jeroboam, set up golden calves at Bethel and Dan to be centres of Israel's worship of God (1 Ki. 12:28ff.). This led to God being identified with Canaanite nature gods, and to a loss of moral purity and social justice in the nation.

CALL, CALLING. The word occurs some 700 times in OT and NT. In the OT, when people 'call on the name of the Lord' (Gn. 4:26), they claim his protection. He also calls them to service (1 Sa. 3:4), indicating a close relationship with him which he initiates. Is. 43:1 shows God calling Israel to be his people, giving them a task and promising them his protection. In the NT the call of God is 'in Christ' (Phil. 3:14) to belong to him (1 Pet. 2:9). In Paul's letters, the call comes from God for salvation (2 Thes. 2:14), fellowship (1 Cor. 1:9) and service (Gal. 1:15); those who respond are 'called' (1 Cor. 1:24). In Mt. 22:14 Jesus distinguishes 'the called' (those who hear) from 'the chosen' (those who respond). See also ELECTION; PREDESTINATION.

CALNEH, CALNO. A city founded by Nimrod, Gn. 10:10. The site is unknown; the name may mean 'all of them' and refer to several cities. It may be that of Am. 6:2 and Is. 10:9, which is 16 km SE of Arpad.

CALVARY: See SKULL, THE.

CAMEL. An animal famous for its ability to cross desert areas, going without water for several days. Two kinds are known in the Near East, the one-humped Arabian dromedary and the two-humped Bactrian camel; they are known to inter-breed and both kinds are depicted on ancient monuments. The hump is a storage organ which is drawn on when food is short. The camel can go for a week without drinking; it can lose up to one-third of its body weight without danger, which is replaced within ten minutes when the animal is given water. Its body temperature rises from 34°C in the morning to 40°C in the afternoon, thus reducing water loss through sweating. It can live on poor vegetation. Freight camels can carry up to 200 kg and a rider; riding camels can cover 150 km in 13 hours. Its winter hair is woven into rough cloth (Mt. 3:4); its droppings are used for fuel; its hide is made into leather; its milk is a valuable food source (the Israelites were forbidden to eat its meat, Lv. 11:4).

Camels are mentioned in the Bible from the days of the patriarchs onwards. Although comparatively rare in ancient times they are known from other sources to have been domesticated by *c.* 2500 BC. They formed part of Abraham's wealth (*e.g.* Gn. 12:16), but were not used for transport except by desert traders (Gn. 37:25). Saul and David fought camel-using Amalekites (1 Sa. 30:17); Hazael brought 40 camel-loads of gifts to Elisha (2 Ki. 8:9). The camel featured in two of Jesus' most striking word pictures, Mt. 19:24 (the eye of a needle) and Mt. 23:24 (straining a gnat and swallowing a camel).

CANA. A Galilean village in the uplands W of the lake, the scene of Jesus' first miracle (Jn. 2:1ff.). The site is uncertain; one possibility is 6 km NNE of Nazareth, but some scholars prefer one 14 km N of Nazareth which

Arabs still call Cana of Galilee.

CANAAN, CANAANITES. *Person:* The son of Ham and grandson of Noah, who laid a curse on him (Gn. 9:24ff.). According to Gn. 10:15ff. and native Canaanite-Phoenician tradition, he was the ancestor of the Canaanites (see below).

Place: In Scripture Canaan usually refers to the coastal area of Syria and Palestine, and especially to Phoenicia proper, the land inhabited by the Canaanites; Nu. 13:29 and Jdg. 1:27ff. also refer to the Jordan valley and the plains and valleys, leaving the hill country to the Amorites. But the term can also cover Syria-Palestine in general, from Sidon in the N to Gaza in the S, and E to the Dead Sea. The Amarna letters (14th cent. BC) also use the term for Egypt's Syro-Palestinian territories generally.

Racial group: The inhabitants of Canaan. The term Caananite is also sometimes used in a stricter sense of 'merchant', trading being a characteristic occupation of people in Canaan ('a land of trade', Ezk. 17:4). The term tends to be overlapped by 'Amorite' which is included in Canaan in Gn. 10:15f. In Nu. 13:17-21 the Israelites prepare to conquer 'Canaan', while in Jos. 24:15, 18 the land they occupy is called 'the land of the Amorites'. There is evidence that the kingdom of Amurru in the Lebanese mountains gained a firm hold of some on the coastal areas and Canaanite seaports in the 14th/13th cents. BC, as well as evidence of Amorite occupation of the hill country (Nu. 13:29).

Just when the Canaanites appeared in Palestine is disputed. Both they and the Amorites were certainly established in Syria-Palestine by 2000 BC, and for the next 1,000 years the land was divided among Canaanite/ Amorite city-states. Between 1500 and 1380 BC these came within Egypt's Asiatic empire, but in the 14th cent. BC the N ones came under Hittite control. At the end of the 13th cent. BC the now decadent city-states were shattered by political upheavals. The Israelites under Joshua defeated some Canaanite kings in the hill country as they began their conquest of a land which God had promised them, expressing his judgment against the Canaanites' wickedness (Dt. 9:5). From the 12th cent. onward, the Canaanites were restricted to the coastal areas and emerged as the more-than-ever maritime Phoenicians, centred on Tyre and Sidon.

Most Canaanite city-states were monarchies; the king had extensive powers to conscript soldiers and to requisition land and lease it in return for taxes and services. This is directly reflected in Samuel's denunciation of Israel's request for a king like the other nations had (1 Sa. 8:10ff., c. 1050 BC). The king directly controlled military, economic and religious matters, and in larger states such as Ugarit his court was elaborately organized. The family was the basic unit of society, and there were also guilds of specialist workers—herdsmen and butchers, smiths, potters, builders. It has been suggested that there were strict distinctions between upper-class patricians and lower-class serfs.

The Canaanites had an extensive pantheon of gods, headed by El. In practice, Baal (*i.e.* Hadad, the storm god) and Dagon were more prominent. Asherah, Astarte (Ashtaroth) and Anath were goddesses of sex and war. Texts from Ugarit mention cattle, sheep and birds being sacrificed to the gods, and there are indications that human sacrifice was also practised. Literature found at Ugarit includes fragments of a Baal epic. The copies date from the 14th/13th cents. BC and the high-flown poetry demonstrates that the similar vocabulary and turns of speech of some Hebrew poetry must also be of very ancient origin.

See also ARCHAEOLOGY (OLD TESTAMENT) for Ugarit; and ASHERAH; ASHTAROTH; BAAL; CALF, GOLDEN for religion.

CANANAEAN (lit. 'Zealot, zealous'). The surname of Simon, one of Jesus' apostles (Mt. 10:4). He is called by the Greek equivalent 'Zealot' in Lk. 6:15, either because of his temperament or because of his previous association with the Zealot party. See ZEALOT.

CANDACE. The title of the Ethiopian queen whose minister was converted through Philip (Acts 8:27). Women rulers, probably queen mothers, bearing this title are well attested in literature from the Hellenistic period (330-37 BC). See ETHIOPIA.

CANNEH. A trading partner with Tyre (Ezk. 27:23), otherwise unknown but possibly in the middle Euphrates area.

CANON (OF SCRIPTURE): See NEW TESTAMENT CANON; OLD TESTAMENT CANON.

CAPERNAUM. The nearest village to the river Jordan on the NW shores of the Sea of Galilee, near a spring which watered Gennesaret; it is the mound now known as Tell Hum. Being near a political border it required a customs post (Mk. 2:14) and a military detachment (Mt. 8:5).

Excavations have shown that it was occupied continuously from the 1st cent. BC to the 7th cent. AD. Until the conversion of Constantine the Great (AD 306-337) it was a flourishing Jewish settlement and Constantine was informed about AD 335 that it was one of several towns which excluded Gentiles. It is uncertain whether a Jewish-Christian group existed there at the time, although a rabbinic story speaks of 'heretics' there in the 2nd/3rd cents. AD. A synagogue has been excavated there, with a colonnaded assembly hall connected to a courtyard. Both were built on a high platform reached by a flight of steps, and this corresponds with a description written by the pilgrim Egeria *c.* AD 383, probably about the time it was being built. She was also shown a church which she says was built from the house of the apostle Peter, using its original walls. A shrine from the early 4th cent. AD has been found, using walls from an earlier date, which had been plastered and decorated in bold colours. Among the graffiti found on fallen pieces of plaster are the words *amen, Lord* and *Jesus*. Clearly this was the traditional house of Peter visited by pilgrims. Houses excavated in the area revealed a village 800 by 250 m in extent. One block of houses could have contained 15 families (130-150 people), and consisted of small rooms opening onto a number of internal courtyards. Steps which survive must have led to terrace-roofs of earth and straw as the walls of basalt fieldstones and earth-mortar could not have supported an upper storey. This fits the incident of the paralytic in Mk. 2:4. The block in question was occupied continuously from the 1st cent. BC and the original walls retained to the 7th cent. AD.

CAPHTOR. The home of the Caphtorim, from which the Philistines came (Gn. 10:14; Je. 47:4); it is presumably the Philistines who are called Caphtorim in Dt. 2:23. It is likely to have been Crete, which controlled much of the Aegean area between 2000 and 1000 BC. See also NATIONS, TABLE OF; PHILISTINES.

CAPITAL. The ornamental top of a pillar (*e.g.* Am. 9:1); the ornamental protrusion in the tabernacle lampstand (Ex. 25:31ff.); and similar items.

CAPPADOCIA. A highland province, much of it around 900 m, in the E of Asia Minor, constituted a Roman province by Tiberius in AD 17. It produced large numbers of sheep and horses and the trade route from Cen-

tral Asia to the Black Sea ports passed through it.

CAPTAIN. More usually translated in modern EVV as 'commander' (but *cf.* Nu. 14:4; Jn. 18:12 RSV), as someone in charge of a group of soldiers. The AV reference to Jesus as 'captain' in Heb. 2:10 is better rendered with RSV as 'pioneer'. See ARMY.

CARCHEMISH. A city which guarded the main ford across the river Euphrates 100 km NE of Aleppo; modern Jerablus. Having been a Syrian city-state, it was incorporated as an Assyrian province *c.* 717 BC. In 609 BC Neco II of Egypt recaptured it (2 Ch. 35:20) but was defeated there by Nebuchadrezzar II of Babylon in 605 BC in a significant battle which led to Babylonian control of the whole region (Je. 46:2).

CARMEL (lit. 'garden land' or 'fruitful land'). A range of limestone hills *c.* 50 km long extending SE from the Mediterranean Bay of Acre to the plain of Dothan, covered with luxuriant scrub and woodland. Strictly, Mt Carmel is the main ridge, rising to 530 m, at the NW end. It was here that Elisha challenged the prophets of Baal and Asherah (1 Ki. 18:20ff.). Baal was still worshipped on Carmel as 'Zeus Heliopolites Carmel' in AD 200. A town in Judah, modern Kh. el-Karmil, some 12 km SSE of Hebron, is also called Carmel in the OT, where the selfish Nabal and his more generous wife Abigail lived when David was fleeing from Saul (1 Sa. 25).

CARPENTER. Both Joseph (Mt. 13:55) and Jesus (Mk. 6:3) followed this skilled trade. Carpenters did all woodwork tasks in housebuilding, and built furniture and agricultural tools. In large cities they made carts (or chariots in time of war). Most joinery used local cedar, cypress, oak and ash; mulberry was commonly used for agricultural implements. The carpenter's tools included a marking tool, compass or dividers, adze, small chopper, iron saw, files, bow-drill and wooden mallet, hammer, chisels and awls. By Roman times wood planes and spoke-shaves were also in use. Wood carving was done by specialists who may also have worked in bone and ivory.

CART, WAGON. In OT times they were 2- or 4-wheeled, could carry one or two drivers with a light load but tended to be unstable (*cf.* 1 Ch. 13:8); they were hauled by two oxen or milch-cows. The wheels could be solid or spoked, and sometimes had a heavy metal tread. Some wagons were covered (Nu. 7:3). See also CHARIOT.

CARVING: See ART.

CASTOR AND POLLUX: See TWIN BROTHERS.

CATHOLIC LETTERS. During the formation of the NT Canon the letters of James, 1 and 2 Peter, 1, 2 and 3 John and Jude were grouped together and called 'Catholic' (meaning 'universal') because they were mostly addressed to a wider audience than a specific church or person. Later, the term was applied to those letters accepted by the church and orthodox in doctrine, and hence meant 'genuine' or 'universally acceptable'.

CATTLE. Domesticated animals of the ox tribe are mentioned over 450 times in the OT alone. They were domesticated in New Stone Age times (10,000 BC) primarily for meat, but later the cows were kept for milk and the bulls were used for haulage. They seem to have been widely kept in Palestine, although they did best in the hill country of Upper Galilee. Several humanitarian rules about oxen are recorded in the Bible. They were to be rested and watered on the Sabbath (Ex. 23:12; Lk. 13:15), should not be muzzled when treading out corn (Dt. 25:4; *cf.* 1 Cor. 9:9); and should be led to safety when found straying (Ex. 23:4).

CAUDA. An island off Crete, modern Gavdho (Gozzo), which Paul's ship was driven close to (Acts 27:16).

CAULDRON: See FLESHPOT.

CAVE. Natural caves are common in the limestone and chalk hill country of Palestine W of the Jordan. From earliest times, they were used as dwellings: Lot and his daughters lodged in one (Gn. 19:30), as did David (1 Sa. 22:1) and Elijah (1 Ki. 19:9ff.). They were also used to hide in (*e.g.* 1 Ki. 18:4), and were common places for the burial of corpses (*e.g.* Jn.

11:38), for which see BURIAL AND MOURNING. See also QUMRAN.

CEDAR: See TREES.

CENCHREAE. A town which served as an outpost for nearby Corinth; modern Kichries. Phoebe was a deacon in the church there (Rom.16:1) and Paul kept a religious vow (Acts 18:18).

CENSER. A small, sometimes portable incense-altar or burner (*e.g.* 2 Ch. 26:19), often made of bronze and conical in shape. Small stone incense-altars with concave bowls on legs are commonly found in excavations.

CENSUS. Two censuses of men of military age give the book of Numbers its name (Nu. 1:26). The high totals—over 600,000 men—are surprising; the word now translated 'thousand' possibly may have meant 'tent group', so that in Nu. 1:21 Reuben consisted of 46 tent groups totalling 500 men, not 46,500 men. David's census in 2 Sa. 24:1ff. and 1 Ch. 21:1ff. earned him God's disapproval.

In the NT, two censuses are mentioned. That of Lk. 2:1ff. raises problems because it is otherwise unknown, but scholars agree that such a census could have taken place in Judaea near the end of Herod's reign (37-4 BC); the custom described is attested from Egypt in AD 104. The census of Acts 5:37 was held by the imperial legate Quirinius for tax purposes in AD 6 when Judaea was incorporated into the Roman provincial system, and was opposed by the Zealots. See also QUIRINIUS.

CHALDEA, CHALDEANS. A land and its inhabitants in S Babylonia, later denoting Babylonia as a whole especially during the last dynasty (626-539 BC). The Chaldeans were a semi-nomadic desert tribe who originally occupied 'Ur of the Chaldeans' (Gn. 11:28; Acts 7:4), and were distinct from the Aramaeans. A Chaldean seized the Babylonian throne in 721-710 BC and 703-702 BC, and Isaiah warned Judah not to support him (Is. 23:13). Nabopolassar began the famous Chaldean dynasty in 626 BC which included Nebuchadrezzar and Belshazzar (Dn. 5:30). The term 'Chaldean' sometimes was applied to priests, astrologers and educated persons (Dn. 2:2, 10). See BABYLONIA.

CHALKSTONES. Used in Is. 27:9 to show that idolatrous altars must be pulverized to dust.

CHAMBERLAIN. The guardian of the royal chambers, usually a eunuch (Acts 12:20); 'personal servant' (NIV).

CHARIOT. Heavy wheeled vehicles drawn by asses were used for war and ceremonial in S Mesopotamia before 2000 BC, but the true chariot did not appear until later when the horse was introduced into the Near East by people from the S Russian steppe. Many of the small Aramaean and Canaanite city-states in Palestine had chariots when the Israelites invaded; the later Assyrian empire used chariots as a major weapon. They were generally light, built of wood and leather, with an open back and fittings for shields, spears and arrows on the outside of the front or side panels. The wheels were generally 6-spoked and stood about waist-high; knives were not fitted to the wheels until Persian times (from about 500 BC). There were usually two horses yoked on either side of a pole which curved up from the floor of the car. The Egyptians had two-man crews, but the Assyrians and Israelites had a third who shielded the driver and warrior.

In the OT, the successful Joseph owned a chariot in Egypt (Gn. 46:29), and Egyptians used them to pursue the Israelites fleeing on foot (Ex. 14:9). In Palestine the Israelites faced the formidable iron-fitted chariots of the Canaanites in the plains (Jos. 17:16) and the Philistines on the coast (1 Sa. 13:5). Joshua was commanded to destroy, and not employ, the chariots he captured (Jos. 11:6ff.), and it was not until Solomon's time that they became part of Israel's army. Solomon became a horse-trader (1 Ki. 10:26ff.), and built 'chariot cities' at Hazor, Megiddo, Gezer and Jerusalem. When the kingdom was divided after Solomon's death, the N had most of the chariots, and the stables unearthed at Megiddo were probably built by Ahab who according to the Assyrian Shalmaneser III brought 2,000 (probably 200) chariots to the battle of Qarqar (853 BC). Chariots hardly feature in the NT; there are two references in Revelation (9:9; 18:13), and one in Acts 8:28.

See also HORSE; WAR.

CHARITY. Giving money or goods to the poor is not explicitly mentioned in the OT, although compassion on the poor was encouraged (Dt. 15:11). The prophets considered charitable help a right which the needy might claim; Ps. 41:1 is a command to take personal interest in the poor. In the NT, Jesus stressed the need for right motives in charitable giving (Mt. 6:1ff.). The early church appointed officers to ensure a fair distribution of gifts (Acts 4:32ff.) and each Christian was encouraged to put money aside for the poor every week (1 Cor. 16:1ff.; *cf.* Rom. 15:25ff.). For the AV use of charity as 'love', see LOVE; for the gifts organized by Paul see COLLECTION (FOR THE JERUSALEM CHURCH); see also COMPASSION; POVERTY.

CHARMS. The habit of wearing a small symbolic object as a charm or protection against evil was common throughout the ancient Near East. The charms were usually ornaments, gems, stones, seals, beads, plaques or emblems, sometimes inscribed with prayers or incantations. The Hebrews were unique in condemning the practice (*e.g.* Is. 3:20ff.). The 'frontlets' or 'phylactery' worn on the forehead, and fringes on garments (Mt. 23:5) were reminders of God's law and meant to be a deterrent to superstition and idolatry. See PHYLACTERIES.

CHASM. A word used to denote the complete separation between believers and unbelievers in both this world and the next; it occurs only in Jesus' parable in Lk. 16:19ff., for which see also ABRAHAM'S BOSOM; LAZARUS AND DIVES.

CHEBAR. A river in Babylonia by which Jewish exiles settled, and the site of Ezekiel's visions (*e.g.* Ezk. 1:1). It may have been a canal E of Nippur.

CHEDORLAOMER. The king of Elam who attacked the rebellious Sodom and Gomorrah and was killed by Abraham (Gn. 14:1ff.). He has not been definitely identified from other texts, but his name is undoubtedly Elamite.

CHEEK. To be struck on the cheek was a sign of humiliation (Mt. 5:39).

CHEMOSH. The god of the Moabites to whom children were sometimes sacrificed (2 Ki. 3:27). Solomon erected a temple to him in Jerusalem, which Josiah destroyed (2 Ki. 23:13). See MOAB.

CHEPHIRAH. A Hivite fortress 8 km W of Gibeon (Jos. 9:17); modern Kh. Kefireh.

CHERETHITES. A people who settled alongside the Philistines in S Palestine and who with the Pelethites formed David's private bodyguard (2 Sa. 20:23). They were probably native Cretans, and the Pelethites were probably Philistines (who had passed through Crete from some other original homeland).

CHERITH. An E tributary of the R. Jordan beside which Elijah was fed when he hid from Ahab (1 Ki. 17:3ff.).

CHERUBIM. The plural of cherub, a celestial being. They guarded the tree of life in Eden (Gn. 3:24), and golden figures of cherubim were placed on the ark of the covenant (covenant box) symbolically to guard its contents and by their outstretched wings to provide a visible pedestal for God's invisible throne (Ex. 25:18ff.). In Ezk. 10 God's chariot-throne was carried by cherubim. Figures of cherubim were included in the Temple decorations (1 Ki. 6:23ff.). Their appearance is not described clearly. One of Ezekiel's visions had them with two faces (Ezk. 41:18f.), another had them with four faces and four wings (Ezk. 10:21). Excavations at Samaria and Byblos (Gebal) unearthed figures with a human face, four-legged animal body and two wings, which may be representations of cherubim.

CHESULLOTH. A town of Issachar in the plain W of Tabor (Jos. 19:18); modern Iksal.

CHILDREN: See FAMILY.

CHILDREN (SONS) OF GOD. *Old Testament.* The expression is used in three ways. First, to denote membership of a class of beings; in Hebrew 'son of God' means 'god' or 'godlike'. In Ps. 29:1 'heavenly beings' is literally 'sons of gods', God's heavenly subordinates. Some see the beings of Gn. 6:1f. in this category as fallen angels, although others relate them to the second use of the expression, which is to describe men who are permitted to exercise God's judgment. Thus in Ex. 21:6, 'God' may in fact be 'judge', God's deputy exercising power of life and death; the statement in Ps. 82:6, quoted by Jesus (Jn. 10:34), also comes into this category. The third use is to describe people who are related to God by covenant. It refers to Israel as a whole ('my first-born son', Ex. 4:22); Israelites generally (Dt. 14:1); and the anointed Messiah-King (Ps. 2:7; cf. 2 Sa. 7:14).

New Testament. There is a parallel meaning to the OT Ps. 29:1 in Lk. 20:36 which refers to people in God's presence who cannot die any more. People who act in ways pleasing to God are also called his children, because they are like him (*e.g.* Mt. 5:9; Lk. 6:35). The idea of Israel as God's children is still prominent (*e.g.* Jn. 11:52; Rom. 9:4). So too is the OT sense of people who reflect God's holiness: *e.g.* Phil. 2:15, which is based on the song of Moses (Dt. 32:5ff.). But the major NT emphasis is the linking of the sonship of God's people with the special sonship of Jesus, as in Heb. 2:10ff.; Rom. 8:29. Paul stresses that because God's children are those who have faith in Christ, Gentiles as well as Jews are included (Rom. 9:4ff.). The child of God receives an inheritance of eternal life, is now controlled by the Holy Spirit, and is therefore no longer a 'slave' in bondage to sin and death (Rom. 8:12ff.). In John's writings, people become children of God by 'spiritual birth' and have the status

conferred on them by God (Jn. 1:12f.). In 1 Jn. 3 and 4 believers born of God are to reproduce the Father's love and righteousness.

See also ADOPTION.

CHINNERETH. A fortified city (Jos. 19:35) which gave its name to the Sea of Chinnereth (OT), known in the NT as Gennesaret, Galilee or Tiberias; the name could be derived from 'harp', the lake's shape.

CHIOS. An Aegean island off the W coast of Asia Minor (Acts 20:15); a free city-state until Vespasian became Emperor (AD 69-79).

CHLOE (lit. 'verdant'). A Greek female name. 'Chloe's people' (1 Cor. 1:11) were possibly Christian slaves of an Ephesian lady visiting Corinth.

CHORAZIN. A town 4 km N of Capernaum, modern Kerazeh, which Jesus denounced because it did not repent (Mt. 11:21).

CHRISTIAN. The three occurrences of the name in the NT (Acts 11:26; 26:28; 1 Pet. 4:16) all imply that it was a generally recognized title although the Christians themselves used, and possibly preferred, other titles. The word appears to be Latin, and may have meant 'soldiers of Christ', 'the household of Christ' or 'partisans of Christ'. The first of the NT occurrences dates from the late 40s AD in Antioch. This was the first church with a significant Gentile ex-pagan membership and so non-Christians would not see the church as a Jewish sect. It was probably the pagans who coined the name, and in the other two occurrences it is a non-Christian (Agrippa, Acts 26:28) and non-Christian public opinion (1 Pet. 4:16) who use it. If it was originally a nickname, it was later adopted by the Christians themselves (as Methodists adopted their nickname). It was appropriate in that it concentrated attention on the centrality of Christ to the person's faith, and the easy confusion between *Christos* and the common name *Chrestos* ('good, kind') could be turned to good effect.

CHRONICLES, BOOKS OF. Two books which together tell the story of Israel up to the division of the kingdom, and then the story of Judah up to the return from exile in Babylon. They concentrate on the nation's religious life.

Contents. Genealogies of Israel from Adam to those who returned from exile (1 Ch. 1-9); the acts of David (1 Ch. 10-29); the acts of Solomon (2 Ch. 1-9); the history of Judah from the rebellion of the N tribes to the return from exile (2 Ch. 10-36).

Authorship and date. It is anonymous, and no conclusions about authorship are possible. The last event recorded in it is the return from exile, and so it could have been written shortly afterwards. However, the listed descendants of Jehoiachin (1 Ch. 3:17-24) cover six generations after the exile to *c.* 400 BC—although the genealogies could have been supplemented after the history itself was compiled. The story

is continued in Ezra, which may indicate that Ezr. 1-6 was originally a continuation of Chronicles; Jewish tradition attributes authorship of Chronicles to Ezra.

Sources. The bulk of Chronicles (1 Ch. 10-2 Ch. 36) is parallel to 1 Sa. 31-2 Ki. 25, and is frequently identical with these earlier books. It is probable that Chronicles is a revised edition of the earlier work, but as it uses a different edition to the one which appears in the OT, it is not always possible to identify where it introduces changes. The author wanted to bring a specific message from God applied to his own day, so he reworked the text, omitted what had then become irrelevant, added new material, and changed what was misleading. Some alterations raise problems, such as the increased military and economic figures; these are perhaps due to copyists' errors or misunderstanding. The author may be like an artist painting people of the past in the dress of his own age, but where his extra material can be checked by archaeology it does have historical value. Its genealogies are dependent on Genesis, Joshua and other OT books, and its thinking reflects that of Deuteronomy and the laws of Leviticus.

Emphases and implications. It is concerned especially with faithful worship rather than military achievement; with showing David's tribe Judah to be the true Israel, which had the temple in its capital city where true worship was rightly offered; and with the people's obedience to God and trust in his power—many of the changes from Samuel-Kings clarify God's justice in Israel's history. The work represents an important stream of post-exilic thinking, concerned to affirm that God can be known, trusted and obeyed in everyday life.

CHRONOLOGY OF THE OLD TESTAMENT. The significance of events and people can be better understood if they can be dated as precisely as possible. The OT itself does not provide all the necessary data, however, and scholars attempt to relate biblical data to that provided by archaeological sources. For example, from 620 BC onwards, classical sources such as the Canon of Ptolemy can be compared with Egyptian and Babylonian texts and the margin of error never exceeds one year. Good dates are available from 1400 BC onwards because the Assyrians kept careful lists of officials appointed annually; by fixing the eclipse of the sun in June 763 BC, for example, it is possible to use these lists to date accurately events and people from 892 to 648 BC. Again, Egyptian sources between 2100 and 1200 BC can be cross-checked with Mesopotamian and astronomical data and dates usually can be fixed within a maximum error of 10 years.

Before 2000 BC, exact dates are less certain—with a margin of error up to 200 years—and before 3000 BC the only sure method of dating is by testing archaeological remains by the carbon-14 method which is accurate only to within 250 years and therefore of little use to biblical chronology. Dating is complicated by slight differences in some king-lists, and by different methods of counting years used in ancient societies, but for Israel's dates the margin of error is only about 10 years in Solomon's day, and almost nil by the fall of Jerusalem in 587 BC.

Dates before Israel's conquest of Canaan. Attempts to use biblical data to date the period from Adam to Abraham are hindered by uncertainty over its correct interpretation. For example, setting Abraham's birth at its earliest possible date of 2000 BC and following biblical genealogies provides a date of 2300 BC for the flood, which is much too late on archaeological evidence. The period of the Patriarchs (Abraham to Joseph) depends for dating largely on archaeological finds which parallel statements or descriptions in the biblical narrative. The names of the kings in Gn. 14 have not been identified with known individuals, but the names are known from the period 1900-1500 BC, as are power-alliances such as that described. Social customs of adoption and inheritance in Gn. 15,16,21 are closely paralleled in documents from Ur and elsewhere from the 18th to 15th cent. BC. On this basis, Abraham can be dated *c.* 2000-1850 BC, and Joseph 1750-1650 BC. It is also possible to relate statements in patriarchal times to later events. For example, Abraham was warned that his descendants would dwell in a foreign land for four centuries (Gn. 15:13ff.), which is recorded later as 430 years from Jacob's entry into Egypt to the Exodus (Ex. 12:40f.).

The entry of Jacob into Egypt would have been about 1700 BC; the next biblical event is the building of the Egyptian cities of Pithom and Raamses by the Hebrews, Ex. 1:11. The latter was largely built by Rameses II (*c.* 1290-1224 BC), so the Exodus is preferably dated after 1290 BC and probably before 1260 BC.

Dates from the conquest to the monarchy. It is important to interpret the biblical data carefully, because the ancient method of recording periods of time differed greatly from today's. 1 Ki. 6:1 says 480 years elapsed between the Exodus and Solomon's 4th year of rule. Subtracting 40 years of desert wanderings, 40 years of David's reign and Solomon's first 3 years gives a total of 397 years for the period from Joshua to Saul. However, if the conquest was indeed *c.* 1240 BC (see above) and David came to power *c.* 1010 BC, that allows only 230 years. But in fact all the biblical data adds up to 470 years *plus* several unknown periods (*e.g.* the length of Saul's reign). This problem is eased when it is realized that some of the records are of concurrent rather than consecutive events, as in the case of some of the judges. So, the difference between the archaeological dating of 230 years and the biblical total of 470-plus years can be absorbed. Ancient scribes did not produce synchronized lists of rulers, as is known from Egyptian sources; one list of dynasties (the Turin Papyrus) which totals 450 years must in fact fit into 234 years between *c.* 1786 and 1552 BC. David's rule lasted 40 years (1 Ki. 2:11), and Solomon's for a

similar period ending *c.* 931/30 BC. Acts 13:21 says Saul had also reigned for 40 years, and this is probably about right; he would have been about 25 when he began to rule, and biblical data shows his son Jonathan was about 40 when Saul died.

Dates from the divided monarchy to the Exile. Dates provided by Assyrian texts fix within narrow limits the reigns of the kings of Israel and Judah from the division of the kingdom (*i.e.* the accession of Jeroboam and Rehoboam) in 931/930 BC down to the fall of Samaria in 722 BC. From Hezekiah's reign in Judah to the capture of Jerusalem by the Babylonians on 15/16 March 587 BC dates can be worked out to the year using Babylonian tablets, although some uncertainty exists over the date of the final fall of Jerusalem, in 587 or 586 BC. The return from exile under Cyrus took place in the first year of his rule over Babylon (Ezr. 1:1) which was technically 538/537 BC (following his conquest of the city and accession in 539 BC). The dates of subsequent events (the rebuilding of the temple, the ministries of Haggai and Zechariah and the work of Ezra and Nehemiah) are all dated in the OT in terms of the reigns of the Persian kings, which have been accurately established. For these dates see EZRA, BOOK OF; NEHEMIAH, BOOK OF.

See also ARCHAEOLOGY (OLD TESTAMENT) for further general information. See EXODUS; ISRAEL; PATRIARCHAL AGE; articles on specific leaders and incidents for more detailed information; the chronological table (number 2 in the centre section) for a summary of OT dates; and the next article for NT data.

CHRONOLOGY OF THE NEW TESTAMENT. The early Christians had little interest in chronology and the NT documents include only scanty data.

Dates in the life of Jesus. Jesus was born before Herod the Great died (Lk. 1:5), hence before 4 BC. Quirinius was governor of Syria after 12 BC, and called a census in AD 6/7, which is too late for Lk 2:2; it is possible however that Caesar Augustus decided on a census after Herod's visit to him in 12 BC, putting Jesus' birth perhaps at 11 BC. Halley's comet was seen in 12 BC, although comets were usually seen as portents of evil, not good; some scholars have suggested that the star followed by the astrologers in Mt. 2 was a conjunction of Saturn and Jupiter, although there is little reason why this should have suggested the birth of a king. A period of about 30 years elapsed before Jesus began his ministry (Lk. 3:23). He began his ministry in AD 27-28 or AD 28-29 (Lk. 3:1). Jn. 2:20 refers to the 46 years taken to build the temple; Josephus dates Herod's decision to build it as 20-19 BC, but Herod spent some time accumulating material before construction began, so the incident could have been later than AD 26-27.

Jesus was crucified when Pontius Pilate was procurator of Judaea, AD 26-36. Several theories have been offered as to which year it was. Lk. 13:1 and 23:12 infer Pilate had been procurator for some time so it could not have been as early as 26-27. Many early authorities date it as 25 March AD 29 (*e.g.* Tertullian, *c.* AD 200); it was certainly a Friday but the Paschal full moon (Passover time) was almost certainly in April that year. The evidence of astronomy—by which the Jewish calendar was calculated—is that 15 Nisan (the Synoptic Gospels' date for the crucifixion) was a Friday only in AD 27, which is too early. But 14 Nisan (the date in John's Gospel) was a Friday in 30 and 33, and the most likely choice is one of these two years.

The length of Jesus' ministry is more important than the precise years of its start and end. Some have suggested it was 1 year, based on a literal application of 'the year of the Lord' (Lk. 4:19). Supporters of a more plausible 2-year theory maintain that the only Passovers between Jesus' baptism and crucifixion were the 3 explicitly mentioned in John (2:13; 6:4; 11:55). However, it is likely that a 4th Passover occurred between the first two mentioned by John. His comment about the time of year in 4:35 must be literal, not proverbial, so his return to Galilee in 4:43 must have been in winter. Because a long interval is implied in 5:1, the unnamed feast of that verse is likely to be the Passover of the following spring. This makes Jesus' ministry a full 3 years long.

Dates in the apostolic period. Paul's conversion occurred 3 years before his escape from Damascus (Gal. 1:18) when the city was governed by an official 'under King Aretas' (2 Cor.

11:32). Aretas took over Damascus between 37 and 40, so Paul's conversion must have been between 34 and 37, probably 34-35. Paul's visit to Jerusalem (Acts 11:30) is dated by Luke as after Agrippa's death in 44 (the narrative of Acts 12:1-24 is a flashback). The famine predicted by Agabus (Acts 11:28) was between 46 and 48, probably 46. Paul's 1st missionary journey began soon after that, returning to Antioch in autumn 47. Early the following year he visited Jerusalem for the Apostolic Council (Acts 15) and began the 2nd missionary journey later in 48. The mention of Gallio as proconsul of Achaia (Acts 18:12) means Paul probably arrived in Corinth early in 50 and may not have returned to Syria until winter 51/52; the expulsion of Jews from Rome (Acts 18:2) is dated by the Roman historian Orosius as 49-50. Paul's 3rd journey therefore could not have begun until 52, and because of sickness possibly not until 53, and as it included a 3-year stay in Ephesus could not have ended until at least 55-56.

It is likely that Paul left Ephesus in 57, crossed to Europe to meet Titus in 58, and returned to Jerusalem in 59. After two years' imprisonment in Caesarea he appealed to Caesar in 61 (Festus, Acts 24:27, was probably in office 57-61). In the autumn (Acts 27:9) he sailed for Rome, arriving there in 62. For at least 2 years until Nero's persecution in 64 Paul remained under house arrest; nothing more is known definitely of him. Irenaeus records that the apostle John lived on to the time of the emperor Trajan (c. 100), which marks the end of the apostolic period.

For more biographical details, see also JESUS CHRIST, LIFE OF; PAUL, LIFE OF. For specific problems in Paul's chronology see COUNCIL, JERUSALEM, and GALATIANS, LETTER OF. For the dating of specific NT books, see articles on those books.

CHURCH. The English word comes from a Greek original meaning 'the Lord's', but in the NT 'church' is used to translate another word meaning a local assembly of people. In Acts, Revelation, Paul's earlier letters and the letters of James and 3 John it always means a specific local congregation. In his later letters, Colossians and Ephesians, Paul uses 'church' also to mean the unified 'body' of all God's people gathered under the one head, Jesus Christ. Like the believer the church is both local on earth and 'in heaven' at the same time. He uses the pictures of a body with its members dependent on one another (1 Cor. 12:12ff.), and a building or temple of God's Spirit being erected (1 Cor. 3:10ff.). Jesus may use 'church' in Mt. 16:18 differently to Paul, meaning the gathering of apostles to form under him the restored house of David by means of which salvation would come to the Gentiles.

The Christian church first appeared in Jerusalem after Jesus' ascension, made up of a predominently Galilean band of Jesus' disciples together with those who responded to the apostles' preaching in Jerusalem. It was regarded as a sect within Judaism (*cf.* Acts 24:5), and in Jerusalem especially its members accepted the obligations of the Jewish law and temple worship. Their distinctive belief was that Jesus was the promised Messiah; their distinctive practices included baptism in the name of Jesus, regular attendance at teaching meetings led by the apostles, and household fellowship. The first leaders of the church were the 12 apostles, but that soon gave way to a Jewish pattern of eldership with James the Lord's brother as president (Gal. 2:9; Acts 15:6ff.). A pattern for the new churches was Antioch, not Jerusalem, however, and it was there that believers were first called Christians.

Paul founded many churches on the pattern of Antioch in the S provinces of Asia Minor, in Macedonia, Greece, W Asia, and Crete. He began where possible in the Jewish synagogue but in time a separate church was formed with both Jewish and Gentile converts, sometimes based on families, and with elders appointed by the apostles. The frequency of church meetings and the pattern and leadership of the Lord's Supper is unknown. The first day of the week (Sunday) could not have been used as a strict sabbath because it was not then a public holiday for Gentiles and meetings may have been at night following the close of the Jewish sabbath on Saturday evening (*cf.* Acts 20:7).

The origin of other churches is a matter of inference. There were Christians in Rome when Paul wrote to them *c.* AD 56; there had been Romans in Jerusalem on the day of Pentecost (Acts 2:10). Possibly Andronicus and Junias took the gospel there (*cf.* Rom. 16:7). The address of 1 Peter shows there were also churches scattered along the S coast of the Black Sea and the areas inland from it.

See also next article. For the concept of the church see BODY OF CHRIST; CONGREGATION. For church leadership see MINISTRY and cross-references there. For information on named churches, see articles on the appropriate places.

CHURCH GOVERNMENT. The NT does not provide a detailed code of regulations. From the NT teaching as a whole, five general principles can be deduced. 1. All authority is derived from Christ, exercised in his name and the Spirit's power. 2. His humility provides the pattern for Christian service. 3. Government is shared rather than autocratic (*cf.* Acts 15:28). 4. Teaching and ruling functions are closely associated. 5. Administrative assistants may be required to help the preachers.

The apostles were chosen to be with Jesus (Mk. 3:14); they were given power over demons and diseases (Mt. 10:1), and Christ's authority to evangelize (Mk. 3:14; Mt. 28:19). They were promised a more specific role as judges of God's people (Mt. 19:28), with power to remit and retain sins (Mt. 18:18; Jn. 20:23). Peter received these powers first (Mt. 16:18f.) as a representative of the others to whom the commission was repeated (Mt.

18:18). The apostles exercised general authority over the churches, for example supervising new developments in Samaria (Acts 8:14). When the pressure of work increased, they appointed assistants to administer the church's charity (Acts 6:1ff.). Church officers with a distinctive name (presbyter) were first appointed in Jerusalem and probably copied from the Jewish synagogue practice. The general pattern of local church government seemed to be a board of elders or pastors, possibly augmented by prophets and teachers, with deacons to help, while apostles and evangelists provided general superintendance of the whole church. It seems likely that in time one elder became permanent president of the board and was then specially designated as 'bishop'. However, there does seem to have been some variety of practice in the NT.

See also APOSTLE; MINISTRY (and cross-references there to specific functions); POWER OF THE KEYS.

CILICIA. A region in SE Asia Minor; the W part, Tracheia, was a wild plateau and the E part, Cilicia Pedias, was a fertile plain. Roman rule effectively began in 67 BC, and the province disappeared in Augustus' time, before Vespasian re-established it in AD 72, so Paul and Luke are thus correct in combining Cilicia (Pedias) with Syria before this date (Gal. 1:21; Acts 15:23, 41).

CIRCUMCISION. It originated with Abraham (Gn. 17) when the covenant between him and God was set out and expressed in the sign of circumcision. The covenant operates on the principle that the household is spiritually united with its head (Gn. 17:7, 26f.). It symbolized the costly demand of obedience and commitment which God makes of those whom he calls to himself. Circumcision was integrated into the religious system inaugurated by Moses in connection with the Passover (Ex. 12:44) and apparently continued throughout OT times (*e.g.* Je. 9:25f.).

It was a foundation feature of NT Judaism, and became the cause of controversies in the early church. Paul emphasized that without the obedience which circumcision demanded (*e.g.* Dt. 10:16) it became 'uncircumcision' (Rom. 2:25ff.). The outward sign is insignificant compared with the reality of keeping the commandments (1 Cor. 7:18f.), but although Christians no longer need such a sign they do need the inner meaning it expresses (Col. 2:11ff.). Paul often rebukes the Jews for having abandoned its primary link with Abraham's faith and equating it instead with the law of Moses (Gal. 5:2f.; Rom. 4:11f.). To Christians who are 'the true circumcision' the enforcement of the now outmoded sign is equivalent to pagan gashing of the body (Phil. 3:2f.).

CISTERN. A pear-shaped reservoir below ground for storing water collected from rainfall or a spring, with a small top opening. Most Palestinian homes had their own; public cisterns also existed, one in the temple area holding over 2 million gallons. Joseph (Gn. 37:22) and Jeremiah (Je. 38:6) almost died in such pits, which were sometimes used as prisons when empty. See also POOL; WELL.

CITIES OF REFUGE. Places of asylum for people who had committed unintentional manslaughter, to prevent the excesses of a blood-feud. The cities (which belonged to the Levites) are mentioned chiefly in Nu. 35:9ff.; Dt. 4:41ff.; 19:1ff.; and Jos. 20:1ff. In the latter passage they are named as Kedesh, Shechem, Hebron, Bezer, Ramoth and Golan. There was already a regulation for asylum in the oldest collection of Israel's laws (Ex. 21:12ff.), probably based on the ancient practice of regarding the altar or religious sanctuary as an asylum (*e.g.* 1 Ki. 1:50f.). But the altar may be at a great distance, and the slayer cannot stay there permanently, so the cities were provided in addition.

According to the regulations of Nu. 35, the 'congregation' in the city pronounces final judgment, according to strict criteria (vv. 12-24). The unintentional slayer is to stay in the city of refuge until the death of the high priest (vv. 25,28). This is sometimes explained as the manslayer's guilt devolving on to the high priest and being atoned for by his death, although it is better to see it as the conclusion of a definite period during which the manslayer was temporarily linked to the tribe of Levi until its head, the high priest, died and so unfastened the link. Nothing is known about the practice of this right

of asylum (except for 1 Ki. 1:50f. and 2:28f.). It is possible that as central authority in Israel became firmly established, the right of asylum became less significant. Christians rightly regard Christ as a 'refuge' but there is no biblical warrant to press further the parallel between him and the cities of refuge. See also AVENGER OF BLOOD.

CITY. *Old Testament.* The words used for city seem to have no regard to the size or rights of the settlement, which could be walled or unwalled. Many of the cities encountered by the invading Israelites were walled. In times of danger such a city would provide shelter for people in the surrounding unwalled villages. In later times some of these cities were quite large; excavations have shown the walls of Nineveh, for example, to have been 16 km in circumference. Many cities had a ring road inside the walls, with houses behind it. The number of gates varied—Jericho appears to have had only one—and these were the places where legal judgments and business deals were executed (*e.g.* 2 Sa. 15:2-6). There was usually a central commercial area too, with agricultural suburbs. In pre-Israel times, many were city-states with their own king, perhaps owing allegiance to one of the great powers such as Egypt. Some cities had specific purposes: Pithom and Raamses in Egypt were store cities, for example (Ex. 1:11), and Solomon had military cities for his cavalry (1 Ki. 9:19). Cities were sometimes used as bargaining counters in treaties between states and were even given as dowries, being transferred from one state to another (*e.g.* 1 Ki. 9:11-16). Of all OT cities, Jerusalem is given a special place as the 'city of David' and 'city of God'.

New Testament. The Greek word for city, *polis*, is often found in the NT. It is a general term for 'village' or 'town' and does not usually refer to the organization of government. Rom. 16:23 is one of few references to political city structures. Paul also speaks of Christians being citizens of heaven (Phil. 3:20). Jerusalem ranked high in Jesus' esteem as the city of the great King (Mt. 5:35) even though he also wept over its sinfulness (Mt. 23:37), and until its destruction in AD 70 it remained a centre of Christian influence and a focus of esteem. In Hebrews and Revelation the emphasis is on the heavenly Jerusalem, prefigured in Ezekiel and Jewish apocalyptic writings. Researchers have discovered similarities in Rev. 21-22 with Greek cities, including its four-sided shape, a central street, a river flanked by avenues, and all adorned with trees. The chief difference is that unlike Greek cities, the 'new Jerusalem' has no temple. Others have noticed the relation to ancient astronomy (the 12 precious stones are well-known counterparts to the signs of the Zodiac; the vast size is patterned on the vastness of space). All these elements bring out the spiritual meaning; the fulfilment of Israel's hopes; the answer to aesthetic yearnings; the manifestation of God's glory already pre-figured in the universe. It is a city of perfected people, not of walls.

See BUILDING (for walls); articles on specific cities.

CLAUDIA. A Roman Christian who greeted Timothy (2 Tim. 4:21). A common name; she has sometimes been considered the wife of Pudens.

CLAUDIUS (EMPEROR). Roman Caesar AD 41-54. He is supposed to have acted against Christians when he expelled Jews from Rome for rioting at the instigation of Chrestus (*cf.* Acts 18:2), but there is no other evidence of Jewish-Christian tension in Rome and Christ may not be meant.

CLAUDIUS LYSIAS. A Roman in charge of the garrison at the Antonia Fortress in Jerusalem who took Paul into custody (Acts 21:31ff.). His letter to Felix (Acts 23:26ff.) subtly rearranges the facts to his own advantage.

CLEAN AND UNCLEAN. Bodily cleanliness was valued and practised in the hot biblical lands; Egyptian priests for example bathed twice each day and twice each night. In the OT, the terms are generally applied to people, creatures and objects which made a person ceremonially 'unclean'.

The distinction between clean and unclean is found as early as Noah (Gn. 7:2), probably defining animals which were suitable for sacrifice. In the law of Moses, a person became temporarily unclean if he or she touched a dead body (Nu. 19:11ff.); had or came into contact with leprosy (Lv. 13-14); was subject to natural (connected with reproduction) or unnatural discharge of fluid from the body (Lv. 12,15); or ate the flesh of any unclean creature. Lists of clean (permitted) and unclean (forbidden) creatures are given in Lv. 11 and Dt. 14. Carnivorous animals and birds of prey were unclean because they consumed the blood of their victims; fish without scales (shellfish and crustaceans) were banned and are now known to have been a likely source of food poisoning; 'unclean' pigs were also potential carriers of disease. Physical disablement was also seen as a cause of 'uncleanness' but only among the descendants of Aaron who ministered at the altar. The distinctions were maintained throughout the OT period. The prophets pointed out that the 'unclean' could not walk in God's way of holiness (Is. 35:8). Hosea (9:3) and Amos (7:17) spoke of foreign lands and their food as being 'unclean'. After the exile in Babylon the distinction between clean and unclean was greatly enlarged into the Pharisaical tradition (see below).

Uncleanness kept a person from the sanctuary and from social contact with others, but provision was made for 'cleansing'. Only the clean person could approach God (*e.g.* Ex. 30:18ff.). The usual form of purification was by washing the body and clothes (*e.g.* Lv. 15:8ff.), but for some ceremonial defilements, a sacrifice was also required (*e.g.* Lv. 12:6f.). Ps. 51:7 provides an example of the ceremonial as a picture of the spiritual or ethical truth behind it. The purpose of these laws

and remedies has been considerably debated; other nations had similar regulations so they were not simply to keep Israel separate from others. The most likely explanation combines hygienic with spiritual purposes; Israel was to be a holy people obedient to God, and the laws emphasized the concept of holiness.

In the NT, Jesus emphasized moral rather than ceremonial purity; a key passage is Mk. 7:1-23 which describes some of the Pharisees' regulations and clearly repeals the ancient laws concerning unclean food and practices. However, Jesus did encourage the healed leper to go through the traditional ceremony (Mk. 1:44), and later Paul was willing to follow a Jewish purification rite in order to make himself (and his message) acceptable to a specific Jewish audience (Acts 21:26, *cf.* 1 Cor. 9:20ff.). Peter was reminded that nothing and no-one created by God is unclean (Acts 10:10ff.), and Paul accepted the point but reminded readers not to offend more scrupulous Christians (*e.g.* Rom. 14:14).

CLEMENT. A Philippian Christian (Phil. 4:3). Some early writers identified him with the Clement who was bishop of Rome at the end of the 1st cent., but this is uncertain.

CLEOPAS (a contracted form of *Cleopatros*). A disciple who met Jesus on the Emmaus Road (Lk. 24:18).

CLIMATE: See CLOUD; DEW; PALESTINE (climate); RAIN; WIND.

CLOPAS. In Jn. 19:25, a woman at the cross is Mary the daughter, wife or mother (the original is uncertain) of Clopas, who was probably a different person from CLEOPAS.

CLOTHES: See DRESS.

CLOUD. Cumulus clouds rising over the sea were recognized as an indication of rain (1 Ki. 18:44; Lk. 12:54), and high rainless cirrus clouds are noted (Jude 12), which form as the hot Sirrocco or Khamsin winds come in from the desert. Clouds brought by sea breezes rapidly dissolve in the hot dry air (Ho. 6:4), a reminder of God's forgiveness (Is. 44:22). A cloud that obscures the sky is a picture of God hidden by people's sins (La. 2:1). God showed his presence by a cloud (Ex. 13:21); and at the transfiguration (Mk. 9:7), the ascension (Acts 1:9) and the second coming (Rev. 1:7) clouds indicate his mystery and hidden glory.

CNIDUS. A free city in SW Asia Minor where Paul's ship changed course (Acts 27:7).

COAL. Several Hebrew words are rendered 'coal' in some EVV; usually charcoal or other fuel is meant, as coal was unknown. See FUEL.

COCK, HEN. Domestic fowl are not mentioned in the OT, unless 1 Ki. 4:23 includes them, but there is evidence that Assyria paid tax to Egypt with hens *c*. 1500 BC. In the NT Jesus refers to the hen gathering her chicks (Lk. 13:34); the cock-crow of Mt. 26:74f.

acted as an alarm clock in eastern lands.

COELESYRIA (lit. 'hollow Syria'). The valley between the Lebanon and Antilebanon ranges (the valley of Aven, Am. 1:5). As a political region it embraced a wider area, and became an administrative division of the province of Syria after the Roman occupation (64 BC).

COLLECTION (FOR THE JERUS-ALEM CHURCH). In the 2 years before Paul's final visit to Jerusalem (AD 57), a collection among the Gentile churches to relieve the poverty at Jerusalem increasingly occupied his attention. He and Barnabas had been encouraged to remember the poor by the Jerusalem Council (Gal. 2:10), and had already taken a gift from Antioch to Jerusalem (Acts 11:30). The later fund is first mentioned in 1 Cor. 16:1ff., which implies Paul had already told the Galatian churches about it. Each householder was to set aside a proportion of his weekly income for 12 months, so that the collection could be taken to Jerusalem the following spring. Evidently he later had some misgivings as to their enthusiasm and responsiveness, because he sent Titus to oversee the collection (2 Cor. 8:16ff.). Paul was in Macedonia at the time, and the Christians there insisted on making their contribution even though they were living at barely a subsistence level. Paul's other reference to this collection is in Rom. 15:25ff. in which it becomes clear that a major motive in organizing it was to strengthen the fellowship between Jewish and Gentile churches. The Gentile mission field had been repeatedly invaded by Jewish Christians seeking to undermine Paul's authority and to impose the Jewish customs observed by the Jerusalem church. Paul wanted the Gentiles to demonstrate their indebtedness to Jerusalem for the gospel itself, and thus to allay suspicions there about the Gentile mission. At the time, Paul was thinking about the relationship of Jews and Gentiles within the church, as Romans (9-11) makes clear.

He took with him to Jerusalem delegates from the contributing churches, probably all those named in Acts 20:4 and perhaps others too (no Corinthian Christians are named there, but Titus may have been their messenger and he is never mentioned in Acts; there is no delegate from Philippi either but that could have been Luke, the author of Acts). But Acts is completely silent about this important event save for recording Paul's reference to it in his speech to Felix (24:17). It is possible that charges of misusing money—by diverting the collection to a 'sect' rather than to the temple—were being prepared by the Jews to be put against Paul when he came before the Emperor, and that Luke is reticent about mentioning the subject before that trial.

For other biblical material on relief for the poor, see CHARITY; POVERTY.

COLONY. A self-governing corporation of Roman citizens settled in foreign lands usually for strategic reasons or for rehabilitating war veterans or the unemployed. Greek republics were sometimes given colonial status as an honour. The self-conscious Romanism of Philippi was probably exceptional (Acts 16:12). See also ROMAN EMPIRE.

COLOSSAE. A city in the Roman province of Asia 15 km up the Lycus valley from Laodicea where the main road E from Ephesus originally joined a route S from Sardis; now uninhabited (near modern Honaz). The church may have begun through Epaphras (Col. 1:7) while Paul was working in Ephesus (Acts 19-20). Paul had not visited the church before he wrote to it (Col. 2:1); the city's mix of Jewish, Greek and Phrygian people would have been fertile ground for the heresies the letter countered. See next article.

COLOSSIANS, LETTER TO THE. *Contents.* Address to the Colossians, with thanks and prayers for them (1:1-12); the glory and greatness of Christ (1:13-23); Paul's own labours (1:24-2:3); warning against and remedies for false teaching (2:4-3:4); instructions on how to 'put on' the new life, with specific exhortations (3:5-4:6); final personal messages (4:7-18).

Authorship, date and origin. Some doubts were expressed in the 19th cent. about the genuineness of Colossians, but the close connection of it with the letter to Philemon reinforces the claim to Pauline authorship. Philemon refers to several people mentioned in Colossians, including Onesimus, Epaphras, Mark, Aristarchus, Demas, Luke and Tychicus. It is hard to imagine either or both of these references to people as inauthentic and fictitious, the alternative being to accept that both were written by Paul at about the same time. It was written from prison (4:3,10,18). This could have been in Ephesus, but Ephesians and Colossians may have been written at the same time, thus ruling this out. Caesarea has been suggested but the list of people in Col. 4 were probably not with Paul in Caesarea. Rome is the most likely choice—the place a runaway slave (Onesimus) would probably flee to—and the personal references seem to fit, giving a date of about AD 60.

Reason for writing. As Paul was writing to Philemon in Colossae about the slave Onesimus he would take the opportunity of sending a letter to the whole church by the same courier. Also, Epaphras had brought him news about a threatened heresy (*cf.* 1:8) which he wanted to counter. For the establishment of the church, see COLOSSAE.

The Colossian heresy. Paul counters it not point by point, but by positive teaching, so its precise nature can only be inferred. It gave an important place to the spirit world at the expense of Christ (*cf.* 1:16; 2:18); to religious festivals (*e.g.* 2:16f.) as the way of discipline (2:20ff.); and to 'higher' knowledge (2:4,8,18). Some have argued this heresy had Jewish roots,

others that it was a forerunner of 2nd-cent. Gnosticism; as syncretism was rife, it could have been a combination of both emphases. Paul counters it by stressing the Lordship of Christ in creation and redemption (1:15ff.); in personal discipleship (3:10ff.); and in giving wisdom and understanding (1:27).

COLOURS. Words for colours appear sparsely in both OT and NT. There are two related reasons for this. One is that the Hebrews were not interested in aesthetic details of creation so much as in the way creation reflected its awe-inspiring Creator. The other is that as a result their language had few words for colours anyway. Even the ones they had tended to be symbolic or descriptive of the material itself; to be 'dressed in purple' for example meant 'to be a king or wealthy person'. 'Purple' in the OT usually means a reddish-purple cloth (normally woollen), dyed with juice from the murex shellfish. The cochineal insect or shield-louse yielded a rich red. The NT writers, although they had access to extensive and flexible Greek words for colours, were even less concerned with them. In any case, the Greeks themselves were more interested in graduations between black and white; 'fields white for harvest' (Jn. 4:35) means simply 'gleaming'. See also DRESS; DYEING; JOSEPH (for coat of many colours).

COMMANDER: See CAPTAIN.

COMMUNION: See FELLOWSHIP;

LORD'S SUPPER.

COMPASSION. The idea is sometimes rendered in EVV as 'pity' or 'mercy'. Bible authors are deeply aware of the wonder of God's compassion to sinful people, and taught that anyone who felt it would regard compassion to fellow humans as a duty (1 Jn. 3:17), especially to the orphan, widow and stranger (*e.g.* Dt. 10:18), and to the poor and afflicted (*e.g.* Pr. 19:17). See also CHARITY; MERCY; POVERTY.

CONCUBINE. Sexual relations with a secondary wife were common in biblical times. In Assyria, for example, a concubine was subject to the wife's authority but her sons could share the family inheritance. Abraham (Gn. 16:2f.) and Solomon (1 Ki. 11:3) are among biblical figures who had concubines. They were protected under the law of Moses (Dt. 21:10ff.) but were more easily divorced than wives (Gn. 21:10ff.). The later prophets emphasized the necessity of monogamy, as did Jesus (Mt. 19:3ff.). The Romans in NT times accepted *concubinatus* as an informal more-or-less permanent union without a marriage ceremony; children of such unions were deprived of citizen status. In the early church, men had to marry their concubines or be refused baptism. See also MARRIAGE.

CONFESSION. In both OT and NT, it has two meanings. It can be a joyful public declaration of a personal relationship with God, and also the more obvious admission of guilt and sin as an outward sign of repentance and faith.

Old Testament. It frequently has the character of praise for and declaration of God's mighty acts, leading naturally to confession of sin (*e.g.* Pss. 32; 116). Confession can lead the worshipper to renewed commitment to God. It is not only personal, but may have a corporate liturgical element, as on the Day of Atonement (Lv. 16:21).

New Testament. It has the basic meaning of acknowledging something in agreement with others, but in the sense of pledging oneself to Christ rather than giving mental assent to an idea. Thus to confess Christ is to acknowledge him as Messiah (Mt. 16:16); Son of God (Jn. 1:34); and Lord (Phil. 2:11). This is linked to confession of sin and the desire for his forgiveness (1 Jn. 1:5ff.). Confession of faith in Christ is to be made to God but openly (Lk. 12:8), by word of mouth (Rom. 10:9), and it may be costly (Mt. 10:32ff.). Confession of sin is similarly addressed primarily to God but also may be made before people in corporate confession or to a group or individual (Acts 19:18; Jas. 5:16). True repentance may involve acknowledging sin to a fellow Christian (Mt. 5:23f.), but there is no suggestion that confession of private sins must be made to an individual minister. It leads to either salvation or judgment because it is the outward manifestation of faith or lack of it (Lk. 12:8).

CONFIRMATION. 1. Used in EVV to mean 'make firm' or 'reaffirm', as in

Heb. 6:16 ('settles all arguments', GNB). In Acts 14:22; 15:32, 41 RSV correctly renders 'strengthen' where AV had 'confirm'. 2. The ecclesiastical rite is presumably traced to Acts 8:14ff.; 19:1ff. where the gift of the Holy Spirit follows the laying-on of hands subsequent to baptism. However, Acts shows no constant sequence of such events.

CONGREGATION, SOLEMN ASSEMBLY. A word used in the OT to render several Hebrew words, signifying the company of people assembled by appointment (*e.g.* Ex. 16:1f.), or for a festival (*e.g.* Is. 1:13). In the NT the Greek equivalent word is usually rendered CHURCH.

CONSCIENCE. There is no word for it in the OT. Scholars have suggested that it came into the NT via popular Greek thought, probably because of the troubles at Corinth where Christians may have been appealing to 'conscience' to justify controversial actions such as eating food which had been offered first to idols. However, the idea is not absent from the OT; RSV renders 1 Sa. 24:5 literally, 'David's heart smote him', which the NIV renders colloquially as 'David was conscience-stricken'; GNB and NEB also introduce the word, which follows the popular understanding of pain suffered by a person when his actions go beyond his moral limits.

Its use in the NT is to be seen against the background of God's character as a holy judge. However, a person's conscience—the faculty by which he perceives God's moral demands—can be inadequately disciplined and become weakened (1 Cor. 8:7,12), and even can be silenced (*cf.* 1 Tim. 4:2). It must therefore be educated by the Holy Spirit (*cf.* Rom. 8:14 with 1 Pet. 3:16) if it is to be a witness and guide to Christian living. In Rom. 2:14f. Paul says that conscience belongs to all people, and through it God's character and will can be actively appreciated; the general revelation of God's goodness faces all people with moral responsibility. The author of Hebrews says that conscience in relation to God could not be perfected under the terms of the old covenant, but through Christ's death it can (Heb. 9:9, 14).

CONTAINERS. Before the invention of pottery (*c.* 6000 BC) containers were made from skins, rushes, wood and stone, which in later times probably remained as important in daily life as pottery. Bottles for water and wine were tightly-sewn skins (Mt. 9:17). Soft stones, limestone, alabaster, and basalt were cut and ground into bowls, jars and dishes. Large stone or earthenware jars were used to store liquids; the porous earthenware absorbed a little of the liquid, hindering evaporation and helping to keep the contents cool. The rich could afford metal, glass and ivory containers (*cf.* Rev. 18:12); metal ones are rarely unearthed in Palestine although bronze bowls of Phoenician workmanship have been found at Nimrud. Gold and silver containers were a convenient method of storing wealth before the introduction of coined money, and formed the bulk of temple and royal treasures and payments of tribute-tax to ruling nations. Precise definition of the various biblical words describing containers is not possible. See also CUP; FLESHPOTS; POTTER, POTTERY.

CONTENTMENT. The positive assurance that God has supplied one's needs, rather than a passive acceptance of the *status quo*, and the consequent release from unnecessary desire or anxiety, as in 1 Tim. 6:6, 8 and Phil. 4:11. The Christian spirit of contentment follows the fundamental commandment against covetousness (Ex. 20:17) and the rebuke Jesus gave to the discontent which grasps for possessions and neglects God (Lk. 12:13ff.). In the OT 'be content' means pleasure or willingness to do something requested by another (*e.g.* Jdg. 17:11).

CONVERSION. A turning round, or turning back, to God. In the OT, for Israelites it meant turning back to God in whole-hearted sincerity after a period of disloyalty (*e.g.* Dt. 30:2, 10). National acts of repentance were frequently marked by the leader and the people 'making a covenant' in the sense of making a fresh commitment to be wholly loyal to God's covenant (as in Jos. 24:25; 2 Ch. 34:31). But the OT stresses that there is more to conversion than outward sorrow and reformation of lifestyle; it also involves a real change of heart and a sincere seeking after God (*e.g.* Dt. 4:29f.). There are a few references to individual conversions (*e.g.* 2 Ki.

23:25; *cf.* Ps. 51:13).

In the NT the word is almost always used of that decisive turning to God of a person which secures entry into the kingdom of God and the forgiveness of their sins (Mt. 18:3; Acts 3:19). Backsliding Christians are exhorted to repentance, not conversion (*e.g.* Rev. 2:5; Lk. 22:32 is the only exception). This conversion is unrepeatable, and includes repentance (a change of heart and mind towards God) and faith (belief in God's word and trust in Christ). The NT records a number of conversion experiences—some were dramatic (*e.g.* Acts 9:5ff.), some quieter (*e.g.* Acts 16:14)—but the writers show no interest in the psychology of conversion. They think of it not as an experience one feels but as an action one does. They interpret it theologically as commitment to union with Christ as Saviour and Lord which brings freedom from the penalty and bondage of sin and death. It is regarded as someone's own freely-chosen act, but also as God's work in the person (*e.g.* Phil. 2:12f.; *cf.* Je. 31:18f.). People respond because God has already worked in them. See also REGENERATION; REPENTANCE.

CONVERT (TO JUDAISM): See PROSELYTE.

COPPER: See MINING AND METALS.

CORD, ROPE. Rope was normally made from twisted hair or strips of skin in OT times. In Jn. 2:15 and Acts

101

27:32 the Greek word is literally 'bulrush cords'.

CORINTH. A city of Greece at the W end of the isthmus between central Greece and the Peloponnesus in control of trade routes. Two harbours were close by and hence the city became a flourishing trade centre; it was also an industrial centre specializing in ceramics. The city is dominated by a steep flat-topped rock 566 m high on which is the acropolis which in ancient times contained a temple of Aphrodite, the goddess of love; worship of Aphrodite gave rise to the city's proverbial immorality. The early Greek city was destroyed by Rome for its opposition in 146 BC but was rebuilt in 46 BC by Caesar Augustus. Paul's stay there (Acts 18:1ff.) is dated by an inscription from Delphi which shows that the proconsul mentioned, Gallio, came to Corinth in AD 51-52. The meat market (1 Cor. 10:25) has been identified by excavators. See also next article for the church there.

CORINTHIANS, LETTERS TO THE.

Contents of 1 Corinthians. Greetings (1:1-9); Christian wisdom and the unity of the church (1:10-4:21); problems in Corinthian church life of sexual sin and litigation (5:1-6:20); answers to questions on celibacy, meat offered to idols, and conduct during worship meetings (7:1-14:40); the resurrection of Jesus and of Christians (15); the collection for famine relief, and closing remarks (16). *Contents of 2 Corinthians.* Greetings (1:1-7);

explanations for Paul's apparently inconsistent behaviour (1:8-2:13); an assertion that he seeks God's glory, not his own (2:14-4:12); the basis of his confidence in Christ (4:13-5:10); his motivation (5:11-21); an appeal for a response of fellowship and purity (6:1-7:4); Paul's confidence in the Corinthians (7:5-16); the collection for famine relief (8:1-9:15); warning against false apostles (10:1-13:10); closing greetings (13:11-14).

The church at Corinth. The city had a reputation for vice of every kind, but this had been foisted on Old Corinth by its trading-rival Athens and despite the worship of Aphrodite in the city the morals there were probably much the same as in any other Mediterranean port. A brief account of the founding of the church in Acts 18 shows Paul stayed with the Jewish couple Aquila and Prisca, who were probably already Christians and had been expelled with other Jews from Rome. After opposition to his preaching in the synagogue, Paul took with him a number of Jewish converts and based his mission next door in the house of Justus. The Jews took advantage of a change of proconsul to attack Paul but were unsuccessful. The church was able to grow unmolested and Paul stayed there for the unusually long time (for him) of 18 months. The church contained both Jewish and pagan converts from varied social backgrounds, among them the wealthy city treasurer Erastus and the domestic slaves of Chloe.

Its problems and their background. A surprising number of errors had developed quickly in the church, despite Paul's long teaching ministry there. This could have been due to several factors. The Jews in the church would have been influenced previously by other, mostly Greek, streams of thought but would have held strongly to their Jewish food laws. The Gentile converts would have been familiar with the excesses of pagan worship which included cult prostitution and speaking in tongues. The pagan temples played a central part in daily life, functioning as restaurants and social centres as well as being significant, but not the only, sources of meat. Gnosticism found a fertile ground here, as many of the religions already regarded matter as illusory and evil and only the objects of thought were concrete and good, leading to a stress on mystical 'knowledge' and the immortality of the soul rather than the resurrection of the body. It is possible that the Corinthian Christians themselves had developed to extremes Paul's own teaching about the next world and return of Christ, believing themselves already to be in 'the new age' in which all things were lawful (1 Cor. 4:8; 6:12). In 2 Corinthians Paul is also facing a personal attack by people whom he describes as false apostles and Satan's servants (2 Cor. 11:13ff.). His defence implies these people stressed their own clever speech, spiritual authority and human strength. These are probably a different group from the 'superlative apostles' (2 Cor. 11:5) from Jerusalem with whom Paul claims equality.

How Paul deals with the Corinthians. It is virtually certain that Paul wrote more letters to Corinth than those now preserved in the NT. 1 Cor. 5:9 refers to one other letter, called here 'Cor. A'. 2 Cor. 2:3ff.; 7:8ff. also refer to a previous letter. It is unlikely that this is 1 Cor. because the implied tone is not that of 1 Cor.; it was followed by a painful visit which does not fit 1 Cor.; and 2 Cor.2:5ff. does not seem to refer to the same incident as 1 Cor. 5:5. So if 1 Cor. is called 'Cor. B', then there must have been a 'Cor. C' before 2 Cor. ('Cor. D'). It has been suggested that rather than being lost, the other 2 letters are contained within the two biblical letters. For example, 2 Cor. 6:14-7:1 looks like 'Cor. A' and if it is taken out 6:13 and 7:2 match up remarkably. Further, 2 Cor. 10-13 even looks like a 'Cor. E' because of the sharp change of tone. But such theories raise as many problems as they solve, and if sense can be made of the letters as they stand, the theories are to be rejected. The probable course of events is as follows:

1. After Paul left Corinth, he must have received reports about actual or threatened immorality in the church.

2. He responded by writing 'Cor. A' warning the church to keep clear of immoral members (*cf.* 1 Cor. 5:9).

3. Three further sources of information prompted him to write 'Cor. B' (1 Cor.). These were: reports from Chloe's servants (or members of her house-church, 1 Cor. 1:11); reports from Stephanas, Fortunatus and Achaicus (1 Cor. 16:17); and a letter from the Corinthians themselves rais-

ing questions which Paul answered in 1 Cor. 7:1-16:4.

4. The letter appears to have failed in its intention; 2 Cor. 2:1 and 13:2 speak of the need for further action which was a 'painful visit'.

5. That also failing, he delivered a stinging rebuke in another letter ('Cor. C') delivered personally by Titus (2 Cor. 7:5ff.). It upset Paul to write it, but Titus returned with good news that the Corinthians had at last repented.

6. Delighted with the news, Paul wrote 'Cor. D' (2 Cor.).

7. Before that letter was sent, more news arrived to the effect that this victory in Corinth was not complete, and that self-styled 'apostles' were challenging Paul's authority and leading the people astray. So he appended 2 Cor. 10-13 ('Cor. E' to those who suggest it was sent separately after 'Cor. D'). The effect is unknown, although in about 96 AD Clement, bishop of Rome, had to write sternly to the Corinthians who were once again split, largely on personality rather than doctrinal grounds.

Authenticity and dates. There is no doubt that the two letters are genuinely from Paul. They can be dated about 53-54 (1 Cor.) and 55 (2 Cor.), on the basis that Gallio became proconsul in Corinth in July 51 or 52, Paul staying perhaps to the end of that year, travelling to Ephesus and Jerusalem, then staying 2 years in Ephesus.

For issues raised in the letters, see IDOLS, FOOD OFFERED TO; MEAT MARKET.

CORNELIUS. A Roman centurion of Caesarea, a Gentile 'God-fearer' who followed Jewish religious customs. He became the first Gentile convert to Christianity through Peter (Acts 10:1ff.). He belonged to the Italian Cohort, an auxiliary cohort of Roman citizens whose presence in Syria in the first century AD is known from inscriptions.

CORNERSTONE. Possibly one of the large stones near the foundations of an ancient building which binds together two or more courses of stones, or more probably the final capstone to complete an arch or the top corner of a building. In Ps. 118:22 a rejected stone is said to have become the cornerstone, given Messianic significance by the rabbis and applied by Jesus to himself (Mt. 21:42 *etc.*) and by Peter (Acts 4:11; 1 Pet. 2:7) to explain Jesus' rejection by the Jews and his exaltation by God. Paul uses the idea to describe the unity of the church held together by Christ (Eph. 2:20). A similar passage in Is. 28:16 symbolizes God's reliable presence among his people.

CORRUPTION. Used in Acts 2:27 (RSV) and elsewhere in AV to describe the temporary nature of the present world and its subjection to decay and death.

COS. A mountainous island off the SW coast of Asia Minor near Halicarnassus, the site of the medical school founded by Hippocrates (5th cent. BC). Paul sailed past it (Acts 21:1).

COSMETICS AND PERFUMERY.
Cosmetics (concoctions of pulverized minerals, vegetable oils and extracts, and animal fats) were widely used in the ancient world to beautify personal appearance or to produce pleasing fragrances. The Egyptians, for example, placed small cones of perfumed ointment on the foreheads of guests at banquets. The body's heat slowly melted the ointment which trickled down the face and on to the clothing. The practice was adopted by the Hebrews (Ps. 133:2) and continued into NT times (*e.g.* Lk. 7:46). In areas where water was scarce, perfumed ointments were used to mask the odour of perspiration, and also to reduce chafing and irritation caused by the heat. Although some ointments were in the luxury bracket (Am. 6:6), their everyday equivalents were common; one papyrus from 13th-cent. BC Egypt mentions 600 *hin* (over 2,000 litres) of 'anointing oil' for a gang of workmen.

In 1 Sa. 8:13 the typical king is pictured as having his own perfumery; one such royal establishment was unearthed at Mari on the middle Euphrates (from 18th cent. BC). The text also associates perfumers with cooks, for their techniques were similar. For example, flowers or other sources of perfume were dipped in hot fats or oils at 65° C (150° F), the most widespread form of manufacture and the closest to cooking. Oil of myrrh and other gum-resins were heated in a greasy fixative, which was strained off as liquid perfume. Such processes are sometimes pictured on Egyptian tomb-paintings of the 15th cent. BC. Several perfumes are mentioned in the Song of Songs (*e.g.* 4:13f.), among them spikenard, probably the root of the gingergrass imported from Arabia; henna, the fragrant flowers of a plant whose crushed leaves produce red dye; saffron, from the saffron crocus and/or tumeric, which also yield a yellow dye; myrrh, a gum-resin from balsam trees; and frankincense, a white gum-resin from trees in S Arabia and Somaliland. The 'pure nard' of Mk. 14:3 and Jn. 12:3 is probably a very expensive perfume related to valerian and imported from India. Perfumes were put on clothes (Ps. 45:8) and furniture (Pr. 7:17) as well as on the body, and were used at the funerals of great people (2 Ch. 16:14).

Cosmetics for decorating the face and body were used from earliest times. Oriental women painted round their eyes and darkened their eyebrows (2 Ki. 9:30; Je. 4:30). Eye-paint was made from a crushed mineral mixed to a paste with water or gum; in Egypt the mineral was generally lead sulphide, and this was probably the main ingredient of most ancient eye-paints rather than antimony as has been suggested in the past. Red ochre (iron oxide) found in Egyptian tombs may have been used as rouge for the cheeks. The crushed leaves of henna produced a red dye for hands, feet, nails and hair, and in Mesopotamia yellow ochre was used for face powder.

Cosmetics and perfumes were contained in a variety of purpose-made boxes, phials and flasks, many of which have been recovered by archaeologists but which are rarely mentioned in the Bible. They were made from wood, ivory or alabaster. According to Pliny, ointments in alabaster containers improved with age and became very valuable after a number of years—adding to the naturally high value of Mary of Bethany's ointment with which she anointed Jesus (Mk. 14:3).

See also HAIR, HAIRDRESSING; HERBS; INCENSE; OIL.

COUNCIL. Used in RSV at Acts 25:12 for the provincial governor's advisory board, and in Mk. 13:9 for a Jewish court lower than the Sanhedrin. See SANHEDRIN.

COUNCIL, JERUSALEM. The meeting (c. AD 48) between delegates from the church at Antioch (led by Paul and Barnabas) and the apostles and elders of the church at Jerusalem to discuss the problems arising from a large influx of Gentile converts (Acts 15:2ff.). This may have been a different meeting from that described in Gal. 2:1ff., although many commentators equate them.

The possibility of there soon being more Gentiles than Jews in the church threatened the maintenance of moral standards. The Jews suggested the simple solution of continuing in the church the Jewish practice of admitting Gentile proselytes by the rite of circumcision and by obliging them to keep the Jewish law. These had not been imposed on the Gentile converts as yet, but zealous Jewish Christians

from Jerusalem had disturbed the Antioch church by pressing for them. Against the Jewish contention, Peter reminded the Council how the Holy Spirit had been given to Cornelius (Acts 10) on the grounds of his faith alone, and then Paul and Barnabas described how God had similarly blessed many Gentiles. James the Just summed up, and said that no conditions should be imposed on Gentiles beyond faith. However, the practical problem of day-to-day relationships in mixed churches remained, and a letter was sent from Jerusalem to Gentile churches urging them to respect some Jewish scruples concerning food and relations between the sexes.

COUNSELLOR. One who gives advice, used of the Messiah in Is. 9:6 and the Holy Spirit in Jn. 14:16, 26; 15:26; 16:7 (RSV, NIV). The Greek word has entered Christian thought as 'paraclete', and it means one who is called to stand by someone, especially in a law-court, hence the translation as 'advocate' (NEB, and 1 Jn. 2:1 RSV). The help of the Spirit is seen in such legal terms in Mt. 10:19f. where Christians are envisaged as being on trial before secular and Jewish authorities. There is little evidence for an active use of the word outside the NT, and early church commentators tended to see it in terms of encouragement because of its context—the disciples' desolation at Jesus' departure. An ambiguous rendering such as 'Counsellor' contains the various meanings which John probably intended. See SPIRIT, HOLY.

COURAGE. A quality of mind with a place among the cardinal virtues (Wisdom 8:7), the opposite of cowardice, one of the mortal sins (Ecclus. 2:12f.). In the NT, it sees every occasion as an opportunity for victory, rather than being a 'grin and bear it' resignation. It shows itself in patient endurance, moral consistency and spiritual faithfulness (2 Cor. 5:6f.; Heb. 13:6).

COURTYARD. There were four courts (courtyards) in Herod's Temple—those of the Gentiles, the Women, the Men (Israel) and the Priests. Private houses and palaces often had courtyards. See HOUSE.

COUSIN. Used in AV in Lk. 1:36, 58 for kinswoman (as RSV).

COVENANT, ALLIANCE. The idea of making a treaty pervades almost the whole history of the ancient Near East. Two main types occurred in the Hittite empire, for example. One was a treaty of equals (parity-treaty) in which the two partners are called 'brothers', with stipulations about borders and the return of runaway slaves. The other was a vassal-treaty contracted between a conquering king and a minor king. It stipulated that the subject-state should have no relationship with a country outside the conqueror's empire; should not be hostile to other vassal-states; should give help to the conqueror when demanded; and the vassal-king should pay taxes personally once a year to the conqueror. The treaty was concluded with a list of witnesses, including gods and natural phenomena. Both types of treaty occur in the OT. The best example of a parity-treaty is between David and the Phoenician Hiram, renewed on a more elaborate scale by Solomon (*cf.* 1 Ki. 5:1). The later marriage between Jezebel and Ahab must be understood as a partial fulfilment of the conditions of the treaty. The best example of a vassal-treaty is that between Israel and the Gibeonites (Jos. 9-10), in which the Gibeonites asked to be Israel's slaves, and Israel offered Gibeon military support—an obligation of the major partner. Little is known about the rites which sealed treaties. The Mari texts and the OT mention animal sacrifice (*e.g.* Ex. 24).

Old Testament covenants (with God). The idea of a covenant between a god and a king or his people is also well attested in the ancient Near East, so it is not surprising that God should use a familiar form to express his relationship with his people. Four major covenants are mentioned.

1. Early covenants between God and Noah (Gn. 6:18; 9:8ff.) contain promises from God and put obligations on Noah, a prelude to later covenants.

2. The covenant with Abraham has a strong emphasis on promise (Gn. 17): the promise that Abraham would have many descendants, and that those descendants would inherit the 'Promised Land' of Canaan.

3. The Sinai covenant with Moses as mediator was formed after the Exodus. The law of God is read, the people respond, make sacrifices, and

have a covenant meal (Ex. 24). The stipulations spelt out in Ex. 21-23, are quite different from those in normal political treaties. When this covenant was broken (Ex. 32) the author demonstrated that the covenant with Abraham was still in force, so the Sinai covenant existed alongside the earlier one and did not replace it.

4. The covenant with David (2 Sa. 7) was not a new covenant but was an extension of that of Sinai to deal with a new historic situation. As the king was now a mediator between God and the people, a covenant with him was necessary. It had profound influence on later expectations in OT and NT times, as Pss. 2 and 110 make clear.

At various times, the OT covenants were renewed after they had been broken (as in Ex. 32-34); and ratified when a fresh commitment to them was made, without their necessarily having been broken (as in Jos. 23-24). Recent research has shown that the idea of the covenant pervades most of the writings of the prophets, although explicit references to it are infrequent. The prophetic threats, for example, are closely linked to roughly contemporary curses in vassal-treaties, implying that on such occasions the prophets considered the covenant to have been broken. Covenant lawsuits can be traced in Is. 1:2f. and Je. 2:4f. Here Israel is accused of idolatry (and hence of breaking the covenant). In Mi. 6:1ff. heaven and earth are called as witnesses to that fact—a striking parallel to the older Hittite vassal-treaties.

Covenant in the New Testament.

About 600 BC there was an upsurge of interest in the covenant, which continued into NT times. Jeremiah had considered the Sinai covenant as so totally broken that it could only be replaced by a new one (Je. 31:31). The word 'covenant' is closely connected with the Lord's Supper (Mk. 14:22ff.; 1 Cor. 11:23ff.). Its reference to Jesus as the 'passover lamb' who must be sacrificed for and 'eaten' by his people and the covenant 'in his blood' is paralleled in the covenant-forming sacrifices at Sinai. With this new covenant containing the promise of forgiveness of sins and eternal life by faith in Christ the curse of the old covenant is removed, according to Paul (Gal. 3:13); the Davidic covenant is also fulfilled as Jesus becomes the new king in David's line on the eternal throne. Indeed the covenant with David, looking forward to the coming Messiah, forms a very important link between OT and NT. With the new covenant of the NT a fresh expectation of the coming return of the Messiah is given.

COVENANT, BOOK OF THE. In Ex. 24:7 Moses read 'the book of the covenant' to the people as the basis for God's covenant with them at its ratification at the foot of Mt Sinai. It is the oldest existing codification of Israelite law. It begins with two religious regulations, forbidding the making of idols and prescribing an altar of earth rather than stone, without steps, for Israel's sacrifices (Ex. 20:22ff.). Then follows a series of judgments in the form of case studies. These cover slavery (Ex. 21:2ff.); murder and manslaughter (21:12ff.); injury done to parents (21:15, 17); kidnapping (21:16); assault and battery (21:18ff.); incidents involving animals (21:28ff.); theft (22:1ff.); damage to crops (22:5f.); deposits and loans (22:7ff.); seduction (21:16f.). There are some similarities in this section with other ancient law-codes, but it reflects a simpler way of life. It presumes a settled agricultural community, and there is nothing of the elaborate and social organization of the Babylonian law-code of Hammurapi, for example. The final section of the book (Ex. 22:18-23:33) contains God's instructions given through his spokesman Moses, for which there is no other ancient parallel except that there is a general similarity here to ancient vassal-treaties (see previous article). The Ten Commandments are the heart of the covenant being formed between God and his people. The religious instructions here are a reminder that Israel knew no clear distinction between civil and religious law.

Another 'book of the covenant' is mentioned in 2 Ki. 23:2, 21; 2 Ch. 34:30f.; for this see DEUTERONOMY.

COVENANT BOX: See ARK OF THE COVENANT.

COVETOUSNESS. The desire to have or to influence other persons or things was banned in the OT (Ex. 20:17). In the NT it is any intense and misdirected desire, as for example for money (1 Tim. 6:9) and possessions (Lk. 12:15). Being essentially worship of self it is reckoned the ultimate idolatry (Eph. 5:5; Col. 3:5).

CREATION. The biblical doctrine is that God created the heavens and the earth. Its purpose is ethical and religious, in contrast to scientific investigation. Reference to the doctrine is widespread through both OT and NT, and according to Heb. 11:3 it is based on divine revelation and can be understood only from the standpoint of faith. The work of creation is variously attributed to the Father (e.g. Is. 45:11f.), the Son (e.g. Col. 1:16) and the Spirit (Gn. 1:2)—i.e. the whole is the work of the triune God. The doctrine emphasizes that matter had a beginning and is not eternal (it was created 'from nothing', Gn. 1:1; Heb. 11:3), and that there is no other kind of power over against God and beyond his control. However mankind and the creatures were formed from already-created materials (Gn. 2:7, 19). Creation was a free act of God; he did not need to do it (cf. Acts 17:25), but chose to do so in order to display his glory. He is thus over and above all he made (cf. Rom. 9:5), and yet also present within creation to sustain it (Acts 17:28; Col. 1:17).

The Genesis account. The basic narrative in Gn. 1:1-2:4a takes the form of a simple account with no attempt to introduce the subtleties which would be appreciated by modern scientific knowledge. There is a depth and dignity in it which is not found in other ancient creation stories. Taking it as a simple account of what can be seen, the author asks first, 'Who caused the pattern of day and night?' and answers 'God' (vv. 3-5). Then he observes the springs in the earth and the clouds above as the source of water (vv. 6-8); the distribution of land and sea across the world (vv. 9f.); the varieties of vegetation (vv. 11-13); the heavenly bodies which mark off the seasons (vv. 14-19); the multitudes of creatures in the sea, on the land and in the air (vv. 20-25). Of each he is saying simply that God made it like it is. Finally he sees mankind, made in God's likeness to have 'dominion' over all the rest, and he made both male and female (vv. 26-28).

The 8 creative acts (introduced by the phrase 'And God said ...') are compressed into a pattern of 6 days. A strict chronological approach to the passage is problematic because the sun and moon do not appear until the fourth 'day'. But Bible writers are sometimes more concerned with stressing the facts themselves than their order (the order of Jesus' temptations is different in Mt. 4 and Lk. 4 for example). This avoids a number of potential difficulties in interpretation.

There is a reasonably consistent scheme in the arrangement but something is lost if the exegesis is pressed to unnecessary limits; the whole is poetic and does not yield to close scientific correlations. Some have sought a more or less exact correlation between science and Bible (the Concordist view) and insisted that the phrase 'after its kind' refutes evolutionary theory. However, the meaning of the Hebrew word thus translated is not clear, and the stress in

the passage is that however life came into being, God was behind it all. Others have suggested that Gn. 1:2 indicates an earlier descent into chaos to which God responded by reforming the creation, but neither the Hebrew nor geological science can support the theory.

The word 'day' has caused difficulties for some, but it should be noted that in the Bible it has several meanings. It is often 24-hours, but also a time of judgment (Is. 2:12f.), an indefinite period (Ps. 95:8), or a long period of (say) 1,000 years (Ps. 90:4). To insist on 24 hour days does not take account of the poetic nature of Gn. 1. To insist on 'long periods of time' may be tied too closely to current scientific theories which are notoriously liable to change. A related problem is that we cannot be sure what the phrase 'evening and morning' means. It could refer to the Jewish way of reckoning days, or to the completion of one phase and the start of another. Some have therefore suggested that the creation was revealed to the writer in 6 days, each vision describing one aspect of God's creative work. Others have suggested each section was written on a separate tablet with a similar literary structure for each, a variation of the idea that Gn. 1 is primarily a literary composition to teach that God made all things but without commenting on the divine way of working.

Ancient Near Eastern stories. No myth has been found which deals with the creation of the universe as a whole, and those which are known concentrate on the origin of the gods, the organization of the universe, the creation of man and the establishment of civilization. They are marked by polytheism and power-struggles among the gods, in contrast to the dignified monotheism of the biblical narratives. Several creation stories came from Babylonia, the best-known being an adaptation of a Sumerian legend. During a divine feud, the god Marduk killed Tiamat and used the dead god's two halves to create the heavens and the earth. To set the gods free from menial tasks he created mankind from the clay mingled with the blood of the rebel god Kingu.

To the Greeks, there was an automatic development, mainly by procreation of gods and earthly things, from undefined beginnings. In their Orphic myth, Zeus swallowed the great creator Phanes and re-created the existing world. He made men out of the remains of Titans who had killed and eaten his son Dionysus.

CREATURES. The word is used to emphasize being alive rather than createdness. It embraces all animals on earth (Gn. 9:16). See separate articles for specific animals; BEAST.

CREED. There is no full-scale creed in the NT which summarizes the essential articles of Christian faith and which had church authority. However there are what appear to be fragmentary creeds set in the context of the church's missionary work, worship, and defence against paganism. For example, there is evidence that the early church had a body of distinctive

teaching entrusted to it by God ('the pattern of the sound words', 2 Tim. 1:13f.). Credal 'statements' appear in such places as Eph. 4:5 and Phil. 2:16. The verbs 'delivered' and 'received' in 1 Cor. 15:3 are the technical terms for the transmission of authoritative teaching. There is also evidence of ceremonial declarations of faith which would have been used in public worship, in Phil. 2:5-11 and 1 Cor. 16:22. Oscar Cullman has suggested that the formulation of early creeds was controlled partly by the need for Christians to declare their faith publicly when on trial before pagans; when required by magistrates to witness to their allegiance (to the state), they would reply, 'Jesus Christ is Lord.'

CRESCENS. A companion of Paul (2 Tim. 4:10) on service in Galatia. The name is Latin.

CRETE. A mountainous island in the Mediterranean lying across the S end of the Aegean, about 250 km long and between 11 and 56 km wide. It is not mentioned in the OT but is the probable origin of the Cherethites; the name Caphtor probably referred to it and adjacent coastlands. In the NT Cretans are mentioned at Pentecost (Acts 2:11). Paul sailed past Crete (Acts 27:7ff.) and evidently re-visited it later (Tit. 1:12, where he quotes Epimenides, a Cretan poet). The peak of Cretan civilization was reached early in the Late Bronze Age (c. 1600-1400 BC), after which it declined. Dorian Greeks came to Crete and ushered in the Iron Age in the 12th cent. BC. The island was then divided among feuding city-states until the Romans subdued it in 67 BC.

CRIME AND PUNISHMENT. The modern distinction between criminal and civil offences was unknown in the ancient Near East. In the first place, every offence was committed against a person or a community and the only way to put it right was to compensate the wronged person. Also, the laws were regarded as having divine sanction (in Israel's case, God's sanction was given when the law was promulgated on Mt Sinai with the accompanying covenant between God and Israel). Hence, a crime against a person or his property was also a crime against God, to be punished by God or the authorities.

Crime. To commit crime is to act in a consciously wrong way. The common Hebrew word had the double sense of an offence against man and God, and its basic meaning was 'to miss something', from which the OT and NT idea of sin missing God's righteous requirements is derived. Laws were devised to protect individuals and communities against injustice, and to compensate people for actual damage done to them. Unique to Israel's codes of laws were the 'apodictic' laws, the direct statements found in the Ten Commandments ('You shall not kill', *etc.*) which became part of Israel's religion at the start of its nationhood.

The most important types of offences in the OT are murder, assault, theft, and negligence. A distinction was made between intentional and unintentional killing (*e.g.* Ex. 21:12ff.). A distinction was also made between a single offence and a whole sinful way of life; Wisdom literature especially regards the way of life as very important. An ungodly life means rebellion against God (*cf.* Ps. 1). In the NT, Paul says that while the law brings knowledge of sin, it cannot take sin away, although the law was intended to restrain offences through its penalties (Rom. 7). Every life not saved by Christ is sinful in nature and has to be punished by God.

Punishment. OT words have a sense of 'reproving' or even 'instructing' as well as the merely legal sense of 'punish', in other words punishment is corrective, like that inflicted by a father on his son. In the NT the concept of divine punishment is fully realized. In Matthew and in Peter especially, God's final punishment in contrast to the gift of eternal life occurs at the 'day of judgment', a later development of the OT concept of the 'Day of the Lord'. In the OT, murder had to be punished by death by the victim's nearest relatives (as is still the case in Islamic law). For lesser crimes, judges, elders or heads of families decided or arbitrated, usually at the city gate. Decisions were designed to maintain the 'social equilibrium', with a given loss being compensated by a fixed penalty. A thief had to compensate for stolen animals by paying several times their value—probably as a deterrent to such crime (Ex. 22:1). There are examples in the OT of people who escaped human punishment none the less being punished by God (*e.g.* Nu. 16). During the OT period the idea shifted from God's punishment being given in this life to a final judgment on the 'Day of the Lord' when each person would be judged for his deeds.

See also DAY OF THE LORD; PRISON; SIN.

CRISPUS (lit. 'curly'). The ruler of the synagogue in Corinth, converted to Christ (Acts 18:8) and baptized personally by Paul (1 Cor. 1:14).

CROSS, CRUCIFIXION. A stake used for punishment and execution. Crucifixion was not practised in the OT (where execution was by stoning) although dead bodies were occasionally hung on a tree as a warning (Dt. 21:22ff.; *cf.* Gal. 3:13). Phoenicians and Carthaginians practised it; the Romans later used it extensively, rarely for Roman citizens but usually for slaves, provincials and the lowest types of criminal. Thus tradition which says Peter (a Jew) was crucified but Paul (a Roman citizen) was beheaded is in line with ancient practice. There were 3 types of cross: the T-shaped St Anthony's cross; the X-shaped St Andrew's cross; and the dagger-shaped cross which is likely to have been the one Jesus was crucified on, because of the inscription nailed to it above his head.

After a criminal was condemned, he was 'scourged' with a whip with leather thongs, and then made to carry the cross-beam like a slave to the scene of his execution outside the city. He was stripped naked, laid on the ground with the cross-beam under his shoulders and his arms or hands tied or nailed to it. This was lifted and secured to the upright so that the victim's feet (which were tied or nailed) were just clear of the ground. The main weight of the body was supported by a projecting peg astride which the victim sat. He was then left to die from exhaustion, with death sometimes being hastened by breaking his legs, which was not done in Jesus' case. The remains of a crucified person dating from between AD 7 and 66 found in Jerusalem had the legs twisted so that the calves were parallel to the cross beam; this would have induced severe pain and spasmodic contractions and rigid cramps, and contributed to a quicker death. Contemporary writers describe this cruel and degrading form of death as very painful, but the Gospels give no detailed description of Jesus' sufferings.

The NT writers are more interested in the theological significance of what happened. Through the cross God reconciled Jew and Gentile to each other and to himself (Eph. 2:14ff.). As the lowest form of execution, it illustrated Jesus' humility (Phil. 2:8), a fact which Jews found hard to understand in the Messiah (1 Cor. 1:23). The familiar, shameful sight of victims carrying cross-pieces was used to illustrate the path of discipleship (Mk. 8:34). See also RECONCILIATION; REDEMPTION.

CROWN. A distinctive head-dress,

often ornate, worn by kings and other exalted persons. In the OT, the high priest wore a crown consisting of an inscribed gold plate fixed to a turban by a blue cord (Ex. 29:6; Lv. 8:9). David's golden crown was an emblem of God-given kingship (Ps. 21:3). David captured a gold stone-inset crown of the king of Ammon which weighed a talent (about 30 kg; 2 Sa. 12:30); Ammonite statues show kings wearing large, high crowns, and Egyptian illustrations show a variety of tall and elaborate crowns. In the NT, Jesus' 'crown' of thorns was a mocking symbol of royalty, although the word more usually described the laurel wreath won at the games, and Paul uses it in this sense to describe the Christian's final, imperishable reward of eternal life (1 Cor. 9:25; 2 Tim. 4:8). He also sees his converts as a 'crown' (Phil. 4:1). Christians are to hold tight to their 'crown' through the trials of this life lest it be taken from them (Rev. 3:11).

CUNNING. RSV, NIV rendering of a Greek word for dice-playing in Eph. 4:14, warning against a plausible mixture of truth and error.

CUP. A bowl, wider and shallower than a modern teacup, usually made of pottery but occasionally of metal, for drinking (2 Sa. 12:3) or for holding, say, the blood of the Passover sacrifice or wine (Ex. 12:22; Zc. 12:2). In NT times the rich had glass and metal goblets. The cup shared at the Last Supper was probably a large earthenware bowl. It is used as a picture of blessings or disasters (*e.g.* Ps. 16:5; 116:13; Mt. 26:39. See CONTAINERS.

CUPBEARER. The butler of Joseph's Pharaoh (Gn. 40:1ff.). Such people were wine-tasters and often foreigners, who became confidants and favourites of the king and wielded political influence. Nehemiah (1:11) was cupbearer to Artaxerxes I of Persia (*c.* 464–423 BC), enjoying royal trust and favour.

CURSE. There are two uses of the term in the Bible. The principle one is the utterance of a curse desiring someone's hurt (Jb. 31:30), confirming a promise (Ne. 10:29) or (when uttered by God) denouncing a sin (Dt. 29:19f.). A curse was considered to be an active agent backed by the power of the soul of the person who uttered it. On the borders of Canaan, Moses set before the people the blessing and curse, life and death (Dt. 30:19). When God's curse falls on disobedient people, it is the fulfilment of his covenant (Lv. 25:14-45). In the NT, the law is a curse to those who do not obey it, but Christ redeemed us by becoming a curse for us (Gal. 3:10, 13). The other meaning of 'curse' relates to things which are deliberately made unavailable to people or are set apart for religious reasons (often translated 'devoted' as in Lv. 27:21). It can also relate to the utter destruction of 'devoted things' (or people) contaminated by sin (*e.g.* Jos. 6:18ff.). See also ANATHEMA; BAN.

CUSH. *Person:* A descendant of Ham,

and father of Nimrod the hunter (Gn. 10:6ff.).

Places: 1. A region probably in W Asia (Gn. 2:13); see EDEN. 2. The region S of Egypt (Nubia or N Sudan); called Ethiopia by classical writers, a usage followed in some Bible translations, but it is not the modern Ethiopia. For part of the OT period it was closely linked with Egypt; in Is. 37:9 both had the same king Tirhaka. Topaz came from this land (Jb. 28:19) of dark-skinned people (Je. 13:23); so did Queen Candace's minister (Acts 8:27). See also ETHIOPIA; ETHIOPIAN EUNUCH; ETHIOPIAN WOMAN.

CUSHAN-RISHATHAIM. The king of Aram-Naharaim (E Syria-N Mesopotamia) who subjugated Israel for 3 years until their deliverance by Othniel (Jdg. 3:8ff.). He is otherwise unknown; the name may mean 'Cushan of double wickedness'.

CUSHION. In Mk. 4:38, a pillow (as GNB) perhaps kept for the seat of honour in the stern of a boat.

CUTH, CUTHAH. An ancient city in Babylonia, the seat of the god Nergal, whose inhabitants repopulated Samaria (2 Ki. 17:24, 30); modern Tell Ibrahim.

CYMBAL: See MUSIC; MUSICAL INSTRUMENTS.

CYPRUS. An island 225 km long and 100 km at its broadest in the E Mediterranean 100 km W of the Syrian coast. It is possibly referred to in Ezk. 27:7 as ELISHAH. In the NT, Barnabas originated from there (Acts 4:36), and some Christians fled there (Acts 11:19f.). Paul and Barnabas began their first missionary journey there (Acts 13:4ff.), and Barnabas later revisited it with Mark (Acts 15:39). The church continued to flourish; it sent 3 bishops to the Council of Nicea in AD 325. In Roman times it gave its name to copper (Lat. *cyprium*), which was probably first extensively mined there in the 14th cent. BC. In the 9th-8th cent. BC Phoenicians settled there. It was then dominated successively by Egypt, Persia, and Greece; it was made a Roman province in 58 BC, governed by a proconsul from 27 BC (*cf.* Acts 13:7).

CYRENE. A port in N Africa, rich in corn, wool and dates, becoming a Roman province in 74 BC. Jews formed one of the four recognized classes; Simon the cross-bearer (Mk. 15:21) and missionaries to Antioch (Acts 11:20) came from Cyrene.

CYRUS. A Persian king. Cyrus I was a contemporary of Ashurbanipal of Assyria *c.* 668 BC. His grandson Cyrus II came to the throne *c.* 559 BC, conquered the Medes in 549 and founded the Persian empire. In 539 BC he conquered Babylon. He allowed the exiled Jews to return to Jerusalem and to restore the temple (Ezr. 6:1ff.). Daniel prospered during the first 3 years of Cyrus' reign (Dn. 6:28; 10:1). For the theory that Cyrus was also called Darius the Mede, see DARIUS.

D

DABERATH. A city of Issachar belonging to the Levites, possibly at the W foot of Mt Tabor (1 Ch. 6:72).

DAGON. In the OT he is the principal god of the Philistines, in Samson's time at Gaza (Jdg. 16:21ff.), in Saul's and David's time at Ashdod and Bethshan (1 Sa. 5:2ff.). His precise nature is unknown; if the common Hebrew word for grain, *dagan*, is connected with him, he would have been a grain god. He was worshipped throughout Mesopotamia from 2500 BC, and his temple at Mari (18th cent. BC) was adorned with bronze lions. His temple at Ugarit (14th cent. BC) had a forecourt, antechamber and probably a tower.

DALMANUTHA. In Mk. 8:10 a district on the Lake of Galilee which has never been clearly identified; the disciples went there after the feeding of the 4,000.

DALMATIA. A Roman province E of the Adriatic mentioned in 2 Tim. 4:10 and identical with ILLYRICUM.

DAMASCUS. The capital city of Syria E of the Anti-Lebanon Mts and W of the Syrian-Arabian desert. The district is famous for its orchards and gardens, irrigated by the Abana (mod. Barada) and Pharpar rivers (*cf.* 2 Ki. 5:12), and the Euphrates. It is a natural communications centre and was head of an Aramaean state in the 10th-8th cents. BC. The centre of the modern city beside the Barada river partly occupies the area of the old walled city. Some streets still follow the lines of Roman times, including Straight Street (Acts 9:11); the great mosque built in the 8th cent. AD is said to cover the site of the temple of Rimmon (2 Ki. 5:18). It was already well-known in Abraham's time (Gn. 14:15) and seems to have been occupied from prehistoric times.

In David's time it became the capital of a newly-formed city-state of Aram (Syria; 1 Ki. 11:24). Ben-hadad, its king, provided 20,000 troops at the indecisive battle of Qarqar (853 BC) when Israel and others joined him in an attempt to throw off Assyrian domination. Both Elijah and Elisha worked among the Syrians (*e.g.* 1 Ki. 19:15; 2 Ki. 5:1ff.; 8:7). Later attacks by Assyria weakened Damascus and Israel recovered border towns it had previously lost to them (2 Ki. 13:25). But Aram joined with Israel to oppress Judah and was crushed by Assyria when Ahaz of Judah appealed to them (2 Ki. 16:5ff.). Damascus was restored as capital of Coelesyria in 111 BC, and was a Roman province 64 BC-AD 33. It was while on his way here that Saul of Tarsus (Paul) was converted to Christ (Acts 9:1ff.). By the time of Paul's escape from it (*c.* AD 37) it was in the hands of Aretas IV, king of Arabia Petraea (2 Cor. 11:32).

See also ARAM, ARAMAEANS.

DAN. *Person:* One of the 12 sons of Jacob, borne to him by Rachel's maid Bilhah (Gn. 30:1ff.).

Place: A city near one of the sources of the Jordan, modern Tell el-Qadi or Tel Dan, previously called Laish. It was the northernmost Israelite city.

Tribe: One of the 12 tribes of Israel descended from the son of Jacob. Its original settlement lay in the SW of Canaan, but when it was pressed into the hill country by the Amorites many Danites moved N to find a new home near the source of the Jordan (Jos. 19:47). Here the exploits of its hero Samson were enacted (Jdg. 13:1ff.). The S remnant was probably absorbed by Judah, the N Danites were deported by Tiglath-Pileser III of Assyria in 732 BC (2 Ki. 15:29).

DANCE. The OT occasionally refers to dance for amusement (*e.g.* Ec. 3:4), but it usually has religious significance, as for example to celebrate the crossing of the Red Sea (Ex. 15:20). In NT times it was a common aspect of life (*e.g.* Lk. 7:32; 15:25).

DANIEL. Several OT people, including the prophet of the book Daniel. An Israelite of noble descent, he was deported to Babylon by Nebuchadrezzar with some companions for royal service there (Dn. 1:1ff.). He was given the Babylonian name Belteshazzar, became an interpreter of dreams, and predicted the future triumph of the Messiah (Dn. 7-12). He may also be the Daniel referred to in Ezk. 14:14, 20; 28:3 coupled with Noah and Job.

DANIEL, BOOK OF. *Contents.* Chs. 1-6 are largely historical, written in the third person, recounting how Daniel and his companions were deported to Babylon, that he became an interpreter of dreams, and that he remained influential and survived a plot against his life. Chs. 7-12 are a series of visions emphasizing Israel's destiny and are written in the first person.

Authorship and date. Most modern scholars reject the traditional view that it is a 6th-cent. BC document written by Daniel despite Jesus' attribution of it to him (Mt. 24:15). It is generally claimed to be by an unknown author *c.* 165 BC, because its prophecies reflect events and needs of that time. However this view is itself dubious. For example, the book was accepted as canonical (authoritative) by Jews in the Maccabean period (152-37 BC) who saw none of the historical errors in it which have been postulated by modern scholars. Daniel proves to be a more accurate historian of the Neo-Babylonian and early Persian period than any since the 6th cent. BC; he knew Nebuchadrezzar could make or alter laws at will (Dn. 2:12f.) while Darius the Mede could not (6:8f). The Aramaic of Daniel closely resembles that of Ezra and the 5th-cent. Elephantine papyrii, while the Hebrew style resembles that of Ezekiel, Haggai, Ezra and Chronicles more than that of Ecclesiasticus which was written *c.* 180 BC.

The prophecies. Among scholars who accept the 6th-cent. origin of the work, there are two main schools of thought concerning the interpretation of the important apocalyptic visions of Daniel which relate closely to Jesus' statements about the last days (Mt. 24-25), Paul's doctrine of the man of sin (2 Thes. 2), and the book of Revelation. Some take them as culminating in Christ's first coming and related events, seeing in the church (the 'new Israel') the fulfilment of God's promises to the old Israel. Thus the stone which strikes the image (2:34f.) is the first coming of Christ and the subsequent growth of the church. The 3-and-a-half 'times' (7:25) and 70 weeks of years (9:24) are symbolical and end with the ascension of Christ. The 'desolator' (9:27) refers to the subsequent destruction of Jerusalem by the Emperor Titus. Others see the prophecies as culminating in the second coming of Christ, with the nation of Israel once more prominent in God's dealings with humanity. Thus the image of Dn. 2 represents the Satan-dominated world represented by Babylon, Medo-Persia, Greece and Rome, with Rome continuing in some form to the end of this age. Ten kings around that time are destroyed by Christ at his second coming and his kingdom is established on earth. The little horn of 7:24ff. is the antichrist; that of 8:9ff. is Antiochus Epiphanes who desecrated the temple in 167 BC. The 70th week is a literal 7 year period of persecution before the return of Christ; the 3½ years of 'great tribulation' begin with Michael's victory over Satan and end with the bodily resurrection of God's people (12:2f.).

DAN-JAAN. Probably a N town in the district of Dan, possibly the Ijon of 1 Ki. 15:20; Joab went there while compiling David's census (2 Sa. 24:6ff.; AV, NIV, RSV mg.).

DARIUS. 1. Darius the Mede, aged 62, became king of Babylonia (Chaldea) after the death of Belshazzar (Dn. 5:30f.). He is not mentioned outside the book of Daniel, and contemporary inscriptions have no king of Babylon between Nabonidus (and Belshazzar) and Cyrus. He is sometimes identified with Cyrus, who was related to the Medes, called 'king of Medes' and became king aged about 60. But there is no evidence that he was a son of Ahasuerus (Dn. 9:1). 2. Darius I succeeded Cambyses as king of Persia and Babylon and reigned 521-486 BC. He enabled the Jews to rebuild the Jerusalem temple (Ezr. 4:5; Hg. 1:1; Zc. 1:1). 3. Darius II (Nothus) ruled Persia and Babylon 423-408 BC, called Darius the Persian in Ne. 12:22.

DATHAN. A Reubenite who rebelled against Moses (Nu. 16:1ff.).

DATING (BIBLICAL EVENTS): See CHRONOLOGY OF THE OLD TESTAMENT; CHRONOLOGY OF THE NEW TESTAMENT.

DAVID. In Scripture only one person is called David, the youngest son of Jesse and second king of Israel, typifying the unique place he has as ancestor, forerunner and foreshadower of Jesus Christ. There are 58 NT references to him, including the oft-repeated title of Jesus, 'Son of David'. His story is found between 1 Sa. 16 and 1 Ki. 2, much of it paralleled in 1 Ch. 2-29.

He was the great-grandson of Ruth and Boaz, the youngest of 8 brothers who were jealous of him; he was brought up to be a shepherd. Samuel anointed him without ceremony as the successor to Saul, to whom David was brought to minister through soothing music (1 Sa. 16). Having killed the Philistine champion Goliath and won Saul's daughter as his reward, David became the object of Saul's jealousy (1 Sa. 17; 18:8f.). David escaped Saul's death-plots, with Saul's children Jonathan and Michal siding with David, and he became an outlaw constantly on the run (1 Sa. 18, 19). People who helped him were cruelly punished by Saul (1 Sa. 22:6ff.). David gathered an armed force which harassed Israel's enemies and protected outlying Israelite communities which kept the fugitives in food and shelter. He made a treaty with the Philistines, who fortunately for him did not trust him sufficiently to fight against Israel in the battle which ended Saul's life; David graciously and movingly mourned Saul, his predecessor: 'How are the mighty fallen...' (2 Sa. 1:19ff.).

At the age of 30 he was anointed king of Judah at Hebron, where he reigned for 7 years; after 2 years of civil war he was anointed king over all 12 tribes and later moved his capital to Jerusalem. He led Israel in a systematic and decisive defeat of surrounding nations, extending his influence from the Egyptian frontier across to the upper Euphrates, and inaugurating a period of material prosperity. He brought the ark of the covenant to a special tabernacle in Jerusalem, thereby laying the foundations for the later religious significance of the city. Yet at the peak of prosperity and religious fervour, David committed the sin for which he is always remembered, his adultery with Bathsheba and the subsequent arranged murder of her husband Uriah (2 Sa. 11, 12). He repented deeply, but the deed was done and stands as an example of how sin spoils God's purposes. Later, David's son Absalom was to die after a bitter and bloody rebellion against his father. The family bloodshed foretold by the prophet Nathan after David's sin ran on to, and beyond, his dying day.

David was renowned as a singer-songwriter (cf. 2 Sa. 23:1), and 73 of the biblical psalms are recorded as 'David's', some clearly implying his authorship. Imperfect as he was, he was also a man of action, poet, tender lover, generous foe, stern dispenser of justice—all that was wholesome and admirable in a man. The Jews saw in him the kingly ideal in the image of which they looked for the coming Messiah, who did indeed appear in David's family tree.

DAY OF THE LORD. Seen in the OT as the occasion when God actively intervenes to punish sin. This may come through invasion (Am. 5-6) or natural disaster (Joel 1-2). In popular thought it meant Israel being made

119

head of the nations, whereas the prophets said it meant judgment for Israel (Am. 5:18). In the NT it refers to the second coming of Christ (*e.g.* 2 Thes. 2:2) which is unexpected but preceded by signs.

DAY'S JOURNEY. The distance one could travel in 7-8 hours; perhaps 30-50 km. For Sabbath day's journey, see WEIGHTS AND MEASURES.

DAYSPRING. Used in Lk. 1:78 AV to compare the Messiah with the rising sun.

DEACON. Although 'deacon' is used rarely in the NT, associated Greek words translated 'minister', 'servant', 'ministry' and 'to minister' occur some 100 times; in most there is no technical meaning of a specialized function in the church. Basically, a 'deacon' is a servant, often a waiter. In Hellenistic times (330-37 BC) it also meant Greek cult or temple official. In Jn. 2:5, 9 it is used for 'waiter' ('servant' in EVV), while Paul the apostle can describe himself, Epaphras and Phoebe as 'deacons' ('servants', 'ministers' of the church) in Col. 1:7, 23, 25. Jesus called himself a 'deacon' in the context of table service (Lk. 22:26f.).

However, the word is sometimes used for an official in the church (*e.g.* Phil. 1:1) or as a special gift (Rom. 12:7, 'service'). Paul provides a list of qualifications for them in 1 Tim. 3:8ff., which are especially appropriate for people engaged in finance, administration and social service. Although some take the appointment of the 7 deacons in Acts 6 to administer charity as a formal institution of the diaconate, the language does not support this. They are never called deacons and the root word of service is applied in the context equally to the 12 (v.4). The significance lies in the event as the first example of the delegation of administrative and social responsibilities to suitable people. Later ecclesiastical usage narrowed the NT conception to a class of deacons whose function was not always specified.

There is no Greek word for 'deaconess' and early Greek writers took 1 Tim. 3:11f. to refer to women deacons rather than deacons' wives. Not until the 3rd cent. is there clear reference to women deacons in the church but many of their functions then (*e.g.* visiting women in pagan households) would have applied in apostolic times.

See also MINISTER; MINISTRY.

DEAD SEA. Sometimes called Salt Sea, Eastern Sea, Sea of the Arabah in OT. The surface of the water is 427 m below sea-level, and the deepest point of the bed some 433 m lower still. It is about 77 km long and stretches 10 or 14 km across from Moab to Judah. Apart from a few streams, the Judaean coast is arid and bare. The concentrated chemical deposits of salt, potash, magnesium and calcium chlorides comprise 25% of the water, making it buoyant but fatal to fish. Ezekiel saw in a vision a river of pure water flowing from Jerusalem to sweeten the sea (Ezk. 47:8ff.).

DEAD SEA SCROLLS. A popular name given to collections of written material found in several places W of the Dead Sea in 1947 and the years following. They fall into three unrelated groups.

Qumran texts. These are the most important, found in 11 caves around the Wadi Qumran NW of the Dead Sea. They are the remains of the library of a Jewish community which occupied a neighbouring building complex now known as Kh. Qumran for most of two centuries prior to AD 70. It was probably a branch of the Essenes who withdrew under the leadership of one they called the 'Teacher of Righteousness' and organized themselves to be the 'righteous remnant' of Israel after the Hasmonaean dynasty had taken the high priesthood as well as civil and military power. They expected the early arrival of the new age, in which the Davidic Messiah, a prophet like Moses, and a priest in Aaron's line would all arise. The library remains comprised 100 books of the OT in Hebrew, representing all OT books except Esther. Their discovery has reduced by 1,000 years the gap separating the time of writing from the oldest surviving copies and has made immense contributions to the textual history of the OT.

The non-biblical scrolls show that the Qumran community practised rigorous self-discipline and interpreted the OT law more severely than the Pharisees. Admission to their fellowship meals was closely guarded. They interpreted biblical prophecies as relating to their own times, and claimed additional revelation from God through the Teacher of Righteousness. They apparently abandoned the settlement during the war of AD 66-73, when the books were probably stored in the caves for safety, and the fate of the survivors is unknown. Some resemblances between them and the early church have been traced, regarding their future expectations, biblical exegesis, remnant consciousness, 'Teacher of Righteousness' and religious practices. But there are also significant differences. The Christians gave sacramental significance to baptism and the fellowship meal, and did not withdraw from society; they saw Jesus alone as Prophet, Priest and King, and as Saviour not just as a leader. The Qumran community did not claim their Teacher rose from the dead, although some may have expected him to.

Bar-Kokhba war texts. In caves in the Wadi Murabbaat, 18 km S of Qumran, material was found belonging to the period of the Jewish revolt by Bar-Kokhbar AD 132-5, whose army used the caves as an outpost. A few biblical fragments have been found, together with letters to and from the commander.

Khirbet Mird. A Christian monastery was here (N of Kidron Valley), and documents dating between the 5th and 8th cents. AD were discovered, including Greek texts of Wisdom, Mark, John and Acts.

See also ESSENES; QUMRAN (for history of the community and the layout of its buildings); TEXTS AND VERSIONS.

DEATH. Death is natural and inescapable (Heb. 9:27) and yet also unnatural, the penalty for sin (Gn. 2:17; Rom. 6:23). As Adam did not die physically on the day he disobeyed God, the promised death was more than physical. However, we do not know whether or not his body would have died before the fall. It is best to understand death as something which involves the whole person; physical death is a symbol and expression of, and is united with, the deeper death which sin inevitably brings. That deeper death is a state as well as an event; Paul says that 'to set the mind on the flesh *is* death' (Rom. 8:6; *cf.* 1 Jn. 3:14). Salvation is only possible for those who pass from this state to the state of (eternal) life in Christ (Jn. 5:24). Sometimes the NT emphasizes the seriousness of sin by using the term 'the second death' (*e.g.* Rev. 2:11; *cf.* Mt. 25:41) for the final condition of unrepentant people eternally separated from God.

The NT is more interested in life, however, and death is treated more or less incidentally as that from which people are saved. Christ destroyed the power of death (Heb. 2:14) and sin (Rom. 6:10), so that believers 'sleep' rather than 'die' (1 Thes. 4:14). The completeness of Christ's victory over death is indicated by his resurrection; he cannot die again (Rom. 6:9). That victory is made available to his people, who will be raised from death to enjoy eternal life (1 Cor. 15:54ff.). Even in this life nothing can now separate us from God (Rom. 8:38f.); the believer has already passed out of the state of death even though the gateway of physical death must still be passed through.

See also BURIAL AND MOURNING; LIFE; RESURRECTION.

DEBIR. *Person:* The Canaanite king of Eglon who fought against Joshua (Jos. 10:3).

Place: A city on the S side of the Judaean hills which became a city of the Levites and is equated with Kiriath-sanna in Jos. 15:49. Among possible sites are Tell Beit Mirsim 20 km WSW of Hebron, and Kh. Rabud 8 km to the E of Tell Beit Mirsim. Different Debirs are mentioned in Jos. 15:7 (in N Judah) and Jos. 13:26 (in N Gad).

DEBORAH. A prophetess among the judges of Israel (*c.* 1125 BC) to whom people came to have disputes settled (Jdg. 4:4f.). When Sisera oppressed Israel, she accompanied the Israelite commander Barak into battle at his request (Jdg. 4:6ff.). The song of Deborah (Jdg. 5:2-31a) has been preserved from the 12th cent. BC with its language practically unmodernized and is thus one of the most archaic passages in the OT. It is an important source of information about the tribal relations in Israel at the time. It has been argued that 'a mother in Israel' (Jdg. 5:7) could be 'a metropolis' referring to the city of Daberath, but this is unlikely.

DEBT, DEBTOR. Loans in Israel were charitable, not commercial (they were commercial in Babylonia by 2000 BC). The debtors in Lk. 16:1ff. were either tenants who paid rent in kind or merchants who had goods on credit. The description of sins as debts in Mt. 6:12 proclaims God's grace and encourages the duty of forgiveness, rather than seeing man's relationship with God as one of creditor and debtor. Charging interest was forbidden by OT laws to all but foreigners (e.g. Ex. 22:25; Dt. 23:20). Jesus approved investment to earn income (Mt. 25:27) but disapproved of charges on private loans (Lk. 6:30ff.). Some personal item was given as security for a loan (Dt. 24) and where there was no security to forfeit debtors could be sold into slavery (e.g. Am. 2:6). All debts were to be cancelled every 7 years (Dt. 15:1ff.). See also BANK, BANKER; MONEY; MONEY CHANGER.

DECAPOLIS. A large area S of the Sea of Galilee and mainly E of the Jordan. About AD 1 ten cities there formed an alliance against the Semitic tribes; they were Scythopolis, Pella, Dion, Gerasa, Philadelphia, Gadara, Raphana, Kanatha, Hippos and Damascus. Jesus visited it at least twice (Mk. 5:1; 7:31).

DECEIT. In the NT it means 'cunning' and 'treachery' (e.g. Rom. 1:29). The devil is the arch-deceiver (Rev. 20:10); Jesus has no deceit in him (1 Pet. 2:22).

DECISION, VALLEY OF. The place of God's judgment on the nations (Joel 3:14), also called the valley of Jehoshaphat (vv. 2, 12), possibly a symbolic name for the valley of Beracah (see 2 Ch. 20).

DECREE. Used in EVV to indicate royal or divine pronouncements, or authoritative decisions.

DEDAN. A city and people of NW Arabia famous for their role in trade caravans (e.g. Is. 21:13), probably involved in Solomon's trading (1 Ki. 10). It may have been a Sabaean trading colony in the 7th cent. BC. The kingdom later seems to have fallen into Persian hands. The modern site is al-Ula, 110 km SW of Taima.

DEDICATION. Used in the OT for consecrated things; see BAN; CURSE.

DEDICATION, FEAST OF. Held on 25 Kislev and lasting 8 days, it originally celebrated the winter solstice but later commemorated the cleansing of the temple by Judas Maccabaeus in 164 BC. Its prominent feature gave it the name Feast of Lights; Jesus' presence is described in Jn. 10. See also FEASTS.

DEER. Three kinds once lived in Palestine. The red deer was the largest, and probably disappeared before the Israelites arrived. The fallow deer (the common park deer with spotted hide) disappeared from Palestine about 1922. The small roe deer, no taller than 80 cm, was last reported near Mt Carmel early in the 20th cent. Deer is also used in AV where later EVV correctly translate GAZELLE.

DEHAVITES, DEHAITES. In Ezr. 4:9 (AV) probably to be translated with RSV as 'that is', not as a name.

DEMAS. A co-worker with Paul (Phm. 24; Col. 4:14). In 2 Tim 4:10 however self-interest led him to leave Paul and go to Thessalonica. The name may be a pet-form of Demetrius (see next article).

DEMETRIUS. 1. A Christian whose witness is commended in 3 Jn. 12; some identify him with Demas (see previous article). 2. A silversmith who stirred up a riot against Paul (Acts 19:24). 3. Also the name of three kings of the Seleucid dynasty; Demetrius I persecuted the Maccabees and was killed by Alexander Balas (1 Macc. 10:50).

DEMON. Although rarely referred to in the OT demons are frequently mentioned in the Gospels. In the classics the demon was a (good) god or being with divine power, but in the Gospels they are always hostile to God. Their leader is Beelzebul (Satan; Mk. 3:22). People possessed by demons display such symptoms as dumbness (Lk. 11:14), epilepsy (Mk. 9:17f.) and strange behaviour (Lk. 8:27, 29). The NT clearly distinguishes between demon-possession and ordinary physical or mental sickness (e.g. Mt. 4:24). Jesus was in constant conflict with evil spirits, and to cast them out was not easy; his opponents attributed his power to Satan (Lk. 11:15). He shared his victory over demons with his followers, giving them power to cast them out (Lk. 9:1; 10:17). Other NT references are few; Paul regards idols as demons in 1 Cor. 10:20f. See also next article; BAAL-ZEBUB; EVIL SPIRITS; SATAN.

DEMON-POSSESSION. Apparent possession by spirits is a world-wide phenomenon. It may be sought deliberately as by a witchdoctor (the prophets of Baal probably sought possession in 1 Ki. 18); it may come on people suddenly, as on watchers of Voodoo rites. The possessed person behaves in a way unnatural to him or her, perhaps speaking in a totally different voice or displaying powers of telepathy or clairvoyance. A case of unsought possession in the OT may be that of Saul; when God's Spirit left him he became depressed by an 'evil spirit' (see 1 Sa. 16:14). The Gospels record many cases of possession and Jesus distinguished between 'casting out' these and 'healing' ordinary cases of physical or mental sickness (Mt. 10:1, 8). Possession (lit. being 'demonized') was not always continuous, but when it came it sometimes produced violent effects (e.g. Mk. 9:18).

Such a diagnosis is often dismissed today, but missionaries especially testify to examples of possession. It is possible to hold that a demon may seize on a repressed facet of the personality, and from this centre influence a person's actions. The demon may induce symptoms of illness, including epilepsy. (The Bible does not link epilepsy as such with demon-possession as some ancient religions did.) The early church cast out demons in Jesus' name (Acts 16:18). The command to test the spirits in 1 Jn. 4:1ff. shows that some false teachers spoke under possession. The Bible never speaks of possession by any good departed spirit or angel; the alternatives are either the Holy Spirit or an evil spirit (*cf.* 1 Cor. 12:1ff.; Mt. 12:44f.).

See also previous article; EVIL SPIRIT; SATAN.

DEPUTY. A vice-regent administering Edom in 1 Ki. 22:47. In NT used by AV for 'proconsul'.

DERBE. (lit. 'juniper'). A Lycaonian city, the most easterly place visited by Paul and Barnabas when they founded the churches of S Galatia (Acts 14:6ff.). It may have lain on the E frontier of Roman Galatia; modern Kerti Huyuk, it was 100 km from Lystra.

DESCENT INTO HADES. Although the doctrine of Christ's descent to the abode of the dead between crucifixion and resurrection is firmly embedded in early Christian creeds, the biblical picture is not clear. It receives explicit mention at 1 Pet. 3:19 (and possibly 4:6), with indirect references at Acts 2:27 and Rom. 10:7. In 1 Pet. 3:19f. the idea is of Christ preaching the gospel to those like the disobedient people of Noah's day who died before Christ and had no chance of repenting. The reference in 1 Pet. 4:6 has been variously interpreted as referring to those who died before Christ; to the spiritually 'dead' generally; or to Christians who died before the Lord's return. The meaning is however more important than the manner of the event described; it is part of Jesus' triumphant activity—he is Lord of hell as well as of heaven. See also HELL; SHEOL.

DESERT: See WILDERNESS.

DESIRE. In the OT, it means more than merely 'longing for'. Hebrew psychology involves the whole personality in desire. Hence it could easily become covetousness, leading to envy and jealousy. When such sinful desire was unchecked, the whole community was at risk (Je. 6:13ff.). In the NT sinful desire is equated with love of money (1 Tim. 6:9), illicit sex (Mt. 5:28), and general 'passions of the flesh' (Eph. 2:3), which can become a consuming fire (Col. 3:5f.).

DESOLATING SACRILEGE. First occurring in Dn. 12:11, the term means an offensive (idolatrous) object, and probably refers to the idolatrous altar which included an image of Zeus placed in the Jerusalem temple by Antiochus Epiphanes (see 1 Macc. 1:54ff.). Something similar may be in view in Mk. 13:14; Mt. 24:15, a sign of the impending destruction of the temple. It has been interpreted as the Antichrist or the Roman army's flags (which had images of the Emperor) brought into the temple (*cf.* Lk. 20:21). See also ANTIOCHUS.

DEUTERONOMY, BOOK OF. The name means 'second law', the first having been given on Mt Sinai.

Contents. Three long speeches given by Moses, the first including an historical résumé of God's mighty acts in Israel's journey between Horeb (Sinai) and Beth-peor (1:1-4:43); the second outlining the nature of covenant faith in God, calling for total commitment and dealing with aspects of Israel's worship (4:44-28:68); the third again re-emphasizing the covenant demands, and Moses' last words and actions (29:1-34:12). See also *Structure* below.

Teaching. Probably no book of the OT gives such profound and continuous expression to the covenant idea. God made a covenant with his people which he promised to keep (*e.g.* 7:12). The people were to express their loyalty to him by obeying the 'law' (*e.g.* 4:1ff.). God is shown as sovereign Lord, King, Judge and Warrior who is able to fulfil his purposes for his people in the face of every enemy. By obeying him, and worshipping him in love and gratitude, the people would find peace and life.

Structure. It seems beyond question that Deuteronomy is related in some way to the political treaties of the ancient Near East, and the structure of the book is an adaptation of the model. For example, M. G. Kline (1963) suggested the following structure: preamble (1:1-5); historical prologue (1:6-4:45); covenant stipulations (5:1-26:19); covenant sanctions and oath (27:1-30:20); covenant continuity (31:1-34:12). G. J. Wenham (1970) sug-

gested the shape of Deuteronomy fell somewhere between ancient treaties and law codes as follows: historical prologue (1:6-3:29); basic stipulations (4:1-11:32); detailed stipulations (12:1-26:19); requirements for recording and renewing the covenant (27:1-26); blessings (28:1-14); curses (28:15-68); recapitulation (29:1-30:20); record of covenant renewal (31-34).

Social and religious background. The society portrayed in Deuteronomy is an early one, with Canaanites, Amalekites, Ammonites and Edomites as enemies. There is no temple and the only reference to a king (17:14ff.) is to one who shall be appointed at a later stage. Many of the laws reflect a background of Canaanite religion (*e.g.* 14:21b) and a simple agricultural community (*e.g.* 23:24f.). It is reasonable to argue that an authentic and ancient period of national existence which pre-dated the monarchy lies behind Deuteronomy. The central sanctuary for worship plays an important part in it, which seems to have changed with the years (*e.g.* Gilgal, Jos. 4:19; Bethel, Jdg. 20:18). Deuteronomy seems to present the ideal of a central sanctuary which was never forgotten by reformers but never realized till post-exilic times.

Authorship and date. Fewer questions have proved more difficult to answer than this. None of the NT references to Moses in the context of the Pentateuch (Gn.-Dt.) permits the conclusion that Deuteronomy as we now have it came completely from Moses' hand. Increasingly scholars are recognizing that although any investigation will lead ultimately to the figure of Moses, it is impossible to decide when Deuteronomy reached its final form. Much in it does seem to go back to him and there is much to be said for the view that Moses provided the heart of it. But at certain key points in Israel's history it became necessary to present his words and to show their relevance to a new situation, as in the newly-established kingdom under Saul, or when that kingdom broke up. While a substantial part of Deuteronomy was in existence some centuries before the 7th cent. BC, when its editing is commonly held to have been completed, we cannot say how much of it comprises Moses' actual words.

See also COVENANT; JOSIAH.

DEVIL: See SATAN.

DEW. Moist air drawn in from the sea is largely responsible for frequent dewfall in W Palestine; the number of yearly dew-nights varies from 250 on the sandy soil of Gaza and the high slopes of Mt Carmel to 100-150 in the Judaean Highlands. There are two types—'downward', dew moistening loose soil in summer, and 'upward', resulting from the condensation of water vapour from damp soil and more frequent in winter. This may explain Gideon's fleece (Jdg. 6:36ff.), first wet from downward dew when the hard soil was dry, then dry when the soil was damp from upward dew. Dew is beneficial to summer crops and permits dry-farming in the absence of rain. It was greatly valued by the ancients (Gn. 27:28; Dt. 33:28), and

was used as a symbol of resurrection (Is. 26:19). See also PALESTINE (climate).

DIBLATH, DIBLAH. In Ezk. 6:14, probably a scribal error for RIBLAH.

DIBON. A city of Moab E of the Dead Sea and 6 km N of the river Arnon; modern Dhiban. It originally belonged to the Moabites, but was captured by the Amorites in pre-Israelite times (Nu. 21:26) and then taken by the Israelites (Nu. 21:30) and given to Reuben and Gad. It was lost later, briefly regained by Omri, and then lost again to Mesha king of Moab; Isaiah (Is. 15:2) and Jeremiah (48:18, 22) knew it as a Moabite town.

DINAH. 'Judgment' or 'judged'. The daughter of Jacob by Leah. She was raped by Shechem, a Hivite prince, and Jacob's sons slaughtered the Shechemites (Gn. 34), an action denounced by Jacob (Gn. 49:5ff.).

DIONYSIUS THE AREOPAGITE. A member of the aristocratic council of Athens who was converted to Christ (Acts 17:34). A 2nd-cent. tradition said he was the first bishop of Athens, and some later mystical writings were long accepted as his. See AREOPAGUS.

DIOTREPHES. An ambitious person who would not recognize John the Elder, publicly attacked him and formally excluded those who did receive him (3 Jn. 9f.).

DISCIPLE. 'Learner'; the pupil of a

teacher; the adherent of a particular outlook in philosophy or religion. The Jews in NT times considered themselves disciples of Moses (Jn. 9:28); the Pharisees had disciples as did John the Baptist (Mk. 2:18). Like John, Jesus was not an officially recognized teacher (Jn. 7:14f.), but he was popularly known as a rabbi and his associates were called disciples. The word is used both of all who responded to his message (*e.g.* Lk. 6:17) and of those who travelled with him (*e.g.* Mk. 6:45). Discipleship was based on Jesus' call and involved exclusive loyalty to him (Mk. 8:34ff.) which might mean literal abandonment of home, business and possessions (Mk. 10:21). The disciples were appointed as Jesus' representatives to preach, cast out demons and heal the sick (the 12, Mk. 3:14f.; the 70, Lk. 10:1ff.).

DISPERSION. A term which can denote either Jews scattered in the non-Jewish world (*e.g.* Jn. 7:35) or the places where they live (*e.g.* Jas. 1:1). Voluntary dispersion may have begun with such colonies as are hinted at in Damascus in Ahab's time (1 Ki. 20:34). The conquering kings of Assyria and Babylon compulsorily removed sections of Israel's population to other parts of their empire (*e.g.* 2 Ki. 15:29; 25:11f.). A sizeable and intensely self-conscious Jewish community remained in Babylon down to mediaeval times. Other Jews, voluntarily and as refugees, also settled in Egypt and elsewhere (*e.g.* Je. 43:7). A new Dispersion began with Alexander

the Great's conquests. In the 1st cent. AD Philo numbered the Jews in Egypt at a million. There were large colonies in Syria and in at least 71 cities of Asia Minor; Jews were expelled from Rome in 139 BC (not for the last time; *cf.* Acts 18:2). But they always came back. For all their unpopularity they established themselves as a kind of universal exception. Their social exclusiveness, their taboos and uncompromising religion were all tolerated. They alone might be exempted from official sacrifices and from military service (they would not march on the sabbath).

The life of most of the communities centred in the law and in the synagogues. One major result was a Greek translation of the OT for Greek-speaking Jews, the Septuagint. The communities paid the temple tax and kept contact with each other and with Jerusalem. Despite Jewish unpopularity, its simple but majestic worship of one God and its high standards brought many Gentiles into the synagogues too; circumcision may have prevented many men becoming full proselytes, but they remained as 'God-fearers'. There is no doubt that the Dispersion prepared the way for the Christian gospel. Paul usually began his work in a place by preaching in the synagogue. The Gentile God-fearers were a vital factor in early church history, coming to faith already knowing the Scriptures and watchful of idolatry and immorality. The Jewish influence on so many leading converts also helps to explain why 'Judaizing' was such a peril in the early church.

DIVINATION. The attempt to predict future events which cannot be perceived by normal means. It is similar to the foreseeing aspect of prophecy, which is a legitimate function, but the term usually is used only of prophets who use magic or occult methods (*e.g.* Mi. 3:6f.). Otherwise the practice is condemned (*e.g.* Lv. 19:26; Dt. 18:9ff.), with the exceptions of casting lots to discover God's will (*e.g.* for allocating territory, Jos. 18f.; for detecting guilt, Jos. 7:14f.), and the use of dreams (though there is no biblical instance of someone deliberately asking for guidance through dreams).

Several forms of divination are mentioned in the Bible. *Rhabdomancy* (throwing sticks in the air and examining their position when they fall); *hepatoscopy* (examining the entrails of an animal); *teraphim* (images of dead ancestors, possibly used in spiritualism), are all to be found in Ezk. 21:21. Also there is *necromancy* (consulting the dead), Lv. 19:31; *astrology* (drawing conclusions from the relative positions of planets), Is. 47:13, *cf.* Mt. 2:9 where the Magi may have been trained in a Babylonian mix of astronomy and astrology; and *hydromancy* (observing pictures in water), Gn. 44:5, 15. In Acts 16:16 a girl had a demonic 'spirit of divination' ('python'). This probably refers to the mythological serpent which guarded the Delphic oracle; it was killed by Apollo but the name applied to anyone who prophesied under his supposed influence, usually speaking uncontrolled words through a closed mouth.

See also MAGIC AND SORCERY.

DIVINER'S OAK. 'Oak of Meonemim' (RV), 'Plain of Meonemim' (AV). This was probably a tree where Canaanite or apostate Israelite soothsayers gathered to practise divination; the site is unknown.

DIVORCE: See MARRIAGE.

DIZAHAB. A place in N Moab named in Dt. 1:1; ed-Dheibe 30 km E of Heshbon is the most likely suggestion.

DOCTRINE. In the OT, the word carries the idea of a body of revealed teaching, usually rendered as 'law'. In the NT there is more emphasis on the body of received teaching used as a standard of orthodoxy.

DODANIM. The name of a people descended from Javan, son of Japheth; probably refers to inhabitants of Rhodes.

DOG. The OT regarded dogs with contempt and disgust, despite being the first animals ever domesticated. In Egypt, they were held in reverence and used in hunting. They are still basically scavengers in the E, therefore 'unclean' and potential carriers of disease. In Dt. 23:18, 'dog' seems to mean 'male prostitute'; in Phil. 3:2 'dogs' are Judaizers and in Rev. 22:15 people of immoral lives.

DOOR-POST, GATE-POST, POST. Wooden planks framed a doorway and supported the lintel. Blood was sprinkled on them at the first Passover (Ex. 12:7); a slave's ear was pierced against one (Ex. 21:6); God's law was written on them (Dt. 6:9).

DOR. A Mediterranean coastal city just S of Carmel. It was given to Manasseh. In Graeco-Roman times it was called Dora.

DORCAS (lit. 'gazelle'). Also called Tabitha, she was renowned for her charitable work in Joppa. When she died, Peter prayed and she returned to life (Acts 9:36).

DOTHAN. The fertile plain of Dothan separates the hills of Samaria from the Carmel range, an easy pass for travellers from Bethshan and Gilead to Egypt. Near the town of Dothan are rectangular cisterns like the pit into which Joseph was thrown (Gn. 37:17ff.). It was probably absorbed by the Israelites but not conquered.

DOVE, PIGEON. Several species are found in Palestine and there is some confusion of names. They include the rock dove, widely used for food and carrying messages in antiquity, and the turtle dove domesticated with the name Barbary dove.

DRAGON. Used figuratively in Rev. 12-13; 16; 20 for Satan. In the AV it also refers to some kind of animal, possibly the jackal (as in Ps. 44:19 RSV) or (different Hebrew original) a sea monster (*e.g.* Jb. 7:12).

DREAM. In the Bible there is no pre-occupation with dreams (which may arise simply from one's daytime activities, Ec. 5:3), but it is recognized that they may become a means by which God communicates to people. Two kinds are mentioned. In one, the sleeper 'sees' a connected series of images which correspond to everyday events (*e.g.* Gn. 41:1ff.). In the other, dreams communicate a specific message from God (*e.g.* Mt. 1:20ff.). Among the Hebrews there was a close connection between dreams and the function of the prophets (*e.g.* Dt. 13:1ff.). Jeremiah censures false prophets for treating the dreams of their own subconscious as revelations from God but admits that a true prophet can have a genuinely prophetic dream (Je. 23:16ff.). The borderline is thin between dream and VISION.

DRESS. The Bible does not give a detailed description of the clothes people wore, but Egyptian, Babylonian and Hittite monuments do provide some illustrations. The origin of dress is associated with a sense of shame (Gn. 3:7ff.), although children in ancient times often went naked up to puberty. The most important garments for both sexes seem to have been a kind of loin- or waist-cloth, a long or short shirt or robe, an upper garment and cloak, together with belt, headdress, and sandals.

Men's dress. The loin- or waist-cloth largely disappeared by 1200 BC except for soldiers (Is. 5:27). Poor people, prophets and penitents wore animal skins (*e.g.* Mt. 3:4). The normal dress was a shirt made from linen or wool, with or without sleeves; it was worn next to the skin and reached to knee or ankle. The cloak was a roughly-square piece of cloth thrown over the shoulders, with openings for the arms; at night it doubled as a blanket and could not be taken as security for a loan (Ex. 22:25ff.). A folded square of cloth was worn on the head as a veil or turban, for protection against the sun. Poor people generally went barefoot, but some had leather or wooden-soled sandals laced by thongs; they were not worn inside the house.

Women's dress. This was much the same, although there must have been noticable differences because the sexes were forbidden to wear one another's clothes (Dt. 22:5). The difference was probably in finer material, more colour, and a veil for the women.

Special dress. Clothes for festivals were more costly, and were often white, although scarlet and purple were appreciated; women added ornaments (Je. 4:30). Such garments were sometimes given as gifts or used for payment (*e.g.* 2 Ki. 5:5).

Religious dress. The oldest sacred dress was a simple loin-cloth (ephod, 2 Sa. 6:14). The high priest's ephod was made of costly byssus worked with purple, scarlet and gold, reaching from shoulder to hip. Ordinary priests also wore a cloth covering hips and thighs, and a long embroidered tunic with sleeves and an elaborately-worked belt (Ex. 28).

For dressmaking, see also BLEACHING; DYEING; SPINNING AND WEAVING.

DRUSILLA. The youngest daughter of Herod Agrippa I, she was per-suaded to desert her husband Azizus and marry the procurator Felix with whom she listened to Paul (Acts 24:24).

DUALISM. The belief that there are two divine powers or spiritual principles set against each other. Thus in some periods of Persian religion there existed a belief that an evil spirit existed independently of the creator of good who did not owe his existence to that creator. The Israelites, although they had contact with these ideas, always saw Satan as subordinated to God. Other world-views saw the creator making the universe from pre-existing matter but the Bible also denies this, saying God made matter itself. Dualism was expressed philosophically by distinguishing between spirit (which was seen as good) and matter (which was seen as evil), but this is denied by the Christian doctrines of creation (God made all things good, Gn. 1:31) and sin (the worst sins relate to spiritual rebellion, Eph. 6:12). God is Spirit (Jn. 4:24), but the Word became flesh (Jn. 1:14). Neither does the Bible distinguish between body and soul; people are regarded as body-soul unities, and they will still have bodies of a new kind in heaven (1 Cor. 15:35ff.).

DUKE. Used in AV for tribal chiefs or 'princes'.

DUMAH. *Person:* Son of Ishmael and founder of an Arab community. *Places:* 1. Capital of a district in N Arabia (modern Dumat-al-Jandal) for the above community. 2. A township in Judah 18 km SW of Hebron.

DUNG. Animal dung was mixed with straw, dried and used as fuel for heating bread ovens, and was also used for manure. The Dung Gate of Jerusalem (*e.g.* Ne. 2:13) was probably the gate through which refuse was taken from the city. The dung of sacrifices was 'unclean'; disobedient priests are threatened with having it smeared on them in Mal. 2:3.

DURA. The place in Babylonia where Nebuchadrezzar set up an image for all to worship (Dn. 3:1). Possibly Tell Der, 27 km SW of Baghdad.

DUST. Mankind was created from the dust of the earth (Gn. 3:19). Dust is used to describe mankind's lowliness (Ps. 103:14); smallness (2 Ki. 13:7); and mortality (Gn. 3:19; 1 Cor. 15:47ff.). Warning of judgment is conveyed by shaking dust off the feet in Mt. 10:14f.

DWARF. Denotes one of the physical disabilities which barred a man from the priesthood in Lv. 21:20; the word's exact meaning is unknown. In the ancient Near East dwarfs were thought to possess special (and magical) powers.

DYEING. The craft of dyeing was known to the Israelites at the Exodus, when they dyed skins scarlet by the juices of cochineal insects (Ex. 26:1). Black-purple or red-violet dye prepared from molluscs found on the E Mediterranean coast was a Phoenician monopoly and used for costly garments; Jesus was mockingly clothed in this (Jn. 19:2) and Lydia traded in it (Acts 16:14). Yellow dyes were made from pomegranate rind, safflower and tumeric, blue from indigo plants. See also COLOUR.

EAGLE, VULTURE. Some true eagles are still found in, or travel through, Palestine, and in the Bible the term may include all birds of prey. Mt. 24:28 should probably be rendered 'vulture' (as most modern EVV), referring to the griffon vulture.

EAR. The OT tends to speak of parts of the body, including the ear, as if they were semi-independent, unlike the inter-dependence assumed in the NT (*e.g.* Is. 33:15). A Hebrew slave was confirmed in perpetual voluntary service by having his ear ceremonially pierced against his master's door (Ex. 21:6), and sacrificial blood was put on the priest's ear (plus thumb and toe, Lv. 8:23f.); both events probably symbolize obedience.

EARTH. Used sometimes to mean the whole world (*e.g.* in Gn. 1:1) and sometimes a more restricted area, a 'land'. It is not always possible to be certain which is meant; the Egyptian word was similarly ambiguous in ancient times. In Gn. 1:10 it means dry land as opposed to sea. Placing earth (soil) on one's head was a token of mourning (*e.g.* 2 Sa. 1:2). See also WORLD.

EARTHQUAKE. Earthquakes are natural to Palestine's geological structure, and are mentioned in the Bible and attested in excavations. Among those mentioned are the one in 1 Sa. 14:15, which caused great panic, and Acts 16:26 which had the effect of releasing Paul and Silas from prison. Earthquakes were symbolic of God's judgment (Is. 29:6).

EAST. A compass bearing often indicated by 'rising of the sun'.

EAST, PEOPLE OF THE. A general term applied to various groups living to the E of Canaan used in association with Amalekites, Ammonites, Kedarites, Midianites and Moabites. See also KADMONITES; NOMADS.

EASTER. Used in Germanic languages to denote the festival of the spring equinox, later used to denote the anniversary of Jesus' resurrection. In the 2nd cent. AD the Roman church always celebrated it on a Sunday, while the Asia Minor churches celebrated it on 14 Nisan, which was the date of the crucifixion; the Roman view eventually prevailed.

EBAL (OBAL). 1. A Semitic family inhabiting S Arabia. 2. A descendant of Esau.

EBAL, MOUNT. The N and higher of 2 mountains which overshadowed Shechem (modern Nablus). It lies N of the Vale of Shechem, 938 m above sea-level. The space between Ebal and its neighbour Mt Gerizim provides a natural amphitheatre with excellent acoustics. After Moses' discourse in Dt. 5-11, stones were set up on Ebal, covered with cement and inscribed with the law (a practice attested elsewhere in Palestine), and then an altar was erected and sacrifices offered. Six tribes stood on Gerizim to utter blessings and six on Ebal to utter curses on disobedience (Dt. 27).

EBED-MELECH. An Ethiopian servant of Zedekiah who rescued Jeremiah from a dungeon (Je. 38:7ff.; *cf.* 39:15ff.).

EBENEZER (lit. 'stone of help'). The site of Israel's defeat by the Philistines when the ark of the covenant was taken (1 Sa. 4:1ff.), and the name of the stone later erected by Samuel to commemorate a victory over the Philistines (1 Sa. 7:12).

EBER. 'One who emigrates.' Several OT people, including the great-grandson of Shem who became father of Peleg and Joktan. The name is the same as 'Hebrew', and is a poetic description of Israel in Nu. 24:24.

ECBATANA. (Achmetha, AV.) Modern Hamadan, the former capital of the Median empire and summer residence of the Persian kings. Cyrus' decree about the temple was filed in

133

the library there (Ezr. 6:2f.).

ECCLESIASTES, BOOK OF. *Contents.* The book's theme is a search for the key to life's meaning. The Preacher (the author's title) examines life from all angles to see where satisfaction can be found. He finds that God alone holds the key and must be trusted. Meanwhile we are to take life day by day from his hand, and glorify him in the ordinary things. Within this general framework, Ecclesiastes falls into two main divisions of thought, the futility of life and the answer of practical faith, which run concurrently through it. The book exhorts the reader to live a God-fearing life realizing that one day account must be rendered to God.

Authorship and date. The author writes as if he were Solomon but nowhere claims to be him. The Hebrew style is later than Solomon, so the book has either been modernized later or is by a later writer who took a comment perhaps made by Solomon ('utterly meaningless, everything is meaningless,' NIV) as his text. It is generally suggested that the book was in its present form by 200 BC. Some suggest that an originally sceptical work was balanced by a later writer, but it is hard to understand why an orthodox writer should do this. The theme of the book should be compared with Paul's comment in Rom. 8:20ff.

ECCLESIASTICUS (SIRACH): See APOCRYPHA.

EDEN. A trading partner with Tyre (Ezk. 27:23) identical with EDEN, PEOPLE OF.

EDEN, GARDEN OF. The place which God made and in which he placed Adam; Gn. 2:8 implies the garden did not cover the whole area of Eden. To a Hebrew-speaker the name would have suggested the similar-sounding word 'delight', but it may be a borrowed word meaning a plain. A river flowed through the garden, then branched into four (Gn. 2:10ff.); Tigris (Hiddekel, RSV) and Euphrates are known but Pishon and Gihon cannot be identified with certainty. An area of arable land was to be cultivated by Adam (Gn. 2:15f.). Two fruit-trees had special meaning: one bestowed eternal life, the other knowledge of good and evil (Gn. 2:9). Adam and Eve were forbidden to eat the latter. As Adam must already have been aware of a distinction between right and wrong, it was possibly an ordinary tree selected by God as an ethical test. By his obedience or disobedience Adam would gain experiential knowledge of doing good or evil. There were also animals there, Gn. 2:19f., implying they were suited for domestication.

Theories of the location of Eden are numerous. The text names three territories in connection with the rivers. Assyria (Gn. 2:14) could refer to the state which began shortly after 2000 BC, or more likely the city of Assur which was flourishing soon after 3000 BC. Cush (Gn. 2:13) normally means Ethiopia but the Kassites came from a region E of the Tigris, and this is probably meant. Havilah (Gn. 2:11) probably refers to part of the Arabian peninsula. So Eden was probably somewhere in S Mesopotamia, with Pishon and Gihon either canals or tributaries connecting Tigris and Euphrates, assuming these rivers flow into one (the Persian Gulf). If however they are branches from a common source (the text could mean either) then a location in Armenia is usually preferred. The Bible's lack of precision about the location is probably intentional; Eden is no longer open to mankind (Gn. 3:24).

There are some similarities between a Sumerian story of an earthly paradise called Dilmun, which has led some scholars to suggest the Genesis account is dependent upon it. It is equally possible, however, that both accounts refer to a real place and the Sumerian story collected mythological accretions during the course of transmission.

See also ADAM; CREATION; EVE; FALL.

EDEN, PEOPLE OF (BETH-EDEN). Probably the Aramaean state of Bit-Adini which lay between the Balih and Euphrates rivers. Its main city Til Barsip was taken by the Assyrian Shalmaneser III and in 855 BC it became an Assyrian province.

EDER. 'flock.' 1. A place where Israel camped between Bethlehem and Hebron. 2. A town of S Judah, S of Gaza.

EDOM, EDOMITES. The term is given to: Esau; his descendants (Gn. 36:1ff.); the land in which they lived. The land was a rugged mountainous area with peaks rising to 1,067 m. It stretched from Wadi Zered at the S end of the Dead Sea to the Gulf of Aqabah, along both sides of the Arabah, the great depression connecting the Dead Sea to the Red Sea. While not a fertile land, there are good cultivable areas. In biblical times, the King's Highway passed through it. The land was occupied before Esau's time, so his descendants presumably migrated there and in time became the dominant group incorporating the original Horites (Gn. 14:6).

After the Exodus Israel was forbidden by the Edomites to travel along the King's Highway (Nu. 20:14ff.) but God also forbade them from abhorring Edom (Dt. 23:7f.). Joshua did not encroach on its land, but Saul fought Edom and David conquered it (1 Sa. 14:47; 2 Sa. 8:13f.). The conquest enabled Solomon to build a port at Ezion-geber and exploit the copper mines in the area (cf. 1 Ki. 9:26f.). When the monarchy was divided, Edom first acknowledged Judah's supremacy but later rebelled against Joram and had 40 years' respite (2 Ki. 8:20ff.). Amaziah won it back briefly (2 Ki. 14:7) but it later rebelled again and became a vassal state of Assyria after c. 736 BC.

EDREI. A chief city of the kingdom of Og, where Israel defeated the Amorites (Nu. 21:33f.). Probably modern Dera, 24 km ENE of Irbid.

EDUCATION. The child has always been of paramount importance in Judaism. Biblical books like Proverbs and Ecclesiastes are sources for the study of education, but there are few details provided about the nature of schooling. Indeed, schools are not mentioned; in Acts 19:9 the AV uses 'school' for a lecture room and there is nothing to say whether this normally was used for elementary schooling for 6–14-year-olds or more advanced study for 14–18-year-olds. Ezra established Scripture as the basis for schooling after the Exile, and his successors made the synagogue the place for education as well as worship—some suggest (and the NT supports them) that the synagogue was primarily a teaching centre. In 75 BC Simon ben-Shetah made elementary schooling compulsory, but it must have been well-established before that time.

In the earliest biblical periods, education was exclusively in the home, and the tutors were parents (*e.g.* Dt. 4:9); home tuition remained important throughout biblical times. With the development of synagogues the young were trained in them or in adjacent buildings and later on in the teacher's own home. Eminent rabbis had their own schools. By the NT period there were three grades of teacher—'sage', scribe and 'officer' in descending order; Nicodemus (Jn. 3:10) was probably of the highest order and the 'teachers of the law' (Lk. 5:17) the lowest. Ideally, they were not to be paid for teaching, but frequently a polite fiction granted them pay for time spent instead of services rendered. Many rabbis learned a trade (*cf.* 1 Cor. 9:3ff.). In earlier times, the prophets also probably gave some instruction (*e.g.* 1 Sa. 10:11ff.); the precise role of 'the wise' is unknown. The 'schoolmaster' of Gal. 3:24f. ('custodian', RSV) refers to a Greek or Roman slave who generally supervised a boy and saw him safely to and from school, which is the point of Paul's metaphor.

The scope of education was not wide. In early times a boy would learn moral instruction from his mother and a trade and some religious knowledge from his father. Education remained primarily religious and ethical with Pr. 1:7 as its motto. Girls' education was wholly in their mothers' hands and included domestic functions, moral instruction, and reading. The chief educational method was repetition (*cf.* Dt. 11:19; Is. 28:10 seems to echo the method). Until comparatively late times, pupils sat on the ground at their teachers' feet (Acts 22:3). The aim of Jewish education was to make people holy, and to translate religion into practice. There were no Christian schools in the early church; parents once more played a vital role (Eph. 6:1, 4), as did the local church meeting.

See also SCRIBE; WISDOM; WRITING.

EGLON. *Person:* King of Moab assassinated by Ehud (Jdg. 3:12ff.). *Place:* A city near Lachish in the S confederacy against Judah, possibly Tell el-Hesi or Tell Eitun.

EGYPT. The ancient kingdom and modern republic in the NE corner of Africa and linked to W Asia by the Sinai isthmus. The present political unit is roughly a square from the Mediterranean Sea to 22° N and from the Red Sea to 25° E. Some 96% of the land area is unusable desert, and 99% of the population lives in the 4% of viable land which is reached by the R. Nile. Historically ancient Egypt consisted of two parts: Upper Egypt from the 1st cataract at Aswan N to Cairo (Memphis), where the Nile valley is never more than 19 km wide, and Lower Egypt covering the Nile Delta area to just S of Cairo. To the W stretches the Sahara, a flat rocky desert of drifted sand, and parallel with the Nile valley is a series of oases—great natural depressions where life and agriculture are made possible by a supply of artesian water. To the E of the Nile is the Arabian desert, a mountainous region with some mineral wealth including gold and ornamental stone. Egypt was thus sufficiently isolated to develop its own culture but sufficiently accessible to receive external stimulus.

Early history to Joseph's time. The first real Egyptians who settled in the Nile valley are called Taso-Badarians and appear to have been of African origin. Communities grew up with local shrines and beliefs in an after life. The first pharaoh of all Egypt was apparently Narmer of Upper Egypt who conquered the rival Delta kingdom and founded Dynasty 1. In Dynasties 3-6 Egypt achieved a peak of prosperity, splendour and cultural achievement. King Djoser's step-pyramid is the first major structure of cut stone in history (*c.* 2650 BC). Sculpture, paintings, furnishings and jewellery reached high standards. The economic powers of the kings weakened in Dynasty 5, and the priests of the sun-god Re wielded power behind the throne.

A period of social and political turmoil followed in Dynasties 9-11, calling forth a series of pessimistic writings that are among the finest and most remarkable in Egyptian literature. Amenemhat I founded the 12th Dynasty ('Middle Kingdom', *c.* 1991 BC), restored order and material prosperity and proclaimed himself the nation's political saviour. This was the golden age of Egypt's classical literature and was probably the Egypt of Abraham's time; a charge like that of Gn. 12:20 is paralleled in an Egyptian text. For the century after 1786 BC the 13th Dynasty ruled Egypt. The state machinery began to fail. Many Semitic slaves were in Egypt and some Semitic chiefs gained power in Lower Egypt, forming the 15th-16th 'Hyksos' Dynasties. Joseph (Gn. 37-50) fits perfectly into this background with its blend of Egyptian and Semitic elements.

History to the Exodus period. The centuries between *c.* 1552 and 1069 witnessed the pinnacle of Egypt's political power and influence and the age of its greatest grandeur and luxury—but also the breakdown of the old Egyptian spirit and the eventual dissolution of Egyptian civilization. The energetic Tuthmosis III of the 18th

Dynasty aimed to conquer Palestine-Syria and made Canaanite/Amorite city-states tax-paying vassals. Until late in the reign of Amenophis III (c. 1360 BC) Egypt was the chief power in the ancient Near East; this pharaoh preferred Aten the sun-god to Amun, the chief national god, and his son Amenophis IV abolished worship of Amun and changed his own name to Akhenaten. People then worshipped Aten by venerating the Pharoah; after his death, Amun was restored.

The Egyptian hold on Syria was reasserted in Dynasty 19 by Sethos I, who probably founded the Delta capital largely built by his son Rameses II who named it after himself. This period apparently witnessed the oppression of Israel and the Exodus. Rameses needed a large building force for the cities Raamses in the Delta and Pithom on the Wadi Tumilat (Ex. 1:8ff.). There is nothing exceptional in the story of Moses being brought up in Egyptian court circles; Asiatics are known to have been brought up in royal *harims* with the purpose of later holding public office. The 19th Dynasty was the most cosmopolitan in Egyptian history; Hebrew-Canaanite loan-words appeared in its language and Semitic deities such as Baal and Ashtaroth had temples there. Thus the Hebrew slaves could hardly fail to hear something of the land of Canaan long before they left Egypt.

Later Egypt and relations with Israel. The general picture is now of decline halted briefly at intervals by outstanding kings. The memory of Egypt's former greatness served Israel and Judah ill when they appealed for help from what had become a 'bruised reed' (Is. 36:6). Dynasty 21 (from c. 1069 BC) pursued a policy of friendship and alliance with neighbouring Palestinian states, partly for commercial reasons, which links up with contemporary OT references. For example, a pharaoh (possibly Siamūn) took 'police' action against Gezer in SW Palestine, then gave it to Solomon as a dowry with his daughter (1 Ki. 9:16). However, Sheshonq I (Shishak in the Bible), the founder of Dynasty 22, regarded Solomon's Israel as a rival, but did nothing until the kingdom split after Solomon's death. Then he invaded and subdued both Israel and Judah according to an inscription recovered from Megiddo and a list of place-names inscribed by Sheshonq at Thebes (*cf.* 1 Ki. 14:25f.). Asa king of Judah ended Egypt's aggressive policy (2 Ch. 14:9ff.), but from archaeological discoveries it appears that Omri or Ahab had links with Egypt.

By the time Hoshea, Israel's last king, appealed to Egypt for help against Assyria (725/4 BC, 2 Ki. 17:4) it was weak and divided. (The Egyptian 'So' was probably Osorkon IV, last pharaoh of Dynasty 22, c. 730-715 BC, who was so powerless that he bought off Sargon of Assyria at Egypt's borders with a gift of 12 horses.) Ethiopian rulers subsequently took control of Egypt, but one of them, Tirhakah, was defeated by the Assyrians when he went to Hezekiah's aid (2 Ki. 19:9; c. 701 BC). Ashurbanipal eventually sacked the ancient Egyptian holy city of Thebes in 664/3 BC, and left garrisons in the country. Psammetichus I skilfully re-united Egypt and established the 26th Dynasty which held a balance of power in W Asia, siding with Assyria against the ascending Babylon (*e.g.* Pharaoh Neco, *c.* 610-595 BC, 2 Ki. 23:29). But after the rout at Carchemish in 605 BC all Syria-Palestine fell to Babylon (Je. 46:2). Nebuchadrezzar marched against Egypt after the latter had supported Zedekiah's revolt against Babylon, but the two nations became allies until both were swallowed up by Medo-Persia. Alexander the Great liberated Egypt in 332 BC. It later fell under Rome, and from the 3rd cent. AD was a predominantly Christian land until the Islamic conquest of 641/2 AD heralded the mediaeval and modern epochs.

Literature and language. The ancient Egyptian language was related to the Libyco-Berber languages of N Africa, swamped at an early pre-historic epoch by a Semitic language. It was written in both hieroglyphic picture-signs and a less pictorial hieratic style. Coptic, the last stage of Egyptian language and the native language of Roman-Byzantine Egypt, was turned into a literary medium by Egyptian Christians (Copts) and survived as the liturgical language of the Coptic (Egyptian) Church to modern times. Stories and propaganda works were outstanding during the 12th Dynasty. They include a biography of a sailor who spent long years of exile in Palestine and exhortations to loyalty to the throne. In the 18th Dynasty some delightful fairy stories appeared (*e.g. The Foredoomed Prince; Tale of the Two Brothers*), and poetry excelled in lyric, royal and religious forms. Countless historical and business texts have been discovered from many periods. The literature shows how universal were concepts of the deity as creator and of a sense of sin, but these similarities to some Hebrew literature do not prove there was ever a direct relationship with it. Some Egyptian proverbs have been suggested as a source for the OT Book of Proverbs, but recent research has shown there is no adequate basis for assuming a direct relationship between them.

Religion. There were always local gods up and down the land; Ptah at Memphis, Thoth at Hermopolis, Amun at Thebes who became the state god, and many others. Then there were the cosmic gods, first among them being Re or Atum the sun-god, Nut the sky-goddess and Shu, Geb and Nu the gods of air, earth and the primordial waters respectively. The nearest thing to a truly national religion was the cult of Osiris, the good king who having been murdered by his brother became ruler of the dead and god of vegetation, connected with the annual rise of the Nile and consequent rebirth of life.

Temples were isolated in their own high-walled estates, and only the officiating priesthood worshipped in them. Only when images of the gods went out in glittering processions on festival days did the general populace actively share in honouring them. Apart from this, they sought spiritual

139

solace in household and lesser gods. The cults treated the great gods like earthly kings who had to be woken each morning with a hymn, (their images) washed and dressed, breakfasted (with an offering); they did a morning's business, had midday and evening meals (offerings) before retiring for the night. The contrast with the God of the OT could hardly be greater.

The Pyramid Texts from the 6th Dynasty include a large number of spells, apparently forming intricate funerary rites. Hymns and prayers to the gods were full of mythological allusions. Egyptian beliefs in an after-life found expression in the concrete, material terms of a more-glorious other-worldly Egypt ruled by Osiris. The body was a material attachment for the soul, and mummification was an artificial means of preserving the body for this end. Egyptian concern over death was not morbid; this cheerful, pragmatic materialistic people simply sought to take the good things of this world with them, using magical means to do so. The tomb was the deceased person's dwelling. The pyramids were simply royal tombs whose shape was modelled on that of the sacred stone of the sun-god Re at Heliopolis.

See also next article; CHRON-OLOGY OF THE OLD TESTAMENT; EXODUS; JOSEPH; MAGIC AND SORCERY (Egyptian); MOSES; PHARAOH; PITHOM; PLAGUES OF EGYPT; RAAMSES; THEBES.

EGYPT, RIVER (BROOK) OF. On one occasion the Hebrew means 'the Nile' (Gn. 15:18); elsewhere it means either 'the torrent-wadi (brook) of Egypt' or 'the Shihor', and the ident-ification of the different Hebrew nuances is problematic. Shihor is clearly part of the Nile (see the parallelism in Is. 23:3), and refers to the lowest reaches of the easternmost of the Nile's ancient branches, flowing into the Mediterranean just W of Pelusium (*cf.* Jos. 13:3). The question is whether this is the same as is meant by 'the brook' or 'the torrent-wadi'. Against the identification stands the fact that nowhere in Scripture is the Nile referred to as a torrent-wadi. If it is not the Nile, the best alternative is the Wadi el-Arish which runs N out of Sinai to the Mediterranean 145 km E of the Suez Canal and 80 km W of Gaza. It would be a practical boundary (Jos. 15:4), thus making Shihor (Jos. 13:3) the uttermost W limit of Israelite activity. Some scholars argue however that 'the Brook' is simply another name of the Shihor-Nile, but this makes no allowances for the Hebrew nuances. Also, Assyrian records show that Sargon II of Assyria reached 'the City of the Brook of Egypt' in 716 BC, and some argue that this is Pelusium at the mouth of the Shihor. But his description fits better the settlement El-Arish, on the Wadi el-Arish, and it is probably this which is to be preferred as an identification of 'the brook of Egypt'.

EGYPTIAN, THE. Paul was mistaken for this agitator (Acts 21:38) who according to Josephus had claimed *c.* AD 54 to be a prophet and that Jerusalem's walls would collapse at his command.

EHUD. Leader of the Israelite revolt against Moab, who killed King Eglon in his private apartments with his left hand (Jdg. 3:12ff.).

EKRON. One of the five principal Philistine cities, the modern al-Muquanna. At its peak the walled city covered 40 acres. It was not possessed by Israel until after Joshua's death (Jdg. 1:18) but was retaken by the Philistines who put the ark of the covenant there (1 Sa. 5:10). Apart from a brief Israelite conquest by Saul (1 Sa. 17:52) it remained Philistine-controlled until 701 BC when its Assyrian-vassal ruler Padi was expelled by rebels and Sennacherib retook it. The city's god was Baal-zebub (2 Ki. 1:2f.).

ELAH. (lit. 'terebinth'). *People:* Several OT people, including the Israelite king who was assassinated during a drunken orgy (1 Ki. 16:6ff.). *Place:* A valley the Philistines used to enter central Palestine, where David killed Goliath (1 Sa. 21:9); modern Wadi es-Sant, 18 km SW of Jerusalem.

ELAM, ELAMITES. The ancient name for the plain of Khuzistan watered by the Kerkh river. Civilization in the area is as old as, and closely connected with, the cultures of lower Mesopotamia. The Elamites cannot be certainly linked with any other known race. Rock sculptures depict Akkadian (ACCAD) figures and bear Akkadian inscriptions and there is archaeological evidence for Semitic influence (*cf.* Gn. 10:22). Its control of trade routes to the SE and the Iranian Plateau made Elam the object of constant attacks. Elam was supreme about the time of Chedorlaomer (Gn. 14:1), then was conquered by Babylon but it re-conquered Babylon *c.* 1300-1120 BC. Later conquered by Assyria (Ezr. 4:9), its capital Susa became one of the chief cities of the Medo-Persian Empire (*cf.* Dn. 8:2). See also MEDES; PERSIA; SUSA.

ELATH, EZION-GEBER. Settlement(s) at the N end of the Gulf of Aqabah. As a stopping-place on Israel's journey (Nu. 33:35f.) it was probably no more than wells and palm-groves near modern Aqabah. Solomon (*c.* 960 BC) developed copper and iron mining and smelting N of Ezion-geber, old Elath, which also served as a terminal port for his trading fleet. Assuming its identification with Tell el-Kheifeh, Ezion-geber was later burned down, then rebuilt by King Jehoshaphat of Judah. The Edomites re-occupied it *c.* 848 BC until Uzziah of Judah recaptured it *c.* 780 and rebuilt it as Elath. Under Persian rule, trade still flourished through it to Arabia.

ELDAD. 'God has loved.' An Israelite elder who failed to appear at the tabernacle when summoned by Moses but who still received the gift of prophecy (Nu. 11:26ff.).

ELDER. *In Jewish practice.* Although also a title given to people with a specific function in OT times, the term 'elder' has the basic meaning of 'an older man'. Throughout the Bible seniority entitles people to respect (*e.g.* Lv. 19:32; 1 Tim. 5:1); old age brings wisdom (Pr. 4:1). Consequently, the leaders of Israel were the elders, who were probably heads of families to begin with. Seventy were chosen to share Moses' burden of government (Nu. 11:16ff.). Along with the priests, they were entrusted with the written law and told to read it to the people (Dt. 31:9ff.). When Israel settled in Canaan, the elders acted as judges in each city (*e.g.* Jos. 20:4). The lay judges of Ex. 18 and Dt. 1 were selected for their wisdom, piety and integrity, not merely for their age. The national body of elders continued to be powerful during the monarchy, *e.g.* approving David's coronation (2 Sa. 5:3).

The link between elders and priests is prominent in the NT (*e.g.* Mt. 21:23). Out of it grew the Sanhedrin, the nation's ruling council and supreme court of justice with the high priest as president. Elders and chief priests were included in its 71 members (Mt. 27:1). In Palestine the task of teaching the law seems to have passed almost entirely to the elders, called thus in Lk. 7:3 but more often called scribes, teachers of the law, lawyers or rabbis. The synagogues had one or more 'rulers' to keep order and lead worship.

Early Christian practice. The apostles sometimes called themselves elders (*e.g.* 1 Pet. 5:1), and they appointed elders in the churches (Acts 11:30) who had responsibilities of teaching and pastoral oversight (1 Tim. 5:17). The Jewish-Christian institution of eldership thus helps to unify the diversities of NT ministry. When the office of bishop became separated from that of elder in the 2nd cent. AD, the teaching, pastoral and sacramental tasks were still shared between them. See also BISHOP; CHURCH GOVERNMENT; MINISTER; MINISTRY; OLD AGE.

ELEALEH. A town E of Jordan always mentioned in conjunction with Heshbon; modern el-Al, 4 km NE of Heshbon.

ELEAZAR. 'God has helped.' The third son of Aaron who succeeded him as chief priest. Even before his father's death he held an important position because of the punishment of his elder brothers Nadab and Abihu (Lv. 10:1f.). He is frequently mentioned alongside Moses and Joshua as a leader (*e.g.* Nu. 26:1; Jos. 14:1), and after the Exile the 'sons of Eleazar' formed one of the two main divisions of priests (1 Ch. 24:4ff.). Note also ELIEZER.

ELECTION. The act of choice whereby God picks an individual or group out of a larger company for his own purpose. The OT expresses the idea of deliberate choice after considering alternatives and sometimes implies positive pleasure in the chosen object. In the NT it means 'to choose out for oneself'.

Old Testament. Israelite faith was founded on the belief that Israel was God's chosen people. He had chosen Abraham by taking him to the promised land of Canaan and he chose Abraham's descendants by redeeming them from slavery in Egypt and renewing with them the covenant he had made with Abraham. The source of this election was God's freely-given love for a nation which was unattractively small and rebellious (Dt. 7:7f.). He made it his delight to do Israel good just because he chose to (Dt. 28:63). Although in rescuing Israel from Egypt he was keeping an earlier promise (Dt. 7:8), that promise was itself an act of free undeserved love. Choice, promise and rescue are all celebrated in Ps. 135:4ff. The object of Israel's election was the blessing and salvation of the people and ultimately God's own glory through Israel's demonstration to the world of his praise (Is. 43:20f.). Their destiny was to enjoy his presence. From the chosen people God also chose individuals for specific tasks (*e.g.* Moses, Ps. 106:23; the prophets, Je. 1:5; and the servant-saviour, Is. 42:1).

This election created obligations to keep God's law and not to conform to the idolatry and wrong-doing of the non-elected world (Lv. 18:2ff.). It gave Israel grounds for hope and trust in God at times of discouragement (*e.g.* Is. 41:8ff.), but they wrongly assumed they could always rely on God no matter how they lived (Je. 5:12). Thus the promised benefits of election were forfeited through unbelief and disobedience. Isaiah foretold that only a remnant would live to enjoy the golden age that would follow God's judgment of the nation's sins (*e.g.* Is. 37:31f.). Jeremiah and Ezekiel looked forward to a day when God would give the people he spared a new heart (Je. 31:31ff.; Ezk. 36:25ff.). These prophecies indicated more of an individualized concept of election, concluding that while God had chosen all Israel for the privilege of living under the covenant, he had chosen only some of them (those made faithful by regeneration) to inherit the riches of the relationship with himself which the covenant held out.

New Testament. The NT announces the extension of God's covenant promises to the Gentile world and a transfer of its privileges to those who are God's true Israel through faith in Christ (Rom. 4:9ff.). The Christian church takes Israel's place as God's chosen 'nation' living in the world as his people. Jesus himself is called 'elect' by the Father (Lk. 9:35), pointing to his unique role. The Christian community is also called 'elect' in contrast to the rest of mankind, having the privileges of access to God and the responsibilities of praising him and guarding his truth like Israel of old (1 Pet. 2:9). And as with Israel, God chose poor and undistinguished people for this momentous task (1 Cor. 1:27ff.). The term is also used of Jesus' choice of his apostles (Lk. 6:13) and the church's choice of deacons (Acts 6:5) for special service.

It is Paul who develops the idea fully. He shows God's election to be gracious (Rom. 11:5), an act of undeserved favour to a fallen race. It is also a sovereign choice prompted by God's good pleasure alone (Eph. 1:5, 9). God selects some sinners to make known to them the riches of his mercy (Rom. 9:21ff.), which invokes no injustice because he owes mercy to no-one. The wonder is not that he withholds mercy from some but that he should be gracious to any. God's sovereign election explains why some people actually respond to the gospel when it is preached, for left to himself no sinner can believe it (1 Cor. 2:14). Election is also an eternal choice (Eph. 1:4), showing that nothing can shake God's resolve to save his people. Finally it is in and through Christ (Eph. 1:4), for his people to bear Christ's image and share his glory (Phil. 3:21); they are redeemed from the guilt and stain of sin (Eph. 5:25ff.), and united with him. Paul sees a threefold significance in election for the believer. It shows that salvation is entirely of God (1 Cor. 1:30f.); it assures the believer of eternal security (Rom. 8:33ff.); and it spurs the believer to live a holy life (Col. 3:12ff.).

See also CALL; COVENANT; PRE-DESTINATION.

ELECT LADY. The person to whom 2 John is addressed. The title is most likely referring to a church although some suggest it refers to an unnamed or named person (Electa, Kyria).

ELEMENTS, ELEMENTAL SPIR-ITS. The NT word which is thus translated is the neuter plural of an adjective meaning 'standing in a row' or 'an element in a series'. It has four uses: 1. An ABC (first principles, Heb. 5:12). 2. The component parts of physical bodies. 3. The heavenly bodies (in 2nd century Christian writings). 4. 'Angels', 'spirits' in Orphic hymns which are later than the 1st cent. AD. All four have been suggested to interpret Paul's use of the term. 2 especially fits with Col. 2:8, 20; 3 with Gal. 4:9f.; and 4 with Gal. 4:8f. and Col. 2:8, 18. The best interpret-ation is to combine senses 2 and 3, but the question has been in dispute since earliest times.

ELHANAN. In 2 Sa. 21:19 he killed Goliath the Gittite; however in 1 Ch. 20:5 he killed Lahmi the brother of Goliath. The context is the same in both accounts, and therefore the 2 Sa. reference illustrates how easily cor-ruption can slip into the text by careless copying. Another Elhanan is listed among David's mighty men (2 Sa. 23:24).

ELI. A descendant of Aaron, and the priest at Shiloh, the inter-tribal sanc-tuary which incorporated the taber-nacle and housed the ark of the covenant. Because of the scandalous conduct of his sons Hophni and Phinehas, which Eli failed to curb, God's judgment was pronounced on them and confirmed by revelation to the child Samuel (1 Sa. 1-4).

ELIAB. 'God is father.' A common OT name including that of David's elder brother (1 Sa. 16:5ff.).

ELIAKIM. 'God establishes.' The name of several OT people, including the son of Hilkiah who became steward of the royal household (Is. 22:20ff.); the name also appears on three seal-impressions of the 6th cent. BC.

ELIASHIB. The name of several OT people, including the high priest who helped to build the wall when Nehemiah returned to Jerusalem (445 BC). He later compromised by forming a marriage alliance with Tobiah, an enemy of Nehemiah (Ne. 13:4f.).

ELIEZER. 'God is help.' A common OT name, including Abraham's chief servant and heir before the birth of Ishmael and Isaac (Gn. 15:2f.). Another important Eliezer was the second son of Moses (Ex. 18:4); and another was a prophet who foretold the shipwreck of Jehoshaphat's fleet (2 Ch. 20:35ff.). Note also ELEAZAR.

ELIHU. 'my God is he.' The name of several OT people, including Job's young friend who appears towards the end of the story. His speeches stress divine sovereignty, prepare the way for God's revelation and promote suspense by delaying it.

ELIJAH. 'Yahweh is God.' A 9th-cent. BC prophet of Israel from Tishbe in Gilead, traditionally identified with a site 13 km N of the Jabbok. His ministry to the N kingdom is recorded in 1 Ki. 17-19; 21; 2 Ki. 1-2 in pure classical Hebrew which must have been written no later than the 8th cent.

BC. All except the last of the six episodes in his life concern the clash between the worship of God and Baal (Baal-melqart, the official god of Tyre who had been introduced into Israel by King Ahab's wife Jezebel, 1 Ki. 16:30ff.).

In the first episode, Elijah announces a drought, during which he is miraculously sustained at the brook Cherith and at Zarephath (1 Ki. 17). In the second, three years later, the drought ends after Elijah overthrows the prophets of Baal in a dramatic confrontation on Mt Carmel (1 Ki. 18). The third describes his escape from Jezebel's anger and a fresh revelation of God on Mt Horeb (Sinai; 1 Ki. 19). Fourthly there is his condemnation of Ahab's theft of Naboth's vineyard in which Elijah upholds the strong property rights of Moses' law (1 Ki. 21). The fifth episode is another judgment by fire, this time on the king's soldiers (2 Ki. 1), and the sixth is Elijah's 'translation' into heaven (2 Ki. 2).

Elijah is important as a link between the earlier 'ecstatic' prophets like Samuel (as a man of Spirit-determined action) and the later 'written' prophets like Amos (in his constant recalling of the people to the worship of God and the standards of righteousness in the community laid down by Moses). There is some parallel between Moses and Elijah in the fiery miracles and in their deaths. His ministry was to be revived before the 'day of the Lord' (Mal. 4:5f.); Jesus applied this to John the Baptist (Mt. 17:12f.). Elijah also appeared with Jesus and Moses at the transfiguration (Mk. 9:4).

ELIM. 'terebinths' or 'oaks'. The Israelites' second stopping-place after crossing the Red Sea from Egypt, an oasis of 12 springs and 70 palm trees. Possibly Wadi Gharandel, a well-known watering place, 60 km SSE of Suez along the W side of Sinai. See EXODUS.

ELISHA. 'God is salvation.' A 9th-cent. prophet of Israel, probably from Abel-meholah in the Jordan valley, of a family of some wealth, and still a young man when sought out by Elijah as his successor. His ministry extended over 50 years through the reigns of Ahab, Ahaziah, Jehoram, Jehu, Jehoahaz and Jehoash, and is recorded in 1 Ki. 19; 2 Ki. 2-9; 13. He emerged as a kind of seer in the tradition of Samuel to whom peasants and kings alike turned for help. He had gifts of knowledge and foresight and the ability to work miracles; he headed a prophetic school and was in frequent demand. He had a home in Samaria but was constantly moving round the country.

He was Elijah's servant until Elijah died when he assumed his former master's role (2 Ki. 2). He then purified polluted water and called down God's judgment on those who deliberately mocked him as a prophet (2 Ki. 2). The Naaman story (2 Ki. 5) cannot be dated with accuracy, but occurred during one of the lulls in hostility between Israel and Syria; it reflects a cosmic view of God's sovereignty over all nations. Elisha is often shown involved in affairs of state, as in the

ascent of Hazael to Syria's throne (2 Ki. 8). The anointing of Jehu (2 Ki. 9) precipitated a prophet-inspired revolt against the previous dynasty of Omri.

ELISHAH. The eldest son of Javan (Gn. 10:4) whose descendants occupied a country near the sea which traded purple cloth to Tyre (Ezk. 27:7). It is probably to be identified with Alasia of Egyptian and Syrian inscriptions. See also CYPRUS.

ELIZABETH. 'God is my oath.' The wife of Zechariah the priest, mother of John the Baptist, and a relative of the Virgin Mary (Lk. 1:5ff., 36).

ELLASAR. A city or kingdom ruled by Arioch (Gn. 14:1, 9). Identification is uncertain; Assyria and Ilansura (between Haran and Carchemish) are among the suggestions.

ELOI, ELOI, LAMA SABACHTANI. ('My God, my God, why hast thou forsaken me?') In Mk. 15:34 (*cf.* Mt. 27:46), one of Jesus' sayings from the cross and a quote from Ps. 22:1. It is a mystery which we cannot fathom; it reflects the intensity of his human feeling and separation from God due to his identification with sinful people.

ELON. 'terebinth, 'oak'. A S Danite town, possibly Kh. W. Alin 2 km E of Beth-shemesh. Also the name of several OT people.

ELTEKEH. A city in Palestine allotted to Dan and later a city of the Levites. Either Kh. el-Muqanna 40 km W of

Jerusalem or Tell-esh-Shalaf 16 km NNE of Ashdod.

ELZAPHAN. 'God has hidden.' a leader of the Kohathites, he helped dispose of the bodies of Nadab and Abihu who had desecrated the altar (Lv. 10:1ff.).

EMBROIDERY. The ornamentation of cloth was of two main types: chequer work (weaving, Ex. 28:39 RSV) and coloured embroidery. The former used, for example, gold thread cut from plates of beaten gold (Ps. 45:13). Coloured embroidery decorated girdles (Ex. 28:39), and even gates (Ex. 27:16) and ships' sails (Ezk. 27:7). Both men and women's clothes could be decorated (Ezk. 16:10, 18). The working methods are not described in the Bible.

EMIM. Early inhabitants of Moab, described as great and numerous and compared in stature to the Anakim (Dt. 2:10). They are unknown outside the Bible.

EMMANUEL: See IMMANUEL.

EMMAUS. A village said to be 11 km from Jerusalem to which Clopas and a fellow disciple were travelling when Jesus appeared to them (Lk. 24:13). The site cannot be certainly identified. The distance is wrong for two possibilities, Amwas (32 km WNW of Jerusalem) and Ammaous (modern Kh. Beit Mizza) 6 km W of Jerusalem. The Crusaders found a fort named Castellum Emmaus at El-qubeibeh,

the right distance, but the name cannot be traced to the 1st cent.

ENDOR. Modern En-dur, 6 km S of Mt Tabor, where Saul consulted a medium (1 Sa. 28:7).

EN-EGLAIM. (lit. 'Spring of two calves.' Mentioned only in Ezk. 47:10, on the shore of the Dead Sea; the site is unknown.

EMEMY OF CHRIST: See ANTI-CHRIST.

EN-GANNIM. 'Spring of gardens.' 1. A town in Judah, possibly modern Beit Jamal, 3 km S of Beth-shemesh. 2. A city in Issachar, SW of Tiberias.

EN-GEDI. 'Spring of the kid.' An important oasis W of the Dead Sea, famous for aromatic plants. David hid there (1 Sa. 23:29).

EN-HADDAH. 'Sharp spring.' A place allotted to Issachar but which has not been identified.

EN-HAKKORE. 'The spring of him who called.' A spring in Lehi where Samson drank after slaughtering the Philistines (Jdg. 15:19ff.) None of the places mentioned in the story has been identified.

EN-HAZOR. A place in Issachar; the site is unknown.

ENOCH. 1. Son of Cain, after whom a city was named. 2. Son of Jared and father of Methuselah, an outstanding

147

man of God who like Elijah was received into God's presence without dying (Gn. 5:24). Pss. 49:15; 73:24 probably reflect the story and thus assisted the origin of Jewish hope for life beyond death. In the NT Heb. 11:5f. attributes Enoch's assumption into heaven to his faith. In the intertestamental period Enoch became a popular figure (*e.g.* Ecclus. 44:16; 49:14). *1 Enoch* is among the most important books from this period. Probably the legend was elaborated in the Babylonian exile as a counterpart to local legend; so Enoch came to be regarded as the initiator of writing and the first wise man. He acquired scientific knowledge on journeys through the heavens with angelic guides, and was also God's prophet against fallen angels. Later tradition (2nd cent. BC) emphasized his ethical teaching and his visions of the course of world history.

ENOSH. Son of Seth who lived 905 years; in his time people began to call on the covenant name of God (Yahweh).

EN-RIMMON. 'Spring of the pomegranate.' A village in Judah re-occupied after the Exile. Modern Umm er-Ramamim, 15 km N of Beersheba.

EN-ROGEL. 'Well of the fuller (bleacher).' A water-source just outside Jerusalem, 200 m S of the junction of the Hinnom and Kidron valleys, known today as Job's well.

EN-SHEMESH. 'Spring of the sun.' A point just S of the Jericho road 4 km E of Jerusalem; modern Ain Haud, sometimes called 'Spring of the Apostles'.

ENSIGN: See BANNER.

ENVY. A grudging regard for the advantages seen to be enjoyed by others. The RSV sometimes substitutes 'jealousy' for the Hebrew word but they are different: jealousy fears to lose what we already possess. Its evil is depicted in Pr. 27:4. In the NT it is characteristic of the unredeemed life (*e.g.* Rom. 1:29); was the spirit which crucified Jesus (Mt. 27:18); and is to be avoided by Christians (Jas. 3:14, 16).

EPAPHRAS. One of Paul's friends and associates, who founded the churches of Colossae, Hierapolis and Laodicea, and whose visit to Paul in Rome prompted Paul to write to the Colossians.

EPAPHRODITUS. 'comely', 'charming'. A Macedonian Christian from Philippi called a messenger (apostle) by Paul (Phil. 2:25) who brought a gift to Paul in Rome. He became seriously ill having literally 'gambled' with his life (Phil. 2:30) in God's service.

EPHESIANS, LETTER TO THE. This letter was not written to deal with particular pastoral needs or theological problems. It therefore stands as a positive proclamation of God's eternal purposes for mankind in Christ (1:1-3:21), and the practical consequences for personal living and relationships (4:1-6:24).

Destination. Although the great majority of texts have 'at Ephesus', in 1:1 several important ones (including papyrus 46 dated AD 200, Codex Vaticanus and Codex Sinaiticus) omit them. The early church writer Basil said they were lacking in the oldest texts known to him, and the heretic Marcion called this letter 'to the Laodiceans'. This evidence is reinforced by the letter's unusual lack of personal greetings, and comments such as 1:15 do not fit easily with Ephesus where Paul had worked intensively for three years. It is likely that the letter was sent to a group of churches in Asia Minor, of which Ephesus was the largest; either one copy was circulated or several copies were sent to different addresses.

Authorship. The evidence of the use of this letter goes back to perhaps AD 95 and it was accepted as Paul's from the end of the 2nd cent. Arguments against Pauline authorship include the unusual lyrical style and absence of controversy; the fact that it contains 42 words not used elsewhere in the NT and 44 more not used elsewhere by Paul himself; the stress on the church; and resemblances to other NT writings especially Luke-Acts. However, the fact that Paul is simply declaring incontrovertible facts accounts for the style and words; the emphasis on the church is relevant to the teaching about God's purposes on earth; and literary dependance on others is unlikely. Indeed the strongest resemblance of content, expression and even order of material is with Colossians, which was written by Paul, almost certainly before Ephesians.

Purpose. It seems unlikely that an imitator tried to present the essence of Paul's theology and quoted Col. 4:7f. to imply that the two were written together, as some have suggested. It is more likely that Paul, having heard of the needs of the Colossian church, wrote to them. That exercise filled his mind with the theme of Christ's glory. Paul's thoughts turned to other churches in the area and, no longer having to deal with specific problems, he expressed in teaching, exhortation, praise and prayer the glory of God's eternal purposes and the responsibility of the church to make them known.

EPHESUS. The most important city in the Roman province of Asia, on the W coast of what is now Asiatic Turkey. Situated at the mouth of the R. Cayster, the city had a magnificent 11 m-wide road, lined with columns, running down to the fine harbour which was a great export centre at the end of the Asiatic overland trade route and a natural landing-point for ships from Rome. The city is now uninhabited and the sea some 10 km away. It possessed a theatre, able to hold 25,000 people, baths, library, agora (market place) and paved streets. Its population in the 1st cent. BC may have reached a third of a million. Its temple dedicated to Artemis (Diana) was one of the 7 wonders of the world before it was destroyed by the Goths in AD 263. It contained an image of the many-breasted goddess which, it was claimed, had fallen from heaven (*cf.* Acts 19:35). Remarkably, Paul had friends among the Asiarchs (Acts 19:31) whose primary function was to foster the Roman emperor cult. Ephesus also had a large Jewish colony.

Christianity arrived there *c.* AD 52 when Paul visited it briefly and left Aquila and Priscilla there (Acts 18:18ff.). His third missionary journey took him there for over two years (Acts 19:10), based first at the synagogue then later in a lecture-hall. He made the city a centre for the evangelization of the province of Asia, the Corinthian correspondence being written from there (1 Cor. 16:8). His preaching caused the famous riot of Artemis' adherents (Acts 19) and he had an experience which he described as fighting with wild animals at Ephesus (1 Cor. 15:32). When he left, Timothy remained behind and the letters to him show the consolidation of the church there.

Later on the city was also the base of the John who had jurisdiction over the 7 leading churches of Asia addressed in Revelation; it was the landing point for a messenger from Patmos and the start of the road which joined the 7 cities in order. By then, the Christians were steady in faith but lacking in love; the image of the tree of life is set against the background of the sacred date-palm of Artemis.

EPHPHATHA. The actual word addressed by Jesus to the deaf man (Mk. 7:34), probably an Aramaic term transliterated into Greek, meaning 'be opened'.

EPHRAIM. *Person and tribe:* The second son of Joseph, blessed by Jacob with his right hand indicating that Ephraim's descendants would be greater than Manasseh's. From the beginning the tribe occupied a position of prestige and significance; Gideon's reply to the complaint that Ephraim had not been called to fight against the Midianites revealed its superior position (Jdg. 8:1f.). It came reluctantly under David's rule, and there was still discontent in this N tribe during Solomon's reign (1 Ki. 11:26ff.). Despite the later revolt of Ephraim, it retained a special place (Je. 31:9), and is often spoken of as representative of all the N tribes (*e.g.* Is. 11:13; Ho. 5:5).

Region: The boundaries of Ephraim are recorded in Jos. 16,17. Most of the places mentioned cannot be precisely located at present. The region in central W Palestine which it occupied was relatively high hill country with better rainfall than Judah and some good soils, hence the biblical references to the area's fruitfulness.

EPHRATH, EPHRATHA. The ancient name for Bethlehem Judah. Rachel was buried near there (Gn. 35:19); it was the home of Naomi's family (Ru. 4:11) and of David (1 Sa. 17:12), and was the Messiah's birthplace (Mi. 5:2).

EPHRON. *Person:* The one from

whom Abraham bought the cave of Machpelah to bury Sarah (Gn. 23:8). *Places:* 1. A hill area on the border of Judah (Jos. 15:9). 2. A place NE of Bethel, to be identified with Ophrah (2 Ch. 13:19). 3. A fort captured by Judas Maccabaeus SE of Galilee (1 Macc. 5:46ff.).

EPICUREANS. Paul encountered some philosophers of this school at Athens (Acts 17:18). Their founder Epicurus was born in 341 BC on Samos island, and studied under Democritus who regarded the world as the result of a random combination of atomic particles. He founded his school in 306 and died in 270. The Epicureans sought happiness by serene detachment and believed the gods had nothing to do with human existence. They found contentment in limiting desire, and in friendship. The pursuit of extravagant pleasure which gives 'epicure' its modern meaning was a later perversion.

ERASTUS. 1. Paul's assistant who shared Timothy's mission to Macedonia (Acts 19:22; 2 Tim. 4:20). 2. The city-treasurer of Corinth who sent greetings to Rome (Rom. 16:23), mentioned in a Latin inscription found at Corinth. He is not likely to be the same person as 1.

ERECH. An ancient Mesopotamian city named in Gn. 10:10 as one of Nimrod's possessions. Known to Akkadians as Uruk and to Sumerians as Unu it was one of the great cities of Sumerian times, and today is a group of mounds known as Warka 64 km NW of Ur and 6 km E of the present course of the Euphrates.

ESARHADDON. 'Ashur has given a brother.' King of Assyria and Babylon 681-669 BC. He succeeded his father Sennacherib who was murdered in 681 BC (2 Ki. 19:37), and his first act was to pursue the murderers and squash the 6-week-old rebellion in Nineveh. He continued his father's policy in the W, taking heavy tribute-taxes from the vassal kings of Syria, Israel and Judah. He sacked Sidon in 676 BC after a 3-year siege, and called for subordinate kingdoms to provide materials for his building projects, which may explain Manasseh's temporary detention in Babylon (2 Ch. 33:11). In May 672 BC he declared Ashurbanipal to be crown-prince of Assyria and called all subject nations to declare their loyalty to the national god Ashur. He died in 669 BC at Haran on his way to deal with an Egyptian revolt. See also ASSYRIA.

ESAU. The elder of Isaac's twin sons, his father's favourite. The supremacy of Jacob over Esau, foretold at their birth, was unwittingly confirmed by the aging Isaac (Gn. 25:21ff.; 27:22ff.). From this duplicity there sprang a deep-rooted animosity between Israel (Jacob's descendants) and Edom (Esau's). The Bible uses Esau to symbolize those whom God has not elected (Rom. 9:13), not because of any difference in his life or character but because of God's eternal choice. In Heb. 12:16f. he also symbolizes those who abandon eternal hope for temporal gain. See ELECTION.

ESCHATOLOGY. The doctrine of the 'last things'; biblical writings understand history as a movement under God leading from Creation towards a goal. Hence eschatology concerns the consummation of the whole world's history as well as individual destiny.

OT perspectives. The prophets looked forward to a final and permanent goal of God's purpose in history. 'The Day of the Lord', an act of God's judgment, does not always refer to the end of time but to an anticipated intervention by God in the prophets' historical context. Increasingly the concept of a final day of judgment and a permanent age of salvation emerges. Then the nations will serve the God of Israel and there will be international peace and justice (Is. 2:2, 4). God's people will be secure (Is. 65:21f.) and the law will be written on their hearts (Je. 31:31ff.). A principal feature of these prophecies is the Messiah who will rule in righteousness.

NT perspectives. The distinctive character of NT eschatology is that God's decisive act has already taken place in Jesus Christ, though the final consummation of it is still to come. Hence there is a present or 'realized' aspect to NT eschatology, and a 'not yet' or 'future' aspect. In some measure, the OT prophets' 'last days' have arrived (1 Cor. 10:11; 1 Pet. 1:20), but they are not complete (2 Tim. 2:18). Jesus modified the purely future expectations of Jewish eschatology by declaring that in him the rule of God

has drawn near and demands response (Mt. 4:17; Lk. 17:20f.), but it also remains a future reality (Mk. 14:25). This was confirmed by his resurrection, an eschatological event showing him to be the first example of what will happen to many (1 Cor. 15:20). So Jesus is both God's own agent of salvation and also the 'eschatalogical man' who defines in his own risen humanity the destiny of all. All the NT writings agree that eschatology is Christ-centred and realized, but there are differences of emphasis; the Fourth Gospel, for example, stresses the 'realized' aspect more strongly than Paul's letters.

Signs of Christ's return. The NT regards the second coming of Christ to be imminent, but qualifies that expectation with the assertion that certain things must happen first. All calculation of dates is ruled out, and so Christians live in daily expectation precisely because the date cannot be known. What is uppermost in the NT is the theological relationship of future fulfilment to the past history of Jesus and the present experience of Christians.

This accounts for the foreshortening of perspective in Jesus' prophecy of the judgment of Jerusalem (Mt. 24; Mk. 13; Lk. 21; often called the 'Olivet Discourse'). Here the disciples asked when Jesus' prediction of the destruction of the temple would be fulfilled and when 'all these things' (referring to the end of the age) would be accomplished. Jesus' reply is that false Christs and many sufferings are the beginning, not the end, of the last days; there will be persecution and the setting up of a 'desolating sacrilege'; there will be cosmic catastrophes; and it will all happen 'in this generation'. Several problems are raised by this. The 'desolating sacrilege' refers in Dn. 11:31; 12:11 to the pagan altar set up in the Jerusalem temple by Antiochus Epiphanes in 168 BC, but Jesus' future meaning is uncertain. The simplest solution is to see the prophecy fulfilled in the events leading up to the fall of Jerusalem in AD 70, although it may refer also to events in the last days. The cosmic disturbances seem to refer directly to the second coming; Paul in 1 Thes. 4:14ff. would seem to support this. The reference to 'this generation' (Mk. 13:28ff.) is especially difficult, and it is best to take it as meaning that the signs, but not necessarily 'the end' itself, will be occurring in the disciples' lifetime. Another common suggestion is that it refers to 'race' or 'kind of people' rather than a strict generation. The fact of the unexpectedness of the second coming is according to some scholars contradicted by the teaching about signs, but this is a common combination in all biblical apocalyptic literature. The point of Jesus' discourse was probably to provide some teaching about the signs of the end but also exhort his hearers to keep ready in the present for his future return.

Indeed, the 'signs' are largely present in every generation, except the strange cosmic disturbances and the appearance of the Antichrist (2 Thes. 2:3ff.). The evil of the last times is seen in the NT to reach a crescendo in this figure who is a false Messiah inspired by Satan to perform miracles and blasphemously to claim divine honours (Rev. 13:5ff.). The second coming of Christ will see the destruction of this figure and all evil (2 Thes. 2:8); the gathering together of all God's people, living and dead (1 Thes. 4:14ff.); and the judgment of the world (Mt. 25:31).

Death and resurrection. The Christian hope for life beyond death is not based on a belief that some part of a person survives death. Immortality is conferred by God and is attained through the resurrection of the whole person. The Bible therefore takes death seriously as the result of sin (Rom. 5:12) and as an enemy of God and man (1 Cor. 15:54f.). It will be destroyed at the end (1 Cor. 15:26). The OT pictures the dead in Sheol, the grave or underworld. It is a place of silence (Ps. 115:17), in which God is not remembered (Ps. 6:5). Only occasionally does the OT attain a hope of real life beyond death (*e.g.* Ps. 73:24). In the NT Hades is the equivalent of Sheol, but there is little evidence provided about the 'intermediate state' between death and the resurrection, except to describe it both as 'sleep' (1 Thes. 4:13f.) and being 'with Christ' (Phil. 1:23). In 2 Cor. 5:2ff. Paul may envisage a bodiless state in Christ's presence.

That changes with the return of Christ to earth, for the Christian dead will be raised and those who are still alive will be transformed (1 Cor. 15:23, 52). The fact of Jesus' resurrection guarantees the Christian's future resurrection (Rom. 8:11). However there is still a present or realized element in this aspect of eschatology, for the risen life of Christ is already communicated to Christians in this age by his Spirit (Jn. 5:24; Eph. 2:5f.). But the Spirit's transformation of Christians into the image of Christ is incomplete because their bodies remain mortal. The final resurrection existence will not be of flesh and blood but of 'spiritual bodies' (1 Cor. 15:20, 44) expressing the personal self which is taken from this life into the next. It follows that the damned will not be raised in the full sense but only for their judgment (Rev. 20:12f.).

Judgment and hell. When God's will finally prevails at the coming of Christ, there must be a separation between the finally obedient and the finally rebellious so that the kingdom of God can include the former and exclude the latter. God judges through his agent Christ (Jn. 5:22ff.). The standard of judgment here is God's impartial righteousness, and there is hope for the person who seeks his justification from God (Rom. 2:7). Believers must face this judgment (2 Cor. 5:10) but may do so without fear (1 Jn. 4:17) for they are already acquitted or justified by Christ (1 Tim. 1:16). The life which is built on that foundation is however exposed to judgment (1 Cor. 3:10ff.). The final destiny of the wicked is hell, pictured as a place of unquenchable or eternal fire (*e.g.* Mk. 9:43). The NT view is very restrained compared with Jewish apocalyptic and later Christian writings. The gospel sets before people their true destiny in Christ and warns them of the consequence of missing it.

The millennium. The interpretation of Rev. 20:1-10 has been long disputed by Christians. It describes a period of 1,000 years (the millennium) in which Satan is bound and the saints reign with Christ before the last judgment. No other Bible passage refers clearly to it. There are three main views. 'Amillennialism' regards it merely as a symbol of the age of the church. 'Postmillennialism' regards it as a future period of success for the gospel in history before the coming of Christ. 'Premillenialism' regards it as a period between the coming of Christ and the last judgment. It may not be a period of time at all but a symbol of the significance of the coming of Christ. Whichever it is, the essential meaning is the same: it expresses the hope of Christ's final triumph over evil and the vindication of his people who have suffered from evil. The principal hope of the Christian is not the millennium but the new creation of Rev. 21f.

The new creation. The final goal of God's purposes for the world includes the elimination of all evil and suffering. God's rule will finally prevail entirely, all things will be united in Christ (Eph. 1:10) and the whole creation will be liberated from the curse of sin (Rom. 8:19ff.). Christians will be like Christ and share in his glory. Among the pictures describing this are the banquet (Mt. 8:11; 25:10), and the new Jerusalem (Rev. 21). Meanwhile, the Christian who lives between the 'already' and the 'not yet' has been transferred to Christ's kingdom by the Spirit (Col. 1:13) while waiting for the final 'hope of righteousness' (Gal. 5:5). The Spirit is the down-payment of what is to come (Eph. 1:14), but the warfare between the old human nature and the new Christ-like nature continues (Gal. 5:13ff.). The Christian life involves suffering because of both physical mortality and the satanic dominion of the world, but is always oriented towards the time when God's rule will finally prevail (Mt. 6:10). Christians wait for that day patiently and vigilantly, acting out the prayer 'your kingdom come' as far as possible without confusing that kingdom with the social and political structures of this age.

See also: APOCALYPTIC; DAY OF THE LORD; DEATH; HEAVEN; HELL; HOPE; JUDGMENT; RESURRECTION; SHEOL.

ESDRAELON. The Greek form of JEZREEL, although usually applied to lowland adjacent to the Valley of Jezreel. It is a triangular alluvial plain NE of the Carmel range where important towns guarded both N-S and E-W trade routes. Esdraelon was a marshy region whereas Jezreel was also agriculturally valuable.

ESDRAS: See APOCRYPHA.

ESHCOL. *Person:* A confederate of Abraham in rescuing Lot (Gn. 14:13ff.). *Place:* The valley where Moses' spies gathered a huge bunch of grapes (Nu. 13:23f.), traditionally a few km N of Hebron.

ESHTAOL, ESHTAOLITES. A lowland city and its inhabitants W of Jerusalem belonging to both Judah and Dan where Samson was first moved by God's Spirit and where he was buried (Jdg. 13:25; 16:21).

ESSENES. A Jewish religious community which flourished in the 1st cent. BC and 1st cent. AD. According to Philo they numbered about 4,000, lived in villages and devoted much time to communal study of moral and religious questions and to ceremonial purity. According to Pliny (*c.* AD 73-9) they lived on the W side of the Dead Sea and renounced both women and money. The most reliable account however is from Josephus, who said they could be found all over Judaea and practised hospitality, but much of his description still implies a separate community life. There was a 3 year novitiate before full membership and admission to the common meal was granted. Morning prayers were addressed to the sun, then the day was spent working, with meals at midday and in the evening. The prayers to the sun may have been the practice of the Sampsaeans, perhaps associated with the Essenes; the term 'Essene' was sometimes loosely applied to a wide range of Jewish sectarian groups. One such group was the Qumran community (its initiation was like that described by Josephus). If it can be shown that the Qumran Jews were Essenes, then the literature found there will take precedence over all other accounts of Essene life; for that community see also DEAD SEA SCROLLS; QUMRAN.

ESTHER. The second wife of

Ahasuerus (Xerxes, 486-465 BC) after his first wife Amestris (probably Vashti in the biblical book) had angered him by mutilating the mother of one of his mistresses. Esther risked her life to save the Jews (Est. 4:11-17). See next article.

ESTHER, BOOK OF. This book tells how Esther, a Jewess, became the wife of a Persian king and was able to prevent the massacre of the Jewish race within the Persian empire.

Contents. Esther becomes wife of the king (1:1-2:18); Mordecai, her cousin, informs her of a plot by Haman, the king's favourite, to kill the king, and the subsequent plot to kill the Jews is hatched (2:19-4:17); Esther arranges a banquet at which Mordecai is honoured (5:1-6:14); at a second banquet she reveals the plot against the Jews and Haman is executed (7:1-10); the Jews protect themselves against their enemies, and Mordecai is given a place of authority (8:1-10:3).

Authorship and date. The book was written after the death of Ahasuerus (Xerxes), which was 465 BC. Some Jews regard Mordecai as the author and 9:20, 32 could suggest this; such details could also have been inserted in the king's original annals (10:2; *cf.* 6:1) which would account for the omission of God's name. The Greek versions of Esther contain 107 extra verses which do mention God and are collected in the English Apocrypha.

Authenticity. A few scholars regard the book as fiction, but others recognize that the nucleus of the story is well-informed on Persian matters. If Ahasuerus is Xerxes, that explains the gap of 4 years between 1:3 and 2:16, because he was invading Greece (disastrously) 483-480 BC. Herodotus names his wife as Amestris but secular historians do not say if he had more than one wife; he certainly had no scruples about taking any woman he chose. In 2:5f. the reference to Mordecai having been taken captive in 597 BC makes him 120 years old, but the Heb. allows the 'who' of v.6 to refer to his grandfather Kish as the original exile.

See also AHASUERUS; APOC-RYPHA (for additions to Esther); HAMAN; MORDECAI; PERSIA; PURIM; and the previous article.

ETAM. 1. A place in the Judaean hill country, 10 km SSW of Jerusalem. 2. A cave where Samson hid from the Philistines somewhere in W Judah.

ETHAM. A camp of the Israelites somewhere on the isthmus of Suez. See EXODUS.

ETHAN. 'Enduring', 'ancient'. A wise man in the time of Solomon (1 Ki. 4:31; Ps. 89 title).

ETHICS, BIBLICAL. Biblical ethics (or 'morals') are not concerned with majority opinion or customary behaviour, but supremely with God's requirements. He alone is good (Mk. 10:18); his will is perfect (Rom. 12:2) and has been revealed through his law (Rom. 2:18). The basic demand of that law is to imitate a holy God (Lv. 11:44f.) and to display the heavenly

Father's perfection (Mt. 5:48), by living out the love of Jesus (Eph. 5:1f.). Therefore, the biblical ethic is God-centred and loses its meaning once the religious undergirding is removed. Even in Paul's letters, Christian behaviour clearly springs from Christian doctrine.

Old Testament ethics. The covenant God made with Israel through Moses (Ex. 24) had direct ethical significance. God's grace is the chief motive for obeying his commands; people are invited to respond gratefully to his prior acts of undeserved love rather than submit to his will in fear of punishment. So, for example, slaves must be treated generously because God treated the Israelites generously when they were slaves in Egypt (Dt. 15:12ff.). The covenant encouraged an intense awareness of corporate solidarity in Israel; unity of 'flesh and bone' applies to one-to-one relationships (Gn. 2:23), the extended family (Jdg. 9:1f.), and a nation declaring loyalty to its leader (2 Sa. 5:1). Hence the OT lays a strong emphasis on social ethics: corporate solidarity led to neighbour-concern. The poor had the same rights as the rich because they all came under the covenant umbrella; the weak were especially protected (*e.g.* Ex. 22:22f.).

The law was given in the context of the covenant and so stressed the maintenance of right relationships. The Ten Commandments set out the basic standards governing belief, worship and life. Their relevance is not exhausted with the coming of Christ (Mt. 5:17ff.; Rom. 13:9), because they have deep roots in the creation-ordinances of responsibility for the earth (Gn. 1:28), of the sabbath (Gn. 2:2f.), of work (Gn. 2:15), and of marriage (Gn. 2:24). After the fall new provisions (such as divorce, Dt. 24:1ff.) were needed as concessions to sin-torn relationships but were not annulments of the original requirements. We must not then confuse God's tolerance with his approval, and we must distinguish between biblical ethics and the equivocal behaviour of some biblical characters.

By the 8th cent. BC social conditions had changed dramatically. Some of Amos' contemporaries had two homes; big business flourished; money-lending was on a large scale; foreign alliances were arranged. The prophets applied the law by going back to its basic concern for social justice. They flayed those who sold the needy, accepted bribes, used false weights, and hid their moral failures behind a facade of religious observances (Is. 1:10ff.; Ho. 6:6; Am. 5:12ff.; Mi. 6:8ff.). They stressed personal responsibility, which may have been blurred by the emphasis on corporate solidarity (Ezk. 18:20ff.). And they saw the solution to the gulf between a holy God and sinful people as a bridge built by God's grace alone and a new kind of law written on people's hearts (Je. 13:23; 31:31ff.; Ezk. 37:1ff.).

New Testament ethics. Jesus showed great respect for the OT moral law which he did not come to abolish but to fulfil (Mt. 5:17ff.). He did not however lay down a comprehensive code of rules for moral living; he was more concerned to set out the general character of God's will. Law deals with actions, and Jesus dealt more with the character and motives which inspire actions. For example, he taught that people nursing hate or lust could not evade moral blame even if they kept the letter of the law (Mt. 5:21f., 27f.). The sins he mostly condemned were those of the spirit, not of the flesh, and on two occasions when sexual sin was brought to his notice he deliberately turned the spotlight on the bad motives of the accusers (Lk. 7:37ff.; Jn. 8:3ff.). His contemporaries generally took the command to love one's neighbour as applying to their fellow Jews; in the parable of the Good Samaritan Jesus applied it to all (Lk. 10:29ff.). Love is also the gateway to God's kingdom (or rule, Mk. 12:34) and he gave implied assurance that all who submit to God's rule can share in his strength to convert their ethical convictions into action.

Because the NT letters were addressed to specific issues, their moral teaching has a slightly different tone. Applications are spelt out in detail (e.g. sexual sin in 1 Cor. 6:9; 2 Cor. 12:21). There are 'household codes' dealing with right relationships in marriage, the home and work (e.g. Eph. 5:22ff.). In Paul's language, union with Christ (2 Cor. 5:17) and the indwelling Spirit (Phil. 2:13) raise the Christian's moral life to a new plane. It is important to notice that Paul used the term 'law' as a shorthand for 'justification by keeping the law' (e.g. Rom. 10:4), which is obsolete, and also for

'the expression of God's will' (e.g. Rom. 7:12) about which he is more positive.

ETHIOPIA. Settled by the people of Cush (Gn. 10:6), biblical Ethiopia is part of the kingdom of Nubia stretching from Aswan (Seveneh) S to the junction of the Nile near modern Khartoum. It was dominated by Egypt for 500 years from c. 1500 BC and governed by a viceroy. About 720 BC Ethiopia conquered Egypt (cf. Na. 3:8ff.), then it came first under Assyrian then Persian domination. In Acts 8:27 'Ethiopia' refers to the kingdom of Candace who ruled at Meroe, where the capital had been moved during Persian times. See also CUSH.

ETHIOPIAN EUNUCH. The royal treasurer of the court of Ethiopia's Queen Candace converted under Philip's ministry (Acts 8:26ff.). He was probably a 'God-fearer'; there was a vigorous Jewish settlement in Upper Egypt. Ethiopian tradition claims him as the country's first evangelist. See also CANDACE; ETHIOPIA; EUNUCH.

ETHIOPIAN WOMAN. Married by Moses, possibly as his second wife after Zipporah died. She may have left Egypt with the Israelites, or, if 'Cushite' is derived from Cushan (i.e. Midian, Hab. 3:7) rather than Cush, she may have been of allied stock to Jethro and Zipporah. See CUSH; ETHIOPIA.

ETHNARCH. An officer in charge of Damascus with a garrison under Aretas IV, king of Arabia (9 BC-AD 39), who was encouraged by the Jews to arrest Paul after his conversion.

EUNICE. Timothy's mother. She was Jewish (Acts 16:1) and a Christian (2 Tim. 1:5), living either at Derbe or Lystra. Her son had not been circumcised because she had married a Gentile, probably through her family's social climbing.

EUNUCH. The primary meaning is 'court officer' but in Hebrew there is a secondary meaning of one who is castrated, and it is not always possible to know which is meant. In eastern courts they were valued as trustworthy. The castrated person was excluded from the assembly of Israel (Dt. 23:1). In the early church it was said that Origen misinterpreted in a literal sense Mt. 19:12 and mutilated himself; Jesus was referring to those who sacrificed legitimate desire for the kingdom.

EUODIA. Probably a deaconess at Philippi. She had been a great fighter for the gospel but needed to be reconciled to another (Phil. 4:2).

EUPHRATES. The largest river in W Asia, often called 'the river' (*e.g.* Dt. 11:24). It rises in E Turkey and runs for 2,000 km to the Persian Gulf. Its level in September is 3 m below that in May. Its course has shifted to the W since ancient times, hence some important cities once on its banks are now E of it.

EUTYCHUS. 'lucky.' The common Greek name of a young man who fell from an upstairs window-seat during Paul's long evening address at Troas (Acts 20:7ff.). Luke (the doctor) was sure he had died; Paul's action in v.10 leading to his recovery is like that of Elisha in 2 Ki. 4:34f.

EVANGELIST. From the verb 'to announce good news', the noun 'evangelist' is mentioned only three times in the NT. Timothy is exhorted to do the evangelist's task (2 Tim. 4:5); Philip is called 'the evangelist' (Acts 21:8) but not an apostle (*cf.* Timothy). The distinction is confirmed in Eph. 4:11, which suggests that the evangelist's role was a distinct gift within the church. In later centuries the term was also applied to the authors of the Gospels.

EVE. The first woman, wife of Adam and mother of Cain, Abel and Seth, formed from one of Adam's ribs (Gn. 2:22). She was the serpent's instrument in persuading Adam to eat the forbidden fruit and as a result was condemned to suffer pain in childbearing and to be ruled over by Adam. She was then called Eve by Adam because she was the mother of all (Gn. 3:20). A Sumerian story concerning a goddess born to heal another god's painful rib may suggest a common original narrative with the Genesis account.

EVIL. The Hebrew (OT) word comes from a root meaning 'to spoil', 'to break in pieces' and so make worthless. It binds together both the evil deed and its consequences. The prophets regarded physical evil (pain, suffering or disaster) as something God tolerates in the world though he overrules it and uses it to punish people or nations (*e.g.* Is. 45:7). Christian suffering is divinely permitted for purposes of spiritual blessing (Jas. 1:2ff.), it is disciplinary, not penal, and cannot separate us from God's love (Rom. 8:38f.). Moral evil arises from mankind's sinful inclinations (Jas. 1:13ff.). Behind all history is a spiritual conflict with evil powers (Eph. 6:10ff.). God's whole saving activity is aimed at dealing with evil. Jesus engaged pain and sorrow (Mt. 8:16f.), and on the cross demonstrated God's love and triumphed over evil powers (Col. 2:15). Both physical and moral evil will be banished eternally in the new creation (Rev. 21:1ff.). See also SATAN; SIN; SUFFERING.

EVIL-MERODACH. The king of Babylon who released Joiachin of Judah from imprisonment. He succeeded Nebuchadrezzar II in 562 BC and was killed two years later in a plot led by his brother Nergal-sharezer.

EVIL-SPEAKING. More usually translated as slander, deceit or false witness, it is condemned in the Bible (*e.g.* Ex. 20:16; Ps. 34:13; Eph. 4:31).

EVIL SPIRITS. These are only referred to in 6 NT passages, but there are 23 references to unclean spirits which seem much the same. On most occasions they are a cause of physical disability (Mk. 1:23), although the sufferer is not regarded as especially evil or polluted. The spirits are part of Satan's forces and Jesus and the disciples resisted and defeated them (Mk. 5:8; Mt. 10:1). Some are concerned with moral evil (*e.g.* Mt. 12:43ff.; Rev. 16:13f.). Such passages underline the biblical view that evil is not impersonal. See also DEMON; DEMON POSSESSION; SATAN.

EXCOMMUNICATION. The exclusion of a member from a church due to a serious offence. When educative discipline fails to prevent offences, offenders must be removed; if private remonstrance fails, it is first reinforced by witnesses, and failing that the church through its representatives exercises the discipline (Mt. 18:15ff.). Public, notorious faults are to be rebuked publicly (1 Tim. 5:20) and very serious offences merit immediate excommunication (1 Cor. 5:3ff.). The ultimate aim of discipline is to bring true repentance to the offender and to stop the evil spreading through the church. See also ANATHEMA.

EXODUS. This event marked the birth of Israel as a nation. The Hebrews had been in the E Delta of Egypt for 430 years (Ex. 12:40f.), and had been made slaves during the 18th and 19th Egyptian Dynasties. God commissioned Moses, with Aaron as his spokesman, to lead them out to the land of promise, Canaan (Ex. 3-4). That a large group of subject people should leave a major state is neither impossible nor unprecedented; in the late 15th cent. BC people of 14 areas decamped from the Hittite kingdom to the land of Isuwa, only to be recaptured. Some non-Israelite people, with both mixed origins and mixed motives, went with Israel (Ex. 12:38).

The sea crossing. The place where the Israelites crossed the Sea of Reeds is much disputed, and is bound up with the location of some of the sites mentioned. There are two basic theories. The 'Southern' theory suggests that they crossed near the present Suez area, and the 'Northern' theory that the 'Sea of Reeds' is in the Lake Serbonis region on the Mediterranean shore. The N route however does not accord with obedience to the command not to go via 'the way of the land of the Philistines'(Ex. 13:17f.). W. F. Albright suggested a third alternative, with the Israelites first fleeing S from Raamses to Pithom and Succoth, then turning back N to Baal-zephon (Ex. 14:2), crossing the Sea of Reeds in that area before making SE into the desert.

The desert wanderings. Once out of Egypt the Israelites spent long years in three areas—the Sinai peninsular, the Arabah rift valley S of the Dead Sea, and the wilderness of Zin S of Beersheba—before entering Canaan. The land away from the Mediterranean coast rises gradually to a limestone plateau S of the route from Egypt to Kadesh, and S of that is a triangular area of granite and other hard crystalline rocks forming mountain ranges including the traditional Mt Sinai, some peaks rising to 2,000 m. Most of the wadis have scanty vegetation, the water table being close to the gravelly surface, and in ancient times

there may have been more vegetation and rain than there is now, not because of climatic change but because tamarisk and acacia groves have since been destroyed for firewood and charcoal.

The precise route taken during the desert wanderings is still uncertain. Almost none of the names of Israel's stopping places survived in the later Arabic names, and the traditional location of Mt Sinai has not been traced back beyond the early centuries AD. The traditional route is, however, still possible. From the desert of Shur they passed S down the W coast of Sinai (Nu. 33:10 mentions a coastal camp). Later they camped at Dophkah (Nu. 33:12), which could mean 'smeltery' and thus refer either to the Egyptian copper and turquoise centre at Serabit el-Khadim (which would not have an Egyptian presence at that time of year) or possibly somewhere across the mining belt of S-central Sinai. From Mt Sinai they moved slowly N to Kadesh-barnea, probably near Ain Qudeirat.

The phenomenon of the earth swallowing Korah, Dathan and Abiram (Nu. 16) has been located by G. Hort in the Arabah Rift Valley where there are mud-flats. A hard crust 30 cm thick forms on the deep mass of mud and ooze and may be walked on safely. However, rainstorms can turn the whole into gluey mud. The crust broke and swallowed up the rebels, and those carrying censers were struck by lightning ('the fire of the Lord'). Other incidents also reflect the natural phenomena of the area. The repeated phenomenon of water coming from rocks tapped by Moses' stick (Ex. 17:1ff.; Nu. 20:2ff.) reflects the water-holding properties of Sinai limestone; an army officer in the 20th cent. accidentally produced a flow of water by hitting such a rock with a spade. The stranded quails (Ex. 16:13; Nu. 10:11 with 11:31) suggest the S route because quails return to Europe at that time of year (spring) and land in the N of the area only in the autumn.

The numbers of Israelites given—over 600,000 men (Nu. 2:32)—would give a total including women and children of over 2 million. Sinai was unable to support so many, as the Bible itself indicates (*cf.* the need for God-given manna, Ex. 16). But the people would in any case be widely spread out in tribal and family groups occupying several neighbouring wadis, and water could be obtained by digging small pits over an area. Various attempts have been made to re-interpret the Hebrew to obtain more realistic figures, but none adequately account for all the data. See CENSUS.

Theological significance. The Exodus is seen throughout the Bible as a prime example of God's redeeming grace, which is to be recalled with gratitude and responded to by obedience. It also illustrated the dangers of rebelling against God (*e.g.* Ps. 95:8ff.; Acts 13:17f.; Heb. 3:7ff.).

See also CHRONOLOGY OF THE OLD TESTAMENT (date); EGYPT; MOSES; NUMBER; PASSOVER; PLAGUES OF EGYPT; RED SEA;

and articles on individual place names.

EXODUS, BOOK OF. The second book of the Pentateuch recording the two foundations of Israel's later history as a nation—the escape from Egypt and the giving of the law. The chronological setting is given only in general terms, consistent with the Hebrew treatment of history as a series of events and not as a sequence of dates.

Contents. The Hebrews' suffering in Egypt (1); the early life of Moses (2-4); Moses' attempts to secure the release of the Hebrews ending in the plagues and the institution of the Passover (5-13); the crossing of the Red Sea (14-15); the march to Sinai (16-18) where God gave the law and made a covenant with Israel (19-31) which was broken (32-33) and renewed (34); instructions for the building of the tabernacle or meeting-tent (35-40).

Authorship. The Jewish view from the time of Joshua (Jos. 8:34f.), subscribed to by Jesus and accepted by the early church, was that Exodus was the work of Moses himself. The book itself also gives that impression. This view has been strongly disputed by many scholars, who have suggested that Exodus is composed of a number of different documents by various authors which were brought together by several redactors (editors) at different periods of time. The suggested documents and their authors are commonly designated by letters: J, E, D, P, L, and apply to all the books of the Pentateuch. Some go so far as to say that 'every successive age found it necessary to manipulate the records' (McNeile). If views of this kind had any objective validity then the narratives in Exodus would cease to have any historical value. However, the theories, by their very nature, cannot be proven. Indeed, it is strange, for example, that the passages which are designated as P documents and allegedly written from a priestly point of view, do little to enhance the priesthood. Instead, the political leader Moses remains the great hero and it is Aaron the priest who allows the people to fall into idolatry. When the literary criteria used to dissect Exodus have been applied to other documents known to have a single author, the criteria have proved worthless. If editing did take place, it probably would have been confined to such things as the modernization of place names, something very different from inserting new material and representing it as a composition of the Mosaic age.

See also the previous article and its cross-references; PENTATEUCH.

EXPIATION. Used in RSV in 1 Jn. 2:2; 4:10 to render the AV word 'propitiation'. Most modern EVV paraphrase it: 'atoning sacrifice' (NIV); 'the sacrifice that takes our sins away' (JB); 'the means by which our sins are forgiven' (GNB). Expiation and propitiation both refer to the removal of guilt, but technically expiation has an object (sin) in mind whereas propitiation more accurately focuses attention on someone's relationship with God. See PROPITIATION.

EYE. In the OT the organs of the body are seen as acting semi-independently and possessing moral qualities. Hence the eye can be proud (Is. 5:15) or have pity (Dt. 7:16). God's watchful care is symbolized by his 'eye' (Ps. 33:18). The practice of blinding defeated enemies was common in the E (*e.g.* 2 Ki. 25:7).

EYE OF A NEEDLE. A phrase used by Jesus (Mt. 19:24 and parallels) to denote something impossible. In the Jewish Talmud the idea of an elephant passing through a needle's eye is used similarly. There is no evidence to support the idea that Jesus was referring to a narrow gateway.

EZEKIEL. 'God strengthens.' He was deported to Babylonia, almost certainly with king Jehoiachin in 597 BC (2 Ki. 24:14ff.). He was called as a prophet five years later, possibly at the age of 30 (Ezk. 1:1f.), and lived at least another 22 years (29:17). His wife died on the day Nebuchadrezzar besieged Jerusalem (24:1f., 15ff.); there is no mention of children. His thought is influenced by priestly symbolism. His message was badly received (3:25; 33:30ff.), but he was still respected (*e.g.* 14:1). See also next article.

EZEKIEL, BOOK OF. *Contents.* In chs. 1-24 Ezekiel is the prophet of doom warning the exiled Jews that their exile and the coming destruction of Jerusalem were God's judgment on their sin. Chs. 25-32 are prophecies about other nations, and mark a division between the two main phases of Ezekiel's activity. After this, Ezekiel begins to look to the future. Chs. 33-39 outline the message by which he sought to build up the exiles as the people of God. Chs. 40-48 are allied prophecies which may have been added later; there is a 13-year gap between 33:21 and 40:1 and a change of style, and the Jewish historian Jesephus mentions Ezekiel's having written two books.

Authorship and date. Ezekiel was well known and accepted early in the 2nd cent. BC (Ecclus. 49:8) but there was an unsuccessful attempt by some Jews in the 1st cent. AD to question its authenticity because ch. 16 was considered repugnant, ch. 1 had been used in mystical speculation, and details in chs. 40-48 were considered contradictory to the law of Moses. Otherwise the unity and authenticity of Ezekiel remained unchallenged until the 20th cent. Although only a few scholars have accepted a late date for it (about 200 BC), many considered it of Palestinian rather than Babylonian origin, but this requires extensive rearrangement of the text and some (unknown) motive for so distorting it. Few scholars now deny the book is basically the work of Ezekiel himself during the 6th cent. BC Exile.

Teaching. Ezekiel stresses God's transcendence to make clear that his sovereign rule and power is not limited by his people's failure. God's promise of restoration is no longer bound to a prior act of repentance, but is an act of God's grace which leads to repentance (36:16ff.). In the final section of the book Ezekiel looks forward symbolically to the time when God's people will conform perfectly to his purposes.

See also previous article.

EZION-GEBER: See ELATH.

EZRA. According to Ezr. 7, Ezra was sent with other exiles to Jerusalem by the Persian king Artaxerxes I in 458 BC; he had probably been the equivalent of Secretary of State for Jewish affairs. He was authorized to enforce the uniform observance of the Jewish law and to make appointments within the Jewish state. He is then not heard of until he read the law publicly (Ne. 8) in 444 BC, after he had presumably returned to Persia for a while. It has been suggested that the author of Ezra and Nehemiah confused Artaxerxes I and II, thus wrongly placing Ezra before Nehemiah. But if he had come to Jerusalem in 398 BC, such an error by an author even as late as 330 BC would have been spotted by others who witnessed the events or heard of them from their parents. See also next article.

EZRA, BOOK OF. *Contents.* The return of Jews to Jerusalem, 537 BC (1:1-2:70); the altar set up and temple foundations laid, 536 BC (3:1-13); opposition hinders the rebuilding work at various times (4:1-24); renewal of the temple building through the prophecies of Haggai and Zechariah, 520-516 BC (5:1-6:22); Ezra sent from Persia to enforce the law, 458 BC

(7:1-8:36); Ezra and the Jews deal with mixed marriages (9:1-10:44).

Authorship. Ezra and Nehemiah probably formed part of Chronicles. Traditionally Ezra is the author, and chs. 7-9 certainly seem to come directly from him. Two sections (4:8-6:18; 7:12-26) have been preserved in Aramaic, the diplomatic language of the day.

Credibility. The decree of Cyrus (1) is in harmony with his favourable references to other gods in contemporary records. In Hg. 2:18 the foundation laying is in 520 BC; in Ezr. 3:10 it is 536 BC—but the former probably marked the revival of work. The Apocryphal book 1 Esdras is similar to Ezra but its history is confused and Ezra is undoubtedly more reliable.

For date, see CHRONICLES. See also EZRA; NEHEMIAH.

F

FACE. The Hebrew word could refer to the front of something or its outward appearance, as well as a human or animal face, and a person's face became a synonym for his presence; hence 'the face of God'. Humility was signed by bowing the face to the ground; fear by falling on one's face; and contempt by spitting in it. To lift a (fallen or bowing) face was a gesture of favour; to 'set one's face' was to be determined.

FAIR HAVENS. Modern Kaloi Limenes, a small bay on the S coast of Crete, protected by small islands but not an ideal winter harbour (Acts 27:8ff.).

FAITH. *Old Testament.* The word itself occurs rarely, and even then only occasionally conveys the familiar idea of trust. However many words do express the idea, including 'believe', 'trust' and 'hope'. In Ps. 26:1, for example, the writer declares his trust in God using his integrity as evidence of it. The OT does have the basic demand for a right attitude of faith in God similar to the NT even though it expresses it in terms of an upright life (*e.g.* Ps. 37:3ff.; Pr. 3:5). Trust in one's own righteousness (Ezk. 32:13), in idols (Is. 42:17) and in human strength (Je. 17:5) is denounced. People regarded God 'the rock' as worthy of trust (*e.g.* Ps. 18:2), and Abraham's faith which was 'reckoned to him as righteousness' (Gn. 15:6) became a model for NT writers to develop.

New Testament. The word in various forms occurs over 300 times, and the stress on faith is to be seen against the background of the saving work of God in Christ. Faith is the attitude whereby a person abandons all reliance on his own efforts to obtain salvation, and relies on Christ alone for all that salvation means (Jn. 3:16; Acts 16:30f.). Sometimes faith is followed by 'that', indicating that it is concerned with facts (*e.g.* Mt. 21:32; Jn. 5:24); a genuine belief that what God has revealed is true will lead to true faith. The characteristic construction for

165

saving faith is to 'believe in' (literally *into*) Christ; the believer cleaves to Christ with all his or her heart and so 'abides in him' (Jn. 15:4). Often, however, the verb is used alone ('many believed', Jn. 4:41), and Christians are called simply 'believers'. The noun sometimes also refers to the body of Christian belief (*e.g.* Col. 2:7).

In the Synoptic Gospels faith is often associated with healing, but the faith is always in Jesus personally. In the Fourth Gospel, however, the verb is used 98 times and the emphasis is on believing into Christ or his name (that is, believing all that he is essentially in himself). Such faith gives the believer eternal life now (Jn. 3:36). For Paul, faith is the typical Christian attitude. There is no substitute for it; faith alone enables a person to receive God's saving power (Rom 1:16). Against the Judaizers, those who emphasized the value of the Jewish law, Paul insists that we can do nothing at all to bring about our salvation; the doctrine of justification by faith lies at the heart of his teaching (Rom. 5:1). It is a trustful acceptance of God's gift in Christ. He also connects the Holy Spirit with faith. The indwelling Spirit is God's mark of ownership given to people only because they believe (Eph. 1:13f.), a 'down-payment' which guarantees that eternal life in the full sense will infallibly follow.

The writer to the Hebrews is concerned to show the contrast between faith and 'sight' in the classic passage of ch. 11; the people he mentions had no outward evidence, only God's promises, to support them. The letter of James appears at first to contradict the rest of the NT when it says 'a man is justified by works and not by faith alone' (Jas. 2:24). But the 'faith' he opposes is not warm personal trust in a living saviour but an intellectual assent to truths not backed up by a life lived in accordance with them (Jas. 2:15-19). Everywhere he presupposes faith in the Pauline sense (1:3; 2:1). Faith is clearly one of the most important concepts in the NT. It implies complete reliance upon God, whom we cannot please without it (Heb. 11:6).

See also GUARANTEE; JUSTIFICATION.

FALL, THE. The account in Gn. 3 describes how mankind's earliest parents, when tempted by the serpent, disobeyed God's command by eating fruit from the tree of the knowledge of good and evil. It shows sin to be human rebellion against God and pride in mankind's supposed self-sufficiency. The couple became aware of guilt and immediate separation from God; true humanity, which conforms to the image of God, was lost, although God's image in mankind was not entirely erased. The efforts of fallen man were cursed with frustration; historically, mankind's greatest achievements have often brought great evils with them through misuse. The result of the fall is that people know in experience good *and evil*.

Paul describes the psychological and moral effects graphically in Rom. 1:18ff. People know the truth of God but suppress it, which leads them into intellectual vanity and futility. Their search for meaning in life becomes ever more foolish and degrading, leading to superstition, idolatry, vice, and social evils. Man's true dignity has been overthrown. The whole Bible shows all mankind to be fallen from perfection, not that the race has risen morally and culturally from humble origins. It is against this background that the saving action of Jesus Christ takes on its proper significance.

The classic controversy concerning the nature of the fall took place in the early 5th cent. AD between advocates of the Pelagian heresy (stating that Adam's sin affected only himself and that each person is born free from sin and capable of a perfect life) and Augustine, who in line with the NT understood the fall as an historic event affecting all creation thereafter. But what was lost through Adam's sin will be restored finally in the return of Christ (Rom. 8:19ff.; Rev. 21-22).

See also SIN.

FAMILY, HOUSEHOLD. *Old Testament.* There is no OT word which corresponds exactly to the modern 'family' of mother, father and children. The nearest equivalent is 'house' which signified a group of people (but could also refer to the whole nation as Is. 5:7). The term often translated 'family' had more the meaning of 'clan' than the smaller nuclear family. In Jos. 7:16ff. Achan is regarded as belonging to his grandfather Zabdi's household, even though he had children of his own (though perhaps significantly only Achan's nuclear family was killed after he sinned).

Marriage with relatives (except certain close ones, Lv. 18:6ff.) was preferred. In most cases the choice of mate and subsequent arrangements for marriage were made by the parents. A price was paid (or service rendered, Gn. 29:15ff.) to the bride's father as compensation to the family for its loss. The woman left her father's house and went to live in her husband's. In patriarchal times this may have meant living in the same group as her husband's father and brothers, although by the time of the Monarchy the smallness of many private houses uncovered by archaeologists suggests that the son probably set up his own home when he married. Although one man, one wife was probably intended at the creation, polygamy is found as early as the patriarchal period. Abraham had one wife but followed the custom of the time by taking Sarah's servant Hagar when Sarah proved childless (Gn. 16:1f.). Jacob had two wives, something which is assumed in Moses' law (Dt. 21:15), but the fact that this was not God's original intention is shown by the prophets' emphasis on Israel as the sole 'bride' of God (*e.g.* Is. 62:4f.).

The woman was the possession first of her father then, on marriage, of her husband; he could divorce her but she probably could not divorce him. The greatest wish of a couple was for children, especially sons (Ps. 127:3ff.). The eldest son inherited a double portion of the estate and became head of the family when his father died. The terms 'brother' and 'sister' were applied to half-siblings with a different mother or father, and uncles and aunts were often of importance to children. Families retained close ties and obligations throughout OT times; of special importance was the 'levirate marriage' of a close relative to a childless widow (*e.g.* Ru. 2:20; 4).

New Testament. Again, 'family' might also mean tribe or nation; the idea of 'household' is however frequent. It was a unit of society common in the Greek and Roman worlds, and consisted of husband (the 'lord' or 'master'), his wife, children, slaves, and also various dependants such as servants, employees and even friends who joined the household for the sake of mutual benefits. The household was an important factor in the growth and stability of the early church, for among the Jews it was already the context of religious exercises such as major festivals, a weekly sacred meal, and prayers and instruction. The 'breaking of bread' took place in the Jerusalem church by 'households' (Acts 2:46). Churches were often formed by and around households (*e.g.* Cornelius, Acts 10; Lydia, Acts 16). Paul instructed the church in household units at Ephesus (Acts 20:20), and regularly set out the mutual duties of each member of a household (*e.g.* Col. 3:18-4:1). Both baptism and the Lord's Supper took place in household contexts, and it was from the ranks of proved heads of households that church leaders were selected (1 Tim. 3:2ff.). Behind every family stands the universal fatherhood

of God (Eph. 3:14f.), and the church is therefore also viewed as God's 'household' (Eph. 2:19).

See also ADOPTION; AVENGER OF BLOOD; BARRENNESS; CAESAR'S HOUSEHOLD; EDUCATION; FIRST-BORN; INHERITANCE; MARRIAGE.

FAMINE. Food shortages are often recorded in the Bible simply as historical facts. For example, the famine in Acts 11:27ff. which affected Judaea *c.* AD 46-7 is attested in other records, and was the first instance of inter-church aid. However, famines are also integrated into the biblical doctrine of divine providence (*e.g.* Rev. 6:8). God withdrew the fruits of nature in times of disobedience as an indication of his displeasure and a warning to repent (*e.g.* Hg. 1:9ff.; 2:16f.). The link between disobedience and famine is clearly expressed in Dt. 28 and poetically illustrated in Je. 14.

FASTING. This generally means going without all food and drink for a period, and not merely refraining from certain kinds of food. In the OT period there was a fast on the Day of Atonement and after the Exile on four other annual occasions. Occasional personal or corporate fasts expressed grief (1 Sa. 31:13) and penitence (1 Ki. 21:27), or were part of seeking God's help (2 Sa. 12:16ff.). But fasting without right conduct was useless (Is. 58:4ff.). There is only one recorded occasion on which Jesus fasted (Mt. 4:1ff.). He assumed his hearers would fast and told them not to make a public show of it (Mt. 6:16ff.), but he declared it inappropriate while he was with his disciples (Mt. 9:14ff.). Church leaders fasted when choosing missionaries (Acts 13:2f.) and elders (Acts 14:23).

FEAR. The word is used in four ways. There is *holy fear* which comes from the believer's awareness of a living God as a result of which he obeys God and avoids evil (Je. 32:40); it is the secret of right living (Pr. 8:13). Although the NT emphasizes God as loving and forgiving, a reverent fear of God's awesomeness remains, stimulating believers to seek holiness (2 Cor. 7:1). *Slavish fear* is felt by those who reject God (Acts 24:25), but it may be used for their conversion (Acts 16:29ff.). *Fear of people* is sometimes due to respect of them (*e.g.* Rom. 13:7) and sometimes blind dread (Pr. 29:25) which can be removed by true love to God (1 Jn. 4:18). 'Fear' may also stand for *an object of fear* (Pr. 10:24); when the Hebrews entered the promised land God sometimes so impressed the Canaanites with his fear that they were unable to withstand the invaders (Ex. 23:27f.).

FEASTS. A day or period of religious celebration. Some were associated with the seasons, but unlike pagan seasonal feasts they acknowledged God as a generous provider and recorded his free favour to his people. Religious commitment was not incompatible with pleasure in earthly things seen as God's gifts, and there was no sharp demarcation between sorrow for sin and the joy of the Lord,

because acknowledgment of sin and devotion to the law were both involved in many feasts. The prophets often denounced feasts (*e.g.* Is. 1:13ff.) because many Israelites had been using them in the wrong way, thinking that simply keeping the feasts could be a substitute for living a godly life. It was never intended that religion should consist solely of external observances.

The main feasts referred to in the OT are: *Unleavened Bread* or *Passover*, a week commemorating the Exodus; *Weeks* or harvest, later known as Pentecost; *Tabernacles* or 'booths' or 'ingathering'; *Sabbath*; *Day of Atonement*, in which sin was dealt with; *Purim*, celebrating the deliverance of the Jews from Haman's intrigues. In the NT the festival of *Lights* or *Dedication* is mentioned (Jn. 10:22), celebrating the restoration of the temple by Judas Maccabaeus in 164 BC.

For details, see ATONEMENT, DAY OF; PASSOVER; PENTECOST; PURIM; SABBATH; TABERNACLES. See also BANQUET.

FELIX. Brother of Pallas, Claudius' favourite, through whom Felix was made procurator of Judaea. He probably arrived in Palestine *c.* AD 52. During his rule unrest increased and was mercilessly crushed. He put down the followers of a Messianic pretender *c.* AD 55 (*cf.* Acts 21:38 and see EGYPTIAN, THE). Felix displayed his well-known avarice and disregard for justice by keeping Paul in prison for two years hoping for a bribe (Acts 24:26). He was recalled by Nero in AD

59. See also DRUSILLA (his wife); FESTUS (his successor).

FELLOWSHIP. In the NT, the terms 'partnership', 'fellowship', 'communion', 'sharing' come from a root meaning to share in something with someone, with the stress on participation in something rather than mere association with other people. The noun *koinonia* is sometimes transliterated into English to describe Christian relationships. There are two main uses of the term in the NT.

Having a share. People may have a share in Christian work (2 Cor. 8:23), secular business (Lk. 5:10), suffering (2 Cor. 1:7), and worship (1 Cor. 10:18). It may signify the corporate Christian life sharing in the body and blood of Christ (1 Cor. 10:16), in a relationship with Jesus (1 Cor. 1:9) and the Holy Spirit (2 Cor. 13:14), and in sharing in relieving others' needs (2 Cor. 8:4) and in the sufferings of Christ (Phil. 3:10).

Giving a share. The word *koinonia* is also used in 2 Cor. 9:13 where RSV translates 'your contribution'. It is similarly used in Rom. 15:26, where it refers to a generosity which clothes itself in practical action. In Acts 2:42 'fellowship' may mean charitable giving, sharing goods, or the inner spiritual bond which joined the early Jerusalem brotherhood and expressed itself in the outward act of pooling material resources.

See also LORD'S SUPPER.

FESTAL GARMENTS: See DRESS.

FIG, FIG TREE. The fig tree is indigenous to Asia Minor and the E Mediterranean. It can grow to 11 m high, although on rocky ground it often grows as a several-stemmed shrub. It is often planted with the vine, its branches and the vine's foliage prompting a symbol of well-being and prosperity (1 Ki. 4:25). A slow-growing tree demanding years of patient labour, its failure or destruction was a national calamity (Je. 5:17). Broad fig leaves are still sewn together in the E and used to wrap fresh fruit (*cf.* Gn. 3:7). Lumps of dried, pressed figs made an excellent food and an acceptable gift, and were easy to carry (1 Sa. 25:18). The bad figs of Je. 24:2; 29:17 could be inedible male caprifigs which are home to the fig-wasp which pollinates the edible female fig; commonly cultivated figs do not need insect pollinators. The incident of Jesus cursing the fig tree (Mt. 21:18ff.) may be explained by out-of-season leafiness before fruits mature. Sycamore-figs were also eaten after being notched to make them swell (Am. 7:14).

FIRE. Starting a fire by artificial means was a skill known to humans from Stone Age times, but great care was taken to preserve a burning fire to avoid the need for relighting it. Abraham apparently carried a piece of burning fire when he went to sacrifice Isaac (Gn. 22:6); Is. 30:14 implies this was normal domestic practice centuries later. Flames were kindled by a wooden fire-drill or by striking a flint on iron pyrites.

Apart from normal uses for cooking,

heating and incineration, fire had religious significance. A continuous fire burnt on the tabernacle and temple altars (Lv. 6:13); children were occasionally 'passed through' fire (not necessarily to their deaths) in dedication to the pagan god Molech (2 Ki. 16:3); and fire sometimes symbolized God's presence (Ex. 3:2), holiness (Dt. 4:24) and anger against sin (Is. 66:15f.).

FIREPAN. A bowl-shaped utensil used in the tabernacle and temple; golden, to hold burnt lamp-wicks; bronze, to carry coals from the altar; and as a synonym for CENSER.

FIRST-BORN. The eldest son's special position was very widely recognized in the ancient Near East, though it was rarely extended to sons of concubines or slave-girls (Jdg. 11:1f.). In OT times his privileges included a larger (sometimes double) inheritance than other sons, a special paternal blessing, family leadership and an honoured position at mealtimes. Such privileges were normally forfeited only by serious offence (Gn. 49:4) or sale (Gn. 25:29ff.). In Israelite ritual the first-born of a family and of an animal belonged to God (Ex. 13:2); sons were 'redeemed' by paying 5 shekels and sacrificing male animals (Nu. 18:15ff.).

Jesus was the first-born of Mary (Lk. 2:7), a phrase which allows, but does not demand, that she had other children later (cf. Mk. 6:3). As such he was offered to God in the temple (Lk. 2:22ff.). Jesus is also described as the first-born of his heavenly Father in the sense of being pre-eminent and the agent of creation but was not himself created (Col. 1:15ff.). Similarly he is the first-born of the new creation by being raised from the dead (Rom. 8:29). God's people are also called 'first-born', sharing in the Son's privileges in heaven (Heb. 12:23).

See also FAMILY; HOUSEHOLD.

FISH, FISHING. According to the law of Moses, fish with scales and fins were 'clean' (edible) and those without (e.g. shellfish) were 'unclean'. The Sea of Galilee contains at least 24 species of fish today, sometimes found in large shoals; one has a large mouth (cf. Mt. 17:27). The creature which swallowed Jonah is called simply 'a great fish' (Jon. 1:17; Mt. 12:40), which has been interpreted widely, as 'whale'.

At least 7 of Jesus' disciples were probably fishermen (Peter, Andrew, Philip, James, John, Thomas and Nathanael). Fishing on Galilee was often done from boats at night with a drag-net; during the day a fisherman wading in the water could throw a large casting-net. Fish were either emptied into the boat or the net towed to the shore. Jerusalem had a Fish Gate through which traders entered, and Tyrian fish merchants lived in the city after the Exile (Ne. 13:16). Fish were eaten roasted, and preserved by salting or drying. Jesus called his disciples to become evangelists 'fishing for men' (Mt. 4:19). The Bible never refers to fishing as a recreation. See also GALILEE, SEA OF.

FLAGON. In Is. 22:24, a large two-handled jar for storing wine. See also CONTAINERS; GLASS.

FLAX. The oldest of textile fibres, used to make linen. The plant grows to 1 m, producing blue flowers; the seeds produce linseed oil. It was cultivated by the Egyptians before the Exodus and by the Canaanites before Israel's conquest.

FLESH. In the OT, the principal constituent of the human or animal body. It can also mean the whole body (Pr. 14:30) and, by extension, the whole person (Ps. 16:9; 'my body' is 'flesh' in Heb.). This leads to the concept of man and wife united as 'one flesh' (Gn. 2:24). Sometimes there is a sense that flesh is weak (*i.e.* physically frail; *e.g.* Ps. 56:4).

In the NT the Greek word also denotes the fleshy part of the body; the whole body (2 Cor. 7:5); the whole of physical existence (1 Pet. 3:18); and as weak (Mk. 14:38). But the word is also used in a special sense to mean the earthly part of human personality with its passions and desires (Eph. 2:2f.). To centre one's life on that is death or separation from God (Rom. 8:5ff.), for it opposes the Spirit (Gal. 5:17ff.). It denotes the whole personality of a person organized with reference to earthly pursuits rather than God's service.

FLESH-HOOK: See FORK.

FLESHPOT. A large household container usually made from metal for placing over a fire (Ex. 16:3). It was used symbolically for Jerusalem (Ezk. 11:3, 'cauldron'); for avarice (Mi. 3:3) and vengeance (Ps. 58:9). See CONTAINERS.

FLOOD. A deluge of water sent by God in the time of Noah to destroy all but a selected few people and animals (Gn. 6-9). Other words translated 'flood' refer to rivers in spate or overflowing.

The flood narrative. God caused it because mankind was constantly planning and doing evil, but Noah was a righteous man whom God wished to save. Gn. 6:3 and 1 Pet. 3:20 imply there was 120 years' respite before it came, during which Noah built an ark according to God's instructions. At the flood, Noah, his three sons, and their wives took refuge in it along with a male and a female of each division of the animal kingdom, adding several more of 'the clean animals used for food'. Vegetable food was taken on board, and they lived in the ark for about a year. The flood was clearly intended to blot out all life, but the Hebrew words used could refer to a severe but localized (rather than world-wide) catastrophe. In that case the high mountains would have been covered by the cloud and mist which would have accompanied the water (Gn. 7:19f; 8:5). Dogmatism on a local or universal flood is not reasonable on textual grounds. The narrative ends with the ark resting on the mountains of Urartu; when a dove released from it failed to return, Noah considered it was safe to leave the ark. He offered sacrifices to God who promised never to flood the earth again and designated the rainbow as a sign of his promise.

Other accounts. Stories of a flood have been found among ancient documents excavated in the Near East. A Sumerian tablet from Nippur in S Babylonia was written *c.* 1600 BC but the story was probably known in Mesopotamia long before; the fact of a devastating flood is part of Sumerian historical and literary tradition. The famous Babylonian flood story, part of the *Epic of Gilgamesh*, derives largely from the Akkadian *Atrahasis Epic.* It tells how Uta-napishtim (Atrahasis) was given immortality after surviving the flood. His boat came to rest on Mt Nesir in NW Persia and he let out birds to determine when to disembark. Scholars have suggested that two sources (J and P) underlie the biblical narrative, but there are many indications of its essential unity.

The flood and research. Archaeologists have uncovered evidence of serious floods in S Mesopotamia, but these are unlikely to be connected with the biblical flood. The four sites each have different flood levels, and the earliest (at Ur) is dated *c.* 4000 BC. Many geographical phenomena previously associated with the flood are more likely to have been vestiges of the Quarternary Ice Age. Such an age would have produced changes in sea-level, and depression and rising of land masses, which might have had effects in keeping with the biblical account. No certain evidence is available, however.

See also ARARAT; ARK; BABYLONIA (for other accounts); GENESIS, BOOK OF; NOAH.

FLUTE: See MUSIC AND MUSICAL INSTRUMENTS.

FLY. They are rarely mentioned in the Bible and could refer to any particular type. The references are Ec. 10:1; Is. 7:18, with swarms in Ex. 8:21ff.; Pss. 78:45; 105:31.

FOOD. *In earliest times.* Grains, vegetables and fruit served as food for man from the beginning (Gn. 1:29f.); after the flood living animals (but not their blood) were also permitted (Gn. 9:3f.). In patriarchal times (*c.* 1800 BC) grain and bread were the staple diet in Egypt, Palestine and Mesopotamia, along with milk, butter, cheese, wine, water and beer. Red lentil soup was probably a common dish (Gn. 25:29; 2 Sa. 17:28). Honoured guests were treated to a fatted calf with curds and milk (Gn. 18:7f.). Meat was not an everyday dish but desert-game was popular in Syria-Palestine (Gn. 27:3f.). Nuts and honey were delicacies (Gn. 43:11); tablets from the 18th-cent. BC palace at Mari refer to honey being provided at banquets. The Israelites in Egypt had food they remembered with nostalgia after they had left the country: fish, cucumbers, melons, leeks, onions and garlic (Nu. 11:5), the list corresponding closely to well-known Egyptian foods in the 13th cent. BC.

Israel's food in Palestine. The three staple foods were grain, wine and olive oil (Dt. 7:13). The grain was barley, wheat and sometimes spelt; vines provided grapes and raisins as well as the general drink of the time. Beer was also made, but was more common in Egypt and Mesopotamia than in Palestine. Olive oil was used as cooking fat. Other fruits included figs and pomegranates (the juice also provided drink). Apples may have been eaten (Pr. 25:11); they were certainly known in Mesopotamia and SE Asia Minor. Honey of wild bees was found in rocks, trees, *etc.* (Jdg. 14:8), but the OT does not say if the Hebrews practised bee-keeping as the Egyptians did. Certainly Palestine was flowing with milk and honey (Ex. 3:8); Tuthmosis III of Egypt once returned home from Syria-Palestine laden with hundreds of jars of honey. Meat was eaten only occasionally except by the very rich. The ox, sheep, goat and seven kinds of venison were regarded as 'clean' animals suitable for food (Lv. 11:1ff.; Dt. 14:3ff.); some of the forbidden animals (*e.g.* pigs) were unsafe in the hot climate. Feasts would feature a fatted calf or ox; vegetables were as in the paragraph above.

Solomon's food supplies. These are detailed in 1 Ki. 4, providing an example of the large scale catering which was typical of ancient royalty. One day's provision included 30 cattle and over 6,500 litres of flour. Solomon's system of being supplied by a different province each month was also later employed by Nebuchadrezzar of Babylon and Cyrus of Persia. The amounts bear comparison too. The

people who benefited from all this food would have been the king's family and chief ministers of state; the courtiers and subordinate officials working under the ministers; and a large number of domestic servants. The ancient Near Eastern palace was not merely a home but the practical focus of the entire central government. The 18th-cent. BC royal archives at Mari in Mesopotamia record hundreds of litres of grain, bread, pastries, honey and syrups each day; preparations for a 13th-cent. BC Egyptian pharaoh's arrival included 9,200 loaves and 20,000 biscuits. It is possible to compute that Solomon's monthly grain supply would have required 424 acres (1.7 sq km) of farmland.

Seasoning and cooking. Bread and cakes were baked, soup or stew was boiled, meat was roasted or boiled. Salt was a major source of flavouring, along with herbs such as dill, cummin and coriander. These plants and seeds have been preserved in some Egyptian tombs from the 14th cent. BC. Honey was used in baking but not in sacrificial cakes (Ex. 16:31; Lv. 2:11). Sweetened or spiced wine is also known (Song 8:2).

Food in New Testament times. A typical Hebrew family's food was mainly vegetarian. The staple diet was bread, poorer people making theirs from barley rather than wheat (Jn. 6:9). Grapes and figs were much prized; olives were eaten as a relish with bread, preserved in brine, and of course crushed for oil. The Passover feast traditionally had a sauce made from dates, figs, raisins and vinegar

(Mk. 14:20). The fruit or pods of the carob tree provided animal fodder and, it seems, food for destitute people (Lk. 15:16). The dietary laws regarding animals were strictly enforced; meat mentioned in the NT includes the calf and kid (Lk. 15:23, 29), but the breakdown of dietary regulations was a feature of the early church (Rom. 14:2f.; 1 Cor. 8; 10). With a fishing industry based on the Sea of Galilee, fish were widely eaten (*e.g.* Mk. 6:41ff.). Birds as food are not mentioned in the NT, but eggs are alluded to in Lk. 11:12.

See also BREAD; FIGS; FISH; GRAIN CROPS; HERBS AND SPICES; HONEY; IDOLS, FOOD OFFERED TO; MEALS; MILK; OIL; OLIVES; SALT; VEGETABLES; VINE, VINEYARDS; WINE AND STRONG DRINK.

FOOL, FOOLISHNESS. Sometimes foolishness is defined as plain silliness (*e.g.* Pr. 10:14) but more often as disdain for God's truth and discipline (Pr. 1:7). The most hardened foolishness is that of the aggressive unbeliever (Ps. 14:1); Paul takes up the theme in 1 Cor. 1:25ff. The fool is primarily someone who wilfully makes a wrong choice (Lk. 12:20).

FOOT. In both OT and NT, the foot is frequently used to indicate a person's activity and also God's watchful care over them, as when he 'guides their feet' (Pr. 6:18; Lk. 1:79). Being stood on symbolizes defeat (1 Cor. 15:25); falling at someone's feet symbolizes homage (1 Sa. 25:41); sitting at them

indicates learning (Acts 22:3). Footwashing was a necessity and a sign of hospitality (Jn. 13:5ff.); removing sandals was a sign of respect (Ex. 3:5); shaking dust off the feet was a sign of scorn (Mk. 6:11).

FOOTMAN, MEN ON FOOT. A military term often denoting soldiers in general, but also used to distinguish infantry from chariot-fighters (2 Ki. 13:7). They also acted as guards and couriers (2 Ch. 30:6).

FOOTSTOOL. Used only once literally (2 Ch. 9:18); occasionally in a metaphorical sense it describes the relationship to God as king of the earth (Mt. 5:35), temple (Ps. 99:5), and his enemies (Ps. 110:1), and implies their total subservience to him.

FOREHEAD, BROW. It may indicate defiance (Je. 3:3) or determination (Is. 48:4). It is the obvious place for a badge or mark (Ex. 28:38; Rev. 7:3); it was where the PHYLACTERY was worn.

FOREIGNER. Distinct groups are given different titles. *Strangers or aliens* do not belong to the community which they currently occupy; they are outsiders and virtually equal to enemies (Is. 1:7). The *foreigner* may refer to one of different race, but also has religious overtones because of other nations' idolatry. Solomon's love for foreign women caused him to turn away from God (1 Ki. 11:1ff.). After the Exile, prohibitions against mixed marriage were enforced vigorously (Ezr. 9-10). *The sojourner* is in permanent residence in another nation; the Israelites were sojourners in Egypt (Dt. 10:19), and this fact governed those who came among them. Sojourners were to be loved (Dt. 10:19), to share in the sabbath (Ex. 23:12), to be allowed to glean from the fields and to be protected (Dt. 24:17ff.). They shared Israel's religious obligations but were allowed to eat unclean meat (Dt. 14:21); if they wished to join in the Passover they first had to be circumcised (Ex. 12:48). In the NT, aliens from Israel are made fellow-heirs of God's promises (Eph. 2:12, 19), but are now aliens in the world (1 Pet. 2:11).

FORERUNNER. A word often used by Christians to describe John the Baptist because of the prophecies in Mal. 3:1 (*cf.* Mt. 11:10) and Lk. 1:76, but used only once in the NT, referring to the ascended Christ (Heb. 6:20), translating a military term for scouts preparing the way for an advancing army. Usually the forerunner is less important than the one who follows, but in the case of Jesus the reverse is true; one of his purposes was to prepare a place for his followers (Jn. 14:2f.).

FOREST. In biblical times much of Palestine's hill-country was forested. Several forests are named (*e.g.* 1 Ki. 7:2f.). See also TREES.

FORGIVENESS. *Old Testament.* Three Hebrew words are used to express aspects of forgiveness; one of them basically means 'lift' or 'carry'

and presents a vivid picture of sin being lifted off and taken away from someone. Forgiveness by God is not automatic (Dt. 29:20). When it is obtained it is to be received with gratitude and awe, for sin merits punishment (Ps. 130:3f.). Forgiveness is sometimes associated with atonement and sacrifices, but the sacrifices have value only because God himself has ordained blood as the means of atonement (Lv. 17:11); the OT knows nothing of forgiveness wrung from an unwilling God or purchased by a bribe. It is possible only because he is 'a God ready to forgive, gracious and merciful, slow to anger and abounding in steadfast love' (Ne. 9:17). To receive God's gracious forgiveness a person must be penitent; when it is received it is total and complete (Ps. 103:12; Is. 43:25; Mi. 7:19).

New Testament. Forgiveness is only occasionally linked directly with the cross (*e.g.* Eph. 1:7; Mt. 26:28). More often it is linked directly with Christ himself (*e.g.* Acts 13:38; Eph. 4:32). During his earthly life, Jesus declared people forgiven (Mk. 2:10), but the person of Jesus cannot be separated from his death on the cross which is often said to be 'for sin'. Therefore, forgiveness is again seen as an act of sheer grace (1 Jn. 1:9), in response to which people must repent (Lk. 24:47; Acts 2:38). Forgiveness is also linked with faith as a means of appropriating (not earning) God's grace (Acts 10:43). Jesus speaks of one unforgivable sin, which is continuing blasphemy against God's Spirit by one who consistently rejects the call of God (Mt.

12:31f.). Those who have experienced God's forgiveness are to forgive others wholeheartedly (Lk. 6:37; Col. 3:13).

See also ATONEMENT; SIN.

FORK. Threshers used a long wooden fork to toss grain into the air so that chaff was blown away, an image used to describe the separation of good and evil in Mt. 3:12. Also a bronze implement used with the altar of burnt offering.

FORTIFICATION AND SIEGE-CRAFT. The words 'City' and 'fortress' are almost synonyms throughout the biblical period. Cities were often located at natural defensible sites; Samaria was on a steep isolated hill, for example. Others, on highways or near water supplies, required artificial defences. The average town covered 5-10 acres (exceptionally, Canaanite Hazor covered 200 acres), and was surrounded by walls averaging 3 m in width; 'casemate' walls were two parallel walls about 1.5 m wide separated by 2 m of infill or storage rooms. Walls were usually 6-9 m high. The walls were to prevent enemies entering the city and to give defenders a protected platform from which to fire arrows or sling stones.

Defensive walls were built from earliest times. Several walls and a 13 m diameter circular tower have been excavated at Jericho dating from 7000-6000 BC, 4,000 years before Abraham. Much later (c. 1700 BC) massive earth banks were sometimes built as well, often with a ditch in front. During the early Israelite monarchy casemate walls were built at a number of cities, such as at Saul's capital Gibeah, and at Beersheba during David's and Solomon's reigns. In intertestamental and NT times one or two solid stone walls usually surrounded a city. The excellent Roman wall at Samaria, apparently built by Herod, enclosed 170 acres. A number of walls from this period are being excavated in Jerusalem.

The weakest point in a city's fortifications was the gate. Towers were built to protect the dead area at the foot of the wall. Chariots needed a straight entrance, so from c. 1700 BC onwards angled gates with two doors provided greater security. At Dan the overlapping walls formed a hollow square in which massive double doors were sited; the wooden doors were often covered with metal to reduce the risk of them being burned down. In Jerusalem up to c. 1000 BC small easily defended gates were used, allowing soldiers quick access to or exit from the city, for open warfare was preferred. Cities were sometimes built with inner fortresses as secondary defences. Water during sieges was supplied either from storage cisterns or by tunnels and shafts down to underground springs; external access points were blocked off from enemies (for an example, see SILOAM).

The least costly way to take a fortified city was of course to persuade it to surrender without fighting, which the Assyrian Sennacherib attempted vainly to do to Jerusalem (2 Ki. 18). Surprise was a valuable weapon, too;

Joab probably entered Jerusalem through a water tunnel (1 Ch. 11:4ff.). Otherwise, an attacker had to assault the defences. To do that he could attempt to climb the walls with ladders, break through them with tools or a battering-ram, or dig under them. In difficult places, armies built an assault ramp by filling in part of the moat and building a ramp to the walls; Assyrian reliefs from Nineveh show that when Sennacherib assaulted Lachish the ramps were surfaced with wood. Attackers worked beneath large shields and were given covering fire from their own archers and slingers; the battering ram had an axe-shaped iron head which was levered sideways to dislodge wall-stones. A bank of earth built round the city prevented people trapped in it from escaping (Je. 6:6). Defenders hurled down arrows, stones, burning torches and boiling water. Sieges could last several years; after capture a city was usually plundered and burnt, but later rebuilt. Survivors were deported, enslaved, or burdened with heavy tribute-taxes.

See also ARMOUR; BOW AND ARROW; SPEAR; SLING; SWORD; WAR.

FORTUNATUS. A member of the Corinthian party which encouraged Paul (1 Cor. 16:17f.). The name is common; he was probably a slave, but is otherwise unknown.

FORUM OF APPIUS. A market town and staging-post in Latium, on the Via Appia route 45 km from Rome, packed with 'barges and extortionate inn-keepers' according to the poet Horace. See Acts 28:15 and TAVERNS, THE THREE.

FOUNTAIN, SPRING. Palestine is a land of many springs because of its geological structure, and many are named or referred to in the Bible. See WATER.

FOX, JACKAL. Both are closely related members of the dog family and are found throughout the Near East. The fox is solitary, whereas jackals go in packs. In Jdg. 15:4 the animals caught by Samson were probably jackals.

FREEDMEN, SYNAGOGUE OF THE. Possibly a synagogue attended by Jewish freedmen or their descendants from the places mentioned in Acts 6:9. The meaning of the name is uncertain. See FREEMAN, FREE-WOMAN.

FREEDOM. The state of having been released from servitude for a life of enjoyment and satisfaction that was not possible before. In Scripture, the idea becomes a significant theological concept.

Israel's freedom. At the Exodus God set Israel free from slavery in Egypt to serve him as his covenant people (Ex. 19:3ff.). This was God's gracious gift, and disobedience towards him would result in its loss; God would judge his people by national disaster and enslavement (Dt. 28:25, 47ff.). Freedom is thus *from* slavery to powers which oppose God *for* the fulfilment of God's purposes; he frees people by bringing them to serve himself (Ex. 19:4). Isaiah looked forward to a new freedom when Israel was released from captivity in Babylon, which would herald a new and unprecedented experience of joyful and satisfying fellowship with God (Is. 35:3ff.; 43:14-44:5). Israelites who became slaves through poverty were therefore not to be treated as foreign slaves were; every 7th year they were to be released in memory of the Exodus (Dt. 15:12ff.).

Christian freedom. The idea is developed in the NT. Christ began his ministry by announcing liberation (Lk. 4:16ff.), but he ignored Zealot hankerings for national liberation from Roman rule and instead declared he came to set people free from slavery to sin and Satan (Jn. 8:34ff.). Exorcisms and healings were part of this work (Mk. 3:22ff.; Lk. 13:16). Paul makes much of the thought that Christ liberates people now from the destructive forces of the sin which leads to spiritual death (Rom. 6:18ff.); from the law as a hopeless system of salvation (Gal. 4:21ff.); and from the demonic powers of darkness (Col. 1:13). In due course complete freedom from indwelling sin and physical death will also be granted (Rom. 7:14, 23f.; 8:18ff.). Those who are thus set free receive God's Spirit and are adopted as his children (Gal. 4:5ff.; Rom. 8:15f.). The proper response to the offer of freedom is willingly to become a self-sacrificing servant of God (Rom. 6:17ff.) and men (1 Cor.

9:1ff.). In his letter to the Galatians, Paul stressed that the Christian is free from the OT obligations to perform certain rituals such as circumcision, because faith in Christ is alone the way to salvation.

Free will. The Bible everywhere assumes that human beings have the spontaneous and voluntary power of moral and psychological choice. It seems neither to affirm nor to deny that people's future actions are indeterminate and therefore unpredictable, but it does imply that God foreknows all things. Theologically it implies that no-one can obey God until they have first been freed from sin's power by God's prior grace. On this, see PREDESTINATION; PROVIDENCE; REGENERATION.

See also LAW.

FREEMAN, FREEWOMAN. A person who has been born a slave but has been freed. Paul uses the term metaphorically in 1 Cor. 7:22 for freedom from sin's bondage, and in Gal. 4:22ff. for Sarah, Abraham's wife, and her descendants.

FRIEND OF THE BRIDEGROOM. The figure of 'best man', applied metaphorically to John the Baptist (Jn. 3:29). Mesopotamian law forbad him to marry a forsaken bride, hence the outcry described in Jdg. 14; 15:1ff. See MARRIAGE.

FRIEND OF THE KING. A phrase applied to several people including David's friend Hushai (2 Sa. 15:37) and Solomon's friend Zabud (1 Ki.

4:5). The title does not seem to have implied a specific function, although the friend was obviously important because there was never more than one at any time.

FRIENDS OF GOD: See RECON-CILIATION.

FRINGE (TASSEL). A border along the edges of a garment, reminding the wearer of God's commandments (Nu. 15:38f.; Mt. 23:5). See DRESS.

FRUIT. Used literally for the fruit of trees; Moses' law decreed that fruit-trees were unclean for three years after planting, were 'the Lord's' in the fourth year, and could only be eaten from in the fifth year, thus preserving the health of the tree. Used metaphorically for the 'product' of human life, as *e.g.* fruit of the Spirit (Gal. 5:22); fruit of the lips (Heb. 13:15); fruit of the gospel (Col. 1:6); fruit of repentance (Mt. 3:8); contrast the 'unfruitful works of darkness' (Eph. 5:9ff.). See also AGRICULT-URE; FIG; FOOD; OLIVE; TREES; VINE.

FUEL. Coal was unknown. The wealthy and smiths used charcoal (Jn. 18:18), the poor used sticks (1 Ki. 17:10) or dried animal dung (*cf.* Ezk. 4:12ff.). Most fuel appears to have been common property and to be charged for it was a great hardship (La. 5:4).

FULLER: See BLEACHING.

FULLNESS. There are two possible meanings of the word in the NT: 'that which fills up (completes)' (as in 12 baskets-full of scraps, Mk. 6:43), and 'that which is brought to fullness or completion' (as in 'the full number of Gentiles', Rom. 11:25; 'the fullness of Christ's blessing', Rom. 15:29). There are some references where the precise meaning is disputed.

In Col. 2:9 it means the totality of the Godhead which dwells in Christ. It probably means something similar in Col. 1:19, that in Christ dwells the full sum of divine attributes which is revealed to mankind, although some scholars have suggested that here it refers rather to the early gnostic speculations about the region inhabited by the full number of intermediary beings between God and the world. Paul is then combating the heresy by saying that Christ is the fullness, the totality, of these beings, but there is little evidence of a gnostic creed in the 1st cent. AD and it is unlikely that Paul would have bor-rowed such an important term from a heretical source. In Ephesians it is sometimes suggested that the term refers to the church as well as to Christ. In 1:22f. it is likely to mean 'One who is designated as the fullness of the Godhead who fills all'; this har-monizes with 4:10 and the teaching of Colossians whereas the alternative interpretation as the church com-pleting Christ or Christ filling the church does not.

FUNERAL: See BURIAL AND MOURNING.

FURNACE. The furnace in Dn. 3 into which Daniel's friends were thrown was a brick-kiln or metal-smelter. In Je. 11:4 and Ezk. 22:18ff. it means a pot for smelting metals and is used metaphorically of God's judgment. Mt Sinai smoked like a pottery-kiln (Ex. 19:18). Copper-refining furnaces have been found in the Arabah and elsewhere; iron-smelting furnaces at Tell Jemmeh. See BRICK-KILN; MINING AND METALS.

FUTILITY: See VANITY.

G

GAAL. The leader of a roving band who came to Shechem to take advantage of people's dissatisfaction with Abimelech. He was expelled, and Shechem destroyed (Jdg. 9:22ff.).

GABBATHA. An Aramaic word meaning 'height', also the local word for an area in Jerusalem known as 'The Pavement' (Jn. 19:13), presumably laid by Herod in front of his palace in the Upper City which was Pilate's official residence. This particular pavement has not yet been found. The pavement which can be seen at the Sisters of Zion Convent in Jerusalem was part of the Antonia Fortress but is almost certainly not the place where Jesus was tried. See also TRIAL OF JESUS.

GABRIEL. 'Man of God' or 'strength of God'. One of the two angels named in the Bible; the other is Michael. He interpreted Daniel's vision (Dn. 8:16; 9:21) and announced the births of John the Baptist (Lk. 1:11ff.) and Jesus (Lk. 1:26ff.). In intertestamental Jewish literature he is one of seven archangels standing before God's throne and interceding for people, whose special responsibility is Paradise.

GAD. 'Good fortune.' *People:* 1. The seventh son of Jacob, his first by Leah's maid Zilpah. Gad had 7 sons by the time Jacob moved to Egypt. Jacob warned that Gad's descendants would have a troubled life but that they would hit back (Gn. 49:19). 2. A prophet, contemporary with Saul and David, who came to David after the census (2 Sa. 24:1ff.) and helped David and Nathan organize worship music (2 Ch. 29:25).

Tribe: The descendants of Jacob's son, who in Moses' time had 7 clans. With Reuben and half Manasseh Gad asked to remain E of Jordan as their share of the promised land, because Gilead suited their livestock. Moses agreed on condition they helped their fellow-Israelites establish themselves in W Palestine (Nu. 32). They were among David's fugitive band and later shared in his administration. They were exiled by Tiglath-pileser III of Assyria (2 Ki. 15:29).

GAD, VALLEY (RIVER) OF. The Arnon is meant (2 Sa. 24:5, AV, RV).

GADARENES, GADARA. The only

181

reference is Mt. 8:28. The sub-district of Gadara lay 10 km SE of the Sea of Galilee. It was one of the Decapolis cities, now marked by the ruins of Umm Qays. See also GERASA.

GAIUS. A Latin name used several times in the NT. 1. Paul's companion to Jerusalem, possibly a delegate from Derbe (Acts 20:4f.). 2. A Corinthian whom Paul baptized and stayed with (1 Cor. 1:14; Rom. 16:23); traditionally the first bishop of Thessalonica. 3. The recipient of 3 John, possibly one of the above.

GALATIA. The ancient ethnic kingdom of Galatia was located in the N of the great inner plateau of Asia Minor. In 64 BC it became an ally of Rome and was made a province in 25 BC. The new province also included parts of Pontus, Phrygia, Lycaonia, Pisidia, Paphlagonia and Isauria. Paul evangelized several towns in the province on his first journey (Acts 13-14).

NT scholars are divided as to which area Paul means by Galatia in Gal. 1:2. He had visited the S of the province (Acts 13-14). It is possible that Phrygia (Acts 16:16) refers to the area of Antioch and Iconium, and Galatia to the ethnic N kingdom, but the terms could also mean only the parts of Phrygia incorporated into the Roman province—Galatian Phrygia—which does not demand a trip further N, especially as the verse says they did not enter (the province of) Asia. In Acts 18:23 the names are reversed, Galatia here probably being 'Galatic Lycaonia' to distinguish it from E

Lycaonia in King Antiochus' territory. It is more likely that Paul visited and wrote to only the S Galatia area. See also next article.

GALATIANS, LETTER TO THE.
Contents. Greetings (1:1-5); the 'new' gospel rebutted (1:6-10); autobiographical details (1:11-2:14); grace does not produce sin (2:15-21); An appeal to personal experience (3:1-16); the covenant of faith with Abraham (3:7-22); Christian maturity (3:23-4:11); an appeal (4:12-20); Christian freedom (4:21-5:1); faith not works, liberty not licence (5:2-26); mutual support (6:1-5); sowing and reaping (6:6-10); postscript (6:11-18).

Authorship and date. Paul's authorship has never been seriously contested. The date depends on two uncertainties. The first is whether the letter was sent to N or S Galatian churches (see previous article). If N, then it could not have been written before AD 49/50, when Paul's second missionary journey began, and more probably after AD 52 when the third journey began (*cf.* Acts 18:23 with Gal. 4:13, which imply two visits to them). If written to the S, it could have been earlier; 1:6 implies a date soon after the first missionary journey (AD 47-8), in which case the 'at first' of 4:13 refers to the first of two visits Paul made to the area during the first missionary journey (Acts 14:6, 21). The second uncertainty relates to the interpretation of Paul's visits to Jerusalem listed in Gal. 1:18 and 2:1. The first is almost certainly that mentioned in Acts 9:26ff. The second is usually associated with that of Acts 15:2ff., but this is problematic. The two accounts are very different; Gal. 2 recounts only a private interview with other apostles and does not record the findings of the Council which would have been directly relevant to the Galatian situation. It is more likely that Gal. 2:1 refers to the famine-relief visit of Acts 11:30; 12:25, thus dating Galatians *c.* AD 48/49. The incident of 2:12 is then likely to be correlated with Acts 15:1.

Arguments of the letter. Paul's converts were obviously in danger of adulterating the gospel of Christian freedom with elements of Jewish legalism, among which were circumcision, observance of the Jewish calendar and possibly food laws as well. Judaizers had visited the church and cast doubts on Paul's apostolic status. When Paul heard about this, he wrote instantly to denounce the teaching as 'no gospel' and to urge the Galatian Christians to stand firm in their new-found freedom. He argues that the gospel he preached was God's revelation and that the Jerusalem apostles recognized this (1:11-2:20). If people could be saved by Jewish observances, then Christ's death was pointless (2:21). Having begun the Christian life in the power of God's Spirit, it is wrong to live it out on the level of legal works (3:2ff.). The true children of Abraham are those who live by faith, not law (ch.3). Lawkeeping belongs to the age of spiritual immaturity (3:23-4:7) and produces a form of slavery (4:8ff.); Christ's freedom is a faith which works by love and fulfills the 'law' of Christ (5:13-6:10). The

arguments are presented more systematically in Paul's later letter to the Romans.

GALEED (lit. 'Witness pile'). Name of the cairn erected by Jacob and Laban as a memorial to their covenant (Gn. 31:47f.).

GALILEE. 'Ring, circle.' The regional name of part of N Palestine, occurring occasionally in the OT (*e.g.* Is. 9:1) and the scene of Jesus' boyhood and early ministry. Owing to pressure from non-Jews all around, its Jewish population was withdrawn to the S for 50 years during the Maccabaean period two centuries before Christ; it was later recolonized. This, and the diversity of its population contributed to the contempt felt for Galileans by S Jews (Jn. 7:52).

In Jesus' time, the province was a rectangular territory 70 km N-S and 40 km E-W, an upland area at the S end of the Lebanon mountains. Upper Galilee was forested and thinly inhabited; Lower Galilee had stretches of fertile land with a dense and prosperous population exporting olive oil, cereals and fish. It was traversed by several important trading routes. Galileans had resisted the Romans even more doggedly than S Jews. See also next article.

GALILEE, SEA OF. A lake in the region of Galilee also called Chinnereth (Nu. 34:11), Gennesaret (Lk. 5:1) and Tiberias (Jn. 21:1). It is 21 km long and up to 11 km wide, 211 m below sea level, and the Jordan flows through it. Its fisheries were famous throughout the Roman empire producing a flourishing export trade. Surrounded by hills, it is liable to atmospheric down-draughts and sudden storms.

GALL. A plant with bitter fruit, probably the colocynth gourd, often associated with the herb wormwood. The drink offered to Christ was wine mixed with stupefying drugs (Mt. 27:34). Metaphorically used for any bitter experience (Acts 8:23).

GALLIO. The son of Seneca the rhetorician and brother of Seneca the philosopher, he was proconsul of Achaia AD 52-3 (*cf.* Acts 18:12ff.). He was executed by Nero in AD 65.

GALLOWS. Mentioned only in Esther. Hanging was not usual in Persia, and the word probably means a stake on which Haman was impaled. See CROSS.

GAMALIEL. 'Reward of God.' 1. A man who helped Moses take a census, and a leader of Manasseh (Nu. 2:20). 2. A member of the Sanhedrin representing the less extreme wing of the Pharisees (the school of Hillel), and Paul's teacher (Acts 22:3). He intervened reasonably at Peter's trial (Acts 5:33ff.).

GAMES. *Old Testament.* In common with their Near Eastern neighbours, the life of the majority of Hebrews left little time or inclination for physical sport. However, hunting, running and throwing would have been practised for recreational purposes on occasion. Like Egyptians and Babylonians, Palestinian people would have enjoyed wrestling; the contest in 2 Sa. 2:14 may have been initiated as a wrestling match. Gaming boards with peg holes and draughts boards with 20 or 30 squares have been found; play was determined by throwing dice, bones or sticks. 'Chinese type' chess was known in Elam and Babylonia before 3000 BC. Egyptian paintings show children in tugs-of-war, juggling and playing ball games; leather-covered balls have been found, as have whistles, rattles, toy pots, chariots and animals. Story-telling, music and dancing were among the commonest forms of adult relaxation.

New Testament. Apart from an obscure reference to a children's street game (Mt. 11:16f.) and a possible allusion to a chariot-race (Phil. 3:13f.) the games mentioned are Greek athletic contests. The festivals were religious in origin and flavour, encouraging discipline, health and fair play. Paul refers to the athlete's vigorous training and the laurel-wreath prize in 1 Cor. 9:24ff.; v. 26 refers to a boxing contest in which hands and arms were bound with studded leather to inflict grave injury. References to foot-racing are found in Gal. 2:2; 5:7; Phil. 2:16; Heb. 12:1f., for which minimal clothing was worn (thus Christians are encouraged to 'strip off' sin). Phil. 3:13f. probably refers to a chariot race, much in fashion among Romans in Paul's day, and Philippi was a Roman colony. He pictures the charioteer stretching out over the horses' backs leaning his weight on the reins; to look back would lead to a fatal crash.

GARDEN. In Egypt the Hebrews had known productive vegetable gardens criss-crossed with irrigation channels (Dt. 11:10). In Palestine they cultivated gardens for fruit and vegetables (1 Ki. 21:2; Am. 9:14); they were sometimes walled, and had to be kept watered (Song 4:12ff.). The 'king's garden' in Jerusalem was a well-known landmark (Je. 39:4); Egyptian and Mesopotamian kings kept fine gardens. God's redeemed people were promised that their lives would be ordered and fruitful as a garden (Is. 58:11). See also EDEN, GARDEN OF; GETHSEMANE.

GATH (lit. 'winepress'). One of the five principal Philistine cities; its inhabitants are often called Gittites in EVV. It was struck by bubonic plague when the ark of the covenant was taken there (1 Sa. 5:6ff.). David lodged there for a while when outlawed by Saul (1 Sa. 27), and later added it to his dominions (1 Ch. 18:1). It may have become a Philistine enclave in Judah (Am. 6:2). It was conquered by Assyria in the 8th cent. BC. The site has not been clearly identified.

GATH-HEPHER (lit. 'winepress of digging'). A town on the border of Zebulun and Naphtali, 5 km NE of Nazareth, the birthplace of Jonah (2 Ki. 14:25) and also traditionally his burial-place.

GAZA. One of the five principal Philistine cities, considered to mark the S limit of Canaan's coastline (Gn. 10:19). Conquered by Joshua (Jos. 10:41) but apparently lost later, because it was there that the Philistines imprisoned Samson. The description of Samson 'making sport' for spectators there is reminiscent of some features of Cretan civilization; the Philistines probably once inhabited Crete. When the Philistines captured the ark of the covenant, Gaza was afflicted with bubonic plague (1 Sa. 6:17). It was on important trade routes from Egypt to W Asia and is frequently mentioned among Assyrian conquests. In Jeremiah's time it was taken by Egypt (Je. 47:1), and in 332 BC by Alexander the Great. It was rebuilt by the Romans in 57 BC, nearer the sea. The ancient city site (Tell Kharubeh) now lies within the modern city.

GAZELLE. Two species of these dry-zone antelopes are still found in Judaean hills and plains, the dorcas and Palestine gazelles. See also DEER.

GEBA (lit. 'a hill'). A town 11 km N of Jerusalem and 5 km from Gibeah, assigned by Joshua to the Levites. Modern Jeba.

GEBAL (lit. 'hill, bluff'). A Canaanite and Phoenician port, modern Jebeil 40 km N of Beirut. By 2500 BC it was an export centre for cedar wood, receiving luxury goods from Egypt in exchange. It was called Byblos by the Greeks. Scribes there invented a simpler script and it may have been there that the alphabet arose. It was never ruled by Israel; Solomon hired masons from it (1 Ki. 5:18).

GEBER. An Israelite prince mentioned as prefect of the area E of the Jordan before Solomon divided it (1 Ki. 4:19; *cf.* vv. 13f.).

GEDALIAH (lit. 'Yahweh is great'). Several OT people, the most important being chief minister and governor of Judah appointed by Nebuchadrezzar II in 587 BC (2 Ki. 25:22). He took care of people remaining in Jerusalem after the Babylonian war (Je. 40:6ff.), but was assassinated (Je. 41:1ff.). A seal impression inscribed 'belonging to Gedaliah who is over the house' found at Lachish almost certainly belongs to him.

GEDER. A S Canaanite town; probably GOSHEN.

GEDERAH. 1. Probably on the N side of the Vale of Elah (Jos. 15:36). 2. A pottery centre (1 Ch. 4:23), possibly Tell ej-Judeideh N of Maresha valley. 3. In Benjamin (1 Ch. 12:4), possibly Judeira NE of Gibeon or Kh. Judeira 10 km farther W.

GEDEROTH. A town in the Lachish district of Judah.

GEDEROTHAIM. Possibly a variant of Gederah in Jos. 15:36.

GEDOR. 1. A town in the Judaean hills (Jos. 15:58); Kh. Jedur 2 km W of

Beit Ummar. 2. A place in the Negeb (1 Ch. 4:39).

GEHAZI. Elisha's servant mentioned by name on three occasions. In 2 Ki. 4 he attempted vainly to resurrect the Shunnamite's son and in 2 Ki. 5 he obtained gifts for himself from Naaman under false pretences, and became a leper as punishment. In 2 Ki. 8 he related the Shunammite's story to king Jehoram.

GELILOTH. Possibly means 'circle' (of stones), mentioned only in Jos. 18:17 and probably identical to GILGAL (*cf.* Jos. 15:7).

GENEALOGY. *Old Testament.* A list of names indicating the ancestors or descendants of a person, or simply a register of people involved in some situation. OT genealogies are chiefly found in Genesis to Deuteronomy, Ezra-Nehemiah, and Chronicles, and are of two forms. 'Ascending' genealogies commonly have the linking formula 'x the son of y' (*e.g.* 1 Ch. 6:33ff.); 'descending' genealogies have the formula 'x became the father of y' (*e.g.* Ru. 4:18ff.). Fequently genealogies miss out some generations; the list of Aaron's descendants in Ezr. 7:1-5 omits 6 names given in 1 Ch. 6:3-14. The formula 'son of' can equally mean 'grandson' and 'descendant', and 'became the father of' can mean 'became the ancestor of'. Where ages of people are given (*e.g.* Gn. 5:6) this need not militate against interpreting these genealogies as abridgments, for the ages may have been to emphasize the Patriarchs' mortality as a result of the fall, as well as their long lives.

Royal family trees were a standard feature of ancient historical tradition; Assyrian scribes listed their kings from remote times following an almost unbroken line spanning 1,000 years, noting the length of each reign and the relationship of one king to another. Records of lawsuits over land ownership show that many other people also retained such knowledge. In both biblical and other ancient genealogies, personal notes were sometimes added, *e.g.* 1 Ch. 5:9f.. Some non-biblical texts also show a similar use of 'son'. Shalmaneser's Black Obelisk refers to Jehu as 'son of Omri', but the two only ruled the same state and were not related. An Egyptian king Tirhaka (*c.* 670 BC) honours his 'father' Sesostris III who lived *c.* 1870 BC and was not a true ancestor. There is no reason to suppose that all biblical genealogies claim to be complete, since their purpose was to trace a line of descent from a specific ancestor. And in view of similar records known to have factual bases, it is also wrong to dismiss them as legendary or as personifications of tribes or gods.

The main OT genealogies are: Adam to Noah (Gn. 5; 1 Ch. 1); Cain's descendants (Gn. 4:17ff.); Noah's descendants (Gn. 10; 1 Ch. 1); Shem to Abraham (Gn. 11:10ff.; 1 Ch. 1); descendants of Abraham by Keturah (Gn. 25; 1 Ch. 1), Lot (Gn. 19:37f.), Nahor (Gn. 22:20ff.), Ishmael (Gn. 25:12ff.) and Esau (Gn. 36); descendants of Jacob (the 12 tribes, Gn. 46; Nu.

26; and various places in 1 Ch.). There are also registers of Levites; registers of David's administrators and soldiers; and registers of families who returned to Jerusalem in the time of Ezra and Nehemiah.

New Testament. Two genealogies give the ancestry of Jesus (see next article). In 1 Tim. 1:4 and Tit. 3:9 the term 'genealogy' is used in conjunction with the words 'fable' and 'foolish questions'. Paul has in mind either mythical OT histories such as are found in the apocryphal book *Jubilees* or family trees of aeons found in Gnostic literature. He is not referring to OT genealogies.

See also next article; CHRONOLOGY; GENERATION; NATIONS, TABLE OF.

GENEALOGY OF JESUS CHRIST. Genealogies are given in Mt. 1:1-17 and Lk. 3:23-38. Luke's goes back to Adam, Matthew's to Abraham; Luke has taken his early material from Gn. 5; 11; perhaps via 1 Ch. 1. From Abraham to David the two lists are practically identical and are based on 1 Ch. 2, but from David to Joseph they diverge. Matthew's list, which clearly omits some generations, traces the line through David's son Solomon, whereas Luke traces it through Nathan, another of David's sons by Bathsheba. Both trace Jesus' ancestry through Joseph even though both make it clear that Joseph was not Jesus' physical father. It has been suggested that Luke's genealogy is in fact through Mary, his physical mother. However, it is strange that if this was

Luke's intention, the otherwise careful historian did not say so. J.G. Machen (1932) suggested that if Matthan (Joseph's grandfather, Mt. 1:15) is the same as Matthat (Joseph's grandfather, Lk. 3:24), it is possible that Joseph's 'father' Jacob (in Mt.) died without issue and that his nephew Joseph (son of his brother Heli, Joseph's father in Lk.) became his heir. If Nathan in Zc. 12:12 is David's son, his house evidently had some standing in Israel and there may be some significance in Luke's showing Jesus to be his descendant. The main purpose of both lists is to establish Jesus' claim to be the son of David and to emphasize his solidarity with mankind and with OT history. See also the previous article (for genealogical methods).

GENERATION. The English word is used to translate several Hebrew and Greek words. One Hebrew word can mean simply 'history' (it divides Genesis into 11 sections, *e.g.* 2:4). Another can mean a class of people (*e.g.* the righteous, Ps. 14:5). The Greek words in the NT correspond roughly with these; one can mean history (Mt. 1:1) and birth (Mt. 1:18); the other can mean people living at a given time (Mt. 11:16) and the components of a genealogy (Mt. 1:17). It is sometimes held that a period of 40 years is to be taken as a round number indicating a generation. See also GENEALOGY.

GENESIS, BOOK OF. *Contents.* The story of creation (1:1-2:3); the story of

early mankind (2:4-11:26); the story of Abraham (11:27-23:20); the story of Isaac (24-26); the story of Jacob (27-36); the story of Joseph (37-50).

Authorship. There is nothing in the book to indicate its author. There are two groups of opinion, one accepting the other denying that Moses was the author or compiler. For the former view, Moses would have learned literary skills in Egypt, and in his position as leader of the Israelites would have been anxious to preserve the records available to him. The creation story may have been received as a direct revelation from God, and Moses certainly had experience of immediate contact with God (*e.g.* Ex. 33:11). Apart from some explanatory footnotes by later copyists up to the time of the Monarchy (*e.g.* 12:6; 13:7) there is nothing that need be dated later than Moses.

For the other view, there are several theories. Scholars have suggested it contains three collections of data (J, E and P) and more moderate versions of this view do not deny the basic historicity of the narratives. More recently the 'documentary' theory has been abandoned by some who speak instead of 'cycles of tradition' collected together by later editors. The exact origin of Genesis remains something of a mystery. (For further detail, see PENTATEUCH).

Historicity. It is difficult to obtain independent historical evidence to compare with Genesis, especially chs. 1-11. In the creation account, it is not possible to discover precisely how God made man, and neither archaeology nor anthropology can give final answers as to the time, place or means of man's origins. Nor is there clear evidence about the flood, although floods did occur in Mesopotamia and the Sumerians also had a detailed account of a great flood (see FLOOD). However, research has shown that the Patriarchal narratives (chs. 12-50) do reflect life in the ancient Near East 2000-1500 BC.

Genesis and theology. It is the book of beginnings, introducing the great drama of redemption; chs. 1-11 are the prologue, and the first act begins at ch. 12 with the introduction of Abraham. The prologue is cast in universal terms showing how mankind rebelled against God who pronounces judgment but who also gives evidence of grace and mercy. God's answer to the persistent sin of mankind was to raise up Abraham as the first step in his calling of an elect people from whom would eventually come the redeemer. The primary value of Genesis (as of all Scripture) is theological. It is concerned to teach lessons about God, his relationship with mankind and his purposes in the world. These lessons remain valid even where corroborative evidence of its historical accuracy or detail is lacking. See also CREATION; FLOOD; MAN.

GENTILES. Originally a general term for 'nations', it received a more restricted meaning of 'non-Israelites'. Israel, conscious of being a nation uniquely separated to God (Ex. 19:6), continually struggled against moral and religious corruption from pagan neighbours. This led to so exclusive an attitude that by the time of Jesus to stigmatize a fellow-Jew as a 'Gentile' was a term of intense scorn (Mt. 18:17). However, the Gentiles were included in the Messiah's mission (Is. 42:6; 49:6), and Jesus came in this tradition (Lk. 2:32; Mt. 12:18). After initial hesitancy (Acts 10:45; 11:18) the church soon accepted Jews and Gentiles as equal before God (Col. 3:11). See also FOREIGNER.

GENTLENESS. A quality of the Christian believer. It suggests the yielding of a judge who, instead of demanding the exact penalty required by strict justice, gives way to circumstances which call for mercy. See, *e.g.*, 2 Cor. 10:1; 1 Tim. 3:3; Jas. 3:17.

GERAR (lit. 'circle'). An ancient city S of Gaza, possibly once inhabited by an advance party of the Sea Peoples (Philistines, Gn. 26:1). Probably modern Tell Abu Hureira, 18 km SE of Gaza, which archaeologists have discovered was prosperous in the Patriarchal period.

GERASA. An important city in Greek and Roman times 30 km E of the Jordan, midway between the Dead Sea and the Sea of Galilee. It is only indirectly mentioned in the Bible (Mk. 5:1). The site today, Jaras, is one of the best-preserved examples of a Roman provincial town. It lies in a well-watered valley with fertile cornfields. In the 1st cent. AD the earlier Greek city was largely rebuilt on a typical Roman plan with a straight colonnaded street leading to a forum; there were two theatres, and temples to Artemis and Zeus. It was a city of the DECAPOLIS.

GERIZIM. The more southerly of two mountains which overshadow the modern town of Nablus 4 km NW of the ancient Shechem, where blessings were uttered by Joshua (Jos. 8:30ff.). It was the Samaritans' sacred mount (Jn. 4:20); a temple was built there in the 4th cent. BC and demolished by John Hyrcanus c. 128 BC.

GERSHOM, GERSHON. 1. Moses' elder son, whose descendants counted as Levites (1 Ch. 23:14f.). 2. Levi's son. His descendants (Gershonites) carried the tabernacle in the desert (Nu. 3:17ff.), and under David the Asaph and Ladan (Gershonite) families had singing and treasury duties (1 Ch. 23:1ff.).

GESHEM. One of Nehemiah's chief opponents (Ne. 2:19; 6:1f.; probably the Gashmu of 6:6). An inscription from Dedan records his fame in N Arabia. An Aramaic text from Egypt shows he was paramount chief (king) in Kedar in N Arabia. The Persian king kept good relationships with Arabians, so Geshem's complaints would be heard.

GESHUR, GESHURITES. A Syrian city NE of Bashan to which Absalom fled (2 Sa. 13:37; 14:23). His mother was the daughter of its king (2 Sa. 15:8). Other 'Geshurites' are attested in Jos. 13:2; 1 Sa. 27:8, living near the Egyptian border.

GESTURES. Oriental people tended to be physically demonstrative. Few natural physical reactions are recorded in the Bible (*cf.* Mt. 12:49; Acts 12:17), but many meaningful conventional actions are recorded. These include bowing, kissing, striking hands to make a bargain (Pr. 6:1 AV), tearing garments and putting ashes on the head. Lk. 7:44ff. records customary gestures of hospitality. Some prophetic gestures were symbolic; *cf.* Jn. 20:22. See also FOOT; HEAD; HAND.

GETHSEMANE (lit. 'an oil press'). A garden E of Jerusalem beyond the Kidron valley and near the Mt of Olives; a favourite retreat of Jesus and the scene of his arrest (Mk. 14:32ff.). His kneeling (Lk. 22:41) prompted the later Christian posture for prayer. The traditional site E of the Jericho road-bridge over the Kidron is questioned by some scholars who locate it NE of St Mary's Church where larger gardens were available for pilgrims in the 1st cent.

GEZER. One of the chief cities of pre-Roman Palestine from at least 1800 BC, on the road from Jerusalem to Joppa 12 km away from the main Egypt-Mesopotamia highway. It was given to Israel by an Egyptian king when his daughter married Solomon (1 Ki. 9:15ff.). Excavations have uncovered typical gates and defences from Solomon's time, also a CALENDAR and HIGH PLACE.

GIANT. A man of great stature. It may mean someone physically large (*e.g.* 2 Sa. 21:20), but one Hebrew word, sometimes translated 'giant', is more correctly equivalent to the English 'hero' (*e.g.* 1 Ch. 1:10). For terms used for giants see ANAK; EMIM; REPHAIM; ZAMZUMMIM; ZUZIM. See also GOLIATH.

GIBBETHON (lit. 'mound'). A city in Dan, probably modern Tell el-Melat, W of Gezer. It saw battles between Israel and the Philistines, and was conquered by Sargon of Assyria in 712 BC.

GIBEAH. Often used in the OT to mean 'hill' but also used as a place-name. One such place was in the Judaean hill country, possibly modern el-Jeba near Bethlehem. A more important one was in Benjamin, N of Jerusalem, destroyed in the Judges period (Jdg. 19-20) and famous as Saul's birthplace and residence (1 Sa. 10:26; 13-15). This is almost certainly Tell el-Ful, 5 km N of Jerusalem, first settled in the 12th cent. BC. In Saul's time, *c.* 1025-950 BC, it was a small fortress, and a tower of it has been uncovered. It was probably abandoned at Saul's death; excavations show it was subsequently rebuilt and destroyed several times.

GIBEON. During the Israelite invasion of Canaan, the elders of this city (modern el-Jib, 9 km N of Jerusalem) tricked Joshua into making a treaty with them, and they were reduced to menial service as a punishment (Jos. 9:3ff.). The city was allotted to Benjamin and set apart for the Levites. It had a high place where the tabernacle and altar of burnt-offering were located and where Solomon worshipped after his accession (1 Ki. 3:4f.; 1 Ch. 16:39). Later, Shishak of Egypt numbered Gibeon among the cities he captured (*cf.* 1 Ki. 14:25). Gibeonites helped Nehemiah rebuild Jerusalem's walls (Ne. 3:7). Excavations have revealed a stepped tunnel leading to an underground water reservoir, possibly the 'pool' of 2 Sa. 2:13 and Je. 41:12.

GIDEON (lit. 'hewer, smiter'). The judge who led Israel to victory over the Midianites, a bedouin people then dominating the centre of Palestine (Jdg. 6-8). He was also called Jerubbaal (perhaps 'Baal strives') following his first act of defiance in pulling down the Baal-altar of his father Joash whose quick-witted reaction saved his son from execution. The defeat of the Midianites came after Gideon's army was reduced at God's command from 32,000 to 300; his sudden night-attack demoralized the enemy and led to a thorough rout. Gideon was invited to set up a hereditary monarchy, but he refused; he did however set up an 'ephod' (probably an image of God) in Ophrah, which became a source of apostasy (Jdg. 8:27). In Heb. 11:32 Gideon, a humble man, is placed among the heroes of faith. For the incident of his 'fleece', see DEW.

GIFT. Many different words are used in the Bible for 'gift'. Sacrifices and other offerings were gifts to God (*e.g.* Ex. 28:38); health, wealth, food and happiness were gifts from him (Ec. 3:13; 5:19). People gave gifts on special occasions (Ps. 45:12), and sometimes the word means 'bribe' (as Ex. 23:8). In the NT, several words describe God's gifts to mankind: salvation (Rom. 5:15, 17); the Holy Spirit (Acts 2:38); eternal life (Rom. 6:23); and spiritual gifts imparted to each believer (1 Pet. 4:10), for which see SPIRITUAL GIFTS.

GIHON (lit. 'stream'). 1. One of four rivers of the Garden of Eden, sometimes identified with the Nile because of the reference to Cush (Ethiopia), but probably located E of Mesopotamia from where the Kassites later descended. 2. A spring E of Jerusalem from which Hezekiah cut a conduit to channel water into the pool of Siloam; probably modern Ain Sitti Maryam. See EDEN, GARDEN OF.

GILBOA (possibly 'bubbling fountain'). A range of mountains (modern Jebel Fukua) in Issachar's territory, the scene of Saul's final and fatal clash with the Philistines (1 Sa. 31).

GILEAD. *People:* Several OT people including the grandson of Manasseh and forefather of the Gileadite clan which was a major part of the Manasseh tribe.

Region: The name applied to the whole or part of lands E of the Jordan occupied by the tribes of Reuben, Gad, and the half of Manasseh. Geographically, Gilead proper was the hilly, wooded country N of a line from Heshbon to the N end of the Dead Sea, separated into N and S halves by the Jabbok river. Such simultaneous use of a term in both wide and restricted senses is common in both ancient and modern times. The balm of Gilead was proverbial (Je. 8:22); its rich woodland was a symbol of luxury (Je. 50:19); and it offered refuge for fugitives (Gn. 31:21ff.; 2 Sa. 17:22ff.).

GILGAL (lit. 'circle (of stones)' or 'rolling'). The name of several OT places, the most important being Israel's base of operations after the crossing of the Jordan into Canaan (Jos. 4:19f.). There, the new generation born since the Exodus was circumcised, the first Passover in Canaan was celebrated, and the manna food ceased to appear. Later, it was at Gilgal that Saul and Samuel parted company (1 Sa. 15). During the 8th cent. BC it became a centre of formal and unspiritual worship (Am. 4:4; 5:5). The exact site is still uncertain; one possibility is Kh. el-Mefijir, 2 km NE of OT Jericho (Tell es-Sultan).

Several references to 'Gilgal' are difficult to locate. In Jos. 15:7 it may be the Gilgal above or another stone circle further W. In Jos. 12:23 (RSV mg.) it may be the capital of a king ruling a mixed population on the edge of the plain of Sharon, possibly Jiljuliyeh 5 km N of Aphek.

GIRDLE. It can be a ceremonial sash (Ex. 28:4), a rough leather belt (2 Ki. 1:8), or an ordinary waistband (Acts

21:11) into which working people commonly tucked their clothes, as is still done in parts of the E today. Girdles were also used to support sword-sheaths (2 Sa. 20:8), and were given as presents or rewards (2 Sa. 18:11). See also DRESS.

GIRGASHITES. A tribe listed among Canaan's descendants (Gn. 10:16), and overcome by Israel (Jos. 24:11). They are indirectly attested in N Canaanite inscriptions from Ugarit (14th/13th cent. BC).

GIRZITES. A little-known semi-nomadic clan in the NW of the Negeb defeated by David (1 Sa. 27:8).

GITTITES: See GATH.

GLASS. Seldom mentioned in the Bible, it was a rare luxury until Roman times, considered precious like gold (Jb. 28:17). Glazing was known and used on beads and brickwork from *c.* 4000 BC, but glass itself is first attested *c.* 2600 BC. By the 14th cent. BC a factory at el-Amarna in Egypt made glass containers. Cobalt and manganese were used as colouring agents, but early glass was not very transparent because of impurities in the basic materials. In Greek and Roman times glass became more common; the container of Mt. 26:7 may have been of glass. The invention of glass blowing resulted in mass-produced table services rivalling pottery and metal in cost. Much of it was translucent, like a highly-polished glaze (*cf.* Rev. 4:6; 21:18, for which see SEA OF GLASS).

GLEANING. A kindly Israelite law allowed the poor, orphans and strangers to gather surplus grain, grapes and olives (Lv. 19:9f.; *cf.* Ru. 2:2ff.). The custom still persists in some E countries. See AGRICULTURE.

GLORIA IN EXCELSIS. A liturgical hymn originating in the early church and inspired by the angelic hymn of Lk. 2:14. It expresses praise for the Messiah's birth and announces the peace which heals the relationship between a holy God and sinful people.

GLORY. In the OT, the root word has the idea of heaviness, and so of weight or worthiness. It is used to describe people's wealth, splendour or honour, but the most important concept is God's glory. This was shown in the cloud which led the Israelites through the desert (Ex. 16:10), rested on Mt Sinai (Ex. 24:15ff.) and filled the tabernacle (Ex. 40:34ff.). God's glory is the revelation of his being, nature and presence, sometimes with physical phenomena.

The shepherds (Lk. 2:9) and disciples (Jn. 1:14; Mk. 9:2ff.) saw God's glory physically reflected in Christ. John sees Christ's death as the 'hour of glory' (Jn. 13:31; 17:5). God's glory is also seen in Christ's resurrection and ascension (Acts 3:13) and it is to be fully revealed at his second coming (Mk. 8:38). The object of the church is to see that the world acknowledges God's glory (Rom. 15:9).

GNAT. An imprecise word given to several groups of two-winged insects sometimes including mosquitos. The phrase in Mt. 23:24 refers to the Pharisees' practice of drinking water through a straining-cloth to avoid swallowing any unclean insect. In Ex. 8:16ff. the 'gnat' is probably a blood-sucking tick.

GNOSTICISM. A term derived from the Greek *gnosis*, knowledge, once applied to a body of heretical teaching denounced in the first centuries of the Christian church but today sometimes applied more loosely to any religious belief which emphasizes dualism and/or the possession of secret knowledge. A difficulty with this wider definition is that the word ceases to have any specific reference and becomes the lowest common denominator of Hellenistic (Greek-cultural) religious thought. On the other hand even early church leaders disagreed on the common factors within groups that actually called themselves Gnostics. However, it is possible to form some idea of basic Gnostic belief.

Beliefs. The foundation belief was that the created world was evil and totally separate from, and in opposition to, the world of spirit where the supreme God dwelt in unapproach-able splendour and without dealings with the material world. Matter had been created by an inferior being, the *Demiurge* who with his aides the *archons* kept mankind imprisoned in physical existence. Only those possessing a divine spark or soul could escape on death from material existence if they also received the enlightenment of *gnosis*, knowledge. In most gnostic systems this enlightenment is the work of a divine redeemer who descends from the spiritual realm in disguise. He is often equated with the Christian Jesus. Within this mythological structure, the Gnostic was trying to discover his own identity; appreciating this, the psychiatrist C. G. Jung based many of his observations on an understanding of ancient gnosticism. Gnostic thought is quite alien to traditional Christianity, its mythological setting of redemption depreciating the historical events of Jesus, and denying the importance of the person and work of Jesus in delivering people from sin rather than leading them to self-realization.

Sources and origins. Our knowledge of Gnostic sects comes partly from the early church Fathers, especially Tertullian, Clement of Alexandria and Hippolytus of Rome, who wrote extensively about Gnosticism from an orthodox Christian standpoint. There are however Gnostic texts which give direct insight into the beliefs. A remarkable discovery occurred in 1945 at Chenoboskion, an ancient town in Egypt 48 km N of Luxor. The documents found there are usually called the Nag Hammadi texts because it was at Nag Hammadi, the nearest modern town to the site, that they were first reported. They formed part of a library collected by an early Christian sect and were abandoned *c.* 400 AD. The texts were not published until

1978, and the task of interpreting them continues.

Among the better-known gnostic documents are the 'Gospels' of Thomas, Philip and Mary, and the *Gospel of Truth*. The texts raise the question whether Gnosticism was a Christian heresy or a non-Christian system overlaid with Christian ideas, and the texts seem to indicate that there were non-Christian forms, although there is no proof that these existed in the pre-Christian era. If Gnosticism was not simply a perversion of Christian ideas, there is no concensus about its origins. It has links with the OT and the Greek philosophers, and with Iranian religion (Zoroastrianism).

Relevance to the NT. Some scholars (Bultmann among them) have suggested that Gnosticism is older than Christianity and that the NT is a form of it. However, there are fundamental differences in outlook; history, for example, was irrelevant to Gnostics but crucial to OT and NT writers, who also saw salvation as a present rather than merely future experience. However, traces of 'Gnostic' belief can be found in the NT. For example, some people in Corinth claimed to have special 'knowledge' and to live in an elevated 'spiritual' existence. The letter to Colossae, and the letters in Rev. 1-3 also confirm the presence of 'Gnostic' ideas in the 1st cent. churches. Such ideas are condemned by NT writers.

See also HERMETIC LITERATURE.

GOAT. Domesticated from ancient times, goats could thrive on poorer ground than sheep. Kids were used for meat, she-goats for milk; goatskins were used for leather and as bottles, and the hair of some varieties was woven into cloth. Goats have done great damage in E Mediterranean lands where they have not been properly controlled.

GOD. God is, and he may be known: these two affirmations form the foundation and inspiration of all religion. The first is an affirmation of faith, because God's existence is not subject to scientific proof. The second is an affirmation of experience through which God makes himself known. The Christian religion is distinctive in that it claims that he can be known as a personal God only in his self-revelation in the Scriptures which reaches its fullness in Jesus Christ his Son. That revelation allows the following affirmations to be made.

God is independent of creation. He is the source of all life; his name given to Moses was 'I am who I am', that is 'I am the one who has "being" within himself' (Ex. 3:14). Jesus clearly expressed this in Jn. 5:26.

God is pure spirit. He is without physical form or presence; when the Bible speaks of his ears, eyes and hands, it is expressing the senses that these physical terms convey. As such, he is essentially 'transcendent', unlimited as to time and space; he is eternal (timeless), ever-present, all-knowing and all-powerful; he is infinitely exalted above the created universe. Even passages which stress

195

his local presence also emphasize his nature as sovereign Creator and Judge (Is. 40:12ff.). At the same time, however, he is 'immanent'; he pervades everything, acting from the centre of every atom and the innermost springs of thought, life and feeling. His transcendence and immanence are affirmed together in Is. 57:15f.; Acts 17:24-31.

God is personal. He is rational, self-conscious and self-determining, an intelligent moral being. God's biblical names (see next article) are expressions of his personal characteristics (or 'attributes'), manifested in specific human situations: compassion in the presence of misery, grace in the presence of guilt, and so on. God is fully present in all his attributes; that is, there is never more love than justice, or vice versa. The one all-pervading attribute is his holiness, which characterizes all the others.

God is sovereign. He makes his own plans and carries them out in his own time and way. His will is not arbitrary, but he acts in complete harmony with his character. Theologians distinguish between his decrees, which determine what will happen, and his precepts, which are the duties he encourages on his creatures; the decrees are always fulfilled, but the precepts are often disobeyed. Hence there is a distinction between God's 'active will' which he fulfils and 'permissive will' in which people are permitted to act freely. The entrance of sin into his perfect world must be seen as a result of his permissive will, since it contradicts his holiness. The sovereignty of God ensures that all will be overruled to serve his eternal purposes, even though we cannot from our standpoint fully reconcile divine sovereignty and human responsibility.

God is a fellowship. This idea is the supreme revelation given in Scripture: God's life is eternally within himself a fellowship of three equal and distinct persons, Father, Son and Spirit. He made that fellowship open to mankind; when mankind surrendered through sin the right to enjoy that fellowship, God made its restoration possible. The grand end of his redemption of mankind was the revelation of himself as three persons acting for our restoration. (See also TRINITY.)

God is Father. 'Father' was Jesus' most used description of God. It has four aspects. He is 'Creational Father', the creator of mankind (*cf.* Is. 64:8; Mal. 2:10). He is 'Theocratic Father', in a special collective relationship with his people Israel (*cf.* Mal. 1:6). He is 'Generative Father' of Jesus Christ, the second Person of the Trinity, God's Son by eternal generation expressing an essential and timeless relationship beyond our understanding. He is, finally, the 'Adoptive Father', expressing the relationship of all believers to him as his 'children' (Gal. 3:26). In living union with Christ they are adopted into his family, become subject to the regenerating work of the Spirit (Jn. 1:13) and are given the privileges which belong to that special relationship (Rom. 8:17).

GOD, NAMES OF. *Basic names.* 1. El is a general name usually qualified in some way, *e.g.* 'the God of Bethel' (Gn. 31:13). 2. Elyon means 'the most high God' (Nu. 24:16). 3. Elohim is the plural of El, but can be treated as singular. In EVV it is rendered simply 'God', and conveys the notion of all that belongs to a concept of deity in contrast to created beings (*cf.* Nu. 23:19). 4. YHWH, Yahweh or Jehovah as it is often wrongly written, is usually translated 'the LORD'. The Jews considered this name too sacred to pronounce, so Adonai ('my Lord') was substituted in public reading. Strictly speaking, this is the only 'name' of God, the name by which the Patriarchs especially knew him (Gn. 12:8; Ex. 3:15). It represents God as a Person, bringing God near to mankind; in Hebrew a name is not a label but signifies the real personality of its owner.

Sometimes the names are used together: 'I the LORD (*Yahweh*) your God (*Elohim*) am a jealous God (*El*) (Dt. 5:9). They are not fully interchangeable. In Gn. 27:20 Jacob speaks of 'Yahweh your God (Elohim)'— Yahweh is the name by which Isaac worships the supreme God.

The revelation to Moses. At the burning bush, God introduced himself as 'the God (Elohim) of your fathers' (Ex. 3:6). When Moses asked for a more specific name, he was told 'I AM WHO I AM' (Ex. 3:14); that is, God was giving him the inner meaning of the name he already knew. It involves a play on words ('I AM' is very similar in Hebrew to Yahweh, which is itself connected with the verb 'to be'), and implies a promise of God's continuing presence and power. Later, God told Moses that he had appeared to the Patriarchs as El Shaddai (God Almighty) and not Yahweh (Ex. 6:3). It seems that the name of Yahweh was known to the Patriarchs but its *significance* was not revealed until God spoke to Moses. The earlier revelations concerned the future which God was capable of fulfilling; the new revelation was more intimate and related to the present.

Particular names of God. A number of titles are given to God at specific times to indicate some relevant aspect of his character. Among them are the following: the LORD will provide (Yahweh-jireh, Gn. 22:1); the LORD is my banner (Yahweh-nissi, Ex. 17:15); the LORD is peace (Yahweh-shalom, Jdg. 6:24); the LORD is our righteousness (Yahweh-tsidkenu, Je. 23:6; 33:16); the LORD of hosts (Yahweh-sabbaoth, Ps. 24:10 and very common in the prophets; the 'hosts' may have been Israel's armies originally but came to comprise all heavenly powers ready to obey God's command); LORD God of Israel (frequent in the prophets, *e.g.* Is. 7:16); the Holy One of Israel (a favourite in Isaiah, *e.g.* 1:4); the Ancient of Days (God the eternal Judge in Dn. 7).

See also NAME (for the concept of names, and prayer 'in God's name').

GODLINESS. Usually means reverence towards God except in 1 Tim. 5:4 where it means proper regard for one's household (RSV 'religious duty'). The word is most often used in the Pastoral Letters and includes the idea of a right relationship with God leading to right modes of action (*cf.* 2 Tim. 3:5). Cornelius' godliness ('devout' in Acts 10:2) was illustrated by his care for his household, his charitable giving and prayers, and his willingness to obey divine instructions.

GOG AND MAGOG. In Ezk. 38:2, Gog could be Gyges, king of Lydia (*c.* 660 BC), and Magog could be Assyrian for 'land of Gog'. But as they are linked with peoples at the extremities of the then known world (Ezk. 38:5f.; *cf.* Rev. 20:8), they are probably to be seen as eschatological figures rather than as historically identifiable.

GOLAN. The N city of refuge E of the Jordan. Possibly Sahm el-Jolan, 22 km E of Aphek (Hippos).

GOLD: See MINING AND METALS.

GOLGOTHA: See SKULL, THE.

GOLIATH. A giant of Gath serving in the Philistine army killed by David in a duel which had religious significance (1 Sa. 17). His height is given as 3.2 m, which though unusual is not impossible as human skeletons of similar size from roughly this period have been found in Palestine. He may have been a descendant of the Rephaim (*cf.* Dt. 2:20f. and 2 Sa. 21:22). In 2 Sa. 21:19 Elhanan is said to have killed Goliath; Elhanan may have been another name for David or, with 1 Ch. 20:5, the victim was a relative of Goliath. See also GIANT.

GOMER (lit. 'completion'). 1. The eldest son of Japheth (Gn. 10:2f.); in Ezk. 38 probably to be identified with the Gimirrai (Cimmerians) from Ukraine who conquered Urartu (Armenia) before the 8th cent. BC. See also ARARAT; NOMADS. 2. Hosea's wife (Ho. 1:3).

GOOD. The OT Hebrew word means that which gratifies the senses and hence that which gives aesthetic or moral satisfaction. The NT Greek words mean moral or physical quality and sometimes that which is noble, honourable, admirable or worthy. The biblical concept of moral and spiritual good however is thoroughly God-centred. It has five elements.

God is good. 'Good' means primarily what God is, then what he does, creates, commands and gives, and finally what he approves in his peoples' lives. So good is defined in terms of God, not vice versa. God alone is therefore fully good (Mk. 10:18), and other people or things are good so far as they conform to his will. God's goodness is often invoked as a theme of praise and an argument in prayer (Ps. 86:5; 106:1). It is seen in what he does (Ps. 119:68), especially in his kindness to the needy (Ps. 25:8f.).

God's works are good. They reveal his wisdom and power (Ps. 104:24ff.). The whole material creation, as God's handiwork, is good (Gn. 1:31; 1 Tim. 4:4).

God's gifts are good. They express his generosity and are beneficial to their recipients. Indeed, all good is God's gift (Jas. 1:17). He showers on all people the blessings of nature (Acts 14:17), and as a perfect Father knows how to give good gifts to those who are his children through Christ (Mt. 7:11). Good on the material level was promised under the old covenant (Dt. 30:15), and in the realm of spiritual privilege is the gift of the new covenant (Heb. 9:11; 10:1). Anything which drives people closer to God, even if it is unpleasant, is for their good and God's glory (Rom. 8:28; *cf.* 2 Cor. 4:17; Heb. 12:10).

God's commands are good. They express his moral perfection and mark out for us the way of blessing (Rom. 7:12; 12:2). Christians are to do good even in the face of evil (Rom. 12:9, 21). Thus *obedience to God's commands is also good.* God approves and accepts such obedience (1 Tim. 2:3) which profits those who do it (Tit. 3:8). God has saved his people for a life of good works (Eph. 2:10); they are to take every opportunity for the good works which are their 'adornment' (2 Tim. 2:21; *cf.* 1 Tim. 2:9f.) and which express their love for both God and other people, fulfilling both the spirit and the letter of the law (Rom. 13:8ff.; *cf.* Mt. 5:18ff.).

Biblical theology identifies the righteous person with the good person by insisting that the law requires love. Love to mankind is shown by doing them good (Gal. 6:9f.), and is illustrated by the early church's poor-relief system (Acts 2:44f.; 4:32ff.).

GOPHER WOOD. The wood of which Noah's ark was built (Gn. 6:14). Some have suggested it was cypress wood, others some resinous tree. See TREES.

GOSHEN. 1. The territory assigned to the Israelites in Egypt. Its exact location is uncertain, but it was within the E Nile Delta near the city of Raamses, suitably near the court at Memphis (near Cairo) or Avaris (in NE Delta) for Joseph (Gn. 45:10). 2. A district in S Palestine (Jos. 10:41; 11:16) probably named after a town in the hills (Jos. 15:51), possibly near Zahiriyeh, 19 km SW of Hebron.

GOSPEL. 'Good news.' In classical literature the reward given for good tidings and also the message itself; originally the announcement of victory. Used over 75 times in the NT, it is the good news that God in Christ has fulfilled his promises to Israel, and that a way of salvation has been opened up to all (Mk. 1:14; Lk. 4:16ff.). The gospel of the coming of Christ was anticipated in God's blessing to Abraham (Gal. 3:8) and was promised by the prophets (Rom. 1:2). It *is* God's power, revealing his righteousness and leading to salvation all who believe (Rom. 1:16). Paul sees it as a sacred trust (1 Tim. 1:11) which he must proclaim (1 Cor. 9:16). It is the word of truth (Eph. 1:13), hidden to unbelievers (2 Cor. 4:3f.).

GOSPELS. The first four books of the NT together were first called 'The Gospels' in the mid-2nd cent. AD. The singular form ('The Gospel according to…') was known earlier, implying that each record contains the good news about Jesus Christ according to its author.

Most of the material now in the Gospels existed in an oral form before it was written in its present form. Jesus took care, in addition to his public ministry, to give to his disciples systematic instruction in a form they could easily commit to memory. His debates with religious leaders led to pronouncements which once heard would not easily be forgotten. There are several NT references to the 'tradition' received by the apostles from Jesus and passed on to new converts (*cf.* Acts 1:1f.). Paul's summary of the church's missionary message in 1 Cor. 15:3ff. does not differ from that in non-Pauline letters and sermons in Acts; Jesus was proclaimed as Lord and Christ, and people were called to repent and receive forgiveness through him. Some teaching is clearly based on Jesus' own words; Paul quotes his sayings on divorce (1 Cor. 7:10) and the maintenance of Christian workers (see 1 Cor. 9:14). There is evidence of systematic instruction of converts, and as the number of converts increased instructors would have been trained and digests of Jesus' teaching inevitably would have been drawn up orally if not in writing. The words and works of Jesus would have been recalled in worship, too, and people who had known or heard him would often have recalled and discussed his teaching.

The beginning of gospel writing coincided with the end of the first Christian generation. As eyewitnesses of Jesus' life and death (Lk. 1:2) died,

a permanent record of their witness became more necessary. All four Gospels probably are to be dated in the decades between AD 60 and 100. Documents probably existed before then (*cf.* Lk. 1:1) but none has survived, except those incorporated into the four Gospels.

Matthew, Mark and Luke are called the 'Synoptic Gospels' because they lend themselves to 'synoptic' study; that is, they can be arranged in parallel columns so their similarities and divergences can be examined. The substance of 606 out of 661 verses of Mark (omitting Mk. 16:9-20) reappears in an abridged form in Matthew; 380 of Mark's 661 verses appear also in Luke. Only 31 verses of Mark have no parallel in Matthew or Luke, while they both have up to 250 verses of common material not contained in Mark. Matthew has about 300 verses of unique material; Luke has 520 verses of unique material. There is no short cut to a satisfactory account of this distribution of common and special material, but some findings do command fairly widespread agreement.

One of these is that Mark was the first to be written and that it was used as a principle source by the other two. For example, where Matthew and Mark have common material, Mark's is always fuller and in most cases the differences are best explained by Matthew abridging Mark than by Mark amplifying Matthew. This is more important because, as C. H. Dodd has shown, Mark appears to have strung his units of material on a thread of apostolic preaching which can be discerned in some NT letters and the speeches in Acts, thus giving a close relation between Mark and apostolic preaching. Mark's material is mostly narrative; non-Marcan gospel material is mostly sayings of Jesus. Mark shows what Jesus did, the others show what he taught; this reflects the distinction between apostolic preaching (what Jesus did) and apostolic teaching of converts.

The non-Marcan material common to Matthew and Luke may conveniently and without prejudice be labelled 'Q', in accordance with a custom dating from the beginning of the 20th cent. It is most likely to have been derived from a common source, and although this source cannot be reconstructed in anything like a complete form, it does look like the general pattern of OT prophetical books. These books contain accounts of the prophet's call, a record of his sayings set in a narrative framework but with no mention of his death. The 'Q' material appears to come from a compilation beginning with Jesus' baptism by John followed by groups of his sayings set in a minimal narrative framework, but with no trace of a passion narrative. It was probably earlier than Mark, and used for teaching in the Gentile mission based in Antioch.

What other sources Matthew and Luke used is much more uncertain. Matthew appears to have used a sayings-collection based on Judaea (labelled 'M'); Luke has distinctive material (largely in chs. 9-18) which may have been derived from Caesarea

(labelled 'L'). But while it is good to consider the writers' sources, it is better to consider the use they made of them. Each Synoptic Gospel is an independent whole, with its own specific contribution to make to the NT picture of Jesus and his ministry.

The Fourth Gospel preserves a quite different tradition with its roots in Jewish Palestine, however much a wider Greek-culture audience was borne in mind when it was finally compiled at the end of the 1st cent. AD. Dodd suggests that the fixed outline of apostolic preaching can be discerned in it as clearly as in Mark.

At an early date after the publication of John all four began to circulate as a collection, but who first gathered them together is unknown. The *Gospel of Truth* (see GNOSTICISM) written *c.* 140-150, presupposes and meditates on the four Gospels. Tatian compiled a Gospel harmony, the *Diatessaron, c.* AD 170, from all four, with occasional intrusions of other material and modifications of Gospel wording. A decade later Irenaeus was declaring the fourfold Gospel as an accepted fact of Christianity, and his contemporary Clement of Alexandria carefully distinguished the four from apocryphal writings. All four were originally anonymous, however. The first reference to Matthew and Mark was made by Papias, bishop of Hierapolis in the early 2nd cent. AD. Irenaeus referred to Luke and John towards the end of that century. There is no doubt that the Gospels preserved the apostolic witness to God's revelation in Jesus Christ.

See also articles on each Gospel; BIBLICAL CRITICISM; NEW TESTAMENT CANON.

GOVERNMENT. *Old Testament times.* In earliest times the Patriarchs (Abraham and his descendants) were semi-nomads and the father was head of the family and its employees. At Sinai, Israel's tribes were organized into a 'theocracy', the rule of God over a nation called to be his people (Ex. 19:5f.). So Moses acted as God's representative, and so the people listened to him. He had elders to help him in administration.

After Joshua, Moses' successor, there were rulers or judges but no central organization. A king was needed but the people asked for one in a way that showed they were rejecting the theocratic ideal (1 Sa. 8). Any king had to be a man after God's own heart. Saul was not, so he was rejected; David was, and became a model of the ideal. David left minor decisions to under-officers. Solomon divided the nation into 12 districts each governed by a prefect responsible for providing the royal household's food (1 Ki. 4:7ff.).

After the Exile, the Jews were subject to Persia represented by a governor (*e.g.* Nehemiah) and with the high priest as local head of state. The same arrangement continued in the Greek period and, with modifications, in the Roman period too.

New Testament times. Palestine was divided into a number of republican states supervised by deputies of the Roman Caesar or by Herodian client-kings. Jewish nationalism was expressed through religious sects, whose attitudes to government included terrorism (Zealots), detachment (Essenes) and collaboration (the Sadducees). Jesus, who was denounced as a royal pretender and claimed a form of kingship (Jn. 18:36f.; 19:21), asserted that his kingdom was not of the same order as temporal states. However, the rights of the temporal state must be conceded, as must God's claims on people (Lk. 20:25).

Outside Palestine, churches were established in republican states which were either Roman satellites or colonies. On only one occasion were Christians accused of opposing Caesar, and this charge was not sustained by the authorities (Acts 17:7f.). Christian writers encouraged a respectful attitude to government (*e.g.* Rom. 13:1ff.; 1 Tim. 2:2) even when they were falsely charged (1 Pet. 2:11ff.). However, Paul had reservations. The rulers of this age crucified Jesus (1 Cor. 2:8); God is the ultimate ruler (1 Tim. 6:15); and demonic powers may well be conceived as the forces behind human government (Eph. 6:12; Col. 2:15). The book of Revelation depicts a struggle for world government between God and satanic powers; and the ruler cult (Rev. 13:15) identifies the enemy as Roman Caesars.

GOVERNOR. The most frequent OT allusion is to the ruler of a district under a king, *e.g.* Nehemiah as governor of Judah (Ne. 5:14). Other governors mentioned include heads of cities (*e.g.* 1 Ki. 22:26). In the NT it often refers to Roman subordinate rulers such as Pilate (Mt. 27:2) and Felix (Acts 23:26).

GOZAN. Ancient Guzana, modern Tell Halaf, on the Upper Habur river, to which Israelites from Samaria were deported in 722 BC (2 Ki. 17:6; 18:11). Excavations have revealed tablets from that time inscribed with W Semitic names.

GRACE, FAVOUR. The idea of grace involves forgiveness, salvation, regeneration, repentance and the love of God, so other words may also convey the theme of grace.

Old Testament. There are two words for grace. *Chesed* (steadfast love, loving-kindness) is often associated with the covenant; 'covenant love' is perhaps the nearest equivalent. *Chen* means totally undeserved favour ('faithfulness' in Je. 31:2) from a superior to an inferior, from God to man or man to man, but never from man to God. Grace is not as fully developed in the OT as in the NT, but it is there, even within the law, which is seen as a provision of God's grace. Israel is called to be God's people by his grace (Dt. 7:7f.). The prophets called for a clear repentance and acknowledged that a new heart was God's gift (Ezk. 18:31; *cf.* Je. 31:31ff.). *Chesed* is found frequently in worship in the Psalms (*e.g.* 5:7, 'steadfast love').

New Testament. The idea of grace is prominent in the Synoptic Gospels; Jesus came to seek and save those who were lost. Many of his parables teach the doctrine of grace: the prodigal son was given a welcome he did not deserve (Lk. 15:20ff.; *cf.* Mt. 20:1ff.). In Acts, the dynamic effect of grace resulting in fearless courage and effective witness is seen in 4:33; 11:23; 13:43. Paul's doctrine, summarized in Rom. 1:16-4:25, is that people are sinful and thus alienated from God, but God in his grace treats them as if they had never sinned. The proper response to God's freely given grace is faith—the kind of faith that involves behaviour and lifestyle as well as belief. This faith too is God's gift, though the believer does turn to God of his own volition.

The letter to the Hebrews uses the most 'grace-words' in the NT. Grace is related to Christ's sufferings (2:9) and viewed as a calling to commitment (12:14f.). The striking phrase 'the throne of grace' (4:16) unites God's majesty and grace. In John's writings, there is surprisingly little directly about grace, but God's love is emphasized throughout, as is faith and its undeserved result of eternal life.

GRAIN CROPS. Wheat and barley were important food crops in the ancient Near East. Barley was a staple food in Palestine, especially for poor families (Ru. 2:17); it has a shorter growing season than wheat and can flourish on poorer soils. It was also used for animal feed (1 Ki. 4:28) and, judging from the evidence of Philistine cups, for brewing. Wheat, because of its importance as a food, was used as a symbol of God's goodness and provision (Ps. 81:16), and its biological process of one grain 'dying' to give birth to several grains was used by Christ to symbolize spiritual fruitfulness through self-denial (Jn. 12:24f.).

The barley harvest came first, in April and May; wheat was harvested up to a month later. The grain was grasped in one hand and cut with a sickle held in the other, then tied into sheaves. Gleaners followed the reapers to take grain left standing at the field edge, then animals were allowed to graze on the stubble. The grain was separated from the straw by laying out the sheaves on a threshing-floor and driving animals or pulling a wooden sled studded with stone and iron fragments over it. The grain was then winnowed by tossing it into the air so that the breeze would blow the lighter chaff or husks into a separate pile—a common sight used symbolically for God's judgment in Mt. 3:12. The grain may also have been sieved to remove grit before being bagged. The straw was added to animal feed, used in brick and pottery making, and thrown onto fires to give instant heat. See also AGRICULTURE; BREAD; GLEANING.

GRASS. Green pastures last only for a while after the rains in Palestine, and wither in the dry season. Grass is therefore a fitting symbol of the temporary nature of human life (Is. 40:6f.), riches (Jas. 1:10f.), and the wicked (Ps. 37:2). The luxuriance of green pastures is like the serenity of spiritual life (Ps. 23:2).

GRASSHOPPER: See LOCUST.

GREECE. The area of Greek settlement was never static; there were republics in the Black Sea area, Sicily, S Italy, Marseilles and Spain. After Alexander, they extended E to India. Greece was never a political entity; the king of Greece in Dn. 8:21 must be one of the rulers who controlled the affairs of many but not all Greek states. However, Greek institutions brought unity at a cultural level. The ideal of free and cultivated life in a small autonomous community became almost universally accepted. The states provided education, entertainment, and health and welfare services. In the NT the term 'Greek' is often equivalent to 'Gentile'. The widespread use of the Greek language opened the gospel to all people. See also ATHENS; HELLENISTS; MACEDONIA.

GREEK: See NEW TESTAMENT LANGUAGES.

GREEKS. Used in the NT to describe inhabitants of Greece in particular (Acts 16:1) and of Gentiles in general (Rom. 10:12). In Acts 6:1 and 9:29 'Hellenists' (RSV) could be Greek speaking Jews originally from outside Palestine, or non-conformist Jews influenced by Greek culture. See also HELLENISTS.

GREETING. There are several biblical forms of social courtesies. Paul sends greetings messages using a formula common in much Greek correspondence, *e.g.* Rom. 16. A formal personal greeting of a monarch, along with obeisance, is recorded in Ne. 2:3. Verbal greetings without physical contact are referred to in Mt. 10:12. A formal cheek-kiss was used (1 Sa. 10:1); the double-cheek kiss is still sometimes used today by males in the east. The more intimate mouth-kiss is recorded (Gn. 29:11).

GRINDING: See BREAD.

GUARANTEE, SURETY. This is a commercial term for a first instalment put down as a pledge that the full payment will follow, used by Paul to describe the Christian's inheritance of the Holy Spirit as a first instalment of coming glory (Eph. 1:14; 2 Cor. 1:22; 5:5). In the OT, people were cautioned against standing as guarantors (sureties) for others' debts (*e.g.* Pr. 17:18). Jesus is our surety of the new covenant (Heb. 7:22).

GUARD. Bodyguards are mentioned on some occasions in the OT, *e.g.* Nebuchadrezzar's, in 2 Ki. 25:8ff. Nehemiah set up guards at various guard-posts to protect the people rebuilding Jerusalem's walls (Ne. 3:7). In the NT, the temple guard arresting Jesus was a group of Levites whose task among others was to keep Gentiles out of the temple (Mt. 27:65).

GUDGODAH. An Israelite encampment in the desert, probably the same as Hor-haggidgad (Nu. 33:32f.), near Bene-jaakan and Jotbatha W of Wadi Arabah.

H

HABAKKUK, BOOK OF. *Contents.* His concern at Judah's lawlessness (1:1-4); God's promise to use the Chaldeans to punish it (1:5-11); Habakkuk asks how a holy God can sanction such brutality (1:12-17); the Chaldeans will perish through pride and the righteous live through faith (2:1-5); a taunt-song against the Chaldeans (2:6-20); a psalm of God's majesty in judgment and salvation (3:1-19).

Authorship and date. Nothing is known about Habakkuk outside the book. Traditions identifying him as the Shunammite's son (2 Ki. 4:16) or associating him with Daniel (Bel and the Dragon 33f.) have little supporting evidence. The only clear historical reference is in 1:6 so the prophecy is usually dated shortly after the battle of Carchemish (605 BC) when the Chaldeans routed the Egyptians and subjugated Johoiakim of Judah.

Message. The answer to the moral problem of God using the Chaldeans to punish Judah is that a person's arrogance carries in it the seeds of its own destruction (2:4). Paul developed the thought of this verse, giving a fuller meaning to its concept of faith (Rom. 1:17; Gal. 3:11).

HABOR. A river in the Assyrian province of Gozan where some of the deported Israelites stayed (2 Ki. 17:6).

HACHILAH (lit. 'drought'). A hill in the Judaean desert where David hid, probably between Ziph and En-gedi.

HADAD. *Pagan god:* The Syrian storm-god also known as Baal. *People:* Among others, the son of Ishmael (Gn. 25:15), and an Edomite of the ruling family who married the Egyptian pharaoh's daughter and plotted against Solomon (1 Ki. 11:14ff.).

HADADEZER (lit. 'Hadad is my helper'). The name of at least two kings of the Damascus region. One was defeated by David but continued to rule his territory and supported the Amorites against David (2 Sa. 8:3; 10:16ff.). Another is also named in Assyrian inscriptions as an ally of Ahab against Shalmaneser III at Qarqar in 853 BC. The latter must be one of the kings of Damascus named BEN-HADAD in the OT.

HADAD-RIMMON. Both elements of the name are local names for a pagan storm-god; Zc. 12:11 may thus refer to mourning associated with it, rather than to a specific place near Megiddo.

HADES: See SHEOL; also DESCENT INTO HADES.

HADRACH. A place on the N boundaries of Syria near Qinnesrin, 25 km S of Aleppo.

HAGAR. An Egyptian servant of Sarah, Abraham's wife. In accordance with the custom of the time, the childless Sarah urged Abraham to have a son by Hagar; Ishmael was born (Gn. 16). Hagar despised Sarah and fled from her anger, only to meet with God who told her to return. After Isaac's birth, however, Ishmael and Hagar were expelled, but God protected them (Gn. 21). Paul used the story as an allegory; Hagar and Ishmael represented the Jews and their futile attempt to keep the law; Sarah and Isaac represented the promise of God received through faith (Gal. 4:21ff.).

HAGGAI, BOOK OF. The book records messages given between August and December 520 BC. Work on restoring the Jerusalem temple had ceased and Haggai (with Zechariah, Ezr. 5:1) roused the people to action again. The structure is accusation (1:1-11), response (1:12-15) and assurance (2:1-9); accusation (2:10-17), response (2:18f.), assurance (2:20-23). The first half looks back on the past, and the unprecedented response is that the people acknowledge Haggai as God's spokesman and they begin the rebuilding work. However, they need encouragement because the new temple lacks the splendour of Solomon's. The second half looks forward to the future, beginning with the need for repentance from past sins. The people respond and are promised prosperity as a sign of God's approval. Then they are assured that the world powers which then dominated the political scene would be overthrown and the Davidic prince Zerubbabel would be the Lord's executive, a promise fulfilled in the descent of Jesus from him (Mt. 1:12; Lk. 3:27).

HAGRITES. A prosperous tribe or confederation E of Gilead attacked by Israel (1 Ch. 5:10, 18ff.). They are mentioned in Assyrian and other inscriptions.

HAIR, HAIRDRESSING. The normal Israelite custom for both sexes was to grow the hair long; Absalom's luxuriant growth is recorded with apparent admiration (2 Sa. 14:26). By NT times, however, long hair was 'a shame' to a man (1 Cor. 11:14), although Paul was writing to Greeks. Baldness was disliked, perhaps because of its association with leprosy; restoratives were eagerly sought. Dark hair was admired in both sexes, but grey hair was very honourable; Herod the Great, however, dyed his when it began greying. Samson had his hair plaited, and women frequently braided or plaited theirs; unkempt hair was a sign of mourning. Barbers and razors were well-known (Ezk. 5:1). The forelock was never cut because this was a pagan custom (Lv. 19:23; Dt. 14:1); orthodox Jews still observe this. The Nazirite left his hair untrimmed then shaved it completely to signify purification after his vow ended. See also BEARD.

HALAH. A place in Assyria to which Israelites were deported, NE of Nineveh.

HALAK (lit. 'smooth, bald'). A mountain in Judaea, the S limit of Joshua's conquests; probably modern Jebel Halaq.

HALLELUJAH. A transliteration of the Hebrew liturgical call 'Praise Yah' (the shortened form of God's name Yahweh). It usually comes at the beginning or end of psalms, suggesting it was a standard call to praise in temple worship after the Exile. The call was taken over into Christian worship (Rev. 19:1, 3f., 6).

HAM. One of Noah's sons, probably the second. From its biblical usage, 'Hamitic' is applied by scholars to a group of languages of which Egyptian is one. Because of intermarriage and migration, Ham's descendants would not have had a recognizable form. See NATIONS, TABLE OF.

HAMAN. The villain of the book of ESTHER, who plots to massacre the Jews but is foiled.

HAMATH (lit. 'fortress, citadel'). A city on the E bank of the Orontes lying on one of the main trade routes S from Asia Minor. In David's time it was friendly to Israel (2 Sa. 8:9f.). Jeroboam II conquered it c. 780 BC (2 Ki. 19:28) as did Sargon of Assyria c. 721 BC who settled some of its people in Samaria. In Greek and Roman times it was known as Epiphaneia.

HAMOR (lit. 'he-ass'). The ruler of Shechem in the time of Jacob, killed by Simeon and Levi after their sister Dinah had been humiliated (Gn. 34). Animal personal names were common in biblical times.

HANANEL (lit. 'God is gracious'). A tower in Jerusalem (Ne. 3:1), which some scholars equate with the Tower of the Hundred or see as another tower in the same fortress. See HUNDRED, TOWER OF.

HANANIAH (lit. 'Yahweh has been gracious'). A common OT name; in the NT it is ANANIAS. Chief among them is a cult-prophet denounced by Jeremiah (Je. 28) for declaring that Judah's restoration would be in two years, not 70, after Nebuchadrezzar's conquest. He broke Jeremiah's yoke as a symbolic gesture.

HAND. In common with most other parts of the body, the hand is described as having apparently almost autonomous functions, although they are never divorced from the actions of the whole person, *e.g.* 'If your right hand causes you to sin...', Mt. 5:30. It is used as a symbol of power (Ps. 31:15). Dropping the hands is a sign of weakness which needs to be remedied (Is. 35:3); lifting them is a gesture of violence (1 Ki. 11:26) or supplication (Ps. 28:2). The touch of a person's hand was believed to communicate authority, power or blessing (Gn. 48:13f.; Mk. 6:5; Acts 8:17ff.); this is one of many indications that in Hebrew thought 'body' and 'spirit' were closely related. See also ARM; BODY; LAYING ON OF HANDS.

HANDKERCHIEF, NAPKIN. In Lk. 19:20; Acts 19:12 probably a cloth used primarily for wiping perspiration.

HANES. Often to be identified with modern Ihnasyeh el-Medineh or Ahnas 80 km S of Cairo, an important city in Middle Egypt, but this does not suit Is. 30:4 which requires it nearer Zoan (Tanis) in the E Delta. It is possible that another city with this name was once in the Delta area; alternatively Hanes may be a transliteration of an Egyptian word for 'king's mansion' in Zoan itself.

HANNAH (lit. 'grace'). The favourite of Elkanah's two wives, tormented by the other (Peninnah) because she was childless. She vowed she would devote a son to God, and she gave birth to Samuel. Her thanksgiving suggests she was a prophetess (1 Sa. 2:1ff.).

HARA. A place to which Tiglath-pileser III of Assyria sent rebellious Israelites in 734-732 BC; the site is unknown.

HARAN. *Person:* Abraham's brother and Lot's father (Gn. 11:26ff.). *Place:* A city 32 km SE of Urfa (Edessa), in modern Turkey, on the main trade route from Nineveh to Aleppo. Terah and Abraham lived there (Gn. 11:31); Isaac's wife Rebekah came from there; Jacob fled there from Esau (Gn. 29:4). It was once a focus for Amorite tribes, later fortified by the Assyrian Adad-nirari *c.* 1310 BC. It rebelled and was sacked in 763 BC (*cf.* 2 Ki. 19:12). It was the last Assyrian capital before the Babylonians captured it in 609 BC.

HARARITE. A term applied to some of David's heroes; it may mean 'mountain dweller.'

HARMON. A place in Am. 4:3 otherwise unknown; NEB suggests 'dunghill', JB 'Hermon'. Possibly Harmel, S of Kadesh.

HAROD (lit. 'trembling'). A spring at the foot of Mt Gilboa E of Jezreel where Gideon reduced his army (Jdg. 7). Possibly modern Ain Jalud.

HAROSHETH. Found only in connection with Sisera, a Canaanite commander (Jdg. 4). It is possibly Tell el-Harbaj SE of Haifa, but the exact location is uncertain.

HARP: See MUSIC AND MUSICAL INSTRUMENTS.

HARROW. A toothed implement dragged along the ground by an ox to break clods of earth after ploughing; there is no known representation to show what an ancient harrow looked like. See AGRICULTURE.

HARVEST: See GRAIN CROPS; OLIVE; PENTECOST; VINE.

HASIDAEANS. In 1 Macc. 2:42; 7:13; 2 Macc. 14:6, a term meaning 'loyal ones' apparently adopted by zealots for the law when Greek-culture ideas flooded Palestine in the 2nd cent. BC. They had little sympathy with the Hasmonaean nationalists. They split into two; the majority became known as PHARISEES, others became ESSENES.

HATE, HATRED. Hatred between fellow Israelites or Christians is condemned (Ps. 55:12f.; 1 Jn. 4:20). Mercy may sometimes temper personal hatred (Ex. 23:5); Christians are called to love their enemies and do positive good to them (Mt. 5:43f.). However, God hates evil (Am. 6:8) and evil-doers (Dt. 32:41), so therefore do his people (Ps. 139:21f.; Heb. 1:9). The world will hate Christians just as it hated Jesus (Jn. 15:18ff.). See also WRATH.

HAVILAH (lit. 'circle', 'district'). 1. An area near Eden, location unknown (Gn. 2:11f.). 2. An area in Sinai and NW Arabia (Gn. 25:18; 1 Sa. 15:7). 3. Possibly a tribe in S Arabia (Gn. 10:7, 29).

HAVVOTH-JAIR (lit. 'The camps of Jair'). Probably in the hills between Mt Gilead and the Yarmuk, which were dotted with settlements, conquered by JAIR (Dt. 3:14).

HAZAEL (lit. 'Whom God beholds'). A powerful king of Syria (Aram) whom God used to scourge Israel during the reigns of Jehoram, Jehu and Jehoahaz. Elijah was commissioned to anoint him (1 Ki. 19:15-17), but he did not become king until, as the emissary of Ben-hadad II to Elisha, he murdered his sovereign and assumed the throne (2 Ki. 8:7ff.). His name occurs in Assyrian inscriptions as an opponent of Shalmaneser III from 841 BC onwards; the Assyrians also knew that he was a usurper and that his predecessor was a victim of foul play. He fought Shalmaneser again in 837 BC, but no further collision between the kingdoms is known until Hazael was cowed into submission by Adad-nirari III *c.* 805-802 BC. Hazael outlived Jehoahaz (814/3-798 BC, 2 Ki. 13:22), so probably died *c.* 797/6.

HAZARMAVETH. The third son of Joktan; probably to be identified with the kingdom of Hadramaut in S Arabia.

HAZEROTH. A desert oasis where Miriam became a leper (Nu. 12), probably Ayin Khodara.

HAZOR. A name meaning 'settlement' or 'village' used of several places in the OT. The most important was a fortified city in Naphtali. When Israel conquered it, it was the royal seat of Jabin. He organized a coalition against Joshua, who killed him and burnt down Hazor (Jos. 11). Later it threatened Israel in Deborah's time under its general Sisera (Jdg. 4) and was crushed by Israel's Barak despite Sisera's force of 900 chariots. Solomon fortified it two centuries later; Tiglath-pileser III of Assyria destroyed it in 732 BC (2 Ki. 15:29).

The large site is Tell el-Qedah, 8 km SW of Lake Huleh in Galilee, and it must have accommodated up to 40,000 people; there is archaeological evidence of its destruction in Joshua's time and of the Assyrian destruction. It figures in Egyptian texts of the 19th cent. BC as a Canaanite city likely to endanger the empire, and in Babylonian texts about 1500 BC as an important city on the route from Mesopotamia.

HEAD. It is regarded not as the seat of the intellect but as the source of life. To lift it up is to grant life in the sense of success (Ps. 27:6), to cover it by the hand or by ashes is to mourn the loss of life (2 Sa. 13:19). Headship symbolizes authority or, in the case of Christ and husbands (Eph. 5:23) the source of life.

HEALTH, DISEASE AND HEALING. The purpose of Scripture is theological, and only those details which are relevant to its over-all purpose are included. For example, the boy whom Jesus healed in Mt. 8:6 was 'paralysed and in terrible distress', but even if the disease was known (possibly poliomyelitis together with respiratory paralysis) it was unnecessary to say so. Contemporary medical knowledge was mostly restricted to what could be seen or felt by the patient or doctor; public knowledge was even more restricted. In the biblical documents sincere and honest people recorded what they saw as they understood it, and the facts they describe can therefore be taken as facts. Of all the writers, probably only Luke had any real medical knowledge, and he occasionally uses known medical terms.

I. Medical terms in the Bible. *Blindness* was common in the ancient Near East. Several diseases would have been responsible including trachoma, and gonorrhoea in pregnant women; Dt. 28:28f. describes the groping gait of the blind. The double healing of the blind man in Mk. 8:22ff. recalls the difficulty of interpreting images which people whose sight is restored surgically sometimes face. *Boils* in the OT refer to different kinds of localized inflammation. Job's sores may have been tuberculous leprosy (Jb. 2:7); Hezekiah's boil was probably a carbuncle (2 Ki. 20:7); the Egyptian boils were probably a specific Egyptian skin disease such as endemic boil or malignant pustule (Dt. 28:27, 35; see PLAGUES OF EGYPT). *Burns* (Lv. 13:24ff.) may have been literal, or a skin disorder.

Childbirth: see BARRENNESS; MIDWIFE. *Consumption* (Lv. 26:16; Dt. 28:22) could be tuberculosis, cancer or some other wasting disease; TB certainly existed in Egypt when the Israelites were there. *Deafness:* The Israelites were told to be kind to the deaf and blind (Lv. 19:14). A deaf man whom Jesus healed also had a speech impediment probably caused by his deafness; he could make sounds but being unable to hear them could not form them into normal speech (Mk. 7:32ff.). The *dropsy* (lit. 'full of water') of Lk. 14:2 was a sign of heart, kidney or liver disease ('whose legs and arms were swollen', GNB). *Dumbness* occurred throughout biblical history and can be attributed to no specific cause; sometimes it was associated with demon possession (*e.g.* Mt. 9:32ff.); for the man in Mk. 7:32 see deafness above.

Dysentery was the infectious disease which Paul healed in Acts 28:8; the technical term was used by Plato, Aristotle and others. It is possible that Jehoram's bowel disease (2 Ch. 21:15ff.) was the chronic amoebic dysentery which when very severe or prolonged can be complicated by prolapse of the rectum or large intestine, which produces intestinal obstruction. *Epilepsy* occurs twice in the NT (Mt. 4:24; 17:15), the latter seeming to be typical grandmal epilepsy as well as demon possession; the conditions are distinguished in 4:24.

Fever is used to cover various ailments which produce a high temperature. Luke's description in Lk. 4:38 indicates he recognized degrees of fever. *Flow of blood, haemorrhage* was probably menorrhagia in Lk. 8:43 (see menstruation below); Lv. 15:2ff. denotes various bodily *discharges* which made a person ritually unclean. *Itch* in Dt. 28:27 was something akin to eczema; in Lv. 13:30ff. it was some irritating skin rash.

Leprosy is a layman's term lacking the precision of the modern term which means a specific bacterial infection. The common Hebrew word describes human skin disease, discoloured fabrics and even walls (Lv. 13) evidenced by pale patches. Some of the features do not occur in true leprosy and suggest such things as infection following a burn (v. 20), ringworm (v. 29) and pustular dermatitis (v. 36). While all ten lepers in Lk. 17:11ff. were 'cleansed', only one was 'cured', which may refer to his spiritual state. There is no clue to the nature of their disease(s). True leprosy did exist in India by 600 BC and in Europe by 400 BC; there is no definite evidence that it existed as early as the Exodus.

Madness, mental illness is described in non-specific ways, but both Saul's and Nebuchadrezzar's attacks are described in some detail. Saul was a gifted but inadequate person who suffered from depression and later had the paranoid ideas and irritability characteristic of aging patients. Nebuchadrezzar had a hypomanic personality which is liable to develop a manic-depressive psychosis, from which he eventually recovered (Dn. 4:28ff.). *Menstruation* rendered women ritually unclean. The woman of Lk. 8:43 probably had menorrhagia, an abnormally prolonged menstrual flow (12 years in her case), which can produce anaemia. The word *paralysis* is non-specific but it clearly describes a non-fatal condition because patients survived for long periods; the boy in Mt. 8:6 probably had a respiratory paralysis associated with poliomyelitis.

Plague, pestilence is used for all sorts of disasters and diseases; in 2 Sa. 24:15 it was a virulent epidemic killing 70,000 people, perhaps the same as that in 2 Ki. 19:35 which killed 185,000 soldiers. *Scab* and *spot* clearly relate to unspecified skin diseases which are rife in the East; the *scurvy* of Dt. 28:27 is not true scurvy but a chronic disease forming a thick crust on the head and sometimes spreading over the whole body. *Tumours* afflicted the Philistines (1 Sa. 5). As models of both tumours and rodents were made, it was pro-

bably a case of bubonic plague which is transmitted by fleas carried by rats and gerbils, and the description of the tumours' spread along lines of communication is consistent with bubonic plague. The *withered hand* of Lk. 6:6ff. denotes one with paralysed and shrunken muscles, possibly a late complication of poliomyelitis.

See also DEMON POSSESSION.

II. Biblical views of disease and its treatment.

God and disease. Suffering and disease in the Bible are closely related to questions of the origin and nature of evil. The nations which obeyed God were promised freedom from disease; if disobedient, they would be afflicted (Ex. 15:25, Dt. 28:22f., 58ff.). But on the whole, disease and suffering is seen as the effect on an individual of the general spiritual malaise of the human society he or she belongs to. God may also use it to punish individuals (*e.g.* Nu. 12:10), and to correct them (Heb. 12:6ff.; *cf.* Jacob in Gn. 32:24ff.). The book of Job shows that the real issue is a person's relationship to God rather than their attitude to their own suffering. See EVIL; SUFFERING.

Hygiene and sanitation. The Israelites had a remarkable sanitary code in Moses' time, without which they might not have survived their stay in the desert. The instructions deal with water supply, sewage disposal, inspection and selection of food, and control of infectious disease. The burning of excrement (Ex. 29:14) and the prohibition on eating animals which had died naturally were especially important in preventing the spread of disease. The quarantine period of 40 days was adopted by Italians in the 14th cent. because of the Jews' relative immunity from certain plagues.

Treatment of disease. Therapies were those known at the time and were not always effective. Hezekiah was recommended a 'cake of figs' to be applied to his boil (Is. 38:21), and some treatment was bound up with superstition, as the attempt to increase sexual fertility by using mandrakes (Gn. 30:14ff.). Wine was used medicinally (1 Tim. 5:23). Doctors existed; Asa was condemned for consulting them probably because these were magicians and because he was not also seeking the Lord (2 Ch. 16:12). The Jewish religion differed from pagan religions in that doctors and priests were generally different people (except in the case of diagnosing 'leprosy'). Medicine throughout the biblical period could hardly be dignified with the name of science, however.

III. Healing and miracles.

Healing means the restoration of an ill person to full health in body or mind (or both). This includes recovery resulting from medical treatment and spontaneous remission of a disease. God is the one who heals all our diseases (Ps. 103:3), whatever method is employed. In biblical times God's people were expected to make use of the means available to assist recovery (1 Tim. 5:23). The features of healing miracles in the Bible are instantaneous,

complete and permanent recovery, usually without the use of external means. They were often dramatized signs along with enacted parables both to authenticate the word of the person who performed them (*e.g.* Acts 2:22), and to illustrate that word (*e.g.* Lk. 5:18ff.). Their purpose, therefore was as theological as it was medical. Many lay ill at the pool of Bethesda but Jesus healed only one to teach a spiritual truth (Jn. 5:3ff.). The church today is generally recovering its healing ministry as an integral part of the gospel of wholeness.

Old Testament healing miracles. They are unusual in the OT, and the few cases mostly cluster around the two critical times of the Exodus (*e.g.* Nu. 12:1ff.) and the ministries of Elijah and Elisha (*e.g.* 2 Ki. 4:1ff., a case either of sunstroke or fulminating encephalitis or even a brain haemorrhage).

Healing miracles in the Gospels. People came in large numbers to be healed by Jesus (Mt. 4:23f.), probably including cases of mental illness as well as organic disease. The Gospels record over 20 stories of healings of individuals or groups. Some were healed at a distance. Luke includes several miracles not recorded by the others (*e.g.* 7:11ff.; 13:11ff.; 14:1ff.). John clearly designates miracles as 'signs' with a spiritual meaning, for which see MIRACLES.

Healing in apostolic times. Christ commissioned the 70 and the 12 (Mt. 10:1; Lk. 10:9) to heal. There are several accounts of healing in Acts (*e.g.* 14:8ff.), but cases of illness are also reported and the apostles' powers

213

clearly were not permitted to be used indiscriminately to keep themselves or their friends free from illness (*cf.* 2 Tim. 4:20). Paul's 'thorn in the flesh' is a handicap which has never satisfactorily been explained but it had a positive spiritual effect on him (2 Cor. 12:7ff.). The classic passage on prayer for the sick (Jas. 5:13ff.) recommends the use of oil, which may have been medicinal or symbolic of the separation of the sickness onto Christ (*cf.* Mt. 8:17). It does not include a promise that all who are sick and are prayed over will recover their health.

See also DEMON POSSESSION, which the NT differentiates from sickness.

HEART. The term is sometimes used metaphorically to mean 'centre', as in Dt. 4:11; Mt. 12:40. References to the actual physical organ are rare, the most explicit being 1 Sa. 25:37. Generally, 'heart' meant the governing centre for the whole man (*cf.* Pr. 4:23). The modern concepts of character, personality, will and mind all reflect something of its meaning. The NT usage is similar; there the heart is the seat of the will (Mk. 3:5), the intellect (Mk. 2:6) and feeling (Lk. 24:32). Heart is thus the nearest NT term to 'person', but 'mind' is the closest modern term to the general biblical use of heart. Ryder-Smith suggests that the great commandment (Mk. 12:30) probably means, 'You shall love the Lord your God with all your heart—that is with all your soul, mind and strength'. But the human heart is not always what it should be

(Je. 17:9) and needs to be changed (Je. 24:7; Eph. 3:17). The right attitude of heart begins when it is broken or penitent (Ps. 51:17); the hard or stony heart does not submit to God (Ezk. 11:19). God searches it (Ps. 139:23) and cleanses it (Ps. 51:10; Je. 31:33), for only the pure in heart can see him (Mt. 5:8).

HEAVEN. The word was used for the physical heavens (the night sky), as in Mt. 5:18. Some passages seem to imply a belief that the sky was a solid dome (*e.g.* Gn. 7:11), but the Hebrews were capable of vivid imagery and the theology of such passages does not demand such an hypothesis. The word also described God's dwelling-place (Dt. 26:15; Mt. 5:45) where angels also dwell (Mk. 13:32) and which believers shall also inhabit (1 Pet. 1:4). References to Paradise (Lk. 23:43) and 'the third heaven' (2 Cor. 12:2) do not imply a multiplicity of heavens but are graphical descriptions of the place of perfection.

HEBER. Several OT people, including the husband of Jael who seemed to be a man of some importance (Jdg. 4:11ff.; 5:24).

HEBREW: See OLD TESTAMENT LANGUAGES.

HEBREWS, THE. The term is used in only a few OT passages, where it seems to be synonymous with 'Israelite'. In most cases it is used to describe Israelites when non-Israelites are being addressed. It may be particularly relevant in situations where the person is not a free citizen on free soil. In the NT, it is an exclusivist term for Jews not decisively influenced by Greek culture (Acts 6:1) and also a term to distinguish Jews generally from Gentiles (2 Cor. 11:22; Phil. 3:5).

The family name 'Hebrew' used for Abraham and his descendants can be traced to his ancestor Eber, a descendant of Shem (Gn. 10:21ff.). The term is used more broadly than for the Israelites who were slaves in Egypt (*cf.* Gn. 40:15 with Ex. 5:3), and it is therefore not surprising that in non-biblical literature of the Abraham-Exodus period non-Israelite and even non-Abrahamic 'Hebrews' appear. The well-attested term 'Habiru' in texts *c.* 2000-1200 BC seems to refer to a social or professional group, although some scholars also regard it as an ethnic group; they cannot be equated with the Hebrew (Israelite) invaders of Canaan. In the OT, 'Hebrew' is always used racially, not generally; Dt. 15:12 refers to a slave as a 'brother Hebrew', and the references in 1 Sa. 13-14 which appear at first to distinguish Israelites and Hebrews in fact equate them (*e.g.* 13:3f.).

HEBREWS, LETTER TO THE. *Contents.* The doctrinal theme: the person of Christ superior to prophets, angels, Moses and Joshua (1:1-4:13); the work of Christ as divinely appointed priest superior to Melchizedek, within the new covenant and centred in a perfect atonement (4:14-10:18). The practical application: encouragement to stand firm (10:19-37); examples of faith from the past (11); advice concerning suffering (12); Christian responsibilities (13).

Authorship and date. The early church writer Origen once said that God alone knew who wrote the letter. He himself believed the thought to be Paul's, but not the words, and said that some ascribed it to Luke. Tertullian believed it was written by Barnabas. Many did hold to Pauline authorship, especially the Alexandrian leaders, with the result that the letter was accepted as canonical Scripture. During the Reformation period Erasmus, Calvin and Luther all doubted Pauline authorship; Luther suggested Apollos, an idea which has commended itself to many modern scholars. Few today support Paul as its author, because the linguistic style is very different from Paul's other letters; its method of argument and manner of introducing exhortations are unlike Paul's; and its acknowledgment of debt to second-hand information (2:3f.) contrasts with Paul's insistence that he received the gospel by revelation.

Theories of alternative authors are at best inspired guesses, and Origen's caution should prevail. Since it was cited by Clement of Rome *c.* AD 95 it must have been written well before that, probably before the fall of Jerusalem in AD 70 because this relevant event is not mentioned. Some prefer to date it *c.* 80-90 because of its use of Paul's letters, but as the author uses only some of those letters and the date of their collection is not known, the argument carries little weight.

Destination and purpose. The traditional title 'to the Hebrews' is not part of the original text but may preserve a genuine tradition. The most widely held theory is that it was written to Jewish Christians to warn them against apostasy to Judaism, based on the warnings in 6:6 and 10:29. The intended readers are clearly Christians (6:4f.), and the thesis of the letter is that Christianity is superior to OT ritual. It was probably not written for Jewish Christians generally because of the personal note in 13:22f., and therefore may well have been addressed to a significant house-community of Christians who were potential teachers not using their gifts (5:12). The language and concepts presuppose an educated group, perhaps an intellectual clique within a local church.

The location of these people has been variously suggested as Palestine, Alexandria and Rome. The latter is most likely because of the allusion in 13:24 and the fact that Clement of Rome was the first to cite it. An interesting conjecture is that the recipients were converted priests, especially those connected with the Jerusalem temple converted through Stephen's ministry (Acts 6:7). Some parallels between the letter and Stephen's speech in Acts 7 have suggested to some scholars that the letter was a challenge to Jewish Christians, who perhaps saw the church as little more than a Jewish sect, to embrace world mission.

Background. The author was clearly and deeply influenced by biblical (OT) teaching, citing the (Greek) text carefully, and expects his readers to accept the authority of Scripture as he does. He also echoes the language and ideas of Philo of Alexandria, a 1st-cent. AD Jewish philosopher, leading some to suppose he was a converted Philonist. However, there are differences as well as similarities, especially in Hebrews' biblical exegesis which is more like that of the rabbis than Philo, and its literal attitude to history as opposed to Philo's allegorical approach. There is plenty of evidence that the letter reflects the primitive Christian tradition—the continuity between old and new covenants, interest in Jesus' earthly life, and the realization that his death needs to be interpreted—as well as new elements such as Jesus' enthronement as a heavenly high priest. While different from Paul's letters (there is no evidence of that wrestling with Jewish law which is central to Paul's experience), the differences are not contrasts and it is possible that the author was influenced by Pauline thought. The letter is best seen as a vital aspect of Christian thought complementary to other streams of primitive tradition.

Theology. The author regards Christianity as the perfect revelation of God, superseding all other faiths but never to be superseded itself. The Sonship of Jesus is considered to be unique for he is the heir of all, agent of creation and the express stamp of God's nature who has been exalted to the right hand of God (1:2f.). He was also fully human (2:14, 17) and thus

apable of sympathizing with our
weakness having been tempted as we
re (4:15). In his earthly life he was
fully obedient (5:8) and endured
hostility (12:3).

Christ's priestly office dominates
the writer's thought. The mysterious
Melchizedek is introduced to stress
that Jesus, although not a priest in the
order of Aaron, is still a true priest, and
is such is in fact superior to the
Aaronic priesthood (5:6ff.; 6:20-7:19).
Against the weakness of this earthly
priesthood the author stresses Christ's
atoning work, including the finality of
his offering (7:27), his offering of
himself rather than a substitute, and
the spiritual nature of that offering
9:14), and the eternal rather than temporary salvation thus achieved (9:12).
The practical application is that Christians can confidently approach God
for mercy and help (10:19ff.). Salvation is seen as deliverance from the
devil's power (2:14f.) and as an eternal
rest (3:1-4:13); the processes of salvation are described as sanctification
holiness, 12:14) and perfection (7:11).
The author describes the active
qualities of faith in action in 11.

HEBRON. The highest town in
Palestine, 927 m above sea level, 30 km
SW of Jerusalem. It was founded c.
1720 BC (cf. Nu. 13:22). Abraham lived
in its vicinity for considerable periods
and was buried nearby. After Israel's
entry into Canaan Hebron's king
joined the anti-Gibeonite coalition and
was killed by Joshua (Jos. 10:1ff.);
Caleb conquered the city (Jos.
14:12ff.). David was twice anointed

king in Hebron (2 Sa. 2:4; 5:3), and it
was his capital for over 7 years;
Absalom set up his rebellion there (2
Sa. 15:7ff.). It was also known as
Kiriath-arba (Ne. 11:25), and under
the name el-Halil is one of the
Muslims' four sacred cities.

HEIFER. Mixed with water, the ashes
of an unblemished red heifer were
used to purify the priest (Nu. 19). A
broken-necked heifer cleansed a city
from the guilt of a corpse killed by persons unknown (Dt. 21:1ff.).

HEIR: See FAMILY; INHERITANCE.

HELAM. A city E of the Jordan, where
David defeated the Syrian Hadadezer
(2 Sa. 10:16ff.); probably modern
Alma.

HELBON (lit. 'fat', 'fruitful'). Men-
tioned in Ezk. 27:18 as trading wine to
Tyre; modern Khalbun, 25 km N of
Damascus.

HELDAI. 1. One of David's commanders appointed over 24,000
soldiers in the 12th month (1 Ch.
27:15), the same as Heled in 1 Ch.
11:30. 2. Someone who returned from
exile and contributed silver and gold
for Joshua's high-priestly crown (Zc.
6:10).

HELEZ (possibly 'strength'). One of
David's heroes called the Paltite in 2
Sa. 23:26; probably the same as Helez
the Peleonite in 1 Ch. 11:27; 27:10, so-
called because he was not from Judah,
but did live in Beth Pelet.

HELKATH. A city in Asher given to the Levites; located in the Kishon valley, possibly Tell el-Harbaj 10 km SE of Haifa.

HELKATH-HAZZURIM (lit. 'field of flints' or 'field of sword-edges'). The location of a tournament between champions of Joab and Abner (2 Sa. 2:14ff.).

HELL. The final destiny of the wicked, translating the Greek word *Gehenna* derived from the Hebrew for the valley of Hinnom outside Jerusalem. It was the place where in OT times child sacrifices were offered to Molech (2 Ch. 28:3), and subsequently became a place for burning refuse. In later Jewish writings Gehenna came to mean the place of fiery punishment for sinners (2 Esdras 7:36), having been used by Jeremiah as a symbol of judgment (Je. 7:31ff.). The general idea of fire expressing God's judgment is also found in the OT (*e.g.* Dt. 32:22; Dn. 7:10).

In the NT hell is pictured as a place of unending fire and the undying worm (*e.g.* Mk. 9:43ff.), of outer darkness with weeping and gnashing of teeth (Mt. 8:12), and as a lake of fire (Rev. 19:20). It is 'the second death' (Rev. 20:14), destroying body and soul (Mt. 10:28). The imagery derives from Is. 66:24, but is markedly restrained compared with Jewish apocalyptic and later Christian writings. It is clearly not intended to be taken literally, but indicates the terror and finality of what elsewhere is simply described as exclusion from the presence of Christ (Mt. 7:23). It probably should not be pressed to prove eternal torment (in the sense of unending inflicted torture) but the NT clearly teaches that it symbolizes a punishment from which there is no release (Mt. 25:46); some scholars see no contradiction between this and a belief that the wicked do not remain conscious for ever but are annihilated.

Hell has been prepared for the devil and his angels (Mt. 25:41); it becomes the destiny of people only because they have refused their true destiny which God offers them in Christ. The NT teaching cannot be reconciled with the 'universalism' which suggests that all people ultimately will be saved; God desires everyone's salvation (1 Tim. 2:4) but not all accept his gracious offer.

See also DESCENT INTO HADES; HINNOM, VALLEY OF; SHEOL.

HELLENISTS. People who were not themselves Greeks but who spoke Greek and adopted the Greek way of life. The earliest occurrence of the term in Greek literature is in Acts 6:1, where it denotes a group of Jewish Christians in the Jerusalem church who were distinguished from the 'Hebrews' who were probably Aramaic-speaking. Many of the Hellenists would have been connected with Jews dispersed outside Palestine. To judge from Stephen and Philip, the Hellenists were more forward-looking than the Hebrews; when persecution broke out the Hellenists were scattered and preached the gospel wherever they went. In Acts 9:29, the

Hellenists were members of a Greek-speaking synagogue. See also GREEKS.

HELMET: See ARMOUR.

HELPER: See DEACON.

HEMAN (lit. 'faithful'). 1. One of the sages whom Solomon excelled in wisdom (1 Ki. 4:31). 2. A Levite and one of David's leading singers (1 Ch. 15:17, 19).

HEN (lit. 'favour'). Possibly a figurative name for Josiah (Zc. 6:10, 14), as RSV, GNB, NEB. For the animal, see COCK.

HENA. A city the Assyrians boasted could not be saved by its gods (2 Ki. 18:34); identified in LXX with Ana on the Euphrates.

HERALD. In Dn. 3:4, an official who relayed Nebuchadrezzar's commands; in Is. 40:9; 41:27 it is literally 'bringing good news'. 'Herald' in 2 Pet. 2:5 is the same word as 'preacher' in 1 Tim. 2:7.

HERBS AND SPICES. Herbs and spices were used in biblical times, as in all ages, in food preparation for flavouring. Herbs were also used medicinally, and spices were used as deodorants in the burial of corpses and as cosmetics. The spice trade from India to the Near East was pioneered in early times; Solomon derived considerable revenue by charging tolls on the merchant caravans passing through his land.

Aloes was probably modern eaglewood, found today in the Far East; from it came a precious spice to perfume garments and beds. (In Jn. 19:39 a different plant is meant, the bitter juice of its leaves being widely used for embalming.)

Balm produced in Gilead was celebrated for its healing properties (Je. 46:11); probably an aromatic gum or spice, it cannot be identified with any plant. Classical authors used 'balm of Gilead' to describe the Mecca balsam still imported into Egypt from Arabia. *Bitter herbs* constituted part of the Passover meal (Ex. 12:8), identified in the Mishna as lettuce, chicory, eryngo, horseradish and sow-thistle, although not all of these may have been available in biblical times.

Cassia and *cinnamon* were used in Roman funerals by which time they probably referred to plant products which come from the Far East. In earlier times, before the trade routes were established, the names probably described similar plants more readily available to the Israelites. *Coriander* does grow in the Mediterranean area, and has grey-yellow seeds known to have been used since 1550 BC for culinary and medicinal purposes. *Cummin* is a plant indigenous to W Asia resembling the caraway in appearance and used to flavour food; it is still threshed with sticks to preserve the brittle seeds which a wheel would crush (Is. 28:27).

The seeds and leaves of *dill* were widely used for culinary and medicinal purposes. The 'dill' of Is.

28:17 however was black cummin or nutmeg flower; the oily seeds are still used for seasoning bread.

Henna is a cultivated shrub favouring warm conditions. Its fragrant white blossoms were given between friends; its pulverized leaves were made into an orange or yellow cosmetic paste which probably had pagan associations.

Mint in biblical times was probably horse-mint, a perennial about 40 cm high with mauve flowers; it was one of the garden herbs scrupulously tithed by the Pharisees. *Myrrh* was a yellow-brown resin from a low shrubby tree native to S Arabia, used as an ingredient in anointing oil and cosmetics; it also formed part of an anodyne offered to Jesus on the cross (Mk. 15:23). The 'myrrh' of Gn. 37:25; 43:11 was probably a resin from evergreen rock roses.

Rue is a perennial herb up to 80 cm high with grey-green leaves giving a strong odour and has been cultivated since ancient times. Highly prized for its alleged disinfectant and antiseptic properties, it was also used to flavour food.

The expensive *saffron* comes from certain crocus flowers, and was used for colouring food and as an aid to recovery from illness. *Spikenard* in the OT was a perfume obtained from the camel grass common in the Arabian desert; in the NT (Jn. 12:3) it was probably obtained from a pleasantly-scented relative of valerian. *Stacte* in Ex. 30:34 is a resin possibly from the storax tree in the Palestinian hills. The *sweet cane* of Is. 43:24; Je. 6:20 was a marsh plant of the arum family used as a tonic and stimulant; sugar cane spread E after OT times.

See also COSMETICS; FOOD, SALT.

HERESY. In the NT the Greek word is usually translated 'party' or 'sect', with the suggestion of self-will or sectarian spirit, but none of the parties thus described is in a state of schism from its parent body (*e.g.* Acts 5:17, 'faction' in 1 Cor. 11:19). The only use of 'heresy' as doctrinal error occurs in 2 Pet. 2:1.

HERMAS. A member of a house-church greeted by Paul in Rom. 16:14. For the (unconnected) *Shepherd of Hermas* see PATRISTIC LITERATURE.

HERMENEUTICS. A term used to denote either the study and statement of the principles on which a biblical text is to be understood or the interpretation of a text in order to express its meaning to someone else. See BIBLE, INTERPRETATION OF.

HERMES. In Greek myth, the son of Zeus and Maia, the patron of commerce, eloquence, literature and youth; in Roman myth he was called Mercury. The close association of Hermes and Zeus at Lystra (Acts 14:12) is known from contemporary inscriptions.

HERMETIC LITERATURE. A collection of writings associated with 'Hermes Trismegistos' ('Thrice-great Hermes'). The writings represent a coalescence of Egyptian and Greek thought often transfused with mystical personal religion, and may go back to the early 2nd cent. BC. Of greater interest are philosophical and religious treatises featuring the god Hermes, written in Greek by unknown authors and usually dated in the 2nd and 3rd cents. AD. The most famous is the *Poimandres*; Poimandres offers to reveal to Hermes things he longs to know about creation, human nature and God. Man is fallen, but those who repent and abandon corruption can escape and at death enter God. Regeneration is seen as purification of the soul from the taint of physical matter.

Apart from Platonic and Stoic philosophy and popular mythology, it also shows evidence of Judaic influence, and there are echoes of the OT. Some writers have pointed to subtle parallels of thought and language with the NT, especially the Johannine vocabulary of rebirth, light and darkness, life and death, belief and witness. Direct influence of the NT on Hermetic literature is not impossible, but neither is it proven; Hermetic influence on the NT would be even harder to substantiate. However, John may have had in mind a public with this *kind* of education and devotion. The Hermetic literature is more concerned with the process of redemption than its nature and the means by which it is effected, and while its ethical teaching is lofty, its other-worldliness does not allow for the concreteness of biblical ethics. See also GNOSTICISM.

HERMOGENES. With Phygelus, an Asian Christian who repudiated Paul (2 Tim. 1:15) in circumstances which are not recorded.

HERMON (lit. 'sanctuary'). A mountain in the Anti-Lebanon range, the highest (2,814 m) in Palestine, also called Sirion. Regarded as a sacred place by the original Canaanites, it is usually capped with snow and the melting ice forms a major source of the Jordan. Because it is near Caesarea Philippi some have suggested it was the scene of Jesus' transfiguration.

HEROD. *Herod the Great.* King of the Jews 40-4 BC, he was born *c.* 73 BC, son of Antipater who had been appointed procurator of Judaea by Julius Caesar in 47 BC. When the Parthians invaded Syria and Palestine and set Antigonus on the Judaean throne in 40 BC, the Roman senate appointed Herod, then military prefect of Coele-Syria, as king and after three years of fighting he made his title effective. He gradually got rid of the rival Hasmonaean (high-priestly) family. His famous building projects included the rebuilding of Samaria (renamed Sebaste), the construction of the harbour at Caesarea and the Jerusalem temple. But not even this endeared him to the Jews; he also built pagan temples and his wiping-out of the Hasmonaeans was never forgiven. He executed three of his sons, and his suspicious nature is well illustrated in the story of the Magis' visit to Jesus and the subsequent slaughter of male children (Mt. 2).

Archelaus. Herod's elder son by Malthace, he ruled Judaea 4 BC—6 AD (Mt. 2:22). His repressive rule was so intolerable that a deputation of Judaean and Samaritan aristocrats petitioned Rome for his removal because of the threat of full-scale revolt. He was deposed, and Judaea became a Roman province administered by prefects appointed by the emperor.

Herod Antipas (the tetrarch, Lk. 3:19). Herod the Great's younger son by Malthace, he inherited the Galilean and Peraean parts of the kingdom. He imprisoned and executed John the Baptist, who had denounced him for divorcing his first wife in order to marry Herodias the wife of his half-brother Herod Philip (Mk. 6:14ff.). He briefly encountered Jesus (Lk. 23:7ff.) who had described him as a fox (Lk. 13:31f.). He built the city of Tiberius (AD 22). He was deposed in AD 39.

Herod Agrippa ('the king', Acts 12:1). Grandson of Herod the Great, he was brought up in Rome. Caligula gave him territory NE of Palestine which Claudius later extended to a kingdom roughly equal to his grandfather's. The Jews approved of him (he was related to the Hasmonaeans through his grandmother). His sudden death in AD 44 is mentioned in Acts 12:20ff.; his daughters Bernice in Acts 25:13ff., and Drusilla in Acts 24:24.

Agrippa, son of Herod Agrippa, born AD 27, received the title king from Claudius. From 48 to 66 he had the prerogative of appointing Jewish high priests. He tried to prevent the Jewish war against Rome in AD 66, and remained loyal to Rome when he failed. He encountered Paul in Acts 25:13-26:32, and died childless *c.* AD 100.

See also PHILIP THE TETRARCH.

HERODIANS. Mentioned in the NT as enemies of Jesus (Mt. 22:16; Mk. 3:6; 12:13), probably a Jewish party which favoured the Herodian dynasty.

HERODIAS. Daughter of Aristobulus (one of Herod the Great's sons) who married first her uncle Herod Philip then her uncle Herod Antipas; her daughter Salome married *her* great-uncle Philip the Tetrarch. The identity of the daughter mentioned in Mk. 6:22f. is uncertain.

HESHBON (lit. 'device'). A city of Moab captured by Israel from Sihon king of the Amorites (Nu. 21:21ff.), given first to Reuben then Gad, and assigned to the Levites. Moab retook it (Is. 15:4; Je. 48:2), but it was in Israel's hands again by the 2nd cent. BC.

HETHLON. Referred to only by Ezekiel (47:15; 48:1); modern Heitela NE of Tripoli.

HEZEKIAH (lit. 'Yahweh is my strength'). The 14th king of Judah, who ruled for 29 years and was outstanding for his piety (2 Ki. 18:5). He was apparently co-regent with his father Ahaz *c.* 729-716 BC; so that Samaria fell in 722 BC, the 6th year of his co-regency (2 Ki. 18:10), and Sennacherib invaded Judah in 701 BC, the 14th year of his sole regency (2 Ki. 18:13). His major religious reform (2 Ch. 29:3ff.) re-established true worship in the renovated temple, reinstituted the Passover on a grand scale, and destroyed pagan shrines. He was restive under Assyrian domination and strengthened the defences of Jerusalem (including digging the Siloam tunnel to safeguard the water supply). Sennacherib of Assyria claimed to have shut Hezekiah up in Jerusalem like a caged bird but did not claim to have conquered the city; the OT describes God's intervention in the siege (2 Ki. 19:32ff.). For the 2 Ki. 20 incident of the sun 'going backwards' see STEPS.

HIDDEKEL. The ancient name of the R. Tigris.

HIEL. His sons were killed during the rebuilding of Jericho, fulfilling Joshua's curse (Jos. 6:26; 1 Ki. 16:34).

HIERAPOLIS. A city in the Roman province of Asia 10 km N of Laodicea, built around hot springs famed for their medicinal powers and forming spectacular lime-encrusted cascades. It was a centre of pagan cults. The church there was probably founded while Paul was in Ephesus (Acts 19:10; *cf.* Col. 4:13). Rev. 3:15f. may contrast its hot water with Colossae's cold and Laodicea's tepid.

HIGH PLACE. Possession of high ground gave control over the land, and this may account for the frequent choice of high places for locating shrines. Loyal worshippers of God used them in the early Monarchy period (1 Sa. 9:25; 10:5), possibly claiming former pagan shrines for God. After the division of the kingdom the high places posed a new threat to the purity of Israel's faith. Jeroboam built some to distract people from focusing on Jerusalem as the national shrine (1 Ki. 12:25ff.). Though nominally dedicated to God, they clearly included many features of Canaanite religion, such as images, standing stones, Asherah poles, and sacred prostitution, and biblical writers saw them as a major source of moral and religious collapse (2 Ki. 17:9ff.). Despite purges in the S kingdom by Hezekiah and Josiah, the high places were soon revived and remained until the Babylonians ended the kingdom; little is known about the high places after the 6th cent. BC. Archaeologists have discovered a variety of such shrines which illustrate the period when Israel was accused of having as many gods as towns (Je. 2:28).

HILKIAH (lit. 'My portion is Yahweh'). Several OT people, including the high priest in Josiah's reign who found the book of the law (2 Ki. 22:8) and helped Josiah's reformation; and Jeremiah's father, probably a descendant of David's high priest Abiathar.

HILL COUNTRY. Sometimes used as a description of Palestine's mountainous backbone. The Hebrew word can mean one hill or a range, and it is not always clear which is meant.

HILL SHRINE: See HIGH PLACE.

HINNOM, VALLEY OF. A valley S of Jerusalem also called 'the valley of the sons of Hinnom'. Muslim tradition identifies it with the Kidron valley but it is more likely to be the Wadi al-Rababi bordering the city on the W and S. In Jeremiah's time it was associated with the worship of Molech, and later it seems to have been used for burning rubbish and the corpses of criminals and animals. Hence it came to be a synonym for HELL.

HIRAM. The king of Tyre in the time of David and Solomon, who reigned *c.* 979/8-945/4 BC. He greatly admired David and sent materials and craftsmen to aid the building of his palace (2 Sa. 5:11). Later he helped Solomon with the temple in return for wheat and oil (1 Ki. 5:2ff.). When the temple was complete, Solomon gave Hiram 20 villages in Galilee and received 120 talents of gold (1 Ki. 9:10ff.) as part of a treaty; the two nations' shipping fleets joined in trade expeditions (1 Ki. 9:26ff.; 10:22). According to non-biblical sources, Hiram warred against Cyprus, built temples to Astarte-Melqart (later Hercules) and enriched older temples. Josephus claimed that Kings Hiram and Solomon exchanged riddles.

HIRELING, HIRED SERVANT. The two main classes of wage-earner in Israel were foreign mercenaries and agricultural labourers. The latter were deprived of their land by an 8th-cent. enclosure movement (Is. 5:8) which forced freehold farmers into slavery. The law said such slaves should be regarded as employees and released in the Jubilee year (Lv. 25:39ff.). See also SLAVERY; WAGES; WORK.

HITTITES. In the OT they are firstly a great nation which gave their name to the whole region of Syria and secondly an ethnic group living in Canaan until after the Israelite invasion. The Hittite empire was founded *c.* 1800 BC by an Indo-European nation which had settled in Asia Minor two centuries earlier. In the 16th cent. BC the Hittite king Mursilis I established a new capital at Hattusas (modern Bogaz-koy) E of the Halys river and the archives discovered there are a major source of knowledge about the Hittites. There are similarities in detail, but not in conception, between Hittite law-codes and the laws of the Pentateuch (Gn.—Dt.); similarities include provisions for levirate marriage (see MARRIAGE). The empire reached its peak in the 14th cent. BC when iron was first smelted in its territory on a scale which marked the beginning of the iron age. It collapsed *c.* 1200 BC as a result of blows from western enemies, but 7 Syrian city-states perpetuated the name Hittite for several centuries. Solomon traded and intermarried with them (1 Ki. 10:28f; 11:1).

The Hittites in Canaan in patriarchal times may have been an early branch of the ancestors of the Hittites above, early migrants from the Hittite empire, or a quite separate group with a similar name; the empire as such never extended so far S. In Gn. 23 they are the residents of Hebron among whom Abraham lived. The last reference to the Hittites of Canaan is in Solomon's reign (2 Ch. 8:7); thereafter they merged into the general population.

HIVITE. A son of Canaan and early inhabitants of Syria and Palestine, located principally in the Lebanon hills and the Hermon range. Hivites were among the conscripts used in Solomon's building projects (1 Ki. 9:20). They are otherwise unattested, and many equate them with the HORITES.

HOBAB (lit. 'beloved'). Referred to ambiguously in Nu. 10:29 suggesting either he or his father Raguel (Reuel) may have been Jethro, Moses' father-in-law (*cf.* Ex. 2:18 and Jdg. 4:11). The evidence is too slight to choose between them.

HOBAH. An otherwise unknown place N of Damascus to which Abraham pursued 4 kings (Gn. 14:15).

HOLINESS, HOLY, SAINTS. The OT word suggests the separation of a person or thing from the common or profane for a divine use. Thus there can be holy ground (Ex. 3:5), holy assembly (Ex. 12:16) and a holy nation (Ex. 19:6), implying consecration to God rather than any ethical purity. The holy nation was called such because it was separated by God from the rest; he then gave them the ethical demands of the law. So holiness comes to be that which has been chosen by God and given a character that conforms to his law.

Holiness belongs to God (1 Sa. 2:2); it refers to his moral perfection and his freedom from all limitation in that perfection (Hab. 1:13); it is the out-shining of all that God is, uniting all his other attributes. As God's revelation in OT times advanced, the application of the term 'holy' to people moved from consecration to a holy God to an ethical quality of life, and this is its main NT connotation. God's people are called to share in his holiness (Heb. 12:10); the divine holiness is imparted to the human soul in spiritual regeneration and becomes the source of a holy character. Jesus is the supreme example of divine holiness, which is more than mere sinlessness. His holiness was positive consecration to God's will and purpose (Jn. 17:19). The apostles called Christians 'saints' ('holy ones') and this term was commonly used until at least the 2nd cent. when it began to develop into an honorific title.

The NT emphasizes the ethical nature of holiness and presents it as the supreme goal of Christian living; it also emphasizes the eternal permanence of moral character (Rev. 22:11). Since the divine holiness could not create a universe in which sin would ultimately prosper, judgment of sin is a consequence of God's holiness. But God's holiness also ensures that there will be a final restoration and regeneration of a moral universe (2 Pet. 3:13).

See also SANCTIFICATION.

HOLY SPIRIT: See SPIRIT.

HOMOSEXUALITY. The Bible says nothing specifically about the homosexual condition but contains explicit condemnation of homosexual conduct, the scope of which needs to be determined carefully. The sin condemned in the Sodom (Gn. 19) and Gibeah (Jdg. 19-20) stories, for example, is attempted homosexual rape, not a consenting homosexual relationship. Historically, homosexual behaviour was linked with idolatrous cult prostitution (*e.g.* 1 Ki. 14:24) and the stern warnings of Lv. 18:22; 20:13 are also primarily aimed at idolatry, using the word 'abomination' which is a religious term often used for idolatrous practices.

In Rom. 1 Paul condemns lesbian and male homosexual acts because they contradict God's creation scheme for human sexual expression. In 1 Cor. 6:9 he says practising homosexuals shall not inherit the kingdom (but with the redemptive note, 'such *were* some of you'). In 1 Tim. 1:9f. he updates the Ten Commandments and includes a condemnation of homosexual acts and heterosexual intercourse outside marriage. To Paul the Lord's condemnation of such behaviour, as Creator, Law-giver and King, was absolutely plain.

HONEY, HONEYCOMB. A favourite food in biblical times, honey was used in cooking (*cf.* Ex. 16:31) and was regarded as having medicinal properties (*cf.* Pr. 16:24). It was not used in meal-offerings to God because of its liability to fermentation. In later times bee-keeping may have been practised by the Jews, otherwise wild bees' honey was gathered (1 Sa. 14:25f.).

HOOK. Hooks were put in animals' noses so they could be led (2 Ki. 19:28). Pruning-hooks (*e.g.* Is. 2:4) were small sickle-shaped knives used by vine-dressers and easily converted into weapons (Joel 3:10). Hooks were also used in fishing (Mt. 17:27).

HOPE. Hope seems to be a general psychological necessity; even if there are no rational grounds for it, people continue to hope. Such hope, even when it appears justified, is often transient and illusory. The Bible sometimes uses the word in its conventional sense; the hope of reward sweetens a farmer's hard work (1 Cor. 9:10). But generally, the biblical writers have a quite different view of hope. Paul said that pagans had no real hope because they were without God (Eph. 2:12). Biblical hope, a confident expectation, becomes possible, regardless of temperament or circumstances, where there is belief in the living God who intervenes in human life and who can be trusted to keep his promises; Abraham's extreme case is an example (Rom. 4:18). Hope is therefore inseparable from faith; because of what God has done through Christ in the past the Christian dares to expect future blessings (2 Cor. 1:10).

This hope is a 'helmet', part of Christian defence against evil (1 Thes. 5:8), and an 'anchor' penetrating deep into the unseen spiritual world (Heb. 6:19); it can therefore never disappoint (Rom. 5:5). Although Jesus never explicitly referred to hope, he taught his followers not to be anxious about a future which was firmly in the hands of a loving Father (Mt. 6:25ff.). Hope makes transient joys satisfying (Heb. 13:14); stimulates purity of life (1 Jn. 3:2f.); enables suffering to be borne patiently (Rom. 5:3ff.); and will be finally realized when Jesus returns (1 Pet. 1:13). Connected with love as well as faith, Christian hope is freed from selfishness (1 Cor. 13:13); faith, hope and love together comprise the Christian way of life.

HOPHNI AND PHINEHAS. The sons of Eli, 'priests of the Lord' at Shiloh, who abused their privileges (1 Sa. 2:12f.) and so led others to treat worship contemptuously. The family was cursed (1 Sa. 2:27ff.; 3:11ff.) and the two were killed (1 Sa. 4:11).

HOPHRA. The 4th king of the 26th Egyptian Dynasty who reigned 589-570 BC. He invaded Palestine during King Nebuchadrezzar's siege of Jerusalem but was repulsed (Je. 37:5ff.). He was killed in conflict with his co-regent Ahmose (cf. Je. 44:30).

HOR. 1. A mountain on the border of Edom where Aaron was buried (Nu. 20:22ff.). Its precise location is uncertain, but biblically is referred to as between Kadesh-barnea and Arad. 2. A mountain on the N border of Israel, probably in the Lebanon range N of Byblos, perhaps Ras Shaqqah.

HORESH. A place in the wilderness of Ziph, possibly Kh. Khoreisa 9-10 km S of Hebron.

HORITES, HORIM. The ancient inhabitants of Edom defeated by Chedorlaomer (Gn. 14:6), and driven out by Esau's sons (Dt. 2:12, 22), but who also apparently occupied some places in central Palestine (e.g. Gilgal, Jos. 9:6f.; 'Horites' in LXX, 'Hivites' in many EVV). They are sometimes identified with the Hurrians, part of the indigenous population of N Syria and Upper Mesopotamia from c. 2300 BC. Hurrian names are found throughout Palestine, but the Horites appear to have had Semitic names in Gn. 36:20ff. and are probably a different group.

HORMAH. An important town in the Negeb, formerly the Canaanite Zephath (Jdg. 1:17). It was linked with but not identical to Arad (cf. Nu. 21:1ff.; Jos. 12:14); excavations at Kh. el-Mesas 6 km W of Tell el-Milh (probably the Canaanite Arad) revealed an Israelite settlement likely to have been Hormah.

HORN. Apart from animal horns (e.g. Gn. 22:13), the Bible uses the term for horn-shaped protuberances on the corners of altars (e.g. Ex. 29:12). Symbolically, 'horn' stands for power (1 Ki. 22:11; Ps. 75:10); in apocalyptic passages it represents the rulers of empires (Dn. 7; 8; Rev. 13; 17). For inkhorn, see WRITING; for the instrument, see MUSIC.

HORNET. A large colonial wasp with a painful or even dangerous sting, still common in parts of Palestine. References such as Ex. 23:28 could be literal or metaphorical; there are records of hornets causing horses and cattle to stampede.

HORONAIM. A town of Moab at the foot of a plateau close to Zoar. Possibly el-Araq or Oronae.

HORSE. Throughout the Bible the horse is regularly associated with war and power, and is rarely mentioned singly. The first record of the horse is on a Babylonian tablet *c.* 1750 BC. Horses were already in Egypt in Joseph's time, and they were used to pursue the Israelites (Gn. 47:17; Ex. 14:9). The nations of Canaan used them against Israel (*e.g.* Jos. 11:4), and the Israelites later ignored the prohibition against accumulating war-horses (Dt. 17:16; *cf.* 2 Sa. 8:4; 15:1). Solomon had many horses, kept, it was once thought, at special stables in Hazor, Megiddo and Gezer (1 Ki. 10:26ff.).

HOSANNA. The Greek form of a Hebrew term used at the triumphal entry of Jesus into Jerusalem (*e.g.* Mt. 21:9); it only occurs in the OT in a longer form in Ps. 118:25 ('save us we beseech thee'). The welcome of Jesus was probably a spontaneous gesture of religious enthusiasm without the original supplicatory meaning.

HOSEA, BOOK OF. The first book in the collection of 12 'minor prophets' which concludes the OT. It addresses the N kingdom Israel, often called Ephraim, in the 8th cent. BC. Hosea loved its people; he wrote with great emotional intensity and the material is arranged in roughly chronological order. *Contents.* His family and children's names (1:1-2:1); unfaithful Israel (2:2-15); the covenant love of the Lord (2:16-3:5); condemnation of pagan worship (4:1-5:7); panic at Assyria's encroachment *c.* 733 BC (5:8-7:16); religious and political disintegration (8); warnings of exile and its consequences (9; 10); the Lord's love recoils from punishment (11:1-11); Jacob the deceiver (11:12-12:14); death is inevitable, exile is imminent *c.* 724 BC (13:1-16); God's promise of forgiveness (14). *Historical setting.* The prophecy covers the last 30 years of the N kingdom. After years of prosperity, decline set in after king Jeroboam II died (753 BC); chs. 4, 5 depict a booming economy and political stability, when prophecies of doom must have seemed incredible. Assyria marched steadily nearer, subduing Damascus in 743 BC, and forcing Israel to pay tribute-taxes two years later. Damascus fell in 732, and Israel was invaded and some citizens taken captive (7:8f.). King Hoshea appealed for help from Egypt (2 Ki. 17:4; Ho. 9:3; 11:5; 12:1) but after a 3-year siege Samaria fell in 722 BC. Hosea blamed Israel's collapse largely on its adoption of an alien lifestyle borrowed from Canaanite neighbours. Every part of life was bound up with Baal-worship, and the nation's leaders had promoted it (5:1ff.). Lawlessness and injustice reigned as a result; Hosea notes burglary, robbery, murder, drunkenness and intrigue (6:7-7:7) as he grieves Israel's rejection of the Lord to whom she was betrothed.

Hosea's personal life. His personal experience prepared him to understand the Lord's undying love for the Israel which had rejected him. It seems his wife Gomer bore 3 children, then left him for her former promiscuous life. Eventually, worn down and no longer attractive, she was abandoned but Hosea bought her back. The story is not told explicitly, because the main purpose of the book is to demonstrate God's consistent love. In addition to his own experience, Hosea meditated on God's dealings with Jacob (12:2ff.), and on the Exodus story (11:1ff.).

Hosea's theology. Hosea concentrates on the covenant relationship between God and Israel. Israel's natural disasters and military defeats he sees as built-in retribution to check abuses and to remind them that even the 'natural' processes of human generation are not under their ultimate control (9:11ff.). The invasion by Assyria was God's way of 'acting like a bear robbed of its cubs', for he had been robbed of his people's love (13:7f.). The apostasy of his contemporaries was the culmination of a long history of such rebellion, and God had called a halt to it. However, Israel would not even admit that she was estranged

from God (8:2), putting great emphasis on public worship (4:13) which bore no fruit in changed lives (6:4ff.). The only future for Israel was exile where people would not have access to their idols. Their poverty would reveal to them their desperate need, driving them back to the Lord (2:6ff.) in true repentance (3:5) and an enduring relationship (2:19ff.). The anguish which the prophet saw in God's love was ultimately to result in the incarnation and death of Jesus Christ to open up the way back to communion with God.

HOSHEA. 1. Joshua's original name changed by Moses (Nu. 13:16). 2. The 20th and last king of the N kingdom of Israel, who conspired against and killed his predecessor Pekah (2 Ki. 15:30). He became a vassal of Assyria and his attempted rebellion led to the final collapse of the kingdom in 722 BC (2 Ki. 17:1ff.).

HOSPITALITY. *Old Testament.* The responsibility to care for travellers and the needy was taken for granted, Abraham's generosity to 3 strangers providing an excellent illustration of it (Gn. 18:1ff.). Generally hospitality demonstrated faithfulness to God (Is. 58:7). Foreign residents (sojourners) were to be loved (Dt. 10:19); failure to provide for a stranger was a punishable offence (Dt. 23:3f.; 1 Sa. 25:2ff.). There was special responsibility to provide for one's own family (*e.g.* Gn. 19:13f.). A stranger would wait at a communal place for an offer of hospitality (*e.g.* Ex. 2:15ff.; Jdg.

19:15). The minimum provision was bread and water (Dt. 23:4); a guest's dusty, tired feet were washed (Jdg. 19:21) and sometimes the best food was prepared (*e.g.* Gn. 18:5). Elisha even received private furnished accommodation (2 Ki. 4:10).

New Testament. Many aspects of OT hospitality reappear; Simon the Pharisee's home appears almost to have been an open house (Lk. 7:36ff.). Jesus was greatly dependent on hospitality (*e.g.* Lk. 10:38ff.), as were the apostles later on (*e.g.* Acts 16:15). Giving or refusing hospitality to a disciple is seen as an indication of one's acceptance or rejection of the gospel (Mt. 25:34ff.; Lk. 10:4f.). The NT letters explicitly command the provision of hospitality for fellow-believers (*e.g.* Rom. 12:13f.), doubtless because persecution had led to some Christians becoming homeless refugees (*cf.* Acts 8:1). Travelling preachers were to be cared for (3 Jn. 5ff.) and letters of recommendation helped distinguish between the genuine and the false (Rom. 16:1f.). Leaders had a special responsibility to welcome guests (1 Tim. 3:2). All hospitality was to be offered without grudging and in brotherly love (1 Pet. 4:9; Heb. 13:1f.).

Biblical inns. Little is known about OT lodging places on trade routes (*e.g.* Gn. 42:27; Je. 9:2). Bethlehem's inn (Lk. 2:7) was possibly a simple lodging place, or a guest room in a private house such as Jesus borrowed for the last supper (Mk. 14:14). The 'good Samaritan's' inn was clearly like a traveller's hostel with shelter and food offered for a recognized charge (Lk. 10:34f.). Many inns in NT times were of low physical and moral standard, hence the Christian responsibility to offer private hospitality.

HOST, HOST OF HEAVEN. Quite often 'host' simply means a crowd of people. 'The host of heaven' usually has pagan worship associations (*e.g.* Dt. 4:19). The senses of 'planets' and 'angels' are interwined, suggesting the spiritual oversight of the physical universe. 'The LORD of hosts' is a title of power and probably refers to God's relationship to the angelic beings rather than to Israel's armies (see also GOD, NAMES OF).

HOUSE. *Biblical references.* The OT word is used for dwellings of all kinds from private houses (Dt. 6:7) to palaces (Je. 39:8) and temples (1 Ki. 8:13), and even for the homes of animals (*e.g.* Ps. 104:17). Over a quarter of the 2,000 references use the word for 'household, family', sometimes but not always including the physical building as well as the people. The NT has similarly wide uses for the Greek word. Jesus also used it to describe heaven (Jn. 14:2) and NT letters apply it to the church (with the sense of household rather than a special building, *e.g.* Eph. 2:19ff.). This undoubtedly owed much to the fact that houses played an important function as meeting places for the first Christians (Acts 5:42; Phm. 2).

Design and construction. Houses were usually built close together, and the majority were within fortified cities and their dependent villages. Larger houses were often on the W side to escape the smoke and dirt carried by the prevailing W winds. Foundations were important because of the danger from erosion by heavy rain (*cf.* Mt. 7:24ff.) and from earthquakes, and sometimes went down to the bedrock; they were built of stones. The walls of private houses were usually built from rough stones or mud bricks. Brick walls were coated with a waterproof plaster on the inside. Walls were up to 1 m thick, sometimes strengthened by stone pilasters. Floors were made from marly clay which could withstand hard use from bare feet, but richer houses had paved floors. Doors, which opened inwards, were fixed in a wood or stone frame which was usually lower than a man's height. Windows were rarely on the ground floor, because the open doorway provided sufficient light. They were always kept to a minimum to keep the house cool in summer and warm in winter, and were frequently latticed (Jdg. 5:28); glazing was rare even in Roman times (see GLASS). Many houses had two floors, and upper rooms were reached by stairs or ladders. The upstairs rooms provided the main living and sleeping accommodation. Flat roofs were made from beams covered with branches and thick mud plaster, which was regularly rolled and annually re-plastered to keep it waterproof. Families might sleep on the roof in summer and use it to dry raisins, figs, flax and so on. Vaulted roofs were in use by Persian times (5th cent. BC), and tiled roofs appeared before NT times.

The earliest houses in Palestine were circular or rectangular one-room structures. Two-roomed houses appeared *c.* 5000 BC in Jericho. During the Middle Bronze Age (2200-1500 BC) the courtyard-based house became common, with rooms built on one or more sides of the yard. Israelite houses were poorer than the Canaanite ones at first, but during the monarchy the 4-roomed house became common; one room ran along the back with three parallel rooms stemming from it, the central one being an enclosed courtyard. Wealthy homes in NT times followed the Roman pattern of rooms round two courtyards, the inner one providing considerable privacy.

Life in the house. It was a store and workshop as well as a dwelling, and in wartime or bad weather the best of the household's farm animals would share the home too. The average family would have bed, table, chairs and lamps (*cf.* 2 Ki. 4:10). The rich had high beds, the poor had mats on the floor. Chests would hold bedding and clothes. In winter, cooking was done indoors, using a rather inefficient brazier filled with burning charcoal; an oven was usually built in the courtyard. Food was stored in large jars; many households ground their own grain and made their own clothes on hand-looms.

See also BUILDING; CONTAINERS; POTTERY; WALL.

HOUSEHOLD: See FAMILY, HOUSEHOLD.

HOUSEHOLD GODS: See TERA-PHIM.

HOZAI. In 2 Ch. 33:19 (AV) to be translated with RSV as 'the Seers'.

HUKKOK. A town on the S border of Naphtali, probably Yakuk 8 km W of the suggested site of Capernaum.

HULDAH. A prophetess consulted *c.* 621 BC on behalf of Josiah following the discovery of the book of the law (2 Ki. 22:14); a contemporary of Jeremiah and Zephaniah.

HUMILITY. This virtue is part of God's character; although incomparably great, he humbles himself to take note of created things (Ps. 113:5ff.). Humanly, it is closely associated with suffering which is calculated to produce humility of spirit; in Mt. 23:12 'humility' expresses both the material penalty for arrogance and the spiritual prerequisite for honour in God's kingdom. Paul regards humiliating circumstances as an opportunity to develop an inner attitude of humility (Phil. 4:12), and gives Jesus' own humility in facing the cross as an example to be followed (Phil. 2:8). False humility can however be an outward show which actually reveals pride (Col. 2:18, 23; *cf.* 3:12).

HUNDRED, TOWER OF THE. Probably near the NE corner of Jerusalem in Ne. 3:1, possibly referring to its height, its steps, or its garrison.

HUNTING, HUNTER. The Israelites seldom engaged in hunting as a pastime, and resorted to it only when faced with hunger or when their life or security was threatened by wild animals (1 Sa. 17:34). Some individuals were renowned hunters, however (*e.g.* Esau, Gn. 25:27). By contrast, Egyptians and Mesopotamians had a long hunting tradition. But hunted game did enhance the Israelite diet on occasions (*e.g.* partridges, 1 Sa. 26:20), and there are references to nets (Jb. 19:6), traps (Ps. 91:3) and bear pits (Ezk. 19:8) as well as hunting bows and arrows (Gn. 27:3) and slingstones (1 Sa. 17:40). Two types of traps or snares were used for birds: one pinned them to the ground, the other caught their neck in a noose and sprang up (Am. 3:5).

There are few NT references to hunting, and they are mostly metaphorical (*e.g.* Lk. 11:54; 21:34); pride and riches are both cunningly set 'traps' for the unsuspecting (1 Tim. 3:7; 6:9).

HUR. Several OT people, including the prominent Israelite who with Aaron held up Moses' arms in battle and helped Aaron judge the people during Moses' absence (Ex. 17:10ff.; 24:14).

HUSHAI. A devoted friend of David who willingly undertook a dangerous spying errand for him (2 Sa. 15:32ff.).

HUSHIM (lit. 'Those who hasten'). Both a male (Gn. 46:23) and female (1 Ch. 8:8) name.

HUZZAB. A word of uncertain meaning in Na. 2:7 AV, RV; 'mistress' RSV; 'it is decreed' NIV.

HYMENAEUS. A pernicious teacher associated with Alexander (1 Tim. 1:19f.) and Philetus (2 Tim. 2:17f.) 'delivered to Satan' by Paul (possibly excommunication, surrender to Satan's sphere, *cf.* 1 Cor. 5:5) with remedial intentions. But it did not apparently evoke repentance. He apparently spiritualized the resurrection (and judgment), doctrines always repugnant to the Greek mind.

HYMN. Spiritual songs were a feature of early church life, as expressions of joy, truth and worship. Jesus and the 12 sang in the upper room (Mt. 26:30) as did Paul and Silas in prison (Acts 16:25). The threefold division of psalms, hymns and spiritual songs (Eph. 5:19; Col. 3:16) must not be pressed far for the terms overlap. But there were psalm-like Christian songs (*e.g.* Lk. 1:46ff., 68ff.; 2:29ff.), and many doxologies (*e.g.* 1 Tim. 6:15f.; Rev. 5:9, 12f.) were doubtless used in worship.

HYPOCRITE. The English meaning is usually someone who deliberately claims to be what he or she is not, but the original Greek word means a play-actor. In the NT only Christ used the term, applying it to scribes and Pharisees who were blind to their own faults (Mt. 7:5), God's workings (Lk. 12:56) and true values (Lk. 13:15), overvaluing tradition (Mt. 15:7) and loving display (Mt. 6:2, 5, 16).

HYSSOP: See PLANTS.

IBLEAM. A Canaanite town in the N borderland of Manesseh whose inhabitants were not expelled by the Israelites (Jdg. 1:27); modern Kh. Bilameh 16 km SE of Megiddo.

IBZAN. An Israelite judge known only from Jdg. 12:8ff. Jewish commentators equated him with Boaz.

ICHABOD. The name given to her child by Phinehas' wife on hearing the Philistines had captured the ark of the covenant (1 Sa. 4:19ff.). The meaning is perhaps 'where is the glory?'.

ICONIUM. A city of Asia Minor where Paul was attacked (Acts 13:51-14:7). Its religion, the worship of a mother goddess with eunuch priests, remained Phrygian into Roman times, when it had become a prestigious city. There is some textual uncertainty as to whether there was one long attack or two shorter ones on Paul, the first by the Jews, the second by the civic authorities.

IDDO. Several OT characters including a seer and prophet (2 Ch. 9:29), and the head of a priestly family who returned to Jerusalem with Zerubbabel (Ne. 12:4).

IDOLATRY. The OT religious picture is of a constant battle between the pure worship of God and the seductions of idolatry which often claimed a majority of the population. Some of the Patriarchs have been accused of idolatry. Rachel stole her father's household gods (teraphim), which does not necessarily implicate Jacob, and these appear to have had as much legal as religious significance, to judge from Laban's attempts to get them back; he was not noted as a religious man (Gn. 31:19ff.). Jacob clearly disposed of Rachel's household gods before building an altar to the Lord (Gn. 35:1ff.) and his pillars were probably simple memorials rather than religious emblems (Gn. 31:13). Moses warned that God could not be represented in any concrete form; the second commandment was unique to the time (Ex. 20:4; Dt. 4:12), but lapses occurred (Ex. 32). When Israel was established in Canaan, Micah made images in the time of the Judges (Jdg. 17-18) and so did Jeroboam during the divided monarchy (1 Ki. 12:28), the latter using familiar Canaanite symbols. This was probably a typical pattern for Israelite idolatry: they fused the trappings of their pagan environment to their own culture and religion.

Images and the underlying realities. There is some doubt as to whether the animal images were meant to represent God or were thought of as a pedestal over which he was enthroned; the analogy of the cherubim (*cf.* 2 Sa. 6:2) suggests probably the latter. The forbidden pillars probably represented the presence of the god at the shrine, and were objects of great veneration, sometimes being kissed by devotees. The wooden asherah were associated with fertility cults. Both OT and NT assert that such images are nothing in themselves but that there are evil spiritual forces which can be evoked through idolatry (*e.g.* Is. 44:6ff.; 1 Cor. 8:4; 10:19f.). Contact with false gods infects a person with deadly spiritual blindness (Is. 44:18ff.). The real spiritual power behind idols makes them an abomination to God (Dt. 7:25), and worship of them is called spiritual adultery (Hos. 1:2). Besides, God is far superior to idols; he alone can act decisively in the universe (Is. 41:26f.).

New Testament perspective. In Rom. 1 Paul says that idolatry is a decline from true spirituality. He also recognizes that it can exist without actual religious symbols. He associates it with sexual sins (Gal. 5:19f.) and covetousness (Eph. 5:5). John warns that any deviation from the truth of the gospel is idolatry (1 Jn. 5:19ff.).

See also ASHERAH; IMAGE; TERAPHIM; articles on named pagan gods; and the following article.

IDOLS, FOOD OFFERED TO. Sacrifices were part of 1st-cent. AD domestic life as well as pagan religious life. Only part of the sacrifice was presented to the god in the temple; the rest was eaten either in the temple precincts or at home, and sometimes food left over was sent to the market to be sold (1 Cor. 10:25). Invitations to such cultic meals would be common in the social life of Corinthian people, and so raised problems for Christians who received them. Christians also faced problems of conscience over attending public festivals which opened with pagan worship and sacrifice, and over membership of trade guilds which included meetings in cult temples (1 Cor. 8:10). What was the Christian housewife to do about buying meat when the best cuts in the market had probably come from sacrificial animals? And should poor believers take advantage of the free meals in the temple precincts?

These were issues which the Christian church faced; it was divided over them and sought guidance from Paul. One group emphasized liberty and superior 'knowledge' and saw nothing wrong in eating such food (6:12; 10:23); they claimed that the social occasions had no religious significance, and that the pagan gods did not exist anyway (8:4). Paul agreed with their monotheism but reminded them that demonic forces also existed. While Christians ought not to be in bondage to them, some had not found that freedom in Christ and therefore would be offended by indiscreet action (1 Cor. 8:4ff.). Indeed, attendance at idolatrous banquets is likely to defile a Christian, he urged, because such gatherings made compacts with the demons (1 Cor. 10:14ff.). But food previously slaughtered at a temple and then bought in the market may be eaten (1 Cor. 10:25ff.); God has made it and declared it clean (*cf.* Acts 10:15; 1 Tim. 4:4f.). However, Christians must still observe the law of love and

waive their due rights if a weaker believer's conscience was damaged by their action, or if a pagan at the same meal pointed out that the food had been offered to idols and was thus confused about the Christian's beliefs (1 Cor. 10:28ff.).

IDUMAEA. After the fall of Jerusalem in 587 BC many Edomites migrated into S Judah (Je. 49:7ff.) and the area they settled in became known as Idumaea (1 Macc. 4:29). About 126 BC John Hyrcanus placed the area under Antipater, grandfather of Herod the Great.

IGNORANCE. It generally has a moral rather than intellectual connotation. It may partly excuse sins which result from it (Nu. 15:22ff.; 1 Tim. 1:13) but may also be culpable when linked to hard-heartedness (Eph. 4:18) or when it is deliberate (2 Pet. 3:5). It is used to describe the condition of people who have not received God's revelation (Acts 17:23, 30). See also KNOWLEDGE.

IJON. A town in N Naphtali taken by the Syrians (1 Ki. 15:20) and Assyrians (2 Ki. 15:29); modern Tell Dibbin, 30 km N of Lake Huleh.

ILLNESS: See HEALTH AND HEALING.

ILLYRICUM. A large mountainous region on the E of the Adriatic. The name derives from one of the first tribes discovered there by the Greeks. The Romans conquered it only in the

1st cent. AD. It was the first Latin-speaking province Paul entered (Rom. 13:19ff.), possibly from Macedonia (Acts 20:1).

IMAGE. The term used to describe a physical representation, usually of a god, without the pejorative overtones of 'idol'. Images of gods were widespread throughout the ancient Near East; they were usually in human form, but sometimes in animal form (especially in Egypt). The image was regarded more as the dwelling-place of the god than as a visual representation of it; hence prayers offered in front of it were not necessarily directed to the image itself. In the OT the manufacture and use of images was forbidden (Ex. 20:4f.) and condemned (Je. 10:3ff.), but was nonetheless widespread in Israel before the Exile (*e.g.* 1 Ki. 11:5ff.). Images of God (Yahweh) may have been erected by the Patriarchs as standing stones or sacred trees (Gn. 21:33; 28:18), but were later forbidden (the Asherah, Dt. 16:21); the golden calves were roundly condemned (Ex. 32:1ff.; 1 Ki. 12:28ff.).

Mankind is also described as being made in the image of God (Gn. 1:26f.; 5:2; 9:6), probably referring to the whole person and not some part of him such as the reason or spiritual nature. As such, mankind is appointed by God as ruler of the earth (Gn. 1:28). The 'image' was not destroyed by the fall (Gn. 9:6), and the NT builds on this teaching: mankind still has its unique position in creation (1 Cor. 11:7; Jas.3:9). The 'new nature'

given to the believer is related to God's image (Eph. 4:24), which is in the process of renewal (Col. 3:10) awaiting final transformation into the likeness of Christ (*cf.* Phil. 3:20f.). Christ himself is described as God's image in a special sense in 2 Cor. 4:4; Col. 1:15. As the eternal son or Word of God, he expresses faithfully and fully in a visible way the glory of the invisible God (*cf.* Jn. 1:1ff.; Phil. 2:6ff.; Heb. 1:1ff.).

See also IDOLATRY; MAN.

IMMANUEL (lit. 'With us is God'). The word is found twice in the OT (Is. 7:14; 8:8; and possibly in 8:10), and once in the NT (Mt. 1:23). The context of Isaiah's prophecy is that Syria and Israel were pressurizing king Ahaz of Judah to join them in resisting Assyria. Isaiah told him not to worry as the power of his enemies was played out. Ahaz refused to believe this good news, and so Isaiah says God will give his people a sign of a virgin bearing a son who will be called Immanuel. The word translated 'virgin' is never used of anyone except an unmarried woman, and if she was immoral the birth could hardly have been a 'sign'; the implication is that the birth was supernatural. The passage also implies that God's presence will be seen in the birth of the child himself, and not (as some have suggested) in the period of his infancy during which Judah would be rid of its enemies. The nation's help does not rest in Assyria, Isaiah is saying, but in God, who is to be found in the birth of a child. Ahaz's rejection of the sign of hope led to Judah's downfall, but for the remnant of Israel the promise of Immanuel in whom they would find their hope and salvation remained. See also VIRGIN.

INCARNATION. It was by his coming in the flesh (incarnation) and his dying in the flesh (making atonement) that Jesus Christ secured our salvation (Rom. 8:3; Col. 1:22; 1 Jn. 4:2). The word 'flesh' basically means a person's or animal's physical organism, and is seen in the Bible as a symbol of the created life which derives from and is dependent upon God. 'Flesh' thus comes to be a generic term for creatures whose life on earth lasts for only a relatively short time (*e.g.* Is. 40:6). Therefore, to say that Jesus Christ came 'in the flesh' is to say that he came and died in the state and under the conditions of created life; in other words, that he was man. The NT also asserts that he was, and continues to be, God, so that without ceasing to be God he was made man (Jn. 1:1ff., 14). Orthodox Judaism has always held such a notion to be blasphemous or nonsensical—that God the creator should become one of his own creatures. Scholars have tried to find some parallel in Jewish speculations about a superhuman Messiah and in pagan myths about redeemer-gods, but the only explanation of the origin of the doctrine is in the impact of Jesus' life, ministry, death and resurrection on the disciples (Jn. 20:28ff.). The first Christians prayed to Jesus as divine Lord (Acts 7:59) and proclaimed him as the one who forgives sins (Acts 5:31). The belief in the incarnation was already there, even if it had not been formulated theologically.

The NT writers do not speculate on questions about the mode of the incarnation or the precise personality of the incarnate Jesus. They do not attempt to dissect the mystery of his person but only to proclaim the incarnation as one of a sequence of mighty works through which God has saved sinners. That is why they do not reflect on the virgin birth; Matthew and Luke, who report it, do not stress the unique Person thus born but the fact that by this miracle God was fulfilling his promises (Mt. 1:21ff.; Lk. 1:31ff., 68ff.; 2:10f., 29ff.). The NT writers all see that Jesus' manhood and deity are both fundamental to his saving work, however. Because he is God, his disclosure of the Father's heart and mind is perfect and final (Jn. 14:7ff.; Heb. 1:1f.); his death is the supreme evidence of God's love for sinners (Jn. 3:16); and he has defeated the forces of evil (Heb. 2:14f.). Only as the 'second man' (Rom. 5:15ff.) could he mediate between God and man (1 Tim. 2:5), and die for mankind's sins—only flesh can die. Hence the NT treats denials of the incarnation as heresies which destroy the gospel (1 Jn. 2:22f.; 4:1ff.; 5:5ff.).

The NT draws out three aspects of the incarnation. First, Jesus is God's Son in a unique sense (Mk. 1:11), taking on his lips as no Jew would the emphatic 'I am' which expressed the self-identification of God (Mk. 14:62; *cf.* Ex. 3:14 and the 'I am' sayings of John., *e.g.* 6:35; 8:12). He was condemned for such 'blasphemy'. As Son of God, he lived in perfect communion with the Father and always did his will (Jn. 8:28f.), thus revealing the Father perfectly (Jn. 14:7ff.). The Father was greater than he in the sense that Jesus acts freely and gladly as a son, not that he is to be considered subordinate to the Father in human esteem or worship. The NT also speaks of his relationship to God as the Word (Jn. 1:1ff.) and the image (Heb. 1:3) of God, emphasizing his full divinity.

The second aspect of the incarnation is that Jesus did not abandon his divinity when he was on earth. His functions of sustaining the physical order were not laid aside (Col. 1:17; Heb. 1:3); he emptied himself of outward glory (Phil. 2:7) but that does not imply that his divine powers were curtailed. His incarnation was not a diminishing of deity but an acquiring of complete manhood (1 Tim. 2:5).

The third aspect is that the incarnation did not change his relationship of obedience and dependence on the Father. His confessed ignorance of the time of his second coming showed that it was not the Father's will for him to know it; as the Son he did not wish to seek or know more than the Father wished. His life was one of sinless perfection (1 Pet. 2:22); he did not have sins of his own to die for (Heb. 7:26) so could die vicariously for the unrighteous (2 Cor. 5:21). He did not wish to deviate from his perfect state yet as man he had to experience and fight intense temptation in order to overcome it; the costliness of his triumphant obedience enables him to offer sympathy and support to tempt-

ed and distraught Christians (Heb. 2:18; 4:14ff.).

See also JESUS CHRIST, LIFE OF; VIRGIN BIRTH.

INCENSE. It was a costly offering by the priests in OT ritual. It is sometimes used as a symbol of prayer (Ps. 141:2; Rev. 8:3f.). The sacred incense was a cosmetic compound. The list of ingredients given in Ex. 30:34ff. includes galbanum, a gum obtained from a plant growing in Persia and known in Mesopotamia from *c.* 3000 BC; and frankincense (the classical olibanum), the whitest of gum-resins used for incense, produced from trees in S Arabia and Somaliland, and a major item carried by traders along the Arabian-Damascus spice route (Is. 60:6). Frankincense was also burnt with other substances during the cereal offering (Lv. 6:15). The gift of frankincense to the infant Jesus has been interpreted as symbolizing his priestly office. The other ingredients in Ex. 30:34ff. were onycha (probably obtained from a mollusc) and stacte or myrrh for which see HERBS AND SPICES.

INCREASE. Multiplication or growth, primarily the natural reproduction of animals and plants but always under God's control (Ps. 67:6). In the NT it also refers to the numerical (Acts 6:7) and spiritual (2 Cor. 10:15) growth of Christians.

INDIA. Trade between India and Mesopotamia via S Arabia is known as early as *c.* 2100 BC by texts and the presence in Mesopotamia of seals from the Indus valley. Many exotic products (including spices) were imported from India; Alexander and his successors used Indian elephants in their Syrian campaigns. In the first 2 centuries AD the Roman market for eastern luxuries stimulated still closer cultural and commercial relations between Mediterranean lands and India, with regular sea routes opened up. Tradition says that Thomas the apostle was the first Christian missionary to India, but while the Syriac S India church is certainly very ancient the question of its foundation remains open. India is mentioned only in Est. 1:1; 8:9.

INHERITANCE. *Old Testament.* Land in OT law belonged to the family, not to the individual. The eldest son received a double portion of the estate, and the other sons equal portions. If a man died without sons, the inheritance went to his daughters; if he was childless, to his brothers or the nearest next of kin (Nu. 27:8ff.). Before the law was given, the Patriarchs were free to overlook the first-born son's rights in favour of younger sons (*e.g.* Gn. 48:8ff.). If a man died childless his brother had to marry his widow (Dt. 25:5ff.) and the first son of that union was regarded as the first-born of the deceased brother. The right to marry the widow could pass to another relative (Ru. 3:9ff.). Wills were unknown in Israel before the time of Herod. Canaan was regarded as a special inheritance from God (Ps. 79:1), and some tribes' portion of land

was determined by casting lots (Jos. 18:2ff.).

New Testament. The idea is narrowed down to Jesus as the true heir of everything (Mk. 12:7; Heb. 1:2). Christians share his inheritance by adoption into God's family (Rom. 8:17); their inheritance is God's kingdom (Mt. 25:34), the earth (Mt. 5:5), salvation (Heb. 1:14) and eternal life (1 Cor. 15:50). The promises will not be completely fulfilled until Jesus' return; the inheritance is reserved in heaven (1 Pet. 1:4). However, the Holy Spirit is the guarantee of that inheritance until we acquire possession of it (Eph. 1:14). See also FIRST-BORN.

INN: See HOSPITALITY.

INNER MAN. Used by Paul to denote the Christian's true self seen by God and known partially in consciousness (*e.g.* Eph. 3:16). He is not however drawing the kind of distinction loved by the Greek Platonists between the immaterial, immortal soul and the material, mortal body. Rather the contrast is between what a person seems to be to human observers and the secret nature of that person's 'heart' (*cf.* 1 Sa. 16:7). This 'inner man' is daily renewed even when the physical body is falling to pieces (2 Cor. 4:16), and desires to keep God's law even when sin frustrates that desire (Rom. 7:22f.).

INSCRIPTION. 1. The silver denarius shown to Jesus (Mt. 22:20 and parallels) was inscribed with the words 'Tiberius Caesar Augustus, son of the divine Augustus' (see MONEY). 2. The placard inscribed with a criminal's name and the offence for which he was being executed was usually hung round his neck on the way to execution then nailed to his cross (Mt. 27:37; Jn. 19:19f.).

INSPIRATION. This word is used to translate the Greek *theopneustos* in 2 Tim. 3:16. The original has the idea of something divinely *ex*-spired, that is 'breathed out from God'. God's breath (or Spirit, the Greek word is the same) is the active outgoing of his power (*cf.* Ps. 33:6). Whether 2 Tim. 3:16 is translated 'All Scripture is inspired by God and profitable...' (RSV) or 'Every inspired Scripture has its use...' (NEB), the point is that all which comes within the category of Scripture is God-breathed and thus profitable for guiding both faith and life. The essential idea is that Scripture has the same character as the prophets' sermons (*cf.* 2 Pet. 1:19ff.); God is its primary author through whose initiative, prompting and enlightenment each writer did his work. Inspired Scripture is thus written revelation, just as the prophets' sermons were spoken revelation. In Scripture, God revealed to the church his saving work through history.

Biblical perspectives. The idea of 'canonical' Scripture, a collection of documents containing a permanent authoritative record of divine revelation, goes back to Moses' writing of God's law (Ex. 34:27f.). The concept of inspiration was there from the beginning, and comprises two convictions.

The first is that the words of Scripture are God's own words. OT passages identify prophets' words with God's own speech (*e.g.* 1 Ki. 22:8ff.; Ps. 119; Je. 25:1ff.). NT writers view the OT as a whole as 'God's oracles' (Rom. 3:2) and prophetic in character (Rom. 16:26). Christ and the apostles quote OT passages as what God said through his spokesmen (*e.g.* Acts 4:25) or simply as what God said (1 Cor. 6:16; Heb. 10:15). Even OT statements not made by God in their contexts are still regarded as his words (Mt. 19:4f.; Acts 13:34f.). And Paul writes in Gal. 3:8; Rom. 9:17 that *Scripture* spoke to Abraham and Pharoah when in context it was God speaking.

Secondly, the human part in the production of Scripture was for the authors to transmit what they received. Each author contributed much to the *form* of Scripture; each book is in one sense its author's literary creation. But the Bible regards the *content* of Scripture as being God's word. Thus the prophets claimed to speak what God said (Dt. 18:15; Je. 1:7); Jesus said he spoke the words his Father gave him (Jn. 7:16); the apostles claimed Christ's authority (1 Cor. 14:37) and maintained that their principles and words were taught them by the Holy Spirit (1 Cor. 2:9ff.; *cf.* Jn. 14:26; 16:13ff.). These are claims to inspiration, and the NT writers claimed the Jewish Scriptures as the Christian Bible designed by God for the instruction of believers (Rom. 15:4; 2 Tim. 3:14ff.) which could not be broken (Mt. 5:17f.; Jn. 10:35) because it was God's word (Lk. 16:17).

Theological perspectives. Four negative points need to be made. First, the divine control of the writers did not detract from, but rather heightened, their freedom, spontaneity and creativeness; 'inspiration' is not mechanical dictation. Secondly, the fact that inspiration did not obliterate personal human style and cultural conditioning does not mean God's control was imperfect but that he chose specific people as the most suitable conveyers of his truth. Thirdly, inspiration is not attached to textual corruptions which entered during transmission, but only to the original text. Fourthly, the inspiration of Scripture is not the same as 'inspiring' literature; 'inspiration' does not relate to literary quality but to divine revelation.

See also AUTHORITY; BIBLE, INTERPRETATION OF; OLD(NEW) TESTAMENT, CANON OF; PROPHECY; REVELATION; SCRIPTURE; SPIRIT.

IOTA AND DOT. In Mt. 5:18 *iota* is the Gk *i* but corresponds to the smallest letter of the Hebrew alphabet, *yod*, the use of which is frequently optional. 'Dot' means a minor stroke which distinguishes one Hebrew letter from another.

IRA. 1. David's priest (2 Sa. 20:26), who was not a Levite although one text says he came from Jattir, a Levitical city; alternatively 'priest' may mean 'chief official'. 2. Two of David's heroes (2 Sa. 23:26, 38).

IRON: See MINING AND METALS.

ISAAC (lit. 'he laughs' or 'laughter'). When Isaac's birth was foretold Abraham (Gn. 17:17) and Sarah (Gn. 18:12ff.) both laughed. When the child was born to the 100-year-old Abraham, Sarah declared God had made laughter for her (Gn. 21:6). In Isaac's birth, God is seen to be fulfilling the promise to Abraham which from a human perspective had seemed impossible (Gn. 12:1ff.). God later tested Abraham by ordering him to kill Isaac, but provided a substitute ram as Abraham demonstrated his obedience (Gn. 22). The story then focuses on Isaac's marriage. Rebekah was called to be his bride from Haran, and their love developed (Gn. 24). For 20 years she too was unable to have children, but eventually became the mother of twins, Jacob and Esau. The latter sold his inheritance as the first-born to Jacob (Gn. 25). Isaac's blessing of his sons is recorded in Heb. 11:20 as evidence of his faith.

ISAIAH. 'Yahweh is salvation.' A prophet who lived in Jerusalem; according to Jewish tradition he came from royal stock. He began prophesying *c.* 740/739 BC when Uzziah died (6:1); his last appearance was in the Assyrian Sennacherib's campaign against Jerusalem *c.* 701 BC. Tradition suggests he was sawn in half by Manasseh (*cf.* Heb. 11:37) but it has no sound historical basis and he may have lived through Manasseh's reign but took no further part in recorded public life. He was married to a prophetess (8:3) and they had two sons (7:3; 8:3). A contemporary of Micah (*cf.* 1:1 with Mi. 1:1), both working in Judah, he was preceded by Amos and Hosea who concentrated on the N kingdom of Israel. In the first half of the century both Israel and Judah had been prosperous (Is. 2-4). But Assyria, under Tiglath-pileser III (745-727 BC), once more began to impose itself on Palestine. During Assyrian domination there were various revolts (*e.g.* 8:16ff.; 14:28ff.), and oracles in Is. 28-31 probably date from Judah's revolt against Sennacherib (705-681 BC), as do chs. 36-39.

ISAIAH, BOOK OF. *Contents.* 1. Prophecies relating to Isaiah's own time (1-35): introduction (1); prophecies mostly from his early period (2-5); his inaugural vision (6); the present world order and the coming kingdom of God (7-12); mainly prophecies about foreign nations (13-23); Isaiah's 'apocalypse' (24-27); Zion's sin, oppression and deliverance, Assyria's downfall and Egypt's vain help (28-33); judgment and salvation in the future (34-35). 2. Historical narratives (36-39). 3. Prophecies which presuppose the Babylonian Exile (40-55): introduction (40); prophecies in which Cyrus of Persia is conspicuous, during which Israel is comforted in its distress and its deliverance from Babylon is promised (41-48); chapters in which the restoration of Jerusalem (Zion) is prominent (49-54); exhortation to accept these promises in faith (55). 4. Various prophecies possibly relating to different times (56-66): non-Jews

have a share in salvation, leaders are rebuked for idolatry (56:1-57:13); comfort for the contrite (57:13-21); false and true religion (58); deliverance depends on repentance (59); Zion's deliverance (60-62); God's vengeance on Edom (63:1-6); penitence and supplication (63:7-64:12); rebels against God and obedient servants (65); Zion glorified and sinners punished (66).

Origin, construction and authorship. Very little information is given about Isaiah's own literary activity. 8:1f.; 30:8; 34:16 and ch. 6 imply his authorship, but ch. 7 speaks of him in the third person. He probably wrote more than these passages indicate, especially in view of the high standard and unity of language throughout. However, if he had had a substantial part in the composition of the book as a whole, its internal structure would presumably have been more straightforward than it is. Chs. 36-39 are essentially parallel to 2 Ki. 18:13-20:19, and Isaiah is described as a historical writer (2 Ch. 26:22; 32:32), but his authorship of chs. 36-39 cannot be established with certainty.

The book has a certain chronological order. Chs. 2-5 are from his earliest time; 7:1-9:7 come from *c.* 734 BC; 18-20 from 715-711 BC; and various prophecies in 28-37 belong between 705 and 701 BC. There is also some arrangement according to subject matter, *e.g.* the prophecies relating to foreign nations in chs. 13-23. However, neither chronological nor subject-matter arrangements have been carried out consistently; for example 28:1-6 contains an early prophecy; ch. 22 is an exception in the foreign section of 13-23; Isaiah's call is not related until ch. 6. It may be taken as certain that the book has been compiled on the basis of shorter collections, but the history of its composition cannot now be reconstructed.

Many scholars today deny that great portions of the book were written by Isaiah and even that the subject matter comes from him. There is wide agreement that 13:1-14:23; 21; 24-27; 34-35 cannot be attributed to Isaiah. Many also assert that none of 40-66 comes from him. Chs. 40-55 are reckoned to be the work of a prophet who is labelled Second Isaiah (or Deutero-Isaiah), to be dated between 550 and 538 BC when Cyrus conquered Babylon and allowed the Jews to return to Jerusalem. Some scholars attribute 56-66 to him as well; others postulate a Third Isaiah (Trito-Isaiah) dated either in the time of Haggai and Zechariah (c. 520 BC) or in the time of Malachi (c. 450 BC). Still others suggest the prophecies in 56-66 come from a wide variety of dates.

However, tradition has always credited Isaiah with the whole book; 1-39 and 40-66 have come down to us as a unity. From Ecclus. 48:24f. it is clear that Jesus ben Sira (c. 200 BC) considered Isaiah to be the author of the whole book. The Qumran copies of Isaiah indicate that when they were copied (2nd or 1st cent. AD) it was regarded as a unity. This does not of course point unequivocally to Isaiah as author, yet it would be surprising indeed if every trace of the great prophet of 40-66 had been completely erased. Jesus and the NT writers see the whole book as a unity, too (e.g. Mt. 3:3; 12:17ff.; Jn. 12:38; Rom. 10:20f.). The strongest argument against his authorship of 40-66 is that it relates to the much later period of the 6th cent. BC. The Spirit of God can of course reveal the future to his prophets, but it is inconceivable that Isaiah could have spoken words of comfort to his contemporaries about a calamity which was not to occur for a century. If he wrote 40-66 privately, it would seem that a very mechanical form of God's inspiration operated, bearing no relation to concepts already existing in Isaiah's conscious mind.

Possibly, however, he could have written them in Manasseh's reign, when he could not appear in public (cf. 2 Ki. 21:16) but could see that judgment was bound to come. The Spirit of prophecy then showed him that the judgment would also come to an end. What he saw in his mind as fulfilled was delayed by Manasseh's repentance (2 Ch. 33:12ff.) and Josiah's reforms (2 Ki. 22-23). It is important to note that in Is. 39:5ff. Isaiah certainly knew a deportation to Babylon would take place.

Finally it should be noted that while there are differences of language and emphasis between 1-39 and 40-66, there are also similarities. It is therefore possible to suggest that while some parts of the book (including passages from 1-39) do not come from Isaiah, 40-66 may well contain a core of Isaiah's work on which the prophet's later disciples worked in the spirit of the original author,

243

especially if the modern emphasis of oral tradition being handed down through a circle of disciples is taken seriously.

The message of the book. From ancient times Isaiah has been regarded as the greatest of OT prophets because of the book's lofty style and spiritual richness. Chs. 1-39 stress especially the character of God as 'the Holy One of Israel' (*e.g.* 1:4; 6:3; 10:17; 29:23). This holy God fulminates in a violent way against Israel's sin, but does not break his covenant promise to it; when judgment comes, always there will be a remnant of God's people left (6:13). God alone is to be trusted; sin is essentially apostasy (30:1ff.). Among the sins Isaiah pointed out were empty rituals (29:13); pagan worship (17:7f.); and social oppression (1:15ff.; 5:7f.).

Judah was to trust God in the political arena too; Isaiah warned against international coalition (*e.g.* 14:28ff.; 18). The judgment Isaiah foretold (3:5) mentions the Assyrians causing great distress to Jerusalem but they would not be permitted to capture it (*e.g.* 8:9f.; 10:5ff.), which is what indeed happened; Jerusalem was only finally destroyed much later by the Babylonians. Although repentance would bring salvation (30:15ff.), people's hearts were so hard that judgment was inevitable and Isaiah's preaching would only harden them further (6:9ff.). Full salvation, Isaiah pointed out, did not consist only of deliverance from political enemies, however, for renewal of the heart (32:15ff.) was also involved, and Isaiah included several prophecies about the future Messiah (7:14; 9:1ff.; 11:1ff.). He also predicted both disaster and blessing for other nations (*e.g.* 18-20).

In chs. 40-55, Jerusalem lies in ruins, its people exiled in Babylonia; there is great distress (42:22). They think God has forgotten them (40:27). The prophet promises that God is about to liberate them, and urges them to believe the promise. 'The Holy One of Israel' is able to help (41:1ff.; 45:5). Trusting other gods is pointless and sinful folly (44:6ff.), for God is creator of all things and director of all circumstances (40:12ff.); his word will be accomplished (55:10f.). Even a world-conqueror like Cyrus is a tool in God's hand (44:24-45:13). God is not only able to help but also willing to, even though Israel is unworthy of it (43:22ff.); he loves Zion like a father and bride (40:11; 50:1). Therefore he certainly will help, and turn away his anger at his people's sin (40:2). Cyrus will defeat Babylon and set God's people free (46-47) to return to Canaan (43:1ff.). This deliverance is described as a new creation (45:8), the beginning of the great era of salvation in which all things will be made new. Isaiah bends his energies to persuade the people to believe the promise (55), appealing to heart, mind and conscience. For the 'Servant Songs' in 40-55, see SERVANT OF THE LORD.

In the final section (56-66) God is presented as the living God fearful in anger (63:1ff.) but bending down in kindness to restore his people (57:15ff.). While he stresses the need to live righteously in order to share in the coming salvation (*e.g.* 56:1ff. on the importance of keeping the sabbath), legalism is condemned (58) and an attitude of humility commended (61:2f.).

ISHBOSHETH. Made a rival king to David after Saul's death, he was assassinated by disheartened supporters (2 Sa. 2-4). His name, which could come from a word meaning 'pride, strength', was probably an alternative to Eshbaal (1 Ch. 8:3; 9:39).

ISHI (lit. 'my husband'). A name for God in Ho. 2:16 (AV).

ISHMAEL (lit. 'God hears'). Several OT people; two are especially important. 1. The son of Abraham by Hagar, Sarah's Egyptian maid. The childless Sarah gave Hagar to Abraham in order to produce a son (Gn. 16); an example of this custom has been discovered on tablets from Nuzi in Iraq. Ishmael was born when Abraham was 86, and was clearly loved by his father (Gn. 17:18f.). After Isaac's birth, Ishmael became jealous and Sarah insisted that he and Hagar should leave home (Gn. 21); they did so, almost dying in the desert. But protected by God Ishmael grew, married an Egyptian, and fathered 12 princes (Gn. 25:12ff.). 2. The son of Nethaniah, of Judah's royal family, who murdered Gedaliah, Judah's Babylonian-appointed governor, 2 months after Jerusalem was destroyed in 586 BC; he escaped arrest (Je. 40:7-41:18).

ISRAEL (lit. 'God strives'). Originally the new name given to Jacob after his night of wrestling at Penuel (Gn. 32:28; *cf.* Ho. 12:3f.); see further JACOB. The name is used most frequently to denote his descendants and the nation which traced its ancestry back to Jacob's 12 sons.

Israel's beginnings.

The earliest reference to Israel in non-Israelite texts is in an inscription of Merenptah, king of Egypt, *c.* 1230 BC, which practically coincides with the beginnings of Israel's history as a nation. It was in the previous reign that the Exodus from Egypt took place and the nation of Israel was born. Some generations previously their ancestors (see PATRIARCHAL AGE) had entered Egypt during a time of famine in Canaan, and had been drafted into forced-labour gangs working on Egyptian building sites.

Their ancestral faith was re-awakened by Moses who led them out of Egypt amid a series of phenomena in which he taught them to see the power of God. They trekked E and at Mt Sinai they were brought into a special covenant relationship with God; he had shown himself to be their God, and now they undertook to be his people. Moses combined the functions of prophet, priest and king, and formed the nation out of an undisciplined company of slaves into a formidable force ready to invade and settle in Canaan. It was organized into a confederacy of 12 tribes united by ancestry and the covenant with God. The visible sign of the covenant was the ark of the covenant, housed in a tent-shrine at the centre of their encampments. The principal centre of the 12 tribes during their period in the desert between Egypt and Canaan was probably Kadesh-barnea, from which they moved N and E conquering lands E of the Jordan. (See EXODUS; MOSES.)

From conquest to monarchy.

After crossing the R. Jordan into the 'promised land', the Israelites quickly captured and destroyed Jericho. They pressed on into the heart of the land taking one fortress after another; Egypt was now too weak to come to the aid of its former Canaanite vassals. Israel soon dominated the central and S highlands and the Galilean uplands. Two menaces perpetually threatened Israelite independence. One was assimilation of Canaanite religious ideas, assisted by intermarriage with the Canaanites, so that God was thought of rather as Baal the nature god than as the great God who had redeemed them from Egypt. The result was that the weakened tribes were regularly attacked by their enemies and called back to God by charismatic 'judges' who rallied them to military victory and religious purity.

The other menace came from the Philistines, bands of sea-rovers from the Aegean who had settled on the W seaboard of Canaan. They intermarried with the Canaanites but retained their military and political traditions; they also retained a monopoly in iron-working which made the Israelites dependent on, and militarily inferior to, them. The Philistines put down an Israelite revolt and destroyed the

national shrine at Shiloh (*c.* 1050 BC), and all visible signs of Israel's unity disappeared. The leadership of Samuel, who like Moses combined the functions of prophet, priest and king, held the nation together. Israel returned to its covenant loyalty, and defeated the Philistines on the same battlefield where earlier they had been routed so shamefully. As Samuel grew old, pressure increased for him to appoint a king as his successor.

Saul was anointed king, and all went well while he accepted Samuel's direction in the religious sphere, but his fortunes declined when the two men split. The Philistine grip on Israel grew firmer by Saul's death *c.* 1010 BC. David, at one time a military commander under Saul and later a mercenary with the Philistines, was made king in his place. He reduced the Philistines to vassal status, and he captured Jerusalem for his capital and the nation's religious centre. His empire stretched from the border of Egypt and the Gulf of Aqaba to the Upper Euphrates. He bequeathed it to his son Solomon, who overtaxed its resources by a grandiose building programme and the maintenance of a splendid court. When Solomon died (*c.* 930 BC) the tribes of Israel split into 2 kingdoms, 10 in the N which renounced the throne of David's family, known as 'Israel', and 2 in the S who remained loyal to David, known as 'Judah'. The subject nations regained their independence. See also JUDAH and articles on individual people and nations.

The N kingdom.

Jeroboam, who founded the N monarchy, created national shrines at Dan and Bethel. Israel's security was threatened both by incursions from the Aramaean kingdom of Damascus to the N and by frequent palace revolts; only two dynasties (those founded by Omri *c*. 880 BC and Jehu *c*. 841 BC) lasted for more than two generations. Omri made Samaria his capital, subdued Moab and entered an economic alliance with Phoenicia. This brought commercial benefits but religious disaster; his son Ahab married a Phoenician princess, Jezebel, who played a leading part in the revival of Baal-worship. Elijah the prophet remained the champion of orthodox faith.

Jehu came to power *c*. 841 BC and suppressed official Baal-worship but experienced increased assaults from Damascus. The Assyrians conquered Damascus in 803 BC, relieving the pressure on Israel which was able to recover some of its lost territory. Elisha the prophet boosted morale and confidence during 40 years of troubles. There followed a period of peace and prosperity early in the 8th cent. BC, but the wealth was concentrated in the hands of a small proportion of the population and an increasing number of poor people were reduced to serfdom. Prophets such as Amos and Hosea denounced the exploitation and called for a return to true social and personal righteousness instead of the punctilious religious observance of the oppressive landowners.

Jehu's dynasty ended in 745 BC, the year that Tiglath-pileser III became king of Assyria. Israel's Menahem (*c*. 745-737 BC) paid tribute-taxes to him, but Pekah (*c*. 736-732 BC) pursued an anti-Assyrian policy, allied with Damascus, and lost some of his land and people to Assyria. In Hoshea's reign, Israel rebelled against Assyria once again, but Samaria was conquered in 722 BC and according to Assyrian records 27,290 people were taken away as captives. Most of the N territory lost its Israelite character at that time; only in Samaria was some semblance of the worship of Yahweh perpetuated.

Josiah of Judah extended his religious reformation and political strength into former Israelite territory but his death in 609 BC at Megiddo ended any hopes of a reunited nation. Under the Babylonian conquest, Judah was also defeated and its people deported, Jerusalem being razed to the ground in 587 BC. In 582 BC, after the assassination of the governor Gedaliah, it was added to the Babylonian province of Samaria. When the S exiles returned in 538 BC the Samaritans' offer to co-operate in the rebuilding of the Jerusalem temple was rejected largely through doubts about their racial and religious purity. The long-standing breach thus became more bitter. The governor of Samaria at this time was Sanballat. His daughter married one Manasseh, a descendant of the Jerusalem high-priestly family, and some time before 400 BC Sanballat installed him as high priest of the ancient holy place on Mt Gerizim, near Shechem, where a new temple was built. The resulting rival cult to that of Jerusalem has survived to the present day.

The Greek (Macedonian) conquest.
When Alexander the Great conquered the Persian empire fresh governors simply took over the administration of Samaria and Judah. The Jews had meanwhile been spread widely around the empire (*cf.* Est. 3:8); some remained orthodox, such as those in Alexandria who translated the OT writings into Greek, while others absorbed Hellenistic (Greek) culture. When Antiochus III (of the Seleucid dynasty which had inherited part of Alexander's empire) was defeated by the Romans at Magnesia in 190 BC, a heavy tax burden fell on his subjects, including the Jews. To his son, Antiochus IV (Epiphanes), Judaea became strategically vital. Not trusting his Jewish subjects he attempted to abolish their religion and install the cult of Zeus Olympios ('the abomination of desolation') in the Jerusalem temple in 167 BC, and the cult of Zeus Xenios into the Samaritan temple.

Some Jews were martyred because they refused to take part in such worship, and others, including the Hasmonaean priestly family headed by Mattathias, took up arms against the occupying power. One of them, Judas Maccabaeus, excelled in guerilla warfare and won from Antiochus a guarantee of religious freedom. He and his followers continued to fight for political freedom, however. Eventually Jonathan, a brother of Judas, was given the high priesthood by Alex-ander Balas who was a successful pretender to the Seleucid throne, which angered other Jews. Under Simon, another brother of Judas, the Jews obtained independence from the Seleucid king Demetrius II in May 142 BC. Simon's son John Hyrcanus succeeded him in 134 BC, and in 128 on the death of the last strong Seleucid king, Antiochus VII, Judaea was freed from its last tax obligations to the Seleucids; Judaea was an independent state at last.

The religious supporters of the Hasmonaean regime then became known as Sadducees; the opponents of it were called Pharisees. Hyrcanus besieged and conquered Samaria and destroyed the shrine at Gerizim; he also defeated the Idumaeans, and Greek cities E of Jordan, and invaded Galilee. His son Alexander Jannaeus (103-76 BC) extended Judaea until he controlled most of the territory which had been Israelite in the nation's greatest days, but at the cost of its spiritual heritage. He was intensely disliked, and put down a revolt with great barbarity. After his death his widow Salome ruled for 9 years, and her death in 67 BC was followed by civil war. The Romans put an end to it, and to Judaea's independence. See also GREEKS; HASIDAEANS; MACCABEES, THE.

The Roman supremacy.
In 66 BC the Roman general Pompey concluded a 20-year war with Mithridates, king of Pontus, who had carved out an empire in W Asia from the lands of the decadent Seleucid

kingdom. Pompey then had to re-organize W Asia, and in 64 BC annexed Syria as a province of Rome and was invited by some Jews to put an end to the civil war in Judaea, which became a tributary of Rome the next year. Samaria was liberated from Jewish control. Hyrcanus II, son of Salome, was confirmed as high priest and national leader or 'ethnarch', strongly supported by the influential pro-Roman, Antipater, an Idumaean. Aristobulus II, Salome's other son and Hyrcanus' civil-war opponent, repeatedly tried to foment rebellion against Rome, but failed. So important was the area strategically that many famous Romans soon played a part in its history: Pompey, Julius Caesar, Cassius, Anthony and Octavian.

When the Parthians invaded Syria and Palestine in 40 BC, Antigonus, son of Aristobulus II, regained the throne by deposing Hyrcanus II. One of Antipater's sons, Herod, escaped the consequent purge, fled to Rome, and such was the esteem of his family there that Anthony and Octavian sent him home as 'king of the Jews'. By 37 BC he had recovered Judaea from Antigonus. When Herod ('the Great') died in 4 BC his kingdom was divided between his three sons. Archelaus, who governed Judaea and Samaria as ethnarch until AD 6, was so brutal that his subjects petitioned Rome to remove him to prevent a revolt. Rome did so (although the revolutionary ideal lived on among the Zealots) and the area once more became a third-grade Roman province. To assess its taxation dues, Quirinius the Roman governor of Syria held a census in Judaea and Samaria, after which the province was governed by prefects, one of whom was Pontius Pilate; among their tasks was the appointment of the high priest. (See also HEROD; PILATE; ROMAN EMPIRE.)

Between AD 41 and 44 Judaea enjoyed a brief respite from Roman administration when Herod Agrippa I was given Judaea and Samaria in addition to his territories to the N and E, but when he died Roman pro-curators were put in although without the power to appoint high priests. There followed a succession of upris-ings led by pseudo-messiahs such as Theudas or by the Zealots. There were fierce riots between Jews and Gentiles in Caesarea when Felix was pro-curator. His successors persistently offended Jewish national and religious sentiment, and a full-scale rebellion broke out in AD 66. The Roman leader Vespasian put it down methodically, beginning in Galilee. Recalled to Rome to become emperor in AD 69, he left the remaining task to his son Titus who in AD 70 completely destroyed Jerusalem except for part of the W wall and its towers. The last centre of Jewish resistance to fall was a Zealot stronghold at Masada, SW of the Dead Sea, in AD 74. Due largely to the work of Yohanan ben Zakkai, head of a new Sanhedrin of Jewish rabbis now governing internal affairs under Roman imperial legates, Israel's national and religious identity once more survived the downfall of its national shrine.

See also ARCHAEOLOGY;

CHRONOLOGY OF THE OLD (NEW) TESTAMENT; TRIBES OF ISRAEL.

ISRAEL OF GOD, NEW ISRAEL. Paul's statement that not all people born Israelites belong to Israel (Rom. 9:6) is in line with prophetic insistence that the true people of God, who are worthy of the name Israel, may be a relatively small remnant of faithful people within the nation. Jesus' calling of a group who were to receive the kingdom (Lk. 12:32) and his designation of the 12 apostles as judges of Israel's 12 tribes (Mt. 19:28) marks him out as the founder of a new Israel. Paul's one use of the term 'Israel of God' (Gal. 6:16) probably refers to both Jewish and Gentile believers (*cf.* 1 Pet. 2:9), but the nucleus of this Israel is Jewish (Rom. 11:18).

ISSACHAR. Jacob's 9th son, the name possibly deriving from words meaning 'hired worker'. The allocation to the tribe of Issachar in Canaan was between Mt Gilboa and the hills of Lower Galilee, at the E end of the Jezreel valley; the tribe was closely connected with Zebulun (*e.g.* Dt. 33:18f.). The judge Deborah probably came from Issachar (Jdg. 5:15); by David's time the tribe had a reputation for wisdom (1 Ch. 12:32).

ITALY. The name had substantially its modern meaning by the middle of the 1st cent. AD. It was Paul's destination on his most famous journey (Acts 27:1, 6). See also ROMAN EMPIRE; ROMANS, LETTER TO; ROME.

ITHAMAR (possibly 'land of palms'). A son of Aaron who became a priest (Ex. 28:1) and directed the building of the tabernacle (Ex. 38:21), he remained mostly faithful at a time of family apostasy (Lv. 10).

ITHIEL (probably 'God is with me'). In Pr. 30:1 probably to be translated with NEB, 'I am weary, O God', and not as a name.

ITHRA (lit. 'abundance'). Husband of Abigail, David's sister, and father of Amasa, one of David's generals.

ITHRITE. A family which originated in Kireath-jearim (1 Ch. 2:53, *cf.* 2 Sa. 23:38).

ITTAI (possibly 'God is with me'). The leader of 600 men from Gath who joined David shortly before Absalom's rebellion; he was probably a Philistine mercenary (2 Sa. 15:18ff.).

ITURAEA. Probably from Jetur, a son of Ishmael (Gn. 25:15f.), and a tribe antagonistic to Israel E of the Jordan (1 Ch. 5:19). The Jewish king Aristobulus I (105-104 BC) fought them, and they appear frequently in classical writings. At the Roman conquest they were known as wild robbers and proficient archers not associated with any precise locality. In Lk. 3:1, possibly part of Trachonitis inhabited by these robbers is called Ituraea.

IVAH (IVVAH). A town conquered by Assyria (2 Ki. 18:34), probably the Ava of 2 Ki. 17:24; the locality is unknown.

IVORY. A form of wealth and a mark of luxury (*e.g.* 1 Ki. 10:18ff.; Rev. 18:12). Although sometimes used for furnishings (1 Ki. 22:39; *cf.* Am. 3:15), its commonest use was in the manufacture of small objects such as boxes and in composite models where it simulated human flesh (*cf.* Song 5:14). Most ivory in Palestine came from Syrian (Asiatic) elephants in the Upper Euphrates until they became extinct in inter-testamental times. Other sources were India or the Sudan.

IYE-ABARIM. A stopping place on the borders of Moab during the Exodus journey; its location is uncertain.

J

JAAR (lit. 'forest'). A poetical abbreviation for Kiriath-jearim (city of forests) in Ps. 132:6, the allusion being to the events of 1 Sa. 7:1f.

JAAZANIAH (lit. 'Yahweh hears'). Several OT people including the Judaean army commander who supported Gedaliah at Mizpah (2 Ki. 25:23); 'Jaazaniah' has been found on a seal there, but it was a common name.

JABAL. The son of Lamech and Adah,

ancestor of nomads (Gn. 4:20).

JABBOK. A river flowing W into the Jordan 32 km N of the Dead Sea, rising near Amman (see RABBAH) in Jordan, and 96 km long. Jacob wrestled with God near it (Gn. 32:22), and it divided Ammorite from Gadite territory (Dt. 3:16).

JABESH-GILEAD. An Israelite town E of the Jordan where Saul proved his kingship (1 Sa. 11) and was buried (1 Sa. 31). Probably an isolated hill, Tell abu-Kharaz, 3 km from the Jordan and 15 km from Beth-shan.

JABEZ (lit. 'He makes sorrowful'). *Person:* A godly head of a Judah family (1 Ch. 4:9f.). *Place:* An otherwise unknown city of Judah (1 Ch. 2:55).

JABIN (possibly 'God perceives'). Name of 2 kings of Hazor. One was killed by Joshua (Jos. 11:1ff.), the other was 'destroyed' after his commander Sisera was killed by Jael (Jdg. 4).

JABNEEL (lit. 'God causes to build'). 1. A city on the SW border of Judah, probably to be identified with Jabneh (2 Ch. 26:6). 2. A town of Naphtali, possibly modern Kh. Yamma.

JACHIN AND BOAZ. The names of decorated bronze pillars or columns which flanked the entrance to Solomon's temple in Jerusalem (1 Ki. 7:21; 2 Ch. 3:15-17). After Nebuchadrezzar had captured Jerusalem in 587 BC they were broken up and taken to Babylon (2 Ki. 25:13). They were 9 m high and 1 m in diameter (1 Ki. 7:15), shortened perhaps when Jehoash or Josiah renovated the temple (2 Ki. 25:17; *cf.* 12:6ff.; 22:3ff.). The capitals appear to have been decorated with four opened and inverted lotus petals beneath an inverted bowl encircled by a network fringed with two rows of pomegranates (1 Ki. 7:17ff., 41f.). The OT description includes them with the furnishings rather than the structure of the temple, so they may have been free-standing rather than roof-supporting. There is considerable evidence of such free-standing pillars at the entrance of ancient temples, but their religious significance is obscure. The names were probably the first words of oracles such as 'Yahweh will establish…' (Jachin) and 'In the strength…' (Boaz).

JACKAL: See FOX, JACKAL.

JACOB. The father of the 12 tribes of Israel, who probably lived during the 18th cent. BC. Born clutching the heel of his twin brother Esau (Gn. 25:26), he twice supplanted his brother. First, he obtained the elder son's larger share of the inheritance (Gn. 25:29ff.). Then he obtained under false pretences from their father Isaac the customary death-bed blessing of the first-born which probably symbolized his social and religious position as head of the family (Gn. 27). Contemporary non-biblical records also imply such customs.

At his mother Rebekah's behest, he fled from Esau's anger on the pretext of going to find a wife from the same clan, 100 km (a reasonable day's journey for a fast camel) to Bethel. As he slept he had a vision of a ladder between earth and heaven and of God standing above it. The promise given to Abraham was confirmed to him and he was promised divine protection which he commemorated by erecting a stone as a memorial (Gn. 28). At Haran he was met by his cousin Rachel and taken to his uncle Laban with whom he agreed to work for 7 years in order to take Rachel as his wife. Laban however gave him Leah, his eldest daughter, and Jacob had to work another 7 years for Rachel. The two women, and their respective maids, bore Jacob 11 sons and a daughter in Haran.

A 12th son, Benjamin, was born as the family travelled S towards Jacob's family home in Canaan. Jacob's management of his father-in-law's livestock had been so successful that Laban both bargained and tricked him into staying longer than he wished, but he eventually walked out. Rachel took with her the household gods, the possession of which probably signified the head of the family, and Laban chased the fugitives seeking the return of his gods if not his daughters. He and Jacob made a pact and a memorial was erected to it (Gn. 31). On his way to meet Esau, Jacob was assailed by a stranger who prevailed only by dislocating Jacob's hip (Gn. 32), an incident regarded as Jacob's redemption from evil (Gn. 48:16). Esau proved friendly but Jacob went away from his territory to settle in Hebron. His descendants called themselves by his God-given name ISRAEL.

In the NT Jacob is regularly placed with Abraham and Isaac as one who is eternally blessed (Mt. 8:11) and with whom God entered into a covenant relationship (Mt. 22:32). Paul uses Jacob to illustrate God's purposes in election (Rom. 9:11ff.), and Hebrews lists him among the great men of faith (Heb. 11:9, 20f.). The background, although not the detail, of the stories is corroborated by archaeological evidence, for which see articles ARCHAEOLOGY OF THE OLD TESTAMENT; PATRIARCHAL AGE.

JAEL (lit. 'wild goat'). She murdered Sisera the commander of the Canaanite forces of King Jabin of Hazor (Jdg. 4:17ff.). The Israelites had already routed the Canaanites, and Sisera was heading N, possibly towards Hazor, when Jael offered him hospitality which according to custom guaranteed her protection. Erecting tents was women's work, which she took advantage of by killing Sisera with a tent-peg, fulfilling Deborah's prophecy (Jdg. 4:9). The victory gave Israel permanent relief from the Canaanites.

JAHAZ. A place in the Moab plains where Israel defeated the Amorite king Sihon (Nu. 21:23f.). Mesha of Moab later regained it, and it remained Moabite in the days of Jeremiah (Je. 48:21, 34). The exact site is disputed.

JAHZEIAH (lit. 'Yahweh sees, reveals'). An opponent of the plan to divorce foreign wives in Ezr. 10:15.

JAIR (lit. 'He enlightens'). Several OT people including: 1. Conqueror of several villages so naming them Havvoth-Jair (Nu. 32:41). 2. A judge of Israel (Jdg. 10:3ff.).

JAIRUS. A ruler of the synagogue in Capernaum whose duties would have included conducting worship and selecting those who would pray, read and preach in it. His 12-year-old daughter was healed by Jesus after she had been pronounced dead; Jesus' response that she was 'only sleeping' was met with scorn (Mk. 5:21ff.).

JAKIN AND BOAZ: See JACHIN AND BOAZ.

JAMES. 1. A Galilean fisherman, a son of Zebedee who with his brother John was called to be one of the inner core of Jesus' 12 apostles (Mt. 4:21; *cf.* Mk. 5:37; 9:2; 14:33). They were surnamed Boanerges, sons of thunder (Mk. 3:17; *cf.* Mk. 10:35ff.; Lk. 9:54). He was killed by Herod Agrippa *c.* AD 44 (Acts 12:2). 2. The son of Alphaeus, another apostle, usually identified with James the younger (Mk. 15:40). 3. An otherwise unknown James, the father of Judas (not Iscariot), Lk. 6:16. 4. The brother of Jesus who did not accept Jesus' authority at first (Jn. 7:5) but to whom the risen Jesus appeared (1 Cor. 15:7) and who became a leader of the Jerusalem church (Acts 15:13ff.; Gal. 1:19; 2:9). According to Josephus he was martyred in AD 61; he is the traditional author of the Letter of James (see the next article and BROTHERS OF JESUS).

JAMES, LETTER OF. *Contents.* Introduction and statement of themes of faith, speech and spirit, piety and poverty (1); development of these themes (2:1-5:6); conclusion and restatement of themes (5:7-20).

Authorship and date. The letter did not receive general acceptance in the W until the 4th cent. AD because of uncertainty about its author. James the son of Zebedee was martyred too early to have written it. Some scholars have suggested it was a homily by an anonymous Jew which was adapted for Christian use, but the many Jewish allusions and few references to Jesus do not demand this explanation. Others have thought of it as a Christian homily written between AD 70 and 130 and given the pseudonym 'James' (the Lord's brother) for authority. But although this accounts for the style of Greek and the argument that it was written to counter an antinomian perversion of Paul's teaching, it does not account for the primitive features such as elders, not bishops (5:14) and the Palestinian colouring (early and late rain, 5:7). It contains striking parallels with Jesus' Sermon on the Mount (*e.g.* 2:13 and Mt. 5:7; 3:12 and Mt. 7:16). The vivid similes, imaginary dialogues and rhetorical questions make it reasonable to suppose it the work of the bi-lingual Palestinian Jewish-Christian James, the Lord's brother;

there are possible supporting parallels between the letter and James' speech in Acts 15. A date before the Jerusalem Council (AD 48/9) would best explain the data.

Teaching. It concerns the Christian's need to resist the pressure to compromise with the world, especially with respect to the use of wealth. Although valued by Roman Catholics as supporting a doctrine of justification by works, it is recognized by evangelical scholars as drawing attention to the destructive social force of improperly used wealth and many aspects of practical Christian behaviour. It also draws attention to God's supremecy and holiness (*e.g.* 1:17f.; 4:11f.). The word 'justification' in 2:21 does not contradict Paul's teaching in Rom. and Gal. because it refers to Abraham's action in Gn. 22 flowing from the faith mentioned in Gn. 15:6.

JANNES AND JAMBRES. Referred to by Paul in 2 Tim. 3:6ff. in the context of false teachers as men who resisted Moses; non-biblical allusions show that he means the Egyptian magicians of Ex. 7-8. Jewish legend made much of them, and pagan sources also refer to them.

JANOAH (lit. 'rest'). 1. A town of Naphtali (2 Ki. 15:29), possibly modern Yanuh, NW of Acco. 2. A town SE of Shechem (Jos. 16:6ff.), modern Kh. Yanun.

JAPHETH. One of Noah's sons who with his wife escaped the flood; the ancestor of a number of tribes and peoples mostly associated in historical times with the regions to the N and W of the Near East, especially Anatolia and the Aegean (for which see NATIONS, TABLE OF). Some connect him with the Greek mythological figure Iapetos, which may be a form of the biblical name.

JAREB. In Ho. 5:13; 10:6 (AV) probably not a proper name but part of a title such as 'the great king' (as RSV, NIV).

JARMUTH. 1. A leading Amorite city before the Israelite invasion, modern Kh. Yarmuk 5 km S of Beth-shemesh. 2. A town for Levites in Issachar, possibly Khokav-hayyarden 10 km N of Beth-shan.

JASHAR, BOOK OF. Mentioned in Jos. 10:13 and 2 Sa. 1:18, and possibly also 1 Ki. 8:12f. (LXX). It was probably a collection of songs with short historical introductions, identified by some scholars with the 'Book of the Wars of the Lord' (Nu. 21:14).

JASHOBEAM. David's leading warrior (1 Ch. 11:11), to be identified with Josheb-basshebeth in 2 Sa. 23:8.

JASON. 1. Paul's host at Thessalonica (Acts 17:5ff.), who was seized by a mob and accused of harbouring seditious agitators; he was probably a Jewish Christian. 2. A Christian at Corinth (Rom. 16:21), possibly identical with the above. The name of the leader of the Argonauts was very com-mon and possibly used by Greek-speaking Jews instead of the similar-sounding Jesus.

JATTIR. A town on the SW escarpment of the Judaean hills, 21 km from Hebron, assigned to priests (Jos. 21:14).

JAVAN. A son of Japheth and father of several groups associated with the N and W of the Near East (Gn. 10:4). The name is identified with the Greek *Iones* which occurs in Homer's *Iliad* and refers to the people who gave their name to Ionia. The OT refers to his descendants as inhabiting coasts and islands (Is. 66:19) and as traders (Ezk. 27:13).

JAZER. A town of the Amorite kingdom of Sihon captured by Israel (Nu. 21:32). The Moabites gained control of it (Is. 16:8f.); Judas Maccabaeus captured it *c.* 164 BC (1 Macc. 5:7f.). Possibly Kh. Gazzir near es-Salt.

JEALOUSY. An exclusive single-mindedness which can be morally blameworthy (if one is selfishly jealous, *e.g.* 2 Cor. 12:20) or praiseworthy (if one is jealous for an external cause, *e.g.* 2 Cor. 11:2). Scriptural usage gives the term more positive connotations than current English usage, especially in the context of jealousy for the exclusiveness of marriage (Ezk. 16:38), and God's zeal for the honour of his name and the good of his people (Dt. 32:16). See also ENVY.

JEBUSITE. The ethnic name of a people descended from Canaan living in the hills round Jerusalem, their principal city, which was also called Jebus (*e.g.* Jdg. 19:10f.). David gained control of it (2 Sa. 5:6). See also JERUSALEM; SALEM.

JEDUTHUN. A Levite appointed by David to conduct with others the temple music (1 Ch. 25:1ff.), also known as Ethan (1 Ch. 6:44). His name appears in the titles of Pss. 39, 62, 77, and his family continued to officiate after the Exile (Ne. 11:17).

JEHOAHAZ (lit. 'Yahweh has grasped'). Three OT kings: the 6th king of Judah (for whom see AHAZIAH); the 11th king of the N kingdom of Israel who reigned *c.* 814-798 BC (2 Ki. 13:1ff.); the 18th king of Judah (called Shallum in Je. 22:11), deported by Pharaoh Neco II to Egypt where he died (2 Ki. 23:30ff.).

JEHOIACHIN (lit. 'Yahweh will establish'). Also called Jeconiah (1 Ch. 3:16); Coniah (Je. 22:24, 28). Aged 18, he was appointed king of Judah by the Babylonians following the death of his father Jehoiakim in 598 BC. His 3-month reign was marked by evil. Jeremiah foretold the end of his dynasty (Je. 22:24ff.); in Babylon Nebuchadrezzar treated him well as a royal hostage according to Babylonian documents, and he was later housed in the royal palace when Evil-Merodach succeeded Nebuchadrezzar (2 Ki. 25:27ff.).

JEHOIADA (lit. 'Yahweh knows'). A popular name in OT times. The most significant OT Jehoiada was chief priest in the Jerusalem temple during the reigns of Ahaziah, Athaliah and Joash. He helped hide Joash for 6 years while Athaliah usurped the throne, then produced the young Joash in a *coup d'état*, virtually ruling on his behalf until the boy grew old enough to reign (2 Ki. 11).

JEHOIAKIM (lit. 'Yahweh has established'). King of Judah (609-598 BC) who replaced his brother Jehoahaz at the command of Pharaoh Neco II of Egypt. His reign is recorded in 2 Ki. 23:34-24:6. He imposed heavy land taxes, and built costly royal buildings using forced labour (Je. 22:13ff.). The prophets Jeremiah and Habakkuk noted the religious decay during his reign; he was a covetous, oppressive and murderous king. He submitted to Nebuchadrezzar of Babylon at first but rebelled in 601 BC, and died on the way to captivity (2 Ch. 36:6).

JEHONADAB (JONADAB) (lit. 'Yahweh is liberal'). 1. David's nephew whose cunning enabled David's son Amnon to rape Tamar (2 Sa. 13:3ff.). 2. A zealous worshipper of God who prohibited the Rechabites from agricultural work and forming settled communities (Je. 35:6ff.).

JEHORAM (JORAM) (lit. 'Yahweh is exalted'). Several OT people including 2 kings. 1. King of (N) Israel 852-841 BC (2 Ki. 1-9). He generally followed the unorthodox religious policies of his predecessors, and was killed and succeeded by Jehu. 2. King of Judah 848-841 BC (2 Ki. 8:16ff.; 2 Ch. 21). He reversed the God-centred policies of his father Jehoshaphat; Arabians and Philistines plundered his kingdom.

JEHOSHABEATH, JEHOSHEBA. Jehoram's daughter who married a high priest (2 Ch. 22:11) and saved the life of Joash (2 Ki. 11:2).

JEHOSHAPHAT (lit. 'Yahweh has judged'). Several OT people, including the 4th king of Judah (c. 873-849 BC). He strengthened Judah's defences (2 Ch. 17) and made a treaty with neighbouring Israel (2 Ch. 18:1). He eradicated much of the pagan worship, provided itinerant teachers of Moses' law (1 Ki. 22:42ff.), and appointed judges in key cities (2 Ch. 19:4ff.).

JEHOSHAPHAT, VALLEY OF. The name given by Joel to the place of final judgment (Joel 3:2, 12). It is probably symbolic of the judgment (Jehoshaphat means literally 'God has judged') and not a current geographical name (cf. v. 14). Some have identified it with the Kidron valley because of its similar associations with God's judgment, the earliest such identification being by the Bordeaux pilgrim AD 333.

JEHU (possibly an abbreviation of 'Yahweh is he'). Several OT people including the 10th king of the N kingdom of Israel (c. 842-815 BC). During a period of religious apostasy the prophet Elisha instigated a revolt by arranging for Jehu to be anointed king. Jehu killed Jehoram of Israel and Ahaziah of Judah, plus Ahab's family and the priests of Baal (2 Ki. 9-10). The Black Obelisk of Shalmaneser II of Assyria shows an unnamed king of Israel, generally believed to be Jehu, paying tribute-tax.

JEHUDI. Normally means 'a Jew' (Zc. 8:23); in Je. 36:14 name of an officer of Jehoiakim's court.

JEPHTHAH. One of the later Hebrew judges (Jdg. 11:1-12:7, c. 1100 BC). The son of Gilead and a common prostitute, he fled to Tob and gathered a gang of renegades who raided settlements and caravans and possibly offered protection to outlying villages. When Israel was threatened by an invasion of Ammonites, he was invited to command Israel's forces, which he agreed to on condition of remaining their head after the battle. He promised God a human sacrifice at a time when pagan ritual included such things and the law of Moses was neglected; he was deeply grieved when the candidate turned out to be his only child.

JERAH. One of the sons of Joktan (Gn. 10:26) whose descendants possibly settled in S Arabia.

JERAHMEEL (lit. 'May God have compassion'). Several OT people including the ancestor of a clan on the S frontier of Judah (1 Sa. 27:10).

JEREMIAH. Jeremiah's ministry covered one of the most fateful periods in the history of the ancient Near East. In 40 years (626-587 BC) he prophesied during the reigns of 5 kings of Judah. The Assyrian empire disintegrated and Babylon and Egypt struggled for supremacy, with Judah caught in the middle. Jeremiah was called to prophesy as a young man (1:6); Hezekiah's religious reforms (2 Ki. 18) had long since been nullified by Manasseh's apostasy (2 Ki. 21) and Judah had sunk into moral decline. Growing up in a pious household (1:1), Jeremiah was no doubt taught Israel's laws and probably imbibed the hopes and anxieties of a faithful minority.

The five kings. Jeremiah began his ministry in the reign of *Josiah* (638-608 BC) who had introduced some religious reforms (2 Ch. 34:4ff.). He began a systematic reform when the book of the law was rediscovered (2 Ki. 23). Je. 1-6 probably describes the period before this second reformation; 11:1ff. may contain hints of Jeremiah's approval of it. *Jehoahaz* (Shallum in Je. 22:11) briefly succeeded Josiah but was deported to Egypt, an event Jeremiah lamented (22:10ff.). The reign of *Jehoiakim* (607-597 BC) saw the significant battle of Carchemish (Je. 46, 605 BC) in which Neco of Egypt was crushed by Nebuchadrezzar of Babylon, thus bringing the whole Near East under Babylonian control (25:15ff.). In 604 BC Nebuchadrezzar sacked Ashkelon (47:5ff.), following which a fast was proclaimed in Judah (36:9ff.). Jeremiah's proposed policy differed from the king's (22:13ff.; 26:20ff.). Jehoiakim rebelled vainly against Babylon; Jeremiah reprimanded him and was persecuted for it (11:18ff.; 12:6; 15:15ff.; 20:2; 26:10f.; 36:27). Jeremiah continued his ministry however, and Jehoiakim finally died a violent death (22:18; *cf.* 2 Ki. 24:1ff.).

Next came *Jehoiachin* (Coniah, Jeconiah) who lasted only 3 months before being deported to Babylon in 597 BC (2 Ki. 24:8ff.), as predicted by Jeremiah (Je. 22:24ff.). Nebuchadrezzar then appointed *Zedekiah*, Josiah's youngest son, to the throne (597-587 BC). He was weak and vacillating, with poor-quality officers of state. Jeremiah opposed him when he mooted rebellion (chs. 27f.), but he persisted and entered treasonable negotiations with Pharaoh Hophra of Egypt. Babylon besieged Jerusalem. Jeremiah predicted a long period of national exile, though false prophets contradicted him (28:1ff.; 29:24ff.). He encouraged submission to the Babylonians (34; 37:3ff.), and was imprisoned for desertion (37:11ff.) and treason (38:1ff.). Looking further ahead, he also proclaimed promises of restoration (31-33). When Babylon finally destroyed Jerusalem in 587 BC, Nebuchadrezzar treated Jeremiah kindly, but after rebels had killed the governor Gedaliah the remainder of the people compelled the prophet to accompany them to Egypt (42-44); his subsequent life—and death—is unknown.

Jeremiah's personality. His personality is the most sharply etched of all the OT prophets. His emotions are vividly displayed. He was a man of marked contrasts, both gentle and tenacious, affectionate and inflexible. In him the frailties of the flesh contended with the energies of the spirit. Those whom he loved hated him because he denounced their sins; a loyal patriot, he was branded a traitor. He was plunged into unimaginable depths of grief (8:18ff.; 9:1). He cursed the day he was born (15:10; 20:14ff.), accused God of having wronged him (20:17) and invoked curses on his tormentors (18:18ff.). Determined to abandon his mission, he found he could not (20:9ff). But in all his conflict he found a refuge in God, and brought to its finest expression the OT ideal of fellowship with him.

Jeremiah's message. God is creator and sovereign Lord (*e.g.* 25:5f.). He knows people's hearts and is the source of life for those who trust him (17:5ff., 13). He demands his people's allegiance and hates idolatry (7); in Jeremiah's time idols were even to be found in the Jerusalem temple (32:34). Moral corruption inevitably followed idolatry and was likewise condemned by Jeremiah (*e.g.* 5:1ff.; 23:10ff.). Before God, he urged, the requirements of the moral law took precedence over the ceremonial laws which the people often kept carefully (*e.g.* 6:19ff.).

Inevitably the theme of judgment was very prominent in Jeremiah's message. God's punishment of Judah was to be seen in drought and famine (14:1ff.) and invasion by a foreign power (6:1ff.). His prophecies against the nations in 46:51 have been shown

to have a clear factual basis following the discovery and publication of a contemporary document *The Babylonian Chronicle.*

The professional priests and prophets were Jeremiah's sworn enemies, as he complained at their policy of making material gain from their office and their contention that the Jerusalem temple would never fall to the Babylonians (14:14ff.; 23:9ff.). Knowledge of the law without obedience to it was worthless, he said (2:8); the law needed to be written on the heart, prompting spontaneous and perfect obedience. Jeremiah recognized that this could happen only if God gave a new covenant (31:31ff.).

His message was not without hope, however. The exile in Babylon would not last for ever (29:10ff.) and Babylon itself would be overthrown eventually (50f.). This hope gave birth to his great act of faith—buying land—in the darkest days (32). But he looked even beyond the return from exile to an ideal future in which Samaria would have a part, abundance would prevail and Jerusalem would be holy to the Lord because its people had repented and he had forgiven them (31), establishing over them the rule of the Messianic Prince (23:5f.).

Jeremiah's oracles. The book is not arranged in chronological order; ch. 36 suggests a rough arrangement according to subject matter. The chapters may be arranged according to the kings ruling at the time in the following order, thus: Josiah, 1-20 (except 12:7-13:27); Jehoiakim: 26; 22-23; 25;

35-36; 45; 33; 12:7-13:27; Jehoiachin: 13:18f.; 20:24-30; 52:31-34; Zedekiah: warnings: 24; 29; 27-28; 51:59f.; promises: 30-33; the siege: 21; 34; 37-39. In addition, there are prophecies after the fall of Jerusalem (40-44); prophecies against the nations (46-51); historical appendix (52).

The disorderly arrangement strengthens the conviction that the oracles were Jeremiah's words put together during days of danger and turmoil. The greatness and importance of Jeremiah is to be seen in his emphasis that religion is essentially a spiritual relation with God, with moral and spiritual demands. Jesus, the 'Righteous Branch' of 23:5, quoted often from it and fulfilled its central theme.

JERICHO. OT Jericho is now the mound of Tell es-Sultan, 16 km NW of the present mouth of the Jordan and 27 km ENE of Jerusalem. Its name is probably connected with the early W Semitic moon-god. Its story is virtually a precis of the whole archaeological history of Palestine *c.* 8000-1200 BC.

Every settlement there owed its existence to the fine perennial spring and the 'oasis' which it waters; in the OT Jericho is sometimes called 'the city of palm trees' (Dt. 34:3). The earliest-known agriculturalists in Palestine built huts by this spring. The oldest town was built there soon after 8000 BC, with a stone wall and round houses which later gave way to rectangular ones. Around 2300 BC, Jericho was violently destroyed by newcomers who eventually resettled

the site and became part of the Canaanite population. Splendid pottery, tables, beds, plates of fruit and joints of meat have been preserved in tombs from this time by peculiar atmospheric conditions.

Jericho was once again destroyed sometime after 1600 BC, probably by the Egyptians, and it was re-occupied *c.* 1400-1300 BC. But from the 13th cent. BC onwards, the time of the Israelite conquest, very little is known about it. In Joshua's time there may have been a small settlement on the E part of the mound, all traces of which have been eroded away. The narrative of Jos. 3-8, telling of the fall of Jericho, reflects faithfully the conditions in, and topography of, the area. For centuries no attempt was made to rebuild the once-important town, in awe of Joshua's curse (Jos. 6:26), but the spring may have supported a tiny hamlet. Eglon, king of Moab, temporarily occupied it (Jdg. 3:13), and David's envoys stayed there till their shaved beards regrew (2 Sa. 10:5). Then in Ahab's reign (*c.* 874/3-853 BC) Hiel the Bethelite refounded Jericho proper and in fulfilment of the curse lost two sons in the process (1 Ki. 16:34). It was frequented by Elijah and Elisha (2 Ki. 2:4f., 18ff.) and near there the Babylonians captured Zedekiah, Judah's last king (2 Ki. 25:5). The remains of this 9th-6th cents. BC Jericho are fragmentary but definite, and include buildings and pottery. The Babylonians destroyed it but a modest Jericho existed after the Exile (*cf.* Ne. 3:2).

In NT times, the town was situated

S of the old mound. Herod the Great and his successors built a winter palace nearby, with ornamental gardens. Jesus healed Bartimaeus (Mk. 10:46ff.) and met the wealthy Zacchaeus (Lk. 19:1ff.) there.

JEROBOAM (probably 'may the people increase'; possibly 'may he contend for the people'). 1. The first king of the N kingdom of Israel (c. 931-910 BC); apparently a wealthy land-owner whom Solomon placed in charge of the N work force (1 Ki. 11:28). He rebelled against Solomon and fled to Egypt (1 Ki. 11:40). When Solomon's successor Rehoboam refused to adopt a less harsh policy, the nation was split and 10 tribes made Jeroboam their king (1 Ki. 12). He fortified key cities such as Shechem, and built rival shrines to Jerusalem at Bethel and Dan (1 Ki. 12:28ff.). They threatened the pure worship of God and drew prophetic rebuke (1 Ki. 13:1ff.)

2. Jeroboam II (c. 793-753 BC) was the 4th king of Jehu's dynasty and one of the N kingdom's most illustrious rulers. He restored Israel's borders almost to what they had been under Solomon (2 Ki. 14:25). Excavations at Samaria have revealed the grandeur of his fortress and the luxury and false religion which so vexed Amos (e.g. Am. 6:1ff.).

JERUEL. In Jahaziel's prophecy (2 Ch. 20:16), possibly part of the wilderness of Tekoa extending W of the Dead Sea N of En-gedi.

JERUSALEM.   One of the world's most famous cities, it is considered sacred by Jews, Christians and Muslims alike. Set high in the hills of Judah c. 50 km from the Mediterranean and 30 km W of the Dead Sea, it rests on an uneven plateau surrounded on three sides by deep ravines. The topography naturally divides the city into E and W halves, both of which can be divided into N and S quarters. The water supply has always been problematic; only the Virgin's Spring (probably the biblical Gihon) and the Bir Eyyub well (probably the biblical En-rogel) are main sources, other pools being filled with rainwater or via aqueducts.

The meaning of Jerusalem is unclear; the name is pre-Israelite, probably meaning 'foundation of (the god) Shalem'. The similar Hebrew word for peace (shalom) became associated with it later. The Greek version of the name in NT times probably conveyed the idea of 'sacred Salem'; to the Jews it was indeed the holy city without a rival (cf. Is. 52:1).

History. Jerusalem is known to have existed in the 19th-18th cents. BC when it is mentioned in Egyptian texts. It is mentioned again in the 14th cent. BC when it was a mountain fortress under Egyptian control. Early biblical references to it are possibly in Gn. 14:18; 22:2; cf. Ps. 76:2. When Israel entered Canaan, the city was called Jebus and controlled by the Jebusites, an indigenous Semitic tribe. Joshua defeated them but did not take the city; from Jdg. 1:8, 21 it seems that the tribe of Judah overcame the city outside the fortress, which Benjamin then occupied peaceably alongside the Jebusites remaining in the fortress. David captured the fortress, possibly by sending his men up the water tunnel (2 Sa. 5:6ff.). He improved its fortifications, built himself a palace and installed the ark of the covenant in the city, thus making it his capital. The name 'Zion' appears at this time, referring originally to the fortress or the area it stood on, but afterwards becoming a synonym for the whole city.

When the kingdom was divided after Solomon's death, Jerusalem remained capital of Judah, but was destroyed by Nebuchadrezzar of Babylon in 587 BC. Fifty years later the Persian conquerors of Babylon allowed Jews to return to Jerusalem and to rebuild the temple, but the walls remained ruined until Nehemiah restored them in the mid-5th cent. BC. In 167 BC Antiochus IV destroyed its walls and plundered and desecrated the temple, but after the revolt led by Judas Maccabaeus the temple was rededicated in 164 BC. The Romans forced their way in a century later, and when the pro-Roman Herod the Great won control from the Hasmonaean dynasty in 37 BC he had to embark on an extensive repair and rebuilding programme. The Jewish revolt in AD 66 concluded when the Roman general Titus destroyed the fortifications and temple in AD 70. Another revolt in AD 132 led to Jerusalem being rebuilt as a pagan city dedicated to Jupiter Capitolinus, from which all Jews were excluded. Con-

stantine (4th cent. AD) allowed them back in. Since then it has been captured by Persian, Arab, Turkish, Crusader, British and Israeli forces. In 1542 the Turkish sultan Suleiman the Magnificent rebuilt the walls as they can be seen today.

Growth and development. There is some uncertainty about the physical history of Jerusalem, partly because it has been continuously occupied and archaeologists cannot always dig where they wish. The earliest city was on the SE hill, an area wholly outside the present city walls, and the Jebusite wall lay down the E slope on terraces which may be referred to by the biblical term Millo (*e.g.* 2 Sa. 5:9). David and Solomon's city extended N; the temple was built on the NE hill. In the prosperous 8th cent. BC the settlement was extended to the NW ridge (the Second Quarter of 2 Ki. 22:14), and opinion is divided as to whether the SW hill was also occupied at this time. Nehemiah's rebuilding works abandoned the W ridge and brought the E wall back to the top of the NE ridge; the circuit described in Ne. 3 begins at the N of the city and is in an anti-clockwise direction. There is little evidence that the city spread to the W ridge again until the 2nd cent. BC. The Jewish historian Josephus says that the Romans penetrated three N walls in AD 70, but the exact location and identification of these is disputed. It has been established, however, that the Church of the Holy Sepulchre, which claims to mark the site of Jesus' crucifixion, does indeed lie outside the Second N Wall, and so may be the authentic site.

The church at Jerusalem. The Christian church was born in Jerusalem on the Day of Pentecost, when the Holy Spirit was first poured out on the disciples of Jesus. To outsiders, it had the character of a Jewish sect (Acts 24:5), but it grew large (Acts 21:20) and included Greek-speaking Jews who were in Jerusalem but not natives of it. The 7 helpers appointed to oversee the church's charitable aid were probably all such 'Hellenists' (Acts 6:5).

After the death of Stephen the Hellenistic elements seem to have disappeared and the church became more strongly Jewish in character. Some of its members disapproved of the gospel being offered to Gentiles without also requiring that they kept details of the Jewish law (Acts 15:1; Gal. 2:12). Officially, however, the Jerusalem church sanctioned the Gentile mission, and a church council agreed not to press circumcision on Gentile Christians but only to ask them to observe certain Jewish scruples to make table-fellowship easier (Acts 15:19ff.). The church was scattered when the Jewish war against Rome broke out in AD 66.

The NT naturally inherits the OT love for Jerusalem, and uses it to picture the ideal heavenly city which the earlier prophets had eagerly predicted in view of Israel's apostasy (Rev. 21; *cf.* Is. 29:1ff.).

JESHIMON (lit. 'waste, desert'). Probably a synonym for the Wilderness of Judaea.

JESHUA. *People:* A late form of the name Joshua which was common at the time the Jews returned from the Exile; little is known of any of the biblical people who bear it (in Ne. 8:17 JOSHUA, the son of Nun, is intended; in Ezr. 3:2 *etc.* the reference is to the high priest JOSHUA, the son of Jehozadek). *Place:* A town in Judah probably identical to Shema and Sheba.

JESHURUN (lit. 'the upright one'). A poetic variant of the name ISRAEL, possibly to be interpreted as 'people of the law'.

JESSE. David's father, from Bethlehem, who had 7 other sons (1 Sa. 16:10f.). His last appearance in Scripture is at the cave of Adullam, from where David sent him to Moab for safety (1 Sa. 22:3f.).

JESUS CHRIST, LIFE OF. *Sources.* The evidence for Jesus is almost entirely restricted to the four Gospels. There are only a few scattered allusions in the rest of the NT (*e.g.* Acts 20:35; 1 Cor. 11:23ff.). The only direct mention by a Roman historian is a bare record written by Tacitus of Jesus' execution by order of Pontius Pilate. The Jewish historian Josephus has a passage about Jesus which may have been re-written by Christians. Most of the other Christian accounts of Jesus life and teaching outside the NT documents are clearly legendary or even written to promote deviant doctrines. But while the Gospel writers exercised considerable freedom in selecting and wording sayings and naratives, they were essentially concerned to pass on a carefully preserved tradition about Jesus. See also GOSPELS.

Setting. Jesus was born shortly before the death of Herod the Great in 4 BC (Mt. 2:1, 13ff.); the exact date cannot be determined. He was about 30 years old when he began his public ministry (Lk. 3:23), some time after John the Baptist had begun preaching *c.* AD 28 (Lk. 3:1ff.). His ministry lasted for 3 years (see CHRONOLOGY OF THE NEW TESTAMENT), taking place mostly in Palestine with a few short journeys beyond its borders (*e.g.* into Phoenicia and Decapolis, Mk. 7:24, 31). The main centre of Jesus' teaching, and his home province, was Galilee, which until relatively recently had had a largely Gentile population and was despised by Jews from the S area of Judaea. Galileans also had a pronounced accent.

For some 60 years before Jesus' birth, Palestine had been under Roman rule exercised through local princes like Herod the Great; Archelaus who inherited from him Judaea and Samaria was deposed and direct rule through a prefect was imposed, the prefect during Jesus' ministry being Pontius Pilate. Roman rule was not popular; the Jews resented being subject to any state because it seemed incompatible with Israel's status as the people of God. Although many people preferred to maintain the relatively peaceful *status quo*, some (often called Zealots) were dedicated to political and even violent opposition to the Romans.

Birth and childhood. Only Matthew and Luke, using different sources, record Jesus' birth. Matthew concentrates more on Joseph's side of the story and Luke on Mary's, but both agree on the fact of the virgin birth. By contrast to his supernatural conception, he was brought up in a very ordinary 'middle class' home in Nazareth, Joseph the 'carpenter' being a skilled craftsman and possibly an employer. But they were not affluent (Lk. 2:24; *cf.* Lv. 12:8). As Joseph is not mentioned again, and as Jesus is called 'Mary's son', Joseph may have died while Jesus was young, leaving him as the eldest son to run the family business and provide for his brothers and sisters (Mk. 6:3). Jesus' knowledge of the Scriptures shows he had a normal Jewish child's education based at the local synagogue. Beyond the one incident which showed his abnormal aptitude for religious debate (Lk. 2:42ff.) nothing else is known about his early life. See also BROTHERS OF JESUS; GENEALOGY OF JESUS CHRIST; VIRGIN BIRTH.

The start of his ministry. A Judaean relative of Jesus, John the Baptist, was preaching repentance and baptizing people. John recognized Jesus as the judge whose coming he had predicted (Mt. 3:11f.) and encouraged his disciples to follow Jesus (Jn. 1:35ff.). Jesus submitted himself first to John's baptism to identify with what John stood for and with those who had responded to John's call, rather than to admit personal sin (*cf.* Jn. 8:46; 1 Pet.

2:22). His calling as the promised deliverer was confirmed by a decisive revelation (Mk. 1:10f.; *cf.* Is. 11:2). This was followed by his temptation (Mt. 4:1ff.; Lk. 4:1ff.); an early exploration of just what it meant to be the Son of God. He was challenged to doubt his Father God's care in his extreme need, to force his Father's hand, and to compromise his total loyalty to the Father. His ministry began with preaching and baptizing in the Jordan valley but he soon moved N to Galilee (Jn. 3:22; 4:1ff.), where he concentrated on teaching and healing.

Lifestyle and disciples. Jesus, like other Jewish teachers, gathered a group of disciples who accompanied him on his travels. From them he selected an inner circle of 12 (often called apostles). Probably all the 12 except Judas Iscariot were Galileans, but they varied widely in temperament from Thomas the pessimist to Peter the extrovert. They accepted Jesus' lifestyle, temporarily abandoning their homes and families and being willing to suffer persecution. Together they lived on the contributions and hospitality of people who supported their mission (Mt. 10:8ff.). Jesus himself was unmarried and had no settled home (Lk. 9:58). At first he began teaching in local synagogues (Mk. 1:21) but soon seems to have taught the crowds mostly in the open air.

Social, political and religious attitudes. Jesus won notoriety among the Jewish establishment for keeping company with the outcasts of respectable society. But his mission was to all in need, whatever their social standing

(Mk. 2:17). His story of the good Samaritan challenged current Jewish taboos (Lk. 10:29ff.), and he placed Gentiles alongside Jews in God's purposes (Mt. 8:11f.). Both the rich (Jn. 19:38ff.) and the poor (Mt. 11:5) responded favourably to him. He sternly condemned a callous neglect of the less fortunate (Lk. 16:19ff.).

He frequently debated with Jewish religious leaders; Jesus lacked the formal education of a scribe but his style of teaching and group of disciples cast him in the role of a rabbi. He paid little attention to the many religious rules not found in the OT but which were strictly emphasized by contemporary religious leaders. For example, he cut through the tangled legislation about sabbath observance (Lk. 13:10ff.). The debates were often heated and strongly worded (*e.g.* Mt. 23:1ff.), and his popularly-acclaimed condemnation of religious legalism was a major factor in the scribes' determination to get rid of him. He was finally condemned on a political charge, however, that of claiming to be king of the Jews (Lk. 23:2). Much of his early support probably did come from people who hoped he would crush the Roman occupation but he resisted an attempt to make him leader of a coup (Jn. 6:14f.). He also refused to adopt the strict nationalist line on paying taxes to Rome (Mk. 12:13ff.), and predicted the downfall of the Jewish nation (Lk. 13:25ff.).

Miracles and authority. Both Christian and non-Christian sources attest that Jesus was known to his contemporaries as a worker of miracles. Most of his recorded miracles are cases of healing and of exorcism and these were a regular feature of his ministry (Mk. 1:32ff.); they also featured in his disciples' independent work (Mk. 6:13). They were integrally related to his preaching, as part of his attack on all the powers of evil manifest physically as well as spiritually. His healings were primarily responses of compassion, as were most of his nature miracles; only the walking on the water and withering of the fig-tree seem to be intended to teach simply something about his person and ministry. He used little or no ritual, relying instead on a mere word of command (Mt. 8:5ff.). This personal authority left a big impression on people (Mk. 1:22). He refused to state openly the source of his authority (Mk. 11:27ff.) but clearly implied it was derived from God. See also MIRACLE.

Final entry into Jerusalem. Jesus knew that his last visit to Jerusalem would lead to a final confrontation with the authorities and result in his own death (Lk. 18:31ff.). It was made at Passover time when the city would be crowded with pilgrims and the themes of death and redemption were in people's minds. One of his first acts on arriving was to throw out the traders from the Temple precincts, reinforcing his Messianic claim (Mk. 11:15ff.). During the week the religious leaders attempted to elicit from him blasphemous or politically subversive statements which could be used against him. At his farewell meal with his disciples, in some sense a Passover meal although

possibly held a day before the official celebration, he gave final instructions to his closest disciples. Then he shared with them the bread and wine as symbols that his coming death was to be redemptive, for the benefit of many.

Trial and death. With his disciple Judas acting as an inside informer, the authorities were able to arrest Jesus quietly in Gethsemane. Jesus refused to resist arrest. Then came a series of hearings before the Jewish authorities. The first (probably unofficial) was before Annas whom the Romans had deposed as high priest (Jn. 18:12ff.), the second and third before the official high priest Caiaphas and the Sanhedrin, one at night the other early the following morning. The last hearing (probably a full meeting of the Sanhedrin) ratified the earlier verdict that Jesus was guilty of blasphemy, probably because of his acceptance of the Messianic title (Mk. 14:53-15:1). Jewish law required the death penalty for blasphemy but the Roman occupiers reserved the sole right to carry out such sentences by crucifixion; Stephen was later martyred by the Jews by stoning (Acts 7:59; *cf.* Jn. 18:31). Therefore Jesus was taken to Pontius Pilate, who realized the charge of being 'king of the Jews' was artificial and that Jesus was not a political revolutionary.

Pilate's attempts to evade the issue by referring Jesus to Herod Antipas (Lk. 23:6ff.), offering to release Jesus in the customary Passover amnesty (Mt. 15:6ff.), by scourging him as a substitute for death and by declaring him innocent (Lk. 23:22; Jn. 19:1ff.) all proved unsuccessful in changing hostile public opinion. On the threat of being reported to his superiors Pilate condemned Jesus to be crucified (Jn. 19:12). His death was unusually quick, and his final cry showed him still in control of the situation (Jn. 19:30). He was buried in a nearby rock-cut tomb even though crucified bodies were normally left unburied (Jn. 19:38ff.). See also CROSS; SEVEN WORDS.

Resurrection and ascension. That Jesus' tomb was found to be empty on the Sunday morning cannot be seriously disputed on historical grounds. The Gospels and 1 Cor. 15 attest to probably 11 separate encounters with the risen Jesus soon after, varying from single people to large groups. Jesus, while free from some of the limits of time and space, was solidly physical. Having convinced his followers of his victory over death, he left them in a way that showed them his physical presence was no longer necessary; they were to continue his mission assured of his continued spiritual presence with them (Mt. 28:18ff.). See also ASCENSION; RESURRECTION.

JESUS CHRIST, TEACHING OF.

Jesus did not deliver his teaching as an orderly treatise; he spoke instead in a wide variety of real-life situations. While he did lecture to crowds, often for long periods (*e.g.* Mk. 6:34f.) the carefully structured discourses in the Gospels bear the marks of having been later compiled from Jesus' sayings than of being *verbatim* transcripts of actual addresses. The form of his

teaching was similar to that of other Jewish teachers, including not only arguments from the OT and rules of conduct but also the rhythmic style and use of parables which aided people's memories. There is no Jewish parallel to the sheer quantity and vividness of his parables and epigrams, however; he could never have been a dull teacher. See also PARABLE; SERMON ON THE MOUNT.

Jesus' use of the OT. His recorded words in the Gospels contain over 40 *verbatim* quotations from the OT, about 60 clear verbal allusions or references to the OT, and well over 100 other possible allusions which he either intended or which arose because his mind was so full of OT words and ideas that he naturally expressed himself in them. He used it in all aspects of his teaching, but especially with reference to his own person and mission. He quoted OT predictions which were fulfilled in him (*e.g.* Mt. 11:5; *cf.* Is. 35:5f.), and OT incidents which were 'patterns' he fulfilled (*e.g.* Mt. 12:40ff. referring to Jonah and Solomon). See also TYPOLOGY.

The kingdom of God. Jesus' first recorded words were a concise summary of his basic teaching: 'The time is fulfilled, and the kingdom of God is at hand' (Mk. 1:15). This note of present fulfilment was of central importance; his coming introduced a new era, the looked-for 'Day of the Lord' and the fulfilment of all the hope of the OT. The 'kingdom of God' meant God's sovereignty, the situation in which God is in control, his rule or reign in human affairs. People could 'enter' or 'receive' it now (Mk. 10:15, 23f.) but its final consummation was still to be in the future. As people responded to his message, so the rule of God would be progressively established. See KINGDOM OF GOD.

God the Father. To accept God's rule involves a new relationship with him. Jesus taught his followers to regard God as a caring Father, one of the most distinctive and novel features of his teaching. They were to rely on their heavenly Father even in practical matters of food and clothing (Mt. 6:25ff.; 7:7ff.); therefore their relationship with him was to be intimate, and not that of formal religiosity. Jesus also claimed his own unique relationship to the Father as Son of God. Most of the 100 references to the Father in John's Gospel are specifically to him as Father of Jesus. The uniqueness of his sonship compared with that of believers is illustrated in Mt. 11:27. In Jesus' teaching there is no sense of a more general Fatherhood of God embracing all people.

Ethics of the kingdom. Although Jesus denounced legalism the ethical standard he gave for his followers was perfection (Mt. 5:48). But instead of proliferating rules for conduct, Jesus gave a more searching critique of motives and attitudes (Mt. 5:21ff.). He gave love a central place, but it was the kind which is expressed in unselfish service (Mk. 10:42ff.). While he did not make specific proposals for social reform, he did tend to undermine the

comfortable acceptance of the socio-economic *status quo*, recommending voluntary poverty and unstinting generosity always (*e.g.* Mk. 10:17ff.). Discipleship involved also the renunciation of reputation and even relationships (Mk. 10:28ff.); its ruling motive was not the prospect of reward but gratitude to God (Mt. 18:23ff.).

The mission of Jesus. While seeing himself playing the central, messianic role in inaugurating the kingdom of God, he hardly ever claimed to be the Messiah in so many words—and when he did, he was outside Jewish territory (Jn. 4:25f.). He regularly substituted the title 'Son of Man' for 'Christ' (Messiah, *e.g.* Mk. 8:29ff.), because popular Jewish conceptions of the Messiah were narrowly political and nationalistic; although 'Son of man' had messianic connotations in Dn. 7:13f., it was not current in mainstream Jewish thought. He also referred to himself as fulfilling some OT pictures of the Messiah, *e.g.* David's lord (Ps. 110:1; Mk. 12:35ff.) and the suffering servant (Is. 53; Mk. 10:45). He constantly emphasized the necessity for suffering and death, seeing its chief purpose as the forgiveness of sins (Mt. 26:28). See also next article; ATONEMENT; MESSIAH: REDEMPTION.

The people of God. Jesus may not have intended to found a formal hierarchical 'church', but his mission inevitably involved the creation of a new community of people who through his redemptive sacrifice entered the kingdom of God. The word 'church' occurs only twice in the

Gospels. In Mt. 18:17 it refers to the local group of Jesus' followers meeting to settle disputes among its members, and in Mt. 16:18 it foreshadows the NT view of the universal church as Jesus' continuing representative on earth. Hitherto Israel had been God's special people, but from now on that title belonged to all who responded to Jesus' call, Jew or Gentile (Mt. 8:11f.), as a result of the 'new covenant' he established (Lk. 22:20).

The future. How and when Jesus expected the final consummation of the kingdom is not spelt out systematically, but some stages are clearly taught. He predicted the destruction of Jerusalem and its temple (Mk. 13:2ff.) as the inevitable result of Jewish rejection of God's final appeal (Lk. 19:41f.). It seems some of his sayings about 'the coming of the Son of Man' relate to this event which many of his hearers would live to see (*e.g.* Mt. 10:23). He looked forward to a final judgment in which he would play a central role (Mt. 25:31ff.).

He also predicted his return to earth which would be as unmistakable and as universally visible as a flash of lightning (Lk. 17:24). To meet such an unpredictable event demanded a lifestyle of constant readiness (Mt. 24:42ff.); even Jesus did not know precisely when it would be (Mk. 13:32). Disagreement over the detailed interpretation of specific passages should not be allowed to obscure the over-all pattern of Jesus' vision about the coming of the kingdom; he did not expect the end of the world in the very near future, and his call for constant readiness is as binding on his followers today as it was when he first uttered it. See also ESCHATOLOGY.

JESUS CHRIST, TITLES OF. A title describes or refers to some function or status of a person and thus may indicate the honour to be ascribed to him. Names and titles are sometimes closely related. Julius Caesar's family name became the title of all succeeding Roman emperors; Adolf Hitler's simple title *Der Führer* ('The leader') can have no future political use because of its associations. Similarly, the titles (such as 'Christ') given to Jesus during his lifetime and later by the first Christians illustrate how their thinking about him was moulded by their experience of him. In differing ways the titles express the supreme worth of Jesus, in whom God acted decisively to judge and save the world.

Titles used for Jesus during his lifetime.

The personal name Jesus (a Greek form of the Hebrew Joshua) means 'Yahweh is salvation' (*cf.* Mt. 1:21) and so *Saviour* was naturally used first as a description of what Jesus did (Acts 13:23) then later as part of his solemn title (2 Tim. 1:10).

As a result of his activity, he was called *Teacher* (Mk. 4:38) and, to distinguish him from other Jewish teachers, *The Teacher* (Mk. 5:35). Like Jewish teachers he was also styled *Rabbi*, literally 'my great one', a mark of respect which came to mean 'the revered (teacher)'; *e.g.* Mk. 9:5 which RSV translates as *Master*, a title which

269

more accurately translates another Greek word suggesting respect (*e.g.* Lk. 5:5). Another respectful term is *Lord* (Mk. 7:8), which probably represents an original Aramaic *rabbi* but which Luke uses in narratives with the post-resurrection allusion to Jesus' divinity (Lk. 7:13).

The fact that he was regarded as more than an ordinary teacher is implied in the title *Prophet* (Lk. 7:16), which Jesus also used for himself (Lk. 4:24). In some cases this title may have been used in a unique sense; the Jews expected Elijah or a prophet like him to come and usher in the End. Jesus claimed John the Baptist was this prophet (Mt. 17:12f.). John's apparent denial of the fact in Jn. 1:21 may be a denial that he was another expected prophet like Moses (Dt. 18:15ff.), which Peter considered Jesus to be (Acts 3:22ff.); Jewish thought did not always separate the two very clearly.

Jewish hopes for the final establishment of God's rule or kingdom were associated with another figure, a king anointed by God and belonging to the family of David. The Hebrew title of this person was transliterated into Greek as *Messiah*, the corresponding Greek word being *Christ*, and each having the meaning of *Anointed One*; *Son of David* was a natural synonym. Jesus was undoubtedly crucified by the Romans on a charge of claiming to be king of the Jews (Mk. 15:26). He also implicitly acted as the Messiah, being anointed by the Spirit (Lk. 4:18), proclaiming the coming rule of God associated with his own activity (Mt. 12:28), and speaking with the authority that suggested he stood in the place of God (Mk. 2:7). But on the few occasions he spoke about the Messiah (*e.g.* Mk. 12:35; 13:21) he did not directly identify himself as the Messiah. However, Peter named him as such and Jesus did not reject the suggestion although he did play it down (Mk. 8:29f.), probably because the popular concept of Jesus' Messiahship was vastly different from his own and he had to guard against misrepresentation.

The Gospels make it clear that Jesus preferred the title *Son of Man* (see the shift of terminology in Mk. 8:29f./31 and 14:61/62). In the language of his time it appears to have been possible to use the phrase as a modest way of referring to oneself in certain situations. It is often assumed, though, that Jesus derived the title from Dn. 7:13f., in which case it refers to the future coming of a heavenly being described with apocalyptic symbolism (Mk. 13:26). But alongside these references are many to the present humiliation and suffering of the Son of Man (Mk. 8:31) and his earthly life and authority generally (Mk. 2:27f.), and it is hard to see how these could be made of the figure in Daniel. Other scholars, therefore, have suggested that Jesus was simply referring to himself as 'man' or that the early church read back the title after the resurrection. It is perhaps most likely that Jesus identified himself with the figure of authority in Dn. 7:13f. who was destined to rule over the world, but recognized too that the way to that rule lay through humiliation, suffering and rejection.

The figure of the suffering *Servant of the Lord* probably contributed to that recognition although Jesus did not use the title himself (*cf.* Mk. 10:45).

The title *Son of God* expressed Jesus' unique relationship with the Father whom he addressed intimately as Abba (daddy: Mk. 14:36; *cf.* Mk. 9:7; Mt. 11:27). He alone was qualified to reveal God to men, yet did not know all the Father's secret's (Mk. 13:32). The Jewish authorities suspected he was claiming to be a unique Son of God (Mk. 14:61). In this title is found the fullest expression of who Jesus was, although he himself was reticent about using it publicly in his lifetime.

Titles in the early church.

Some 20 years separates the death and resurrection of Jesus from the earliest NT documents (some of Paul's letters). It is therefore difficult to trace the use of various titles and their associated theological understanding in this pre-literary period, which must have been a time of unparalleled creative thinking about the person and work of Jesus.

Clearly terms such as *Teacher* and *Prophet* were no longer appropriate. Surprisingly, however, the title *Son of Man* also seems to have dropped out of use. It is found only on the lips of the dying Stephen (Acts 7:56), as a quotation from the OT (Heb. 2:6; *cf.* Ps. 8:5), and as a description of Jesus in Rev. 1:13 and 14:14 which also resembles Dn. 7:13f. The thought was still alive, though, for the Gospels record Jesus' use of it, and Paul's comparison of Jesus as 'the Man' with

Adam may reflect it (Rom. 5:15; 1 Cor. 15:21). It was probably regarded as appropriate only as a self-designation of Jesus, and it never found its way into confessional statements (Jn. 9:35 being a possible exception). The *Servant* motif reappears in 1 Pet. 2:21ff. and the title in Acts 3:13; 4:27. It was probably used in the Palestinian church but dropped out of use because of its ambiguity (it is the same word as 'child' in Acts) and because its related term 'slave' implies subordination in the Godhead.

According to Peter's speech on the day of Pentecost, God had made Jesus both Lord and *Christ* (Acts 2:36), and this gives the key to the development of Jesus' titles. The resurrection had led the disciples into a new evaluation of Jesus and this was confirmed by the outpouring of the Holy Spirit from the exalted Jesus (Acts 2:33). Jesus' claims to be a Messianic figure had been vindicated. The term *Christ* tended to lose its sense of 'anointed one' and took on the meaning 'saviour', being used especially in connection with Jesus' death and resurrection (*e.g.* Rom. 5:6ff.; 6:3ff.).

The associated title *Lord* was used from the earliest days in the Palestinian church, to judge from the Aramaic phrase *Maranatha*, 'our Lord, come' or 'our Lord has/will come', preserved in 1 Cor. 16:22. The resurrection demonstrated the fact that God had made Jesus Lord (Acts 2:34f.), and Peter quoted Ps. 110:1 to illustrate it, a passage Jesus himself had used to show the Messiah was David's Lord (Mk. 12:36; *cf.* 14:62). New converts became members of the church by confessing Jesus as Lord (Rom. 10:9). The Roman emperor was also called 'Lord' and successive emperors increasingly claimed total allegiance, a fact which was to cause Christians problems (1 Cor. 8:5f.).

The title *Son of God* may be especially associated with Paul, for it is linked with his early preaching in Acts 9:20 but appears only once again in Acts, again on Paul's lips (13:33), where he stresses that God raised Jesus from the dead because he was the Son. The thought of Jesus' pre-existence is to be associated with the title Son, and it is expressed clearly but without the use of the word in the pre-Pauline hymn quoted in Phil. 2:6ff. The picture is of a divine figure who exchanged his heavenly mode of existence for an earthly one. Also relevant is the idea of God giving up his Son to die in Rom. 8:32, which may be connected with Abraham's call to sacrifice Isaac (Gn. 22); the use of the term Son here makes the greatness of the divine sacrifice all the more plain.

Titles used by Paul.

Unexpectedly, perhaps, Paul does not describe Jesus as *Servant* although he does see the Servant's role being fulfilled by the church (Rom. 15:21). The name *Jesus* is rare on its own, too, although frequent in combinations (Lord Jesus, Jesus Christ). His main designation of Jesus is *Christ*. His message was 'the gospel of Christ' (Gal. 1:7). He uses it in many traditional ways but introduces a distinctive emphasis in the phrase 'in Christ',

by which he means that Christ determines the believer's life. He does not mean so much a mystical union with a heavenly figure as that the historical facts of Jesus' death and resurrection condition our existence (*e.g.* 2 Cor. 12:2).

His use of *Lord* was similar to that of the pre-Pauline church. If 'Christ' meant primarily 'Saviour' then 'Lord' expressed the exalted position of Jesus and his rule over the universe and especially over believers. Hence he uses it especially when writing of the Christian duty to obey Jesus (*e.g.* Rom. 12:11), but also for the earthly Jesus (1 Cor. 9:5) especially with reference to 'the Lord's supper' (1 Cor. 10:21). In his phrase 'the God and Father of our Lord Jesus Christ' (2 Cor. 1:2), he is giving Jesus an equality of status with God the Father, and is probably reflecting OT usage of 'Lord' for 'God'. For example, Phil. 2:10f. take up the language of Is. 45:22ff. and apply to Jesus what is said there about God.

Despite Paul's infrequent use of *Son of God* he does reserve it for important summaries of his message (Rom. 1:3f.) and in describing how believers are adopted into God's family (Gal. 4:4ff.). He also describes Jesus as God's *image* (Col. 1:15), and the *firstborn* of all creation (Rom. 8:29). But by the later pastoral letters (1 and 2 Tim., Tit.) the title is not used at all.

Titles of Jesus in John's writings.

The title *Lord* in the Gospel is usually on other people's lips and not in the narrative, although Jesus does describe himself as 'master' (Jn. 13:13f.). On several occasions he is confessed as *Messiah* (*e.g.* Jn. 1:41; 4:29; 11:27) but he does not use the word himself. The title *Son of Man* figures prominently but with a stress on his heavenly origin, his descent into the world, his glorification on the cross and his significance as the giver of life, which is absent from the other Gospels (3:13; 6:27; 12:23).

The fundamental title for Jesus is *Son of God*, indicating the closeness of his loving relationship with the Father (3:16f., 35; 5:20), a relationship of obedience (5:19) and fellowship (12:27f.). The same ideas are expressed by the title *Word* in the Gospel's prologue; Jesus the Word is so closely identified with God that he is called that by Thomas in 20:28. In the letters, John is apparently dealing with opponents who have denied a true and lasting union between the Messiah or Son of God and Jesus, and so *Jesus* is often the subject of statements which express his significance as *Christ* or *Son of God* (1 Jn. 2:22). In Rev. Jesus is seen as *King* and *Lord* (17:14), but most distinctive is the title *Lamb* using 28 times a Greek word not used in other NT allusions to the 'lamb of God'. The slain Lamb is worthy of worship (5:6ff.) and leads God's people in battle (17:14).

Titles in other NT writings.

Hebrews is distinctive in its use of titles. It reverts to using the simple *Jesus* to designate the One who died and has been exalted (Heb. 2:9). But it introduces the title *High priest* and expounds Jesus' work in terms drawn from OT legislation. Underlying this title is Jesus' status as *Son* (of God) who alone can mediate between people and God (Heb. 5:5).

See also INCARNATION; KENOSIS; MESSIAH.

JETHRO. Another name for Moses' father-in-law Reuel, who held a thanksgiving to God for Israel's escape from Egypt and advised Moses to delegate administration (Ex. 18).

JEW. Originally a member of the state of Judah (Ne. 1:2). In the NT it is used of members of the Jewish faith or their leaders; in modern usage it sometimes denotes ethnic birth but not necessarily religion.

JEWELS AND PRECIOUS STONES. Jewellery was worn and valued by people in ancient times, and before the use of coins was a form of transferable wealth (2 Ch. 21:3). Among the types of jewellery mentioned in the Bible are bracelets and ear-rings (Gn. 24:22), necklaces and rings for fingers (Gn. 41:42). Since many types of stone occur in varied colours and because scientific terminology had not been developed, identification of biblical precious and semi-precious stones is not always easy.

Two important lists of stones are given in the Bible. One lists the 12 stones in the high priest's breastplate, each engraved with the name of a tribe of Israel (Ex. 28:17ff.); an abbreviated version found in Ezk. 28:13. Rev. 21:19f. (*cf.* Is. 54:11f.) also lists 12 stones but does not seem to be an exact parallel with the OT list. Nor has any satisfying symbolic relationship between the stones and the 12 tribes (or apostles) been identified. (See illustration no. 25.)

The following alphabetical list is based on RSV renderings.

Agate was probably modern agate, a type of translucent quartz with layers of different colours. In Rev. 21:19 (*chalcedony* in NEB, NIV) it is a green stone, the name being used today for various types of translucent quartz. *Alabaster* was a banded variety of calcium carbonate (modern alabaster is a softer stone, a variety of gypsum), and also described a long-necked perfume flask made of any material (Mk. 14:3). *Amethyst* was the well-known purple transparent crystalline quartz.

Beryl in the OT was probably Spanish gold topaz, but in Rev. 21:20 ordinary green beryl is meant. *Carbuncle* in Ex. 28:17 is probably green felspar (as NEB) but in Is. 54:12 a red stone is meant. For *carnelian* see sardius. *Chrysolite* (Rev. 21:20) is the ancient term for yellow topaz or quartz. *Chrysoprase* (Rev. 21:20) is uncertain; modern chrysoprase is an apple-green chalcedony. *Coral:* black or red marine coral in Ezk. 27:16 but a red stone in La. 4:7. *Crystal* was applied to any hard, transparent colourless substance.

Diamond was probably a white opaque stone; modern diamonds apparently were not known until the 1st cent. AD. *Emerald* was probably a green stone like the modern emerald. *Jacinth* was a blue stone, the word in classical Greek meant hyacinth or bluebell. *Jasper* was a translucent green stone; in Rev. 21 possibly green quartz. For *lapis lazuli* see sapphire.

Onyx may have been a green stone or true onyx (translucent agate with black and white layers). *Pearl* in the NT is undoubtedly the modern pearl noted as ornaments (1 Tim. 2:9); the gates of the New Jerusalem may have been seen as mother-of-pearl (Rev. 21:21). In the OT its meaning is unclear. *Sapphire* was the ancient name for lapis lazuli, a deep blue stone with golden flecks of iron pyrites. *Sardius* was a red stone, possibly modern sard, a form of carnelian which is how RSV renders it in Rev. 21:20. *Topaz* was probably yellow rock crystal or chrysolite.

See also MINING AND METALS; ORNAMENTS.

JEZANIAH. A Judaean military commander who sought Jeremiah's advice (Je. 40:8; 42:1ff.); in 2 Ki. 25:23 he is called JAAZANIAH.

JEZEBEL. The daughter of the priest-king of Tyre and Sidon, she married king Ahab of Israel to ratify an alliance between the two states. She continued worshipping her native god Melqart, the Tyrian Baal, and her staff included 450 of his prophets and 400 prophets of the goddess Asherah (1 Ki. 16:31ff.; 18:19). Her desire to make her gods equal to Israel's God led to the contest on Mt Carmel (1 Ki. 18:17ff.). Her concept of absolute monarchy was alien to Israel and was illustrated by her unscrupulous requisitioning of Naboth's vineyard (1 Ki. 21). She remained in power for 10 years after Ahab's death before being killed by Jehu in 842 BC. In the NT her name had become a byword for apostasy (Rev. 2:20).

JEZREEL (lit. 'God sows'). 1. A city in Issachar and the plain on which it stood; modern Zerin, 90 km N of Jerusalem. Israel assembled there before fighting the Philistines at Gilboa (1 Sa. 29:1); there Naboth had his vineyard (1 Ki. 21:1) and Joram and Jezebel were slain (2 Ki. 9:24ff.). 2. A town in the mountains of Judah (Jos. 15:56).

JOAB (lit. 'Yahweh is father'). The son of Zeruiah, David's half-sister, he led David's forces to victory over the rebels under Abner (2 Sa. 2:12ff.), killing Abner personally probably because he saw him as a potential rival for the king's favour. Later Joab became commander-in-chief of Israel's forces. He could sometimes be magnanimous (2 Sa. 12:28) but also cruel (2 Sa. 11:6ff.); he reconciled David and Absalom (2 Sa. 14:31ff.) but later had a hand in Absalom's death despite the king's injunction that he should be kept alive (2 Sa. 18:14ff.). He also killed a rival commander (2 Sa. 20:3ff.). Later his loyalty to David faltered, he supported the wrong side, and he was killed with Solomon's connivance (1 Ki. 2:28ff.).

JOANNA. A woman healed by Jesus who helped to maintain his travelling disciples, and announced the resurrection. Her husband was a responsible official of Herod Antipas (Lk. 8:1ff.; 24:1ff.).

JOASH, JEHOASH (lit. 'Yahweh has given'). Several OT people, including 2 kings. 1. Son of Ahaziah and 8th king of Judah (c. 837-800 BC). He was hidden by his aunt Jehosheba and uncle Jehoiada the high priest after his family was assassinated, and proclaimed king when aged 7 (2 Ki. 11). He repaired the temple (2 Ki. 12:4ff.) but later misappropriated the Temple treasures (2 Ki. 12:18f.) and was killed in a plot to replace him (2 Ki. 12:21f.). 2. Son of Jehoahaz, 12th king of (N) Israel who reigned c. 801-786 BC. He was under pressure from Assyria, the Aramaeans and Judah; he defeated Judah and sacked Jerusalem (2 Ki. 14:8ff.).

JOB. Apart from the book bearing his name and passing references in Ezk. 14:14, 20; Jas. 5:11, no reliable information about him is available. The land of Uz where he lived may have been in Bashan. He was a rich, respected man who lost his wealth, children and health; the symptoms of his disease are described uncertainly in poetic language. People interpreted his misfortunes as divine punishment for gross sin and threw him out of town. During a long discussion with three friends Eliphaz, Bildad and Zophar, and a later dialogue with the young man Elihu, he maintained his innocence. A revelation of God's sovereignty restored his peace; his wealth doubled and family multiplied again. See also next article.

JOB, BOOK OF. *Contents.* The encounter between God and Satan in heaven (1-2); Job's 'why am I suffering?' (3); the first round of discussion from Eliphaz (4-5), Job (6-7), Bildad (8), Job (9-10), Zophar (11), Job (12-14); the second round from Eliphaz (15), Job (16-17), Bildad (18), Job (19), Zophar (20), Job (21); the incomplete third round from Eliphaz (22) and Bildad (25) with Job's replies in 23-24, 26-27; interlude and Job's summary (28-31); Elihu's intervention (32-37); God's reply (38-42:6); prose epilogue (42:7-17).

Authorship and date. The book is anonymous. One Jewish tradition assigned it to Moses, but this was merely a pious pronouncement not to be taken seriously. Most scholars now date it between 600 and 400 BC, although some still favour a date from Solomon's time, but the book is unique in Jewish literature and no objective dogmatism is possible.

Text and integrity. Job contains the most difficult poetry of the OT and 100 words not found elsewhere. Part of the original MS may have been lost; because it is virtually impossible to ascribe 27:7-23 to Job it may be part of Zophar's missing third speech. Most scholars separate the prose prologue and epilogue from the poetry, but there is no evidence that the prose was added later; it is quite possible that the poetry transformed the heart of an old story into verse. Being highly original, this book does not fit neatly into any category of ancient literature, but it is generally aligned with the Wisdom literature (34:2).

The problem of Job. Job's problem is not so much his sufferings as such, but why God had not acted as the theory of the time said he should, by rewarding the righteous with health, wealth and happiness. The statements of Job's friends are rejected by God not because they are untrue, but too narrow (42:7). Job does not have his questions or charges fully answered, however. Instead, he realizes that his concept of God collapsed because it also was too small. The book does not answer 'the problem of suffering' but proclaims a God so great that no answer is needed, nor possible for finite minds.

JOCHEBED (probably 'Yahweh is glory'). A daughter of Levi and the mother of Moses, Aaron and Miriam (Ex. 6:20; Nu. 26:59).

JOEL, BOOK OF. *Contents.* Four main topics are discussed. 1. The locust plagues (1:1-12), while literal enough, have deeper symbolic meanings concerning Israel's apostasy. 2. The land would become fruitful again when the nation repented (1:13-2:27), genuine sorrow being symbolized by solemn sacrifice and fasting. The locust swarm is likened to the Day of the Lord; the description of locusts reflects first-hand experience of them and they could symbolize the Gentiles before their judgment. The locust devastation will eventually be surpassed by the plenty granted by the Lord after repentance. 3. The outpouring of the Spirit is the apex of the prophecy (2:28-32). Vv. 28f., 32 were clearly ful-

ackground

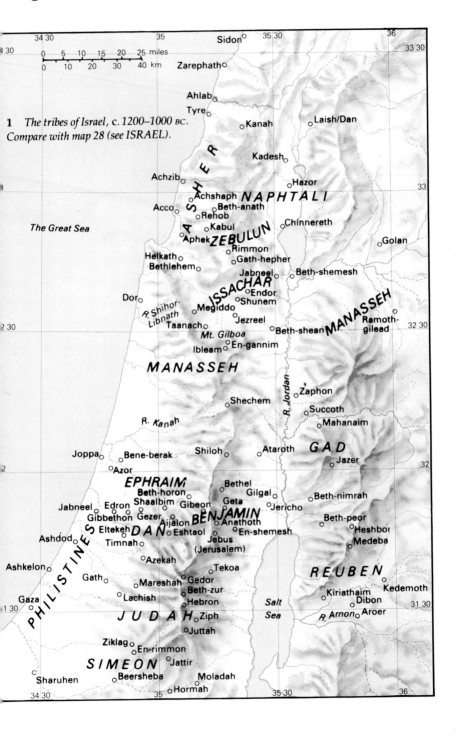

1 *The tribes of Israel, c. 1200–1000 BC.*
Compare with map 28 (see ISRAEL).

34 30   35   35 30   36

33 30

Sidon

Zarephath

Ahlab

Tyre

Kanah

Laish/Dan

Kadesh

A S H E R   N A P H T A L I

Achzib

Achshaph

Hazor   33

Acco   Beth-anath

Rehob

Kabul

Aphek   ZEBULUN

Chinnereth

Golan

The Great Sea

Rimmon

Helkath   Gath-hepher

Bethlehem

Jabneel   Beth-shemesh

I S S A C H A R

Endor

Dor   Shunem

R. Shihor-   Megiddo

Libnath   Jezreel

Taanach   Beth-shean   MANASSEH

Ramoth-

Mt. Gilboa   gilead   32 30

Ibleam   En-gannim

M A N A S S E H

Zaphon

Shechem   Succoth

R. Jordan

Mahanaim

R. Kanah

Joppa   Bene-berak   Shiloh   Ataroth   G A D

Jazer   32

Azor

E P H R A I M   Bethel

Beth-horon   Gilgal   Beth-nimrah

Jabneel   Edron   Shaalbim   Gibeon   Geta

Gibbethon   Gezer   Aijalon   Jericho

Eltekeh   BENJAMIN   Beth-peor

Ashdod   D A N   Eshtaol   Anathoth   Heshbor

Timnah   En-shemesh   Medeba

Azekah   Jebus

(Jerusalem)

Ashkelon   Tekoa

Gath   Gedor   R E U B E N

Mareshah   Beth-zur

Gaza   Lachish   Hebron   Kiriathaim   Kedemoth

Salt   Dibon   31 30

J U D A H   Ziph   Sea   R. Arnon   Aroer

Juttah

Ziklag   En-rimmon

S I M E O N   Jattir

Sharuhen   Beersheba   Moladah

34 30   35   Hormah   35 30   36

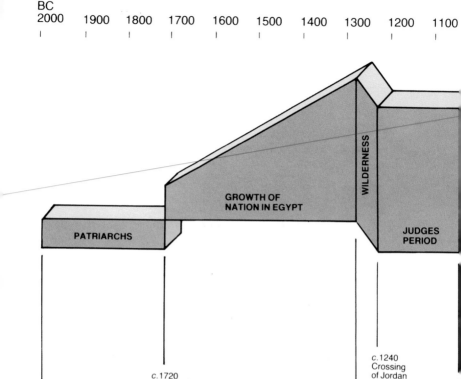

| 2000 | 1900 | 1800 | 1700 | 1600 | 1500 | 1400 | 1300 | 1200 | 1100 |

PATRIARCHS

GROWTH OF NATION IN EGYPT

WILDERNESS

JUDGES PERIOD

c.1240
Crossing
of Jordan

c.1720
Entry into
Egypt

c.2000 BC

c.1280
Exodus

2 *Simplified diagram, showing the history of Israel from patriarchal times to the
fall of Jerusalem in AD 70.*

*Abraham arrived in the promised land around 2000 BC. His great-grandson, Joseph,
brought the whole family to Egypt, where they and their descendants lived and
multiplied for 400 years or so. After the plagues and the passover (see PASSOVER;
PLAGUES OF EGYPT) the whole nation crossed the Red Sea, wandered for forty
years in the desert and finally crossed the Jordan to claim the promised land as their
God-given right.*

*After a period of rule by 'judges' the nation demanded, and got, a king so that they
could be like the other nations round about them. Saul, David and Solomon
successively built a strong military and commercial empire, but Solomon's
successors, Jeroboam and Rehoboam, quarrelled and the land was divided in 930 BC
between Israel in the north and Judah in the south.*

*The Assyrians and then the Babylonians conquered the land and the latter deported a
large proportion of the influential inhabitants into exile. They were restored by the
Persians who allowed them to rebuild Jerusalem's walls and temple in the time of
Ezra and Nehemiah (see EZRA; NEHEMIAH).*

*Israel was never again to be independent in biblical times, falling successively under
Macedonian, Egyptian, Syrian and Roman rule (see CHRONOLOGY OF THE
OLD TESTAMENT).*

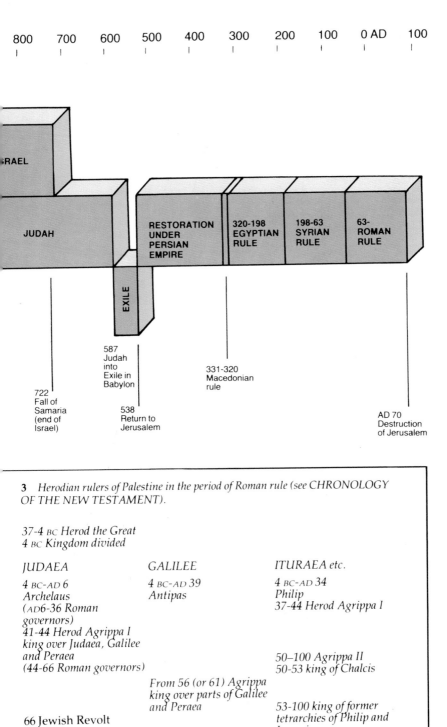

| 800 | 700 | 600 | 500 | 400 | 300 | 200 | 100 | 0 AD | 100 |

ISRAEL

JUDAH

EXILE

RESTORATION UNDER PERSIAN EMPIRE

320-198 EGYPTIAN RULE

198-63 SYRIAN RULE

63- ROMAN RULE

722
Fall of Samaria (end of Israel)

587
Judah into Exile in Babylon

538
Return to Jerusalem

331-320
Macedonian rule

AD 70
Destruction of Jerusalem

---

3 *Herodian rulers of Palestine in the period of Roman rule (see CHRONOLOGY OF THE NEW TESTAMENT).*

37-4 BC *Herod the Great*
4 BC *Kingdom divided*

JUDAEA

4 BC-AD 6
Archelaus
(AD6-36 Roman governors)
41-44 Herod Agrippa I
king over Judaea, Galilee
and Peraea
(44-66 Roman governors)

66 Jewish Revolt

GALILEE

4 BC-AD 39
Antipas

*From 56 (or 61) Agrippa
king over parts of Galilee
and Peraea*

ITURAEA etc.

4 BC-AD 34
Philip
37-44 Herod Agrippa I

50–100 Agrippa II
50-53 king of Chalcis

53-100 king of former
tetrarchies of Philip and
Lysanias

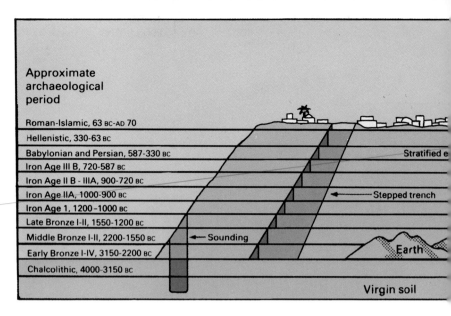

Approximate archaeological period

Period	
Roman-Islamic, 63 BC-AD 70	
Hellenistic, 330-63 BC	
Babylonian and Persian, 587-330 BC	Stratified e
Iron Age III B, 720-587 BC	
Iron Age II B - IIIA, 900-720 BC	
Iron Age IIA, 1000-900 BC	Stepped trench
Iron Age 1, 1200-1000 BC	
Late Bronze I-II, 1550-1200 BC	
Middle Bronze I-II, 2200-1550 BC	←—Sounding
Early Bronze I-IV, 3150-2200 BC	Earth
Chalcolithic, 4000-3150 BC	
	Virgin soil

5 *The tell, or ruin mound, of Arpad (modern Tell Rif'at) (see ARCHAELOLOGY, OLD TESTAMENT PERIOD).*

Photo: A.R. Millard

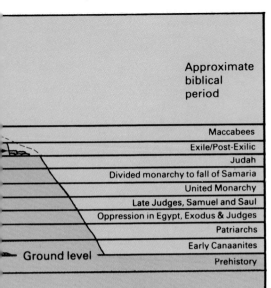

Approximate biblical period
Maccabees
Exile/Post-Exilic
Judah
Divided monarchy to fall of Samaria
United Monarchy
Late Judges, Samuel and Saul
Oppression in Egypt, Exodus & Judges
Patriarchs
Early Canaanites
Prehistory

Ground level

4 *Diagram of a tell (ruin mound) showing successive levels of occupation, each buried by a later one. The most recent is, of course, at the top.*

In reality a tell is much more complex than this and not all periods will be represented. The diagram shows, however, what a valuable source of information the tells provide.

The vertical scale is exaggerated (see ARCHAEOLOGY, OLD TESTAMENT PERIOD).

Uncovering ivories during excavations at Calah (Nimrud) (see ARCHAEOLOGY, OLD TESTAMENT PERIOD).

Photo: D.J. Wiseman

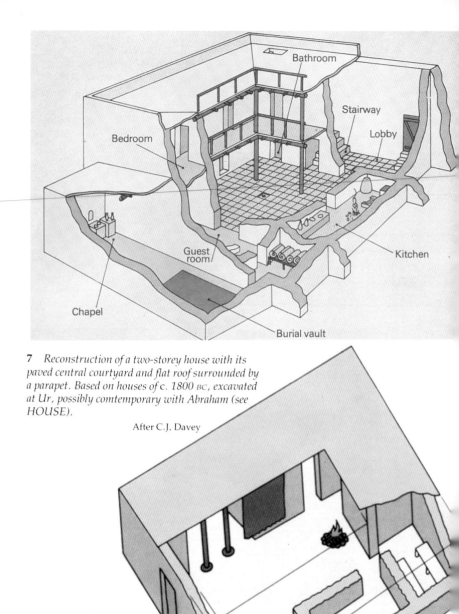

7   *Reconstruction of a two-storey house with its paved central courtyard and flat roof surrounded by a parapet. Based on houses of c. 1800 BC, excavated at Ur, possibly comtemporary with Abraham (see HOUSE).*

After C.J. Davey

8   *Cutaway reconstruction of a typical Israelite house with four rooms grouped round a central courtyard. Excavated at Tell el-Farah (see HOUSE).*

After C.J. Davey

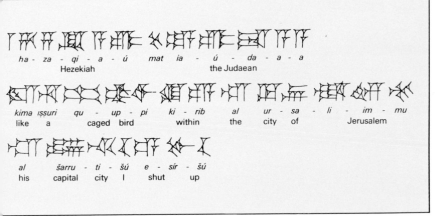

ha - za - qi - a - ú   mat ia - ú - da - a - a
Hezekiah   **the Judaean**

kima ıṣṣuri   qu - up - pi   ki - rib   al   ur - sa - li - im - mu
like   a   caged bird   within   the   city   of   **Jerusalem**

al   šarru - ti - šú   e - sír - šú
his   capital   city   I   shut   up

9 *Above: Hezekiah 'the Judaean', named on a clay prism. 7th century BC (see WRITING).*

10 *Left: Hebrew letters y (ᴧᴠ 'jot'), r and d. The d is distinguished by a small extra stroke or 'tittle' (compare IOTA AND DOT).*

מלך היהודים

REX IVDAEORVM

OBACIΛEYC TⲰNIOYΔAIⲰN

11 *Central panel: 'The King of the Jews', the title written on the cross, in Hebrew, Latin and Greek characters of the 1st century AD (see SUPERSCRIPTION).*

12 *Lower panel: The writing on the wall at Belshazzar's feast (Dan. 5:25) in the Aramaic script of the 6th-5th century BC (see MENE, MENE, TEKEL, PARSIN).*

Old Testament times

13 *Above: Restored interior of the temple of the goddess Ninmah at Babylon (see BABYLON).*

Photo: D.J. Wiseman

14 *Below: Part of the ruins of Babylon with the reconstructed Ninmah temple in the background (see BABYLON).*

Photo: D.J. Wiseman

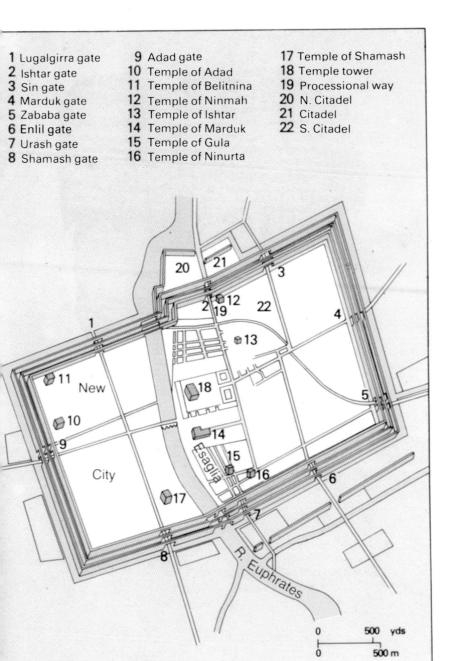

1 Lugalgirra gate
2 Ishtar gate
3 Sin gate
4 Marduk gate
5 Zababa gate
6 Enlil gate
7 Urash gate
8 Shamash gate
9 Adad gate
10 Temple of Adad
11 Temple of Belitnina
12 Temple of Ninmah
13 Temple of Ishtar
14 Temple of Marduk
15 Temple of Gula
16 Temple of Ninurta
17 Temple of Shamash
18 Temple tower
19 Processional way
20 N. Citadel
21 Citadel
22 S. Citadel

New City

Esagila

R. Euphrates

0   500   yds
0   500   m

5   *Plan of Babylon at the time of Nebuchadrezzar II, 605–582 BC (see BABYLON;
NEBUCHADREZZAR).*

16 *Probably the oldest 'map' yet found. This tablet dates from the 7th-6th centuries* BC *and depicts the world as a circle, surrounded by water and with Babylon at its centre, as it was in c. 2400* BC *(see BABYLON).*

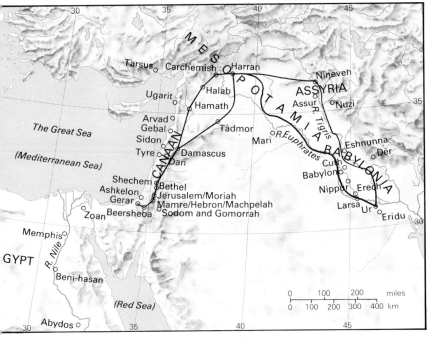

Above: Possible routes for Abraham's journey from Ur to Canaan (see ABRAHAM).

Below: This modern Bedouin tent is probably similar to those used by Abraham, though materials have changed (see ABRAHAM; PATRIARCHAL AGE, PATRIARCHS).

Photo: Sonia Halliday

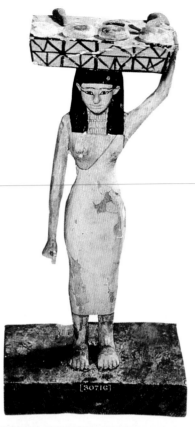

19 *Left: An Egyptian servant girl carr* *a basket of loaves as provision for the dea* *Wooden tomb model,* c. *1900* BC *(see EGYPT; JOSEPH).*

Photo: British Museum

20 *Below: Wooden model of an Egypti* *ship,* c. *1800* BC *(see EGYPT; SHIPS AND BOATS).*

Photo: British Museum

1 *Above: Brickmakers, including Syrian slaves, working under an Egyptian taskmaster, c. 1450 BC (see EGYPT; MOSES).*

2 *Below: Part of an Egyptian papyrus (c. 1200 BC) recording the Wisdom of Amenemope some of whose sayings are similar to the proverb collections in the Old Testament (see PROVERBS).*

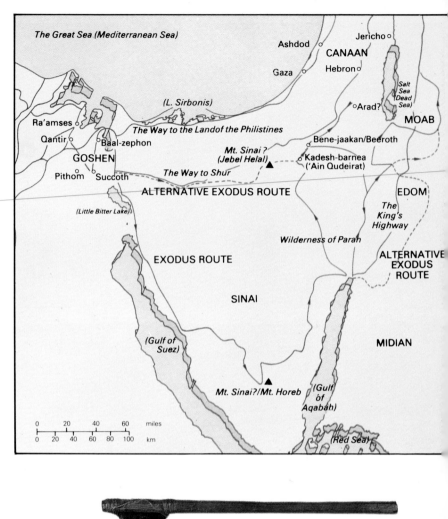

23 *Above: Possible route of the Exodus (see EXODUS).*

24 *Below: Egyptian weapons: a bronze hand-axe with its original haft from 1475*
BC *and below, a copper battle-axe of about 1800* BC *(see EXODUS).*

Photo: British Museum

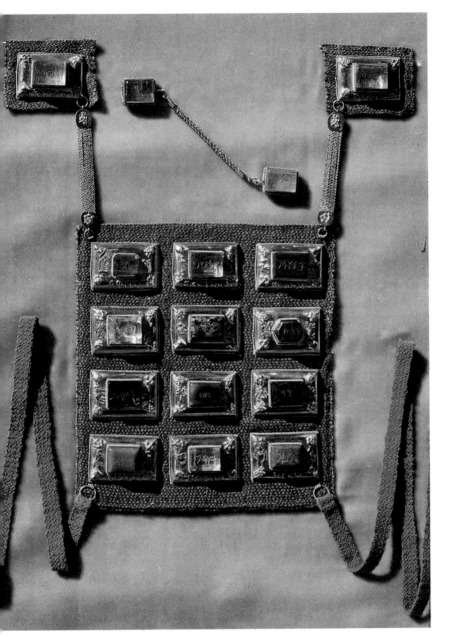

5 *Modern replica of Aaron's breastpiece, showing the stones, each with a symbol of one of the twelve tribes of Israel (see AARON; BREASTPIECE OF THE HIGH PRIEST).*

Photo: Green Lake Center, Wisconsin

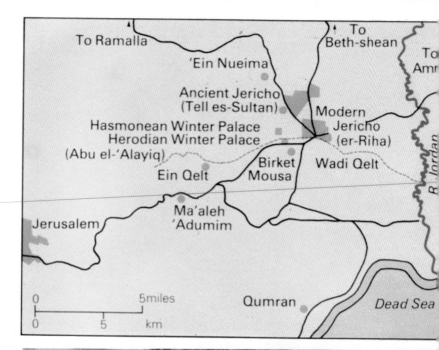

26 *Above: Jericho and adjacent ancient sites (see JERICHO).*

27 *Below: Aerial view of Tell es-Sultan, OT Jericho (see JERICHO).*

Photo: Sonia Halliday

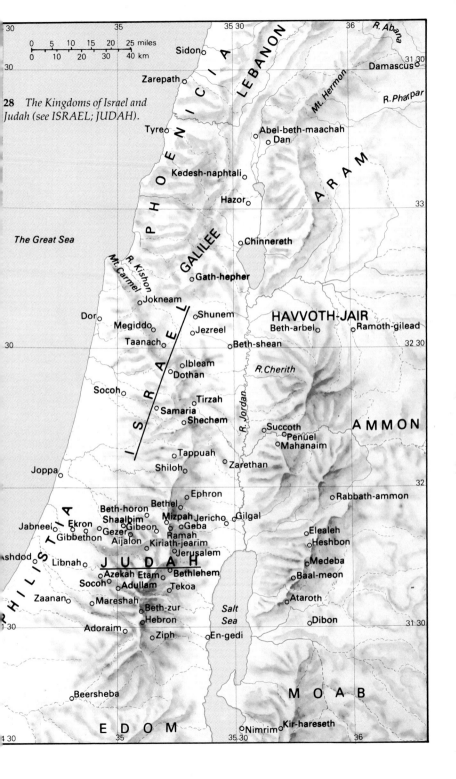

28 *The Kingdoms of Israel and Judah (see ISRAEL; JUDAH).*

0 5 10 15 20 25 miles
0 10 20 30 40 km

Sidon

Zarepath

Tyre

Kedesh-naphtali

Hazor

The Great Sea

PHOENICIA

LEBANON

Mt. Hermon

Damascus

R. Abana

R. Pharpar

Abel-beth-maachah
Dan

ARAM

GALILEE

Chinnereth

Gath-hepher

R. Kishon

Mt. Carmel

Jokneam

Shunem

HAVVOTH-JAIR

Dor

Megiddo

Jezreel

Beth-arbel

Ramoth-gilead

Taanach

Beth-shean

Ibleam

Dothan

R. Cherith

Socoh

Tirzah

R. Jordan

Samaria

Shechem

Succoth

Penuel

Mahanaim

AMMON

ISRAEL

Tappuah

Shiloh

Zarethan

Joppa

Ephron

Rabbath-ammon

Bethel

Beth-horon

Mizpah

Jericho

Gilgal

Shaalbim

Gibeon

Jabneel

Ekron

Gezer

Geba

Ramah

Elealeh

Gibbethon

Aijalon

Kiriath-jearim

Heshbon

Jerusalem

Ashdod

Libnah

JUDAH

Bethlehem

Medeba

Azekah Etam

Baal-meon

Socoh

Adullam

Tekoa

Zaanan

Mareshah

Ataroth

Beth-zur

*Salt
Sea*

Adoraim

Hebron

Dibon

Ziph

En-gedi

Beersheba

MOAB

EDOM

Nimrim

Kir-haresheth

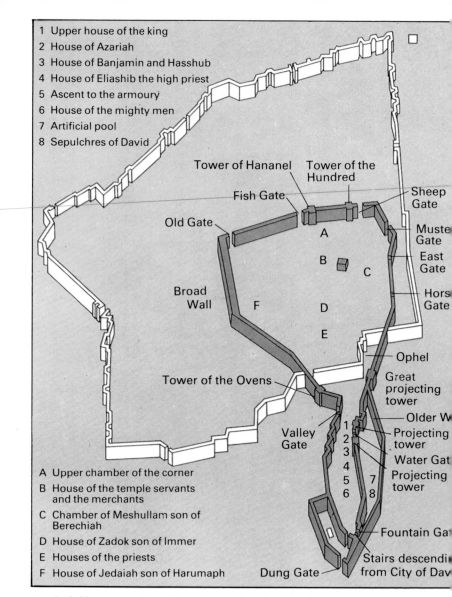

1 Upper house of the king
2 House of Azariah
3 House of Banjamin and Hasshub
4 House of Eliashib the high priest
5 Ascent to the armoury
6 House of the mighty men
7 Artificial pool
8 Sepulchres of David

Tower of Hananel
Tower of the Hundred
Fish Gate
Sheep Gate
Old Gate
Muste Gate
East Gate
Broad Wall
Hors Gate
Tower of the Ovens
Ophel
Great projecting tower
Older W
Valley Gate
Projecting tower
Water Gat
Projecting tower
Fountain Gat
Stairs descendi
from City of Dav
Dung Gate

A Upper chamber of the corner
B House of the temple servants
  and the merchants
C Chamber of Meshullam son of
  Berechiah
D House of Zadok son of Immer
E Houses of the priests
F House of Jedaiah son of Harumaph

29 *Probable reconstruction of Jerusalem as rebuilt by Nehemiah in the 5th century* BC. *Compare with map 32 (see JERUSALEM; NEHEMIAH).*

30 *Athenian vase-painting showing a seated youth studying the alphabet, c. 440 BC (see WRITING).*

31 *A typical Hebrew scroll of the Law (Torah), the five books of Moses (Pentateuch). This example, with modern handles, was in use in a synagogue in Jerusalem for at least 200 years until withdrawn in 1924 owing to wear and the fading of the ink (see LAW; PENTATEUCH).*

Photo: D.J. Wiseman

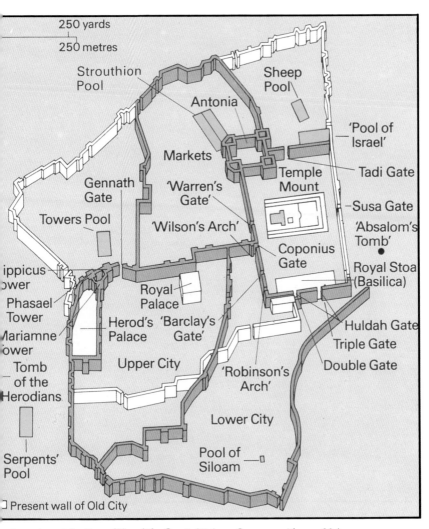

250 yards
250 metres

Strouthion
Pool

Sheep
Pool

Antonia

'Pool of
Israel'

Markets

Temple
Mount

Tadi Gate

Gennath
Gate

'Warren's
Gate'

Susa Gate

Towers Pool

'Wilson's Arch'

'Absalom's
Tomb'

Coponius
Gate

ippicus
ower

Royal Stoa
(Basilica)

Phasael
Tower

Royal
Palace

Herod's 'Barclay's
Palace   Gate'

Huldah Gate

Mariamne
ower

Triple Gate

Tomb
of the
Herodians

Upper City

'Robinson's
Arch'

Double Gate

Lower City

Serpents'
Pool

Pool of
Siloam

⊐ Present wall of Old City

Jerusalem at the time of Herod the Great, 37-4 BC. Compare with map 29 (see
RUSALEM).

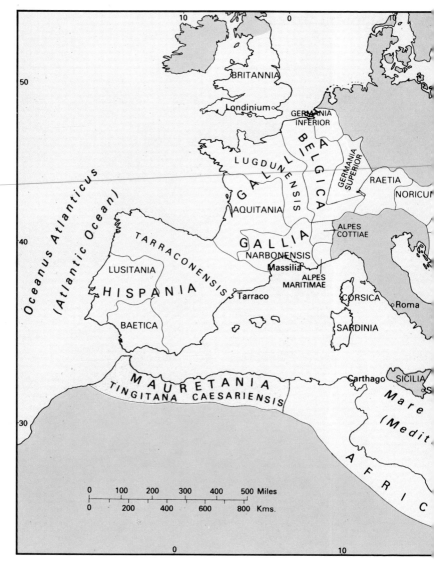

33 *The Roman Empire. This diagrammatic map shows the extent of the Roman Empire, with additions of territory made during the first hundred years of the Christian era, roughly the period covered by the New Testament.*

It is clear that Judaea was ideally placed to be a centre for the spread of the gospel. (Jerusalem is labelled by its Latin name, Hierosolyma.) The Holy Land lay astride trade routes between Africa and Arabia and the north and east. Travel on the Roman road network made journeys to Cilicia, Galatia, Asia and Greece (Macedonia) if not easy, at least practicable.

Latin, the language of government, and Greek, the language of daily business, were spoken throughout the Empire. The New Testament was written in Greek and it is easy to see that the Christian faith arrived on the scene at exactly the right place and

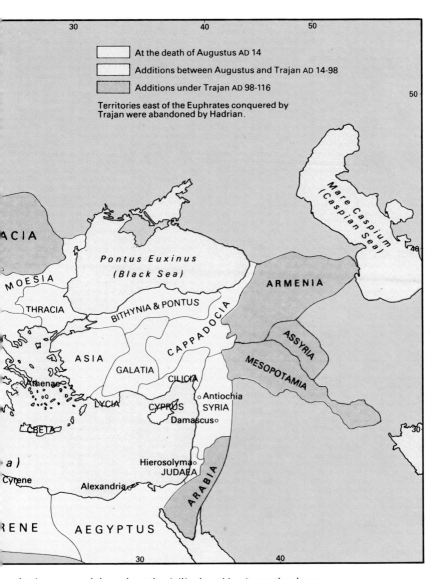

At the death of Augustus AD 14

Additions between Augustus and Trajan AD 14-98

Additions under Trajan AD 98-116

Territories east of the Euphrates conquered by
Trajan were abandoned by Hadrian.

...right time to spread throughout the civilized world as it was then known.

...mmunication was relatively easy but the map shows that the distances involved in
...velling were immense. From Jerusalem to Damascus even is over 150 miles. Paul,
...as and Barnabas must have travelled thousands of slow miles as they founded the
...v churches.

...e description of Paul's sea voyage in Acts 27 and 28 provides a graphic picture of
... dangers and privations of first-century travel (see PAUL; ROMAN EMPIRE).

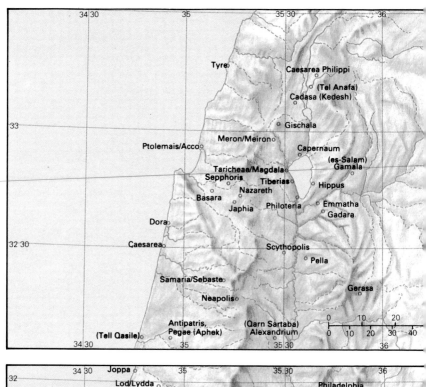

Tyre

Caesarea Philippi

(Tel Anafa)
Cadasa (Kedesh)

Gischala

Ptolemais/Acco
Meron/Meiron

Capernaum

(es-Salam)
Gamala

Taricheae/Magdala
Sepphoris
Tiberias
Hippus

Nazareth
Basara
Emmatha
Japhia
Philoteria
Gadara

Dora

Caesarea
Scythopolis

Pella

Samaria/Sebaste

Gerasa

Neapolis

0   10   20

Antipatris,
Pegae (Aphek)
(Qarn Sartaba)
Alexandrium

(Tell Qasile)
0   10   20   30   40

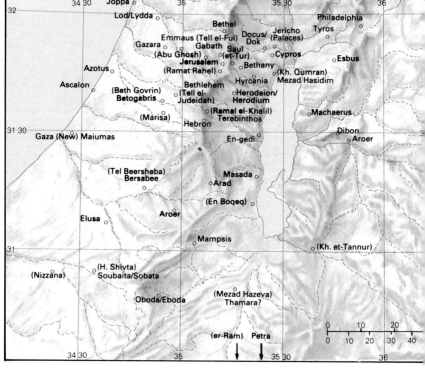

Joppa
Philadelphia

Lod/Lydda
Bethel
Docus/
Jericho
Tyros
Emmaus (Tell el-Ful)
Dok
(Palaces)
Gazara
Gabath
Saul
Cypros
(Abu Ghosh)
(et-Tur)
Esbus
Azotus
Jerusalem
Bethany
(Ramat Rahel)
(Kh. Qumran)
Mezad Hasidim
Ascalon
Bethlehem
Hyrcania
(Beth Govrin)
(Tell el-
Herodeion/
Betogabris
Judeidah)
Herodium
(Marisa)
(Ramal el-Khalil)
Terebinthos
Hebron
Machaerus

Gaza (New) Maiumas
En-gedi
Dibon
Aroer

(Tel Beersheba)
Bersabee
Masada
Arad

Elusa
Aroer
(En Boqeq)

Mampsis
(Kh. et-Tannur)

(Nizzana)
(H. Shivta)
Soubaita/Sobata

Oboda/Eboda
(Mezad Hazeva)
Thamara?

(er-Ram)
Petra

0   10   20

0   10   20   30   40

Left: Some important excavated sites from Herodian (New Testament) times
e ARCHAEOLOGY, NEW TESTAMENT PERIOD).

Above: Part of a model of ancient Jerusalem, showing buildings of the New
stament period on the Ophel, between the temple and the area of the earliest city.
mpare with map 32 (see JERUSALEM).

Photo: J.P. Kane

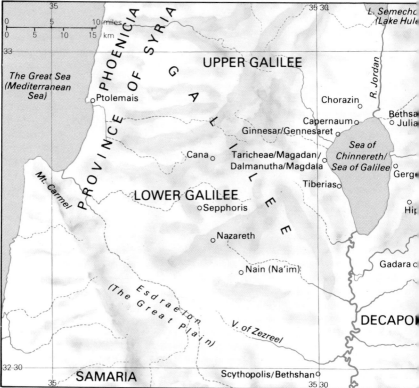

36 *Above: Herodium, site of one of the fortified places built by Herod the Great in Judaea in the 1st century* BC *(see HEROD).*

Photo: J.P. Kane

37 *Below: Galilee in New Testament times, the scene of Christ's childhood and early ministry (see GALILEE).*

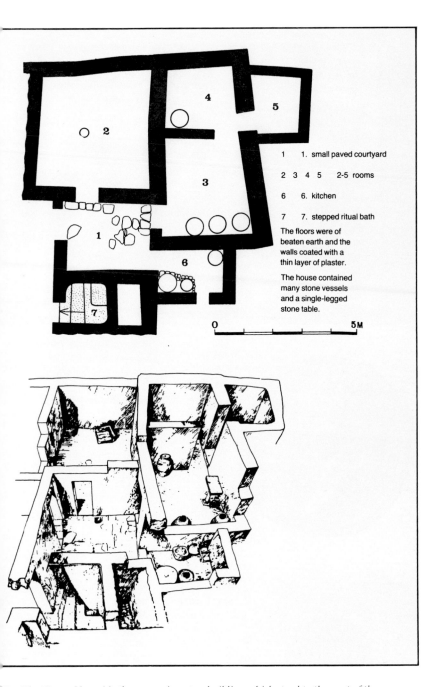

1. small paved courtyard

2 3 4 5   2-5 rooms

6. kitchen

7. stepped ritual bath

The floors were of beaten earth and the walls coated with a thin layer of plaster.

The house contained many stone vessels and a single-legged stone table.

0   5M

38   The 'Burnt House' is the name given to a building which stood to the west of the Temple area in Jerusalem and was destroyed by fire in AD 70 along with the rest of the city. The lower walls still stand up to about a metre in height (see JERUSALEM).

After N. Avigad

39 The New Testament makes no reference to metal working, but this marble relief of a coppersmith's workshop from Pompeii shows several of the processes involved.

In the centre the smith steadies a lump of hot metal on the anvil while his assistant prepares to strike it with a heavy hammer. Above them are the double doors of the furnace. On the left the smith weighs small items and on the right he engraves or embosses a large circular dish. Completed wares decorate the walls.

A child (left) and a watchdog (right) complete the scene which appears to be an example of home-based industry (see METALWORK).

Photo: Robert Hare

40 Gold 'aureus', a coin of Claudius, Roman emperor AD 41–54 (see CLAUDIUS; MONEY).

Photo: British Museum

41 Silver 'tetradrachm' (the equivalent of a shekel) showing the Jerusalem temple with inside, a shrine containing a scroll of the law. AD 132–135 (see MONEY).

Photo: British Museum

*Above: The synagogue at Masada, built by the Zealots c. AD 70, had benches
around the walls and a roof supported by two rows of columns (see SYNAGOGUE).*

Photo: J.P. Kane

*Below: Reconstruction of the synagogue at Meiron in Palestine, showing the
galleries and the Ark of the Law (at the far end) common in synagogue buildings.
3rd–4th centuries AD (see SYNAGOGUE).*

After E.M. and C.L. Myres and J.F. Strange

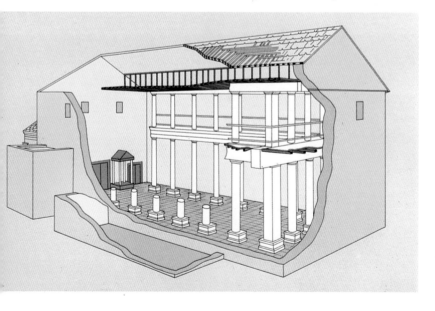

44 *Above: Ruins of Corinth. The Acropolis dominates the city (see CORINTH).*

Photo: A.R. Millard

45 *Below: View across the Kidron Valley showing the Mount of Olives with tomb monuments of the 1st century AD (see BURIAL AND MOURNING; KIDRON; OLIVES, MOUNT OF).*

Photo: Ronald Sheridan

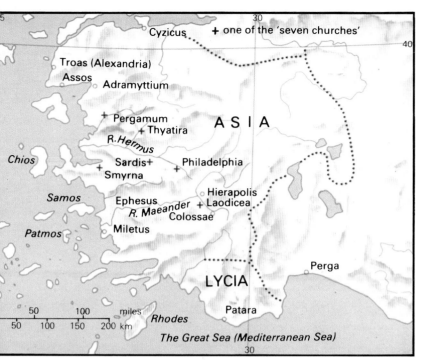

46 *Above: The 'Seven Churches of Asia' of Revelation 1-3, showing also the island of Patmos where John received the revelation (see REVELATION).*

47 *Left: Greek papyrus of part of the book of Revelation (12: 12 – 13:1) from the 3rd century AD (see REVELATION).*
Photo: Chester Beatty Library

COMPARATIVE MEASUREMENT

Biblical term	Biblical equivalent	Approximate mo‹ equivalents	
WEIGHTS			
Old Testament			
Talent (light)	3,000 shekels	30 kg	66 lt
Mina	1/60 talent; 50 shekels	0.5 kg	1.6 ‹
Shekel (royal)		13 g	0.5 (
Shekel (common)		11.5 g	0.4 (
Shekel (temple)	1/2 or 1/3 shekel	5 g	0.2 (
Pim		7.5 g	0.25
Beka	1/2 shekel	6 g	0.25
Gerah	1/20 shekel	0.5 g	0.02
New Testament			
Pound (*litra*)	(Latin *libra*)	327 g	7.5 ‹
Talent	125 libra	40 kg	88 lt
LIQUID MEASURES			
Old Testament			
Bath	Ephah (dry measure)	22 litres	38.5
Hin	1/6 bath	3.6 litres	6 pi
Log		0.3 litre	0.5
New Testament			
Measure (*batos*)		39.5 litres	9 g‹
Firkin (*metrētēs*)		39.5 litres	9 g‹
Pot (*xestes*)		500 cc	1 pi
MEASUREMENT OF LENGTH			
Old Testament			
Cubit		44.5 cm	17.5 in
Span	1/2 cubit	23 cm	9 in
Palm		7.37 cm	3 in
Digit	1/4 palm	1.85 cm	0.75 in
Gomed	2/3 cubit	29.6 cm	11.75 i‹
Reed	6 cubits	266.7 cm	8 ft 9
Hellenistic times			
Schoinos		184.9 cm	196.5 y
Stadion		6.1 km	3.75 m‹
New Testament			
Cubit		44.4 cm/52.5 cm	17.5 in.
Fathom (*orgyia*)		1.8 m	6 ft
Furlong (*stadium*)	100 fathoms	185 m	202 yd
Mile (*milion*)	8 furlongs	1478 m	1,618 y

48 *A selection of comparative measurements of weights, liquid measures and length (see WEIGHTS AND MEASURES).*

filled at Pentecost and aspects of 30f. were fulfilled in Jesus' death. The pillars of smoke could be sand columns raised by desert whirlwinds or the destruction of doomed cities; a solar eclipse can turn the moon blood-red. Paul applies v. 32 to Jesus (Rom. 10:13). Everything here has both an historical meaning and a deeper meaning belonging to the last days. 4. God's enemies will be judged (3:1-21); the references of vv. 3-8 are clearly historical but the full horror of vv. 15ff., 19a, and the full benediction of v. 18 have yet to be realized.

Authorship and date. It betrays a Judaean background but dating is difficult; various scholars assign it anywhere between 800 and 200 BC and all stress its timelessness. If an early date is admitted, then some prophetic battle-cries get their first airing in Joel (3:10; *cf.* Is. 2:4). It is one of the briefest yet most heart-searching OT books, showing how the eternal meets the temporal.

JOGBEHAH. A town in Gilead (Nu. 32:35), modern Jubeihat 10 km NW of Amman.

JOHANAN (lit. 'Yahweh is gracious'). Several people in the OT, most notable of whom was a Jewish leader who supported Gedaliah the governor of Jerusalem after the city fell, and rescued people captured by Gedaliah's murderer Ishmael (Je. 40-43).

JOHN THE APOSTLE. Probably the younger son of Zebedee. His mother was probably Salome who is regarded as the sister of Jesus' mother Mary (*cf.* Mk. 16:1 with Mt. 27:56 and Jn. 19:25); if so, he was Jesus' cousin. His family seems to have been well-off; Zebedee had hired labourers (Mk. 1:20) and Salome helped to provide for the disciples (Lk. 8:3). He may have been the unnamed disciple of John the Baptist in Jn. 1:35ff. He and his brother James were nicknamed 'sons of thunder' by Jesus (Mk. 3:17), probably because they were high-spirited and impetuous Galileans and whose undisciplined zeal was sometimes misdirected (Lk. 9:49, 54). They also seem to have been ambitious (Mk. 10:37), and with Peter formed an inner circle within the 12 apostles (*cf.* Mk. 5:37; 9:2; 14:33).

John is almost certainly the 'disciple whom Jesus loved' in John's Gospel, in which he is never named (Jn. 13:23; 19:26f.), who with Peter discovered the undisturbed grave-clothes in the tomb of Jesus (Jn. 20:3-8). In Acts he remained closely associated with Peter and they bore the brunt of early Jewish hostility to the church (Acts 4:13; 5:33, 40). He and Peter laid hands on Samaritan converts (Acts 8:14), and he was described by Paul as a pillar of the Jerusalem church (Gal. 2:9). Assuming he wrote Revelation, he was exiled to Patmos (Rev. 1:9), but the date of this is uncertain.

Some late (5th cent. AD) and probably unreliable evidence suggested he was martyred about the same time as his brother James (Acts 12:2). Jesus' prophecy in Mk. 10:39 need not imply both met with a simultaneous and violent end. Much stronger is the tradition reflected by Polycrates, bishop of Ephesus (AD 190), that John 'fell asleep' in Ephesus, and by Irenaeus that John lingered on there till the time of the Emperor Trajan (AD 98-117), even though some writings from Ephesus in the early 2nd cent. do not mention him.

JOHN THE BAPTIST. Born *c.* 7 BC to an elderly couple, Zechariah a priest and his wife Elizabeth, he grew to manhood in the Judaean desert (Lk. 1:80) where he received his call to be a prophet *c.* AD 27 (Lk. 3:2). He quickly gained widespread fame as a preacher calling for national repentance. Crowds flocked to hear him, and many of his hearers were baptized in the Jordan confessing their sins. He condemned the established order (Lk. 3:9) and denounced religious leaders. He looked forward to the Coming One whose ministry would be a baptism with the Holy Spirit and fire (Lk. 3:16f.). Among those who came to him for baptism was Jesus, whom John apparently hailed as the Coming One, although later when in prison he began to doubt (Jn. 1:35f.; *cf.* Lk. 7:18ff.).

He seems to have left the Jordan valley for a while to work in a Samaritan area (Jn. 3:23), which could explain Jesus' statements of 4:37f.; he was reaping what John had previously sown. Then he returned to the territory of Herod Antipas, probably Peraea; Herod imprisoned him at Machaerus being the leader of a dangerous movement who had denounced his second marriage. Some months later, he was beheaded (Mk. 6:14ff.).

In the NT, John is presented as the forerunner of Christ. In Jesus' estimation he was the promised Elijah of Mal. 4:3f. (Mk. 9:13) and the last and the greatest of the prophets (Lk. 16:16). His disciples stayed together as a group for some time after his death (*cf.* Acts 19:1ff.).

JOHN, GOSPEL OF. *Contents.* 1. The revelation of Jesus to the world: Prologue (1:1-18); the manifestation of Jesus (1:19-2:11); the new message (2:12-4:54); Jesus the Son of God (5); the bread of life (6); conflict with the Jews (7-8); the light of the world (9); the good shepherd (10); the resurrection and the life (11); the shadow of the cross (12:1-36a); epilogue (12:36b-50). 2. The revelation of Jesus to his disciples: The last supper (13:1-30); the farewell discourses (13:31-16:33); Jesus' prayer (17). 3. The glorification of Jesus: Jesus' trial and death (18-19); Jesus' resurrection (20); the commission to the disciples (21).

Author and date. Fragments of John's Gospel have been found which date from before AD 150. Traditions which attribute it to John the apostle are given by Irenaeus (*c.* AD 180) and Clement of Alexandria (*c.* 200). However, others are silent on the matter, including Papias who had close access to apostolic traditions and Polycarp who according to Irenaeus was an associate of John. The traditional view is that it was written by a Palestinian Jew who was an eyewitness of the events recorded and 'the disciple whom Jesus loved', identified with John the apostle and the son of Zebedee.

The identification has been challenged by some who suggest John was incapable of writing such a Gospel (on the basis of Acts 4:13), but this ignores such analogies as the 'unlearned' Bunyan who wrote *Pilgrim's Progress* and does not take into account the fact that no other Gospel was written by one of the Twelve for comparison. The church was slow to accept the Gospel as authentic, however. This might be explained if John used an amanuensis, or if a disciple (or group of disciples) of John wrote it using the apostle's memoirs and theology as its basis. But the tradition that John dictated it is widespread and bears the marks of genuineness; there are good grounds for maintaining a close association between him and the actual writing of the Gospel. Ephesus has traditionally been accepted as the centre of John's ministry and the writing of the Gospel. The Gospel is usually reckoned to have been composed in the 90s, largely because the thought it contains seems to have developed from both that of the Synoptic Gospels and of Paul's letters.

Purpose and theological structure. The purpose is clearly stated in 20:30f.: it is a selection of some of Jesus' 'signs' to bring readers to the belief that he is the Messiah and Son of God and thus to an experience of eternal life. Hence it is primarily evangelistic, and written for a Jewish audience probably outside Palestine; while not writing simply to counter the current dangers of Gnosticism, John probably also had such deviant views of the person of Christ in mind.

As an historical work it is selective. Unlike the Synoptic Gospels, it concentrates less on Galilee and much more on Jerusalem where the incidents often relate to Jewish feasts (2:13; 5:1; 6:4; 7:2; 10:22; 11:55). While the narrative of the last week or so of Jesus' life follows the Synoptists' lines, it also includes fresh material such as the farewell discourses and prayer (14-17), and details of the trial before Pilate and the resurrection appearances. John's main purpose is to reveal Jesus' glory as Son of God; this is claimed by Jesus (17:5, 24), seen by his disciples (1:14) and evidenced in his signs (5:41; 7:18). This Jesus has brought God's truth (18:37; 14:6), leading people into true worship (4:23f.) and freedom (8:32ff.).

The signs of Jesus authenticated his character and mission (3:2; 9:16), and are usually quoted to illustrate something of spiritual significance. He also gave verbal 'signs', such as the 7 'I am' sayings (6:35; 8:12; 10:7, 11; 11:25; 14:6; 15:1; with possibly 8:24 in addition) which were veiled claims to deity. John emphasizes that Jesus' words and deeds were witnessed by the crowds (12:17), the disciples (15:27) as well as the Scriptures (5:39) and the Father (5:37).

He described Jesus as the Word (1:14, 17) at a time when Jews were beginning to see the Word as a somehow separate being from God, and when educated pagans saw the Word as the principle of order and rationality in the universe. He also described Jesus as the awaited Messiah (11:27), the Son of Man who reveals God (3:13), and the Son of God through whom people may receive salvation (3:36). This latter title ascribes full deity to Jesus (*cf.* 1:1 and 20:28). Jesus came to bring life (John's favourite word for salvation), which people receive by believing in him (6:29) who is 'the life' (14:6). Or, using another picture, people are in darkness until Jesus brings the light of life (12:46).

Through Jesus' sacrificial death (10:11) as saviour of the world (4:42) sin is removed (1:29), life is given (6:51) and people are drawn to God (12:32). When a person believes in Jesus, the Holy Spirit creates a radical change known as the new birth (3:1ff.) by which he becomes a child of God (1:12). From the human side this change is the product of faith, which is self-commitment to him (3:16). This new relationship with God (10:14f.) is characterized by love (14:21ff.) and described as 'abiding' in Jesus (15:4ff.). It automatically makes the believer a member of Jesus' 'flock' or a branch of his 'vine' (10:10f.; 15:1ff.), within which relationships are to be based on loving service (13:1ff.). This 'church' is no closed fellowship for others are to believe and enter it (17:20). It will continue after Jesus has been glorified (14:12) for he will be present through his Spirit (14:18).

Background to John's thought. It is possible that a source of Aramaic sayings may be behind the Gospel, Aramaic being Jesus' mother tongue. John's thought is often expressed using very similar features to Jewish writing, and most of its key ideas are taken from the OT (*e.g.* word, life, light, shepherd, bread, vine). John shows some parallels of thought to some mystery religions; it therefore would have been intelligible to pagans as well as Jews. There must have been 1st cent. beginnings of 2nd cent. Gnosticism, and as in Colossians and 1 John there are indications of an awareness of it in the Gospel although it was probably not written under their influence or directly to counter them, as some have suggested. (See GNOSTICISM; HERMETIC LITERATURE.)

Relation to the Synoptic Gospels. The question as to whether John knew the other three Gospels is still open. The closest contacts are with Luke, although they probably do not prove literary dependence. Clement of Alexandria claimed that John was urged to write 'a spiritual Gospel' at a time when he perceived 'that the external facts had been made plain'. The Synoptic and Johannine historical narratives can be made to fit together in a convincing manner, and of course none of the Gospels claims to give an exactly chronological account. However, real problems do remain, such as the date of the cleansing of the temple and of the last supper and crucifixion, although even these do not affect the substance of the records.

The teaching ascribed to Jesus in John differs markedly from that in the other Gospels in both style and content. John, for example, has no parables, whereas the long discourses in John are not paralleled in the others. There are sufficient similarities, however, to believe that the new material is as authentic, and Mt. 11:25ff. is a reminder that 'Johannine' language is not entirely absent in the Synoptic Gospels. The impression is that John interprets Jesus' life rather than giving a strictly literal account of it; it does not contradict the other Gospels but interprets the Person who is depicted in them.

As William Temple put it, the Synoptists provide a photograph of Jesus, and John provides a portrait.

JOHN, LETTERS OF. *Background and contents of 1 John.* Although called a letter, it is more like a tract needed because of the activities of false teachers who had left the church to which John is writing and who were trying to seduce the faithful (2:18f., 26). They believed they had superior knowledge to ordinary Christians (2:20, 27). They were the forerunners of later heretics known as Gnostics. They appear to have denied that Jesus was the Messiah (2:22), the pre-existent (1:1) Son of God (4:15; 5:5, 10) come in human flesh (4:2) to bring salvation through his death (4:9f.)—something repugnant to the Gnostics' clear distinction between 'evil' flesh and 'pure' spirit. The false teachers also claimed to be sinless (1:8, 10) but were in fact morally indifferent (2:4, 15).

After stating his purpose as explaining what he has seen and heard of Jesus Christ and encouraging joyful fellowship between himself, his readers and God (1:1-4), he asserts that God is light (1:5-2:6), assuring those who admit their sin that God offers forgiveness through Christ. Christians are then to follow him faithfully (2:7-17). But false teachers have arisen (2:18-27). True believers must therefore abide in Christ and test themselves and their teachers by their likeness to him (2:28-3:3). Since Jesus came to take away sin (*cf.* 1:8), his people cannot consciously pursue sinful ways; by contrast, the false teachers make no attempt to emulate the perfect ideal of Jesus (3:4-10). Christians, whose mark is love and self-sacrifice, will be hated by the world (3:11-18), but their deeds of love will help to reassure them that they belong to God, and give them greater confidence in prayer (3:19-24).

Correct belief about Jesus having come in the flesh shows whether people speak by the Spirit of God or by the spirit of antichrist (4:1-6). God himself is love and loving relationships indicate that God dwells within his people (4:7-12). So the grounds of Christian assurance are possession of the Spirit, confession of Jesus and practice of love, and all who are born of God can overcome the forces of evil (4:13-5:4). God himself has testified to the Christ who submitted to baptism and shed his blood on the cross, as has the Spirit (5:5-12; *cf.* Jn. 15:26). Those who belong to God can be assured of eternal life; they are to win back their erring brethren through prayer and they have the power not to sin

(5:13-21).

Background and contents of 2 and 3 John. These are real letters each long enough to be written on a standard sheet of papyrus (25 by 20 cm) and conforming to the pattern of letter writing at the time. 2 John was probably addressed to a church symbolized as 'the elect lady'. False teachers were denying that the Son of God had been incarnate in human flesh, but their teaching abandoned true faith in God. Such teachers were not to be given hospitality. 3 John is a private letter (like Paul's letter to Philemon) addressed to the author's friend Gaius, a leading member of another church. He is commended for his attachment to truth and hospitality offered to travelling preachers. He is contrasted with Diotrephes, who may have been aspiring to be 'bishop' in his own church and resented any outside interference. (See also ELECT LADY.)

Place of writing, authorship and date. All 5 Johannine writings probably emanate from the province of Asia. The heretics of 1 John resemble the Cerinthians who were in Asia Minor at the end of the 1st cent., and tradition connects their author with Ephesus. It is certain that the same person wrote all three letters, and reasonably certain that this author also wrote the Gospel of John; the Gospel and the letters certainly represent the same mind at work in different situations. However, there are considerable stylistic differences between these writings and Revelation, which is ascribed to John the Apostle. Some have suggested that a different John wrote Revelation, others that John's disciples wrote the Gospel and letters and John himself wrote Revelation, but it is still plausible that John the Apostle (or one of his close disciples) wrote the Gospel and letters. The date of the letters cannot be determined except that the heresy they attack suggests a date between AD 60 and 90.

JOKNEAM, JOKMEAM. A city of Zebulun, modern Tel Yoq-neam 12 km NW of Megiddo; it was given to the Levites (Jos. 21:34). There was another levitical Joknean, in Ephraim (1 Ch. 6:68).

JOKSHAN. A son of Abraham and Keturah, father of Sheba and Dedan (Gn. 25:2f.).

JOKTAN. The father of several people whose names are associated with tribes and places in S Arabia (Gn. 10:25ff.). The name is unknown outside the Bible but modern S Arabian tribes claim pure Arabs descend from him.

JONAH (lit. 'dove'). A Hebrew prophet during the 8th cent. BC from the vicinity of Galilee. He predicted the territorial expansion of Jeroboam II (2 Ki. 14:25) and is the hero of the OT book of Jonah. See next article.

JONAH, BOOK OF. *Contents.* Jonah, told by God to go to preach against Nineveh, rebels and during a storm at sea is thrown overboard and swallowed by a fish (1). He prays from the fish and is disgorged onto the shore (2). He goes to Nineveh, and the city repents (3). He is angry at their repentance, and God teaches him to have compassion on people (4).

Authorship and date. It does not use the first person and does not claim to have been written by Jonah, but gives no clue as to its author. It is probably later than the 8th cent. BC because 3:3 implies Nineveh is no more (it was destroyed in 612 BC) and probably not earlier than the 6th cent. It was known and venerated by the end of the 3rd cent.

Interpretations. It has been variously explained as mythology, allegory, commentary, parable and history. Most modern commentators see it as primarily a parable but also partly a commentary, *i.e.* relating traditions about Jonah to the bare details of 2 Ki. 14. Regarding it as parable is not merely to avoid believing the miracle of the great fish; such parables are frequent in Scripture, but no others are so long (*cf.* 2 Sa. 12:1ff.; Lk. 10:30ff.). Jewish tradition accepted it as historical, and Jesus probably did too (Mt. 12:39f.). The fish, and the rapid growth of the gourd in ch. 4 may have been genuine miracles, and the size of Nineveh which is apparently unhistorical (see 3:3) could relate to a larger area than the city itself. Both the view of it as historical and as parable are possible.

However, it is agreed that the purpose of the book is didactic, ending with a challenging question (*cf.* Lk. 10:36). It stresses the universal power and mercy of God; it may have been a challenge to avoid narrow Judaism, or to missionary work.

JONATHAN (lit. 'Yahweh has given'). Several OT people, including Saul's eldest son and heir to the throne, which made his friendship with David, who eventually succeeded Saul, the more remarkable (1 Sa. 20:31ff.). He was an able and courageous warrior (2 Sa. 1:22), illustrated by his lone attack on a Philistine garrison (1 Sa. 14:6ff.). Jonathan's pact of friendship with David (1 Sa. 18:1ff.) led him to defy his own father and endanger his own life (1 Sa. 19-20), making him a model of loyalty to truth. He died in the same battle as his father (1 Sa. 31:2).

JOPPA. The only natural harbour between Haifa and the Israel-Egypt border. After Israel's occupation of Canaan it belonged to Dan but soon fell into Philistine hands. Simon Maccabaeus annexed it to Judaea in the 2nd cent. BC (1 Macc. 13:11); it features in Acts 10. It is now the S part of Tel Aviv-Jaffa.

JORAM: See JEHORAM.

JORDAN. The name aptly means 'the descender'; the Jordan depression, formed from a rift valley, is the lowest on earth. From Lake Huleh 70 m above sea level the valley drops to 200 m below sea level in just 10 km to Lake Tiberias (Galilee); at the N end of the Dead Sea (120 km from Lake Huleh) the river has plunged to 393 m below sea level.

The Jordan valley was one of the earliest sites of urban settlement in the world. The Natufians changed from hunting to urban life at Jericho c. 7000 BC, and a pottery-making people arrived c. 5000 BC. Amorites destroyed many urban centres in the valley c. 2200 BC, but after 1900 BC the Hyksos invasion led to elaborate urban defences being built. The Egyptians defeated the Hyksos and rebuilt the fortress towns before the Israelite invasion c. 1220 BC, which may be evidenced archaeologically by the destruction of Hazor, Debir and Lachish.

At the N end of the valley a dense population clustered around the Sea of Galilee in NT times, and the town of Capernaum especially features in the Gospels (e.g. Mk. 1:21; Lk. 7:1ff.). The surrounding hills also featured in Jesus' ministry (Mt. 5:1; 28:16; Lk. 9:10ff.). See also GALILEE, SEA OF.

S of Galilee the river's flood plain (the Zor) is covered with vivid green vegetation and stands in sharp contrast to the deeply dissected and arid slopes on either side; the luxuriant growth, once the haunt of wild animals, is frequently mentioned in the OT (e.g. Je. 12:5; 49:19). Nine perennial streams enter the Jordan on the E between the Yarmuk and Jabbok rivers; Elijah's brook Cherith may have been a seasonal tributary of the Jabesh (1 Ki. 17:1ff.). Near the mouth of the Jabbok the Jordan could be crossed (e.g. Jdg. 8:4f.; 2 Sa. 19:15ff.). Israel appears to have crossed it in this area at Adam (modern Tell Damiyeh) 26 km N of Jericho (Jos. 3:1ff.); S of the Jabbok the swift current makes crossings more difficult.

JOSEPH (lit. 'May he (God) add (sons)'). *Old Testament*. Joseph was the 11th and favourite son of Jacob, his 1st son by Rachel (Gn. 30:24). A spoilt boy, he is famous for his 'coat of many colours' (RV) or 'long robe with sleeves' (RSV, Gn. 37:3; either translation is possible) which evoked his brothers' jealousy. Instead of killing him as they had first planned, they sold him as a slave to travelling traders. Reuben, who wanted to rescue Joseph, was probably absent guarding the flocks (a necessary precaution to take when strangers approached) and returned only after Joseph had been taken away (Gn. 37:22, 29). The traders are described as both Ishmaelites and Midianites; the terms overlap (cf. Jdg. 8:24 where the Midianites are also called Ishmaelites) and such usage of multiple terms is typical of Near Eastern documents. Joseph was sold by them to the Egyptian Potiphar (Gn. 37:36); his own story of having been kidnapped (Gn. 40:14f.) was a desperate plea of innocence which frank admission of having been sold by his blood brothers would have rendered suspect.

He was one of many Semites who became servants (some of them in high and trusted positions) in Egyptian households between 1900 and 1600 BC; one record from c. 1740 BC indicates that 45 out of 79 servants listed were 'Asiatics' (Semites like Joseph). Some Egyptian documents also indicate that Potiphar's wife was not the only such person to attempt to seduce a servant, but when she accused Joseph of the sin he was flung into prison (Gn. 39). His fellow prisoner the butler (Gn. 40:1) should be rendered 'cup-bearer'; bakers were well-known in Egypt although 'chief bakers' were not apparently so called. Dreams were considered important in the East and his God-given ability to interpret them led to Joseph's eventual release and elevation to high office (Gn. 40-41). To appear in court he had to be properly shaved and robed in linen (Gn. 41:14), and was invested into office in traditional Egyptian manner (Gn. 41:42). It seems probable that he was vizier, second only to the Pharaoh, but some scholars suggest he was minister of agriculture. Egypt was famed for its agricultural wealth but it did experience periodic famines.

Pharaoh invited Joseph's family to settle in Egypt, and the brothers were re-united and reconciled (Gn. 43-46); Pharaoh sent wagons for them which were probably the 2-wheeled ox carts featured on Egyptian paintings 200 years later. Differences of custom explain why the family was given a secluded area to live in (Gn. 46:34). Joseph in his administration made Egypt in fact what it had always been in theory: Pharaoh's land of which the people were tenants (Gn. 47:16ff.). He moved people to the nearest cities which had granaries; the RSV emendation about making them slaves (Gn. 47:21) is unnecessary. Joseph and his father were embalmed in the Egyptian manner (Gn. 50:2f., 26) and placed in wooden coffins which would have had a face portrait at the head end. The tribes of Ephraim and Manasseh, Joseph's sons, are sometimes called the tribe or house of Joseph. See also EGYPT, and separate articles on the people and places mentioned.

New Testament. Joseph was the husband of Mary the mother of Jesus; from Mt. 1:20 he seems to have been a descendant of David. Matthew and Luke record that Mary and Joseph were engaged but that she became pregnant before they had sexual intercourse (Mt. 1:18; Lk. 1:27, 34f.). Joseph acted as a father to Jesus, fleeing for safety to Egypt before returning to Nazareth (Mt. 2); Jesus' words in Lk. 2:49 may indicate he knew Joseph was not his natural father. There is no reference to Joseph during Jesus' ministry, and the word to John from the cross would imply that Joseph had died (Jn. 19:26f.). It is natural to assume that Jesus' brothers in Mk. 3:31; 6:3 were subsequent children of Joseph and Mary born after Jesus. See also GENEALOGY OF JESUS CHRIST.

JOSEPH OF ARIMATHEA. A secret disciple of Jesus (Jn. 19:38) and a member of the Jewish Sanhedrin who provided linen and a tomb for Jesus' burial (Mt. 27:57ff.). A legend, unlikely to be authentic, says that he founded the first Christian settlement in Britain, at Glastonbury.

JOSEPHUS, FLAVIUS. A Jewish historian born AD 37/38 and died early in the 2nd cent. He became a Pharisee when aged 19, and strongly opposed the Jewish revolt against Rome in AD 66. He surrendered to the Romans with the only other survivor at the stronghold at Jotapata, and joined the Roman headquarters during the siege of Jerusalem as interpreter. He settled in Rome after the fall of Jerusalem, where he devoted himself to literary activity. His best known works are *Jewish Antiquities* and *History of the Jewish War*. For the period 175 BC-AD 74 Josephus is of incomparable value, and he provides useful background material to the NT period.

JOSHUA. 1. The son of Nun, a young man at the time of the Exodus who became Moses' personal assistant (Ex. 33:11). He was one of the spies sent into Canaan and he backed Caleb's minority report recommending invasion (Nu. 13-14). He was formally consecrated as Moses' successor to military leadership in the plains by the Jordan (Nu. 27:18ff.), when he was about 70 years old. He fought successful campaigns against the Canaanites and allocated the land to the 12 tribes at Shiloh, where the national sanctuary was set up. See also the next article. 2. The name of the high priest when the altar was repaired and the Jerusalem temple dedicated in 537 BC. In 520 BC he was encouraged in the work by the prophets Haggai and Zechariah; he was named prophetically 'Branch' or 'Shoot' (Zc. 6:12).

JOSHUA, BOOK OF. *Contents.* It records the invasion of Canaan by Israel and its partition among the 12 tribes. The invasion: Joshua assumes command and the Jordan is crossed (1-4); a bridgehead is established from Gilgal to Ai (5-8); the S campaign (9-10); the N campaign (11). The settlement: list of defeated enemies (12); the early settlements (13-17); later settlements, cities of refuge and towns for the Levites (18-21); the way ahead (22-24).

Structure and author. In the Hebrew Scriptures, Joshua heads the historical section known as 'Former Prophets' covering the period from the invasion to the Exile. Chs. 1-11 form a continuous narrative providing a broad picture of events. In the second half the author uses many sources in telling Joshua's story and showing how Israel fulfilled God's promise that they would possess the land. There are strong echoes of the style and concerns of Deuteronomy in the book, and this has led to theories about its author coming from a 'deuteronomic school' of thought; its dating would then depend on the view taken about Deuteronomy itself. But the book gives no indication of who was responsible for the final compilation, nor when it took place.

Historical and spiritual content. Archaeological evidence for the period is very incomplete but there is sufficient proof of the destruction of Canaanite society (*e.g.* at Hazor) to allow the account of the invasion to be taken seriously. The importance of the book for Christianity is that it shows God's faithfulness to his covenant, records the development of his purpose for the nation, gives reasons for failures and provides analogies for discipleship. Israel needed to be rid of the Canaanite culture which would jeopardize its own faith in God; the 'rest' it attained in Canaan (Ps. 95:11) is used in Heb. 4:1ff. as prefiguring the rest and victory provided by Christ.

JOSIAH (lit. 'may Yahweh give'). The 17th king of the S kingdom of Judah. He became king aged 8 after the assassination of his father Amon and then reigned *c.* 640-609 BC (2 Ki. 21:24-23:30). He turned the nation back to God, freeing it from Assyrian and other pagan religious practices. Taking advantage of the weakening power of the Assyrians he extended his reforms into Israel too (2 Ch. 34:3ff.). In 622/1 BC the 'book of the law' was found in the temple (2 Ki. 22:8ff.). Normally considered to be Deuteronomy, this led to further reform. The covenant was renewed and the Passover celebrated in a grand way (2 Ki. 23). Josiah was killed in battle with Pharaoh Neco II of Egypt in 609 BC.

JOTBAH. Manasseh's wife's birthplace; possibly Kh. Jefat 20 km E of Sea of Galilee.

JOTBATHA. A stopping place in the Israelites' desert wanderings, possibly Tabeh on the W shore of the Gulf of Aqabah.

JOTHAM (lit. 'Yahweh is perfect'). 1. The youngest of Gideon's (Jerubbaal's) 70 legitimate sons and sole survivor of Abimelech's massacre (Jdg.

9). 2. Son of Uzziah and 12th king of Judah. He feared God and was co-regent from *c.* 750 BC and sole ruler *c.* 740-732 BC.

JOY. In both OT and NT, a quality and not simply an emotion founded upon and derived from God (Ps. 16:11; Rom. 15:13). In the OT it is especially expressed in noisy excitement at religious festivals and enthronements of kings (*e.g.* Dt. 12:6f.; 1 Ki. 1:39f.). In the Psalms it is a mark of both corporate worship (Ps. 42:4) and personal adoration (Ps. 43:4). Isaiah associates joy with the coming fullness of God's salvation (Is. 49:13).

In the NT, joy is associated with major events in Jesus' life (Lk. 2:10; 19:37) and the gift of the Spirit (Acts 13:52); it is the result of a deep fellowship between Christ and his church (Jn. 16:22ff.). Joy may be the outcome even of suffering (Col. 1:24); it is closely associated with love as the fruit of the Spirit (Gal. 5:22); and is to be a mark of discipleship (Phil. 3:1).

JOZACHAR (lit. 'Yahweh has remembered'). A servant of Joash who took part in his assassination (2 Ki. 12:21f.) and was later executed (2 Ki. 14:5).

JUBAL. A son of Adah and Lamech and the ancestor of musicians (Gn. 4:21).

JUBILEES, BOOK OF. A Jewish book probably written in the late 2nd cent. BC and popular in the Qumran community. It is a midrash or legendary re-writing of Genesis and part of Exodus, giving a detailed chronology calculated in jubilee periods of 49 years. Its solar calendar has festivals falling on the same day of the week every year; to solve the problem of the date of the Last Supper some scholars suggest Jesus followed this calendar.

JUDAEA. The Greek and Roman designation of Judah. After the Roman conquest (63 BC) it appears both in a wide sense denoting all Palestine including Galilee and Samaria and in a narrow sense excluding them.

JUDAH. The 4th son of Jacob by Leah, who took a leading role among his brothers, and the tribe and area named after him. After the Babylonian Exile the name became popular among the Jews and several different Judahs are mentioned in Ezra and Nehemiah.

The tribe of Judah. Judah played no special part in Israel's Exodus or desert wanderings. Achan, who was one of its members, caused the defeat of Israel at Ai after it had entered Canaan (Jos. 7). Judah's territory was allocated before the conquest; it was in the S of Palestine bounded on the W by the Mediterranean and on the E by the Dead Sea. Judah overran the coastal plain but quickly lost it to the Philistines and voluntarily abandoned good areas inland from the sea to Simeon, presumably hoping Simeon would act as a buffer between Judah and the plain (Jos. 19:1, 9).

The failure to hold Jerusalem (Jdg. 1:8, 21) created a psychological (although not a communications) barrier between Judah and the central Israelite tribes. Judah would have looked S to Hebron rather than N to Shiloh as a religious centre, and although it provided the first of Israel's judges (Othniel, Jdg. 3:9ff.), Judah appears to have become increasingly isolated from the other tribes. David was first crowned king of Judah (2 Sa. 2:4), then of 'all Israel' (2 Sa. 5:1ff.), and Judah probably maintained its separate identity under David and Solomon.

The kingdom of Judah. After the death of Solomon Judah had separate kings to Israel (the 10 N tribes); apart from Jeroboam Israel's kings never sought to destroy Judah, and the S prophets never questioned Israel's right to exist. Solomon's riches which Judah inherited gave it an initial advantage over Israel but the wealth seems to have been lost and the evidence suggests that for some while Judah needed a prosperous and strong Israel if it was to maintain its own prosperity and strength. A measure of parity between the two kingdoms was restored by Abijah (king *c.* 913-911 BC, 2 Ch. 13). Later, Jehoshaphat (*c.* 870-848) probably used Israel as a buffer between Judah and Damascus and therefore did not join it in the fight against the Assyrians at Qarqar. The relative equality of the kingdoms is also seen by the fact that Israel's Jehu, who killed Ahaziah of Judah (*c.* 841 BC, 2 Ki. 9:27), did not carry his anti-Baal campaign into Judah and Ahaziah's mother Athaliah did not attempt to avenge his death.

Judah was not initially threatened by the advances of Assyria. Ahaz (who reigned *c.* 732-716) accepted Assyrian sovereignty and Judah remained a vassal state for the next 100 years. It was caught up in Egyptian intrigues, for which it suffered; Hezekiah's revolt in 705 BC was crushed by the Assyrian Sennacherib 4 years later. Judah was reduced to a shadow of its former self and at least two-thirds of its population was killed or taken away. As Assyria was weakening, Judah experienced a revival of religious and nationalistic feeling; Josiah's reforms were both religious and political (2 Ch. 34:3, 8). He was virtually independent of Assyria by 621 BC. However, Judah was soon crushed by Egypt in 609 BC, and Josiah was killed in battle. Egypt's domination was short-lived and the rising power of Babylon defeated it at Carchemish in 605 BC (2 Ki. 24:1). After 3 years as a vassal of Babylon Jehoiakim of Judah rebelled (2 Ki. 24:2), but Jerusalem surrendered to Nebuchadrezzar on 16 March 597 BC. Zedekiah, the last king of Judah, revolted in 589 BC; in July 587 the walls were breached and Zedekiah was deported (2 Ki. 25:6f.). A month later Jerusalem was destroyed.

Nebuchadrezzar had already deported the cream of the population in 597 (2 Ki. 24:14); two other deportations occurred after the fall of Jerusalem and the subsequent murder of Jerusalem's governor Gedaliah (Je. 52:29f.; *cf.* 2 Ki. 25:11, 25f.). The land of Judah remained relatively empty. Only the Edomites moved into parts of it, remaining until John Hyrcanus

Judaized them after 129 BC.

Judah after the Exile. Babylon fell to Cyrus the Persian in 539 BC; the year following he ordered the rebuilding of the Jerusalem temple and granted the deportees permission to return (Ezr. 1:2ff.; 6:3ff.). But Judah remained part of the Persian empire, and it was clear by the mid-4th cent. BC that hope for political independence and a restored Davidic monarchy still lay far in the future; however, the relatively peaceful conditions favoured the people's religious development.

The campaigns of the Greek Alexander the Great hardly affected Judah but did open up possibilities for (mostly voluntary) emigration to Alexandria in Egypt, where the Jews flourished. When Alexander's empire was divided up, Palestine was controlled by Egyptian Ptolemies until 198 BC and then by Syrian Seleucids. Reacting against the pressure of Antiochus Epiphanes (175-163 BC) to introduce Greek culture, Judah attained first religious autonomy and then political freedom in 140 BC. This was limited by the Romans, then in AD 70 completely lost. After Bar Kochba's revolt in AD 135 Judaea ceased to be a Jewish land, but the name of Judah in its form of 'Jew' became the title of the people who, dispersed through the world, adhered to the Mosaic law. For details of the final centuries of Judah, see ISRAEL.

JUDAISM. The religion of the Jews. It should be regarded as beginning with the Babylonian Exile, but for the period up to AD 70 the term is best reserved for those elements which modify or extend OT concepts. Judaism came into full existence only after the destruction of the temple in AD 70, and was fully developed by AD 500, about the same time as Catholic Christianity.

The rise of Judaism. Josiah's reforms in the 7th cent. BC meant that legitimate sacrifices could be offered only at the Jerusalem temple. For people who could not reach the temple religion had to develop some other focus, and when, during the Exile, the temple was removed altogether, the modification of OT religion into Judaism became inevitable. The Torah, or Law of Moses, as a set of principles, became the focus of life. Ezra's policies were largely responsible for this. Jews in Alexandria in the 2nd cent. BC began assimilating Greek modes of thought, and the Jerusalem priests also became 'Hellenized'. temple worship became a duty rather than a joy. The Pharisees exalted the synagogue as the chief means of worshipping God and discovering his will through the Torah; by the time of Christ there were hundreds of synagogues in Jerusalem itself. This synagogue-centred religion adapted rapidly to the conditions after the destruction of the temple in AD 70; by AD 90 other Jewish religious groups had been destroyed or reduced to impotence, and by 200 ordinary people were forced to conform to Pharisaic requirements if they wished to remain Jews.

The doctrines of Judaism. A deep similarity between Jesus' teaching and that of early Jewish rabbis has long been recognized. Therefore other than in matters mentioned here there was little essential difference between Christian and Jewish thought down to AD 500, although more significant shifts of emphasis have taken place since.

Basic to Judaism is Israel's call to be God's people. Within Israel all were regarded as brothers. Rabbis were recognized simply by their acquired knowledge of the Torah. Women's dignity was maintained although they were always under their husband's authority. The Torah was for the Pharisees the perfect and final revelation of God's will; the prophetic books they regarded as commentaries upon it. Keeping the Torah became the explanation and justification of Israel's existence. The Pentateuch (Gn.-Dt.) was only the written Torah, and the oral Torah developed out of the need to apply the law's principles to everyday life. The written Torah was found to have 613 commandments (248 positive, 365 negative) which were protected by new laws, the keeping of which guaranteed the keeping of the basic commandments. They received their definitive form in the Talmud. The tendency towards legalism was tempered by an emphasis on right intention. Judaism knows nothing comparable to the Christian doctrine of original sin, and there was an invariable tendency to decrease the burden of any enactment which seemed too heavy on the masses. The development of Judaism was shielded from Greek influence at its most critical stage and as a result preserved a more even balance between the individual and society than is evident in much Christian practice.

Judaism's concept of God had less emphasis on his absolute holiness than the Christian concept does, since the Jewish hope for a world to come on earth does not demand such close contact with the Eternal as does a hope for life in heaven. So the problem of atonement is rarely met, and the concept of incarnation is ruled out, although the often negative descriptions of God have driven pious Jews into forms of mysticism to compensate. The Messiah was generally regarded as the great deliverer from foreign oppression and the enforcer of Torah observance. Bodily resurrection was always considered necessary for true life after death, the world to come being on this earth and linked with the present world by the limited period of 'Days of the Messiah'.

See also JEW; TALMUD AND MIDRASH.

JUDAS. Several NT people including: 1. Jesus' brother (Mk. 6:3), possibly the author of the letter of Jude. 2. One of the 12 apostles also named Thaddaeus (Mk. 3:18; Jn. 14:22), regarded by some as the author of Jude. 3. A Galilean who led a rebellion in AD 6 (Acts 5:37). See also next article.

JUDAS ISCARIOT. One of Jesus' 12 apostles who always appears last in the Synoptic Gospels' lists, usually with the description 'who betrayed him' (*e.g.* Mk. 3:19). The surname

Iscariot probably derives from 'a man of Kerioth', which according to Je. 48:24 and Am. 2:2 is in Moab, but there is another possible identification, Kerioth-hezron (Jos. 15:25) 19 km S of Hebron. He was the treasurer of the apostolic band and pilfered the money (Jn. 12:6; 13:29). Following his criticism of Mary's generous anointing of Jesus on the specious grounds that the money could have been used for charity, he went to the chief priests to betray Jesus secretly (Mk. 14:4ff.; Jn. 12:3ff.), for which he was paid.

His opportunity came the night of the Last Supper. After a whispered dialogue with John, Jesus offered the traditional Passover morsel to Judas as a final appeal for his loyalty. Judas did not change his mind, and Satan took control of him (Jn. 13:27ff.). He betrayed the secret of the meeting-place in Gethsemane, where a band of soldiers arrested Jesus; Judas identified him with a kiss (Mk. 14:43ff.). Two versions of his gruesome end are preserved (Mt. 27:3ff.; Acts 1:18f.), which Acts 1:25 goes to the heart of: the apostate went to the destiny reserved for him.

Jesus undoubtedly viewed him as a potential disciple, and he repeatedly appealed to him. The fact that Jesus could foresee the betrayal does not mean that Judas could not avoid becoming the traitor. Nonetheless, he probably never really belonged to Christ; he is an example of an uncommitted follower who keeps the company of Jesus but does not share his spirit (*cf.* Rom. 8:9f.).

Many suggestions have been made

about his motives. They include greed; jealousy; fear of the outcome of Jesus' ministry and a desire to save himself; a desire to force Jesus to declare himself Messiah; a bitter spirit which turned to hate when he saw his ambitions being thwarted.

JUDE, LETTER OF. *Contents.* Greeting (vv. 1-2); purpose of writing (vv. 3-4); false teachers denounced (vv. 5-16); exhortation to Christians (vv. 17-23); doxology (vv. 24-25).

Authorship and date. The author calls himself 'brother of James', and there was only one James who could be referred to without further description, the brother of Jesus (Gal. 1:19). As one of Jesus' other brothers was called Judas (Mk. 6:3), it is likely he wrote this letter. The date of writing cannot be fixed other than sometime in the second half of the 1st cent. AD.

Occasion and purpose. Jude was apparently planning another treatise when the advances of an incipient gnosticism threatened the Christians he wrote to (v. 3). It was probably a form of lawlessness which misinterpreted as licence Paul's teaching on liberty (v. 4; *cf.* Gal. 5:13).

Argument. False teaching must be exposed and truth contended for (v. 3). The doom of false teachers has been announced of old; vv. 8-10 may refer to a now-lost passage in the book *Assumption of Moses.* False teachers introduce trouble and disgrace into the church (vv. 12-13), but true believers need not be alarmed by them; instead they should grow in faith, pray, live in loving fellowship with God, look for-

ward to Christ's return and seek to rescue those who are led astray (vv. 17-23).

JUDGES. People who dispense justice. When Israel was in the desert between Egypt and Canaan, Moses appointed deputies to judge ordinary cases (Ex. 18:13ff.). Israel's law also provided for such people when they had settled in Canaan; they were to be scrupulously fair and honest (Dt. 16:18f.). Texts from Mari in Syria (*c.* 1800 BC) show judges keeping order, collecting the taxes and providing information.

After Joshua's death there followed a period of tribal discord and defeat, in answer to which God provided battle-leaders and peace-time rulers called 'judges' (Jdg. 2:16); the first mentioned was Othniel and the last Samson (Jdg. 3:9; 16:31). In the period just before the monarchy Eli the priest and Samuel the prophet judged Israel (1 Sa. 4:18; 7:15). Under the kings and after the Exile there were once more judges with judicial or administrative roles (*e.g.* 1 Ch. 26:29; Ezr. 7:25). See also next article.

JUDGES, BOOK OF. Describing the history of Israel from the death of Joshua to the rise of Samuel, it takes its name from the leading characters who were empowered by God to deliver and preserve Israel.

Contents. 1. Events following the death of Joshua, including further conquests and failure, especially toleration of evil (1:1-2:5). 2. Israel's history under the judges, beginning with the author's prophetic understanding of how God recompenses the nation in accordance with its faithfulness (2:6-3:6); the book exhibits a repeated cycle of sin, conquest by foreigners, prayer of repentance, and salvation through God's appointed judges. It describes 6 periods of oppression and the careers of 12 judges (3:7-16:31): Invasions of Cushan-rishathaim, a Hittite, and Othniel's deliverance followed by 40 years' peace (3:7-11); oppression under Eglon of Moab and deliverance through Ehud, followed by 80 years' peace (3:12-31); deliverance by Deborah from local Canaanite opposition led by Jabin II of Hazor and his commander Sisera, followed by 40 years' peace (4-5); deliverance by Gideon from nomadic Midianites and Amalekites (6:1-8:32); the rise and fall of Abimelech, Gideon's son who sought to make himself Israel's king, Tola and Jair rescuing Israel from the resulting turmoil (8:33-10:5); oppression under Ammon and the Philistines, relieved by Jephthah, 3 minor judges, and finally Samson (10:6-16:31). 3. An appendix giving details of Israel's earlier apostasy before Othniel, to illustrate the depth of its sin in which almost every one of the Ten Commandments was broken and everyone did what was right in his own eyes (17-21).

Authorship and date. The song of Deborah (5:2ff.) claims to have been written at the time of the events it celebrates, but the rest of the book could not have been finally compiled until 2 centuries later. It refers to the destruction of Shiloh (18:30f.; *cf.* 1 Sa. 4; *c.* 1080 BC), and records the death of Samson a few years before Samuel's inauguration as judge (16:30; *c.* 1063 BC). The repeated phrase 'there was no king' (17:6; 18:1; 21:25) suggests it was written after Saul's accession *c.* 1043 BC, but before David's capture of Jerusalem in 1003 BC (2 Sa. 5:6f.; *cf.* Jdg. 1:21). The author was therefore active during Saul's early reign and a prophet (the Hebrew Bible includes the book in the 'former prophets'). The most likely candidate is Samuel, as the Jewish Talmud suggests, or one of his close prophetic associates, perhaps relying on oral and written sources that are now lost, such as the hero-anthology mentioned in Jos. 10:13.

Background and chronology. (What follows assumes the early date for the Exodus, *c.* 1450 BC.) Joshua had subdued Canaan but its inhabitants had not lost their potential for resistance. At the time of Joshua's death *c.* 1400 BC, Egyptian control over Palestine was weak, and soon after there was a revival of Hittite activity from beyond Syria and complaints from Canaanites about marauding *Habiru*. Palestine returned to Egyptian control *c.* 1318 BC. The Philistines, driven back from Egypt *c.* 1191, consolidated their position in Canaan towards the end of the Judges period. Confirmation of Deborah's victory in 1216 BC has come from Hazor. Jdg. 11:26 claims Israel had been in Palestine for 300 years; the period from the first oppression to Samuel's rise seems to be 1382-1063 BC, 319 years, suggesting a date for the

293

conquest of 1406-1400 and allowing for the fact that some judges worked concurrently.

Teaching. There are three main emphases: God's anger at sin; his mercy shown to those who repent; and human depravity illustrated by the constant return to the old sinful ways. The author was not simply recording history, but interpreting it.

JUDGMENT. People today tend to reject out of hand the idea that one day they must render account to God for their lives and decisions. Moral issues, for example, tend to be related to the present moment and to considerations of personal happiness rather than to an after-life and to the unchanging character of God. The Bible counters this attitude with the assertion that judgment is inevitable and awaits us all.

Biblical summary. In the OT God is portrayed as a judge who takes vigorous action against evil (*e.g.* Ps. 94:2). His judgment is not impersonal, but related to his character of mercy, righteousness and truth (*e.g.* Ps. 36:5f.). So it brings rescue for the righteous as well as doom for the wicked (Dt. 10:18; 32:41). This stress on judgment as part of God's total character which is already active in the world continues in the NT (*e.g.* Rom. 1:18); Jesus exercised the Father's judgments in his ministry (Jn. 3:19; 5:30). The main NT emphasis however is on the future judgment which will accompany the return of Jesus (Mt. 25:31ff.; Rom. 2:15f.), also prefigured towards the end of the OT period in the expectation of the coming 'Day of the Lord' (Am. 5:18ff.; *cf.* 1 Cor. 1:8). Jesus himself will judge (Jn. 5:22); no-one will be exempt (1 Pet. 4:5), including the angels (Jude 6; *cf.* 1 Cor. 6:3) and even, in a rather different manner, Christians (Lk. 19:12ff.; 1 Pet. 4:17; see below). The future existence of those acquitted is called heaven, that of those not acquitted is called hell.

The basis of judgment. The basis on which God judges a person is that person's response to his revealed will. Hence it includes the entire range of human experience and allows for different degrees of knowledge of, and ability to fulfil, that will (Mt. 11:21ff.; Rom. 2:12ff.). It will be utterly just and convincing (Rom. 3:19). In face of the injustices in the present world, God has appointed a day when he will judge it righteously (Acts 17:31).

The apparent conflict between the biblical assertion that people are justified before God by faith yet judged according to their works can be understood as follows. Justification is being declared righteous before God at his judgment seat and stems from trusting faith in the *work* of Jesus Christ (Rom. 5:1; 8:1). But the declaration is not merely judicial; the believer is also incorporated into Christ's death and resurrection (Rom. 6:1ff.), and therefore there can be no genuine faith which does not result in works of obedience (Jas. 2:18ff.). Justification leads to sanctification (2 Cor. 3:18). And, as Jesus explained, to believe in him is itself to be doing the work God requires (Jn. 6:28f.).

The parable of the sheep and goats (Mt. 25:31ff.) seems at first to teach justification by charitable works, leading some commentators to write of 'anonymous Christians' including agnostics who are unconsciously following Christ and will be acquitted because of their practical ministry to the needy. However, Jesus refers to such acts as being 'to one of the least of these my brethren', hence as part of the Christian's mission. The disciple is seen as being intimately united with the Lord; service to a believer is service to the Lord (*cf.* Mt. 10:40). The good works of non-Christians are evidence of God's 'common grace' in the world and are to be received thankfully and even identified with, but they are not grounds for being justified before God; there are no 'anonymous Christians' (Acts 4:12). Some also suggest that only *explicit* rejection of Christ incurs God's judgment (*cf.* the assertions in Jn. 3:18, 36). However, unbelief is not the only ground of judgment; the Bible indicates that people are already under God's condemnation before they hear the gospel (Rom. 2:12; 5:18). But Scripture also recognizes that people have different opportunities to hear and respond to the gospel and that God will take this into account at the judgment (Rom. 2; *cf.* Lk. 12:48); that does not alter the fact that Jesus Christ is the sole author of salvation (Jn. 14:6; Eph. 2:12f.).

The judgment of Christians. Christians will be judged according to their stewardship of the talents, gifts, opportunities and responsibilities granted to them (1 Cor. 3:12ff.; 1 Pet. 1:17). It will be a fatherly judgment and will not place in peril the Christian's place within God's family, but it is not thereby to be treated lightly.

See further ESCHATOLOGY; HEAVEN; HELL; JUSTIFICATION.

JUDGMENT SEAT. The image of God's judgment seat (Rom. 14:10; 2 Cor. 5:10) was probably prompted by Greek state assemblies which met in front of a dais from which business was conducted, and by the Roman magistrates' platform erected in a public place to administer justice (*cf.* Jn. 19:13; Acts 12:21).

JUDITH: See APOCRYPHA.

JULIUS. The centurion who escorted Paul to Rome (Acts 27:1). His Augustan cohort is known from archaeological evidence and was an auxiliary force of non-citizens; Julius, however, was probably a new citizen of Rome.

JUSTICE. Justice is closely associated with righteousness in both OT and NT, and received several shades of meaning as the biblical revelation developed chronologically. In the patriarchal age justice often means conformity to an accepted standard of values; *e.g.* Jacob's honesty in keeping his contract (Gn. 30:33). The law speaks of 'just' weights and measures (Lv. 19:36).

From Moses' time onwards justice distinguishes God's will and those activities which result from it. He acts in ways which are always perfect and right (Ps. 89:14; *cf*. Rev. 15:3). By a natural transition justice then comes to identify the moral standard by which God measures human conduct. People must 'do justice' (Gn. 18:19), which is the outworking of true holiness (Mi. 6:8) and the opposite of sin (Ec. 7:20). It was a characteristic of the Messiah (Is. 9:7; Acts 3:14).

Justice describes God's punishment of sin. God cannot remain indifferent to evil (Hab. 1:13; Heb. 12:29); his condemnation is just (Rom. 3:8). From the time of the Judges justice also describes God's acts which vindicate or deliver his people (*cf*. his 'triumph', Jdg. 5:11, using the Hebrew word for justice). This leads to the sense of justice or righteousness seen in God's undeserved pardon and acceptance of a sinner (as in Ps. 103:17).

In Is. 45:21 God is seen as a saviour because he is righteous (just); this idea is found also in 1 Jn. 1:9, although the NT continues at the same time to use justice (righteousness) to describe God's judgment of sin (Rom. 3:25f.). God's righteousness can be granted, by his grace, to the believer (Is. 45:24f.), whose natural righteousness is quite inadequate to please God (Is. 64:6); he is made just by the imputed righteousness of Christ (Phil. 3:9).

Therefore God's people are called on to seek mutual justice in their social relationships (Is. 1:17; Je. 22:16); righteousness became, from the Exile on, a synonym for giving charitable gifts (*cf*. Ps. 112:9). Jesus' lofty ethical demands (Mt. 5:20, 48) were applied in his own life (Heb. 4:15). He also brought to mankind God's redempt-

ive justice and imputed it to those who believe, thus uniting in himself the many shades of meaning of 'justice' (*cf*. 1 Cor. 1:30).

See also next article; RIGHTEOUSNESS.

JUSTIFICATION. 'Justify' is a legal term meaning 'acquit' or 'declare righteous'; justifying is the judge's act. God, the Judge of all the earth (Gn. 18:25), requires people to be righteous, that is to live in accordance with his law, and he shows his own righteousness as Judge by condemning those who fall short of it (Rom. 2:5). When God does acquit someone, he actively implements that justification by showing favour to the person and publicly reinstating him; in Paul's writings terms such as 'adoption' describe this subsequent favour and reinstatement.

The nature of justification. Of the 39 occurrences of the verb 'justify' in the NT, 29 are in Paul's letters or recorded words. Justification is God's act of remitting the sins of guilty people, and accounting them righteous freely by his grace through their faith in Christ, not because of their own works but of the representative law-keeping and redemption of Jesus Christ on their behalf (Rom. 3:23-26; 4:5f.; 5:18f.). The gospel, says Paul, discloses God's righteousness (Rom. 1:17). God gives his righteousness to believing sinners (Rom. 5:17), and he acts righteously both by judging sinners and also by providing for their salvation in a way which meets his just demands (Rom. 3:25f.); God acquits them in the court of heaven without denying his justice as Judge.

This concept of justification was central to Paul's personal religion; he described his missionary call in terms of it (*e.g.* Gal. 2:15ff.; Phil. 3:4ff.). Justification brings an end to hostility between the believer and God (Rom. 5:9f.). The believer then inherits all God's blessings promised to the just (Rom. 8:14ff.), and is assured that nothing can ever separate him from God's love or rob him of his justified status in this life or the next (Rom. 8:30ff.). From this view of justification flows Paul's thought about the equal footing of Jew and Gentile (Gal. 3:8ff.), redemption (Gal. 3:13), faith (Rom. 4:23ff.), and the gift of the Spirit (Gal. 4:6ff.). It is the key to his view of history, too. After the fall of the first representative man, that is Adam, condemnation was brought on the human race (Rom. 5:12ff.). God made a covenant with Abraham and his family, justified him through his faith and promised that through one of his descendants all nations would be blessed (Gal. 3:6ff.). Moses' law gave Abraham's descendants knowledge of sin and thus taught them their need of justification (Gal. 3:19ff.). Through Christ, the second representative man, justification became available to all nations (Gal. 3:26ff.).

The ground of justification. Because all have sinned, all are doomed; none can be justified by keeping God's law (Rom. 3:9ff.). But God justifies sinners on the just ground that Jesus Christ, acting on their behalf, has satisfied the claims of God's law upon them (Rom. 3:21ff.; 5:9ff.). Believers are 'made righteous' before God because he admits them to share Christ's status; in other words, God treats them according to Christ's desert. They are justified 'in Christ' (Gal. 2:17) not through a false judgment that pretends they have kept the law personally, but by the true judgment which accounts them as being 'in' the One who has kept the law representatively. So in accepting sinners on the grounds of Christ's obedience and death, God still acts justly.

The means of justification. Believers receive justification through faith. Paul does not regard faith as the ground of justification, for then believing would be a work earning merit from God, and justification would not be by God's grace alone (Rom. 4:5, 16; 11:6). Rather, as in the case of Abraham, faith is wholehearted reliance on God's promise through which the believer secures the already-offered justification (Rom. 4:18ff.).

Paul and James. Some have thought Jas. 2:14-26 contradicts Paul's insistence on justification through faith alone, because he considered Paul's teaching might encourage believers to live carelessly (*cf.* Rom. 3:8). But Paul uses 'justify' in a narrow technical sense for God's acceptance when people believe. James uses it in the broader sense of being proved genuine by demonstrating in practical works the reality of the inner faith. Paul would have agreed wholeheartedly that bare orthodoxy unaccompanied by good works provides no sufficient ground for inferring that a person is saved (*cf.* Eph. 2:10; 5:5f.).

See also ATONEMENT; REDEMPTION.

JUSTUS. A Latin name popular among Jews and converts to Judaism, probably because it implied obedience and devotion to the law. Among those so named are Joseph Barsabbas (Acts 1:23), suggested as a possible successor to Judas Iscariot; and the Gentile owner of a house Paul used as a base in Corinth (Acts 18:7), possibly the same person as GAIUS (Rom. 16:23).

JUTTAH. A walled town 8 km S of Hebron assigned to the priests (Jos. 21:16).

K

KABZEEL. A town in S Judah resettled after the Exile (Jekabzeel in Ne. 11:25); possibly Kh. Hora, 13 km E of Beer-sheba.

KADESH (KADESH-BARNEA). A well, a settlement and a desert area apparently in the NE of the Sinai peninsula. There, Chedorlaomer subdued the Amalekites (Gn. 14:7), but it is best known as a stopping place for the Israelites as they wandered between Egypt and Canaan (Nu. 13:26; 20:1; Dt. 1:19, 46). There they doubted God's ability to bring them into the promised land, and were condemned to 40 years' wandering (Nu. 14:32ff.). Miriam was buried there, Moses disobeyed God there by striking the water-bearing rock, and from there vainly sent envoys to secure transit rights through Edom (Nu. 20). It became the SW limit of Judah's territory. It is often identified with Ain Qudeis 80 km SW of Beer-sheba, but Ain Qudeirat 8 km NW of it seems more suitable, having more water and vegetation; possibly the whole group of springs in the area was used by the large number of Israelites.

KADMIEL (lit. 'God is the first ancient one'). A Levite who returned to Jerusalem after the Exile. He was associated with the temple rebuilding (Ezr. 3:9), national repentance (Ne. 9:4f.) and sealing the covenant (Ne. 10:9).

KADMONITES. Occurs only once as a tribal name (Gn. 15:19) and may mean simply 'Easterners'; see EAST, PEOPLE OF THE.

KAIN. A town S of Hebron, its identity uncertain; see also ZANOAH (2).

KAIWAN. In Am. 5:26 probably represents the Assyrian Ninurta, god of the planet Saturn.

KANAH. 1. A wadi from the head of the Michmethath valley forming the Ephraim-Manasseh border. 2. A town of Asher, probably Qana 10 km SE of Tyre.

KEDAR (probably 'black, swarthy').

A son of Ishmael and forebear of a nomadic tribe of the Syro-Arabian desert from Palestine to Mesopotamia. They had large flocks (Is. 60:7), traded with Tyre (Ezk. 27:21) and had a reputation for barbarism (Ps. 120:5); Isaiah prophesied their downfall (Is. 21:16f.). By the Persian period they controlled a realm astride the vital Palestine-Egypt land-route. See also NOMADS.

KEDEMOTH. A city given to the Levites in Reuben's territory. Probably modern ez-Zaferan 16 km N of the Arnon.

KEDESH. 1. A former Canaanite royal city which became a principal town in Naphtali, and a city of refuge, assigned to the Levites (Jos. 12:22; 19:37; 20:7; 21:32). It was one of the first cities to fall to Assyria (2 Ki. 15:29). Modern Tell Qades NW of Lake Huleh. 2. A town of Issachar, modern Tell Abu Qedes SSW of Megiddo. 3. In Jos. 15:23, probably KADESH.

KEILAH. A town David saved from the Philistines while fleeing from Saul (1 Sa. 23); modern Kh. Qila, 10 km E of Beit Guvrin.

KENATH (lit. 'possession'). A city E of the Jordan usually identified with ruins at Qanawat 25 km NE of Bozrah.

KENAZ. Several OT people including an Edomite chief (Gn. 36:11, 15, 42), possibly the ancestor of the KENIZ-ZITES; another was brother of Caleb and father of Othniel (Jos. 15:17; Jdg.

1:13).

KENITES. A Midianite tribe whose name means 'smith', an interpretation confirmed by the presence of copper in the region SE of the Gulf of Aqabah which they inhabited. Moses invited one, his nephew, to join the Israelites in the desert because of his nomadic skills (Nu. 10:29ff.); Kenites accompanied Judah into its territory (Jdg. 1:16); Saul spared them (1 Sa. 15:6) and David befriended them (1 Sa. 30:29). They remained prominent after the Exile (Ne. 3:14; Rechabites were of Kenite stock). See also NOMADS.

KENIZZITES. A leading Edomite family descended from Esau's eldest son Eliphaz. Caleb was one; possibly some of his father Jephunneh's ancestors had joined it (Nu. 32:12). The sons of Kenaz are mentioned in 1 Ch. 4:13ff., but some names may be missing, so making relationships difficult to identify.

KENOSIS. A Greek term from a verb meaning 'he emptied himself' and used in Phil. 2:7. The theological 'kenotic theory' seeks to show how the Second Person of the Trinity could share genuine human experience, by divesting himself of his divine attributes of omniscience and omnipotence; in its classical form it goes back no further than the mid-19th cent. However, it is open to serious objections, because Paul says nothing about divine attributes in the context. Some have suggested a link with Is.

53:12, so that in Phil. 2:7 the kenosis is the final surrender of Jesus' life. But the context makes it more likely that we should understand the term as referring to Jesus' chosen renunciation of the glory of his oneness with the Father (*cf.* Jn. 17:5, 24; Phil. 2:6), becoming a 'servant' in human flesh to make the humble sacrifice on Calvary.

KERCHIEFS. In Ezk. 13:18, 21 (AV), possibly veils or caps used in divination. See MAGIC AND SORCERY.

KEREN-HAPPUCH. Job's youngest daughter after his fortunes were restored; the name means 'painthorn', *i.e.* 'beautifier'.

KERIOTH. 1. A town in S Judah, possibly Kh. el-Qarytein and the home of Judas Iscariot. 2. A city of Moab, probably El-Qereiyat S of Ataroth.

KETURAH (lit. 'perfumed one'). Abraham's second wife, whom he married after Sarah's death (Gn. 25:1ff.).

KEY. Used literally only in Jdg. 3:25, for a flat piece of wood with pins which correspond with the holes in a hollow bolt. The key raised locking-pins which held the bolt in place.

KEYS OF HEAVEN (PETER): See POWER OF THE KEYS.

KIBROTH-HATTAAVAH (lit. 'graves of craving'). A campsite of the Israelites where many died of disease after craving meat and having been sent quails by God (Nu. 11:31ff.).

KIDNEYS. The kidneys together with the fat and part of the liver of sacrificial animals were burnt on the altar as 'God's portion'. Along with the blood and other internal organs kidneys were held to contain life. The same Hebrew word is also used figuratively for human emotions, as in Ps. 73:21 (heart, RSV); Pr. 23:16 (soul, RSV).

KIDRON. The brook Kidron, modern Wadi en-Nar, is a torrent-bed starting N of Jerusalem, passing between the temple mount and Mount of Olives *en route* to the Dead Sea. Its modern name means 'Fire Wadi', describing its dry sunbaked nature for most of the year. There is an intermittent spring on its W side called Gihon ('Gusher'), the flow of which was diverted by tunnel into Jerusalem (see SILOAM). The valley was used as a place to destroy pagan artefacts (1 Ki. 15:13), and is sometimes identified with the valley of JEHOSHAPHAT; see also HINNOM.

KIN, KINSMAN. Many of Israel's family relationships are to be understood in terms of tribal customs known the world over. Kinship describes relationships by blood; strong ties existed through the original 'father' of a tribe between all the families descended from him. Brothers within the same family were distinguished depending on whether they shared one or both physical parents. Men were expected to take wives from their kindred (Gn. 24:38ff.)

but not from among very close relatives (Lv. 18). Kinsmen had certain obligations. If a man died without leaving a son, his brother (or close relative) was to marry the widow in order to raise up a son for him (Dt. 25:5ff.; *cf.* the book of Ruth). Kinsmen had to redeem a relative's property if he went bankrupt (Lv. 25:25ff.), and in some circumstances to avenge the murder of a relative (*cf.* Gn. 9:5f.). See also FAMILY, HOUSEHOLD.

KING, KINGSHIP. The office of king was common in the Near East from earliest times. Such a ruler controlled a settled region often centred on a city (*e.g.* Gn. 14:1f.); his authority was hereditary and reckoned to have been derived from the god of the land. In Egypt the king (pharaoh) was usually regarded as identical with the god, in Assyria as the god's representative. In classical Greek times the king's power was traced back to Zeus; later the idea of king-benefactor grew leading to the concept of the divine king in Alexander and the Roman Caesars.

When Israel left Egypt it was ruled by Moses and then Joshua as non-hereditary leaders called by God and acknowledged by the people. After Joshua tribes were ruled by village fathers who called on 'judges' to lead a united army when necessary. Eli and Samuel resumed a religious-judicial leadership, and Samuel became the king-maker at the people's insistence, regarding their request as a measure of apostasy (1 Sa. 8). Saul became Israel's first king but never established a dynasty. David, his successor, was more successful and established a dynasty lasting over 400 years, based on the 'Davidic covenant' (*cf.* Ps. 132:11f.); he assumed some religious leadership as well (2 Sa. 6:13ff.). The chief responsibility of the king was to maintain righteousness (Is. 11:1ff.) but after the division of the kingdom into Israel (N) and Judah (S) many kings encouraged injustice and wickedness (*e.g.* 1 Ki. 14:16; 2 Ki. 21:16). The failure of such people fuelled hopes for a future righteous ruler which later crystallized into the hope for the Messiah. During the period 104-37 BC some of the high priests assumed the title of king and some were proclaimed as the fulfilment of the Messianic hope, but it was only truly fulfilled in Jesus Christ. He came from David's family (Mt. 1) and proclaimed the kingdom of God (Mk. 1:15; see next article); ultimately all would bow before him as Messiah-king (Phil. 2:9ff.).

The OT kings appointed priests but not prophets (1 Ki. 2:27), yet both often took leading roles in the affairs of state (*cf.* 1 Ki. 19:15f.). Kings also had army commanders (2 Sa. 19:13), secretaries (2 Sa. 8:17), recorders and other ministers (1 Ki. 4:3ff.) to assist them.

KINGDOM OF GOD, KINGDOM OF HEAVEN. According to the Synoptic Gospels the kingdom, the sphere of God's rule or authority, was the central theme of Jesus' preaching. Matthew prefers 'kingdom of heaven', probably because of the Jewish tendency to avoid using God's name; Mark and Luke prefer 'kingdom of God'. There is no distinction between the two terms.

John the Baptist first announced it (Mt. 3:1ff.). The Jews had for some while expected a decisive intervention by God to restore Israel's fortunes and to liberate them from their enemies; the promised Messiah would pave the way for the kingdom of God. The future manifestation of God's kingship is one of the central concepts of the OT prophets. John announced that this long-hoped-for time had arrived, emphasized that it was a time of judgment from which no-one was exempt, and pointed to the coming Messiah, Jesus, who would pour out God's Spirit on those who repented. Jesus, at the start of his ministry, took up John's cry (Mt. 4:17). His teaching has two aspects:

The kingdom is present. For Jesus, the kingdom was already present in his own person and ministry, and appeared visibly in the casting out of demons; Satan's power had been broken (Lk. 11:17ff.). It was also signified by the many other works which Jesus did, as he reassured John the Baptist (Mt. 11:2ff.). Thus the forgiveness of sins was part of the proclamation of the kingdom and also a reality offered now, not just in the future (Mk. 2:1ff.). Jesus' Messiahship was proclaimed as a present reality at his baptism and transfiguration (Mk. 1:11; 9:7); he was invested with God's full authority (Mt. 21:27); he came to fulfil the law (Mt. 5:17ff.), to seek and save the lost (Lk. 19:10), to serve and to give his life as a ransom for many

(Mk. 10:45). The secret of belonging to the kingdom lay in belonging to him (Mt. 7:23).

The kingdom is future. As yet, the kingdom is present in the world only in a provisional way. Jesus' miracles are tokens or signs of another order of reality yet to come when the powers of evil will be delivered to eternal darkness (Mt. 8:29). In several of his parables, Jesus taught that the kingdom grows secretly and can be partially frustrated by others (Mt. 13). The kingdom could only fully come via the cross, he taught; only through his humble obedience (Mt. 3:15) could he later exercise authority over the world's kingdoms (Mt. 4:8; 28:18) when the present world order ends.

The kingdom and the church. Kingdom and church are connected but they are not identical. The kingdom is the whole of God's redeeming activity in Christ in this world; the church is the assembly of those who belong to Jesus Christ and have accepted the gospel of his kingdom. The kingdom takes visible form in the life of those who live by the King's commands (Mt. 11:28ff.). But the kingdom is not confined to the frontiers of the church. Where Christ's kingship prevails not only individual lives are changed but the whole pattern of living is changed too, as seen when Christianity affects communities once dominated by nature religions. But as the book of Revelation shows, however far the kingdom invades world history with its blessing and deliverance, it is only through the final and universal crisis of Christ's return that the visible, all-conquering reign of peace and salvation will be established.

The kingdom in theology. Roman Catholic theology has tended to equate the church and the kingdom. In reaction to this, the 16th-cent. Reformers emphasized the spiritual and invisible significance of the kingdom by a misapplication of Lk. 17:20f.; they said it was the spiritual sovereignty of Christ exercised through the preaching of his Word and the operation of the Holy Spirit. Later liberal theologians viewed the kingdom moralistically as a kingdom of love and peace, or in terms of the growth of social justice and communal development. NT scholarship today is re-emphasizing the original significance of the kingdom in Jesus' preaching, with its present aspect seen against the background of the progress of God's dynamic saving activity in history and with the final consummation as its goal.

See also JESUS CHRIST, TEACHING OF.

KINGS, BOOKS OF. The closing part of the narrative which begins in Genesis and focuses on the story of Israel from its origins to the ending of its political independence by the Babylonians. The division of Kings from the books of Samuel, and the division of Kings into two books, is artificial.

Contents. The story of the Israelite monarchy written from a theological perspective. It falls into three main sections: the reign of Solomon (1 Ki. 1-11); the divided kingdom, including the involvement of the prophets Elijah and Elisha and the increasing paganism resulting in exile for the N tribes (1 Ki. 12-2 Ki. 17); the (S) kingdom of Judah up to its exile (2 Ki. 18-25).

Origin. As the last event referred to is King Jehoiachin's release from prison in Babylon in 561 BC (2 Ki. 25:27), the final form of the books must date from after this time. The main composition can be dated earlier, perhaps in the early years of the Exile; there is little evidence for a 'first edition' as early as, say, Josiah's reforms. The identity of the author(s) is unknown; it is sometimes suggested that they were 'Deuteronomists' concerned to show how the principles declared in Deuteronomy worked out in history, although the emphases of Dt. and of Kings do not coincide exactly.

Structure and historicity. Kings gives a reign-by-reign treatment of the history, and after the division of the nation the stories of N and S kings are interwoven to give a roughly chronological narrative. Alongside the summaries of kings' reigns there is detailed material about royal and political matters and the careers of Elijah and Elisha. It is history with a message rather than a simple 'objective' account; some periods of great historical importance such as the reign of Omri are passed over briefly because they are not relevant to the author's concern about Israel's relationship with God. Some sources of historical data are referred to (*e.g.* 1 Ki. 11:41; 14:19, 29), and these are generally regarded as of genuine

303

historical value, although problems over the dating of the kings does arise (for which see CHRONOLOGY OF THE OLD TESTAMENT; many excavations are also relevant to the period, for which see ARCHAEOLOGY.)

Emphases, message and purpose. David's faithfulness to God is often used as a standard by which other kings are judged (*e.g.* 1 Ki. 9:4; 2 Ki. 22:2). The well-being of the people as a whole is bound up with the righteousness or sinfulness of the king (2 Ki. 21:11-15). The temple is used as a touchstone for evaluating kings; Jeroboam I is condemned for devising alternative shrines (1 Ki. 12-13) while Josiah is commended for his destruction of other shrines and reforms of temple worship (2 Ki. 22-23). More important still is God's law; Manasseh disobeys the law (2 Ki. 21:2ff.; *cf.* Dt. 17:2ff.; 18:9ff.), and Josiah restores the terms of the covenant. The spoken words of prophets support the written law (*e.g.* 2 Ki. 22:13ff.), and Elijah and Elisha especially are seen as bringing God's word into specific historical situations. A king's attitude to the prophet was another index of his attitude to God.

The books explain why, because of many kings' apostasy, God has good reason to judge Israel and Judah by exiling them. There are hints of hope for the future, that God's commitment to David still holds true. Prayer is possible even when the temple is pillaged, because God hears prayer; the covenant which sanctions the punishment also contains promises

for restoration upon repentance (1 Ki. 8:22ff.). In teaching this, Kings also challenged the people in Exile to renewed repentance, faith and obedience towards God.

Biblical context. Kings is one of several biblical responses to Judah's fall and Exile, and especially bears comparison with Jeremiah and Lamentations. Within Scripture its particular emphasis lies in picturing God's involvement in political life, warning against both under- and over-valuing it, and in showing the interplay between human free will and the outworking of God's purposes through, or despite, human decisions.

KING'S GARDEN. An open space in Jerusalem near the Pool of Siloam (Ne. 3:15).

KING'S HIGHWAY. A road running from the Gulf of Aqabah to Damascus, E of the Jordan valley. It was used as early as 2300 BC, and perhaps later by Chedorlaomer and Abraham (Gn. 14). Edomites and Ammonites prevented the Israelite invaders from using it (Nu. 20:17; 21:22). It was an important trade route in Solomon's time, and was incorporated into a Roman road in the 2nd cent. AD.

KIR, KIR OF MOAB, KIRHARE-SETH. 1. Kir was the place of exile of the Syrians (2 Ki. 16:9; Am. 1:5) and a country (not necessarily the same) from which God had originally brought them (Am. 9:7). In Is. 22:6 it is parallel to Elam; no ancient place of this name is known but it means 'city' so may not be specific. It cannot be identified at present. 2. Kir of Moab (Kir-hareseth) was a fortified city of S Moab. When besieged there, its king offered his son as a sacrifice (2 Ki. 3:25). Generally identified with Kerak, a hill 1,027 m above sea level 18 km E of the Dead Sea and 24 km S of the Arnon, topped today by a medieval castle.

KIRIATHAIM. 1. A place in Reuben's territory, later in Moabite hands according to Je. 48:1 and a 9th-cent. BC inscription of Moab's king Mesha. Possibly modern El Quraiyat 10 km NW of Dibon in Jordan. 2. A city of Levites in Naphtali, possibly the Kartan of Jos. 21:32; the site is unknown.

KIRIATH-ARBA (lit. 'city of four'; 'tetrapolis'). An earlier name for Hebron which appears to have fallen out of use after Israel's conquest of Canaan; for details see HEBRON.

KIREATH-JEARIM (lit. 'city of forests'). A chief city of the Gibeonites on the Judah-Benjamin border, also called Kiriath-baal (Jos. 15:60), Baalah (Jos. 15:9f.), Baale-Judah (2 Sa. 6:2) and Kiriath-arim (Ezr. 2:25). The ark of the covenant was kept there for 20 years (1 Sa. 7:1; 2 Sa. 6:2). Probably Abu Ghosh (Kuriet el-Enab) 14 km W of Jerusalem on the Jaffa road.

KIRIATH-SEPHER. A name for DEBIR (Jos. 15:15ff.; Jdg. 1:11ff.).

KISH (lit. 'bow', 'power'). Among

others, King Saul's father (1 Sa. 9:1).

KISHON. A river rising in the N Samaria hills, draining the plain of Esdraelon and entering the Mediterranean at the bay of Acre; modern Nahr el-Muqatta. The name is not used often in Scripture, the river being described by reference to a nearby town (*e.g.* Jos. 19:11). The high-running river made the plain too boggy for Sisera's chariots (Jdg. 4-5); when at a low level it was the scene of Elijah's execution of pagan prophets. The subsequent rains washed away traces of the deed (1 Ki. 18).

KISS. A common greeting in the E (*e.g.* Gn. 29:11; 33:4; Lk. 15:20), and a token of homage (1 Sa. 10:1). The holy kiss (Rom. 16:16; 1 Pet. 5:14) was an expression of Christian love presumably restricted to one's own sex. See also GREETING.

KITTIM. One of the sons of Javan (Gn. 10:4) whose descendants settled in Cyprus and gave their name to the town of Kition (modern Larnaka). They were sea traders (Nu. 24:24) and the name later applied to all Cyprus. In Dn. 11:30 'ships of Kittim' must refer to Rome in the context. See also CYPRUS.

KNEADING-BOWL. A large shallow bowl (wooden or pottery) for preparing dough. See BREAD.

KNEE, KNEEL. Weakness is described as 'feeble knees' (Is. 35:3); fear as 'trembling knees' (Dn. 5:6).

Most NT references are in the context of bowing in respect (Mk. 1:40), subjection (Rom. 11:4; 14:11; Phil. 2:10), religious worship (Lk. 5:8), and occasionally as a posture for prayer (Lk. 22:41).

KNIFE. Flint-knives were used in the Near East, along with the metal knife, until recent times. Flint was specified for circumcision, perhaps for hygienic reasons (it could be discarded, Ex. 4:25). Abraham's knife was a short sword (Gn. 22:6), as was the Levite's in Jdg. 19:29.

KNOWLEDGE. The Hebrew thought of knowledge as actively relating to the experienced world. This made demands on the will as well as the understanding; by contrast the Greek ideal of knowledge was a contemplation of static and abiding reality, a much more abstract idea. Hence the OT speaks of 'knowing' grief (Is. 53:3) or a marriage partner through sexual union (Gn. 4:1). Knowing God (e.g. Je. 16:21) is recognizing him as the sovereign Lord who makes demands on human obedience. God himself knows completely his creation (Ps. 139) and his agents (Je. 1:5).

This Hebrew conception is largely retained in the NT. Knowing God is a dynamic and eternal relationship (Jn. 17:3; Phil. 3:10); spiritual enlightenment is 'coming to know the truth' (1 Tim. 2:4). Paul and John sometimes oppose the systems of esoteric 'knowledge' embraced by the cults of their day (e.g. 1 Tim. 6:20; Col. 2:8), stressing that true knowledge of God comes

from commitment to the historic Christ.

KOA. A people which will attack Jerusalem according to Ezk. 23:23, identified with the Qutu of Assyrian texts who lived E of the Tigris and associated with the Sutu, possibly the Shoa in Ezk.

KOHATH, KOHATHITES. The second son of Levi and his descendants, one of the three major Levite families. In the desert, they carried the tabernacle (Nu. 3:27ff.; 4:26). They later continued to be associated with temple worship (1 Ch. 6:31ff.).

KORAH. Several OT people, the most famous of whom rebelled with others against Moses and Aaron (Nu. 16). They felt the leaders had grown proud, failed in their duty to enter the promised land and wrongly kept the priesthood to themselves. They were killed by a sudden natural disaster; for a possible explanation of it see EXODUS.

LABAN (lit. 'white'). A descendant of Abraham's brother Nahor (Gn. 22:20ff.), Rebekah's brother and father of Jacob's wives Leah and Rachel, who lived in Haran. He spoke Aramaic (Gn. 31:47), practised marriage customs unknown to Jacob (Gn.

29:26), worshipped other gods (Gn. 31:19ff.) but did acknowledge the Lord (Gn. 24:50f.; *cf.* 31:53). He took advantage of Jacob's love for Rachel by tricking him into 14 years' work (Gn. 29-30); the two men later made a peace-treaty (Gn. 31:44ff.).

LACHISH. A large fortified city, modern Tell ed-Duweir 40 km SW of Jerusalem. It was first settled *c.* 2500 BC and was strongly fortified by *c.* 1750 BC. Temples found there illustrate the religious practices of Canaanites between 1550 and 1200 BC; they had altars of unhewn stones approached by steps (*cf.* Ex. 20:24ff.; Jos. 8:31). Bones of young sheep or goats were found, mostly the right foreleg (*cf.* Lv. 7:32). Joshua captured the city (Jos. 10:31f.); however, evidence for its destruction *c.* 1200 BC may be due to an Egyptian raid (*cf.* Jos. 11:13). The Israelites probably occupied the site throughout the time of the Judges. King Rehoboam rebuilt it (2 Ch. 11:5ff.) to a completely new plan as part of his defences against Egypt. The city had a large administrative building, and was surrounded by two walls. It was captured and destroyed by the Assyrian king Sennacherib (2 Ki. 18:17; 19:8; 2 Ch. 32:9). It was later administered by an Assyrian governor, and must have been partially rebuilt, but was destroyed again, this time by the Babylonians in 588-587 BC (Je.34:7). Returning exiles resettled it (Ne. 11:30); the site was later walled in the Persian and Greek periods but then abandoned for good.

Numerous inscriptions have been found there. Those relating to the Judaean monarchy are important for the history of the Hebrew alphabet. One seal bore the name of Gedaliah the royal steward, possibly the person appointed governor of Judah by Nebuchadrezzar (2 Ki. 25:22). A number of fragments of letters shed light on the last days before the fall of Judah, one of them referring to 'the prophet', possibly Jeremiah or Uriah (Je. 26:20ff.), testifying to the fact that prophets were actively participating in political affairs.

LAHMI. The name of Goliath's brother, killed by Elhanan, found only in 1 Ch. 20:5.

LAMB OF GOD. The actual term appears only twice in the NT (Jn. 1:29, 36), although other words for 'lamb' are applied to Jesus elsewhere. John the Baptist probably had in mind the lamb used as a sin offering. Others have suggested the Passover lamb or the horned ram who led the flock (but neither of these had sin-bearing roles), or an allusion to the sin-bearing servant of Is. 53. The author of John probably wanted readers to think of the sacrificial and Passover lambs, and the servant, combined.

LAMECH. 1. The descendant of Cain who introduced polygamy; one of his sons was Tubal-cain the first metalworker. He boasted of '77-fold' vengeance killings (Gn. 4:17ff.;*cf.* Mt. 18:22). 2. A descendant of Seth and father of Noah, probably not the same as 1 because this one expresses pious hopes (Gn. 5:29).

LAMENTATIONS, BOOK OF. *Contents and structure.* Chs. 1-4 are acrostic poems, 1-3 containing 66 lines each and ch. 4 containing 44. Chapter 3 is noteworthy because each of the 22 Hebrew letters is used for 3 successive one-line verses. The alphabetical pattern is usually an aid to memory, but in this case the carefully worked and highly artificial style also has the purpose of 'speaking' to the eye as well as the ear, of conveying an idea and not just a feeling; it expresses desperate grief with dignity. Chapter 3 is an individual lament rather than a funeral dirge, although the author speaks for the nation, and ch. 5, in a different style, closely resembles psalms of communal lament (*e.g.* Pss. 4; 80).

Authorship and date. Traditionally it has been ascribed to Jeremiah (although the book is anonymous) because of the similarity in temperament and belief concerning God's judgment of Jerusalem. However, some scholars consider the differences in style, and possible differences of attitude to Egypt (4:17; *cf.* Je. 37:5ff.) and to Zedekiah (4:20; *cf.* Je. 24:8ff.) rule out Jeremiah. The arguments are inconclusive. No part of the book need be dated later than the return from Exile in 538 BC.

Message and significance. It continues the prophets' emphasis that God has destroyed Jerusalem to punish his people's sin (1:18); a deep-seated sense of guilt runs through the book. The picture of God's wrath makes Lamentations a key source for study-

ing this aspect of God's nature (*e.g.* 2:1ff.). But a covenant-keeping God also gives cause for hope (3:19ff.); suffering can be disciplinary and related to God's goodness (3:25ff.).

LAMP, LAMPSTAND, LANTERN. Small open pottery bowls with one or more slight lips, which can be identified as simple oil lamps, first appear in Middle Bronze Age remains (2200-1550 BC) and continue through the Iron Age (1200-587 BC), with the lip becoming more pronounced. In the Hellenistic period (330-37 BC) the Greek style of lamp with an inward-curving rim became completely enclosed, with a small central filling hole, and a long spout for the wick. These lamps were mass produced from moulds, and lids were often impressed with floral and other designs.

The standard Palestinian lamp in NT times was round, plain, with a fairly wide flanged filling hole and a flared nozzle for the wick, sloping downwards. Some multi-wicked lamps have been found, and a few were made from metal (*cf.* Ex. 25:31ff.; 1 Ki. 7:49). Lamps burnt coarse olive oil or fat, and could stay alight for 2-4 hours. The wick was made from flax or other fibre, or rags. Pottery carriers for lamps are known from the Roman period (37 BC-AD 324); the lanterns of Jn. 18:3 may have been these.

In the OT, lamps symbolized life (Pr. 24:20), joy, prosperity and guidance (2 Sa. 22:29; Ps. 119:105). In the NT serviceable lamps symbolized readiness to serve God (Mt. 25:1ff.), and in Rev. 1-2 lampstands symbolize the churches 'shining' in the world. See also LIGHT.

LANDMARK. The boundaries of family land were defined by pillars or cairns. To remove them was tantamount to removing someone's claim to the land, and was a punishable offence (Dt. 19:14; 27:17).

LAODICEA. A city in the Roman province of Asia founded by Antiochus II in the 3rd cent. BC and named after his wife Laodice. Lying in the fertile Lycus valley at important crossroads, it became a prosperous commercial centre; when it was destroyed by an earthquake in AD 60 it was rich enough to refuse aid from Nero. Its products included glossy black wool; it was a specialist centre for eye-treatment; but its poor water supply was piped from hot springs some distance S and probably arrived lukewarm. The letter to Laodicea in Rev. 3:14ff. contains pointed allusions to these features. The church was possibly founded by Epaphras (Col. 4:12f.), probably while Paul was at Ephesus (Acts 19:10); there is no record that Paul visited it. The 'letter from Laodicea' (Col. 4:16) is often thought to have been a copy of Ephesians. See also HIERAPOLIS.

LAPPIDOTH (lit. 'torches'). The husband of Deborah (Jdg. 4:4).

LASEA. In Acts 27:8, probably Lasos, 8 km E of FAIR HAVENS.

LASHA. In Gn. 10:19 the furthest inland limit of Canaan, somewhere near the SE shore of the Dead Sea. The site is unknown.

LASHARON. In Jos. 12:18, possibly 10 km SW of Tiberias.

LASHES: See STRIPES.

LAST THINGS: See ESCHATOLOGY.

LATIN. Mentioned only twice in the NT (Lk. 23:38, RSV mg.; Jn. 19:20). An Indo-European language, it was spoken first in Rome and the Latian plain by people who entered Italy from the N before 900 BC. Latin expanded with Rome and became the second language of the W Mediterranean; 27 Latin words appear in the NT.

LAW. *Old Testament.* Discoveries of ancient Near Eastern material show that the legal tradition found in the OT started before 2000 BC. A legal code from Eshnunna, in the Akkadian language and dated *c.* 1800 BC, has several close similarities to the Covenant code of Ex. 21-23. The legal code of Hammurapi, king of Babylon *c.* 1700 BC, is the largest known and throws light on some OT legal practices. Some of Israel's specific laws have their roots in Mesopotamia and point to a common heritage.

There are three types of Hebrew law: the *apodictic* ('you shall/shall not'); *participial* laws consisting of participle clauses commanding the death of a criminal ('one doing this shall be put to death'); and *casuistic* laws ('if someone does...then the following action is taken'). The apodictic laws might be given by anyone in authority, including God, the king, and a father, and are sometimes mixed with religious material which has nothing in common with legal material (*e.g.* Ex. 22:27b). It is thus probably better to regard the Ten Commandments as the Lord's 'policy' than simply as a collection of laws. The participial laws possibly originated in, and governed, tribal conduct; the sentences were pronounced by tribal chiefs. The casuistic laws were probably legal examples to be followed by judges in dealing with civil disputes.

There are four Israelite codes of laws. *The Covenant code* (Ex. 21-23) is the oldest with its core going back to Moses, and some parts perhaps even to the Patriarchs; it was, however, naturally altered and adapted in later times. These laws were part of God's covenant with Israel, but do not cover all the possible judicial areas. *The Deuteronomic code* (Dt. 12-25) is a later codification of old Hebrew law. It contains undeniably ancient material but some was also added later, perhaps at the time of Josiah's reformation (*c.* 622 BC). *The Holiness code* (Lv. 17-26) is so-called from Lv. 21:8 and concerns the relationship of the sanctuary, priests and covenant community to the Lord. It is clearly very archaic and may well go back to Moses' time. The *final compilation* of the laws was made during and after the Exile in Babylon, the final form of the Pentateuch (Gn.-Dt.) being reached by *c.* 450 BC (*cf.* Ne. 8).

For more detailed discussion of views about dating and compilation of the law, see also OLD TESTAMENT, CANON OF; PENTATEUCH.

The distinction between civil and criminal law common today does not seem to have existed among the Hebrews; for example, laws about the 'crime' of theft concern the 'civil' need to redress the owner of the stolen property. There are seven clear categories of laws. *Murder and assault:* a distinction was made between premeditated murder and unintentional manslaughter (Ex. 21:12ff.). Assault was treated seriously; because of the emphasis on family solidarity the son who assaulted his parents was sentenced to death (Ex. 21:15). People incapacitated by assault had to be recompensed by the attacker (Ex. 21:18ff.). *Theft* included kidnapping which was punishable by death (Ex. 21:16). The penalty for stealing animals (the possession of which was very important in a semi-nomadic society) was a four- or five-fold restitution (Ex. 22:1ff.), although other laws specify only double repayment. *Moral and religious offences* included seducing a virgin, bestiality, cursing parents, idolatry and ill-treatment of foreigners; widows and orphans were especially protected against exploitation (Ex. 22:21ff.). *Family law* limited marriage between very close relatives (Lv. 18), provided for childless widows (Dt. 25:5ff.) and prescribed the conditions for divorce (Dt. 24:1ff.). *Slavery laws* provided for the automatic release of Hebrew slaves after 6 years' service (Ex. 21:2ff.), and for the protection of women slaves (Ex. 21:7ff.). The law of *retaliation* (*lex talionis*) restricted blood-revenge and wilful acts of assault in revenge for crimes (Ex. 21:23ff.); the temptation was always to exact more than an eye for an eye. Finally, there were *international laws*. Scores of tablets inscribed with treaties between nations have been recovered; the Israelite legal basis for such treaties is contained in Dt. 20:10ff. Israelite laws had a strong religious element. They were intended to promote love to God and to one's neighbour, as Jesus indicated in Mt. 22:35ff.

New Testament. The term has a rather different connotation to that of the OT. Sometimes, 'law' denotes the whole of the OT itself (*e.g.* Rom. 2:17ff.), or more frequently that part of the OT not included in 'the prophets' (*e.g.* Mt. 5:17), and sometimes called more specifically 'the law of Moses' (*e.g.* Acts 28:23). It may also mean God's law as the expression of God's will (*e.g.* Rom. 7:22). Paul uses it frequently to denote the law given to Moses on Mt. Sinai (*e.g.* Rom. 5:13). Closely related to this is his expression 'under the law' (Gal. 4:4f.), which means to be governed by the Mosaic institutions which God himself sanctioned. Confusion sometimes arises because Paul also uses the same phrase 'under law' to denote a person who regards the keeping of the law as a way to be accepted by God (Rom. 6:14f.). This person is in bondage to guilt and sin, which was not the automatic consequence of living within the Mosaic structures before the time of Christ. Law as a command-

ment demanding obedience cannot justify the ungodly, and it is from this 'bondage' that the believer has been set free (Rom. 7:4ff.). Paul tends to move from one meaning to another very quickly; for example in Rom. 3:19 'law' means the whole OT and 'under the law' means the laws of God given through Moses; in v. 21 'apart from the law' refers to the system which cannot justify the ungodly and 'the law (and prophets)' refers to the Pentateuch (Gn.-Dt.)

Therefore, in one sense being 'under law' means the opposite of being 'under grace'; it means being excluded from God's salvation revealed through Christ (Rom. 6:14). Thus believers are discharged from the law (Rom. 7:4, 6). But, says Paul, in another sense the gospel *upholds* the law (Rom. 3:31). The law is good (Rom. 7:16, 22, 25) and it is to be fulfilled by those who live by the power of the indwelling Spirit (Rom. 8:4). In Rom. 13:9f. he gives concrete examples to show that being controlled by love leads to conformity to God's law.

John does not speak about fulfilling the law, but he does emphasize the necessity for believers to keep God's commandments (1 Jn. 2:3f.; 5:2f.), because that expresses their love for him. James, well aware of the 'royal law' (Jas. 2:8), conceives of neither love nor law apart from concrete expressions of love in commandments (2:11). In other words, the law reflects God's own perfections; believers are to be holy because God is holy (1 Pet. 1:15f.). Salvation is to be saved from breaking the law and from conformity to it (1 Jn. 3:4). Obedience, for a Christian, is a joy, for he is destined to conform to the image of God's Son (Rom. 8:29), who is even characterized as a lawgiver (Mt. 5:22ff.) whose demands of inner holiness are even greater than the demands of outward conformity.

LAWYER: See SCRIBE.

LAYING ON OF HANDS. The symbolic action of laying hands on someone to invoke divine blessing or to symbolize spiritual blessing flowing from one person to another. In the OT, Jacob blessed Joseph's sons by laying his hands on their heads (Gn. 48:8ff.). Aaron laid his hands on a goat to symbolize the transference of the people's sin to it (Lv. 16:21). The Levites, who as priests represented the people before God, were ordained by the people placing hands on them (Nu. 8:10); Joshua was appointed Moses' successor in this way, receiving both authority and added spiritual gifts as a result (Nu. 27:18ff.; Dt. 34:9). In the NT, Jesus laid his hands on children (Mk. 10:16) and the sick (Mk. 6:5), as did the apostles (Acts 9:12). Baptism and reception of the Spirit were sometimes accompanied by laying-on of hands (*e.g.* Acts 8:14ff.; *cf.* Heb. 6:2). It was also an ordination or commissioning rite for ministry (Acts 6:5f.; 13:3; *cf.* 1 Tim. 5:22), as an outward sign that God gave his gifts for the task. See also HAND.

LAZARUS AND DIVES. In Lk. 16: 19-31 Dives (Lat. 'rich man') ignored the plight of Lazarus the beggar. After death, Dives departed to Hades and Lazarus to heaven. Contact between the two after-lives was impossible, for the irrevocable decision concerning eternal destiny had been taken on earth. The story also illustrated the danger of wealth blinding people to others' needs. See also CHASM.

LAZARUS OF BETHANY. Although his sisters Mary and Martha are better known, Lazarus appears in the Gospels' narrative only because Jesus raised him from the dead (Jn. 11). The early part of the story reads like an eyewitness account with striking detail (*e.g.* vv. 6, 8f., 12ff.). The quiet sobriety of the account of the resurrection itself is in marked contrast to the fantastic inventiveness of, say, the account of Jesus' resurrection in *The Gospel of Peter*, and also bears the marks of an eyewitness account. A fictional story would almost certainly have revealed something of Lazarus' experience in the realm of the dead and/or his words on being raised. It is possible that the Jewish plot to kill Lazarus (Jn. 12:10f.) might have provoked Jesus' comment about resurrection in the parable of Lazarus and the rich man (Lk. 16:31), but no other identification between the two can be made.

LEAH. The elder daughter of Laban who through her father's deception became Jacob's first wife (Gn. 29:21ff.). She bore 6 of the 12 founders of Israel's tribes, allied with Rachel and Jacob against Laban (Gn. 31), and was buried at Machpelah (Gn. 49:31).

LEATHER: See TANNER.

LEAVEN (YEAST). Leaven was used as a raising agent in bread. It was made originally from fine white bran kneaded with must; from the meal of fitch or vetch; or from barley mixed with water and then allowed to stand until it turned sour. Later, it was produced from bread flour kneaded without salt and kept until it began to ferment. In ordinary bread-making, leaven was probably a piece of dough left over from one baking, allowed to ferment, and then kneaded into the next batch. It has been suggested that the Jews also used the lees of wine as yeast, but this is uncertain.

Leaven was prohibited in the Passover (Ex. 12:15ff.; 23:15) to remind Israelites of their hurried departure from Egypt; leavened bread was used in the thank-offering, however (Lv. 7:13). Fermentation may also have symbolized disintegration and corruption; leaven was used as a symbol for human sinfulness by the later rabbis. Jesus used it to symbolize the hypocrisy, scepticism and guile of Pharisees, Sadducees and Herodians (Mt. 16:6; Mk. 8:15), and Paul used a similar picture (1 Cor. 5:6ff.; Gal. 5:9). But Jesus also used leaven on one occasion to symbolize the growth of his kingdom (Mt. 13:33). See also BREAD.

LEBANON. Biblically, a mountain range in Syria, the name also being loosely applied to adjoining regions

(*e.g.* Jos. 13:5); today it is the name of a republic. The name derives from a root word meaning 'white', referring to the white limestone and to the peaks which are snow-capped for 6 months of the year (Je. 18:14). The range is 160 km long, a direct continuation of the N Galilee hills, and is marked by a series of peaks, the highest being *c.* 3,000 m (Qurnet es-Sauda, ESE of Tripoli), with Mt Hermon *c.* 2,800 m. The W flanks of the range sweep down to the Mediterranean leaving at most only a narrow coastal plain, originally providing the Phoenician coastal cities with a natural barrier against invaders from inland.

Well watered by both rain and streams, the coastland and lower mountain slopes supported olive groves, vineyards, fruit orchards and small cornfields. The famous and once-dense forests higher up consisted of myrtles and conifers, culminating in the majestic cedar groves of which only a handful survive today. Its fertility is reflected in Scripture (*e.g.* Ps. 72:16), its cedars became symbols of strength (*e.g.* Ps. 92:12) or pride (Ps. 29:5f.). The trees provided the finest building timber in the Near East, used for temples (1 Ki. 5) and ships (Ezk. 27:5). The timber trade dates to earliest times; the Egyptian pharaoh Snofru imported 40 shiploads of cedar *c.* 2600 BC. Later Egyptian rulers conquered Syria and exacted tribute-taxes of cedar; a relief of Sethos I (*c.* 1300 BC) depicts the Syrians felling the trees. The Assyrians followed suit; Tiglath-pileser I *c.* 1100 BC and Esarhaddon *c.*

675 BC both levied cedar-taxes for temple building.

See also BASHAN; HERMON; SENIR; SIRION.

LEB-KAMAI. An artificial word used in Je. 51:1 (RV, NIV) as a word play. The consonants represent the Chaldeans and the vowels give the quasi-meaning of 'the heart of those that rise up against me'.

LEES. The dregs at the bottom of wine-jars (*e.g.* Is. 25:6).

LEG. Sometimes used symbolically for 'strength' (*e.g.* Ps. 147:10). The thighs of sacrificial animals were usually considered the choicest cut and were reserved for the priests (*e.g.* Lv. 7:32ff.).

LEGION. The main division of the Roman army, comprising 4,000-6,000 men and divided into 10 cohorts of 6 centuries each. Palestine saw few legionaries until the Jewish rebellion in AD 66; policing was previously done by auxiliary cohorts. In the NT the word suggests 'a great number' (*e.g.* Lk. 8:30).

LEHABIM. The third son of Mizraim (Gn. 10:13). The name is otherwise unknown but may be equated with Libyans (2 Ch. 12:3) or LUDIM.

LEHI (lit. 'jawbone'). The place in Judah where Samson killed 1,000 men; the site is unknown (Jdg. 15).

LEMUEL. King of Massa whose mother's instructions are recorded in Pr. 31:1-9. Rabbinic tradition held it referred to Solomon.

LETTER (EPISTLE). Private or official letters are part of the heritage of all literate peoples; examples in the OT include 2 Sa. 11:14 and 1 Ki. 21:8. The earliest known Greek letters already show a tendency to use the letter form for larger purposes. Some of Isocrates' letters (368-338 BC) are set speeches; Plato's Seventh Letter (*c.* 354 BC) is a refutation of popular misconceptions about his ideas and behaviour. Both aim at other readers than just those addressed, and hence are a form of publication. The theory and practice of this kind of letter-writing was a subject treated by teachers of rhetoric. G. A. Deissmann attempted to divide Paul's letters into personal, direct un-literary 'letters' and impersonal literary 'epistles'. The distinction cannot be maintained sharply; Galatians and Ephesians are composed on a rhetorical plan, but they all contain rhetorical elements and most contain personal greetings. Even Philemon, the most intensely personal, contains rhetorical elements comparable to some in Isocrates' *Epistle 8*. Hebrews, James, 1 and 2 Peter and Jude are mostly literary, like sermons. For NT letters, see under separate titles.

LEVI. The third son of Jacob and Leah, whose only recorded action (apart from events common to all Jacob's sons) was his treacherous attack with Simeon on the city of Shechem in revenge for the rape of their sister Dinah (Gn. 34). They were cursed by Jacob for a life of violence (Gn. 49:5ff.), but later descendants of Levi turned the curse into a blessing through their loyalty to God; although scattered through the tribes they were God's representative priests. For Levi in the NT, see MATTHEW.

LEVIATHAN. A transliteration of a Hebrew word occurring only 5 times in the OT, where it indicates some form of water monster. In Ps. 104:26 it may indicate the whale or dolphin. The symbolism of Is. 27:1 and Ps. 74:14 make identification difficult; it may be a reference to a mythological 7-headed monster. In Jb. 3:8 it is generally believed to refer to the mythological dragon which caused solar eclipses by wrapping its coils round the sun. In Ezk. 29:3ff. the description is that of the crocodile (dragon, RSV). In the longest description, Jb. 41, it is also probably the crocodile (*cf.* vv. 13, 15). There are crocodiles in the Nile, and Crusaders reported seeing crocodiles in the Zerka river which enters the Mediterranean near Caesarea and is still called locally Crocodile R.

LEVITICUS, BOOK OF. *Contents.* It consists mainly of laws relating to the Israelites' religious ritual, but it also continues the narrative of Israel's experiences at Sinai (1:1; 4:1; *etc.*). The contents can be divided thus: laws concerning offerings (1-7); the tabernacle service put into operation (8-10); laws concerning purity (11-15); the Day of Atonement (16); various laws (17-25); promises and warnings (26); appendix on valuation and redemption (27).

Unity. In the form in which we now possess Leviticus, it forms a well-knit and coherent whole. It is possible that the laws about offerings (1-7) once existed separately, but they fit well into their context in the Pentateuch (Gn.-Dt.) and in Leviticus itself. The ban on eating blood (17:10f.) had already been imposed in 3:17 and 7:26f. without the accompanying explanation; the laws of purity (11-15) point to the necessity of keeping sin at a distance, and as sin separates people from God so the sacrificial means of approaching him have to be explained first (1-7). 20:25 provides a close link between 11-15 and 18-20, and does not therefore encourage the view that 17-26 form a separate 'Holiness Code' as has been suggested. Indeed, the whole book can be called 'the book of God's holiness' (*cf.* 20:26).

Authorship and composition. The author is not named. God is said to speak often to Moses and/or Aaron but he gives no command to write down his laws. Moses may have set them down, or a later writer may have set in order Moses' original material. In the documentary hypothesis, Leviticus is usually assigned to the Priestly Code (P), for a discussion of which see PENTATEUCH.

Significance. Leviticus provides a background to all the other Bible books with its detailed descriptions of offerings and ceremonies. Jews still find within it their regulations about food and other matters. But of special interest to Christians is its explanation of the way God deals with sin through sacrifices, promises and warnings. It is the book of sanctification and consecration of the whole of life, the book of avoidance of and atonement for sin. The inmost significance of the sacrificial offerings was fulfilled by the obedient death of Jesus Christ, and hence the book points forward to him as the ultimate means whereby people are made acceptable to God.

LIBERTY: See FREEDOM.

LIBNAH. 1. An important town taken by Joshua (Jos. 10:29f.). It revolted against Jehoram (2 Ki. 8:22) and was besieged by Sennacherib (2 Ki. 19:8, 35). The identification of the site is disputed. 2. An unidentified campsite in the desert (Nu. 33:20f.).

LIBNI. A son of Gershon; Ladan in 1 Ch. 23:7f.; 26:21.

LIBYA. During the 12th-8th cents. BC Libyans entered Egypt as raiders or settlers, hence were prominent in Egyptian forces (e.g. 2 Ch. 12:3; Na. 3:9). See also LEHABIM; PUT.

LIE, LYING. A statement of what is known to be false with intent to deceive (cf. Jdg. 16:10, 13). Biblical writers severely condemn lies which perpetrate fraud (Lv. 6:2f.), achieve undeserved condemnation (Dt. 19:15), or are false words claimed to be from God (Je. 14:14). Lying expresses evil (Ho. 12:1; Nu. 23:19). Satan is the 'father of lies' (Jn. 8:44); habitual liars

forfeit eternal life (Rev. 21:27); thus all falsehood is forbidden among Christians (Col. 3:9). 1 Sa. 16:2 does not justify expedient lies; the prophet had no obligation to divulge his mission but he did have an ostensible reason for his visit. See also TRUTH.

LIFE. *Old Testament.* Life is that which is active (Ps. 69:34) in contrast to that which is inert, hence faith as well as people can be alive or dead (Jas. 2:17). Both the words 'soul' and 'spirit' can be virtual synonyms for life; man is a living soul or 'self' (Gn. 2:7) whose dying soul can be restored (1 Ki. 17:21) or flagging spirit revived (1 Sa. 30:12). But mankind is mortal (Jb. 4:17), barred from the tree of eternal life (Gn. 3:24); human life is as temporary as that of cut grass or morning dew (Pss. 39:4f.; 90:5f.). Anything which threatens life is seen as an invasion of death (Ps. 30:2f.); to incur God's displeasure is to die (Gn. 2:17; 20:3); to live a long time is a sign of God's blessing (Dt. 5:16). In death, people return to the dust (Gn. 3:19), although they may live on in their children or reputation (Ps. 72:17); like water spilt on the ground they cannot be gathered up again (2 Sa. 14:14). Death (Sheol) is a state of sleep with no memory or thought (Jb. 3:16ff.; Ps. 6:5). The OT has only occasional glimpses of any life in the grave (e.g. Ezk. 31-32); the hope of overcoming the apparent victory of death lies only in God.

He is the living God, which distinguishes him from the powerless idols (Is. 46:5ff.). He is the source of life (Je. 17:13), who delivers people from

Sheol and leads them along the path of daily life (Ps. 16:10f.). Human dependence on God is such that our breath or spirit can be called God's (Gn. 6:3; Is. 42:5; *cf.* Jb. 34:14). Life is thus on loan from God and true life consists in God-centred conduct (Ps. 73:23ff.). Although not always apparent, righteousness leads to life (Pr. 11:19). The living God rules over death to heal (2 Ki. 5:7, 14), to raise the dead (1 Ki. 17:20ff.), to cause life to bud in a childless woman (1 Sa. 1:19f.; 2:6). Rarely is God seen as delivering people from death itself but the conviction was not absent (*e.g.* Jb. 19:26; Ps. 16:8ff.); Jesus appealed to the OT witness that God continued to be Abraham's God after the Patriarch had died, and therefore it could be inferred that he would raise him from Sheol (Mt. 22:31f.). Resurrection life in the OT belonged to the reign of the Messiah (Is. 26:19).

New Testament. As in the OT, life is seen as something transitory, dependent on and at the disposal of God (Mt. 4:4; 10:28). The moral quality of life as a relationship to God is more sharply focused. A person related to God is 'alive' and the person not so related is 'dead' (Eph. 2:1f.). All life is seen as under imminent judgment (Lk. 13:3); the NT makes a clearer distinction than the OT between soul or natural life which is under judgment (Lk. 12:20) and resurrection life which is the only true life and which outlasts death. Christ laid down his own life, and took it up again, in order to remove the death-threat of Sheol for all (Jn. 10:17; Acts 2:31). The person

who gives up their natural life to him will be caught up in his resurrection life (Mk. 8:35f.).

The resurrection life, being the only true life, is often called simply 'life' (Acts 5:20; Rom. 5:17). It is abundant (Jn. 10:10), immortal (2 Tim. 1:10) and holy (Rom. 6:22f.). It is God's property (1 Tim. 6:13) and was made visible in Jesus Christ who assures his followers that they will inherit it too (Mk. 10:29f.). He is life itself (Jn. 14:6), the author of all life (Acts 3:15), the sustainer of life (Jn. 6:35), and by his resurrection has shown himself the judge of all life (Mk. 14:62; Jn. 11:25). Our resurrection is to be understood in terms of his (1 Cor. 15). His life is mediated to the Christian through repentance and faith (Acts 11:18; Jn. 3:16). The individual cannot determine this life, only enter or receive it (Mk. 10:17, 30); Christ gives it impartially to whomever he wills (Jn. 5:21).

In the Synoptic Gospels this life is always seen as a future inheritance associated with the coming kingdom of God (*e.g.* Mt. 25:46). This view continues in John and in Paul's letters (*e.g.* Jn. 5:28f.; 2 Cor. 5:4), but resurrection life is also seen as the believer's present possession (1 Jn. 3:14; Eph. 2:5f.). The Holy Spirit comes as a 'down payment' or 'first instalment' of future life (2 Cor. 5:5). This is realized in renewal of life and transformation of attitude (Rom. 12:1f.; Gal. 5:22ff.), but the body must still pass through the gate of physical death, which Jesus will finally abolish at his second coming (1 Cor. 15:51ff.). The NT view of death is summed up by the believer's cry,

'Come Lord Jesus', not Bach's plea, 'Come sweet death'. Resurrection life will still be bodily, the life of the whole person (Phil. 3:21), in the presence of Jesus (Jn. 14:3) with a full vision of God (1 Cor. 13:12).

See also DEATH; RESURRECTION; SOUL; SPIRIT.

LIGHT. Used symbolically in the Bible to describe God's presence and favour (*e.g.* Ps. 27:1; 2 Cor. 4:6). This gave rise to an ethical contrast between light (good) and darkness (evil), as in Jn. 3:19ff.; 2 Cor. 6:14. God's holiness is expressed as 'unapproachable light' (1 Tim. 6:16; *cf.* 1 Jn. 1:5); his people are thus 'children of the light' (Eph. 5:8) called to reflect his light in the world (Mt. 5:14ff.). In John's Gospel light refers more especially to God's revelation of his love in Christ; Jesus is the light of the world (Jn. 8:12). See also LAMP.

LIGHTNING. Lightning and its accompanying thunder was well-known in Palestine, especially in November-December; at times 'fire' is used when 'lightning' is meant (*e.g.* Ex. 9:23; 1 Ki. 18:38; Ps. 148:8). It is sometimes employed to describe someone's striking appearance (Mt. 28:3), is associated with God's appearance (Ex. 19:16; Rev. 4:5) and regarded as an instrument of his judgment (Ps. 144:6). See also THUNDER.

LILY: See PLANTS.

LIME, LIMESTONE. Limestone is abundant in Palestine. Lime was made from it by heating it in a kiln. It was used for plaster (Dt. 27:2); in Is. 33:12; Am. 2:1 it is a symbol of total destruction.

LINE. Measuring lines were used to mark out buildings or land (*e.g.* 2 Sa. 8:2; Is. 34:17), and hence used symbolically to denote God's testing of a place or nation's integrity (*e.g.* Is. 28:17).

LINEN. Linen is made as a thread from the rind of flax, then spun into material. Although flax was cultivated in Palestine, Egypt was the chief producer in ancient times (*cf.* Pr. 7:16). Israel's priests wore linen coats, turbans and girdles (Ex. 28:39) for coolness (Ezk. 44:17f.). The Israelites used the linen they took from Egypt to make the curtains, veil and screen for the tabernacle (Ex. 26:1, 31, 36). Samuel and David wore linen ephods (1 Sa. 2:18; 2 Sa. 6:14), and it often seems associated with special or holy persons (*e.g.* Dn. 10:5; 12:6f.). Linen was regarded as a fine gift and was highly valued (Pr. 31:22; Is. 3:23).

In the NT the word is little used. The rich man in the parable and the young man in the garden wore linen (Lk. 16:19; Mk. 14:51); Jesus' body was wrapped in linen (Mt. 27:59); and the saints in heaven are seen as clothed in linen to represent their righteous deeds (Rev. 19:8, 14). See also DRESS; EMBROIDERY.

LINUS. A Roman Christian who greeted Timothy (2 Tim. 4:21). Irenaeus identified him with the first bishop of Rome after the apostles, but this is not proven.

LION. Lions similar to those found in Africa lived across the Near East through Persia to India. The last lion in Palestine was killed probably near Megiddo in the 13th cent. AD; they were still known in Persia early in the 20th cent. The 130 references in the Bible suggest they were common and well-known; they were frequently kept in captivity (Dn. 6:7ff.). They are used as symbols of God acting in judgment (Ho. 13:7f.) and of a prowling, hungry Satan (1 Pet. 5:8).

LION OF JUDAH. One of Jesus' Messianic titles (Rev. 5:5), with an allusion to Gn. 49:9 and to courage, might and ferocity. Emperors of Ethiopia, convinced they were descended from Solomon and the Queen of Sheba, used the title until Haile Selassie's overthrow in 1974.

LIP. The lips are sometimes described, like other parts of the body, as if they act independently of the rest. They speak (Jb. 27:4), shout for joy (Ps. 71:23), guard knowledge (Pr. 5:2), offer praise (Ps. 63:3) and possess truthfulness or sin by lying (Pr. 12:19). See also MOUTH; TONGUE.

LIVER. The word occurs only in the OT; 11 of its 14 occurrences are in Ex. and Lv. and refer to the liver of a sacrificial animal, where it appears that the fat on it, or the pancreas, rather than the liver itself, was burned (Ex. 29:13). Livers were also used in divination (Ezk. 21:21), for which see DIVINATION; MAGIC AND SORCERY.

LIZARD. Some 40 species are known in Palestine, the most common being the rainbow lizard and the rock gecko. Six kinds are listed as forbidden for food in Lv. 11:29f., but they are hard to identify precisely. The 'land crocodile' is probably the desert monitor, and the 'sand lizard' probably the skink. The chameleon is uncommon, and so the difficult word thus translated may refer to something else.

LOCUST. The most important biblical insect with 9 Hebrew and 1 Greek names, probably referring to different species, stages of growth (as in Joel 1:4) or nicknames. They were the only insects allowed for food (Lv. 11:21); for desert tribes at certain seasons they could have been a major source of protein. Locusts are in fact highly gregarious grasshoppers, although swarms may be a response to local conditions; swarms are largely wind-driven and can devastate crops. The female lays packets of eggs beneath the soil's surface where they may stay for many months until moisture allows them to hatch. They are sometimes used biblically as symbols of judgment.

LO-DEBAR. Where Mephibosheth lived (2 Sa. 9:4); probably DEBIR.

LOGOS: See WORD.

319

LOIS. Timothy's grandmother (2 Tim. 1:5), a godly woman, almost certainly a Christian. The name is unusual.

LORD'S DAY: See SABBATH.

LORD'S PRAYER. The prayer which Jesus taught his disciples as a model for their regular use. In Mt. 6:9-13 it is in the context of teaching disciples the principles of prayer: the shorter form in Lk. 11:2-4 is given in response to a disciple's question as a prayer to be used.

The first three petitions focus on God's glory. *Our Father who art in heaven* teaches the correct attitude for prayer; we look to God our Father in love and faith, and express reverence to the one who is ruler over all. *Hallowed be thy name* asks God to enable us and all people to recognize and honour him as holy. ('Name' refers to his revelation of himself and his character.) *Thy kingdom come* requests that his rule will be extended in people's lives and present world affairs, and looks forward to the final establishment of his rule when Jesus returns. *Thy will be done on earth as it is in heaven* elaborates the previous request; heaven is where God's will is gladly and unconditionally accepted.

The next three petitions are concerned with believers' physical and spiritual well-being. *Give us this day our daily bread* asks God for all the basic things we need for physical life so that we can most effectively honour him, work for his kingdom and do his will. It is not therefore a selfish prayer but a petition which confesses utter dependence on God. *Forgive us our debts, as we also have forgiven our debtors* is both a prayer and a confession—asking for forgiveness is to admit one's faults. Sin creates a moral and spiritual debt to God, who alone can remit that debt for we can never earn our own forgiveness. In order to pray for forgiveness sincerely, we must be free of all hatred against, and desire for revenge over, others; Jesus expanded on this in Mt. 6:14f. and 18:23ff. The petition does not mean that by forgiving others we merit or earn God's forgiveness for ourselves. *And lead us not into temptation but deliver us from evil* confesses that we are prone to sin and thus pleads that the God who has control over our lives will not allow us into situations which bring with them grave temptations; God himself cannot tempt us (Jas. 1:13). In addition, we ask to be shielded from the devil's onslaughts, and to be kept from failing when our faith is challenged by some supreme test (*cf.* Mk. 14:38).

In some MSS a doxology follows: *For thine is the kingdom and the power and the glory, forever. Amen.* It is a suitable and worthy ending and has been used since earliest times but is not part of the original text; vv. 14f. follow naturally from vv. 12f. The Lord's Prayer is unique in Jewish religious literature. It is Jesus' message of the kingdom of God summarized as a prayer to be used regularly by his people so they may be enabled to live more completely for him until he finally establishes his kingly rule.

LORD'S SUPPER. *Jesus' 'Last Supper'.*

The traditional explanation of this meal is that it was the celebration of customary Passover feast, and the Gospels support this (Mk. 14:1f., 12ff.; Jn. 13:21ff.). There are certain clear similarities, not least the 'sop' dipped in the special sauce as a memorial of Israel's bitter captivity in Egypt. But the evidence is not so clear as to exclude all other interpretations, largely because John's Gospel apparently dates the meal a day earlier than the others. Jn. 13:1; 18:28; 19:14, 31, 42 date the crucifixion as the day before 15 Nisan, with Jesus dying as the Passover lambs were being butchered. On this dating the Last Supper could not have been a Passover meal, and scholars who prefer John's dating thus suggest it was a sabbath *Qiddush*, a simple service with a prayer of sanctification over a cup of wine. The debate is currently deadlocked. Some light may be shed on it by research into separate calendars used for calculating feast days. The Dead Sea Scrolls have revealed that different calendars were in use at the time among Jewish sects, and Jesus may have celebrated Passover according to one of these rather than according to Pharisaic reckoning. What is certain is that whatever the exact nature of the meal, Jesus' had Passover ideas in mind as he sat down to it. The Exodus and Israel's 'redemption' from Egypt form indispensable background to the NT understanding of Jesus' death.

The exact form of words Jesus used over the bread and wine vary in the Gospels and 1 Cor. Some scholars consider Paul's version 'this cup is the new covenant in my blood' (1 Cor. 11:25) more likely to be original on the assumption that Jesus would never have suggested that his disciples should drink his blood (Mk. 14:24). Others suggest that the harsher Semitic phrasing of Mark is more primitive, and again the debate is inconclusive. There is however little doubt that a literal interpretation— 'this *is* (literally) my blood'—is ruled out on linguistic grounds. Jesus was speaking figuratively; some suggest he was pointing to his broken body and shed blood on the cross, others that the bread was pointing to his real 'self' which after his resurrection would continue to be present with his disciples in their table fellowship. The most valuable clue to Jesus' meaning is that the 'words of institution' over the bread and wine added to the order of the Passover liturgy at two vital points before and after the main meal. Jesus was saying by word and symbolic action that the original meaning of the Jewish rite had now been transcended, for he had fulfilled the OT symbolism (1 Cor. 5:7). He was announcing a new significance for the bread, as his body given up in the service of God's redeeming purpose (*cf.* Heb. 10:5ff.), and for the cup, as the memorial of a new 'Exodus' he accomplished (Lk. 9:31; 'departure', RSV). The function of the elements was thus parallel to that of the Passover dishes.

The breaking of bread. The phrase is used in Acts (*e.g.* 2:42, 46) in contexts where the cup is not mentioned. It may have been a title for the whole meal, which continued the sense of joy associated with the post-resurrection appearances of Jesus often at meal-times (*e.g.* Lk. 24:30ff.; Jn. 21:9ff.). There is no need to presume that it was simply a continuation of the disciples' fellowship meals with Jesus.

The eucharist in Paul's letters. The fellowship meals more probably were continued in the love-feast (*Agape*) of 1 Cor. 11:20ff. The common meal (for nourishment) was followed by the solemn rite of the Eucharist. Because of the excesses of some people, Paul seems to have wanted the two parts kept separate; feast at home, reverent self-examination at the Lord's table. The Supper proclaims Jesus' death (v. 26) and is communion of unity with both Jesus and fellow believers (1 Cor. 10:16).

The rest of the NT has little witness to the sacrament. There may be allusions in Heb. 6:4; 13:10; and many scholars relate Jn. 6:22ff. to it. 2 Pet. 2:13 and Jude 12 refer to the *Agape* meal. Evidence of its development comes no earlier than in 2nd-cent. writings. For *Agape* see LOVE FEAST.

LOT. The son of Haran, Abraham's youngest brother, and so Abraham's nephew. He travelled with Abraham from Ur to Canaan, choosing the well-watered Jordan valley for himself (Gn. 13:8ff.). He was twice rescued from evil people in Sodom (Gn. 14; 19). His daughters contrived to have children by him (Gn. 19:30ff.), and the story of his wife (Gn. 19) was recalled by Jesus in his teaching about the last days (Lk.

17:28ff.).

LOVE. *Old Testament.* It is the deepest expression of the personality and of the closeness of personal relationships (Gn. 22:2; 37:3). In its non-religious sense the word is most commonly used for the love of man and woman, reaching its most sublime expression in the Song of Solomon. God is said to love his people, usually in a collective sense (*e.g.* Dt. 4:37). Only on three occasions are individuals said to be personal objects of his love (2 Sa. 12:24; Ne. 13:26; Is. 48:14). God's love is deeper than that of a mother (Is. 49:15), his faithfulness being illustrated in the story of Hosea and Gomer (Ho. 1-3). Love is part of his character so he cannot be swayed by passion or diverted by disobedience (Ho. 11:1ff.). His love is selective; he especially chose Israel to be his people for no other reason than his love (Dt. 4:37; 7:6ff.). In response he demands love from the whole human personality (Dt. 6:5), a relationship of personal devotion created and sustained by God's work in the human heart (Dt. 30:6). It consists of communion with God (Ps. 18:1) worked out in daily obedience (Jos. 22:5). Love is also to be the norm for human relationships (Lv. 19:18); even enemies, while not loved, are still to be helped (Ex. 23:4f.). See also LOVING-KINDNESS.

New Testament. The commonest word for all forms of love, *agape*, was one of the least frequent in classical Greek where on the few occasions it was used it denoted the highest and noblest form of love which sees something infinitely precious in its object. It was used by the LXX for 95% of the Hebrew occurrences of love. Another word, *phileo* (friendship), is also used, with some overlap of meaning.

Love describes the relationship between God the Father and God the Son (Jn. 3:35; 14:31; 15:9). Jesus himself did not use the word to express God's love for people, but revealed it in his compassionate healing (Lk. 7:13), his teaching about God's acceptance (Lk. 15:11ff.), and by showing himself a friend to the outcasts (Lk. 7:34). John declares Jesus' saving activity to be a demonstration of God's love (Jn. 3:16). As in the OT, his love is selective, its object being the 'new Israel', the church (Eph. 5:25), and under the new covenant his love is extended to the individual members of the church (Gal. 2:20).

God's love for mankind is intended to transform man's natural state of being God's enemy (Rom. 5:10) into a loving relationship (1 Jn. 4:19). Jesus expected people to love God (Lk. 11:42) but he preferred to speak of the man-God relationship in terms of faith (Mt. 9:22), perhaps because 'love' did not convey sufficiently the attitude of humility and trust. Love for one's neighbour, said Jesus, was not to be limited (Lk. 10:25ff.); even enemies were to be loved (Mt. 5:44). This new attitude springs from the work of God's Spirit within a person (Gal. 5:22f.). Christians are to love one another with 'brotherly love' (Rom. 12:10), which is not so much brother-like as a special relationship of unity with fellow-members of God's family (Lk. 22:32; Jn. 13:34; 15:12). It is an outworking of Jesus' love (Eph. 5:1f.), revealed in common ways of thinking (Rom. 15:5f.) and in helping one another (Rom. 12:9ff.). It proves the genuineness of the Christian's faith (1 Jn. 2:9ff.; 3:10; 4:20).

LOVE FEAST. Fellowship meals, or love feasts (*Agape*), are mentioned in Jude (v. 12) and possibly in 2 Pet. 2:13. The 'breaking of bread' (Acts 2:42, 46) may have included both *Agape* and Eucharist, and Paul's account of the Eucharist sets it in the context of a fellowship supper (1 Cor. 11:17ff.). His farewell speech at Troas was at a fellowship meal which included the Eucharist (Acts 20:7ff.). For the sacrament itself, see LORD'S SUPPER.

LOVING-KINDNESS. A rendering of a Hebrew word mostly occurring in the Psalms, frequently rendered by RSV as 'steadfast love'. It is closely connected with the ideas of covenant and faithfulness. See also MERCY.

LUCIFER. The Latin name for the bright planet Venus, applied in Is. 14:12 (AV) to the king of Babylon and by extension to Satan as a fallen star (*cf.* Lk. 10:18; Rev. 9:1; 12:9). The true 'morning star' is Jesus (Rev. 22:16).

LUCIUS. 1. A Cyrenian prophet and teacher at Antioch, probably one of its first missionaries (Acts 13:1; *cf.* 11:19ff.). 2. Paul's companion in Corinth (Rom. 16:21). Both were Jews and thus unlikely to be identified with the

Gentile Luke (whose name is a shortened form of Lucius).

LUD, LUDIM. A descendant of Shem; his descendants were identified by Josephus as Lydians (see LYDIA). In Is. 66:19 (*cf.* Gn. 10:13; Je. 46:9) Lud is a Gentile nation of archers (not true of Lydia), but like Lydia was an ally of Tyre and Egypt (Ezk. 27:10; 30:5).

LUHITH, ASCENT OF. A place in Moab placed by Josephus between Areopolis and Zoar (Is. 15:5; Je. 48:5).

LUKE. A companion of Paul described as 'the beloved physician' (Col. 4:14) and a 'fellow-worker' (Phm. 24), who on one occasion provided Paul's only company when others had left him (2 Tim. 4:11). On the basis of the exclusion clause in Col. 4:11 he is usually believed to have been a Gentile. Irenaeus (*c.* AD 180) first named him as the author of the third Gospel and Acts, although the tradition is probably earlier. There are several passages in Acts written in the first person from the viewpoint of one of Paul's companions (16:10-17; 20:5-21; 18; 27:1-28:16) and of the possible companions known from the letters but not named in Acts, Luke stands out as the probable author of Acts and hence also of the Gospel (*cf.* Lk. 1:1-4 with Acts 1:1f.). No other author has ever been suggested. The literary style of Lk.-Acts demonstrates their author was well educated, and the traces of medical language and interest reinforce the identification with Luke the physician. He had ample opportunity to gain first-hand knowledge about Jesus' life and the early church on his visits to Jerusalem and Caesarea.

LUKE, GOSPEL OF. *Contents.* Preface (1:1-4); the birth and childhood of Jesus (1:5-2:52); John the Baptist and Jesus (3:1-4:13); Jesus' ministry in Galilee (4:14-9:50); progress towards Jerusalem (9:51-19:10); Jesus' ministry in Jerusalem (19:11-21:38); Jesus' death and resurrection (22-24).

Sources. Much of the content is shared with Matthew and Mark, and it is generally agreed that Mark was one of Luke's major sources. Almost all Mark is included in Luke but it has been rewritten in Luke's more developed literary style. Luke also includes much of Jesus' teaching which is in Matthew but not in Mark, and it is generally assumed that this came from a common source or collection of sources, rather than one of the Gospels being dependent on the other. Luke also has some unique material; this and the preface (1:1-4) suggests that he was well acquainted with a variety of written and oral witnesses to the life of Jesus. See also GOSPELS.

Author and date. Luke and Acts are two parts of the same work, and it is most probable that Luke, 'the beloved physician' and companion of Paul, wrote both; for reasons supporting this view see LUKE. The Gospel is not a Pauline re-interpretation of the story of Jesus, however, for Luke had his own distinctive slant on the Christian faith. The date of composition depends on the date assigned to Mark and whether Luke was writing before or after the fall of Jerusalem which Jesus prophesied. As Acts finishes before Paul's death and has no interest in Jerusalem's fall, Lk.-Acts was probably complete before AD 70.

Purpose and character. Luke was concerned to show the significance and reliability of the story of Jesus to people who believed in him. He wrote for people removed from the ministry of Jesus by both distance and time. The dedication to the otherwise unknown Theophilus suggests it was meant for church members, but it could also be used as a handbook in evangelism, and a wider audience than the single named individual was intended. The author was a well-educated historian who produced a work which would commend the gospel by its literary quality, but he had conscious theological purposes too. His two key words are the verb 'to preach the gospel' (*e.g.* Lk. 1:19; 3:18; 4:43; Acts 8:4), which is virtually absent from the other Gospels, and 'salvation' (Lk. 1:47, 69; 2:11, 30). He shows how Jesus fulfilled OT prophecy (Lk. 4:18ff.; 10:23f.) and how through him God has begun to rescue people from the powers of evil (Lk. 11:20). Jesus is God's anointed King who will reign in the future kingdom (Lk. 22:29f.; 23:42); he is 'Lord' (Acts 2:36) and Son of God (Lk. 1:32).

Luke draws special attention to Jesus' concern for society's outcasts (*e.g.* 14:15ff.), for women (*e.g.* 7:36ff.) and for Gentiles (7:1ff.). He shows that in God's kingdom the human values of wealth are to be reappraised radically (12:13ff.; 16:19ff.); it is reserved for the spiritually poor who repent and trust only in God whatever the cost (9:23). Luke also presents Jesus as an example to be followed; as Jesus worked in the power of the Spirit (Lk. 4:14, 18), so must the disciples (24:49), and as he was a man of prayer (Lk. 3:21; 6:12), so must the church continually be in prayer (Acts 1:14). In bringing the story of Jesus up to date for his own generation, Luke also aimed to present Jesus as Saviour and to show how the Spirit of God constituted the church as the witness to Jesus. In so doing he created a reliable historical record which became the means of equipping the church for evangelism.

LUST. The English word was originally a neutral description of any strong desire and in AV is used in this way. The restricted modern meaning of sexual passion is found in RSV in 1 Jn. 2:16, and in a broad sense of all selfish physical desire in Eph. 4:22. Otherwise modern EVV use DESIRE or PASSION.

LUZ. The ancient name of the place near which Jacob dreamed of a ladder between earth and heaven and which he re-named BETHEL (Gn. 28:19). It was still known as Luz by its Canaanite inhabitants when the Israelites conquered it (Jdg. 1:22ff.).

LYCAONIA. A territory in S-central Asia Minor named after the Lykaones who inhabited it. In the NT it denotes that part of the territory which formed a region within the Roman province of Galatia (*cf.* Acts 14:6), known as Lycaonia Galatia, in contrast to the region of Phrygia Galatia where Iconium was situated. The inhabitants had their own language (Acts 14:11); an inscription found nearby at Sedasa records the dedication to Zeus of a statue of Hermes (*cf.* Acts 14:12).

LYCIA. A small district on the S coast of Asia Minor. It had been greatly influenced by Greek culture before the Roman conquest. It contained the seaports of MYRA and PATARA (Acts 21:1; 27:5).

LYDDA. A town 18 km SE of the Jaffa coast, probably the OT (and modern) Lod. It was reclaimed by the Jews in 145 BC (1 Macc. 11:34), burnt down in Nero's reign, and became a rabbinical centre after AD 70.

LYDIA. *Person:* A woman from Thyatira in Lydia who at Philippi became Paul's first European convert and gave him hospitality (Acts 16:14f., 40). She was head of a household, hence either widowed or unmarried, a convert to Judaism, and traded in the renowned Lydian purple dye. *Place:* A district on the W slope of Asia Minor, fertile and highly cultivated. Trade routes made its cities, including Sardis, Thyatira and Philadelphia, commercially important. Ruled successively by Persians, Greeks and Romans it was the first state to use coined money and was the home of some musical innovations.

LYE: See SOAP.

LYRE: See MUSIC AND MUSICAL INSTRUMENTS.

LYSANIAS. In Lk. 3:1 the tetrarch of Abilene *c.* AD 27-8, referred to also by Josephus and mentioned on an inscription in Abila dated between AD 14 and 29.

LYSTRA. An obscure town on the high plains of Lycaonia near modern Hatunsaray chosen by Augustus to be a Roman colony to consolidate the new province of Galatia. Its remote security attracted the fugitive Paul and Barnabas (Acts 14:6); they were attacked there too but a church was established (Acts 14:19ff.).

M

MAACAH, MAACHAH. *People:* It is used as both a man's name (*e.g.* the father of one of David's commanders) and a woman's name, *e.g.* Caleb's concubine (1 Ch. 2:48), one of David's wives who was mother of Absalom (2 Sa. 3:3), and Absalom's daughter who became Rehoboam's favourite wife (2 Ch. 11:20ff.). *Place:* A small state SW of Mt Hermon which attacked, and was defeated by, David's army (2 Sa. 10:6ff.). It was later absorbed into the kingdom of Damascus.

MACCABEES. 'Maccabaeus' comes

from the Greek form of the surname of the Jewish hero Judas ben Mattathias (1 Macc. 2:4), possibly meaning 'the hammerer'. The family were called Hasmonaeans in rabbinic literature. Tension between the pro-Syrian (Seleucid) and the pro-Egyptian (Ptolemaic) factions in Judaea after the division of Alexander's Greek empire led the Seleucid king Antiochus IV (Epiphanes) to intervene. He sold the Jewish high priesthood to the highest bidder (Menelaus), attacked Jerusalem in 168 BC, began an intense religious persecution and set up pagan images and sacrifices in the temple. Many Jews (the Hasidim, 'men of the covenant') endured heroic suffering (1 Macc. 1:60ff.; 2:29ff.). At Modein, 30 km from Jerusalem, the aging Mattathias killed a Jew who had come to sacrifice at the royal altar, and its Syrian military supervisor, and called on all who loved the Law to follow him and his 5 sons into the mountains. The Maccabaean revolt had begun.

Judas Maccabaeus, Mattathias' third son, led a guerilla army against the numerically superior Syrians with such success that Antiochus' regent Lycias made a peace treaty with him. The temple was solemnly cleansed in 164 BC, later commemorated by the Feast of Hanukkah or Dedication (1 Macc. 4; cf. Jn. 10:22). This led to persecution of Jewish minorities in some cities, which the Maccabees tried to suppress. Judas was killed in battle in 161 BC, and Jonathan his brother took over leadership of the guerillas now restricted to the hills. In time he became the effective ruler of Judaea,

being appointed high priest in 153 BC and civil governor in 150; he was murdered in 143. Under the last of Mattathias' sons, Simon, Judaea became virtually independent with Simon as high priest and civil ruler. By the time his son and successor John Hyrcanus died in 104 BC, the Jewish state had reached its greatest extent since Solomon. A period of internal intrigue followed which led to Roman intervention in the 1st cent. BC.

A rift had been opened between the Maccabees and Hasidim when Jonathan became high priest, and the Pharisees, later heirs of the Hasidim, were wholly alienated from the Hasmonaean priest-kings. But the Maccabees had set the pattern for the Jewish nationalism and Messianic thought of the NT period. The Zealots have often been linked with Maccabaean ideals.

See APOCRYPHA for the Books of Maccabees.

MACEDONIA. A rich tract of land centred on the plains of the gulf of Thessalonica and famous for its timber and precious metal. Its kings dominated Greek affairs from the 4th cent. BC. Subsequently its federations of republics were incorporated into a Roman province with a proconsul at Thessalonica. After his vision of a man of Macedonia (Acts 16:9) Paul began to take advantage of his high social status (Acts 16:37), and proved himself an independent missionary leader. He regarded Macedonia with affection (Phil. 4:1), being eager to return (2 Cor. 1:16); the Macedonians willingly contributed to his Jerusalem fund (2 Cor. 8:1ff.).

MACHAERUS. A fortress E of the Dead Sea (modern el-Mekawar), rebuilt by Herod the Great, near hot springs. According to Josephus, John the Baptist was imprisoned here.

MACHIR (MAKIR). 1. A grandson of Joseph and father of Gilead (Gn. 50:23; Nu. 26:29). 2. A man who protected Mephibosheth and provided for David (2 Sa. 9:4f.; 17:27ff.).

MACHPELAH. The name applied to the field, cave and surrounding land bought by Abraham as a burial place for his wife Sarah (Gn. 23). Abraham himself, and later Isaac, Rebekah and Jacob, were also buried there. The modern site at Hebron is venerated by Jews, Christians and Muslims, and surrounded by massive walls possibly from Herodian times, but the antiquity of the cave itself is unconfirmed.

MADMANNAH. A town in SW Judah, also known as Beth-marcaboth (*cf.* Jos. 15:31 with 19:5).

MADMEN. A town of Moab prophesied against by Jeremiah (Je. 48:2), otherwise unknown but possibly modern Kh. Dimneh.

MADMENAH. Mentioned only in Is. 10:31, believed to be Shufat, 2 km N of Mt Scopus.

MADON. A city in N Canaan possibly identical to MEROM.

MAGADAN, MAGDALA. Mentioned only in Mt. 15:39, although some MSS also read it for Dalmanutha in Mk. 8:10. Magadan was the locality on the W shore of the Sea of Galilee; Magdala was a town there between Tiberias and Capernaum (modern Kh. Mejdel). The home area of Mary Magdalen (see MARY).

MAGBISH. Either a town in Judah or the name of a clan (Ezr. 2:30).

MAGI. The name given to the wise men, probably non-Jewish religious astrologers, who brought gifts to the infant Jesus (Mt. 2:1ff.). The writer Herodotus used the term to describe a tribe of Medes who were priests in the Persian empire. Dn. (1:20; 2:27; 5:15) uses the original word for a class of wise men and astrologers who interpret dreams and messages of the gods. For Matthew, the visit to Jesus represents the Messiah's relationship to the Gentile world. Later Christian tradition called them kings (*cf.* Ps. 72:10; Is. 49:7) and numbered them 3 (because of the gifts) or 12. For the star of Bethlehem, see STARS.

MAGIC AND SORCERY. The attempt to influence people and events by supernatural or occult means. 'Black' magic attempts to produce evil results through curses, spells and alliance with evil spirits; 'white' magic tries to undo curses and spells and to use occult powers for the good of oneself or others. There is no doubt that it is not always mere superstition but has behind it a spiritual reality which must and can be resisted and overcome by the power of God in the name of Jesus Christ.

Biblical judgment on magic. The Bible describes magic and sorcery by reference to a variety of occult practices. Sorcery is roughly equivalent to 'witchcraft' (*e.g.* Ex. 22:18; Rev. 21:8); 'magician' had a technical meaning usually associated with pagan priests (Ex. 7:11; and see MAGI). Magic practices of all kinds are constantly condemned in Scripture, for they rival the true religion of living in humble dependence on God. Among the practices explicitly condemned is the wearing of charms. In Is. 3:18ff. several kinds are listed; 'crescents' were moon images, 'headbands' probably denotes sun-pendants. There are few direct allusions to sorcerers or witches in Israel; the 'witch' of Endor (1 Sa. 28) was a medium, not a magician, but Jezebel practised sorcery (2 Ki. 9:22) and Mi. 5:12 suggests it was not rare in Israel. Hebrew prophetesses are depicted as practising magic to preserve or destroy people in Ezk. 13:17ff.; the details are hard to follow but clearly involved the use of veils impregnated with spells.

Some biblical incidents which seem at first sight to countenance magic do not necessarily do so. The use of mandrakes to ensure conception (Gn. 30:14ff.) was common and may have been a primitive herbal medicine rather than magical rite, for example. Samuel's action of pouring out water has been interpreted as sympathetic magic to induce a storm but is more likely a symbol of humiliation (1 Sa. 7:6; *cf.* 2 Sa. 14:14). There is a great stress in the OT on the power of blessings and curses; Isaac could not reverse his, for example (Gn. 27:33, 37). But it does not envisage anyone pronouncing an effective blessing or curse contrary to God's will; the Patriarchs believed they discerned God's will and were declaring it. God can turn the undeserved curse into a blessing (Ps. 109:28).

Finally, the Bible never treats miracles in the same category as magic; no formulae are attached to them. Moses silenced Pharaoh's magicians not by being better at magic but by being God's agent through whom God's power was displayed. Magical beliefs and practices were common in Israel from the earliest times, and right from the start of Israel's history they were prohibited. The biblical attitude to sorcery and magic is summed up for all periods in such passages as Ex. 22:18; Lv. 19:26; 20:27; Dt. 18:10ff.

Egyptian magic. Magic, the exploitation of occult powers to achieve otherwise unattainable ends, was closely linked to religion. Egypt's greatest magicians were the scholar-priests, experts in rituals and spells. Joseph's pharaoh called on them to interpret his dreams (Gn. 41:8); dreams and their interpretations were collected in manuals, and it was reckoned that anything one saw oneself doing in a dream would happen in the future. In Gn. 44:4f., 15 Joseph suggests that the cup he planted in his brothers' grain-sacks was used for divination. Two interpretations are possible. One is that he knew of the art of cup divination by which omens were obtained by watching the movement or configuration of drops of oil on water in the cup; it was certainly known at the time in Mesopotamia, but it was apparently extremely rare in Egypt. The other possibility is that his statement should read not '*by* this he divines' but '*concerning* this he will divine'; *i.e.* be sure the theft will be unmasked. Joseph then pretends to have found out the theft by divination in v. 15, because he can hardly admit to his deceit. Later, in Moses' time, the magicians aped some of God's miracles. An Egyptian cobra can be made immobile and stick-like, for example; the account in Ex. 7-9 returns an open verdict on whether they used occult powers or good conjuring to turn water to blood and produce frogs. They failed to produce lice and were themselves overcome by boils (see also PLAGUES OF EGYPT).

Assyrian and Babylonian magic. Magic was used to obtain cures from illness and demon possession, the exorcist using spells from a handbook. Divination was used because it was believed that any event was announced or accompanied by some observable portent. There were manuals with lists of omens and their meaning; they included natural phenomena such as eclipses, conjunctions of planets and actions of animals, and techniques such as observing sheep's liver and using cup divination (see previous paragraph). Magicians were priestly scholars attached to the temples. Balaam (Nu. 22-24) was apparently a diviner in this tradition, going to meet Balak with unspecified omens (24:1); a seal found at Jezreel dating from the 13th cent. BC (Balaam's time) tells of 'Manum the diviner', and diviners texts have been found in N Syria (Balaam's home area). Much later, the educational procedure for Babylonians which is summarized in Dn. 1:4 accurately reflects the training of scholar-magicians. Daniel's skill (Dn. 5:12, 16) was highly valued; if a dream could be interpreted then its benefits could be accepted and its bad effects averted by magic.

See also CHARMS; DIVINATION.

MAGISTRATE. In Ezr. 7:25 the word translates the Hebrew 'judge'. They were among officials summoned by Nebuchadrezzar in Dn. 3:2f. In Acts 16:20ff. the title is given to leading men of the colony. See also POLICE.

MAGNIFICAT. The Latin name for Mary's prophecy-song in Lk. 1:46-55. It is modelled on OT psalms and has a special affinity with Hannah's song in 1 Sa. 2:1ff. The narrative is modelled by Luke's theme and the song need not therefore be regarded as Mary's spontaneous or exact reply. Divided into four strophes it describes Mary's gratitude and praise, God's gracious character, God's sovereignty and special concern for lowly people, and his unique mercy to Israel. The last part of the poem is a virtual paraphrase of OT passages in which

God's deliverance through his Messiah is seen in terms of political deliverance from human oppressors; the NT transfers this specific hope to the return of the Messiah and the inauguration of the age to come. See also ANNUNCIATION; BENEDICTUS; MARY.

MAGOR-MISSABIB (lit. 'terror on every side'). A symbolic name for Pashhur in Je. 20:3 AV, NIV.

MAHANAIM (lit. 'two camps'). A place in Gilead where Jacob saw the angels of God before he met Esau (Gn. 32:1f.). It was David's refuge from Absalom (2 Sa. 17:24) and a district administrative centre under Solomon (1 Ki. 4:14). It is probably to be located overlooking the N bank of the Jabbok, perhaps in the Jerash area.

MAHANEH-DAN (lit. 'camp of Dan'). The place where Samson experienced the stirring of God's Spirit, and the first staging post in Dan's quest for territory (Jdg. 13:25; 18:12), probably two different, temporary sites of which no trace remains.

MAHER-SHALAL-HASHBAZ (lit. 'speed the spoil, hasten the prey'). A symbolic name of one of Isaiah's sons to signify Assyria's swift removal of Judah's enemies (Is. 8:3f.).

MAHLI (lit. 'weak, sickly'). A grandson of Levi (Ex. 6:19), and one of his nephews (1 Ch. 6:47).

MAHOL (lit. 'dance'). In 1 Ki. 4:31 possibly meaning 'sons of the dance' in worship; in 1 Ch. 2:6 the same people are sons of Zerah (a proper name).

MAKKEDAH. A town in the Lachish district captured by Joshua (Jos. 10:16ff.). The exact location is disputed.

MAKTESH. In Zp. 1:11 (AV), probably part of the Tyropoeon valley or 'lower city' (NEB).

MALACHI, BOOK OF. *Author and date.* Some consider the title not to be a proper name but a common noun, 'my messenger' and hence an anonymous work, but this is not necessarily the case; the Hebrew Targum attributes it to Ezra. The abuses which Malachi condemns, such as mixed marriages (2:10ff.) and neglect of tithes (3:8ff.), are those which Nehemiah sought to correct, and the book can be dated from his time, possibly composed during his visit to Susa *c.* 433 BC.

Contents. The book falls into 2 parts. Chs. 1-2 deal with Israel's sin; chs. 3-4 with judgment for the guilty and blessings for those who repent. God declares his love for Israel (1:2-5). Israel's sin is outlined in the form of a dialogue (1:6-2:9): it has not loved its Father God and priests have despised the Lord's name; the lessons of the Exile have not been taken to heart; blemished sacrifices have been offered contrary to the law. 1:11 looks forward to the time when the true gospel is spread through all the world; if there is no repentance, there will be a curse on the priests. Mixed marriages are condemned (2:10-17); Israel had a common Father God and should therefore have demonstrated and maintained its unity; mixed marriages, and divorce, are sins which have been rationalized. The day of the Lord is coming (3:1-6); God's messenger will appear as a refiner to purge the nation; judgment will come on those who oppress others, but Israel will not be fully wiped out because God loves it. True repentance would be demonstrated by the restoration of tithing and God would respond by pouring out his visible blessing (3:7-12). The godly will be saved and will become God's own possession; on the day of judgment they will rise like the sun (3:13-4:3). The prophecy closes with an exhortation to obey the Law of Moses and a promise that Elijah will come before the Day of the Lord.

MALCAM: See MILCOM.

MALCHIJAH (MALCHIAH) (lit. 'Yah is king'). A common OT name including the owner of the pit in which Jeremiah was imprisoned, probably a member of the royal household (Je. 38:6).

MALCHUS. The high priest's servant whose ear was cut off by Peter in Gethsemane, named only in Jn. 18:10 thus confirming the author's close acquaintance with the high priestly family (*cf.* 18:15). It was a common Arab name.

MALICE. It generally means spitefulness or ill will. Malice is a characteristic of people who stand under God's wrath (Rom. 1:29). For believers it belongs to the old life (Tit. 3:3) which must be stripped off (Col. 2:8).

MALTA. An island in the Mediterranean 100 km S of Sicily. Paul was shipwrecked there, the traditional site being St Paul's Bay 13 km NW of modern Valetta. He spent 3 months there before continuing his journey to Rome (Acts 28). It had come under Roman control in 218 BC; Publius, the 'chief man' (v. 7), probably served under the propraetor of Sicily; his title is attested by inscriptions.

MAMMON. The word occurs only in Mt. 6:24; Lk. 16:9, 11, 13, and is a transliteration of an Aramaic word meaning wealth or profit. Jesus sees in it a self-centred covetousness which claims people's hearts and thus alienates them from God. When a person 'owns' something, in reality it owns him.

MAMRE. A place near Hebron, W from Machpelah; associated with Abraham, who lived there for some time, and Isaac (Gn. 23:17ff.; 35:27). It is identified with Ramet el-Khalil 4 km N of Hebron.

MAN (MANKIND). Throughout the Bible mankind is seen as part of nature. Man's mortality and his biological and physical similarity to the animal creation is obvious (Ps.

103:14ff.). Between man and nature there are deep and mysterious bonds. The natural world falls under the curse of corruption because of man's sin (Gn. 3:17f.), and now awaits its redemption along with man's (Rom. 8:19ff.). Man must respect nature's limitations (Dt. 22:9f.), and find in it his own sustenance (Gn. 3:17; 9:1ff.). But the true meaning of life is not to be found in this close relationship with nature; rather, being made in God's image (Gn. 1:27), man is placed in a unique relationship with the Creator. God's word, by which he lives (Mt. 4:4), lifts him above the rest of creation and confers on him the dignity of being a child of God.

Various words are used to describe man in his relationship to God and his environment, such as spirit, soul, body and flesh. They do not describe separate parts of the human constitution, but rather draw attention to different aspects of a person's activity. Hence the 'soul' may emphasize individuality and personal consciousness, and 'body' the historical and outward aspects of his life, but the two are forever inseparable; the Bible does not teach the immortality of the soul but the resurrection of the body, that is the salvation and renewal of the whole person. 'Heart' is often used to describe the seat of a wide range of activities including thinking and choosing as well as feeling emotion.

The fall of man (Gn. 3) involved the refusal to respond to God's word and man's attempt to find his destiny only in the context of the immediate environment (Rom. 1:25). Hence life becomes bondage to the fear of death (Heb. 2:14f.) and conflict with evil (Eph. 6:12). Yet despite this man remains in God's image (Ps. 8; Jas. 3:9), and is still of infinite value to God (Mt. 10:31). Jesus Christ is the true image of God (Col. 1:15), whose victory over death and sin promises life and freedom for those who trust him (Rom. 5:12ff.). Thus the believer, 'in Christ', is being changed into his perfect image (2 Cor. 3:18), 'putting it on' by faith in this life (Eph. 4:24; Col. 3:10).

In the historical development of the Christian doctrine of man an exaggerated distinction was suggested by some writers between 'image' and 'likeness' (Gn. 1:26), likeness being defined as original righteousness which was lost at the fall and image as free will and rationality which could not be lost. Luther, at the Reformation, denied the distinction, showing that man in every part of his personality was affected by the fall. Since then scholars have continued to attempt to define precisely what was lost at the fall. Karl Barth took a different line by suggesting that sin has not so changed man's nature that we cannot still see analogies in human behaviour with God's nature, but emphasized that only in Christ can man know God and be related to him in the divine image.

See also BODY; FALL; FLESH; HEART; IMAGE; SOUL; SPIRIT; WOMAN.

MANAEN. The Greek form of the Hebrew name Menahem ('comforter'). The foster-brother of Herod Antipas who became a Christian leader at Antioch (Acts 13:1).

MANAHATH, MANAHATHITES. *Person:* The ancestor of a clan of Mt Seir later absorbed by Edom (Gn. 36:23). *Place:* The city to which some captured Benjaminites were taken (1 Ch. 8:6) in the vicinity of Bethlehem, probably modern Maliha SW of Jerusalem. Its inhabitants were descendants of Caleb (1 Ch. 2:52ff.).

MANASSEH (lit. 'making to forget'). 1. The elder son of Joseph, born in Egypt, he lost the right of the first-born to his younger brother Ephraim (Gn. 48:5, 14). 2. The tribe of Manasseh derived from 7 families, one from Machir, the others from Gilead, and occupied land on both sides of the Jordan. The E half occupied all Bashan and part of Gilead, the W half had good land N of Ephraim. The tribe was renowned for its bravery; among its heroes was Gideon in the W (Jdg. 6:15) and Jephthah in the E (Jdg. 11:1). 3. The son of Hezekiah who ruled in Jerusalem from the age of 12 for 55 years probably as co-regent with his father, *c.* 696-686 BC, then as sole ruler 686-642 BC. His long reign was marked by bloodshed, tyranny and religious apostasy. He introduced illegal altars into the temple, and encouraged Baalism, astral worship, spiritism and divination. He was deported to Babylon by the Assyrians, where 1 Ch. 33 says that he repented, and was released.

MANGER. The feeding trough for animals in a stall or stable, which served as a makeshift cot for the infant Jesus (Lk. 2:7, 12, 16). If Jesus was born in a cave, as Christian tradition suggests, the manger may have been cut into the walls.

MANNA. The Israelites' chief food during their 40 years stay in the desert (Ex. 16:13ff.). It was found on the ground in the morning. It did not keep overnight, but a double portion was collected on the sixth day and cooked, because none appeared on the sabbath. It was white and looked like coriander seed with a honey taste. Its exact nature has been the subject of much speculation. To the present time, some insects in Sinai secrete honeydew on tamarisk twigs every June, which overnight drops to the ground and is collected by the ants. It fits the biblical description quite closely, but ultimately the provision remains in the realm of the miraculous. Manna was used to teach the Israelites the spiritual lesson of dependence on God (Dt. 8:3, 16). Jesus took it as a picture of himself, the bread of life from heaven (Jn. 6:26ff.); in Rev. 2:17 it represents his spiritual sustenance of believers.

MANOAH. Samson's father, the name identical in form with a word meaning 'resting place' and the Wadi el-Munah from which it may be derived. Samson's birth was announced to him by an angel (Jdg. 13:2).

MAON, MAONITES. 1. Descendants of Caleb's branch of the tribe of Judah. Maon was the son of Shammai (1 Ch. 2:45); it was also the name of a town where David sheltered (1 Sa. 23:24f.), modern Kh.-el-Main 14 km S of Hebron. 2. A hostile people E of the Jordan who oppressed Israel (Jdg. 10:12).

MARAH (lit. 'bitter'). The first named camp of the Israelites after they had crossed the Red Sea, so called because only bitter water was found there (Ex. 15:23); often identified with Ain Hawarah 75 km SSE of Suez.

MARANATHA. An Aramaic formula used without explanation in 1 Cor. 16:22 (AV), meaning 'Our Lord come' (so most EVV).

MARESHAH. A town in the Shephelah, modern Tell Sandahanna, fortified by Rehoboam (2 Ch. 11:8). It was destroyed by the Parthians in 40 BC.

MARK, GOSPEL OF. *Contents.* Prologue (1:1-13); Jesus' earlier ministry in Galilee (1:14-6:44); Jesus' later ministry in Galilee (6:45-9:50); the road to Jerusalem (10); his Jerusalem ministry (11-13); his death and resurrection (14-16).

Author. This Gospel, the shortest and simplest of the four, has been regarded traditionally as the work of John Mark of Jerusalem who at various times was a companion of Paul, Barnabas and Peter. The earliest statement about the Gospel is that of Papias (*c.* AD 140), who said that Mark was 'the interpreter of Peter' who 'wrote down accurately all that he remembered...of Christ, but not in order. For he was neither a hearer nor a companion of the Lord; but afterwards...he accompanied Peter.' The anti-Marcionite prologue to Mark some 40 years later also called Mark Peter's interpreter and added that he was nicknamed 'stumpy-fingered', and Irenaeus said that Mark wrote down 'the substance of Peter's preaching' after the apostle's death. To judge from the incidents chosen and the way they are treated in the Gospel, the claim to be the written record of Peter's teaching seems strong. This would date the Gospel probably between Peter's death *c.* AD 65 and the fall of Jerusalem in AD 70. It may well have been written in Rome, and it seeks to explain Jewish customs as if written initially for a non-Palestinian Gentile readership (see also next article).

Relationship to Matthew and Luke. A close link obviously exists between these three Gospels, often called 'Synoptic Gospels' because their similar content can be compared, contrasted and analysed in parallel columns. Most Protestant scholars believe that Mark (or an earlier draft of it possibly containing only chs. 1-13) was the originator of the gospel form by setting unconnected sayings and actions of Jesus in a theological and/or chronological structure. If this is true, then Mark underlies Matthew and Luke as one of their two main sources, the other being a collection of Jesus' sayings (usually dubbed 'Q') from which Matthew and Luke drew the material which is clearly common to them but not included in Mark. Roman Catholic scholars, for many years, insisted on the primacy of Matthew largely because of its place in the NT, but apart from the fact that little is known about the reasons for the eventual order of the NT books this creates a major problem. Matthew 'tones down' Mark, an understandable procedure for a sophisticated Jewish readership; there can be little reason why Mark should reverse such a process.

The scholarly debates of the 20th cent. have led to many theories about the complex relationships between oral and written traditions and the Synoptic Gospels. There have been some constructive suggestions as well as some negative and at times contradictory theories. For example, it now seems likely that the oral traditions used by Mark were 'church traditions' not merely individual recollections; they had, in other words, already been accepted and believed as authentic. The discovery of the Dead Sea Scrolls at Qumran in 1947, a collection of mostly pre-Christian Jewish writings and OT Scriptures, has shown that there can be no valid reason why there were not also early documentary sources for Mark as well; people, it seems, did collect teachers' sayings and testimonies of events. Further, it would seem possible that Mark's 'translation Greek' which includes frequent Semitisms could be explained by sug-

gesting that he worked from Aramaic documents (as well as Peter's Aramaic mother-tongue), again pointing to early and thus probably reliable origins of the stories about Jesus. For more detail about such debates, see GOSPELS; NEW TESTAMENT LANGUAGE.

Characteristics of Mark. Mark is the most blunt and clipped of the Gospels, although its abrupt ending is probably due to textual loss and is not a theological problem as such. The matter was raised as early as the 2nd cent.; if Mark knew more about Jesus' life and teaching why did he not include it? Why does he omit much that the other gospels include? And is Mark the chronological biography it seems at first sight? The answer may be found in the oral tradition underlying Mark. Constant oral repetition leads not to diversity but to uniformity; stories told with the purpose of teaching a truth are boiled down to their simplest minimum. In this light, Mark appears not as 'primitive' but as highly developed in that it has been pared of all but the significant facts; it is the record of teaching forms that have stood the test of time, a teacher's handbook in effect, which is what Papias claimed it to be. By contrast, Luke was primarily a work of literature (Lk. 1:1-4). Mark was probably not nearly so well educated, but then neither were his readers, and his main purpose was to communicate the truth simply. The principle of arrangement thus seems to be that which could most easily be memorized; stories and sayings are linked by keywords or similarity of subject rather than by strict chronological accuracy.

MARK (JOHN). The traditional author of the second Gospel, apparently a Jew and a native of Jerusalem. 'John' was his Hebrew name, 'Marcus' a Latin addition; it was not unusual for 1st-cent. Jews also to take a Latin (or Greek) name. He was nicknamed 'stumpy-fingered' in the anti-Marcionite prologue to Mark's Gospel, referring possibly to some physical deformity or to the abbreviated style of his gospel, or confusing the name Marcus with the Latin word for 'maimed' (*mancus*). His mother Mary was related to Barnabas (Col. 4:10). She seems to have been a wealthy Christian, probably a widow; her house was large enough to serve as a meeting place (Acts 12:12). Mark is often assumed to be the young man who fled naked from Gethsemane, where perhaps he was guarding the family's fruit (Mk. 14:51; *cf.* Jn. 21:24 for another deliberate anonymous reference to an author).

Mark was taken to Antioch by his uncle Barnabas (Acts 12:25) and he travelled with Barnabas and Paul on their first missionary journey (Acts 13:5). But he later left them for home, an action Paul regarded as desertion, and he refused to take him on the next journey (Acts 15:38). Mark is then lost to view but he is back with Paul in Rome in Col. 4:10, and with Timothy on a mission in 2 Tim. 4:11, possibly in Ephesus. 1 Pet. 5:13 describes the paternal relationship between Peter and a Mark in Rome ('Babylon'), which may support the tradition that John Mark was with Peter and wrote the Gospel there. See also previous article.

MARKET, MARKET PLACE. The trading centre of an E town which in NT times was also a public gathering-place (Mt. 23:7) and often ornamented with statues and colonnades. Children played there (Mt. 11:16), the unemployed looked for work there (Mt. 20:3), and in Gentile towns preliminary trials and public debates were held there (Acts 16:19; 17:17f.).

MARKS. The English word translates a variety of biblical expressions. In Lk. 14:7 Jesus 'marked' in the sense of 'observed closely'. Usually it means a sign, as the mark on Cain's forehead (Gn. 4:15), using a word which also means a pledge or promise, whereas the similar use in Ezk. 9:4, 6 means a seal which signifies that the people so marked belong to the Lord (*cf.* Rev. 14:1; 22:4). Paul says he bears 'the marks of Jesus' (Gal. 6:17), which probably refers to his having been 'branded' as Jesus' servant by his sufferings. By contrast those who do not follow Christ are pictured as being branded by the mark of the antichrist-beast (Rev. 13:16). In 1 Sa. 20:20 'mark' is an archery target (*cf.* Jb. 16:12); in Lv. 19:28 a tattoo with forbidden religious associations.

MARRIAGE. The state in which a man and a woman live together in a sexual relationship with the approval of their social group. Sexual relations outside the marriage bond are regarded in OT and NT as immoral, but polygamy constitutes a recognized marital state in the OT. Marriage was regarded as normal in biblical times, and there is no OT word for bachelor or spinster. Jeremiah's call to remain unmarried was unusual (Je. 16:2) but the NT recognizes celibacy as God's call for some Christians (Mt. 19:10ff.; 1 Cor. 7:7ff.). The story of Adam and Eve describes the unique husband-wife relationship as 'one flesh' (Gn. 2:18ff.), and this illustrates the intimate relationship between God and his people (Ho. 1-3) and between Christ and his church (Eph. 5:22ff.).

Although monogamy is implicit in the story, polygamy is not specifically forbidden in Scripture, although it is clearly shown to be a cause of trouble and often results in sin (*e.g.* Gn. 21; 1 Ki. 11:1ff.); Hebrew kings were warned against it (Dt. 17:17). It was natural, too, that the husband would be drawn to one wife more than the other (Gn. 29). Polygamy continues today among Jews living in Muslim countries. Since children were important to carry on the family name, a childless wife might also allow her husband to have children by her slave. This was legal in Mesopotamia, and practised by some Patriarchs (Gn. 16; 30). The Bible says nothing about the commonly-assumed sexual rights of a master over a female slave, although Ex. 21:7ff. and Dt. 15:12 distinguish between the rights of ordinary female slaves and those who have been taken as concubines who could not claim

automatic release after 7 years. Concubines were in an inferior position compared with wives, but their children could inherit property (Gn. 25:6).

Marriage customs. In the Near East, betrothal, or engagement, was almost as binding as marriage itself. The Babylonian law code of Hammurapi (18th cent. BC) said that if a future husband broke an engagement the bride's father retained the bridal gift, and if the father changed his mind he had to repay double the value of the gift. It was usually the man's parents who chose his wife (Gn. 21:21; Gn. 38:6), although the man could choose and let his parents negotiate the details (Jdg. 14:2f.). The husband or his family gave a gift to the wife's family (Gn. 34:12), but this was more of a seal of a covenant between two families rather than a slave-like deal. The bride was given a dowry by her father, perhaps of servants (Gn. 24:59ff.) or land (Jdg. 1:15), and a wedding present from her husband, perhaps of jewellery or clothes (Gn. 24:53). Partners were usually chosen from the wider family, but restrictions were placed on the marriage of very close relatives (Lv. 18).

The wedding. A number of varied ceremonies are mentioned in the Bible; not all would have featured in every wedding. The couple wore embroidered garments (Ps. 45:13f.; *cf.* Rev. 19:7f.) or jewels and garlands of flowers (Is. 61:10). Companions may have accompanied both partners, and the groom and his friends processed to the bride's family house; the wedding supper might be held there (as seems likely in Jesus' parable, Mt. 25:1ff.) or the bride would be taken back to the groom's house for it. The feast was a well-attended and festive occasion (Jn. 2; Mt.22); the celebrations might last for a week (Gn. 29:27). The groom may have covered the bride with a cloak as a symbol that he took her into his care (Ru. 3:9; Ezk. 16:8), and the marriage formalized by a written contract (Tobit 7:13f.). A special nuptial room was prepared where the marriage was consummated, perhaps after prayer (Ps. 19:5; Tobit 7:16f.); a blood-stained cloth might prove the bride's virginity in case of later dispute (Dt. 22:13ff.).

Levirate marriage. When a married man died without leaving a child, his brother (or nearest relative) was expected to marry his wife; children born to her counted as children of the first marriage, thereby perpetuating the family name. The book of Ruth illustrates the custom. The rule only applied in cases of childlessness; Lv. 18:16 and 20:21 forbid marriage to one's brother's wife in all other circumstances.

Divorce. Moses regulated the existing practice in Dt. 24:1ff. (*cf.* Mt. 19:8). The grounds for divorce are given in general terms and no precise interpretation is possible. Shortly before the time of Christ the Jewish school of Shammai interpreted it as referring only to unfaithfulness while the school of Hillel extended it to anything which displeased the husband. Divorce was forbidden if the husband accused his wife falsely of pre-marital unfaithfulness (Dt. 22:13ff.) or when a man had been compelled to marry because he had seduced a girl (Dt. 22:28f.). Ezra commanded divorce in the case of pagan wives (Ezr.9-10; Ne. 13:23ff.). In the NT, Jesus brands divorce and remarriage as adultery. He does not say a man *cannot* put asunder what God has joined but that he *should not*. Matthew's account allows for divorce on the grounds of 'fornication', usually interpreted as adultery (Mt. 19:3ff.; *cf.* Mk. 10:2ff.; Lk. 16:18). There is a strong body of opinion today that 1 Cor. 7:10ff. gives another ground for divorce if a pagan partner insists on leaving a Christian; the deserted Christian is then free to remarry. In the present tangle of marriage and divorce, the Christian church in dealing with converts and repentant members is often compelled to accept the situation as it is. A divorced convert cannot return to the previous marriage and the second marriage cannot be branded as adulterous (*cf.* 1 Cor. 6:9ff.).

See also BRIDE, BRIDEGROOM; CONCUBINE; FAMILY; FRIEND OF THE BRIDEGROOM.

MARSHAL. In Je. 51:27, an official like a scribe, so translated in Na. 3:17. In AV elsewhere, a military officer.

MARTHA. The name derives from an Aramaic form not found in Hebrew, meaning 'lady' or 'mistress', and is found only in the NT where it refers only to one person, the sister of Lazarus and Mary (Lk. 10:38ff.; Jn. 11;

12:2). The family lived in Bethany, 4 km from Jerusalem. Because Jesus was anointed in Bethany (and assuming that there was only one anointing; see next article), because Matthew and Mark say the anointing took place in the house of Simon the Pharisee, and because Martha served the supper in Simon's house, it has been supposed she was Simon's wife. Jesus rebuked her for impatience and excessive concern about practical details, but she responded faithfully to Jesus at the tomb of Lazarus.

MARY. The name refers to 6 individuals in the NT. *1. The mother of Jesus.* She lived in Nazareth and was engaged to the carpenter Joseph when an angel announced she would have a child. She was descended from David's family, assuming the genealogy of Lk. 3 is traced through her. After conception she visited her cousin Elizabeth who greeted her as 'mother of my Lord' to which Mary replied in a song of praise (Lk. 1:39ff.). She was with Jesus at the wedding in Cana (Jn. 2), and presumably on other occasions too (*cf.* Mk. 3:31ff.), and at the foot of the cross (Jn. 19:25). After the ascension she joined the praying disciples (Acts 1:14). Otherwise nothing is known of her from the NT. See also VIRGIN BIRTH.

2. The sister of Martha and Lazarus. She is named only in Lk. 10:38ff., where she sat listening to Jesus rather than helping her sister prepare a meal, and anointed Jesus with perfume, and in Jn. 11-12. All 4 Gospels have an account of an anointing, but it is unclear if they are of an identical occasion. Luke's account, which has the greatest differences, describes the anonymous woman as 'a sinner' (Lk. 7:37). Medieval scholars identified her with Mary Magdalene, and hence equated Mary Magdalene and Mary of Bethany, but there is no textual justification for either conclusion. It is more likely that Jesus was anointed twice by different people; the early church writer Origen even suggested there were three anointings.

3. Mary Magdalene. Her name probably derives from the Galilean town of Magdala. In Lk. 8:2 she is said to have been delivered of evil spirits, and this is a reason for doubting the suggested identification of her with the 'sinful woman' who anointed Jesus (Lk. 7); Luke would have surely made the connection explicit rather than use very different descriptions. She is mentioned at the crucifixion, and Jesus appeared to her after the resurrection (Jn. 20:1ff.) when he emphasized to her that their relationship was to be of a quite different kind from then on.

4. The mother of James; 'the other Mary'; 'the wife of Clopas'. These are probably the same person. She accompanied Jesus to Jerusalem, was present at the crucifixion (Mt. 27:55f.) and was with Mary Magdalene at the tomb on the resurrection morning (Mt. 28:1; *cf.* Mk. 15:40ff.; Lk. 24:10; Jn. 19:25). According to the writer Hegesippus, Clopas was the brother of Joseph, the husband of Jesus' mother.

5. The mother of Mark. The sole reference to her is Acts 12:12, where her home is the meeting place for the Jerusalem church.

6. *A Roman Christian*. Paul greets her as a hard worker (Rom. 16:6), but nothing else is known of her.

MASON: See STONEMASON.

MASSA. The 7th of 12 princes of Ishmael (Gn. 25:14) who settled in N Arabia; the tribe is probably to be identified with Masa who paid tribute-tax to Assyria and the Masanoi located by Ptolemy NE of Duma. Some biblical proverbs are attributed to Massaites (Pr. 30:1; 31:1).

MASSAH (lit. 'testing'). A place in the desert where Israel put God to the test (Dt. 6:16; 9:22), coupled in Ex. 17:7 and Ps. 95:8 with Meribah ('quarrel'). Because the name Meribah has legal connotations it has been suggested that the name existed before the incident described, the place being one where legal disputes were settled, but this can be no more than an interesting hypothesis. Both names also occur in Dt. 33:8 and Ps. 81:7, where there is no allusion to the original incidents and where it is God who is doing the testing. Possibly, later amplification of the original account in Ex. 17 led to the introduction of the word-play.

MASTER. A variety of Hebrew and Greek words are sometimes translated thus in EVV. The most common OT word means simply 'lord' or 'sir', and the most common NT word is that for 'teacher' or 'instructor'. Of particular interest is Luke's use of the Greek

epistates which means 'superintendent' or 'overseer' (*e.g.* Lk. 5:5). The term 'rabbi', applied to Jesus, means 'my master' (Jn. 4:31).

MATTHEW. One of Jesus' 12 apostles, described in Mt. 10:3 (*cf.* 9:9) as a tax collector. In Mk. 2:14 (*cf.* Lk. 5:27) the tax collector called to follow Jesus is Levi the son of Alphaeus; it is generally assumed that Levi and Matthew are the same. Papias in the 2nd cent. AD said Matthew 'compiled the oracles' in Hebrew, believed to be a collection of Jesus' sayings later included in the Gospel which was then styled 'according to Matthew'. See also next article.

MATTHEW, GOSPEL OF. *Contents.* Jesus' parentage and birth (1-2); Jesus' baptism, temptation and the start of his ministry (3-4); teaching on the ethics of the kingdom of God (5-7); demonstrations of Jesus' power (8:1-9:34); the 12 commissioned (9:35-10:42); Jesus' teaching about John the Baptist and himself (11-12); 7 parables about the kingdom (13:1-52); the rejection of Jesus and martyrdom of John (13:53-14:12); miracles and the transfiguration (14:13-17:27); teaching on humility and forgiveness (18); the journey to Jerusalem (19-20); triumphal entry, cleansing of the temple, attack on religious leaders (21-23); prediction of the fall of Jerusalem and Jesus' second coming (24); parables of judgment (25); betrayal and crucifixion (26-27); resurrection (28).

Characteristics, author and sources. The gospel preached by the apostles is combined with Jesus' ethical teaching to a greater extent in Matthew than in any other NT book, and this and its orderly presentation made it the most widely read and influential of the four Gospels in earliest times. Modern scholars hesitate to ascribe its present form to Matthew because of its heavy dependence on the non-apostolic Mark, which seems an improbable thing for a member of the 12 apostles to do (see also previous article). Most of Mark is included, although often abbreviated to make room for numerous sayings which seem to come from a source common to Matthew and Luke. The added material which is unique to Matthew is mostly elaborations of Christian defences against Jewish slanders. The Gospel originated in the Greek-speaking Jewish-Christian community. No other Gospel links the OT and NT so closely, no NT document sets out so clearly the person, life and teaching of Jesus as the fulfilment of the OT. It was probably written in its present form in the early AD 80s.

Main emphases. Matthew can be called an early Christian apology as it seeks to answer many natural questions or accusations. The incidents are not recorded in chronological sequence (except for the narrative of Jesus' last days on earth). Matthew adds traditions about Jesus' infancy, and a genealogy, to show that Jesus came from the royal line of David and was not an illegitimate child. He also adds material of an apologetic nature to Mark's resurrection narrative, helping to answer such questions as why

Judas betrayed Jesus, why Pilate condemned him, and to counter slanders by stressing that the tomb was sealed and guarded, that the guards were terrified by an earthquake and bribed to say the body had been stolen.

Matthew sees the chief consequence of Jesus' life and death as the inauguration of the universal church of God, the new Israel. God is with his disciples in all nations (1:23; 28:19f.); the infant is worshipped by Gentiles (2:1ff.); Jesus ministers in Gentile areas (4:15) and is proclaimed as the Gentile hope (12:18, 21). The church is the old Israel transformed and widened because Jesus was rejected by many of the Jews to whom he was first sent (15:24); a Roman centurion had greater faith than any Jew and the Messianic banquet would be thrown open to believers of all races (8:10ff.).

The call to repent, in view of Jesus' promised return as Judge, is strong in Matthew, especially in the parables (*e.g.* 25:31ff.). The words of 21:41 and 22:7 had probably already been fulfilled in the fall of Jerusalem (AD 70) by the time the Gospel was written. The coming of Jesus is not seen as imminent; instead he exercises his reign in the church, which is probably the context in which the difficult sayings of 10:23 and 16:28 are to be understood.

Ethical teaching. There are 5 special groups of teaching (chs. 5-7, 10, 13, 18, 24-25). Jesus is the great Teacher who like Moses proclaimed a revised law for the new Israel from the mountain (5:1). He came to fulfil the old law and correct the current misinterpretations of it (5:17). The changes he proposed were not to the old law itself, but to what people thought it meant. His authority as Messiah is uppermost, and as Messiah Jesus makes the unique and gracious invitation of 11:28ff.

MATTHIAS. The successor of Judas Iscariot as one of the 12 apostles (Acts 1:15f.). Casting lots had an OT precedent (1 Sa. 14:41) and its basis was that God had already chosen the person. The early church historian Eusebius said Matthias was one of the 70 (Lk. 10:1; *cf.* Acts 1:21f.). Nothing is known of his later career.

MATTOCK. In 1 Sa. 13:21, a cutting instrument. In Is. 7:25 (AV), 'hoe' is to be preferred (as RSV).

MEADOW. In Gn. 41:2, 18 (AV), a loan-word from Egyptian should be rendered 'reed grass' as RSV.

MEALS. Probably the oldest banquet scene in the world was found on a cylinder seal at Ur in Mesopotamia dating from *c.* 2600 BC. It shows royal guests seated on low stools being served beakers of wine by attendants wearing fleece skirts. A harpist plays, while other servants fan the guests. A later Assyrian illustration shows King Ashurbanipal reclining on a pillowed couch and his wife sitting on a small chair in the garden, both drinking from bowls. Ancient Egyptian palace meals are depicted on tomb paintings. Guests sit on couches near low tables spread with roast fowl and beef, vegetables, pastries and confectionary. Beer brewed from barley, and wine, was drunk until guests fell to the floor. The biblical book Esther describes 5 Persian feasts, one lasting 180 days (Est. 1:3ff.). By contrast Hebrew palace meals were austere until the days of Solomon, who initiated the elaborate feasts of neighbouring kings and possibly had his summer meals served in a garden such as that described in the Song of Solomon.

The situation was very different for ordinary citizens. The working day began early, without formal breakfast. Instead people carried bread, cheese and fruit with them, eating as they walked to work. Egyptians apparently had their main meal at midday (Gn. 43:16) but Hebrews had a snack and a rest then (Ru. 2:14), with supper at the end of the day (Ru. 3:7). The family dined together, and on festive occasions there was music (Is. 5:12) and dancing (Lk. 15:25). In NT times, meals were often eaten on the upper floor, people reclining on their left elbow on couches arranged round 3 sides of a low table. The guest of honour was on the right of servants as they entered to serve the meal; the guest who reclined next to him always seemed 'lower'. The meal was a relaxed affair. Guests washed their hands first, then ate from a common pottery bowl filled with meat and vegetables. Jesus often gave thanks before the meal began (*e.g.* Mt. 15:36). Small pieces of bread held between the thumb and two fingers absorbed the gravy from the dish (Jn. 13:26), and were used as spoons to scoop up and sandwich a piece of meat. The women prepared the meal, and may not therefore have eaten at the same time as the men (Lk. 10:40; but *cf.* 1 Sa. 1:4f.; Jb. 1:4). An ordinary meal would have only one course. For special meals there would be a footbath for guests (Lk. 7:44) and even special clothing (Mt. 22:11). The guests were seated according to their social rank.

The NT records several meals which Jesus attended. There was the wedding party at Cana (Jn. 2), and a banquet at Matthew's house (Mt. 9:10) which followed the more formal Graeco-Roman pattern. The room would have been open to the street, shielded from view only by curtains which passers-by could part; hence the Pharisees could see what company Jesus kept (Mt. 9:11) and a woman could walk in uninvited to anoint Jesus (Lk. 7:36ff.). Other meals attended by Jesus are recorded in Lk. 10:40; 19:5f.; 24:30.

Meals sometimes carried religious significance, for which see FEASTS; LORD'S SUPPER; LOVE FEAST. See also FOOD and articles on separate food-stuffs.

MEANINGLESS: See VANITY.

MEAT MARKET. Jewish law forbade all dealing at pagan markets, but Paul advised the Corinthians to be less rigorous (1 Cor. 10:25); see IDOLS, FOOD OFFERED TO.

MECONAH (MEKONAH). A town near Ziklag occupied by Jews under Nehemiah (Ne. 11:28). The site is unknown.

MEDAN. A son of Abraham and Keturah (Gn. 25:2). His descendants probably settled in N Arabia but the name is otherwise unknown.

MEDEBA (possibly 'water of quiet'). A plain and city of Reuben N of the Arnon. Its ownership switched regularly between Moab and Judah. The site is Madaba, 10 km S of Heshbon, where a 6th-cent. AD mosaic map of Palestine was found.

MEDES, MEDIA. Media was the name for NW Iran, SW of the Caspian Sea and N of the Zagros Mountains; Medes were its inhabitants descended from Japheth (Gn. 10:2). They were first mentioned by name by the Assyrian Shalmaneser III who raided their plains in 836 BC to obtain their famous, finely-bred horses. His successors all claimed to have conquered 'the land of the Medes and Persians'; Sargon II deported Israelites to Media (2 Ki. 17:6; 18:11). Medes rebelled against the declining Assyria and controlled all lands to the N of Assyria by 600 BC. In 550 BC Cyrus of Persia conquered Media, the customs and laws of the two nations being combined (Dn. 6:8). The history of Jews in Media is recounted in the book of Esther. Median Jews were in Jerusalem at Pentecost (Acts 2:9).

MEDIATOR. The term is rare in the Bible, occurring only in Gal. 3:19; 1 Tim. 2:5; Heb. 8:6; 9:15; 12:24 and in the LXX in Jb. 9:33 ('umpire', RSV). The idea, however, is common. The function of a mediator is to intervene between two people (or groups) in order to promote harmonious relationships between them or to reconcile them. In the OT both priests and prophets were mediators in different ways. The priest acted on behalf of people in the presence of God (Heb. 5:1ff.). The prophet acted for God in the presence of people (*cf.* Dt. 18:18ff.), delivering his message to them. Moses was the greatest mediator, for through him God made his covenant with Israel at Sinai (Ex. 19:3ff.).

In the NT, Christ is the mediator of the new covenant (Heb. 9:15; 12:24), bringing God and people together in a new relationship (1 Tim. 2:5). He was the mediator in creation because he is the pre-existent Son of God (Jn. 1:3; Col. 1:16; Heb. 1:2). Through his death he achieved reconciliation between God and mankind who had formerly been alienated from each other (Eph. 2:12ff.), an achievement often described as 'salvation' (Jn. 3:17; Acts 15:11) through which people are 'justified' before God (Rom. 3:24f.). Those who by believing receive the benefits of this mediation still require his continued mediation, however. He introduces them into God's presence (Eph. 2:18), and through him their prayers and praises are presented to God (Jn. 14:14; Rom. 1:8; Col. 3:17; Heb. 13:15), as too is their service (1 Pet. 2:5). Jesus is a 'priest for ever' (Heb. 7:21, 24) who intercedes for them and out of his own experience of weakness sends them his gracious help (Heb. 4:15; 7:25). He reigns over all (Eph. 1:20ff.) and will defeat all his enemies (1 Cor. 15:25).

Hence his mediating work has as many facets as his person, status and work, and demands that we give to no-one else the title or role of mediator between us and God.

MEDICINE: See HEALTH AND HEALING.

MEEKNESS. The spiritual quality of patient submission and humility. In the OT its basic meaning is 'poor and afflicted' (*e.g.* Pss. 22:26; 25:9). It was exhibited by Moses (Nu. 12:3) and would be a quality of the Messianic King (Zc. 9:9). In the NT it is an inner attitude produced by the Spirit (Gal. 5:23, AV), exemplified and encouraged by Jesus (2 Cor. 10:1; Mt. 5:5) and underlying good relationships between Christians (Eph. 4:2).

MEGIDDO. An important OT town on the N of the Carmel mountain ridge 30 km SSE of modern Haifa. It was captured by Joshua (Jos. 12:21) and allotted to Manasseh (Jos. 17:11). Solomon made it one of his fortified cities where he housed horses and chariots (1 Ki. 9:15ff.). It was the scene of Josiah's death (2 Ki. 23:29f.). In Zc. 12:11 it appears in Hebrew as *megiddon*, which reoccurs in the NT as Armageddon (Rev. 16:16) from the Hebrew meaning 'hill of Megiddo'.

The site has been identified with the deserted mound of Tell el-Mutesellim and has been extensively excavated. The earliest settlement dated back to soon after 4000 BC; a millennium later it was an extensive city with some form of sacrificial 'high place'. There is evidence of Egyptian influence in the Middle Bronze Age (2200-1550 BC). In the Late Bronze Age (1550-1200 BC) N cultural influence is seen in a hoard of 200 carved ivory objects, and there was a tunnel bringing water from a spring into the city. There are signs of destruction towards the end of the 12th cent. BC, some time after the arrival of the Israelites, but the people who resettled it do not appear to have been Israelites which accords with the biblical claim that the inhabitants were not driven out (Jdg. 1:27f.). An extensive series of stables, capable of accommodating up to 450 horses, was once thought to have been built in Solomon's time but is now known to date from the later reign of Ahab. Altogether, the excavations reveal what a formidable civilization the Israelites encountered when they invaded Canaan.

MELCHIZEDEK. The king of Salem (probably Jerusalem) and 'priest of God most high' who greeted and blessed Abraham when he returned from defeating Chedorlaomer and his allies; in return Abraham gave him a tenth of the spoils of battle (Gn. 14:17ff.). In Ps. 110:4 a king in David's line is said to be 'a priest for ever after the order of Melchizedek'. The background is David's conquest of Jerusalem *c.* 1000 BC by which he became heir to Melchizedek's dynasty of priest-kings. The writer of Hebrews develops the theme by comparing Melchizedek's superiority over Abraham with Jesus' superiority to the OT priesthood (Heb. 5:6ff.; 6:19-7:28).

MELZAR. In Dn. 1:11ff. (AV) the name is now usually regarded as a title ('steward', RSV).

MEMPHIS. An Egyptian city on the Nile 24 km from the apex of the river delta. It remained important down to the conquest by Alexander the Great (332 BC). Foreign gods such as Astarte and Baal were imported by Asiatic immigrants, and Jews settled there after the destruction of Jerusalem in 587 BC (Je. 44:1). The city is also mentioned by other prophets (*e.g.* Is. 19:13; Ezk. 30:13; Ho. 9:6).

MENAHEM (lit. 'comforter'). The military governor of Tirzah, the older capital of (N) Israel (2 Ki. 15:14ff.), who became the N kingdom's 17th king by capturing the throne from a usurper, Shallum, and strengthened his position by a disastrous alliance with Assyria which led to Assyria annexing Israel.

MENE, MENE, TEKEL, PARSIN. The writing on the wall which appeared at Belshazzar's feast (Dn. 5:25). Daniel's interpretation is taken from similar Aramaic words meaning numbered (*mene*), weighed (*tekel*) and divided (*parsin; peres* in v. 28 is the singular form); on the surface the words simply stood for units of weight or money— mina, shekel and half-shekel. Some scholars have also tried to identify each word with a later ruler of Babylon, but such suggestions are not relevant to the basic message.

MEPHIBOSHETH. The name

originally may have been Meribbaal ('Baal is advocate' or 'hero of Baal'). 1. The son of Jonathan who was crippled during a dash for safety when he was 5 years old (2 Sa. 4:4), whom David cared for (2 Sa. 9; 21:7) and who was apparently the innocent pawn in his servant Ziba's treachery (2 Sa. 16:1ff.; 19:24ff.). 2. Saul's son by the concubine Rizpah (2 Sa. 21:8).

MERAB. Saul's daughter promised to David but given to Adriel (1 Sa. 18:17ff.); RSV puts her in 2 Sa. 21:8 instead of Michal to correct a probable scribal error.

MERARI, MERARITES. Merari was Levi's 3rd son and founder of one of the 3 great Levite families. In the desert Merarites carried the tabernacle framework (Nu. 3:36f.), and were assigned portering and singing duties in the temple (1 Ch. 6:44ff.; 25:3, Jeduthan being a Merarite). They also served under Ezra (Ezr. 8:18f.).

MERATHAIM. In Je. 50:21, a term meaning 'double bitterness' or 'double rebellion'; it is probably not a proper name.

MERCY, MERCIFUL. The concept is expressed by several biblical words which are rendered in EVV by a variety of terms. The chief OT word, *chesed*, means kindness or grace; it denotes God's faithfulness to his graciously established covenant which leads to merciful treatment of his people. In RSV it is most often rendered 'steadfast love' (*e.g.* Ps. 89:28). In the NT, the idea of *chesed* is rendered by *charis*, 'grace', which implies God's concern for man in his guilt; other words for mercy are concerned for man in his despair. God is the 'Father of mercies' (2 Cor. 1:3), who through mercy saves us (Eph. 2:4). Christians are to be merciful like him (Lk. 6:36), for then they will be blessed by him (Mt. 5:7).

MERIBAH: See MASSAH.

MERODACH. The Hebrew form of the primary Babylonian god Marduk. He was later known by his epithet Bel (Baal) (Is. 46:1); his people's defeat was also his defeat (Je. 50:2). The name occurs in several personal names including Mordecai in Esther.

MERODACH-BALADAN. The king of Babylon who sent an embassy to Hezekiah (Is. 39:1ff.; 2 Ki. 20:12ff.). He supported the Assyrians when they entered Babylon in 731 BC but in 721 BC claimed the throne. He remained king until 710 BC when Sargon entered the city unopposed, but even then seems to have continued as local ruler. He worked for independence from Assyria when Sargon died in 705 BC, hence his attempt to encourage Hezekiah to rebel; Merodach was deposed soon after.

MEROM, WATERS OF. The site of Joshua's victory over the Hazor confederacy (Jos. 11:5ff.), either Meiron 5 km WNW of Safat or Maroun er-Ras 15 km to the N.

MERONOTH(ITE). Believed to be

347

Beituniyeh, NW of Gibeon (*cf.* Ne. 3:7).

MEROZ. A community cursed by Deborah for not fighting Sisera (Jdg. 5:23); possibly Kh. Marus 12 km S of Kedesh-naphtali.

MESHA. *Person:* The king of Moab who rebelled against Israel after Ahab's death, *c.* 853 BC, possibly to gain direct control of his wool trade with Tyre (2 Ki. 1:1; 3:4f.). *Place:* Possibly in S Arabia, a boundary point of Joktan's territory (Gn. 10:30).

MESHACH. The Babylonian name given to Daniel's companion Mishael, possibly meaning 'I have become weak' (Dn. 1:7).

MESHECH. One of the sons of Japheth, associated with Tubal (Gn. 10:2), called Mash in Gn. 10:23. His descendants are known as warlike slave and copper traders (Ezk. 27:13; 32:26), and as typical of a barbarous society (Ps. 120:5). They are probably to be identified with the Muska mentioned in Assyrian annals and with the Moschoi mentioned by Herodotus. They seem to have spoken an Indo-European language, and entered the Near East from the N Steppe to rule an area in E Anatolia.

MESOPOTAMIA. Meaning 'between the two rivers', it was a fertile land covering the upper and middle Euphrates, modern E Syria-N Iraq. After the 4th cent. BC Greek and Roman writers extended its definition to describe the whole Tigris-Euphrates valley, that is modern Iraq; hence Stephen included Ur in it (Acts 7:2) which would not have been true in OT times. It was the original home area of Balaam (Dt. 23:4), and provided charioteers and cavalry for David (1 Ch. 19:6) which fits with the known occupation of it by horse-rearing Mitanni and Hurrians (Horites).

MESSIAH.

1. Old Testament. The word describes the person ('anointed one') whom the Jews expected God to send as their liberator; it is mainly a product of the period after the Exile and is found only twice in the OT. The best example of the anointed person happens also to be non-Jewish: the Persian king Cyrus who in Is. 45:1 is called 'God's anointed'. He is chosen by God (41:25); appointed to redeem God's people (45:11ff.) and judge them (47); he is given authority over the nations, and in all his actions is God's agent (45:1ff.). These factors were also to be true of Jesus Christ, who saw himself as the fulfilment of OT Messianic hopes. However, despite the late historical development of the hope for a specific Messiah who would liberate his people and inaugurate the last days, it is possible to trace throughout OT history a hope or expectation of a 'figure of salvation' as part of the whole plan and purpose of God.

Messiah as symbolized by historical figures. Three people are seen in the OT as 'types' of the way God acts through his Messiah. The first is

Adam. The Messianic future is in some respects reminiscent of the Garden of Eden as a time of peace and prosperity (*e.g.* Is. 4:2; 11:6ff.; 32:15ff.; Am. 9:13). The curse on the world is reversed by the salvation figure (*cf.* Gn. 3:15), not as a piece of wishful thinking but as a logical outworking of the doctrine of creation by a holy God. The first Adam had dominion over the rest of creation but fell when he allowed his dominion to be usurped (Gn. 1:28; 2:19f.; 3:13). The NT doctrine of Christ as the 'second Adam' has its roots in these passages which all concern the Messianic King.

The second historical figure is *Moses*. The first Exodus was an eternal revelation of God, not simply an historical event (Ex. 3:15). There grew a belief that there would be a second Exodus. Sometimes no man is mentioned as leader (as in Je. 31:31ff.; Ho. 2:14ff.; Ezk. 20:33ff., note the word 'king' here and *cf.* the possible allusion to Moses as king in Dt. 33:5). On other occasions the forecast of the second Exodus appears to include a Messianic figure (*e.g.* Is. 51:9ff.; 52:12). The prophecy of a Moses-like prophet is explicit in Dt. 18:15ff.; although the passage is considered by some scholars merely to promise a continued line of prophets, some of the features can only be satisfied by the Messiah. For example the promise of guidance (v. 18) in the context of a warning against pagan religious practices is a promise of God's regular revelation. But according to Dt. 34:10, Moses is unique; at the time of writing no-one like him had appeared so

18:15ff. seems also to be Messianic. This is stressed by the fact that the future prophet will be like Moses in his specific work at Sinai (Horeb, 18:16). All succeeding prophets were propagators of God's revelation to Moses, not originators of fresh doctrine; that was to be the Messiah's role. The implication of this dual emphasis seems to be that each prophet must be as like Moses as possible until the (unspecified) time in the future when the Messiah would come as prophet, lawgiver and mediator of a new covenant.

The third historical 'type' of the Messiah is *David*. The tribe of Judah was expected to provide a great ruler (Gn. 49:9f.) and this was fulfilled in some sense by David with whom all succeeding kings were compared (*e.g.* 1 Ki. 11:4ff.; 15:3ff.). It seems that as time went on, David's days glowed brighter in Israel's memory and Nathan's general prophecy (2 Sa. 7:12ff.) became crystallized into a hope for a single 'Davidic' king (*e.g.* Ezk. 34:23). Some of the Psalms focus on this person. He meets world opposition victoriously (Pss. 89:22f.; 110:1); by God's activity he establishes world rule (18:43ff.; 110:1ff.) based on Zion (2:6) and marked by a concern for morality (72:2f.); his rule is everlasting, peaceful and prosperous (72:5, 7, 16); he is called by an everlasting name and is the object of unending thanks (72:15, 17); he is the heir of David's covenant (89:28ff.) and Melchizedek's priesthood (110:4); he belongs to God (89:18), is his son (2:7) seated at his right hand (110:1) and is himself divine (45:6). Either this is blatant flattery or the expression of a great ideal.

A sustained treatment of the Davidic-Messianic theme is also found in Is. 1-37, especially in the self-contained unit of chs. 7-12. Isaiah sees the approaching threat of Assyria as transitory (7:7) yet also decisive for God's people. He calls for reliance on God (7:4), offers a sign that would virtually compel faith (7:10f.), and when this is rejected offers the still greater sign of Immanuel (7:14ff.). This figure would be born of a virgin; some scholars argue that the word used means simply a young woman of marriageable age, but the inference of virginity in its other biblical uses is strong. As Isaiah's teaching develops, Immanuel becomes the royal deliverer (9:1ff.) and the righteous king (11:1ff.), a world ruler (9:7; 11:10) on David's throne (9:7) who is also the 'mighty God' (9:6; *cf.* the description of God himself in 10:21). Isaiah seems to make his own son an immediate sign (8:1ff.) but contrasts the child with the one who comes 'in the latter time' (9:1).

Other OT Messianic figures. Six are important to note. *The Servant* in Isaiah is God's anointed judge (42:1); he is prophetic (49:1f.), the agent of worldwide revelation (42:1ff.) and salvation (49:6), not as a priest but as a victim (53). The first 'Servant Song' (42:1-4) concentrates on his task; before the second (49:1-6) Isaiah exposes Israel's plight (42:18-25) and asserts that its political (43:1-21) and spiritual needs (43:22-44:23) will be met by God. He focuses on Israel's sin (48), and in 49:1-6 the Servant inherits the name which Israel has lost and brings both Israel and the Gentiles back to God. The third Song shows the Servant utterly obedient (50:4-9) even to the point of suffering. He is clearly seen as an individual in the fourth song (52:13-53:12), rejected and bearing sin innocently. The person of this Servant is shrouded in mystery; he is a man (53:2f.) and also 'the arm of the Lord' (53:1), God himself acting as at a new Exodus (51:9f.; 52:10).

The anointed Conqueror in the latter chs. of Isaiah is brought by God himself to Zion (59:16-20); he is endowed with God's Spirit and speaks God's words (59:21). His work is worldwide (60:1ff.), and he himself puts on the 'garments of salvation' (61:10f.) which God had formerly done (59:16f.); Isaiah thus introduces the Messianic motif of a figure both identical to and separate from God. *The Branch*, called 'Yahweh our righteousness', is foreseen by Jeremiah (Je. 23:5ff.; 33:14ff.). The image is interpreted in Zc. 3:8 to be a priest who will remove the sin of the land in a single day, a fulfilment of Ps. 110 and its eternal king-priest. In Is. 4:2ff. the Branch belongs to David yet also is God's, again repeating the Messianic motif of divinity and humanity.

The seed of the woman in Gn. 3:15 is reflected in Is. 7:14 and 49:1 where the Messiah's humanity is traced through his mother. The passage has Messianic overtones because biblically the serpent of the story is ultimately Satan (Rev. 20:2) whom the woman's seed will destroy, being bruised in the process, in order to reverse the calamity of the fall. *The Son of Man* in Dn. 7 is portrayed in the context of the Ancient of Days disposing of his enemies. The beast-kings are personal enemies of the saints and involve their kingdoms in opposing the saints; the one 'like a son of man' personally receives a universal dominion which includes that of his people. Again, he is man, but he comes as God with the clouds of heaven (*cf.* Ps. 104:3). Finally, *the anointed Prince* of Dn. 9:24-27 has attracted many interpretations. The meaning of the whole passage has been summarized thus by S.R. Driver: 'The messianic age is to be marked by the abolition and forgiveness of sin, and by perpetual righteousness.' Such a purpose can hardly be attributed to the period following Antiochus Epiphanes' desecration of the Jerusalem temple and the high-priesthood of Onias III in 175 BC who, anointed though he was, was 'cut off' by assassination. It is more satisfactorily fulfilled by the Messianic figure of Jesus Christ.

See also ANOINTING; SERVANT OF THE LORD.

2. New Testament.

'Christ' is the Greek equivalent of the Hebrew 'Messiah'. In the Gospels (especially John) it denotes the expected deliverer in a general sense (*e.g.* 1:20, 41; 4:25, 29). The dominant popular hope of the time was for a king like David who would be a political conquerer and liberator, and a nationalistic element is present in some passages (*e.g.* Mt. 2:2ff.; Mk.

15:32). Jesus was however reluctant to apply the term to himself, the only clearly explicit reference being in Jn. 4:25f. But he did not deny it either, and constantly stressed his fulfilment of OT hopes; in response to John the Baptist's request, he pointed to an unambiguously Messianic passage (Mt. 11:2ff.; *cf.* Is. 61:1f.). Yet when Peter declared Jesus to be the Christ, he swore him to secrecy, teaching that contrary to popular ideas the Messiah must suffer and die (Mk. 8:29ff.). Here, and when challenged by the high priest (Mk. 14:61f.), he did not deny the title but went on to speak of his role as 'Son of man'. He also played down the titles 'son of David' and 'king of Israel' which others used of him (*e.g.* Mk. 10:47; 15:2). The Messianic demonstration of the 'triumphal entry' was deliberately staged to bring to mind Zechariah's picture of the humble king bringing peace (Zc. 9:9f.), and Jesus deliberately ran from the crowd which wanted to make him a nationalistic king (Jn. 6:15). Jesus preferred to use the title 'son of man', not then in current usage for the Messiah, to carry his own ideas of Messiahship without importing alien ideas not already there in Dn. 7:13f.

The declaration that Jesus was the Messiah lay at the heart of the earliest Christian preaching, using the resurrection to validate the claim (Acts 2:36). Because this did not accord with popular views of Messiahship, the teaching in Acts stresses the scriptural grounds for Messiah's rejection, death and resurrection (*e.g.* 2:25ff.; 13:27ff.). The term Christ was used openly because since Jesus' death and resurrection it was no longer likely to be interpreted politically. The message was that Jesus, now exalted to God's 'right hand' was enthroned as Messianic King (Ps. 110:1; *cf.* Mk. 14:62; Acts 2:34ff.). 'Christ' therefore quickly came to be used as a second name for Jesus, and the disciples became known as Christians (Acts 11:26). Paul used Christ as a name in his earliest letters, and of the almost 400 occurrences of the term in his writings only one (Rom. 9:5) is clearly meant in the technical sense. That does not mean that the church lost interest in Jesus' fulfilment of OT Messianic hopes. The church searched the OT for passages to throw further light on his Messianic role and his saving work (*e.g.* Acts 7; Rom. 10:5ff.; Heb. 2:6ff.). Hebrews especially is largely an exposition of such OT themes.

See also JESUS CHRIST, TITLES OF; QUOTATIONS IN THE NEW TESTAMENT.

METAL, METALWORKERS: See MINING AND METALS.

METHEGH-AMMAH. Apparent textual corruption in 2 Sa. 8:1 makes this difficult to understand. It could be a place-name near Gath; a figurative name for Gath ('bridle of the mother city', RV); or a phrase meaning Philistine control was ended (as GNB).

METHUSELAH. The son of Enoch and grandfather of Noah, who according to Gn. 5:27 lived 969 years.

MEZAHAB (lit. 'waters of gold'). The grandfather of Hadar's wife Mehetabel (Gn. 36:39); perhaps the name of a place with which he was associated.

MICAH, MICAIAH (lit. 'Who is like Yahweh?'). A common Hebrew name. Among OT people so named are Micah of Moresheth, the prophet (see next article); Micah of Mt Ephraim whose story explains the origin of the sanctuary at Dan (Jdg. 17-18); Micaiah the prophet in Ahab's day (1 Ki. 22), possibly the unknown prophet of 1 Ki. 20:35ff.

MICAH, BOOK OF. *Contents.* The coming judgment on Israel (1); Israel to be punished, then restored (2); condemnation of princes and prophets (3); the coming peace and glory of Jerusalem (4); the suffering and restoration of Zion (5); prophetic and popular religion contrasted (6); corruption of society; concluding statement of trust in God (7).

Author and date. The book claims to be the work of Micah of Moresheth in the Judah lowlands. A younger contemporary of Isaiah, he prophesied between 742 and 687 BC. Some scholars have suggested only 1:2-2:10 and parts of chs. 4 and 5 are from Micah himself, because of differences in style, but others assert that the descriptive style and consistent revelation of God's judgment, compassion and hope testify to the book's unity and an 8th-cent. date.

Background and message. Although Micah lived in a rural area, he knew of and denounced the corruptions of city life in Jerusalem, including oppression of the poor (2:1f.), apostasy of the religious leaders (2:11), and injustice practised by those who were supposed to uphold the law (3:10f.). God's righteousness, however, demanded ethical righteousness from his people, Micah argued. Like Amos, Hosea and Isaiah he believed God would use a foreign nation to punish Israel (1:6ff.; 2:3ff.). A century later, his words concerning Jerusalem's downfall (3:12) were still remembered (Je. 26:18f.). Social and religious corruption would have to go (5:10ff.) before God's saving grace could be experienced (not earned, 6:6ff.); this would be in the form of a new universal religion to be centred on Jerusalem (4:1ff.). Micah prophesied the birth of the Messiah in Bethlehem (5:2). The closing verses of the book are read each year by Jews in the afternoon service on the Day of Atonement.

MICHAEL. The name of 11 biblical people, only one of whom, the angel Michael, gets more than a passing reference. In Dn. he is 'a prince' (10:13, 21) who guards the Jews from the godless menace of Greece and Persia (12:1); in Jude 9 and Rev. 12:7 he contends with Satan.

MICHAL. Saul's younger daughter married to David (1 Sa. 18:20ff.). During his exile she was given to Paltiel (1 Sa. 25:44), but she was later restored to him (2 Sa. 3:14ff.). She despised him for his religious dance and remained childless because of it (2 Sa.

6:12ff.); in some versions the sons in 2 Sa. 21:8 were Merab's (as RSV) not Michal's.

MICHMASH (MICHMAS). A city of Benjamin E of Bethel and 12 km N of Jerusalem on the pass from Bethel to Jericho, the modern ruined village of Mukhmas. In Geba, just S of the pass, the Israelites and Philistines fought and Jonathan made a daring personal raid (1 Sa. 13-14). Jews returning from Exile lived here (Ezr. 2:27; Ne. 7:31), as did Jonathan Maccabaeus (1 Macc. 9:73).

MIDIANITES. These desert nomads consisted of 5 families linked to Abraham through Midian, son of his concubine Keturah, sent, with the sons of his other concubines, away to the E (Gn. 25:1ff.). Moses' wife and father-in-law were Midianites (Ex. 2:21), as was his brother-in-law Hobab whom he asked to guide Israel through the desert (Nu. 10:29ff.). Later the Midianites, along with the Moabites, hired Balaam to curse Israel (Nu. 22ff.), and led Israel into sin for which they were defeated (Nu. 25; 31). The references in Jdg. 6-9 about their camels are the earliest known references to camels used in war; they were still famous in Is. 60:6. See also NOMADS.

MIDRASH: See TALMUD AND MIDRASH.

MIDWIFE. The midwife helped at childbirth by taking the new-born child, cutting its umbilical cord, washing the baby in water, salting and wrapping it (Ezk. 16:4). Midwives are first mentioned in the Bible attending Rachel (Gn. 35:17) and Tamar (Gn. 38:28). Women giving birth in the ancient Near East often crouched on a pair of bricks or stones, or a birthstool (*cf.* Ex. 1:16).

MIGDOL (lit. 'tower'). A Canaanite fort mentioned as a place-name several times (*e.g.* Ex. 14:2; Ezk. 29:10). There were several Migdols built near the Egyptian border and none can be located accurately.

MIGRON. A place near Gibeah where Saul stayed (1 Sa. 14:2), possibly the same as in Is. 10:20, modern Tell Miryam N of Michmash.

MILCAH (lit. 'counsel'). 1. The daughter of Haran, wife of Nahor, and grandmother of Rebekah (Gn. 11:29). 2. One of Zelophehad's daughters who inherited their father's estate (Nu. 26:33; 27:1ff.).

MILCOM. The name of the Ammorites' national god (*cf.* 1 Ki. 11:5). Also referred to as Malcam in AV, and probably identical to MOLECH.

MILETUS. The southernmost of the great Greek cities on the W coast of Asia Minor, it was a flourishing commercial and woollen centre in the 8th-6th cent. BC but was destroyed by the Persians in 494 BC. It was rebuilt but in Paul's time (Acts 20:15) it was declining commercially because its harbour was silting up.

MILK. Part of the staple diet of the Hebrews from earliest times; Canaan was seen as 'flowing with milk and honey' (*i.e.* of rich pasturelands, Ex. 3:8). Cows, goats, sheep and possibly camels were all sources of milk for human consumption. It may have been mingled with wine as a delicacy (Song 5:1). It was used as a symbol of prosperity (Is. 60:16) and the nourishment of God's word (Is. 55:1; 1 Pet. 2:22; but *cf.* Paul's different use in 1 Cor. 3:2). The prohibition of Ex. 23:19; Dt. 14:21 is applied by orthodox Jews to prohibit milk consumption at any meal where meat is eaten, and to use separate equipment for preparing milk and meat dishes.

MILL, MILLSTONE. In earliest times, grain was spread on a flat stone slab (quern) and rubbed with a round stone muller. In the Iron Age (from 1200 BC) rotary querns were used consisting of two circular stone slabs 50 cm across, the upper one revolving on the lower; the grain was poured into the pivot-hole at the top and the flour spilled out between the stones. Women (Mt. 24:41) and prisoners (Jdg. 16:21) did the grinding; animals powered larger mills. The handmill, on which families depended, could not be given as surety for a loan (Dt. 24:6). The cessation of the steady sound of grinding was a sign of destruction (Je. 25:10). See BREAD.

MILLO. A place-name derived from the Hebrew 'to fill', used principally to describe part of Jerusalem already in existence in David's time (2 Sa. 5:9) and rebuilt by Solomon (1 Ki. 9:15). It may have been a system of terraces built on the E slope of Ophel Hill.

MINING AND METALS. *Gold* is the first metal mentioned in Scripture (Gn. 2:11) and is thereafter closely associated with silver; the two metals are often alloyed with each other in their natural state. Gold was especially abundant in the alluvium of Egypt's E desert, but also occurred in Arabia, Persia and W Asia Minor. It was used for ornaments as early as the Stone Age (10,000 BC) and for important furnishings in the tabernacle (Ex. 25) and temple (1 Ki. 6). *Silver* was plentiful in biblical times, usually extracted from the sulphide ore of lead (*cf.* Je. 6:29f., which uses the refining process symbolically). It occurred in Asia Minor, S Greece, Persia, Armenia and in Egypt's E desert. Goldsmiths and silversmiths used blow-pipes to ventilate small furnaces and cast their products in steatite or clay moulds.

Copper was smelted and cast in Palestine from *c.* 3200 BC. It was used more or less pure at first, but from *c.* 2000 BC was generally alloyed with tin and used as *bronze*. Some examples of *brass* (copper and zinc) are known but were probably produced accidentally until the Romans began using it for coins in *c.* 20 BC. Copper ores were widespread throughout the ancient Near East (including Cyprus, which takes its name from the metal). Copper was used for tools, weapons and many household items including basins, musical instruments and mirrors.

Tin and *lead* were often confused in ancient times, and occur biblically only in lists. *Iron* was preferred to copper for tools and weapons, but it required more sophisticated manufacturing techniques. The Hittites were the first to use it consistently, although on a small scale. The Philistines brought the art of making it to Palestine, and long retained a monopoly in it (1 Sa. 13:19ff.). Iron ore was plentiful in the Wadi Arabah S of the Dead Sea, where it could be mined with copper (*cf.* Dt. 8:9), and elsewhere in Palestine.

Mining was at first a matter of digging ores out of surface outcrops. Large scale copper workings in Egypt have been found with shafts over 35 m deep. Tunnels were driven into hillsides, supported by pillars left in broad excavations and ventilated by shafts. Stone and (later) bronze tools were used. The rock was split by wedges, and the ore separated by crushing, washing and hand-picking.

Copper *smelting* involved feeding finely-ground ores and fluxes (iron oxides, limestone or sea shells) mixed with charcoal into the charcoal-fuelled furnace supplied with draught from bellows (Is. 54:16). Copper globules sank to the bottom; the slag above was drawn off while liquid and the copper left inside to solidify into an ingot, which was then remelted and cast in stone or clay moulds. *Smiths* worked iron by beating it on anvils (Is. 41:7). They used soldering, riveting and casting-on techniques to make intricate objects as well as tools, weapons, images and pins.

For stone quarrying, see STONEMASON.

MINISTER: See DEACON; SERVANT.

MINISTRY. The characteristic NT term for ministry is 'service', from which comes the word 'deacon'. It is not found in the Greek translation of the OT, implying a clear change of doctrine. The Greek word for the Jewish priesthood is extended only to Christ's more excellent ministry (Heb. 8:6) and metaphorically to the general self-denying service of prophets and preachers (as in Rom. 15:16). Otherwise the NT employs the idea of priesthood only for the body of believers as a whole (*e.g.* 1 Pet. 2:9).

The pattern for Christian ministry is supplied by Jesus who came not to be served but to serve (Mk. 10:45), using the word for waiting at tables ('deaconing'; *cf.* Jn. 13:4ff.), which was the purpose of the first recorded 'ordination' of Christian ministers (Acts 6:2). Service done to others is reckoned also to be done to Christ (Mt. 25:44). Rendering such service is a gift of God (Col. 4:17; *cf.* Rom. 12:7). Even when the diaconate is a recognized office of the church (1 Tim. 3:8ff.) it is still used in a wider sense (2 Tim. 4:5).

Pastoral care is an important aspect of ministry (Jn. 21:15ff.; 1 Pet. 5:2) and is closely associated with preaching and teaching (1 Cor. 3:1f.). But the NT has little to say about sacramental duties. Paul regarded the administra-tion of baptism as a subordinate activity which he usually delegated to his assistants (1 Cor. 1:14ff.). The celebration of the Lord's Supper was a corporate activity (1 Cor. 10:16f.), although there must have been a president, probably a local presbyter or bishop (synonymous terms).

The earliest form of Christian ministry was the exercise of spiritual gifts. In Paul's three lists of gifts, he includes administrative functions alongside the more obviously 'spiritual' ministries (Rom. 12:6-8; 1 Cor. 12:28; Eph. 4:11). They are all ways of serving, rather than being stereotyped offices; indeed all Christians are called to minister (*cf.* 1 Cor. 12:11), and the 'ministers of the word' are called to equip them for it (Eph. 4:11f.). Apostles might decide policy with elders (Acts 15:6ff.) or superintend new developments (Acts 8:14ff.). Evangelists also had a roving commission but lacked the same authority as apostles. Prophets not only foretold (Acts 11:27f.) but also edified and comforted Christians with their inspired teaching (1 Cor. 14:3). Pastors and teachers (Eph. 4:11) were presumably ministers serving their local congregation, assisted by administrators, while 'helpers' undertook charitable work. The NT does not indicate how any of its ministries are to be passed on; its main preoccupation is that ministers teach orthodox doctrine.

See also APOSTLE; BISHOP; CHURCH GOVERNMENT; DEACON; ELDER; SERVANT; SPIRITUAL GIFTS.

MINNI. A people summoned by Jeremiah to fight Babylonia (Je. 51:27). To be identified with the Mannai from SE of Lake Urmia who are often named in 9th-7th cent. texts; they are known to have allied with the Assyrians against Babylon in 616 BC.

MINNITH. In Jdg. 11:33, the limit of Jephthah's invasion of Ammon; the site, between Amman and Heshbon, is unknown.

MIRACLES. Several words are used to refer to God's intervention in history or nature, such as 'sign', 'wonder', 'mighty act' and 'miracle'. In such events, God's activity is seen as distinctive or wonderful, powerful and significant.

Miracles and the natural order. Scripture does not distinguish sharply between God's constant sovereign providence and his particular acts. Belief in miracles is set in the context of a world-view which regards all creation as continually sustained by God and subject to his will (*cf.* Col. 1:16f.). Hence wonder, power and significance are already present in nature (Rom. 1:20), and biblical writers do not distinguish God's 'mighty acts' from 'the course of nature'. The discovery of, say, a repetition of the blocking of the Jordan or causal connections between the plagues of Egypt could not of itself contradict the biblical assertion that these events were mighty works of God. Miracles reveal God as living and personal, active in history as a Redeemer who saves and guides his people; they contradict the belief that

he is only an impersonal force. He is changeless in the sense that he is faithful, not in the sense that he cannot change things in a world of responsible—and irresponsible—people.

Miracles and revelation. Miracles do not simply authenticate God's revelation but are integral to it; they are God's way of speaking dramatically to nourish faith in those who already trust him. Jesus refused to do miracles just to authenticate his teaching, and pointed out that wonders can be worked by those who oppose God (Mt. 24:24). The true miracle is congruous with the rest of the revelation being given; Israel was to reject wonder-workers who denied the Lord (Dt. 13:2f.). Miracle stories are concerned with the faith of observers or participants (*e.g.* 1 Ki. 18:39; Jn. 20:30f.), but an individual's faith is not a necessary condition for a miracle because God can act without it. In Mk. 6:5 Jesus did some miracles but could not do more because his whole mission (or revelation) was rejected. A notable feature of a miracle, even when it can be 'explained' by natural events, is that it is predicted by or associated with God's word through his agent (*e.g.* Jos. 3:7ff.). Miracles also cluster around the crises of sacred history: the Exodus; the period of Elijah and Elisha when Israel seemed about to sink into complete apostasy; the coming of Christ and the pioneering days of the Christian mission.

Miracles in the NT. There is some evidence for regarding Jesus' and the apostles' miracles as different to those in the OT. In Jesus God himself confronts us, freely acting in his own world. The continuity with the past is there (*cf.* the question in Mt. 11:5) but there is an intimate connection between Jesus' words and actions: people receive spiritual sight and the power to walk in God's way as well as being healed of blindness or paralysis. In Jesus' powerful authority (Mk. 2:9ff.) and humble dependence on the Father (Jn. 5:19) is seen the perfect unity of divinity and humanity. The decisive miracle of the NT is the resurrection of Jesus, on which rests the whole structure of NT faith (1 Cor. 15:17). The miracles worked by others in the NT spring from their solidarity with and dependence upon Jesus; they are done in his name. They are part of the proclamation of the kingdom of God and are not an end in themselves.

See also DEMON POSSESSION; HEALTH AND HEALING; SIGN; WONDER.

MIRIAM. A prophetess, the sister of Moses and Aaron; she probably watched over Moses in the bulrushes (Ex. 2). She led the women in praise after the Exodus (Ex. 15:20f.) but subsequently rebelled against Moses and became temporarily leprous (Nu. 12). Traditionally she was the wife of Caleb and mother of Hur.

MIRROR. During the OT period mirrors were made from polished metal; bronze examples have been found in Palestine. Glass mirrors were probably introduced in the 1st cent. AD; neither bronze nor glass gave a perfect reflection (1 Cor. 13:12).

MISHAEL (lit. 'who is what God is?'). 1. A Levite who buried rebels (Lv. 10:1ff.). 2. One of Daniel's friends; his name became MESHACH (Dn. 1:6f.).

MISHREPHOTH-MAIM. A border (Jos. 11:8; 13:6); possibly the R. Litani.

MITHREDATH (lit. 'given by Mithra', the Persian god of light). 1. Cyrus' treasurer who handed back the temple equipment (Ezr. 1:8). 2. A Persian officer who objected to the rebuilding of Jerusalem's walls (Ezr. 4:7).

MITYLENE. An ancient Greek republic and the principal state on the island of Lesbos, valued by the Romans as a holiday resort. It was a natural overnight stop for Paul's ship returning to Palestine (Acts 20:14).

MIZAR. A hill in Ps. 42:6, presumably near Hermon. Some scholars believe that it may refer to Zion.

MIZPAH, MIZPEH. The name means 'watchtower' or 'place for watching' and is used for several different locations in the OT. Two are of special interest. 1. The original Mizpah was so called by Laban where he and Jacob made a covenant and set up a cairn as a monument to it; God was the 'watcher' between them (Gn. 31:43ff.).

2. A town in Benjamin near Gibeon and Ramah (1 Ki. 15:22). It was an important assembly point throughout Israel's history. Israelites gathered there to avenge the Levite's concubines (Jdg. 20:1ff.), after the ark of

the covenant was returned (1 Sa. 7:5f.), and to receive Saul as king (1 Sa. 10:17). After the fall of Jerusalem in 587 BC it was the place of the Babylonian governor's residence (2 Ki. 25:23ff.) and the scene of Ishmael's attempted coup (Je. 41). In the Maccabaean period Judas Maccabaeus called men of Judah there for prayer and counsel (1 Macc. 3:46). The site is probably Tell en-Nasbeh on the top of an isolated hill 13 km N of Jerusalem. It was occupied in the Early Bronze Age (3150-2200 BC), abandoned then re-occupied continuously 1100-400 BC. In the days of the kings, and in the Babylonian and Persian periods (587-400 BC), Mizpah was prosperous; relatively rich tombs, a massive gate, water cisterns, dye plants, and many spinning whorls, loom weights, wine and oil presses, and semi-precious stones have been found there.

MIZRAIM. The second son of Ham (Gn. 10:6 AV); see NATIONS, TABLE OF. Also the regular Hebrew term for EGYPT (as RSV).

MNASON. A Jewish Cypriot who was Paul's host in or near Jerusalem, probably converted at Pentecost (Acts 21:16). The allusion possibly identifies him as a source of information for Luke's writings.

MOAB, MOABITES. Moab was the son of Lot by his eldest daughter (Gn. 19:30ff.). The core of the land of Moab was the gorge-cut plateau E of the Dead Sea between the wadis Arnon and Zered. It was occupied with settled villages until *c.* 1850 BC when its inhabitants became nomadic. Lot's descendants must have intermarried with them until they emerged as the dominant group and gave their name to the whole population and area. Moab emerged *c.* 1300 BC as a highly organized kingdom with good agriculture, splendid buildings, strong fortresses along the border. It produced distinctive pottery. Moabites overflowed from the plateau N of the Arnon, sharing lands there with the closely-related Ammonites (*cf.* Dt. 2:10ff.). Moab was unfriendly to the Israelite invaders (Jdg. 11:17). Moses was forbidden to attack it (Dt. 2:9), although Moabites were excluded from Israel (Dt. 23:3ff.).

The king of Moab sought to curse the invaders through Balaam (Nu. 22-24), and seduced them into idolatry (Nu. 25). They attacked Israel in the days of the Judges (Jdg. 3:12ff.), and warred against Saul (1 Sa. 14:47). David hid in Moab for a while (1 Sa. 22:3f.), from which his ancestress Ruth had come (Ru. 4:18ff.). He subdued Moab (2 Sa. 8:2ff.) but it struggled for freedom from later kings of Judah (*e.g.* 2 Ch. 20). In the 8th cent. BC Assyria subdued it (Is. 15-16); it became free again before being subdued by Nebuchadrezzar of Babylon. Moab ceased to be an independent nation but was still known as a race after the Exile (Ezr. 9:1; Ne. 13:1). The prophets often pronounced judgment on it (*e.g.* Is. 15-16; Je. 9:26). See also next article, and NOMADS.

MOABITE STONE. A black basalt

inscription left by Mesha king of Moab at Dibon to commemorate his revolt against Israel and the subsequent rebuilding of many important towns (2 Ki. 3:4ff.). As archaeologists competed to buy it in the 19th cent. local residents broke it up; less than two-thirds of the pieces have been recovered. It tells of how Mesha honoured his god Chemosh, and began breaking free from Israel before Ahab's death, a process not complete till Joram's failure to re-subdue Moab (2 Ki. 3). The importance of the stone lies in its close relation to the OT. Its language is closely akin to Hebrew; it mentions Israel's God Yahweh; and it provides insights into Moabite beliefs which were similar to some of Israel's. It dates from the latter part of Mesha's reign; he died *c*. 830 BC. See also previous article, and MESHA.

MOLADAH. A town of Simeon near Beersheba occupied by returning exiles (Ne. 11:26); probably Khereibet el-Waten, E of Beersheba.

MOLECH, MOLOCH. The national god of the Ammonites (1 Ki. 11:7), to be identified with the god Muluk worshipped at Mari (SE Syria) *c*. 1800 BC and Malik known from Akkadian (ACCAD) texts; in Je. 32:35 it seems to be connected with Baal. Molech is usually associated in the Bible with child sacrifice (*e.g.* 2 Ki. 23:10), a practice condemned in ancient Israel (Lv. 18:21; 20:2ff.) but which nonetheless seems to have continued (*e.g.* 2 Ch. 28:3, *c*. 730 BC). Josiah destroyed Molech's high places (2 Ki. 23:10ff.)

but Ezekiel was still condemning the practice in the 6th cent. BC (Ezk. 16:20ff.; 20:26ff.). These practices lingered on in N Africa among the Carthaginian Phoenicians into the Christian era. It is possible that in some OT passages the term Molech may not refer to the god but could be a general term for child offerings (*e.g.* Lv. 18:21). See also MALCAM.

MOLID. In 1 Ch. 2:29, possibly connected with MOLADAH.

MONEY. *Old Testament.* Coinage was introduced in the late 8th cent. BC. Before that commercial transactions involved a modified form of barter for which staple food and other commodities such as wool and wood served as units of exchange. Wealth was often measured in terms of cattle and precious metals (*e.g.* Gn. 13:2). Silver was the commonest precious metal in the ancient Near East and often served as money (so translated by RSV in Gn. 17:13), but was reckoned by weight (as in 1 Ki. 10:29); it was a suitable medium of exchange for real estate (Je. 32:9) or as a dowry (Ex. 22:17). Gold was used likewise by weight, especially for tribute-taxes to occupying powers (*e.g.* 2 Ki. 18:14) and also in international border agreements (1 Ki. 9:10ff.). The standard of weight was that in force locally (Gn. 23:16). Precious metals were kept in the form of jewellery, objects of daily use, or in characteristic shaped ingots. Abraham gave Rebekah gold in the form of bracelets (Gn. 24:22), and Achan found gold bars at Jericho

(Jos. 7:21). Silver was used in small lumps (1 Sa. 2:36). Small pieces of metal were carried in leather or cloth pouches or bags (Pr. 7:20).

The first known coins—metal pieces struck with a seal to authenticate their weight and title—were struck in electrum (a natural gold-silver alloy) in Lydia in the 6th cent. BC, although references to minting are known from c. 701 BC in Assyria. In Persia gold coins were introduced by Darius I (521-486 BC) who called them *darics* after himself. They portrayed him with a bow and arrow, weighed 130 g, and were known to the exiled Jews (Ezr. 2:69) and to the editor of 1 Ch. 29:7 who gave 'modern' equivalents for ancient quantities. It is suggested that Hg. 1:6 (520 BC) is the earliest biblical reference to coined money. Later Jewish governors issued small silver coins from c. 400 BC, and included the name 'Judah'; one bears the name Hezekiah, perhaps the high priest at the time of Alexander the Great. Simon Maccabaeus had the right to strike coins but apparently did not (1 Macc. 15:6); the first known coins struck by a Jewish ruler bear the name of Alexander Jannaeus (103-76 BC).

New Testament. Money from three different sources was available in Palestine: the official Roman coinage; provincial coins minted at Antioch and Tyre based mainly on the old Greek standard; and local Jewish money perhaps minted at Caesarea. Hence the need for money-changers at the Jerusalem temple (see next article). Jewish coins were mostly minted in bronze; the earliest ones had horticultural designs, because of the second commandment, although coins minted under the Herods depicted either them or the emperor. The only such coin mentioned in the NT was the *lepton*, the 'widow's mite' of Mk. 12:42, equivalent to half the Roman *quadrans* (see below). During the First Revolt (AD 66-70) Jews coined their own silver shekels (plus halves and quarters) for the first time.

Greek coins included the silver *drachma* of which there were 100 to the *mina* (the 'pound' of Lk. 19:11ff.) and 6,000 to the *talent*, which was only a unit of reckoning, not a coin. About 300 BC a sheep cost one drachma; this coin is mentioned only in Lk. 15:8f. (RSV 'silver coins'). The 2-drachma piece (*didrachmon*) was used for the half-shekel Jewish temple tax (Mt. 17:24) which had developed from Ex. 30:11ff. into a regular poll tax. Only coins minted in Tyre were used for this; those from Antioch did not contain enough silver. The *stater* (4 drachmas) is the 'shekel' found by Peter in Mt. 17:27; it was a more common coin than the didrachmon so it was probably usual for people to pay the tax in pairs. It was probably this that Judas received (Mt. 26:15).

The basic Roman coin was the silver *denarius*, 25 of which equalled the gold *aureus* which weighed 126.3 g in 49 BC, devalued to 115 g by Nero's time (AD 60; possibly the 'gold' of Mt. 10:9). The *quadrans* (a quarter of the copper *as*) was the 'penny' (or smallest coin) of Mt. 5:26. The *as* (the 'penny' of Mt. 10:19) was a quarter of the *sestertius* and one-sixteenth of the silver *denarius*, the latter getting its name originally as being 10 copper asses, but it was fixed at 16 in 217 BC. An idea of its purchasing power is gained from it being a day's wage (Mt. 20:1ff.) and a hotel bill (Lk. 10:35). The denarius used in the attempt to trick Jesus (Mt. 22:19) carried the head of the emperor Tiberius, with his mother in the role of Pax on the reverse.

See also next article, and MAMMON; WEIGHTS AND MEASURES.

MONEY-CHANGERS. A specialized class of money-changers operated in the temple precincts (probably in the Court of the Gentiles) because the money paid to the temple had to be in Tyrian standard coin (Mt. 21:12ff.). See previous article, and BANKER; DEBT.

MOON. Its regular phases provided the basis for ancient calendars; its commonest Hebrew name is closely related to the word for 'month'. The first day of each new month (new moon) was considered holy (Is. 1:13) and marked by special sacrifices (Nu. 28:11ff.); the new moon in the 7th month was a day when no work should be done (Lv. 23:24f.). The moon is a symbol of permanence (Ps. 72:5). Ps. 121:6 implies a belief in its ability to affect the mind; in Mt. 4:24; 17:15 the RSV 'epileptic' is literally 'moonstruck'. The moon was worshipped in ancient W Asia (*cf.* Jb. 31:26) and was the chief god at Ur in Mesopotamia and Haran in Syria.

MORDECAI. A Jewish exile in the Persian capital of Susa where he worked in the palace. He exposed a plot against King Xerxes and opposed a plot to kill the Jews, succeeding the evil-minded vizier Haman as a result. Some identify him with a known finance officer of the time. His story and that of his orphaned cousin whom he brought up is contained in the book of ESTHER.

MOREH. 'Teacher', 'diviner'. 1. A place near Shechem in Gn. 12:6 which may be translated 'teacher's oak'; Abraham pitched camp there. 2. The hill of Moreh at the head of the N side of the Jezreel valley, modern Jebel Dahi, where Gideon encountered the Midianites (Jdg. 7:1).

MORESHETH-GATH. Home town of the prophet Micah, probably Tell ej-Judeieh 32 km SW of Jerusalem; in Mi. 1:14 a word-play likens it to a dowry given by the doomed Lachish.

MORIAH. The mountain area to which Abraham was to take Isaac, 3 days' journey from the land of the Philistines, clearly visible from a distance (Gn. 21:34; 22:4). It was probably what was later the temple mount in Jerusalem (2 Ch. 3:1f.), although Samaritan tradition holds it to have been Mt Gerizim.

MORTAR AND PESTLE. A hollowed stone or deep wooden bowl (mortar) in which grain could be ground with a stout wooden pole (pestle), Nu. 11:8. See also MILL.

MOSERAH, MOSEROTH. A desert campsite of the Israelites where Aaron died (Dt. 10:6), possibly close to Mt Hor.

MOSES. The great leader and lawgiver through whom God brought the Israelites out of Egypt, made them a nation, and brought them within reach of the land promised to their ancestors. His name was probably given by his mother, not the Egyptian princess as the Hebrew word-play suggests; *masa* means 'to draw forth' (Ex. 2:9f.), and was also similar to the Egyptian word for 'child'.

Early life. Born to descendants of Levi, Moses was hidden in a basket of pitch-caulked reeds or papyrus in rushes by a stream bank, to protect him from an Egyptian edict that Hebrew male children should be slaughtered. One of the pharaoh's daughters found him, accepted the offer of a temporary wet-nurse (in fact Moses' own mother), then adopted him into the royal household (Ex. 2). Pharaohs of the New Kingdom period (1550-1070 BC) kept *harims*, and children of the *harim*-women were educated by the overseer, and princes were later given a personal tutor. Semites and other Asiatics were found at every level of Egyptian society at that time; some Semites became wealthy merchants, some married into the royal family. At the end of the 19th Dynasty a Syrian actually controlled Egypt for a short while. Moses would therefore have been unexceptional in his social position. But he felt for his enslaved fellow-countrymen,

killed an Egyptian overseer who was beating a Hebrew, and fled for safety over the border to Midian, where he married Zipporah the daughter of the shepherd-priest Jethro (Reuel), Ex. 2:10ff. His call to serve God came many years later at a flaming but not burnt-out bush, and after some hesitation he accepted the call (Ex. 3-4).

Moses and the Exodus. After meeting his brother and the elders of Israel (Ex. 4:27ff.), Moses went with Aaron to ask the pharaoh to release the people for a religious festival; he refused, contemptuously (Ex. 5:1ff.). It is not surprising that Moses was able to gain easy access to the pharaoh, especially if he was Rameses II; a contemporary document describes many people bringing him their requests. The pharaoh's accusation of workers' idleness (Ex. 5:9) is also paralleled in contemporary documents. A series of plagues (Ex. 7-12) demonstrated to the pharaoh the power of Israel's God. On the eve of the last plague, the killing of all non-Israelite first-born male offspring, the Israelites killed a spotless lamb and smeared its blood on their doorways as a protective sign, the origin of the Passover festival. Then Moses led them out of Egypt. They seemed trapped by the sea of reeds and the Egyptians sent 600 charioteers to recapture them (a not unreasonable number when compared with the 730 and 1,092 captured by Egypt from Syria in two of Amenophis II's campaigns). But God led his people across the marshes to safety (Ex. 14-15). Then Moses went into Mt Sinai to receive God's instructions for the national, social and religious life of Israel which formed the basis of a covenant between God and the nation (Ex. 20-23). However, the people quickly lapsed into idolatry, abetted by Aaron (Ex. 32-34). Moses supervised the construction of the tabernacle and the ark of the covenant which were to be the focus of Israel's religious life for generations to come (Ex. 35-40; Nu. 1-10).

Moses and the desert wanderings. In the second year after leaving Egypt, Moses sent 12 spies into Canaan, the 'promised land'. The majority report sent the Israelites into spasms of fear; they rebelled, and God sentenced them to 40 years' desert wandering instead of taking them straight into the land (Nu. 10-14). The laws God had given to Moses related to a settled agricultural community, such as the one the Israelites had left and the one they had expected to form quickly in Canaan; the implementation of them now had to wait. There is thus no need to see the laws of Moses as having been read back from a later, settled period. More revolts followed, led by Korah and Dathan, bringing the nation to the brink of total rebellion against Moses' leadership (Nu. 16). In desperation and frustration Moses overreached his own authority as God's servant at Kadesh-barnea and was himself punished by being banned from Canaan, something he naturally felt very keenly (Nu. 20; Dt. 3:24ff.). In a later rebellion, Moses was cast once more in the role of an intercessor for the people (Nu. 21). As his life drew to its end he led the nation to

military victory after an unprovoked attack by the Ammonites (Nu. 21), and against the Midianites. He prepared Israel for its entry into Canaan, saw the covenant with God renewed, and had a glimpse of Canaan from the distance before he died (Dt. 29-34).

Moses' work and significance. He was an outstanding leader in view of the fact that he constantly had to counter the negativism of the nation; his enduring faith in the invisible God alone can explain his achievement (Heb. 11:24ff.). As a teacher and the lawgiver he was the model for all the prophets who were to follow until the coming of Christ (Dt. 18:18; Acts 3:22f.). His special calling was to make known God's will; in Ex. 19:3 God spoke to Moses, and Moses to the people. He was a man of prayer (Ex. 33:7ff.) and the mediator of the covenant which later prophets called the people back to and expected to see renewed (Je. 31:31ff.). The covenant or treaty in which God (the King) bound himself to his vassal-people was a familiar procedure in international political life at the time, and Moses gave it a religious significance. But the laws he promulgated were not simply a civil code of social conduct but were rooted in the moral framework of the Ten Commandments; Israel's life was to be marked by holiness and righteousness in every part.

Moses was also a writer, and a number of passages in the Pentateuch (Gn.-Dt.) are clearly attributed to him (*e.g.* Ex. 17:14; 24:4-8; Nu. 33:1f.; Dt. 31:9f.; 32:1ff.). The ability of one man to write laws, narrative and poetry is not unknown in ancient times; the Egyptian Khety (or Akhtoy) *c.* 1991-1962 BC had similar gifts. In the NT, Moses as the representative of the law stood with Elijah, the representative prophet, with Christ the Messiah on the Mount of Transfiguration (Mt. 17:3f.).

See also CHRONOLOGY OLD TESTAMENT; EXODUS, OF THE; PLAGUES OF EGYPT.

MOTH. Palestine has many varieties of butterfly and moth but the only biblical reference is to the atypical clothes moth (Jb. 4:19; Lk. 12:33). It is the larvae which do the damage; the adults do not feed.

MOUNT, MOUNTAIN. The backbone of Palestine is formed from the rounded hills carved out of the hard and folded arches of Cenomanian limestone, distinct from the deeply dissected, softer Senonian limestone flanking the Judaean highlands. In the OT the Hebrew words for mountain (which may mean a range or a single peak) and hill are used almost interchangeably, and the same is sometimes true in the NT (in Lk. 9:37 the word 'mountain' is actually 'hill'). It is not always possible to identify mountains such as those in Lk. 4:5; Mt. 5:1. But mountains do have considerable significance in Scripture apart from important incidents which take place on them. They symbolize eternal continuity (Dt. 33:15), the Creator's strength (Ps. 65:6) and majesty (Ps. 68:16); they 'leap' into the

air in praise of God (Ps. 114:4ff.). They also symbolize the difficulties of life (Je. 13:16; Mt. 21:21) which can only be overcome by faith and prayer (Mt. 17:20). See also HIGH PLACE; PALESTINE; and articles on individual mountains.

MOURNING: See BURIAL AND MOURNING.

MOUTH. The hand over the mouth was a sign of shame (Mi.7:16); the mouth can sin (Ps. 59:12) or be filled with praise for God (Ps. 40:3). The biblical usage is similar to that of LIP and TONGUE.

MULE. A hybrid offspring of a horse and donkey. Such breeding appears to be forbidden in Lv. 19:19 which may explain why mules are not mentioned in Scripture until David's time (2 Sa. 13:29). Mules are valuable because they combine strength with endurance and are able to live on poor food.

MUSIC AND MUSICAL INSTRUMENTS.

1. Music.
Music played an important part in Hebrew culture; although closely associated with religious worship it had secular use also from earliest times (Gn. 31:27), and was linked with dance (Ex. 15:20ff.). Music and dance featured at feasts (Is. 5:12), vintage festivals (Is. 16:10), marriages (1 Macc. 9:37ff.), and also at funerals (Mt. 9:23). Kings (2 Sa. 19:35), ordinary workers

(1 Sa. 16:18), youths (La. 5:14) and prostitutes (Is. 23:16) alike used and enjoyed music. For the worship of the temple David organized a choir and orchestra (1 Ch. 15:16ff.). The kind of music they played is unknown. It is uncertain whether the Hebrews had even a system of notation; accents in the Hebrew biblical text were for recitation, not singing, and are of a late date. Some psalms were clearly meant to be sung antiphonally by two choirs (Pss. 13; 20) or by choir and congregation (Ps. 136).

2. Musical instruments.

Knowledge of these is also slight, but instruments have been found belonging to other ancient Near Eastern nations. The original names are variously translated in EVV. It is therefore difficult to identify them all. RSV names are used in the following descriptions.

The *lyre* is the only stringed instrument mentioned in the Pentateuch (Gn.-Dt.) and may have originated in Syria (Gn. 31:27). It was portable (*cf.* 1 Sa. 10:5) and according to an Egyptian wall painting was played with a plectrum. The historian Josephus thought it had 10 strings; some suggest it had 8 based on the Hebrew term 'sheminith' as in 1 Ch. 15:21. It was made from cypress wood (and later almug) and evidently was valuable. The *harp* is first mentioned in 1 Sa. 10:5 and seems to have originated in Phoenicia. The word suggests it may have bulged at its lower end; like the lyre it was made from cypress or almug. It probably had 10 strings and

supplied the bass sound.

The biblical words translated *flute* give no clue as to its exact nature; the balance of opinion is more in favour of it being an oboe. It was a reed-box for such an instrument which Judas used as a money box (Jn. 12:6). The *pipe* (NIV 'flute') of Gn. 4:21; Jb. 21:12; 30:31 and Ps. 150:4 cannot be more closely identified. The *trumpet* however is mentioned often. The Israelites' national trumpet was a long ram's horn with a turned-up end, and is still used in synagogues today. A trumpet of beaten silver was used by Moses (Nu. 10).

Among the percussion instruments were *castanets* (perhaps like the Egyptian rattle made from rings which jangle together), and *bells* which were probably metal discs or cups. *Cymbals* (which occur in the NT at 1 Cor. 13:1) existed in two forms. One consisted of two shallow metal plates held in the hands and struck together. The other was a cup-shaped instrument held stationary while struck sharply by a similar one. The *timbrel* was similar to the *tambourine*, a hand-held instrument struck with the hand and always associated with joy.

MUSTARD: See PLANTS.

MYRA. A chief city of Lysia on the SW tip of Asia Minor with a port 4 km away; Paul boarded a corn ship there (Acts 27:5f.).

MYRRH: See PLANTS.

MYSTERY (SECRET). In the OT the

word occurs only in Dn. (*e.g.* Dn. 2:29), where it means that which is hidden and needs to be made known. It is not unrelated to the NT usage, because the mysteries of which Daniel speaks are contained within God's eternal plan. In the NT, it means a divine truth which needs to be made known to people by God through his Spirit. The knowledge of God's kingdom is 'secret' in the sense that it is reserved for those to whom it is revealed (Mk. 4:1). This is its only use in the Gospels.

Paul uses the word frequently, and gives it a fourfold character. The mystery of God is *eternal in its scope*. It is the good news of God's revelation (Eph. 6:19) with its focus on Christ (Col. 2:2); it was 'decreed before the ages' and now awaits disclosure (1 Cor. 2:7f.). It is *historical in its announcement*. It was announced by God in the historical life of Jesus (Eph. 1:9; 3:3), and Paul was commissioned to proclaim it (Eph. 3:8f.); in Christ new life is available to Jew and Gentile alike. It is *spiritually perceived*, being revealed to the apostles and prophets by the Holy Spirit (Eph. 3:4f.), and through them to others similarly given spiritual understanding. Finally it is *eschatalogical in its out working*: the mystery which has been revealed in history awaits its fulfilment in eternity (*cf.* 1 Cor. 15:51ff.). The use of 'mystery' to describe the sacraments is post-biblical.

MYTH, MYTHOLOGY. In the NT the word appears only in the Pastoral Letters and 2 Peter, and always in a disparaging sense. Timothy is told to discourage interest in myths (1 Tim. 1:4); these are perpetrated by false teachers (2 Tim. 4:4) or Jewish tradition (Tit. 1:14). Such beliefs may have been a mix of gnostic speculation and Judaism, and are contrasted with the gospel in 2 Pet. 1:16.

In modern theological usage, 'myth' is sometimes thought of as the story which religious ritual enacts dramatically; hence Ex. 1-15 is said by some to be 'myth' which the Passover enacts. Some scholars such as R. Bultmann have attempted to 'demythologize' the gospel by removing features such as the involvement in the world by transcendent powers which are said to belong to a former world-view. Still others use 'myth' to mean an imaginative presentation of some abiding reality. More helpful than these is C.S. Lewis' approach which suggests that the human aspirations expressed in mythology have been given a satisfying response in the historical events of the gospel.

N

NAAMAH. A city in Judah, probably Naneh 10 km S of Lydda. Also a woman's name in the OT.

NAAMAN (lit. 'pleasant'). A common Syrian name in OT times. The military commander of the Syrian army during Ben-hadad's reign. At the suggestion of an Israelite prisoner of war he sought healing for his leprosy from Elisha, and took home two mule-loads of earth which he saw as necessary for him to worship God on (2 Ki. 5; *cf.* Lk. 4:27).

NABAL (lit. 'fool'). A wealthy inhabitant of Maon SE of Hebron who rudely refused to offer hospitality to the outlawed David in return for the protection David had already given him. Abigail, Nabal's wife, intervened to prevent the otherwise inevitable blood-bath; Nabal died soon after (1 Sa. 25).

NABATAEANS. Possibly descended from Nebaioth, son of Ishmael and brother-in-law of Edom (Gn. 25:13; 28:9), they enter biblical history at the end of the OT period. According to non-biblical sources they were desert nomads who attacked merchant caravans in the vicinity of Petra S of the Dead Sea. They built villages and irrigated previously uncultivated desert areas. By the time of King Aretas I (*c.* 170 BC, see 2 Macc. 5:8) Nabataeans were prosperous traders themselves. Later kings held territory in the Negeb in the S and round Damascus in the N, thus completely controlling E–W trade. An officer of Aretas IV attempted to detain Paul at Damascus (2 Cor. 11:32). The rise of Palmyra in the 2nd cent. AD diverted the trade which had gone through Petra, and the Nabataeans became absorbed into the surrounding population.

NABOTH. The owner of a vineyard desired by King Ahab who at his wife Jezebel's suggestion had Naboth judiciously murdered on contrived charges (1 Ki. 21); Naboth's family may have been executed with him (2 Ki. 9:26). The incident brought divine judgment on Jezebel and Ahab's family (1 Ki. 22:34ff.; 2 Ki. 9:33ff.; 10:1ff.).

NADAB (lit. 'generous', 'noble'). Several OT people including Aaron's eldest son who died for offering incense either at the wrong time or in the wrong place (Lv. 10:1ff.); and a king of Israel *c.* 915-914 BC who was assassinated and succeeded by Baasha (1 Ki. 15:25ff.).

NAHALAL, NAHALOL. A town in Zebulun held by Canaanites (Jdg. 1:30), probably near modern Nahalal 9 km W of Nazareth.

NAHALIEL (lit. 'valley of God'). Now Wadi Zerka Main, N of the Arnon, famous in Roman times for its warm springs.

NAHASH. 1. An Ammonite king who attacked Saul but was friendly with David (1 Sa. 11-12; 2 Sa. 10:2). 2. The father of Abigail and Zeruiah, David's sisters, possibly Jesse's step-daughters (2 Sa. 17:25; 1 Ch. 2:13ff.).

NAHOR. 1. Abraham's grandfather (Gn. 11:22ff.). 2. Abraham's brother (Gn. 11:26ff.) who probably travelled from Ur to Haran with Abraham. He was the ancestor of 12 Aramaean tribes (Gn. 22:20ff.), and apparently worshipped false gods (Jos. 24:2).

NAHSHON. Aaron's brother-in-law (Ex. 6:23), an ancestor of David (Ru. 4:20) and Jesus (Mt. 1:4).

NAHUM, BOOK OF. *Authorship and date.* The capture of Thebes is already regarded in the book as having taken place (3:8), and this occurred in 664/663 BC. Nineveh however is still standing, but it fell in 612 BC, so the prophecy may be placed between these dates. Nahum came from Elkosh, presumably in Judah, but no more is known of him.

Contents. Each of the 3 chapters is a unit in itself. Ch. 1 is an acrostic poem and declaration of judgment. Nahum describes God's jealousy: although slow to anger (v. 3) he will punish his (Assyrian) enemies. For those who trust him, God is a stronghold; for those who refuse to believe in him, he is a judge. The enemy will be destroyed, but Judah will be saved. Ch. 2 foretells the siege and sack of Nineveh by the Medes. The queen is captured (v. 7), the city becomes a pool of water as the river sluices are opened (vv. 6, 8). Nineveh, which once plundered others, is now itself plundered because God is acting against it in judgment. In ch. 3 Nineveh is described in all its wickedness; it was a cruel and warmongering city. Thebes had been similarly strong and arrogant; as surely as its end had come, so too would Nineveh's. In other words, the God of Israel controls the destinies of all nations.

NAIL (PEG). Finger-nails of women captives had to be pared (Dt. 21:12). During his madness Nebuchadrezzar let his grow till they became like claws (Dn. 4:33). Iron nails were used for securing objects to walls (1 Ch. 22:3; Ec. 12:11) and in crucifixion (Jn. 20:25). The AV also uses 'nail' where RSV uses 'peg', as for wooden tent pegs (Jdg. 4:21); bronze pegs for fixing the tabernacle (Ex. 27:19); and a pin in a loom (Jdg. 16:13f.).

NAIN. A place mentioned only in Lk. 7:11, generally assumed to be the village still so named in the Plain of Jezreel S of Nazareth; it was never fortified but 'gate' (v. 12) could refer to where the road entered the village.

NAIOTH. A place or quarter in Ramah where Samuel supervised a community of prophets (1 Sa. 19:18ff.); when Saul sought David there, he and his retinue all prophesied.

NAME. The Bible reveals that the custom of giving children names simply because they appeal to the parents is as ancient as it is modern; nothing else can lie behind naming a girl Deborah ('bee') or Esther ('myrtle'). Even though a name such as Ahikam ('my brother has risen') may indicate a tragic earlier bereavement in the family, it is a pleasant-sounding name and may have been chosen for that reason alone. However, there is also a strong and dynamic link made in the Bible between some people and their names. For example, it is not surprising that the great prophet of salva tion, Isaiah, should have a name which means 'Yahweh saves'. The general evidence of Scripture points to the providence of God directing the course of life, and it sees the name as embodying a word of God which would henceforth mould its bearer into someone whose life embodies what the name declared.

There are 7 main categories of dynamic name-giving. The *status-name* confers dignity, as in Adam's calling his new-found wife 'woman'. The *occasion-name* celebrates some happening; Eve named her first child Cain, a word-play on 'gained possession', in recognition of God having fulfilled his promise. The *event-name* encapsulates a whole situation; 'Babel' ('confusion', Gn. 11:9) was in effect a word of God, as divine judgment imposed on mankind the disability it feared (Gn. 11:4). The *circumstance-name* reflects an incident related to the child. Isaac was so called because of his parents' laughter at the thought of having him (Gn. 17:17; 18:12; 21:3ff.). Moses was so called because he was drawn from the water (Ex. 2:10)—and the victory at the Red Sea made Moses pre-eminently the man who came out of the water. The *transformation-name* indicates that something new has entered a person's life. Abram ('high father') became Abraham which implies (but does not exactly mean) 'father of many nations'. In the NT Simon became Peter the rock (Jn. 1:42; *cf.* Mt. 16:18). The *prediction-name* was used by Isaiah for his sons to signify his certainty about God's word (Is. 7:3; 8:1ff.), and

by Jesus for James and John as a warning about their fiery temperaments (Mk. 3:17; *cf.* Lk. 9:54). *Prayer-names* expressed the parents' pious wish. Nabal ('fool', 1 Sa. 25:25) can only have been so named by a mother who prayed, 'Let him not grow up to be a fool'; unfortunately, he lived up to the literal meaning. King Ahaz was probably named Jehoahaz ('Yahweh has grasped'); maybe the politically astute and spiritually inept 'grasper' deliberately dropped the divine element in his birth-name. Jesus' name does not fit these categories; it was a fulfilment name as he came to complete God's purposes.

Most nations had names for their gods. The Patriarchs knew God by titles (*e.g.* Gn. 14:22; 17:1), among which was the so-far unexplained 'Yahweh', the meaning of which was disclosed to Moses as a personal name, 'I reveal my active presence as and when I will' ('I am who I am', Ex. 3:14). It still retains an element of secrecy, for full revelation of his character and purpose was to be spread over a long period of time. The knowledge of this name brings people into a new personal relationship with God (Ex. 33:12, 18f.; Jn. 17:6). God's name then becomes a summary of all that he is in himself and what he is to others, and so he is said to act 'for the sake of his name' (*e.g.* Ezk. 20:9, 14). Hence in the NT Christians 'believe in the name' of Jesus (Jn. 3:18) in the sense of committing themselves personally to him, and are 'kept in the name' (Jn. 17:11), the name-summary of God's character being their security. God's name 'dwells among his people'; his glory has to be verbalized by his name (Ex. 33:18ff.; Dt. 12:5). The holiness of his name led the Jews to avoid the use of Yahweh altogether (and it is avoided in most EVV except JB), but throughout the Bible it is a ground for prayer (Ps. 25:11; Jn. 16:23f.). See also GOD, NAMES OF.

NAOMI (lit. 'my delight'). A Jewess who had moved to Moab with her husband; after his death and the deaths of her sons she returned to Bethlehem with her Moabite daughter-in-law Ruth, where she planned Ruth's marriage. See RUTH.

NAPHISH. The eleventh son of Ishmael, possibly referred to in 1 Ch. 5:19; Ezr. 2:50; Ne. 7:52.

NAPHTALI (lit. 'wrestler'). A son of Jacob and Bilhah (Rachel's maid), often associated with his older brother Dan (Gn. 30:5ff.), and ancestor of the tribe of Naphtali which usually comes last in OT administrative lists (*e.g.* Nu. 1:15). It was allotted a broad strip of land W of the Sea of Galilee (defined in Jos. 19:32ff.). It contained the Canaanite city of Hazor which controlled a vital trade route and was not fully vanquished until the Judges' period (Jdg. 4:2, 23f.). It also contained some of the most fertile tracts of the whole land. From it came heroes such as Barak (Jdg. 4) and Gideon (Jdg. 6-7), but it was vulnerable to attack from the N and in 734 BC was the first tribe W of the Jordan to be deported by the Assyrians (2 Ki. 15:29). Jesus spent the greater part of his public life in the area which, because of its history of deportations and infusions of foreign settlers, was despised by the Jews of Jerusalem.

NAPHTUHIM. Classed with Egypt (Gn. 10:13). Its identity is uncertain but the Nile Delta area would seem likely.

NAPKIN: See HANDKERCHIEF.

NARCISSUS. His household (probably slaves) were greeted by Paul (Rom. 15:16). A rich freeman called Narcissus had committed suicide before Romans was written, but his slaves were still a recognized group, and it is tempting to see a Christian group within it.

NARD: See HERBS AND SPICES.

NATHAN (lit. 'he (God) has given'). Some 11 OT people are so named. The most significant is a prophet involved with David over temple arrangements (2 Sa. 7; 2 Ch. 29:25), the affair with Bathsheba (2 Sa. 12) and the appointment of Solomon to succeed David (1 Ki. 1:11ff.).

NATHANAEL (lit. 'gift of God'). He is mentioned only in Jn. 1:45ff.; 21:2. He seems to be one of Jesus' 12 apostles, having been brought to Jesus by Philip, and is usually identified with Bartholomew who comes next to Philip in the lists in Mt. 10:3 and parallels. 'Bartholomew' is a family name and its bearer would have had an additional name. He was initially sceptical that the Messiah should come from Nazareth.

NATIONS, TABLE OF. An account of the descendants of Noah via his three sons Shem, Ham and Japheth in Gn. 10 and (with minor variations) in 1 Ch. 1:5-23. It is arranged in reverse order, leaving Shem, the eldest, until last. Gn. 10 may be summarized thus:

Heading (or postscript to previous section) (1)
  Japheth's descendants (2-4)
  Details concerning Javan (5a)
  Postscript (5b)
Ham's descendants (6-7, 13-18a)
  Details concerning Nimrod (8-12)
  Details concerning Canaan (18b-19)
  Postscript (20)
Shem's descendants (22-29a)
  Details concerning Shem (21)
  Details concerning Joktan (29b-30)
  Postscript (31)
Postscript to the whole (32).

Some names have been adopted for use in modern times. In language studies, for instance, 'Semitic' and 'Hamitic' refer to language groups.

Contents. The names were probably those of individuals, which later came to be applied to their descendants and, in some cases, to the territory they inhabited. It is not possible to identify all the names listed here with any degree of certainty. Names might be included on the basis of race, language or geography. Even so there is sufficient agreement on a number of them (see table), when compared with sources outside the Bible, to be confident that the list represents the state of geographical knowledge *c.* 2000-1000 BC.

Sources, authorship and date. A common culture existed in the area from the Persian Gulf to the Mediterranean before 3000 BC and trade contacts are recorded with the Arabian peninsula, Anatolia, Iran and India. In the first half of the second millennium BC Assyrian merchants were in Cappadocia and other N people, such as

---

Indentification. The follwing are generaly, though not universally, agreed:

Japheth	Ham	Shem
Gomer = Cimmerians	Cush = Ethiopia	Elam (SE Mesopotamia)
Ashkenaz = Scythians	Sheba = Saba	Asshur = Assyria
Madai = Medes	Mizraim = Egypt	Hazarmaveth = Hadramaut
Javan = Ionians	Ludim = Lydia	Sheba = Saba
Elisha = Cyprus	Caphtorim = Cretans	Lud = Lydia
Dodanim = Rhodes	Put = Libya	Aram = Aramaeans
Meshek = Muski	Zidon = Sidon	
	Heth = Hittites	
	Hivites = Hurrians	

Dedan (in N. Arabia), Philistines, Canaan, Amorites and Hamathites retain their names

---

Kassites, arrived in Mesopotamia. Egyptians had early trade contacts with the Red Sea, Nubia, Libya and Syria, expanding after 2000 BC to Cyprus, Cilicia and Crete.

The contents of these lists would not therefore have been beyond the knowledge of someone educated in Egypt in the mid-2nd millennium BC. Many modern scholars have argued for a date in the Monarchy or after the Exile but it is quite possible that the table could have been composed by Moses during the 13th cent. BC.

NATURE, NATURAL. Four biblical words are translated thus. In Dt. 34:7, 'natural force' means the freshness or vigour usually associated with youth. In Jas. 1:23 and 3:6 the reference is to the cycle of birth, decay and new birth characteristic of the created world. In 1 Cor. 2:14; 15:44, 46 (all AV), the word refers to the life of physical sensation. But the most common use of 'nature' or 'natural' has the sense of that which comes into being by the process of growth. So in Rom. 11:21, 24 the naturally growing branch is contrasted with a grafted branch. Paul uses the term in two special ways. He contrasts the perversions of the world without Christ with the 'natural' or normal behaviour of created people (Rom. 1:26f.). He also contrasts the 'natural' life with the free grace of God and its effects on someone's life (Eph. 2:3), although at times even the Gentile may be able to do 'by nature' the works of the Jewish law (Rom. 2:14, 27).

NAZARENE. Used to describe Jesus

in Mt. 2:23 and through him the Christian church in Acts 24:5. The same term is often translated 'of Nazareth', his home town, in the Gospels (e.g. Lk. 18:37); it was common Jewish practice to identify a person by his place of origin. In Mt. 2:23 the Messianic title is frequently taken to refer either to 'the Branch' (Hebrew *neser*) in Is. 11:1 or to the Nazirite (*nazir*, cf. Jdg. 13:7) in his character as God's holy one. In the early centuries AD there were some Jewish-Christian groups still calling themselves Nazarenes.

NAZARETH. A town of Galilee which was Jesus' home for about 30 years until he was rejected (Lk. 2:39; 4:16, 28ff.), and he was therefore called Jesus of Nazareth. The earliest Jewish reference to it dates from AD 135; it is not mentioned in the OT, the Apocrypha, the Jewish Talmud, nor by the Jewish historian Josephus. Lower Galilee was outside the mainstream of Jewish life until Roman rule in NT times brought security to the area. It is situated in a high valley in the limestone hills of the Lebanon range, near important trade routes which gave it both easy access to the outside world and a certain aloofness as a frontier town which drew scorn from strict Jews (Jn. 1:46). The mild climate in the valley allows wild flowers and fruit to flourish. The early town was higher up the hill than the present one. See also GALILEE.

NAZIRITE. From a Hebrew term meaning 'to separate, consecrate, or abstain'; the Nazirite was someone who separated himself from others by consecration to God with a special vow. The rules for a Nazirite are outlined in Nu. 6. He (or she, Nu. 6:2) was to abstain from wine and intoxicating drinks, vinegar and raisins, perhaps to protest against surrounding Canaanite culture. He could not cut his hair for the period of consecration; the hair was regarded as the seat of life, to be kept in its natural state. He could not go near any dead body, and if he did so he had to go through elaborate purification rites and begin the vow all over again. At the completion of his vow, he made special sacrifices and was released from it by the priest. Although the vow was intended to be for a limited period only, there are examples of parents dedicating their children to be lifelong Nazirites (*e.g.* Samuel in 1 Sa. 1:11). As Samson clearly did not abstain from wine, the term may have been applied more loosely to people devoted to God. It is difficult to find evidence for temporary Nazirites before the Exile, but they were more common later (*cf.* Paul's Nazirite vow in Acts 18:18).

NEAPOLIS (lit. 'new city'). Modern Kavalla in Macedonia, the port for Philippi 16 km inland. Paul visited it on his 2nd missionary journey (Acts 16:11).

NEBAIOTH. Ishmael's eldest son whose descendants are possibly to be identified with the NABATAEANS.

NEBAT. The father of Jeroboam, a rebel against Solomon (1 Ki. 11:26).

NEBO. *Pagan god:* The Babylonian Nabu, son of Bel (Marduk), descriptive of the power of Babylon itself (Is. 46:1), the god of learning and thus of writing, astronomy and science. *Places:* Chiefly Mt Nebo, from which Moses viewed Canaan (Dt. 32:49), usually identified with Jebel en Neba 16 km E of the N end of the Dead Sea. Also, a town in Moab (Nu. 32:3), possibly Kh. Ayn Musa or Kh. el Mukkayet; and a town in Judah (Ezr. 2:29).

NEBUCHADREZZAR, NEBUCHADNEZZAR. The king of Babylon (605-562 BC) frequently mentioned in the OT. According to the Babylonian Chronicle he commanded the Babylonian army as crown prince against Assyria in 606 BC, defeated Egypt at Carchemish the following year (*cf.* 2 Ki. 23:29f.) and conquered Syria and Palestine (*cf.* 2 Ki. 24:7). There he heard of the death of his father Nabopolassar and rode across the desert to claim the throne. In 604 BC he received tribute-tax from Syria and Judah (2 Ki. 24:1); Jehoiakim later transferred his loyalty to Egypt despite Jeremiah's warning (Je. 27:9ff.). Nebuchadrezzar then marched on Jerusalem and captured it and Jehoiakim in 597 BC (2 Ki. 24:10ff.). A decade later he directed from his HQ at Riblah the campaign against the rebel king Zedekiah in Jerusalem, destroying the city and taking many captives including Zedekiah in 587 BC (Je. 39:5f.). Little is known of the last 30 years of his reign and there is no corroboration of the insanity recorded in Dn. 4:23ff. He rebuilt and embellished Babylon, erecting many religious shrines. His architectural works such as the Ishtar gate and the sacred processional way were world-famous. He was succeeded by his son Amel-Marduk (EVIL-MERODACH).

NECK. To be stiffnecked was to be stubborn (Is. 48:4). To be described as wearing a yoke on the neck (like a working animal) symbolized servitude (Je. 30:8). Paul uses the phrase 'risking the neck' to refer to the danger from the Roman punishment of beheading (Rom. 16:4).

NECO, NECHO. The Pharaoh (king) of Egypt *c.* 610-595 BC. He marched to help Assyria against Babylon in 609 BC but was delayed by Josiah of Judah at Megiddo. Josiah was killed and Neco appointed Jehoiakim as vassal-king of Jerusalem (2 Ki. 23:29ff.). In 605 BC Nebuchadrezzar defeated the Egyptians at Carchemish (Je. 46:2) and took Palestine from their control. He met Neco again in open battle in 601 BC, both sides sustaining heavy losses. At home Neco began to cut a canal from the Nile to the Red Sea, which Darius the Persian later completed, and he commissioned the Phoenician fleet which first circumnavigated Africa.

NEGEB. The geographical, not political, term used to describe the S lands of Palestine. It extends from S of the Gaza-Beersheba road roughly along the line (isohyet) where the rainfall is 20 cm a year to the highlands of the Sinai Peninsula, although politically the S frontier is now S of the

Wadi el-Arish. Biblical references to the Negeb are almost entirely confined to pre-exilic times. The Amalekites, among others, lived there at the time of Israel's invasion (Nu. 13:29). It was an important area strategically and economically. The 'way of Shur' trade route crossed it from central Sinai to Judaea, a route followed by the Patriarchs (Gn. 24:62; 26:22). It contained valuable copper ores and Saul's wars against the Amalekites and Edomites probably were over the control of the copper industry and trade (1 Sa. 14:47f.). It was also a convenient area for migrants from the overcrowded Fertile Crescent to settle in. The Nabataeans created a rich civilization based on small irrigated areas there between the 4th cent. BC and 2nd cent. AD. See also PALESTINE.

NEHELAM. The family name or place of origin of the false prophet Shemaiah (Je. 29:24). The name is otherwise unknown.

NEHEMIAH. Unknown except for the book which bears his name, he was the cupbearer, probably a eunuch, of Artaxerxes I, the Persian king (465-424 BC). He was allowed to return to Judah and was appointed governor despite opposition. He led the Jews to rebuild Jerusalem's walls in 52 days, and to pledge themselves again to the covenant. After a spell back in Persia (5:14; 13:6), he returned to Jerusalem again (13:7) to direct further reforms. He was a man of prayer, action and devotion to duty. See also next article.

NEHEMIAH, BOOK OF. *Contents.* Nehemiah's mission: news of Jerusalem (1); return to Jerusalem (2); list of wall-builders (3); opposition (4); economic difficulties (5:1-13); Nehemiah's behaviour (5:14-19); completion of the wall (6); preparations for resettling Jerusalem (7:1-73a). Ezra's work (continued from Ezr. 7-10): Ezra reads the law (7:73b-8:12); the feast of booths (8:13-18); a day of repentance (9:1-37). Nehemiah's community: the pledge of reform (9:38-10:39); the population listed (11); the clergy listed (12:1-26); the wall dedicated (12:27-43); an ideal community (12:44-13:3); more reforms (13:4-31).

Composition. The books of Ezra and Nehemiah are generally considered to have originally formed part of the work of the author of Chronicles. There are two important sources: Nehemiah's own memoirs (1:1-7:73a; 11:1f.; 12:31-43; 13:4-31); and the Ezra narrative (8-9), possibly inserted by the Chronicler because the careers of the two men overlapped. This raises the problem of why Ezra, sent to proclaim the law in 458 BC, did not read it publicly until Nehemiah's arrival in 444 BC. Perhaps the Chronicler saw the work of Ezra and Nehemiah as a whole, arranging the narrative thematically, not chronologically, to show how the community was united in its allegiance to the law. See also CHRONICLES, BOOKS OF.

Message. The Chronicler's purpose was to show that the Judaean community of the 4th cent. BC was the legitimate heir to the promises made by God to Israel and David's dynasty. In his view the chief purpose of David's kingship had been to establish the temple; now it had been restored worship could continue even though there was no king. Nehemiah is a finale of hope and encouragement to the often sad chronicle of Israel's failures and consequent judgment.

See also previous article.

NEHUSHTA. The wife of Jehoiakim and mother of Jehoiachin, taken prisoner by the Babylonians in 597 BC (2 Ki. 24:8ff.).

NEIGHBOUR. The command to love one's neighbour as oneself (Lv. 19:18) is quoted 8 times in the NT (*e.g.* Lk. 10:27). The term in the OT is used generally of people to whom one should behave in an appropriate friendly manner. The Bible praises those who were 'neighbours' to people they might have hated (*e.g.* Rahab, Jos. 2:1, and the story of Ruth's refusal to leave her widowed mother-in-law; Ruth's name in fact comes from the same root as the Hebrew for 'friend' or 'neighbour'). In the parable of the good Samaritan Jesus showed that a 'neighbour' is anyone who acts in a neighbourly manner to someone else, regardless of social or racial status (Lk. 10:29f.).

NEPHILIM: See GIANTS.

NEPHTOAH. Mentioned only in Jos. 15:9; 18:15; possibly Lifta, a village 4 km NW of Jerusalem.

NEREUS. A Christian greeted in

Rom. 16:15. The name (a Greek sea-god) was common, especially among freedmen and lower orders of society.

NERGAL (lit. 'lord of the great city', *i.e.* the underworld). A Babylonian god with its cult centre at Cuthah (modern Tell Ibrahim NE of Babylon). The god of hunting, it was also associated with plague, war, flood and havoc. It was worshipped by exiles in Samaria (2 Ki. 17:30).

NERGAL-SHAREZER. In Je. 39:3, 13 a Babylonian official at Jerusalem in 587 BC. If 2 people of the same name are included in v. 3, one was perhaps an army commander known from outside the Bible, the other (see RAB-MAG) a lower official.

NERO. The son of a distinguished Roman family, he was adopted by the Emperor Claudius as his heir and succeeded to the title in AD 54. A youth of exquisite taste, he scandalized and fascinated his contemporaries with his artistic pursuits. His atrocities (which included the murder of his own mother) and weakness destroyed his family's name, and he committed suicide in the face of revolts in AD 68. It was Nero to whom Paul appealed (Acts 25:10f.) and whose authority he upheld (Rom. 13:1ff.); ironically the Roman Christians were rewarded for their loyalty by one of history's most barbaric pogroms. In AD 64 Rome was badly damaged by fire and Nero diverted suspicion that he had started it himself by mass arrests and executions of Christians, leaving legal precedent for translating popular dislike into official action; 1 Peter reflects this kind of situation.

NEST. Used of birds' nests (*e.g.* Ps. 104:17), it is also a metaphor for a lofty fortress (*e.g.* Je. 49:16), and Job's lost home (Jb. 29:18). Jesus contrasts his own homelessness with the birds' secure nests (Lk. 9:58).

NETHANIAH (lit. 'Yahweh has given'). Several OT people including the father of Gedaliah's murderer (Je. 40:14f.). See also NATHANAEL.

NETHINIM: See TEMPLE SERVANTS.

NETOPHAH. A city or group of villages near Bethlehem, in which returning exiles settled (Ezr. 2:22). The site is unknown.

NETS. Nets were used in biblical times for fishing and hunting. Fishing nets were let down (Lk. 5:4) or cast (Jn. 21:6) from a boat. Hunting nets were used both for birds (Pr. 1:17) and animals such as antelopes (Is. 51:20). Symbolically, they refer to the plots and actions of evil men (Ps. 9:15; Mi. 7:2) or to God's judgments (Ps. 66:11). Around the base of the altar of burnt offering there was a net design (Ex. 27:4f.), probably for practical reasons (it was lighter than solid metal and created a draught for the fire) as well as decorative. The pillars of Solomon's temple also had net designs at the top (1 Ki. 7:17).

NEW TESTAMENT APOCRYPHA.

The term is limited here to writings outside the Bible which are attributed to, or claim to give information about, Jesus Christ and the apostles. Many remain only in fragments, or in quotations in other writers, and some which are known to have been influential have been lost altogether. Most fall into one of the NT categories—Gospel, Acts, Letter, Apocalypse—but the similarity of form is often accompanied by a great difference of conception. For example, many of the apocryphal gospels focus on some aspect of Jesus' life (such as his infancy) and have very little interest in the works and words of him as incarnate Lord. An additional class of literature in this group is the collection of canons on church discipline; one, the *Testament of our Lord*, claims to contain post-resurrection teaching from Jesus.

Reasons for the literature. The creation of apocryphal literature had begun in apostolic times; Paul apparently had to authenticate his signature because of forgeries (2 Thes. 3:17). It continued to be written right down to the Middle Ages. There was a natural desire to satisfy people's curiosity about matters on which the NT is silent, such as Jesus' childhood. Some are bizarre and even offensive, packed with wonders and anecdotes, and written in an attractively animated style. For many early Christians, they must have replaced erotic pagan literature and some were clearly intended to be edifying. It was heretical teachers—especially Gnostics and Montanists—who first made extensive use of this kind of literature, and many writings aim to promulgate sectarian beliefs and behaviour, and to supplement or even supersede the recognized Christian Scriptures.

The Gnostic emphasis on secret knowledge finds clear expression in the gospels which purport to record Jesus' teaching after the resurrection, about which the NT says little. Such writings thus went to great lengths to establish their alleged apostolic credentials, without which they would be disregarded by orthodox church leaders. Sects often attributed writings to James the Just, and to Thomas, Philip, Bartholomew and Matthias. Some genuine words of Jesus must have been passed down in addition to those recorded in the NT Gospels, and people would have desired to collect them together. In the 2nd cent. AD Papias made such an attempt, doing his best to discern the genuine from the spurious yet not, it would seem, always succeeding. Some of his contemporaries may not have been so scrupulous, and the apocryphal gospels thus may contain some genuine sayings mixed in with a lot of worthless material.

Examples of the literature. Among the gospels was the *Gospel according to the Hebrews* which apparently contained a story about a woman accused before Jesus of many sins, which has often been identified with the story of the adulteress found in many MSS of Jn. 8. This gospel has a strong Jewish-Christian tone, records a resurrection appearance to James the Just, and has some points of contact with Matthew. The mid-2nd cent. *Gospel of Peter* heightens the miraculous element in the death and resurrection narratives; three men emerge from the tomb whose heads reach the sky, and are followed by a cross. The *Gospel of Nicodemus* includes a lurid account of Jesus' descent into hell as well as a section 'The Acts of Pilate', an allegedly official report on Jesus' trial, death and burial, which virtually vindicates Pilate; as the stories passed into later Byzantine legend Pilate became a saint and his martyrdom is still celebrated in the Coptic Church. The *Protevangelium of James* was very popular and deeply influenced later beliefs about Mary the mother of Jesus. It dates from the 2nd cent., promotes theories about Mary's perpetual virginity, and is supposedly written by James the Just. In the Gnostic library which was found at Chenoboskion (the 'Nag Hammadi' writings) there was a *Gospel of Thomas*, a collection of 114 sayings of Jesus. Many of them resemble sayings in the Synoptic Gospels but with significant differences and such typically Gnostic themes as the minimizing of the OT and the stress on the necessity to obliterate consciousness of sex.

A large number of 'Acts of the apostles' are known. 5 were gathered by the Manicheans into a corpus. They are all attributed to specific apostles. The *Acts of John* (c. AD 150-60) contains definitely Gnostic sermons. The *Acts of Paul* (c. AD 160-90) was said to have been written by an Asian church elder 'for the love of Paul'; he was deposed for it. It contains a legendary account of Paul's martyrdom and was used to justify women preachers. The *Acts of Peter* (late 2nd cent.) tells how the apostle defeated Simon Magus (the sorcerer of Acts 8) in a series of public encounters in Rome where Simon had led the church into heresy. It sees the Roman Church as founded by Paul, in common with other 'Acts'. The *Acts of (Judas) Thomas* comes from Syria in the 3rd cent. and describes how the apostles divided up the world by lottery and how Judas Thomas the Twin was appointed to India. It contains some Gnostic themes and has a shrill call for virginity. The *Acts of Andrew* (c. AD 260) describes missions among cannibals, miracles, exhortations to virginity and his martyrdom in Greece. It has a clear Gnostic flavour.

Among other apocryphal works are some letters, including the *Letter to the Laodiceans* in Latin, which uses Pauline language and is evoked by Col. 4:16. The *Apocalypse of Peter* is the only strictly apocryphal work for which there is any positive evidence that it was regarded as canonical by some orthodox leaders for a while. But it was not universally accepted and by the time of Eusebius (4th cent.) its authority was not an issue. It appears to have been substantially orthodox but included vivid descriptions of the Lord's transfiguration and the torments of the damned.

How the church reacted. The existence of many writings allegedly from the apostles created an urgent need for authoritative discernment between the genuine and the spurious. It is striking how few of the apocryphal books were ever offically excluded; they just never entered the race. The letter of Serapion, bishop of Antioch, to the church at Rhossus *c.* AD 190, is of special interest because after a cursory glance he sanctioned the public reading of the *Gospel of Peter.* Trouble ensued, the bishop read it more thoroughly, and he found that it was accepted by suspect churches and reflected the Docetic heresy that denied the true manhood of Christ. He wrote: 'We accept Peter and the other apostles as Christ, but as men of experience we test writings falsely ascribed to them, knowing that such things were not handed down to us.' In other words the list of apostolic writings was already traditional but other books might be read provided they were orthodox. There is nothing to suggest that it was an accepted part of catholic practice in the 1st and 2nd cents. to compile books in the name of an apostle. If 2 Peter—the NT writing most often assigned to the 2nd cent.—is apocryphal, then it is unique among apocryphal writings; the NT writings inhabit a quite different world even from that of the best apocryphal works.

See also next article, and APOCRYPHA; GNOSTICISM; PATRISTIC LITERATURE; PSEUDEPIGRAPHA; PSEUDONYMITY; TEXTS AND VERSIONS.

NEW TESTAMENT CANON

'Canon' comes from a Greek word meaning a reed (used for measuring), and which came to mean a list in a column, and also a rule or standard. So the canon is the list of books which the church uses in public worship, with the secondary meaning of the list of books which is recognized as inspired Scripture on which faith and conduct is to be based. To understand inspiration fully, we must also trace the development of the canon as accurately as possible.

New Testament views of Scripture. The early church looked to the OT for its authoritative Scriptures, although the OT canon was itself not finally fixed at the time. The church also had its own body of sacred tradition; the account of the Lord's Supper was regarded as derived 'from the Lord', as was some ethical teaching (*e.g.* 1 Cor. 7:10, 12, 25; 11:23ff.). The preservation of tradition continued in the making of the Gospels. It is likely that Paul's letters were gathered together as a 'corpus' or body of literature not long after his death (perhaps AD 80-85) and would have been given a high status by the churches, but there is no evidence of any other 'scriptural' collections at such an early date. Revelation is the only NT book which claims to be directly inspired; none of the others even claim to be the sole preservers of the true tradition.

The apostolic Fathers (early 2nd cent.). Clement (*c.* AD 90) quoted material similar, but not identical in form, to the Synoptic Gospels; John was unknown to him. Papias left ambiguous information about the Gospels and Polycarp is the first writer to show clear knowledge of Matthew and Luke *c.* AD 115-35. The Fathers know the corpus of Paul's writings but do not often quote from it as Scripture, and a number of passages indicate that a distinction was drawn between OT writings and Christian writings. Along with the material from the canonical Gospels the Fathers also used what we now regard as apocryphal material. The NT writings were therefore not clearly demarcated from other edifying material at this stage.

Beginnings of the canon (2nd-3rd cents.). It was the challenge of heretical teachers which stimulated thought about scriptural status for Christian writings. For example, Marcion of Sinope broke with the Roman church in *c.* AD 150, teaching that the OT Creator-God was the harsh judge, lower and different from the good God who sent Jesus Christ to free people from bondage to the lower God; the 12 apostles failed to keep this gospel uncorrupted and Paul became the sole preacher of it. Marcion naturally rejected the OT, and developed his own canon which included one Gospel which bore some relationship to Luke, and Paul's 10 letters (excluding Hebrews and the Pastorals). The Gnostics, too, were active in the 2nd cent. and documents discovered at Chenoboskion (Nag Hammadi) show that the Gnostics knew most of the books which later constituted the NT but mingled the material with that of their own teachers. Hence the need was growing to distinguish between early apostolic material and later teaching which could not be validated even if it claimed to be inspired.

By the latter half of the 2nd cent.

there is clear evidence for an emerging canon. Irenaeus of Lyons shows the fourfold Gospel was accepted, he quotes Acts as Scripture and implies the Pauline Letters, Revelation and some of the 'Catholic' (or general) Letters were regarded as primary sources of doctrine to which disputes should be referred. Hippolytus of Rome speaks of the fourfold Gospel and of the two Testaments. The Muratorian Canon (*c.* 170-210) is a list of books including the four Gospels, Pauline Letters, some Catholic Letters, Revelation, Acts, and the *Apocalypse of Peter* and *Wisdom of Solomon*. In the 3rd cent., the majority of books in the present NT were given canonical status by writers such as Tertullian, Clement of Alexandria and Origen. But they also cite other works such as the *Letter of Barnabas, Shepherd of Hermas* and the *Letters of Clement*. Eusebius made a distinction between acknowledged books, disputed books and spurious books, including James, Jude, 2 Peter, 2 and 3 John in the disputed category.

The fixation of the canon. In a pastoral letter from Athanasius in AD 397 there is a list of the NT as it is known today; other books such as the *Shepherd of Hermas* and the *Didache* were permitted to be read but the NT was the sole source of religious instruction. In the Syriac-speaking churches the canon developed more slowly and did not come into line with that of the Greek-speaking churches until the 5th cent. The acknowledgment of specific books as canonical clearly proceded at an uneven pace. John's Gospel was still being disputed late in the 2nd cent. by some church leaders, and Hebrews was disputed for several centuries; Origen's suggestion that its thought was Pauline but written by an anonymous author helped towards its eventual acceptance. The corpus of Catholic Letters was established after the essential canon was fixed in the late 2nd cent.; the status of James and Jude fluctuated from place to place. Revelation was opposed in both the 2nd and 3rd cents.

The Canon today. In the 16th cent. both Roman Catholic and Protestant Churches reaffirmed their adherence to the traditional canon. More recent scholarship has suggested that some NT documents may not have been written directly by apostles, which seems at first to challenge the concept of canonicity. But in the 2nd-4th cents. there were 3 criteria for assessing a book: its apostolic authorship (which clearly did not apply to Mark and Luke, but these Gospels were accepted because of the authors' close association with the apostles); its ecclesiastical usage, that is recognition by a majority of churches; and its compatibility with the standards of sound apostolic doctrine. On these criteria orthodox Protestant Christianity today finds no reasons to reject earlier decisions; in the NT we have a full and authoritative record of the divine revelation declared by people dedicated to and chosen and inspired by God.

See also APOCRYPHA; BIBLE; INSPIRATION; OLD TESTAMENT CANON; PAPYRI AND OSTRACA; PATRISTIC LITERATURE; PSEUDE-PIGRAPHA; PSEUDONYMITY; TEXTS AND VERSIONS.

NEW TESTAMENT LANGUAGE. The NT documents have been preserved in 'common' Greek, the universal (but not necessarily the first) language of people in Near Eastern and Mediterranean lands in Roman times, much as English has tended to be a universal language in the 19th and 20th cents. It is the direct ancestor of modern Greek. The NT is not moulded by formal literary education but uses the kind of language and style with which technical material and practical philosophy would have been presented. Contemporary parallels to NT Greek are found in the popular philosophical discourses of Epictetus, in business documents, and in medical books. It was the language non-Greek speakers learnt when they entered Graeco-Roman culture and society; it was neither the property of the educated elite nor was it the colloquial daily speech, but it did have both a literary tradition and close links with colloquial speech. During the NT period, dominated by the Romans, common Greek absorbed some Latin vocabulary which it transliterated (such as 'centurion') and idioms which it transposed into literal translations.

The NT also includes words and phrases which possess a Semitic (Hebrew or Aramaic) source. Hebraisms come mainly from the Septuagint (LXX), the Greek OT, in which some Hebrew phrases are rendered as literally as possible. Some NT authors were influenced by the LXX expressions; others, like the author of Revelation to use a common Greek which has been moulded by their Semitic mother-tongue. It is likely that many of Jesus' original sayings were uttered and preserved in Aramaic, but there is no Aramaic translation of the OT to compare possible phrases with. The speeches and sayings of the Synoptic Gospels and Acts are generally believed to have been translated into common Greek from Aramaic sources. Some suggest that John is entirely the product of a bi-lingual author, which is certainly the case of Paul's letters; his rugged Greek is marked throughout by a close acquaintance with the LXX and perhaps too with his native Aramaic. Behind important Greek words such as 'righteousness' there lies therefore a Hebrew concept which also needs to be considered along with the Greek word itself.

Each NT book has its own style. Mark, for example, is written in the Greek of the ordinary person, which Matthew and Luke correct; Mark also retains many Aramaisms, such as the impersonal use of the third person plural of active verbs to express general action or thought. Luke writes with a sober, cultivated grammatical Greek, sometimes achieving high classical style but failing to maintain it consistently. Paul's forceful Greek has a noticable development of style from his earlier to his later Letters; the development in Ephesians and the Pastoral Letters is so striking that some

scholars doubt Paul wrote them at all. Hebrews is written in the highly polished Greek style of someone acquainted with the philosophers, although affected by the LXX. James and 1 Peter show close acquaintance with the classical style, whereas Jude and 2 Peter display a highly tortuous and involved Greek—2 Peter is sometimes said to be the only NT book which is improved by translation. See also PAPYRI AND OSTRACA.

NICODEMUS. A Greek name (lit. 'conqueror of the people'). He is mentioned only in John's Gospel as a Pharisee and member of the Sanhedrin who visited Jesus at night, and failed to understand Jesus' spiritual metaphors (Jn. 3). In Jn. 7:50f. he protested against Jesus' being condemned without trial; in Jn. 19:39f. he assisted in the burial of Jesus. Nothing more is known of him.

NICOLAUS, NICOLAITANS. Nicolaus, one of the 7 (Acts 6:5), is supposed to have given his name to a Christian group which compromised with paganism to allow Christians to take part in common customs. But Nicolaitan may be a Greek form of Balaam and therefore allegorical, describing the policy of a sect in Rev. 2:6, 15; in this case Nicolaitans are also found in 2 Pet. 2:15 and Jude 11.

NICOPOLIS (lit. 'city of victory'). A Roman colony built by Augustus on a peninsula of the Ambraciot Gulf. Paul spent a winter there (Tit. 3:12), possibly planning to evangelize the

Epirus area from it.

NIGHT HAG, NIGHT CREATURES.
In Is. 34:14, a word variously
translated (*e.g.* 'screech owl', AV),
which seems to be a loan word from
the Assyrian female demon of the
night. But as most of the creatures in
Is. 34 are real, it seems unlikely that a
mythological figure is meant, but
possibly a night-jar (NEB) which is
found in waste land.

NILE. The R. Nile begins at Lake Vic-
toria in Tanzania, and flows through
the vast swamps in S Sudan to
become the White Nile. It is joined by
the Blue Nile at Khartoum and by the
Atbara a further 320 km NE, before
flowing 2,700 km through the Sudan
and Egypt to the Mediterranean. Its
total length is 5,600 km. Six sills of
hard granite rocks cross the river between Khartoum and Aswan, creating
cataracts which impede navigation. In
Nubia and Upper Egypt it flows
through a narrow valley no more than
20 km wide bounded by rocky cliffs
and the desert beyond. Some 20 km N
of Cairo it divides into 2 branches, between and beyond which stretch the
flat swampy lands of the Delta.

Heavy spring rains and melting
snows in Ethiopia and S Sudan have
caused the Nile to flood annually and
deposit fine fertile red earth on the
lands on either side. These annual
floods are now controlled by dams
such as that at Aswan, but without
such floods Egypt would have been
completely desolate. The vital importance of the Nile and its regular inun-

dations was familiar to the Hebrews
(Is. 19:5ff.; 23:10), and judgment on
Egypt was sometimes pronounced in
terms of a dried-up Nile (Ezk. 30:12).
The river also provided fish (Is. 19:8)
and papyrus (for writing), and was
Egypt's main arterial highway. See
also EGYPT; EGYPT, RIVER OF.

NIMRIM, WATERS OF. Mentioned
in Is. 15:6; Je. 48:34, which suggest
somewhere in S Moab; probably Wadi
en-Numeirah 16 km S of the Dead
Sea, and distinct from Nimrah (Nu.
32:3, 36) 16 km N of the Dead Sea.

NIMROD. The son of Cush, a warrior
or hero who lived in Babylonia (Gn.
10:8ff.); the land adjacent to Assyria
was later called 'the land of Nimrod'
(Mi. 5:6). The name is preserved in
Babylonian place-names, and
Sumerian legends about him also
exist. Many scholars compare him
with Sargon of Agade, *c.* 2300 BC, who
was a great warrior, hunter and ruler
of Assyria; his time was looked back to
as a 'golden age'.

NINEVEH. A principal city, and the
last capital, of Assyria. The ruins are
marked by the mounds Kuyunjik and
Nabi Yunus on the R. Tigris opposite
Mosul in N Iraq. The name is an
Assyrian translation of an early
Sumerian name for the goddess
Ishtar. According to Gn. 10:11 it was
one of the cities founded by Nimrod or
Ashur. The site has been occupied
since pre-historic times, and Assyrian
texts claim a temple of ishtar was built
there by Sargon's son *c.* 2300 BC (see

previous article). The town expanded under Shalmaneser I (*c.* 1260 BC) and by the reign of Tiglath-pileser I (1114-1076 BC) it was an alternative royal residence to Assur and Calah. It was probably to Nineveh that Israelite tribute-tax and spoil were brought (2 Ki. 15:20, 744 BC; Is. 8:4, 722 BC). Sennacherib rebuilt Nineveh with administrative buildings, parks and a 48 km-long canal and 2 dams to control the water supply (*cf.* 2 Ki. 19:36). The tribute-tax he exacted from Hezekiah of Judah was sent there (2 Ki. 18:14).

At the height of its prosperity Nineveh was enclosed by an inner wall 12 km round, containing an area which could have housed 175,000 people. The book of Jonah referred to 120,000 people there (4:11); the prophet's 3 days' journey (3:3) may have been a day's journey in from the suburbs followed by a day's business and the return journey. There is no external evidence of the city's repentance (3:4f.) but a solar eclipse followed by flood and famine in 763 BC would have been interpreted as an omen (*cf.* 3:6), and this was around the time of Jonah (2 Ki. 14:25). The fall of Nineveh predicted by Nahum and Zephaniah occurred in August 612 BC. Medes, Babylonians and Scythians besieged it and entered through flood-damaged defences (Na. 2:6ff.); it has remained desolate ever since (*cf.* Na. 2:10; 3:7).

NISROCH. The god, possibly the same as Ashur, in whose temple the Assyrian king Sennacherib was murdered by the swords of his sons (2 Ki. 19:37).

NOAH. The hero of the flood. He was a man of faith, righteous in God's eyes and blameless in the eyes of his contemporaries (Gn. 6:9; Heb. 11:7). The people of the time had sunk to a low moral level (Gn. 6:1ff.; *cf.* Mt. 24:37ff.), and God told Noah that he would destroy the earth. God gave a period of grace during which Noah built an ark to house his family and a representative selection of animals during the flood (Gn. 6:11ff.). The flood duly came and the occupants of the ark were the only survivors (Gn. 7-8). After it, God made a covenant with Noah, giving a new significance to the rainbow as a sign of it, in which God promised never to destroy all flesh with a flood again (Gn. 9:1ff.). Noah planted a vineyard, got drunk and behaved immodestly, apparently evoking some disrespect from his grandson Canaan who was subsequently cursed (Gn. 9:20ff.). Noah is said to have lived for 950 years (Gn. 9:28f.), and from his three sons Shem, Ham and Japheth and their wives the earth was repopulated (Gn. 9:19; 10:1ff.). Other Near Eastern cultures also have similar stories, for which see FLOOD; see also ARK.

NOB. A place mentioned in 3 OT passages, as a city of priests to which David fled (1 Sa. 22), a place Assyrian invaders would reach (Is. 10:32) and a village resettled after the Exile (Ne. 11:32). It was probably the modern Ras Umm et-Tala on the E slopes of Mt Scopus NE of Jerusalem.

NOBAH. An Amorite locality resettled and renamed by the Israelite Nobah (Nu. 32:42), possibly E of Lake Tiberias; Nobah in Jdg. 8:11 is in Mt Gilead.

NOD. A land E of Eden to which Cain was banished after he had murdered Abel (Gn.4:16). The name (lit. 'wandering') is otherwise unknown but suggests an area where nomadic life was customary.

NODAB. A tribe in 1 Ch. 5:19, otherwise unknown.

NOMADS. A human group which changes the area it lives in seasonally, within a larger territory. The word does not occur in the Bible, for nomadic groups are given specific names. Cain was the first 'wanderer' mentioned (Gn. 4), and ancestors of several nomadic groups are named in Gn. 10, such as Gomer (Cimmerians) and Ashkenaz (Scythians). Abraham may have been settled in Ur before he began his nomadic life, but as he is called a Hebrew he could have been one of the nomadic Habiru who lived outside the city. Some would class him as a semi-nomad, because his migrations were not seasonal and not contained within one territory. The Israelites took up temporary nomadic life in the desert after they fled the settled existence of Egypt at the Exodus; it clearly left its mark on the national memory for even in the settled life of Canaan Israelite homes were sometimes called 'tents' (*e.g.* Jdg. 20:8), and Isaiah portrayed prosperity as enlarged tent-space (Is. 54:2). Once settled in Canaan, the Israelites had contact with many nomadic groups including Midianites, Amalekites, Moabites, Edomites, Ammorites and Kedarites.

The two main areas supporting nomads in ancient times were the Arabian peninsula and the Russian steppe. Mesopotamian records tell of nomadic invasions from Arabia, and some of these groups, such as the Amorites, established themselves as ruling dynasties in the cities of Babylonia some time after 2000 BC. Documents describe nomadic groups variously as raiders, settlers, mercenaries and labourers, and an Egyptian wall painting from the 19th cent. BC depicts them as travelling craftsmen. The nomads from Russia were among the first to introduce the horse and chariot into W Asia. The predecessors of the Hittites, who established an empire in Asia Minor after 2000 BC, came from the N, speaking an Indo-European language.

Nomadic groups depend for their livelihood on their flocks and herds of animals, and hence their movements are determined by the need for pasture. Most nomadic groups return to the same areas each year. They live in tents made from skins or wool, and carry only a limited amount of equipment. Semi-nomads live in settlements around oases, growing crops as well as raising animals, and they move out to the plains only when pasture runs short. An increase in population can easily disturb the balance of power as stronger groups encroach on the territory of weaker groups.

Nomadic life encourages members of a tribe to mutual dependence, and this combined with a consciousness of descent from a common ancestor breeds a strong sense of group solidarity. Experience of the harshness of the life encourages the practice of hospitality to other travellers, and a lack of possessiveness over property which is not easily moved. In the Bible, the ideal of nomadic life is used as a picture of spiritual health. The prophets condemned the idle luxury of city life and called for a return to the simplicities of Israel's spell in the desert (Ho. 2:14f.; Am. 3:15). In the NT Jesus warned against the danger of accumulating possessions (Mt. 6:25ff.) and the apostles pictured the Christian church as a travelling band of nomads with no fixed abode in the temporary physical world (1 Pet. 2:11; Heb. 11:13ff.; 13:14).

NOSE, NOSTRIL. Noted in the Bible as the organ for breathing (Gn. 2:7), but the Hebrews had no word for lung. Breath condensing as it was blown out was used as a symbol of inner emotion and anger (Ps. 18:8; *cf.* Jb. 4:9). The word is not used in the NT.

NUMBER. Israel and most of its neighbours used a decimal system of counting. In the OT and NT numbers are usually written as words, not figures. Aramaic inscriptions from the 6th-4th cents. BC provide evidence for a system of figures; vertical strokes were used for digits and horizontal strokes for tens. It has been suggested that the lists of Ezr. 2 and Ne. 7 originally used figures and that the differences between them can be explained because of this. The use of letters of the alphabet for numbers is first found on Maccabaean coins 2 centuries before Christ and is a result of Greek influence; the first 9 letters were used for 1-9, the next 9 represented the tens from 10 to 90, and the last 4 represented the hundreds from 100 to 400. (The number 15 was made up of 6 and 9, because the letters for 10 and 5 formed the consonants of Yah, a form of God's sacred name.) The elements of arithmetic are occasionally illustrated in the Bible (*e.g.* multiplication in Lv. 25:8). Numbers are sometimes used in an approximate sense, as in Is. 17:6; 10 often meant 'quite a lot' (*e.g.* Gn. 31:7), 40 stood for a generation-like length of time (*e.g.* Jdg. 3:11; 5:31), and figures such as 1,000 and 10,000 stood for an indefinite large number (*e.g.* Dt. 32:30).

Problem numbers. Some of the very large numbers recorded in the OT clearly create difficulty in interpretation, especially when different texts and versions give different figures. For example, the Hebrew text has the period from the creation to the flood as 1,656 years; the LXX puts 2,262 and the Samaritan text 1,307. The number of people on board Paul's ship (Acts 27:37) is variously given as 276 and 76; the 'number' of the beast in Rev. 13:18 as 666 and 616. Archaeology indicates that, given that the Israelites were numerically less than the Canaanites (*cf.* Ex. 23:29; Dt. 7:7, 17, 22), the census figures implying a population of 2-3 million require some investigation and interpretation. The word 'thousand' can also mean 'family' or 'clan', and J. W. Wenham has suggested that it should sometimes be repointed (that is different vowels inserted, which were absent from the original Hebrew text) to mean 'officer' or 'warrior', reducing the number of fighting men to 18,000, making a male population of about 36,000 (*cf.* Nu. 3:43) and an adult population of 72,000. This also assists understanding of the 'thousands' said to have been killed in battle, for it is consistent with the ancient practice of selected warriors doing most of the fighting (as in the David-Goliath incident).

Significant numbers. Numbers often have symbolical or theological significance in the Bible. *One* conveys God's uniqueness and unity (Dt. 6:4); both sin and redemption came into the world by one person (Rom. 5:12, 15). *Two* may indicate unity (Gn. 2:24) and co-operation (Lk. 10:1). *Three* is associated with the Trinity (*e.g.* Mt. 28:19), and the 'third day' seems to imply something completed and perfected (Lk. 13:32). *Four* is also a symbol of completion in Eden (Gn. 2:10), in heaven (Rev. 4:6), and in history (four kingdoms in Dn. 2; 7). *Five* and *ten* occur frequently because of the decimal system used; in one parable Jesus spoke of 10 pounds, 10 servants and 10 cities (Lk. 19:11ff.). Ten also has a sense of completeness; 10 powers cannot separate the believer from God (Rom. 8:38), 10 sins can (1 Cor. 6:10). *Seven* is eminent among symbolic numbers. God's rest on the 7th day provided a pattern for human life (Ex. 20:10; Lv. 25:2ff.); the Day of Atonement was in the 7th month (Lv. 16:29). The priests marched round Jericho 7 times (Jos. 6:4), Daniel spoke of 7 'years' to complete God's purposes (Dn. 4:23), and John saw 7 lampstands and stars, and 7-headed beasts, in his heavenly vision (Rev. 1:12, 16; 12:3; 13:1). *Twelve* is linked with God's elective purposes—12 tribes, 12 apostles, and of course 12 months and 12 hours (Jn. 11:9). *Forty* is associated with almost every new development in the history of God's mighty acts—the flood (Gn. 7:17); Moses on the mount (Ex. 24:18); the spies in Canaan (Nu. 13:25); Elijah's journey (1 Ki. 19:8); Jesus' temptation (Mt. 4:2); and the resurrection appearances (Acts 1:3). *Seventy* is connected with God's administration of the world—Noah's 70 descendants peopled the world (Gn. 10); 70 went to Egypt (Gn. 46:27); Judah spent 70 years in Exile (Je. 29:10). Two numbers in Revelation are especially symbolic: *666* (13:18) stands for chaos and has been identified with Roman emperors, and *144,000* (7:4; 14:1) is the number 12 (of election) squared and multiplied by 1,000 (an infinitely large number), thus symbolizing the full number of believers from old and new covenants preserved by God.

NUMBERS, BOOK OF. The 4th book of the Pentateuch so-called because its early chapters contain many census numbers.

Contents. The numbering of the Israelites (1-4); various laws (5-6); consecration of the tabernacle and priests (7-8); the second Passover and departure from Sinai (9-10); complaints and rebellion against Moses (11-12); the 12 spies (13-14); miscellaneous laws (15); Korah's rebellion (16-17); regulations for priests and Levites (18) and purification from sin (19); deaths of Miriam and Aaron, and refusal of passage through Edom (20); the struggle at Hormah (21); the Balaam saga (22-24); apostasy with Baal of Peor (25); second numbering of Israel (26); regulations concerning women and offerings (27-30); vengeance on the Midianites (31); allocation of land E of Jordan (32); desert campsites listed (33:1-49); instructions for the conquest (33:50-35:34); more inheritance laws (36).

Authorship and date. The traditional view that Nu. is the work of Moses is questioned by many scholars. His literary activity is mentioned only in ch. 33 (*cf.* Dt. 31:9), and he is referred to in the 3rd person (15:22f.) which with other passages implies another, possibly later, author. However, the agency of Moses in receiving and teaching the laws is repeatedly asserted (1:1), and the impression is given that they were enacted during the desert wanderings (15:32ff.). So it is possible to assume that they originated in Moses' time, while acknowledging that there are signs of later development to fit altered circumstances. The time when the book received its final form is unknown, but the main contents were probably in writing before the monarchy; scholars are increasingly accepting the probability that much of Nu. contains very ancient material. (See also PENTATEUCH.)

Structure and message. Nu. forms a unity with the other books of the Pentateuch—its division into 5 books is not original. The narrative of Nu. covers a period of 38 years after the Exodus; the 1st part tells of the time at Sinai, the 2nd about the desert wanderings in which Kadesh was probably a sort of national centre. The book also contains numerous laws, and the intended connection between laws and history is not always plain; it is probably chronological. Most of the laws concern religious ritual. Moses emerges as the dominant figure both as lawgiver and national leader, whose failings (11:10ff.; 20:10ff.) are revealed alongside his godliness (12:3, 13). The book reveals God's care for his people through the laws he gives. His holiness is stressed (20:12f.) and he punishes sin (11:1ff.) but does not abandon his rebellious people. He is unchangeable in his faithfulness but is not an unmovable being (14:11ff.), and he shows himself in control of minute detail. In many of these incidents, the coming Christ casts his shadow before him (*cf.* Jn. 3:14; 1 Cor. 10:1ff.; Heb. 3:7ff.; 9:13f.).

NUNC DIMITTIS. The 'song of Simeon' in Lk. 2:29-35. According to an ancient custom Jewish babies were brought to an old doctor or rabbi in the temple for a blessing at the rite of purification a month after circumcision. This may have been the setting for Simeon's utterance over the infant Jesus. He is said to have been 'inspired by the Spirit' (v. 27), which in Jewish tradition is equated with the spirit of prophecy, the return of which was indicative of the Messianic age. Simeon rejoices to God (vv. 29-32) then warns Mary about the suffering the Messiah will experience and the division he will cause.

NURSE. This usually means a wet-nurse who fed someone else's child with her own milk (*e.g.* Ex. 2:7). Suckling an infant usually continued for 2 years and the nurse sometimes remained in the family as a trusted servant (Gn. 35:8). It may also mean the equivalent of a 'nanny' or governess looking after children (*e.g.* Ru. 4:16).

NYMPHA, NYMPHAS. The owner of a house in Laodicea (or somewhere else near Colossae) in which a church met (Col. 4:15); whether male or female is unclear. The reference shows how Paul's circle of friends extended even to areas he had not visited.

OATHS. They were sometimes used as curses to reinforce commands (*e.g.* 1 Sa. 14:24), and they formed a regular part of treaties and covenants (Gn. 26:28; Ezk. 17:13ff.). Such a curse was not irrevocable (*cf.* 1 Sa. 14:45), but

owed its power to God's sovereign response (1 Ki. 8:31f.). The law of Moses emphasized the seriousness of oaths (Ex. 20:7; Lv. 6:1ff.; 19:12). Jesus taught that they were binding and that a Christian's daily conversation was to be as sacred as an oath; in his kingdom oaths will become unnecessary (Mt. 5:33ff.). God bound himself by an oath to fulfil his promises (Heb. 6:13ff.), which he did in Christ (*e.g.* Lk. 1:68ff.). See also ANATHEMA; CURSE.

OBADIAH. At least 12 OT men are called by this name, which means 'servant (or worshipper) of Yahweh'. Two are especially significant. 1. The steward of King Ahab's palace who hid 100 genuine prophets from Queen Jezebel's purge and who acted as intermediary between Elijah and Ahab before the contest on Mt Carmel (1 Ki. 18:3ff.). 2. A prophet who lived probably in the 5th cent. BC (after the Exile), about whom nothing else is known but after whom a biblical book is named (see next article).

OBADIAH, BOOK OF. *Contents.* The judgment of Edom (vv. 1-14); universal judgment (15f.); restoration of Israel (17-21).

Background. Jewish tradition placed Obadiah in the 9th cent. BC in Ahab's time (see previous article), and some scholars suggest that the prophecy reflects Philistine and Arab attacks (2 Ch. 21:16f.) or Edomite attacks (2 Ch. 28:17) on Judah. Others, however, consider the Jerusalem disaster of vv. 11-14 reflects the city's destruction by Babylon in 587 BC, the only such capture in which Edomites participated (*cf.* Ps. 137:7; 1 Esdras 4:45). Also, after the fall of Jerusalem, Edomites were forced by Arabs out of their own land into the area of the Negeb later called Idumaea (v. 7; *cf.* 1 Esdras 4:50). The territory occupied by the Jews in vv. 19f. is similar to that of Nehemiah's time (Ne. 11:25ff.), thus dating the book in the mid-5th cent. BC, about the time of Malachi. There are some parallels between Ob. and Je. (*e.g.* vv. 1-9 and Je. 49:7-22), and Joel (*e.g.* v. 17, apparently quoted in Joel 2:32).

Style and message. Ob. is the shortest book in the OT, and is marked by vivid poetic language and metaphors. Four times (vv. 1, 4, 8, 18) Obadiah claims God's inspiration. His main message is of God's moral judgment of nations. The final goal of history is that Israel will again become 'the Lord's'; he emphasizes the universal and holy nature of the kingdom, themes taken up in the NT.

OBED (lit. 'servant'). Several OT people including the son of Ruth and Boaz, the grandfather of David (Ru. 4:16f.).

OBED-EDOM (lit. 'servant of Edom'). Among other OT people, a Philistine living in Judah whose household was blessed when the ark of the covenant was left there (2 Sa. 6:10ff.).

OBEDIENCE. The biblical words suggest yielding to the authority of a speaker and thus complying with his commands. Mankind's obedience to God thus presupposes both God's authority and his revelation of his requirements; often the OT speaks of obeying God's voice or commands. The Bible regularly insists that isolated acts of religious devotion cannot make up for a lack of consistent heartfelt obedience to God (*cf.* 1 Sa. 15:22). The old covenant emphasized that God's blessing could not be received unless a person obeyed him (Ex. 19:5); the promised new covenant included God's gift of obedience so that his people could enjoy his favour (Je. 31:33). In the NT, faith is obedience, unbelief is disobedience (Rom. 6:17; 10:16). Christian obedience means imitating God's holiness (1 Pet. 1:15f.) and Christ's humility and love (Jn. 13:14f., 34f.), and submission to divinely instituted authority structures (Rom. 13:1ff.; Eph. 6:1ff.).

ODED. 1. Father of Azariah the prophet (2 Ch. 15:1). 2. A prophet of Samaria who persuaded the victorious Israelites to release slaves captured from Judah (2 Ch. 28:9ff.).

OFFERING: See COLLECTION; SACRIFICE AND OFFERING.

OFFICERS. A term used of various subordinate officials, whether civil, judicial or military. It is used to translate a number of Hebrew terms, one of which originally meant people who could write on behalf of their superiors, like the 'taskmasters' whom Egyptian inscriptions show to have recorded the work of slaves (*cf.*

Ex. 5:6, 14), and the 'officers' used by Moses to be judges (Nu. 11:16). Another term describes subordinates in temple administration and other specific spheres (Je. 20:1). In the NT it is used of prison guards (Lk. 12:58), the bailiffs sent by the chief priests to arrest Jesus (Jn. 7:32), and by Paul of himself ('steward', 1 Cor. 4:1).

OG. An Amorite king of Bashan with 60 fortified cities (Dt. 3:4f.). His defeat was one of Israel's vital victories. A giant of a man, his bed was made from black basalt (Dt. 3:11). Some assume that this referred to a sarcophagus.

OHOLIAB. A man specially gifted by God to assist in the design and construction of the tabernacle (Ex. 31:6; 35:34f.).

OHOLIBAMAH, OHOLAH, OHOLIBAH. Oholibamah (lit. 'tent of the high place') was a male and female Edomite name, borne by Esau's daughter (Gn. 36:1ff.) and an Edomite chief (Gn. 36:41). Oholah and Oholibah (lit. 'tent worshipper') were allegorical names given to the N and S kingdoms (Ezk. 23). They imply unfaithfulness to God, the sexual imagery of the passage recalling the fertility rites of neighbouring religions.

OIL. By far the most common kind of oil referred to in the Bible is olive oil; olive trees were cultivated in Palestine and the oil made by crushing the fruit was an important trading item. It was used in food preparation (1 Ki. 17:12ff.) and also as fuel for lamps (*cf.*

Mt. 25:1ff.), Medically it was a valuable internal remedy for gastric disorders, and was also a popular external application for bruises and wounds (Lk. 10:34). Olive oil was produced by grinding the olives with a pestle in a stone mortar (bowl) or by squeezing them in a stone press; the Garden of Gethsemane received its name from oil presses processing fruit gathered on the Mount of Olives. See also OLIVE.

Cosmetic ointments are also sometimes called oil (2 Sa. 14:2; 'oil of myrrh' in Est. 2:12), used for anointing the body. See further COSMETICS AND PERFUMERY.

Oil was used in religious rituals. Olive oil was offered among 'firstfruits' (Ex. 22:29) and mixed with some meal offerings (Lv. 8:26). The anointing oil for consecrating priests was a special mixture. Few of the ingredients in Ex. 30:22-33 can be identified clearly. 'Liquid myrrh' was certainly the volatile essence of gum resin from balsam trees in S Arabia, probably heated with a fixative fat or oil to make a runny perfumed ointment. The 'sweet cinnamon' was probably made from an aromatic bark or wood; the 'aromatic cane' was some kind of root or stem; and the 'cassia' may be an aromatic bark.

OINTMENT: See COSMETICS AND PERFUMERY.

OLD AGE. Throughout the ancient Near East older people were held in honour for their experience and wisdom (Jb. 12:12). This was especially true in Hebrew society because old age (or long life) was a sign of God's blessing for keeping his commandments (Dt. 30:19f.). Older men were expected to lead in positions of authority; failure to respect age was a sign of decadent society (Is. 3:5). The disabilities of age are portrayed pictorially in Ec. 12:2ff., and those mentioned elsewhere include hypothermia (1 Ki. 1:1ff.) and bad sight (Gn. 27:1).

OLD TESTAMENT CANON.

'Canon' comes from a Greek word meaning a reed (used for measuring), and which came to mean a list in a column, and also a rule or standard. Since the 4th cent. it has been used by Christians to mean an authoritative list of books belonging to the OT and NT. There has long been some difference of opinion about which books should be included in the OT; even in pre-Christian times the Samaritans rejected all except the Pentateuch (Gn.-Dt.). In the early church there were disputes over whether the Apocrypha was to be regarded as inspired, which came to a head in the 16th-cent. Reformation when the Roman Catholic church accepted it on an equal footing with the OT and the Protestant churches regarded it at best as edifying (but not authoritative) reading. A book qualifies for the canon only if it has God's authority for what it says; it is part of God's permanent revelation to mankind.

The early development of the canon. Far back in Israel's history some writings were recognized as having divine authority, such as the book of the law which Moses read (Ex. 24:7), and that which was found in the Jerusalem temple and read to King Josiah (2 Ki. 22-23). These writings became parts of the Pentateuch (Gn.-Dt.) which is frequently referred to and treated with reverence by other OT books (*e.g.* Jos. 1:7f.; Ezr. 3:2ff.). The Pentateuch presents itself as basically the work of Moses, through whom God often spoke orally, but who was also a writer (*e.g.* Ex. 17:14; 24:4; Dt. 31:9ff.). Prophets who followed him wrote as well as spoke (1 Sa. 10:25; Je. 36). This was both to send God's word to other places (Je. 36:1ff.) and to preserve it for future generations (Ex. 17:14; Is. 30:8). It is not possible to be certain when the Pentateuch reached its final form, but part of it at least was laid beside the ark of the covenant in Moses' lifetime (Dt. 31:24ff.), an action parallel to the ancient practice of keeping treaties in sacred places, and was regarded as canonical, in the wider sense of authoritative. There is no doubt that the Pentateuch was complete and canonical by the time of Ezra and Nehemiah (5th cent. BC) and may have been so some time earlier. By the 2nd cent. BC all 5 books were being attributed to Moses, and this section of the OT canon was beyond dispute.

The development of the second and third sections. The rest of the Hebrew Bible is structured differently to the English. It is divided into 'the Prophets', consisting of 8 books (Joshua, Judges, Samuel, Kings, Jeremiah, Ezekiel, Isaiah and the Twelve Minor Prophets), and the Hagiographa ('the (other) writings'), consisting of eleven books (Psalms, Job, Proverbs, Ecclesiastes, Song of Songs, Lamentations, Daniel, Esther, Ezra-Nehemiah, Chronicles and Ruth). The more poetic Hagiographa also contains history (Daniel and Chronicles, the latter rounding off the biblical narrative). Both sections have early material (such as some Psalms and elements of Chronicles in the Hagiographa) and late material (such as Haggai and Malachi in the Prophets), so the recognition of the canonicity of both sections very probably developed simultaneously rather than consecutively.

There are references to mixed collections of these books (2 Macc. 2:13; *cf.* Dn. 9:2). Only when books like Ezra had been completed and recognized as canonical, and when it was realized that the prophetic gift had ceased (*cf.* 1 Macc. 9:27), could the firm division between Prophets and Hagiographa, and the arrangement of their contents, be made. It was probably done in about 165 BC by Judas Maccabaeus who collected together the scrolls scattered by Antiochus Epiphanes' persecution (1 Macc. 1:56ff.) and made a list of them (they could not have been bound as a volume) in the order which came to be traditional (*cf.* 2 Macc. 2:14). There is evidence from the 1st cent. AD that the now traditional order of the Hebrew Bible had been accepted as canonical for some while. Some doubts about this have arisen among scholars because of later Jewish disputes about some of the books, leading some to suppose that

disputed books were added to the canon later. However, it is more likely that some rabbis wanted to remove books which were already in the canon.

Christian developments. In the NT Jesus accepted the Jewish Scriptures and the 3 sections of the canon. The first Christians thus shared with the Jews a full knowledge of the identity of the OT canon but the breach with Judaism and the spread of Christianity into Gentile areas led to doubts about it. New lists were drawn up, arranged on different principles. Doubts about the canonicity of books can be resolved only by returning to NT teaching and seeing it in the context of its Jewish background.

See also APOCRYPHA; AUTHORITY; INSPIRATION; NEW TESTAMENT CANON; SCRIPTURE.

OLD TESTAMENT LANGUAGE.
Chiefly Hebrew and Aramaic.

Hebrew belongs to the W group of the Semitic languages ('Semitic' comes from the name of Shem, Noah's eldest son), and is probably descended from Canaanite (*cf.* Is. 19:18). The designation 'Hebrew' for the language first occurs in the prologue to Ecclesiasticus (*c.* 180 BC). Its alphabet has 22 consonants, and it is written 'backwards', from right to left. Characteristic of the Semitic languages is a three-consonant structure to words with a pattern of two vowels inserted between them. There is no indefinite article ('a') and the definite article ('the') is a prefix to the relevant noun or adjective, creating structures different from English; 'the fat man' would be literally 'the man, the fat' in Hebrew. Nouns are distinguished by gender and number, and verbs are either dynamic ('substantival') or static ('adjectival' or 'stative'). Wide use is made of singular nouns for collective items; possessive pronouns ('my', 'your') are suffixes to nouns ('the-hat-mine'). Verbless sentences are common; *e.g.* 'the servant of Abraham (am) I'.

Compared with English, Hebrew may seem less abstract. Physical attitudes are used to describe psychological states; bodily organs are often associated with mental attitudes. The imagery is drawn from everyday life and therefore is readily translatable. Some metaphors employ human images for things and for God; waters 'walk' (*i.e.* 'move') but there was never a literal belief behind such images. There are traces of dialects in some biblical books (*e.g.* Ruth). The high literary style of much of the OT seems to indicate an early existence of a 'grand style'; examples in other Near Eastern languages are known. OT Hebrew made some impact on NT Greek in the form of loan-words and literal (loan) translations. Among many Hebrew loan-words in English usage are sabbath, sack, Satan, shekel, jubilee, hallelujah and myrrh, and the use of 'heart' for emotion and will and 'soul' for person are probably loan-translations.

Aramaic is closely related to Hebrew, but is not derived from it. It is the language of Dn. 2:4-7:28; Ezr. 4:8-6:18; 7:12-26; Je. 10:11; two words in Gn. 31:47; and of the TARGUMS (Aramaic translations of parts of the OT). From the 9th cent. BC Aramaic became the international language of trade and commerce. It steadily came into use in Assyria from *c.* 730 BC; the note in Dn. 2:4 (RSV mg) fits perfectly the known Assyrian-Babylonian court's use of Aramaic. The script is the same as Hebrew but some arbitrary consonant changes have occurred (*e.g.* Hebrew *z* = Aramaic *d*). The definite article is a suffix to nouns, unlike Hebrew; but in common with Hebrew there are two genders, two verbal forms and frequent verbless sentences. Aramaic word order is less rigid than that of Hebrew. Although earlier scholars dated the Aramaic parts of the OT after the Persian period, advancing knowledge of the language shows many such arguments to be groundless, and that what were considered to be late variations in the language actually existed at much earlier times.

See also APOCRYPHA, LANGUAGE OF; NEW TESTAMENT LANGUAGE; TEXTS AND VERSIONS; WRITING.

OLD TESTAMENT QUOTATIONS (IN NT): See QUOTATIONS.

OLIVE. One of the most valuable trees of the whole biblical period, the olive flourished in W Asia where it originated and in Mediterranean lands to which it was introduced. It grows to about 6 m high with a contorted trunk and many branches. It develops slowly and may live for several centuries. If it is cut down new shoots spring up from the old roots. It was valued most for the oil pressed out of the fruits (which were also eaten fresh or pickled, with bread); olive groves also provided cool shelter from the burning sun. The berries ripened in early autumn and were harvested towards the end of November; the primitive harvesting method of shaking or beating the branches (Dt. 24:20) is still widely employed. The berries were crushed in a shallow rock by a large upright millstone rolled over them, and then the oil was allowed to stand to separate out any foreign matter in it. Olive oil was used in cooking, and for medical and cosmetic purposes. Olive wood is still used for fine cabinet-work; after being well seasoned the amber-grained wood can be highly polished. Olive branches were used to construct temporary shelters (Ne. 8:15). Olive trees became symbols of the fruitfulness of righteous people (Ps. 52:8); the association with the dove in Gn. 8:11 has made both continuing emblems of friendship and peace. Paul uses the image of wild stock being grafted on a good olive as contrary to nature, but describing the relationship between Israel and the Gentile church (Rom. 11:17). See also FOOD; OIL; TREES.

OLIVES, MOUNT OF (OLIVET). A small range of 4 summits, the highest being 830 m, which overlooks Jerusalem and the Temple Mount from the E across the Kidron Valley and the Pool of Siloam. It was thickly wooded in Jesus' day, but was deforested later in the 1st cent. AD. OT references to the Mount are few. Jews used to light a series of beacons, starting at the Mount of Olives, to signal the new moon (month) to their compatriots in Babylonia, and it was believed that the Jewish dead would be resurrected there. In NT times the Garden of Gethsemane was near its base, and tradition suggests Jesus' 'ascension' took place on its peak, although Luke's Gospel favours a site nearer Bethany (Lk. 24:50).

OLYMPAS. An otherwise unknown but influential Christian greeted by Paul (Rom. 16:15); the name was common across the empire.

OMRI. The 6th king of (N) Israel. An army commander, he was proclaimed king after Zimri's coup c. 885 BC (1 Ki. 16:15ff.). He besieged the capital Tirzah until the rebel Zimri committed suicide, and then reigned for 12 years and founded a new dynasty. He built a new capital at Samaria (1 Ki. 16:24) and buildings attributed to him have been found at Megiddo and Hazor. He condoned pagan worship (1 Ki. 16:25f.) and in a political alliance obtained the Sidonian princess Jezebel as wife for his son Ahab. Assyrian and Moabite inscriptions attest his international importance.

ON. An Egyptian city, the Greek Heliopolis, the modern Tell Hisn and Matariyeh 16 km NE of Cairo. It was a great centre of Egyptian sun-worship, where the solar gods Re and Atum were especially honoured. Its prominence is reflected in Gn. 41:45, where Joseph is given the high priest of On's daughter. It is also referred to in Ezk. 30:17 and as Heliopolis (Heb. Beth-shemesh) in Je. 43:13.

ONAN (lit. 'vigorous'). The 2nd son of Judah. He refused to consummate the traditional Levirate marriage with his brother's wife Tamar whose husband had died leaving her childless (Gn. 38:8ff.). For the custom, see MARRIAGE.

ONESIMUS. A runaway slave belonging to Philemon, an influential Christian at Colossae. He was converted through Paul (Phm. 10) and became a trustworthy disciple (Col. 4:9). Paul would have liked him to stay with him as a helper (Phm. 12) but returned him to Philemon with the letter now preserved in the NT, requesting tactfully that Philemon receive Onesimus not as a slave but as a fellow Christian (Phm. 15f.). Mention of Onesimus in both Colossians and Philemon suggests the letters were written at the same time. See also PHILEMON.

ONESIPHORUS. A person and household mentioned and greeted by Paul in 2 Tim. 1:16ff.; 4:19. He had been a true friend to the apostle at times of need.

ONO. A town rebuilt by the Benjaminites (1 Ch. 8:12); modern Kafr Ana, near Lydda. It gave its name to the surrounding area (Ne. 6:2).

ONYCHA. In Ex. 30:34 a pungent component of holy incense made from mollusc shells; see INCENSE.

OPHIR. *Person/Tribe:* A son of Joktan whose tribe, known from pre-islamic inscriptions, lived between Saba in the Yemen and Havilah (Gn. 10:29). *Place:* The country from which fine gold was imported to Judah (*e.g.* Is. 13:12), sometimes in large quantities (1 Ch. 29:4) and with other valuable products (1 Ki. 10:11, 22). The site is unknown; among the suggestions are the area of S Arabia inhabited by the tribe of Ophir; present day Oman in SE Arabia; the E African coast (Somaliland); and Supara N of Bombay in India.

OPHRAH. 1. A Benjaminite town (Jos. 18:23), modern et-Tayibeh 9 km N of Michmash. 2. Ophrah of Abiezer in Manasseh, Gideon's home (Jdg. 6:24); the exact site is disputed.

ORACLE. The word is used occasionally in EVV with several shades of meaning. In 2 Sa. 16:23 it refers simply to God's word or utterance with no indication as to how this might be transmitted. In Acts 7:38 it refers to part or all of the law of Moses, and in Rom. 3:2 to all the OT written utterances of God with special regard to his promises made to Israel. In 1 Pet. 4:11 preachers are told to treat their words as carefully as if they were inspired Scripture. See also WORD.

ORCHARD. A plantation of fruit trees (Song 4:13), a common feature in Bible lands.

ORDINATION. The word is not used in the NT; where AV puts 'ordain', RSV more correctly translates 'appoint' (*e.g.* Acts 14:23). There is no record of any ceremony when Jesus appointed the 12 (Mk. 3:14), even though it was clearly a solemn occasion after Jesus had spent the night praying. It is difficult to see 'ordination' in the symbolic sign of receiving the Spirit in Jn. 20:22, and Matthias was simply 'enrolled' as a replacement apostle (Acts 1:26). The Seven were appointed with the laying-on of hands and prayer (Acts 6:6), but as the action was used frequently for circumstances other than initial appointment and as the precise 'office' of the 7 is disputed, it is difficult to see in this event a prototype ordination. Some kind of ordination is recorded in Acts 14:23, but no information is offered as to how it was done. Paul reveals that Timothy's ordination resulted in his being given a spiritual gift, confirmed by prophecy and through the laying-on of hands (1 Tim. 4:14). The essential thing is the gift itself, but the outward act is still considered important. Timothy is told not to lay hands on people hastily (1 Tim. 5:22), which may refer to the solemnity of ordination but is more likely in the context to refer to receiving penitent people back into fellowship. See also LAYING-ON OF HANDS; MINISTRY; SPIRITUAL GIFTS.

OREB. A rock named after a Midianite prince routed by Gideon at the fords of Jordan (Jdg. 7:25).

ORIGINAL SIN: See FALL.

ORNAMENTS. Wood and ivory carving, weaving and embroidery, and fine metalwork were all practised to high standards in biblical times. Egyptian tomb paintings depict brightly coloured costumes (see DRESS) and many examples of personal jewellery have been discovered. The wearing of jewellery is regarded as right and proper in the Bible on certain celebratory occasions (*e.g.* Is. 61:10), but the immoderate or ostentatious use of such personal ornaments is condemned (Is. 3:18ff.; 1 Tim. 2:9). The list in Is. 3:18ff. gives some idea of the kinds of ornaments worn; 'crescents' and 'pendants' would have been some kind of chain ornament. The high priest's robes were ornate, with embroidered decorations and bells (Ex. 28). See also CHARMS; JEWELS AND PRECIOUS STONES; SEAL.

Movable objects were decorated from earliest times, but it was often small items such as boxes for cosmetics which were most ornamental, sometimes having handles or inlays made from ivory or carved bone. The tabernacle—the mobile shrine of the Israelites—was exquisitely adorned by people gifted in such work by the Spirit of God (Ex. 31:1ff.). Pagan religious shrines were highly decorated too; incense and offering stands have been found which were decorated with birds, animals, serpents (symbols of fertility) and human figures.

Buildings, especially palaces, were decorated inside and out. For example, the interior walls of the Assyrian palaces at Nineveh and Khorsabad were adorned with carved bas-reliefs, and doorways were 'guarded' by composite beasts. In Egypt the great temples at Luxor and Karnak were decorated with murals and ornamental inscriptions. In Nebuchadrezzar's Babylon, some exterior walls were covered with coloured glazed bricks with animals and rosettes at intervals. No doubt at times of prosperity the kings and people of Israel and Judah followed many of the decorative customs of surrounding nations.

ORPAH. Naomi's Moabite daughter-in-law. Unlike her sister-in-law Ruth, Orpah returned to her former home after the death of her husband (Ru. 1).

ORPHAN. The Jews were commanded to care for the fatherless (Ex. 22:22; Dt. 24:17), protecting their rights of inheritance and ensuring they shared in the regular feasts. God is said quite specifically to work on their behalf (Dt. 10:18), and condemnation awaits those who oppress them (Dt. 27:19). Sadly, these commands were often broken (Je. 5:28; Ezk. 22:7) but always the unfailing care of God for them is emphasized (*e.g.* Ps. 146:9).

OSTRACA: See PAPYRI AND OSTRACA.

OTHNIEL. A brother (or possibly nephew) of Caleb who married Caleb's daughter. He was a distinguished warrior and Israel's first Judge (Jdg. 1:13; 3:9ff.).

OVERSEER: See BISHOP.

OWL. Owls are referred to several times in the OT by different words which probably denote different species. For the 'owl' in Is. 34:14 (AV), see NIGHT HAG.

OX: See CATTLE.

OXGOAD. A long-handled pointed instrument used to urge on the oxen pulling a plough; it was used as a weapon in Jdg. 3:31. Paul realized that to resist God's direction was as fruitless as an ox resisting the goad (Acts 26:14).

P

PADDAN, PADDAN-ARAM. An area around Haran in Upper Mesopotamia (Gn. 11:31; 25:20), where Abraham settled before reaching Canaan, and from which he obtained a bride for Isaac.

PAHATH-MOAB. Literally 'governor of Moab', so perhaps an ancestor of this Jewish clan had been a governor when Moab was subject to Israel. The clan's 2 families returned to Jerusalem after the Exile (Ezr. 2:6; Ne. 10:14).

PALACE, CITADEL. A large residential building or group of buildings accommodating a ruler and his administration. A large portion of a nation's wealth was contained in such a place, so it was often heavily fortified to resist capture. One of the most complete citadels in Syria/Palestine has been excavated at Zinjirli. It was used *c.* 900-600 BC, had 3 palaces and many storehouses, and was surrounded by walls and towers with a double gate. In Jerusalem, Solomon's citadel enclosed the temple and his palace (1 Ki. 3:1), a huge wooden storehouse, halls, porches, a palace for Pharaoh's daughter, and courts (1 Ki. 7:2ff.). The royal residence would have been several floors high to accommodate the king's large family, with his advisers and servants.

The palaces of Assyria and Babylonia housed the entire administration for large empires and also considerable quantities of tribute-taxes (paid in goods or precious metals). The wealth of the king was suitably displayed for visitors. Senior officials had their own houses; schools were provided (*cf.* Dn. 1:4); and some palaces had gardens of exotic plants (Est. 7:7f.). The palace of the high priest (Mt. 26:3) was probably a large Greek-style residence built around colonnaded courtyards. The present-day Citadel in Jerusalem is founded on the N end of a strongly fortified palace with 3 towers built by Herod the Great.

PALESTINE. The name given to the land between the Mediterranean Sea and the R. Jordan where much of biblical history is centred. It was first used by Herodotus as a name for S Syria; the older term Canaan similarly referred to all the lands W of the Jordan. The term 'Holy Land' was adopted in the Middle Ages (*cf.* Zc. 2:12). The mediaeval belief that Jerusalem was the centre of the world was not entirely absurd; the thin Syrian corridor bounded by the Mediterranean, Black, Caspian and Red Seas and the Persian Gulf unites Europe, Asia and Africa, and all important international and intercontinental routes must pass through it. The 3 great N–S routes in ancient times were the Trunk Road running along the coast from Egypt to the Vale of Esdraelon then skirting the Lake of Galilee to Damascus; the King's Highway following the edge of the Transjordan Plateau from the Gulf of Aqabah to Damascus; and another through central Palestine linking all the major cities. A number of minor E–W routes cross these 3. Perched between the sea and the desert which they feared, the Hebrew highlanders sought to be independent from both environments and their peoples.

Geographical structure. The region, which runs 675 km from the Egyptian borders to Asia Minor, contains 5 geological zones: the coastal plain, the W mountain chain, the rift valleys, the E mountains, and the deserts of Syria and the Negeb. These vary in character from N to S; for example N of Acre the mountains run almost into the sea, creating natural harbours, whereas S of Mt Carmel the coastal plain is broad and almost harbourless. The rocks of Palestine are notably chalk and limestone (the central highlands), volcanic rocks (around Galilee), and recent deposits such as marls, gravels and sands. The Rift Valley (which is traceable S to the E African Lakes) has acted like a hinge; areas W of it are formed of rocks laid down under the sea, whereas the E (Arabian) block has been formed of continental rocks. The earth's crust is unstable in the area, and volcanic eruptions occurred until the 13th cent. AD. The fate of Sodom and Gomorrah was some kind of volcanic action probably associated with the intrusion of sulphurous gas and liquid asphalt (Gn. 14:10; 19:24f.). There are also biblical records of earthquakes (*e.g.* 1 Sa. 14:15) and geological faulting (Nu. 16:31ff.; *cf.* EXODUS for an alternative explanation). Under the semi-arid conditions, badland relief is typical, with hilly areas deeply dissected by wadis.

Physical features. The coastal plains stretch for 200 km from Lebanon to Gaza. Inland from them the Plain of Esdraelon or the Jezreel valley was of major significance for Israel where strategic cities such as Megiddo, Jezreel and Bethshan were located. The Central Hills run 300 km from Galilee down to Sinai. In the S, Judah has gently undulating folds except in the E, rising to 1,000 m; in the N the hills of Samaria fall to 300 m with Ebal (945 m) and Gerizim (890 m) towering above them. NW of Galilee, the mountains reach 900 m. The Jordan follows the Rift Valley, entering the

Sea of Galilee 200 m below sea-level. To the E are desert tablelands of rock and sand blasted by hot winds.

Climate and vegetation. There are 3 climatic zones, each with its own distinct vegetation—Mediterranean, steppe, and desert. The coastal plain as far S as Gaza enjoys mild winters (12°C in January at Gaza) and hot summers (26°C in July at Gaza); more centrally in Jerusalem the corresponding temperatures are 6° and 23°C. Less than one-fifteenth of the annual rainfall occurs in the summer (June-October), and varies from 35-40 cm on the coast to 75 cm on the Judaean and Galilean mountains. Around Beer-sheba and parts of the Jordan valley the steppe climate produces only 20-30 cm of rain. The deep trough of the Jordan has sub-tropical temperatures; at Jericho in summer the daily average is over 38°C. There is no evidence that the climate has changed since biblical times; for example, Roman gutters excavated near the Gulf of Aqabah still fit the springs for which they were constructed.

The flora of Palestine is very rich (about 3,000 plants) for such a small area because of the great variation in land height. There were few dense forests but much of the woodland in OT times (Jos. 17:18) has disappeared. Pastoral farming has been partly to blame for deforestation, leading to serious deterioration of once-fertile land into poor scrub in some areas. One estimate suggests that since Roman times 2,000-4,000 million cu m of soil have been eroded from the E side of the Judaean hills—sufficient for

4,000-8,000 sq km of good farmland. See also DEW; PLANTS; RAIN; TREES; WIND.

Water supply and agriculture. Apart from the Jordan, a few of its tributaries and some coastal streams fed by springs, all the rivers of Palestine are seasonal. There is a sudden spate after the autumn rains (*cf.* Mt. 7:27). Wells were common and irrigation well known; cisterns were built for water storage. Wheat and barley, figs, grapes and olives were the main crops in biblical times, for which see AGRICULTURE and separate articles.

Settlements. Some 622 place names W of the Jordan are recorded in the Bible, and they are sometimes difficult to identify with certainty. The Jordan valley seems to have been occupied since earliest times. A semblance of urban life existed at Jericho by *c.* 8000-6000 BC. Of 70 settlements in the valley many were established over 5,000 years ago but only 35 were still inhabited in Israelite times. Until about 1200 BC there were relatively few settlements in the central hills, perhaps because of forestation, but they included important towns such as Hebron, Jerusalem, Bethel, Shechem and Samaria. The coastal plain S of Carmel favoured fairly dense settlement but further N where water was more abundant the thick woodland made settlement difficult. Location of towns was largely determined by water supply, and the strategic value of occupying important crossroads such as those at Hebron, Jerusalem, Megiddo, Hazor and Samaria.

PALTITE, THE. The name given to inhabitants of Beth-pelet in the Negeb (*e.g.* 2 Sa. 23:26).

PAMPHYLIA. A coastal region of S Asia Minor on the great bay of the Mare Lycium, lying between Lycia and Cilicia, mentioned in Acts 13:13; 14:24; and 15:38 in connection with Paul's 1st missionary journey. One of the chief towns, Attaleia, was probably Paul's landing-place. It was successively under Persian, Greek and Seleucid rule until the Roman conquest in 102 BC. The church at Perga is the only one in the region mentioned in the 1st cent. AD.

PANNAG. In Ezk. 27:17 (AV), a word probably meaning 'meal' (NEB) or baked products ('confections', NIV).

PAPHOS. Two settlements in SW Cyprus; 'Old' Paphos was an ancient Phoenician settlement slightly inland; 'New' Paphos was the centre of Roman rule where Paul met Sergius and Elymas (Acts 13:6ff.).

PAPYRI AND OSTRACA. *Papyrus* is the name of a large aquatic plant, the writing material obtained from it, and of individual manuscripts made from it. In ancient times the plant grew in marshes and lakes throughout Egypt (*cf.* Jb. 8:11) but today is rarely found in its wild state anywhere N of the Sudan. The stems grow to 3-6 m high, ending in graceful bell-shaped flowers. It was also used for reed boats and baskets (Ex. 2:3; Is. 18:2), sandals, clothes, and ropes; its roots were food for the poor. To make paper, the pithy inner stem was cut into thin strips which were laid (overlapping) on a board, with other strips laid across them at right angles. The two layers were welded together by being beaten with mallets. The whitish sheets were pasted end to end to form a papyrus roll. The standard length was 20 sheets; the longest known—40 m—is the Egyptian *Papyrus Harris I* (*c.* 1160 BC) in the British Museum. The side showing the horizontal fibres (the recto) was usually written on first. Sometimes the reverse side (the verso) was used as well, or old writing washed off so the roll could be used again.

Ostraca is the plural of a Greek word originally meaning 'oyster shell' but applied by the Greeks to the fragments of pottery on which they recorded their votes (from which comes the English 'ostracize'). They were used extensively in ancient times because they were the cheapest and most readily available writing material, although because of their limitations tended to be used for recording less important information. Inscriptions were either written on them in ink or scratched onto the surface.

Egyptian papyri and ostraca. Papyrus was used from 3000 BC to after AD 600. Large quantities were made from 2000 BC, and before 1000 BC papyrus was being exported to Syria-Palestine. It was used for all kinds of written records. Ostraca mostly date from 1550 to 1070 BC (the New Kingdom) and the majority come from around Thebes in Upper Egypt. They were the equivalent of memo pads, jotters and scrap paper and reflect every aspect of daily life: rosters of workmen, accounts, bills of sale and letters.

Hebrew, Aramaic and Greek papyri and ostraca. The oldest *Hebrew* papyrus was found by the Dead Sea dating from 8th-7th cents. BC, containing a list of personal names written over an erased letter. Of the 'Dead Sea Scrolls' found at Qumran some are papyrus though most are of parchment. Some papyri are fragments of OT books. Among the most important Hebrew ostraca are those found at Samaria dating from the 9th-8th cents. BC recording payments for oil and wine. They help to reconstruct the administration of the period. Those found at Lachish can be dated with certainty to 587 BC and reflect the desperate plight of Judah as the Babylonians defeated city after city; there are several points of contact with the book of Jeremiah.

The most valuable *Aramaic* papyri come from Elephantine in Egypt. They were written by Jews in the 5th cent. BC and include legal documents and letters. These colonists had their own temple and compounded God's name with those of Canaanite gods. Many *Greek* OT papyri still exist, although often only as fragments. For example one containing parts of Dt. 23-28 dates from the 2nd cent. BC. The scrolls from Qumran include some OT fragments in Greek, mostly from the 1st cent. BC. The Chester Beatty papyri include parts of various OT books ranging from the 2nd-4th cents. AD.

Papyri and ostraca relating to the NT. Several portions of NT books and other Greek documents found in Egypt in the late 19th cent. had important results for NT studies—not least in that they revealed that the NT writers used the common (and rapidly evolving) Greek of the day. The papyri give examples of the secular use of most NT words. For example, the word *arrhabon* in Eph. 1:14, translated 'earnest' in AV, is 'guarantee' in RSV and 'a deposit guaranteeing…' in NIV, because the secular usage in the papyri showed it to be a deposit paid in a transaction. Many apparently new word formations in the NT have been paralleled, and only about 50 words—1 per cent of the total—are now believed to be unique to the NT. Even though the NT documents contain many Hebrew and Aramaic terms which affect the Greek, the language is still very akin to that of the Egyptian papyri. The Egyptian discoveries also reveal that Christians there developed the codex (leaves of papyrus-paper folded and arranged in quires like a bound book) much earlier than people in the rest of the Roman world, where papyrus codices did not replace rolls until the 3rd cent. AD. A single codex could contain the Gospels and Acts, or all of Paul's letters, an important consideration in the preservation and transmission of the biblical text. The collections of papyri have scholarly names which often occur in biblical studies; among the most important are Codex Sinaiticus, Codex Vaticanus and the Chester Beatty Papyri. Other papyri are simply known by numbers—P4, P37, and so on.

It was the discovery of Sinaiticus and Vaticanus in the 19th cent. which made possible real advances in NT textual study. Westcott and Hort published a revised Greek text of the NT in 1881 which was used extensively in the RV. The scholars postulated 4 main 'families' of texts (Syrian, Neutral, Alexandrian and Western). Later research on papyri showed these families were distinguished too sharply. Some papyri, such as the John Rylands fragment of John's Gospel, take scholars to the early 2nd cent. AD, *i.e.* within a single generation of the last writings of the NT. Copies of texts were obviously made from the beginning both by scribes and by untrained Christians, and the need for a standard text did not arise at first. Many early papyri must have been destroyed during persecutions.

A few ostraca with NT fragments have been discovered (*e.g.* verses from Mk. 9 and Lk. 22), but most from post-NT times are letters, contracts and tax receipts. But nonetheless a few linguistic discoveries have been made among them; for example the phrase 'in the name' turns out to have been a regular legal formula of the authority under which something was done.

Some apocryphal writings have also been recovered among the papyri, which have helped scholars to understand the form and content of NT writings. For example, the *Gospel of Thomas* found near Nag Hammadi (Chenoboskion) had an important collection of sayings in which Gnostic influence mingled with Synoptic, Johannine and other traditions.

See also NEW TESTAMENT LANGUAGE; OLD TESTAMENT LANGUAGE; TEXTS AND VERSIONS; WRITING.

PARABLE. The word is derived from a Greek word which literally means 'putting things side by side', that is, 'saying something in a different way'. A parable is usually a protracted simile or a short story designed to teach a single truth or answer a single question. Although it is closely related to 'allegory', the latter denotes a more elaborate story in which most or all of the details have their counterparts in the application. Many of Jesus' parables embody messages which could not be conveyed in any other way. He expresses the unfamiliar message and images of the kingdom in appropriate and familiar forms.

Interpretation. A simple 'proverb' (as RSV describes Lk. 4:23) in the Greek is actually called a parable; so too is the allegory of the sower (Mt. 13:3ff., 18ff.). The word is used for almost any non-literal utterance. Christian preachers have tended to allegorize small details which were not allegorized in the original parable and to hang on such details truths which they cannot support, and this has caused some scholars to stress strongly the 'one point only' purpose for all parables. However, some parables clearly do illustrate several things. The lost (prodigal) son parable stresses the joy of God the Father in forgiving his children, the nature of

repentance, and the sin of jealousy and self-righteousness (Lk. 15:11-32). Some of the parables have been remembered long after their original setting has been forgotten and the Gospel authors fitted them where their teaching was appropriate to the narrative; others are clearly associated with specific events (*e.g.* the good Samaritan, Lk. 10:25ff.). Often their aim was to jolt listeners into seeing things from a different point of view, to force them to decide about their attitude to Jesus, and thus to bring them into a new relationship with him. No one parable can contain the whole of Jesus' gospel—not even the prodigal son, for it says nothing about a doctrine of atonement.

Characteristics. Jesus took his illustrations from nature (Mt. 13:24ff.), everyday life (Mt. 13:33), recent events (Lk. 19:14), and occasional or likely happenings (Lk. 18:2ff.). Sometimes the parable's lesson was obvious from the story and left without comment. In others, even the obvious story of the rich landowner who died before he could enjoy his wealth (Lk. 12:16ff.), Jesus added a brief dictum or 'moral'. Sometimes he drew out the meaning with a question (Lk. 7:42). Many parables related specifically to the kingdom of God, its nature, coming, value, growth, and the sacrifices it demanded. Their interpretation depends partly on how commentators regard the kingdom itself, and it is important to note that they contain both elements of future hope (Mk. 13:28ff.) and of present fulfilment (Mt. 9:37f.). Many are intended to show

God's grace revealed through Jesus in the present and to indicate that the 'new age' has already dawned; others show how God's people are to live until its final consummation, by being persistent in prayer, forgiving and serving others, and using the gifts God has given them.

Purpose. In Mk. 4:10ff. Jesus seems to be saying that his parables were intended to harden people in unbelief rather than to enlighten them. But hardening may be a consequence of hearing the parables, not a purpose (as in Mt. 13:13). To fail to understand Jesus is to fail to understand his parables, so inseparable are they from him. For those who do not or will not view his ministry as that of the Messiah, his parables remain on the level of earthly stories devoid of deeper significance.

See also KINGDOM OF GOD.

PARADISE. A loan-word from ancient Iranian, it means a walled garden. In the OT it occurs in Ne. 2:8; Ec. 2:5; Song 4:13, rendered in RSV by 'king's forest', 'park' and 'orchard' respectively. In later Jewish thought it was used to describe both primeval times and the wonderful Messianic age to come. The Jews believed paradise existed already but was concealed. In the NT the word is used only in Lk. 23:43; 2 Cor. 12:3; Rev. 2:7. Jesus used it to designate the place people go to immediately after death, Paul to describe the glory of heaven. In Rev. 2:7 it will come at the end of time, and the idea of a garden of God in the next world is strong in later chapters of

Rev. (*cf.* ch. 22).

PARAN. A desert in the E central region of the Sinai peninsula, to which Hagar and Ishmael went after their expulsion from Abraham's household (Gn. 21:21). From here Moses sent spies into Canaan after the Exodus (Nu. 13:3). Mt Paran (Dt. 33:2; Hab. 3:3) may have been on the W shore of the Gulf of Aqabah.

PARBAR. In 1 Ch. 26:18, a room or partly-roofed gateway or courtyard building W of the temple, where gatekeepers were stationed. The exact meaning is unknown; NIV has 'court'.

PARTHIANS. Parthia was a district SE of the Caspian Sea and part of the Persian empire conquered by Alexander the Great. In the 3rd cent. BC the Parthians rebelled and extended their empire. They were formidable cavalry-bowmen, ruled by land-owning aristocrats who controlled vital trade routes. Those in Jerusalem at Pentecost may have been Jews living in Parthia, possibly proselytes (Acts 2:9).

PARVAIM. In 2 Ch. 3:6 a source of gold; it may be a general term for E regions.

PASHHUR. Probably a name of Egyptian origin, it is used of several OT people including a priest who imprisoned Jeremiah (Je. 20:1ff.); and someone sent by king Zedekiah to inquire of Jeremiah (Je. 21:1) and who later threw the prophet down a pit (Je.

38:1ff.).

PASSION. In Acts 1:3 it refers to Jesus' suffering and death, and is still used in that way. The RSV uses it to translate a word meaning 'evil desire' (*e.g.* Rom. 1:26) and the bad sense of another word for desire; see LUST.

PASSOVER. The name given to the incident in Ex.12 when the first-born males of Egypt died but those of the Israelites were 'passed over' (the name comes from a verb meaning 'to spare'), and of the special meal instituted that night and held annually by Jews ever since as a memorial to the Exodus. The Israelite families were each commanded to sacrifice an unblemished lamb, or possibly kid. In Dt. 16:2 the choice of animal is clearly wide, and in Ex. 12 the word traditionally translated lamb could also refer to a young goat; however, throughout Jewish history the lamb has always been preferred. They were to smear the doorposts and lintels with the animal's blood. The meal, eaten with bitter herbs and unleavened bread, was open only to Israelites and proselytes; Gentiles were—and are—excluded. The prohibition of leaven (yeast) symbolized the hasty departure from Egypt when normal baking procedures had to be abandoned; it is possible that Moses adapted more ancient ceremonies, Unleavened Bread being an agricultural festival and Passover nomadic and pastoral. The month of the Passover (Abib, later called Nisan) became the first month of the Jewish year (Ex. 12:2).

The Passover of Dt. 16 differs in detail from that of Ex. 12. For example the animal is boiled, not roasted; Passover and Unleavened Bread are integrated more closely; and the blood emphasis has declined. This development approximates better to the NT evidence concerning Passover. In the reforms of Hezekiah (2 Ch. 30:1ff.) and Josiah (2 Ch. 35:1ff.) the proper place for the celebration was reckoned to be Jerusalem, and this continued to be assumed through NT times. After the fall of Jerusalem in AD 70 the Passover inevitably became a family festival because there could be no centralized slaughter. The Samaritans still celebrate their Passover on Mt Gerizim, and keep it separate from the feast of Unleavened Bread.

In NT times, in keeping with Dt. 16:16 *etc.*, all Israelite males were expected to appear in Jerusalem 3 times a year, for the Passover, Pentecost and Tabernacles (Booths) feasts. The temporary population of Jerusalem at such times could be as high as 3 million according to the historian Josephus, although modern scholars reduce this to a more realistic figure of 180,000. The supper was eaten with symbolic elements of roasted lamb, bitter herbs, unleavened bread, four cups of wine at specific points, and ritual hand washings. After the 1st cup of wine, the Exodus story was recounted followed by part of the Hallel hymn and the 2nd cup. Then came the symbolic breaking of bread, the 3rd cup, and the completion of the Hallel hymn with the 4th cup (*cf.* Mt. 26:30). The symbolism of 'Christ our Passover lamb' (1 Cor. 5:7) and 'Lamb of God' (Jn. 1:29) was taken up by NT writers to indicate that Jesus' death completed and fulfilled the Jewish ritual by bringing about God's new and universal rescue of his people.

See also FEASTS; JUDAISM. For the debate over whether Jesus' Last Supper was a Passover meal, see LORD'S SUPPER.

PASTORAL LETTERS. A common name for 1 and 2 Timothy and Titus, although their content is only partially 'pastoral' in the sense of giving instruction about care for church members. See separate articles.

PATARA. A seaport of SW Lycia which, because of the prevailing winds, was a suitable starting place for the passage to Phoenicia; Myra further E was probably more suitable as a terminal for the return journey. Paul trans-shipped there (Acts 21:1).

PATHROS, PATHRUSIM. A name for Upper Egypt, the long Nile valley between Cairo and Aswan (*e.g.* Is. 11:11; Je. 44:1). The name is also attested in Assyrian inscriptions.

PATIENCE. A God-given restraint of anger or resentment in the face of opposition or oppression, which is not mere passivity. It is a characteristic of God's dealings with sinful people (Is. 48:9), illustrated by his many restorations of disobedient Israel (Ho. 11:8f.), his repeated pleadings with

Jerusalem (Mk. 12:1ff.), and his deferment of Christ's second coming (2 Pet. 3:9). It is thus an opportunity for repentance (Rom. 2:4). Christians are to show a similar character (Mt. 18:26ff.; Gal. 5:22; Eph. 4:2) as exemplified by Jesus (Heb. 12:1ff.). Their patience is to be not only with people but also with trying circumstances (Jas. 5:7ff.), and their patience will result in certain eternal life (Lk. 21:19; Rev. 3:10).

PATMOS. A rugged volcanic island 55 km off the SW coast of Asia Minor to which the apostle John was banished from Ephesus for some months *c.* AD 95 and where he wrote Revelation (Rev. 1:9).

PATRIARCHAL AGE, PATRIAR-CHS. The patriarchal age covers the life-spans of Abraham, Isaac and Jacob. It is difficult to date, but estimates generally fall within the period *c.* 1900 BC to 1500 BC; the biblical data are insufficient to settle the issue and only tentative dates can be obtained by comparing the narratives of Gn. 12-50 with other data from the period 2000-1000 BC. A further difficulty is created by the fact that the biblical record focuses on a few people even though their kinsfolk were probably quite extensive, and that the record itself is probably only a selection of the ancient traditions about them.

The biblical picture. The Patriarchs moved from Mesopotamia to Egypt via many places known to archaeologists, such as Ur, Haran, Shechem and

Salem (Jerusalem), for which see separate articles. It is clear that there were open villages or walled towns across the area, but outside them lived semi-nomads including the patriarchal families, sometimes moving great distances with their flocks and herds, searching for pasture and water, frequently camping close to towns (*e.g.* Gn. 13:12ff.). Occasionally they even practised agriculture (Gn. 26:12f.) and dwelt in towns as resident aliens for a while (*e.g.* Gn. 20:1; 33:18-34:31). The patriarchs also clashed from time to time with settled groups (*e.g.* Gn. 21:25ff.; 26). None of the kings or chiefs they encountered can be identified from other historical records at present—although some of them must have been very insignificant and are included in the narrative simply because they were met by one of the Patriarchs.

The Patriarchs were organized into interrelated social units comprising families or clans (*e.g.* Gn. 24:1ff.). The father, as head of the family, had wide powers and his eldest son was normally heir to the position and property. In Abraham's case his heir (Isaac) was the eldest son by his first wife, not his actual eldest son (Ishmael) who had been born to Hagar, Sarah's maid, in a customary attempt to produce a male heir by a form of surrogate motherhood. Marriage was a complex affair. Jacob and Esau each had more than one wife of equal status (Gn. 26:34f.; 29).

They were aware of the need for a personal faith in the God who guided them through life and encouraged them with his promises (Gn. 12:1ff.; 28), and to whom was owed the response of obedience (Gn. 22). Each Patriarch seems to have had his own name for God (*e.g.* Gn. 31:42; 49:24). Sacrifices and prayer were part of their regular worship (Gn. 12:8) and circumcision was a religious rite to mark those who belonged to the covenant family. The concept of the covenant or agreement is deeply significant in patriarchal religion, in which God solemnly bound himself to Abraham and his descendants (Gn. 12:1ff.; 17:5ff.) through whom God would reach out to all mankind.

Modern discoveries about the period. There are strong reasons for placing the patriarchal age within the Middle Bronze Age, *c.* 1900-1550 BC, on the basis of archaeological research. There were considerable movements of peoples in the ancient Near East at this time which the patriarchal narratives reflect in a general way. Rootless groups known as the Hapiru were widely known, and Abraham may have been associated with them in people's minds (*cf.* 'Hebrew' in Gn. 14:13). Travel was often associated with trade, which is known to have flourished during this period. There are also many sociological parallels between the Patriarchs and the Binyaminites known from documents found at Mari. Many of the towns mentioned in the Bible are known to have existed at the time, although of course they were inhabited over many centuries. Similarly the name-patterns of the Patriarchs are known over a long period from shortly after 2000 BC.

Many clay tablets have been recovered which reflect the legal, commercial, religious and private life of the times, including lists of laws such as those of Hammurapi (*c.* 1750 BC). Those discovered at Nuzi are later than the proposed patriarchal period (they date from the 15th and 14th cent. BC) but may reflect some practices established earlier. They include parallels to patriarchal practices such as adoption, marriage to a second wife if the first proved barren, inheritance, and performance of service before being allowed to marry. The value of these late parallels is clearly limited, but earlier ones have also been discovered. For example a Babylonian letter states that a childless man could adopt his own slave as heir (Gn. 15:2). It is important to bear in mind, however, that some patriarchal customs might never be fully paralleled in history simply because they were peculiar to this one, very small, group of people. Some scholars have doubted the value of seeking any parallels at all and have questioned the historical value of the biblical narratives, but this would seem to be an over-reaction. The very strength of the theological ideas of promise and covenant required that the Patriarchs were more than mere literary inventions. Few scholars today would deny at least that such doctrines have been the foundation of Israel's faith and have played a significant role in Christian faith.

See also ABRAHAM; ARCHAEOLOGY; CHRONOLOGY OF THE OLD TESTAMENT; ISAAC; JACOB.

PATRISTIC LITERATURE. A term which describes the orthodox and non-sectarian ancient Christian writings. These writings are of considerable value in studying the NT text and such things as the development of the canon (the authoritative list) of NT books; they show how doctrines were interpreted and throw light on unwritten traditions. The literature dates from the late 1st cent. AD to the latter half of the 2nd cent., a period of intense persecution and pernicious anti-Christian and sectarian propaganda (as predicted in 2 Tim. 3 and elsewhere). The church was spread through the Roman empire, and the Jerusalem church no longer exercised any primacy (as it did in Acts 15). The writings of the 'Apostolic Fathers' are largely practical, and while not of the same class as NT documents, neither are they as tortuously intellectual or fantastical as many of the apocryphal writings.

Among the writings are *1 and 2 Clement*, letters written by a leader of the church in Rome to Corinth where legitimately appointed presbyters had been rejected; the letters appeal for a return to peace and order, and date *c.* AD 95-6. The 7 *Letters of Ignatius* were written by the bishop of Antioch as he travelled to martyrdom in Rome late in Trajan's reign (AD 98-117). He wrote sublimely but hurriedly about the mysteries of incarnation and salvation and was consumed with the desire for martyrdom and the necessity to stick closely to one's bishop. Polycarp's earnest and gracious *Letter to the Philippians* is the one surviving document from a man who knew the apostles, and John in particular. He was a revered bishop of Smyrna, martyred in the mid-2nd cent. AD. The *Didache* appears to be Syrian and deals with church order, fasting, prayer, prophets and the eucharist among other things, but cannot be dated accurately since it reflects neither the known NT period nor the known 2nd cent. churches. Unfortunately only fragments in other writers survive of Papias' 5-volume *Exposition of the Oracles of the Lord*, c. AD 130, for he was in contact with people who heard the apostles (see MARK, GOSPEL OF; MATTHEW, GOSPEL OF). The anonymous *Epistle of Barnabas* (the name was added later) may have been read in some churches for a while, as was the *Shepherd of Hermas*, a symbolic work intended to arouse a lax church and clarifying what must have been a disputed point, that sins committed after baptism were not necessarily unforgivable.

See also NEW TESTAMENT APOCRYPHA; NEW TESTAMENT CANON; TEXTS AND VERSIONS.

PAUL, LIFE OF. *Background and early ministry.* There is little information about Paul's life before he appeared in Jerusalem as a persecutor of Christians. He was a Pharisee (Phil. 3:5), although born in Tarsus, a centre of learning, as a Roman citizen (Acts 22:25ff.). He studied under Gamaliel in Jerusalem, however (Acts 22:3), and as a young man (Acts 7:58) and a violent opponent of Christianity (Gal. 1:13f.) was given official authority to direct the anti-Christian campaign. The Bible suggests he did not have an impressive personal appearance (1 Cor. 2:3f.; 2 Cor. 10:10); an ancient tradition portrays him as 'little of stature, thin-haired upon the head; crooked in the legs, of good state of body, with eyebrows joining, and nose somewhat hooked, full of grace: for sometimes he appeared like a man, and sometimes he had the face of an angel'.

There is no evidence that Paul had contact with Jesus during his ministry, although Christian relatives (Rom. 16:7) and Stephen's radiant martyrdom (Acts 8:1) must have made some impression on him as Jesus' statement in his conversion vision implies (Acts 26:14). The importance of his conversion is underlined by the fact that Acts gives 3 accounts of it (chs. 9, 22, 26). Apart from a period in the desert E of Jordan, he spent the next 3 years preaching in Damascus (Gal. 1:17; Acts 9:19ff.). Introduced to the Jerusalem Christians by Barnabas, he was forced to leave the city after only 2 weeks because of death-threats and for the next decade disappeared from the biblical record in his native city of Tarsus (Acts 9:30). Barnabas called him to help the flourishing church at Antioch which later sent them to Jerusalem with a famine-relief gift (Acts 9:26ff.; 11:20ff.; Gal. 1:17ff.).

Missionary journeys. About AD 46 Paul and Barnabas were commissioned by the church in Antioch to undertake an evangelistic mission which took them through Cyprus and 'S Galatia'. They began by preaching in synagogues, but when the majority of Jews rejected them they turned their attention to the Gentiles (Acts 13:46ff.); they established churches at Pisidian Antioch, Iconium, Lystra, Derbe and possibly Perga. Zealous Jews began insisting that such Gentile converts must be circumcised and observe the Mosaic law if they were to be received by the church as full Christians. Back at Antioch Paul rebuked Peter for duplicity on the issue (Gal. 2:14), and was sent by the church to a council of apostles and elders at Jerusalem to decide the matter (Acts 15). The outcome supported Paul's contention that Gentiles were not obliged to keep the law of Moses, and the council asked only that certain dietary and moral scruples be observed locally to assist Jewish-Gentile relations.

Paul took Silas on his 2nd tour (Acts 15:40-18:22) because Barnabas had stuck by John Mark whom Paul refused to have, following a previous defection. They travelled through Galatia, adding Timothy to the party at Lystra, before being called into Macedonia where churches were established at Philippi, Thessalonica and Beroea. They also went to Athens and then Corinth where Paul stayed for two years. After a brief return to Antioch, he prepared for his 3rd journey and a shift of base to Ephesus. This 'Aegean period' (c. AD 53-8, Acts 18:23-20:38) was in many ways his most important. During it he wrote Romans, the Corinthian letters, and possibly one or more of Ephesians, Philippians, Colossians and Philemon. It was a mixed time of triumph and defeat. In Ephesus disciples of John the Baptist (and presumably of Jesus) came into fuller experience of the risen Christ and saw miracles and church growth; the public interest led to a riot by opponents. Paul revisited Macedonia, came back to Miletus near Ephesus to say a final farewell to his friends there, and sailed towards Jerusalem and almost certain arrest.

Imprisonment and death. Falsely accused of violating temple rituals, he was arrested and for his own safety removed by the Romans to Caesarea, where he was imprisoned for 2 years by the governor Felix (c. AD 58-60, Acts 23-26). Felix's successor Festus wanted to put Paul on trial. Paul, knowing that it would lead to his execution, exercised his citizen's right of appeal and applied for trial in Rome (Acts 25:10f.). Any Roman citizen was protected against all summary magistrates' punishment in cases which did not involve breach of statute law, which Paul's case did not. Festus was probably relieved, but he first arranged an interview between Paul and Agrippa and his sister Bernice.

Paul's concern in appealing to Caesar was not so much his own safety as the interest of the gospel. He had some hope of a favourable outcome (cf. the verdict by Gallio in Acts 18:12ff.), which might win recognition of Christianity as a religion in its own right and not as a sect of Judaism as it had been regarded hitherto; Judaism was no longer a safe umbrella for it to shelter beneath. The case would probably not have been heard by Caesar himself, but of that fact and its outcome there is no certain knowledge. He had reached Rome via a shipwreck off Malta (Acts 27-28), and apparently spent 2 years in Rome under house-arrest teaching about Jesus. He may have been released in AD 63 and visited Spain and the Aegean region before his re-arrest and death at the hands of Nero c. AD 67, as some early Christian texts imply.

For details of dating and the 'Galatian problem' see CHRONOLOGY OF THE NEW TESTAMENT; GALATIA; GALATIANS, LETTER TO THE.

PAUL, TEACHING OF. Historical research since the 16th-cent. Reformation has recognized that Paul's theology is concerned above all with redemption. Jesus, by his death and resurrection, defeated for all time the powers of this age—sin, death and demonic forces (Eph. 6:12; Col. 2:15). Christians enter the 'resurrection age' through conversion (*cf.* Rom. 6) by which they are united with Christ in his death, resurrection and glorification (Gal. 2:20; Eph. 2:5f.). In the present life this means they are transformed through the indwelling Holy Spirit, who brings to them a foretaste of the resurrection life (Rom. 8:23; 2 Cor. 5:5). Their behaviour is thus changed (Col. 3), and so is their whole world-view (Rom. 12:1ff.).

Despite this renewal, Christians remain mortal beings subject to the limitations of this age. Although no longer 'in Adam', 'in Christ' they have their share of suffering (2 Cor. 1:5); they must still die, but do so hopeful of resurrection 'in Jesus' (1 Thes. 4:14; 2 Tim. 4:6ff.). Then shall they be fully conformed to the likeness of Jesus (Rom. 8:29), and the damage caused by sin shall be finally repaired. This salvation taught by Paul is not a spiritual escape of the soul at death, but a physical redemption which results in the deliverance of the whole person at Jesus' second coming. The future has become present within the 'body of Christ', the church, but at Jesus' coming the realities of the new age will then become individually actualized in all their glory, both in Christians and in the created order (Rom. 8:19ff.).

The Reformation emphasis on a person being justified or made righteous in God's sight by faith, not by good works (Rom. 1:17), continued in the following centuries to control the interpretation of Paul's doctrine. With the development of literary criticism the absence of this motif led some scholars to question the authenticity of some traditionally Pauline letters. An important strand of 20th-cent. scholarship has emphasized Paul's teaching on union with Christ as the central theme in his doctrine. The scene for modern discussions was set by Albert Schweitzer, who attempted to answer questions about the sense in which Christ's death and resurrection can be repeated in a believer and about how a Christian can be 'a new creation' yet outwardly appear unchanged. He offered the following synthesis: (1)

Paul interpreted Jesus' death as an end of the world event, bringing God's kingdom and resurrection to all the elect. (2) The world did not end and the period between Christ's resurrection and believers' resurrection became problematic. (3) Paul put forward a 'physical mysticism'; through the sacraments the Holy Spirit mediates Christ's resurrection to believers. (4) This present union with Christ in the Spirit ensures to the believer a share in the 'Messianic resurrection' at Jesus' second coming.

Schweitzer's great contribution was to recognize the vital importance of eschatology (the doctrine of the 'last things') in Paul, but his weakness was to regard Paul's eschatology as a makeshift expedient. The dominant theme in Paul's eschatology is not the delay in Jesus' coming but the exalted status of Jesus to whom all shall pay homage (*cf.* Phil. 2:9ff.). By contrast, C.H. Dodd recognized and emphasized the immediate or 'realized' eschatology of Paul in which the believer already experiences the kingdom (Col. 1:13), although Dodd then played down Paul's future emphasis as a hangover from apocalyptic Judaism and foreign to Jesus' teaching.

The background to Paul's thought. The scholarly debate was put into sharp focus by W. Wrede in 1905; he claimed that Paul was not truly a disciple of Jesus but was the second founder of Christianity. The individual piety and future salvation of Rabbi Jesus had been transformed by theologian Paul into a present redemption through the death and resurrection of a Christ-god. Subsequent scholars such as Bultmann have examined Paul's relation to the Gentile world, and have suggested that he was strongly influenced by Greek and especially Gnostic ideas. R. M. Grant viewed Paul as a man whose spiritual world lay somewhere between Jewish apocalyptic and the later fully-developed Gnosticism of the 2nd cent., seeing the spiritual mysteries of Gnosticism as the logical outcome of a failure of apocalyptic hope. A major weakness of this kind of suggestion is that it tends to convert pagan parallels to Paul's thought into influences on it, and influences into sources for it. However, it is his 1st-cent. Jewish background which Paul himself makes reference to. And scholars such as W. D. Davies have shown that the Qumran sect and Rabbinic Judaism do indeed form the background of many of Paul's concepts which had formerly been labelled as Hellenistic. Paul views mankind in the OT-Jewish framework, not in terms of the dualism of Greek thought, and it is from this that his doctrines of redemption and eschatology have developed.

The development of Pauline criticism. The Tubingen school of thought under F. C. Baur in the 19th cent. dominated Pauline studies for some time. It suggested that only 5 NT documents were definitely from the apostolic period, Revelation and Paul's letters to the Romans, Corinthians and Galatians, and that the early church had Pauline-Gentile and Petrine-Jewish factions which were synthesized into Catholic Christianity only late in the 2nd cent. Such views naturally came under considerable attack from other scholars, and the British and Americans especially were rarely persuaded by them. The pendulum of majority opinion swung back to an acceptance of all but the Pastoral letters, 2 Thessalonians and Ephesians as Pauline. But Bauer had at least brought NT studies out of an unhelpful bondage to tradition and had brought into prominence an inductive historical approach.

In the 20th cent., some of the Tubingen historical reconstructions have continued to be assumed, even when its literary conjectures have been discounted. But it is possible to see Paul's mission not as something different to that of others, but in terms of his conflict with opponents such as the Judaizers (Acts 11:2f.; Gal. 2:12) who sought to impose Jewish rituals on Gentile believers. Paul sought to maintain the unity of the whole church by consulting with Jewish-Christian leaders (Gal. 2), working with Jewish-Christian colleagues (Col. 4:11), and taking gifts to the Jerusalem church (Acts 11:27ff.).

The authorship, date and place of origin of some of the NT letters traditionally ascribed to Paul has come under close scrutiny. These issues are dealt with in articles on the separate Letters, but the major discussions have been as follows. The prison Letters (Eph., Phil., Col., Phm.) have been assigned traditionally to Rome but scholars have found attractive the suggestion that they were written from Ephesus. An Ephesian imprisonment is only implied, never reported in the NT (*e.g.* 1 Cor. 15:32), but the setting, journeys and people mentioned in the Letters fit Ephesus better than Rome; the issue is not fully resolved. Earlier efforts to determine the authorship of the Letters by appeal to literary criteria have been questioned because Paul did use amanuenses to write his thoughts down and they probably influenced the style and vocabulary (*cf.* Rom. 16:22; 2 Thes. 3:17). Besides, Paul incorporated pre-formed pieces into his letters, such as hymns (Phil. 2:5-11), expositions (1 Cor. 2:6-16) and creeds (1 Cor. 15:3-7). Paul is the author of the letters in the sense that they were written under his supervision, partly by his own hand or at his dictation, and so literary criteria (vocabulary, style, *etc.*) used to determine Pauline authorship can be given little weight.

Among other matters relating to the Letters is the suggestion that Romans was originally 2 letters (chs. 1-15 were a circular to which ch. 16, an introduction of Phoebe to the Ephesians, was attached to the copy for Ephesus), but the scholarly support for its traditional unity remains strong. Ephesians has continued to be doubted by some as authentically Pauline but arguments based on literary criteria are weak in view of the comments above, and parallels to some of his thoughts or expressions have been found in the Dead Sea Scrolls, which allow an earlier date for Ephesians than scholars previously believed possible.

See also articles on Paul's major

doctrines such as ESCHATOLOGY; REDEMPTION. For information about the incorporation of Pauline letters into the NT, see NEW TESTAMENT CANON.

PAULUS, SERGIUS. The proconsul of Cyprus in AD 47/8 when Paul visited the island (Acts 13:7). His name suggests he belonged to an old Roman senatorial family, and was possibly one of the Curators of the Banks of the Tiber under Claudius. Commentators disagree over the reality of his profession of Christian faith.

PAVILION. In Jb. 36:29 (RSV, NIV) a difficult phrase is translated 'thunderings of (or from) his pavilion'. NEB takes clouds as a carpet under God's pavilion (*i.e.* tent); GNB simply has 'where God dwells'. In AV the word is also used for army tents (1 Ki. 20:12), and elsewhere metaphorically for the place of divine protection (Ps. 27:5).

PEACE. The OT word *shalom* means 'completeness', 'soundness' and 'well-being'. It may mean material prosperity (Ps. 122:6ff.) or physical safety (Ps. 4:8), but it may also mean spiritual well-being associated with righteousness and truth (Ps. 85:10; Is. 57:19ff.). It was seen as the gift of God, so the Messianic age would be one of peace (Is. 11:1ff.). The NT shows the fulfilment of this hope; Jesus brought peace (Lk. 1:79) and bestowed it on his disciples (Lk. 7:50). The NT word has the full force of *shalom*, and is linked with righteousness (Rom. 14:17). Christ's sacrifice for sin brings people peace with God (Rom. 5:1) followed by inner peace (Phil. 4:7) unhindered by the world's strife (Jn. 14:27). Jesus died partly to create peace between people (Eph. 2), but they must actively promote it (Eph. 4:3) as the Spirit fills them with it (Gal. 5:22).

PEARL: See JEWELS AND PRECIOUS STONES.

PEDAIAH (literally 'Yahweh has redeemed'). Seven OT people, none particularly well known. They are referred to in 2 Ki. 23:36; 1 Ch. 3:18; 27:20; Ne. 3:25; 8:4; 11:7; and 13:13.

PEG: See NAIL.

PEKAH (lit. 'opening'). He seized the throne of (N) Israel after murdering Pekahiah and reigned 737-732 BC (2 Ki. 15:23ff.). He adopted an anti-Assyrian policy, allied himself with Syria and attempted to persuade King Ahaz of Judah to join them (2 Ki. 16:5ff.). In response to Ahaz's plea, Tiglath-pileser III of Assyria invaded N Israel in 732 BC. Pekah was assassinated by Hoshea who took over the throne with Assyrian approval. Pekah's reign followed the evil tradition of Jeroboam (2 Ki. 15:28).

PEKAHIAH (lit. 'Yahweh has opened (his eyes)'). The king of Israel who succeeded his father Menahem *c.* 742/1 BC (2 Ki. 15:23ff.). The fact that he was assassinated implies that he continued his father's pro-Assyrian policy (see previous article).

PEKOD. A small Aramaean tribe E of the lower Tigris which among other Mesopotamian peoples was expected to rise against Jerusalem (Ezk. 23:23).

PELATIAH (lit. 'Yahweh delivers'). Several OT people including a leader whom Ezekiel pictured as devising mischief and giving bad advice in Jerusalem and who fell dead while Ezekiel spoke (Ezk. 11:1ff.).

PELEG (lit. 'water-course, division'). The grandson of Shem and brother of Joktan, in whose lifetime the world was 'divided' (a play on his name). This may perhaps mean division into geographical and linguistic groups or refer to the development of cultivation using irrigation canals (Gn. 11:1ff.).

PELETHITES: See CHERETHITES; PHILISTINES.

PELONITE. A name given to 2 of David's heroes, Helez and Ahijah (1 Ch. 11:27, 36).

PELUSIUM. In Ezk. 30:15f., a key Egyptian fortress city, Tell Farama, on the coast, 32 km SE of Port Said.

PENTATEUCH. The name given to the first 5 books of the OT (Gn., Ex., Lv., Nu. and Dt.). Sometimes called 'the book of the law', it was the most important of the 3 sections of the Jewish canon. The 5-fold division is ancient, determined both by the topics of the books and the practical possibility of containing only about one-fifth of the whole on a single papyrus scroll. Jewish tradition requires a portion of it to be read every week in the synagogue, covering the whole in a year. In the NT (and in other parts of the OT) it is referred to by such titles as 'the book of the law' (Gal. 3:10), the book of Moses (Mk. 12:26), the law (Mt. 12:5), the law of Moses (Lk. 2:22) and the law of the Lord (Lk. 2:23f.).

Contents. It narrates God's dealings with the world, and especially with Abraham's family, from the creation to the death of Moses, in 6 sections: the origin of the world and nations (Gn. 1-11); the patriarchal period (Gn. 12-50); Moses and the Exodus from Egypt (Ex. 1-18); legislation given at Sinai (Ex. 19:1-Nu. 10:10); the desert wanderings (Nu. 10:11-36:13); the final instructions of Moses (Dt. 1-34).

Message. It reveals God's will concerning Israel's task in the world. It testifies to the saving acts of God who is the sovereign Lord of history and nature, seen especially in the Exodus in which he revealed himself as Israel's redeemer. His grace is also seen in his giving of the law and the initiation of the covenant. Even Israel's response of pledging loyalty to God is a gift of his grace, for he himself has arranged the sacrificial system as a means of spanning the gap between himself and his people.

Authorship and unity: views before 1700. For many centuries the tradition was unquestioned that Moses wrote the entire Pentateuch, with the possible exception of the account of his own death in Dt. 34:5ff. which the Jewish Talmud attributed to Joshua.

But there was a tradition in the 2nd cent. BC that Ezra re-wrote it after the scrolls had been burned during Nebuchadrezzar's siege of Jerusalem (2 Esdras 14:21f.). This appears to have been accepted by some of the early Christian writers including Irenaeus, Tertullian, Clement of Alexandria and Jerome, although they did not thereby reject Moses' authorship of the original books. During the Middle Ages Jewish and Muslim scholars began pointing out supposed contradictions and anachronisms in the Pentateuch. For example, it was said that Gn. 36 was not written earlier than Jehoshaphat's reign (c. 873-849 BC) because it mentions Hadad (cf. 1 Ki. 11:14). Some Roman Catholic scholars in the 16th cent. credited Ezra with adding some interpolations to the Pentateuch. Thomas Hobbes in *Leviathan* (1651) said parts of the Pentateuch were more about Moses than by him, and Benedict Spinoza (1670) suggested Ezra wrote Deuteronomy and compiled the other books from several documents, some of them Mosaic.

Authorship and unity: documentary theories. In 1753 the French doctor Jean Astruc suggested that Moses compiled the Pentateuch from 2 main ancient *memoires* and a number of shorter documents; the *memoires* were distinguished by their respective use of Elohim and Yahweh as names for God. J. G. Eichhorn developed this, between 1780-83, abandoned Mosaic authorship and credited the final books to an unknown, later, redactor. Alexander Geddes, a Scottish Roman Catholic, yet further suggested (1792-1800) that the Pentateuch was compiled by a redactor who used fragments which represented 2 schools of thought, 'Elohistic' and 'Yahwistic'. The theories were developed by many other scholars, and notably K. H. Graf, into a belief that 4 documents were incorporated in the Pentateuch, labelled J (Yahwist), D (Deuteronomist), E (Elohist) and P (Priestly).

The documentary theory was given its most cogent and popular form by J. Wellhausen from 1876 to 1884. He suggested that J (c. 850 BC) and E (c. 750 BC) were combined by a redactor about 650 BC. When subsequently D (the Deuteronomic laws, c. 621 BC) was added by a second redactor (c. 550 BC) and P (c. 500-450) by yet another redactor c. 400 BC, the Pentateuch was complete. Wellhausen not only analysed the text, he also linked his critical studies to an evolutionary approach to Israel's history which minimized the historical nature of the patriarchal period and played down Moses' importance. The religion of Israel, he suggested, had evolved from simple sacrifices on family altars to the intricately legalistic structure of Lv. (P) which stemmed from Ezra's era. This theory had such a profound effect on later studies that it has been likened to Darwin's theories in the natural sciences.

The documents are said to have the following characteristics. J, dating from the early monarchy (950-850 BC), tells of God's dealings with man from creation to Israel's entry into Canaan.

It is an intensely nationalistic document, and God is portrayed in quasi-human terms. E, written a century later, has moralistic and religious emphases and rationalizes the sins of the Patriarchs. It includes the story of Abraham's willingness to sacrifice Isaac (Gn. 22) to convey the inwardness of true sacrifice. D corresponds roughly to the book of Deuteronomy, and essential to the theory is the assumption that Josiah's book of the law was at least part of it (2 Ki. 22-23). Worship is centred on Jerusalem, and stress is laid on God's love for Israel and the nation's obligation to respond. P draws together laws and customs from various periods and codifies them to organize the legal structure of Judaism after the Exile. It emphasizes holiness and the transcendence of God.

Authorship and unity: reactions and developments. While some 20th cent. scholars developed the Graf-Wellhausen theories even further, atomizing the Pentateuch into still smaller sources, others took issue with the principles. The use of the divine names as a basis for distinguishing documents has been questioned because there is textual evidence of greater variety even within the alleged documents than was originally recognized. Interestingly, the Muslim Quran, the unity of which is rarely questioned, prefers one name in some sections and another elsewhere; in the Pentateuch names may be chosen to stress the character of God relevant to the narrative.

More problematic for the theory is that the combination name Yahweh Elohim is used (Gn. 2:4-3:24). Similarly, the theory pays too little attention to the fact that different types of literature call for different vocabularies and styles which can be composed by the same person. Even the repeated stories (*e.g.* Gn. 1:1-2:4a; 2:4b-25), an important factor in the documentary theory, can be explained not by different authors or sources, but by the characteristic Hebrew use of repetition for emphasis. Scholars who do not hold conservative views about Mosaic authorship have also been critical of the theory. B. D. Eerdmans, for example, defended the authenticity of the patriarchal narratives and the antiquity of the ritual institutions in P. E. Robertson suggested Dt. was compiled under Samuel's influence for all Israel and was rediscovered in Josiah's reign when 'all Israel' could be treated once more as a religious unit.

The 'form critics' laid stress on the long oral tradition which underlay the narratives and shaped them into literary masterpieces. Some such scholars rejected the documentary theory altogether and suggested that reliable oral traditions were shaped into 2 main traditions, a 'P'-circle and a 'D'-circle, although the actual writing of the books did not take place until exilic times or after. Others have suggested the 'Elohist' was in fact an editor, not an author (or circle). Today, scholars are generally giving more attention to the forms of the narrative than to alleged sources. Indeed, archaeological discoveries have led to serious questioning of the 'evolutionary' view of Israel's religious history, for much of the 'P' material can be shown to have had ancient counterparts.

Though not discarded, the documentary theory has been modified by many scholars. The development of each document is seen to be complex and generally taken to represent the work of a 'school' rather than a single author, and the growth of the traditions is seen as parallel rather than consecutive. It is necessary to identify material in the Pentateuch which clearly does not come from Moses (*e.g.* Gn. 14:14; 36:31; Ex. 11:3; 16:35; Nu. 12:3; 21:14f.; 32:34ff.; Dt. 2:12; 34:1-12) and to recognize that neither Testament ascribes the whole work (although they do ascribe substantial parts) to Moses. It is credible to assume that final editing took place in the early monarchy. But whatever the detailed origins of the Pentateuch, it stands today as a document possessing rich internal unity. It records God's revelation in and Lordship over history. It records both Israel's faithful and rebellious responses to him. It reveals God's holiness which separates him from mankind, and his gracious love which binds them to him on his terms.

See also BIBLICAL CRITICISM; and articles on individual pentateuchal books.

PENTECOST, FEAST OF. The name comes from the '50 days' from the offering of the barley sheaf at the beginning of the Passover; the 50th day was the Feast of Pentecost (Lv. 23:16). Since the time elapsed was 7 weeks, it was also called the feast of weeks (Dt. 16:10). It marked the completion of the barley harvest. It was to be a holiday when bread offerings and animal sacrifices were made (Lv. 23:17ff.), a day of joy and thanksgiving, reminiscent of deliverance from Egypt (Dt. 16:12). In later times Pentecost was regarded as the anniversary of the giving of the law at Sinai, and the Sadducees counted it from the first Sunday of Passover, a practice which was normative until the temple was destroyed in AD 70. In Acts 2:1ff. it was the day on which the Holy Spirit descended upon the disciples giving them new life and power, accompanied by the signs of fire and wind.

PENUEL. The place Jacob called 'the face of God' where he wrestled with the angel (Gn. 32:22ff.). It was the site of an important pass (*cf.* Jdg. 8:8f.); possibly Tulul ed-Dahab 6 km E of Succoth.

PEOPLE. Different original words are thus translated to describe any ethnic group (*e.g.* Gn. 25:23); the Gentiles (Joel 1:6); and the people of Israel (Ezr. 9:1f.).

PEOR. *Pagan god:* Baal-peor, to whom the Israelites were fatally attracted in Shittim (Nu. 25:3ff.). *Place:* A mountain N of the Dead Sea, opposite Jericho, from which Balaam blessed Israel (Nu. 23:28); its exact location is uncertain.

PERAEA. A district E of the Jordan roughly corresponding to OT GILEAD. It is the NT district 'beyond the Jordan' (*e.g.* Mt. 19:1), so named after the Exile. A highland region, it had adequate rainfall for fruit and cereal cultivation. In Jesus' time it was ruled by Herod Antipas and was regarded by Jews as of equal status with Judaea and Galilee.

PERDITION. 'Loss', 'destruction'. A word used in the NT with reference to the final destiny of the wicked (Rev. 17:8, 11). Judas is called 'son of perdition' (Jn. 17:12), a common Jewish phrase which literally means 'son of the perishing'. See also ESCHATOLOGY; HELL.

PEREZ, PEREZITES. The first-delivered of Judah's twin sons by Tamar, despite the fact that his brother Zerah put out his hand first (Gn. 38:28f.). 'Perezites' refers to his descendants; not to be confused with PERIZZITES. In AV the name is often spelt Pharez or Phares.

PERFECTION. A state of wholeness or completeness in which any disabilities, shortcomings or defects which may have existed before have been removed or left behind. The main NT word thus translated includes the idea of reaching the appropriate or appointed end; what that end is varies in different cases. God himself is perfect (Mt. 5:48); so too are his ways and his laws (Ps.

18:30; Jas. 1:25). The thought is that God is wholly free from faults and worthy of all praise. Jesus is described as having been made perfect through suffering (Heb. 2:10), not as if he had been previously on probation but in the sense of being fitted through his experience for the high-priestly ministry (Heb. 5:7ff.).

The OT demands—and ascribes to individuals such as Noah (Gn. 6:9)—a perfection which is wholehearted and loyal obedience to the known will of God. It is faith at work maintaining a right covenant relationship with God by reverent worship and service, an inner attitude rather than mere outward conformity to God's commands (1 Ki. 8:61; 2 Ch. 25:2). In Heb. Jesus is seen as creating this covenant perfection of people. The old covenant of Moses was replaced by the new covenant, for the old could never perfect people in their relationship to God (Heb. 10).

The NT also speaks of God perfecting his people in the image of Christ (Col. 3:10). They are to grow until they are 'complete' (*cf.* 1 Pet. 2:2), 'perfect' (Phil. 3:12). This is a divine gift which will not be enjoyed until Christ's coming, although relative perfection in insight (Phil. 3:15), behaviour (Jas. 1:4) and love (1 Jn. 4:12) is feasible. Absolute sinlessness is a goal to be sought (Mt. 5:48), but which is not yet found fully (1 Jn. 1:8-2:2). Perfection is not only a matter of sinlessness, but of strong faith, joyful patience, and overflowing love.

See also SANCTIFICATION.

PERFUME: See COSMETICS AND PERFUMERY.

PERGA. An ancient city, it was the religious capital of Pamphylia with a temple of Artemis. It was here that John Mark deserted Paul and Barnabas (Acts 13:13).

PERGAMUM. A city of the Roman province of Asia. Although probably settled from a very early date, it became important only after 282 BC when it was made the capital of the Attalid kingdom, bequeathed to the Romans in 133 BC. The first temple of the imperial cult was built here c. 29 BC, referred to in Rev. 2:12ff. as 'where Satan's throne is'. Worship of the divine emperor was the touchstone of civil loyalty, and marked a crisis for the church in Asia. The passage blames the church for tolerating teachers who would lead it into idolatry (see NICOLAUS). The white stone offered by Jesus to his faithful people there may refer to a pebble used as a token of acquittal or as a ticket.

PERIZZITES. Occupants of Canaan who seem to have lived in villages in the hills (*e.g.* Jos. 11:3); their name probably comes from a word for 'hamlet'.

PERSECUTION. This was nothing new for the first Christians, because it was part of their Jewish heritage. A theory of martyrdom rewarded by personal immortality dominated the Jewish attitude towards the Romans. Despite official religious toleration, their cohesiveness, non-co-operation and uncanny financial success had won the Jews widespread hatred and spasmodic persecution. Opposition to Christians came first from the Jews themselves. The first persecution began after Stephen had taught that the Jewish law had been superseded (Acts 6:14; 8:16). In AD 44 James was executed by Herod Agrippa (Acts 12:1f.), and c. AD 80 Christians were officially excommunicated by the Jews. Paul consistently fell foul of Jewish leaders on his missionary journeys.

At first, the Roman authorities were tolerant of the new faith, but this soon gave way to fierce opposition. Christians in Rome were so unpopular that Nero could make them scapegoats for the city fire in AD 64. By AD 112 persisting in Christian belief in the province of Bithynia was a capital offence, although the emperor Trajan did not encourage 'witch hunts'. Christians were sometimes prosecuted for specific offences such as cannibalism and incest (arising from misunderstandings about their eucharists and 'love feasts'), and for magic, illegal assembly and refusal to sacrifice to the emperor's name. From 1 Pet. 2:12; 4:14ff. and later writings it is clear that simply being a Christian was a punishable offence, although there is little evidence for a general law proscribing the faith throughout the empire. Persecution was probably at the discretion of the local governors (*cf.* Gallio's refusal to prosecute in Acts 18:14ff.), and for this reason Tertullian addressed his 2nd-cent. *Apology* to a governor and not to the emperor. Governors generally do seem to have been concerned at punishing only genuine offences and not religious opinions, and they only accepted public and substantiated charges, so the majority of Christians were protected long enough for the church to become firmly established.

PERSEVERANCE. On the few occasions this word or idea is used in the NT (*e.g.* Eph. 6:18), it relates simply to the continual and patient dependence of Christians on Christ, illustrated especially in the parable of the persistent widow (Lk. 18:1ff.). It is only by God's power that Christians are guarded for final salvation (1 Pet. 1:5).

PERSIA, PERSIANS. The Persians were nomadic pastoral people from S Russia who entered the Iranian plateau probably about 1200 BC. The dynasty of kings was apparently founded by Achaemenes *c.* 680 BC; some generations later Cyrus II rebelled against his Median overlord and took over his capital at Ecbatana in 550 BC. From then on the customs and language of the Medes strongly influenced those of the Persians. By 540 BC Cyrus was strong enough to attack Babylon and entered the city in triumph in 539. The empire was divided into large regions ruled by Persian or Median satraps with native officers under them (*cf.* Dn. 6). Various statues of gods collected by the last native Babylonian king Nabonidus were returned to their former shrines;

as the Jews had no image of God Cyrus allowed them to take back the sacred vessels which Nebuchadrezzar had looted from the Jerusalem temple (Ezr. 1:7ff.). He also authorized the rebuilding of the temple by any Jew who wished to return to Judah. The governor of the province which included Judah was clearly unaware of the edict when in 520 BC he attempted to stop the rebuilding, but it was confirmed by Darius I (Ezr. 5-6).

Darius expanded the empire still further. His reorganization gave considerable autonomy to subject peoples, thus allowing such a small community as Judah to survive. Under Artaxerxes I, Ezra became 'Secretary of State for Jewish Affairs' (Ezr. 7:12), and accredited as a special envoy to reorganize temple worship in 458 BC. The Jews exceeded their rights by attempting to rebuild the city walls, but Nehemiah was able to gain permission for the work to resume under his governorship in 445 BC.

The luxury of the Persian court described in the book of Esther is attested by objects and bas-reliefs found at several sites. The Persians revered gods of nature, fertility and the heavens. The tribe of the Magi had a virtual monopoly of priesthood. Some time after 1000 BC Zoroaster proclaimed a religion of lofty moral principles, for whom there was one god, Ahura-Mazda, the Good, opposed by a power of Evil.

PETER. Apparently originally called Simeon (Acts 15:14), he may have adopted the similar Greek name

Simon. John's Gospel gives his place of origin as the strongly Gentile Bethsaida (Jn. 1:44), but he also had a home at Capernaum (Mk. 1:21ff.). Both were lakeside towns, and he worked as a fisherman; he spoke Aramaic with a strong N country accent (Mk. 14:70). He was not trained in the law (Acts 4:13, which does not relate to literacy), but probably had been influenced by John the Baptist (*cf.* Acts 1:22; Jn. 1:39f.). He was married (Mk. 1:30), and his wife accompanied him on missionary journeys (1 Cor. 9:5).

Peter's call. He was introduced to Jesus by Andrew (Jn. 1:41), probably before Jesus' Galilean ministry, which makes his 'instant' lakeside decision more understandable (Mk. 1:16f.); the call to the 12 came later (Mk. 3:16ff.). Jesus named him *Kepha* ('Cephas', a rock or stone) which appears in the NT as 'Peter'. He was one of the inner circle of 3, was frequently impulsive and acted as the spokesman for the group (*e.g.* Mk. 9:2, 5; 14:29). His rejection of Jesus was catastrophic (Mk. 14:66ff.), but he was specifically reinstated after the resurrection (Mk. 16:7; Lk. 24:34; Jn. 21:15ff.).

Peter's commission. Peter's confession and Jesus' response in Mt. 16:16ff. is one of the most discussed passages of the NT. Some scholars reject it completely on the ground that Jesus never intended to start a church, others place it after the resurrection, but such arguments hardly do justice to the distinctiveness of the passage. There is still no unanimity in interpreting it; there are two main approaches. One suggests that 'the rock'

is what Peter has said in confessing Jesus as Messiah; in other words, the apostolic doctrine of Christ. It has the merit of fitting well in the context. It touches the core of the apostolic function; Peter, first among the apostles, has a name which proclaims it. The second approach suggests that Peter himself is the foundation-rock of the church, because v. 19 is addressed directly to him. Even so, the passage refers to the foundation of the church and does not allow for the transfer of its provisions to any successors of Peter. But there is no doubt that here and elsewhere there is primacy of Peter among the apostles. For the words about keys, see POWER OF THE KEYS.

Peter in the early church. It is Peter who takes the lead in the community before Pentecost (Acts 1:15ff.) and as the principal preacher (2:14ff.), spokesman (4:8ff.), and administrator of discipline (5:3) after. He was also the first apostle associated with the Gentile mission (10:1ff.), from which he withdrew after opposition (Gal. 2:11ff.), but was still the first to urge full acceptance of Gentiles on faith alone (15:7ff.). His preaching had the same stress on the cross and resurrection as did Paul's, although he gave it a different expression.

His career after Stephen's death is hard to trace. He clearly led missions in Palestine (Acts 12), and went to Antioch (Gal. 2:11ff.) and possibly Corinth (1 Cor. 1:12). He is closely associated with Christians in N Asia Minor (1 Pet. 1:1). He almost certainly wrote 1 Peter from Rome, and Clement implies that Peter died there during Nero's persecution. The tradition that he was crucified upside down cannot be accepted as reliable.

See also next two articles.

PETER, FIRST LETTER OF. The letter is sent in the name of the apostle Peter to whom there is a modest allusion in 5:1; a certain scribal function is also attributed to Silvanus (5:12), almost certainly Silas of Acts. The address to 5 provinces (1:1) is the widest in the NT.

Contents. Address and greeting (1:1f.); thanksgiving (1:3-12); the implications of salvation (1:13-2:10); Christian relationships (2:11-3:12); suffering and the will of God (3:13-22); holy living (4:1-11); the trials of suffering (4:12-19); address to elders (5:1-4); general address, benediction and personal greetings (5:5-14).

Authorship and place of writing. It was undoubtedly used by Polycarp and Papias (early 2nd cent. AD) and was universally known in the Greek-speaking church from the mid-2nd cent. Nothing suggests it was ever attributed to anyone except the apostle Peter. It conveys greetings from 'Babylon', and this is almost certainly a cryptogram for Rome (*cf.* Rev. 14:8; 17:5).

The Greek of the letter is good and rhythmic, the style not pretentious but with a certain delicacy; some grammatical features are best explained by underlying Semitic (Hebrew or Aramaic) influence. The OT quotations mostly follow the LXX, suggesting the author's familiarity with it. This has led some scholars to deny that it could have been written by an Aramaic-speaking Galilean. But Greek was widely understood and spoken; Peter's brother had a Greek name; and Peter, brought up in a Gentile area, would have been at home in the language. Also, the LXX was the 'Authorized Version' of the OT used by most 1st-cent. Christians. It is also quite likely that Silvanus the secretary influenced the dictated style; such people in the Roman world were entrusted with considerable powers, and Silvanus had been chosen for the delicate task of communicating the resolutions of the Jerusalem Council (Acts 15:22ff.), so was clearly skilled.

There are important parallels in language and thought between 1 Peter, Mark (believed to have been strongly influenced by Peter) and the early speeches in Acts. All set forth Jesus as the suffering servant; the rare ransom motif appears in both Mk. 10:45 and 1 Pet. 1:18. There is a parallel stress on prophetic fulfilment (Acts 2:16ff.; 1 Pet. 1:10ff.); a link of repentance with faith-baptism (Acts 2:38, 40; 1 Pet. 3:20ff.); and a joyous recognition of the Gentile mission expressed from a Jewish viewpoint (Acts 10:9ff.; 1 Pet. 1:1-12; 2:3-10). 1 Peter also includes a number of apparent reminiscences of the words of Jesus (*e.g.* 1 Pet. 1:16 = Mt. 5:48).

Historical background and date. There are 4 references to persecution: 2 seem to refer to current trials (1:6f.; 3:13-17) and 2 to an imminent and more serious ordeal (4:12-19; 5:9). The distinction in 4:12ff. between suffering for wrongdoing and as a Christian has attracted comparison with a letter from Pliny, the governor of Bithynia-Pontus, to the emperor Trajan *c.* AD 110/111. The governor gave Christians a free pardon if they sacrificed to the emperor's genius, and executed them if they did not, and reported that Christians took an oath of abstention from crime. This has led some scholars to suggest that 1 Peter dates from this time, because the only intense persecution beforehand by Nero and Domitian was localized in Rome. But there is no evidence that Pliny's policy was enforced in the other areas to which Peter had written. The alleged parallel between Pliny's concern about the *name* Christian and the emphasis in 1 Peter on the name of Jesus is best explained by the early significance of 'the name' in the apostolic age (*e.g.* Acts 3:6; 4:12). As it is almost certain that Peter died in Rome under the Neronian persecution which was quite literally a fiery trial, he would have had good reason to expect it to spread further E as he saw it approaching him. The letter could well have been written at or shortly before Nero's outburst against the Christians, AD 63/4, perhaps after Paul had died leaving his colleagues Silvanus and Mark in Rome.

Nature and purpose. The agreement between the theology of Paul and 1 Peter is close. There are also close literary resemblances between 1 Peter and other NT writings, including Romans, Ephesians, Hebrews and James. A pattern of instruction for new converts is reflected in 1 Peter,

James and Ephesians especially. There are calls to put away the old life (1 Pet. 2:1, 11); to be humble and selfless (2:11-3:9); to watch and pray (4:7; 5:8); and to resist the devil (5:8f.). For this reason 1 Peter has sometimes been regarded as a baptismal sermon written as a letter; others have suggested it forms the president's part for an Easter baptismal eucharist. However, many of the details used to support these theories can be called into question. The stress on baptism in the letter is not strong; there is only one explicit reference (3:21). And the use in 1 Peter of the Exodus as a 'type' for Christian experience is not restricted to baptism, and can simply stress the spiritual transition which converts have made. 1 Peter can be read as what it purports to be, a general letter of encouragement in the face of suffering.

See also previous article; NERO; PERSECUTION; and the following article.

PETER, SECOND LETTER OF. *Contents.* Greeting (1:1f.); the reliability of Christian faith (1:3-11); the testimony of eyewitnesses (1:12-18) and inspired ancient prophecy (1:19-21); condemnation of false prophets who will be judged at the certain end of the world (2:1-3:10); Christians must live upright lives in anticipation of Jesus' return (3:11-18).

Occasion. The recipients are not defined, but the faith equal 'with ours' (1:1) and 'the corruption in the world' (1:4) suggest they were Gentiles with whom the author had been long and intimately acquainted (1:12f.; 3:1). He writes to warn them of false teachers who are immoral in behaviour and radical in belief (2:10ff.), and to explain their main problem, the second coming of Jesus. If the author was Peter, the date would be the mid 60s (he anticipates death in 1:14); if not it may have been written in the late 1st or early 2nd cent.

Authorship. No other NT book is so poorly attested by early church writers, but on the other hand no book excluded from the NT canon can claim so much support from such writers as 2 Peter does. Origen (early 3rd cent.) is the first to cite it by name. It was however used much earlier; Clement of Alexandria had it in his Bible, and Valentinus in the *Gospel of Truth*, Aristides in his *Apology* (AD 129) and Clement of Rome (AD 95) all appear to allude to it.

This is considered by many scholars to be sufficient attestation of its early date, but often they reject it as written by Peter for several reasons. It appears to borrow from Jude, although both letters may draw on a common document denouncing false teachers. There is a marked change in style between 1 and 2 Peter, although this could be due to two different amanuenses writing down the apostle's message. The subject matter is very different, too, but both draw on the lessons of the flood; both emphasize prophecy; and both stress the tension between being members of both this age and the age to come, something which was neglected in the 2nd cent. Some themes appear to be of 2nd-

cent. origins. Among them are the destruction of the world by fire (3:7), but 2 Peter could have been the source for this later emphasis, and the inclusion of Paul's letters among the 'other scriptures' (3:16). However, Paul claimed that the apostles were inspired by the Holy Spirit just like the OT writers (1 Cor. 2:13), so Peter could have had good reason to claim such for Paul.

The evidence does not therefore justify dogmatism on the question of authorship. Despite the problems it is not impossible for Peter to have written it. Alternative views have their own problems; 2 Peter just does not fit neatly into the setting, and alongside other anonymous works, of the 2nd cent. The early church did investigate its claims to authenticity, and did ultimately decide in favour of it, and this decision has yet to be conclusively shown to be wrong.

PETHOR. A city of N Mesopotamia, S of Carchemish, and the home of Balaam who was called by Balak to curse Israel (Nu. 22:5; Dt. 23:4).

PHARAOH. The common biblical title for the kings of Egypt. It was originally a name for the Egyptian royal palace and court, but by *c.* 1450 BC was applied to the king himself, as a synonym for 'His Majesty'.

Many pharaohs are mentioned in the OT. The contemporary of Abraham would have been one of the kings of the 12th Dynasty *c.* 1991-1778 BC (Gn. 12:15ff.). Joseph's pharaoh was perhaps one of the Hyksos kings of the 15th Dynasty *c.* 1700 BC (Gn. 37-50). The pharaoh of the Exodus was probably Rameses II (Ex. 5-12). The one who received Hadad from Edom (1 Ki. 11:18ff.) could well have been Amenemope or Siamun of the 21st Dynasty, and the one who destroyed Gezer (1 Ki. 9:16) was also probably that Siamun. Several references to pharaohs are found in the prophets. Is. 19:11 reflects the internal fragmentation which took place in Egypt in the 22nd-24th Dynasties (*c.* 750-715 BC). The apparent strength and actual inability of Egypt to help Israel against Assyria is reflected in Is. 30:2f., in Jeremiah (46:25f.) and Ezekiel (30:21ff.; 31:2, 18; 32:31f.) prophesied that Babylon would defeat Egypt. Babylon's Nebuchadrezzar did fight Egypt's Ahmose II, but the outcome is not known.

For pharaohs named in the Bible see HOPHRA; NECO; SHISHAK; TIRHAKAH. See also EGYPT.

PHARISEES. The work of the OT leader Ezra, seeking to master the text and teaching of the law, was continued by the people who became known as scribes. Their wider circle of supporters were known as Hasidim (Hasidaeans), 'God's loyal ones'. The Pharisees were a minority group of Hasidim who separated themselves from the majority's political and religious attitudes in the 2nd cent. BC. They were given governing power by Alexandra Salome (76-67 BC), and from then on were dominant in the Sanhedrin. In NT times they were pro-Roman. By the 2nd cent. AD they were the unquestioned leaders of the Jews. Always a minority group, they numbered only about 6,000 in Herod the Great's time. They came mostly from the middle ranks of society and, understanding the ordinary person, tried to make the rigorous law bearable.

They stressed individual fulfilment of the law (as against the Sadducees' emphasis on temple worship), and resurrection, which the Sadducees denied. The law was adaptable to changing conditions, and decisions about its contemporary application were binding on all. It contained 613 commandments (248 positive, 365 negative). These were hedged by other supplementary commands so that no-one should break the principles; *e.g.* there were 39 prohibited groups of activities on the sabbath. They were convinced that their traditions (Mk. 7:3), being correct applications of the law, came from Moses. The Pharisees, who strongly stressed tithing, undoubtedly stood ethically higher than most others, and Jesus' condemnation of them must be seen in that light.

See also HASIDAEANS; HYPOCRITE; SADDUCEES; SCRIBES.

PHARPAR (lit. 'swift'). A tributary of the Abana (Barada), modern Awaj, S of Damascus (2 Ki. 5:12).

PHILADELPHIA. A city in the Roman province of Asia in the W of modern Asiatic Turkey. Founded in the 2nd cent. BC, it lay at the threshold of a fertile tract (*cf.* the open door of

Rev. 3:8) which was subject to frequent earthquakes; one destroyed it in AD 17 and it was rebuilt and renamed Neocaesarea (*cf.* Rev. 3:12). It had many temples and religious festivals and its inhabitants were known for their loyalty (*cf.* Rev. 3:8ff.). The church had met Jewish opposition (Rev. 3:9).

PHILEMON. The owner of the slave Onesimus and probably resident in Colossae. Philemon was converted through Paul and had become his colleague (Phm. 1, 19). See also the next article.

PHILEMON, LETTER TO. *Contents.* Greetings (vv. 1-3); introduction to themes of love, fellowship and refreshment (vv. 4-7); the request for Onesimus (vv. 8-21); a request for hospitality (v. 22); greetings from Paul's friends, and blessing (vv. 23-25).

Significance. The earliest lists of the corpus of Pauline letters contain Philemon and its authenticity has never been responsibly questioned. Most generations have valued its grace, tact, affection and delicacy of feeling. Although a personal letter, it is carefully composed and follows traditional literary forms.

Purpose and occasion. The core of the letter is an appeal by Paul on behalf of Onesimus, a slave from Colossae (Col. 4:9) who had run away after robbing his master Philemon (Phm. 15, 18). He had been converted through Paul, and a strong affection grew between the two men. Under contemporary law

Philemon could wreak almost unlimited vengeance on Onesimus, hence Paul begged him to receive the slave back as he would receive Paul, and he promised to pay anything Onesimus owed (17-19). However, Paul really wanted Onesimus to stay with him, so sought his release for Christian service (11-16).

The letter was written from prison on the same occasion as Colossians, for Onesimus was to accompany Tychicus who carried the letter (Col. 4:9). Paul's friends in 23f. are almost the same as Col. 4:10ff. The place of imprisonment is debated; it could have been Rome, a haven for displaced persons, or Ephesus, nearer Onesimus' home but large enough to be anonymous in.

See also previous article; ONESIMUS.

PHILETUS. A teacher who undermined orthodox belief in the resurrection (2 Tim. 2:17); see HYMANAEUS.

PHILIP (lit. 'horse lover'). Four people are thus named in the NT. 1. A son of Herod the Great and Mariamne, whose wife Herodias, mother of Salome, left him to live with his half-brother Herod Antipas (Mk. 6:17). 2. A son of Herod the Great and Cleopatra of Jerusalem, who was tetrarch of Gaulanitis, Trachonitis, Auranitis, Batanaea and Ituraea (*cf.* Lk. 3:1), ruling moderately and justly for 37 years until his death in AD 33/34. He rebuilt Panias (modern Banyas) as Caesarea Philippi (*cf.* Mt. 16:13ff.). He married Salome, daughter of

Herodias. 3. Philip the apostle, who brought his brother Nathanael with him (Jn. 1:43ff.). He came from Bethsaida, a fishing village on the W side of the Sea of Galilee. He figures only rarely in the Gospels (Jn. 6:5; 12:21f.; 14:8). 4. One of the Seven chosen as officials ('deacons') of the Jerusalem church (Acts 6:5). He later became an evangelist (Acts 8), and settled with his prophetess daughters in Caesarea (Acts 21:8f.). Luke specifically distinguishes him from the apostle, although they were confused by some early church writers.

PHILIPPI. A city of Macedonia (Acts 16:12), captured by and named after Philip of Macedon *c.* 360 BC. Gold was mined in the area, and gold coins with Philip's head were struck and widely recognized. It was incorporated into the first of 4 districts of Macedonia after the Roman conquest in the 2nd cent. BC. After the battle of Philippi in 42 BC, in which Antony and Octavian fought Brutus and Cassius, the town was enlarged. After the battle of Actium in 31 BC Octavian, who defeated Antony and Cleopatra, gave the Philippians the same rights as they would have had if their land had been in Italy. Their civic pride is reflected both in Acts and Paul's letter to the Philippians (*cf.* Acts 16:21; Phil. 3:20). Paul evangelized the city after a vision calling him to Macedonia (Acts 16:9ff.).

PHILIPPIANS, LETTER TO THE. *Contents.* Greetings (1:1-2); Paul's thanksgiving and prayer (1:3-11);

Paul's ambition and joy (1:12-26); exhortation and example (1:27-2:18); anticipated future plans (2:19-30); digression about false teachers (3); encouragements, appreciations and greetings (4).

Purpose. The church at Philippi was founded during Paul's 2nd missionary journey (Acts 16:12ff.). The letter is personal and tender, written while Paul was in prison (see below) to commend Timothy and Epaphroditus to the church, preparing the way for their proposed visit (2:19ff.). He also wrote in appreciation of a gift brought from the church by Epaphroditus (4:10f., 14ff.), who also carried news of disunity among church members (2:ff.; 4:2). Paul gently rebuked them. There were some perfectionist teachers in Philippi who seemed to restrict all Christian hope to this life, and Paul refuted them in ch. 3. There is also evidence of some persecution in 1:29f.; 2:15. The letter reveals Paul's own attitude to suffering, by God's grace being able to rejoice despite his troubles and likely death; the word 'joy' and its related forms occurs 16 times. Its secret is fellowship with the Lord who is the centre of Paul's life (1:20f.). The letter also contains the great statement on the person of Christ and the nature and scope of salvation in 2:5-11.

Date and place of writing. Acts records three imprisonments which Paul experienced (16:23ff. at Philippi; 21:32-23:30 at Caesarea, following brief internment in Jerusalem; and 28:30 in Rome). The church community Paul refers to (1:14ff.) does not tally with what is known of Caesarea; that incident of imprisonment did not promise imminent death and Paul was hoping to visit Rome at the time whereas in Philippians he hopes to visit Philippi (2:24ff.).

The traditional view is that he wrote the letter from Rome. He alludes to Roman society (1:13; 4:22). The gravity of charges and impending verdict suggest he is on trial at the highest court from which there can be no appeal (1:20ff.; 2:17; 3:10f.); from any lesser court he could have appealed to Rome. The picture of the church at the place of writing fits with a city as large as Rome. However, there are problems with the view. The journeys proposed in the letter could not have been so far from Philippi as Rome was. And his impending martyrdom hardly fits with the relaxed house arrest of Acts 28:30f. More important, 2:24 looks forward to a return to Philippi while Rom. 15:23f., 28 considers his work in the E complete and he is looking W to Spain. If the letter comes from Rome (*i.e.* is later than Romans), he must have changed his plans; that is not impossible but it weakens the theory of Rome as the place of writing.

Another hypothesis which has much to commend it suggests that Philippians was written from an otherwise unknown imprisonment in Ephesus. The journeys would be feasible, and the requirements of 1:13 and 4:22 have been shown to exist by ancient inscriptions discovered in the ruins. But this is speculative and it is surprising that there is no mention of an appeal to Rome. The evidence is finely divided and it is impossible to make a final decision between Rome and Ephesus; the latter would command much wider support if there was internal biblical evidence that Paul was actually interned there (Acts 19-20).

PHILISTINES, PHILISTIA. According to the OT the Philistines were descended from Casluhim, the grandson of Ham (Gn. 10:14). They seem in historical times to have been a 'Sea People' who came from the Aegean area. They migrated to Palestine (which derives its name from the Philistines' territory of Philistia) via Crete (Caphtor, Am. 9:7) and Cyprus. Their territory comprised the coastal strip S of Carmel, extending inland to the foothills of Judah. There were 5 principal Philistine cities: Ashdod, Ashkelon, Ekron, Gath and Gaza (for which see separate articles).

They are first mentioned outside the Bible in the annals of the Egyptian king Rameses III *c.* 1185 BC who campaigned against them. Carved reliefs show the Tjekker, closely associated with the Philistines, wearing head-dresses of feathers rising vertically from a horizontal band. They are also mentioned in Assyrian annals from the late 9th cent. BC onwards. Pottery attributed to them has marked affinities with that of the Aegean. They used lances, round shields, long broadswords and triangular daggers. They appeared in Palestine at the transition from the Bronze Age to the Iron Age, so the reports that they bound Samson with bronze chains

(Jdg. 16:21) and in Saul's time controlled the iron industry (1 Sa. 13:19ff.) are quite consistent. Their language is unknown; they seem to have adopted the Semitic languages of the peoples they dispossessed, and only a handful of apparent Philistine loan-words appear in the OT. Three Philistine gods are mentioned in the Bible: Ashtoreth, Baalzebub and Dagon; the Philistines probably accommodated their ancestral religion to the gods they found in the lands they conquered. They offered sacrifices (Jdg. 16:23) and took charms into battle (2 Sa. 5:21).

According to the OT, Abraham and Isaac dealt with the Philistine king of Gerar, Abimelech (Gn. 20-21, 26), who proved a reasonable man unlike his more aggressive successors. Because the Philistines are not mentioned so early elsewhere, some scholars take the patriarchal references to be later additions. There is evidence, however, for a major expansion of Aegean trade *c.* 1900-1700 BC, and objects of Aegean origin dating from this time have been found in Syria, Hazor in Palestine, and at several sites in Egypt. Ethnic names were not used with great precision in ancient times, so specific members of a mixed group such as the Sea Peoples may not have been significant enough in other nations' annals to have warranted special mention, but were more significant in the small-scale history of Abraham's family.

By the time Israel left Egypt, the Philistines were already settled along the Palestinian coast (Ex. 13:17; 23:31). The Israelites did not encounter them during the conquest of Canaan but the Philistines were later used by God regularly to punish Israel (Jdg. 3:1ff.) which even adopted their gods on occasions (Jdg. 10:6f.). In Samson's time there were social links between the two peoples (Jdg. 13-16), but it was probably constant Philistine pressure (*e.g.* 1 Sa. 4) which prompted the Israelites to ask for a king. Saul drove them out of the hill country (1 Sa. 14), but they continued to assert themselves (1 Sa. 17-18). David, who hid from Saul among the Philistines (1 Sa. 27), had a Cherethite (Philistine) bodyguard when king, so he must have remained friendly with them until a final conflict in which he effectively ended the Philistine menace (2 Sa. 5:17ff.). They were occasionally troublesome during the divided monarchy, however (*e.g.* Is. 9:12).

PHINEHAS. A name of Egyptian origin. 1. Aaron's grandson who killed an Israelite and the Midianite woman he had wrongly taken (Nu. 25), assisted Joshua (Jos. 22:13ff.), and was a priest in the early Judges period (Jdg. 20:28). 2. The younger of Eli's two disreputable sons killed by the Philistines (1 Sa. 1-4).

PHOEBE (lit. 'radiant'). A deaconess and hospitable patron of many Christians including Paul, commended by him in Rom. 16:1f. She seems to have carried Paul's letter.

PHOENICIA, PHOENICIANS. The territory on the E Mediterranean coast (modern Lebanon to S Latakia) and its inhabitants. It was sometimes called by the Hebrews in OT times 'Canaan' (Is. 23:11), although it was general practice at all times to refer to it by its principal cities such as Tyre and Sidon, for there was usually little political cohesion between them. The history of the seafaring Phoenicians is obscure, although the ancient historian Herodotus said they came originally from the Persian Gulf area. They had settled along the E Mediterranean coast by the 18th cent. BC, choosing easily defensible natural harbours. They were under Egyptian domination until the arrival further down the coast of the Sea Peoples (PHILISTINES), when Tyre became the principal Phoenician port. David and Solomon had commercial links with Hiram king of Tyre (2 Sa. 5:11; 1 Ki. 5:1ff.); Hiram also loaned ships and navigators to the Judaean fleet (1 Ki. 9:26f.). Hiram's successor Ethbaal gave his daughter Jezebel as wife to Israel's Ahab (1 Ki. 16:31), and as a result the worship of Phoenician Baals in Israel increased (1 Ki. 18:19).

The Assyrians brought pressure on the Phoenician coast. Ashurnasirpal II (884-859 BC) received tribute-tax from Tyre, Sidon and other Phoenician cities, and by the middle of the next century these cities were under direct Assyrian supervision. In the 7th cent. BC, Phoenicia became an Assyrian province. It later recovered some autonomy during Babylonian and Persian times (cf. Ne. 13:16). Alexander the Great captured the island city of Tyre by building a causeway to it, but once again it recovered and in

NT times was with Sidon a prosperous place (cf. Mt. 15:21); the area's inhabitants were then called Syro-Phoenicians (Mk. 7:26). For the early Christians fleeing from persecution, Phoenicia became a refuge (Acts 11:19).

Elijah condemned Phoenician idolatry (1 Ki. 18-19), as did later prophets (Is. 65:11 refers to its cult practices). The polytheistic religion was centred on Baal, also called Melek. Fertility cults honoured Anat (Astarte). Phoenician art combined Semitic, Egyptian and Hurrian elements, introduced by the flow of trade. Phoenicia exported silk, linen and wool which was dyed, woven and embroidered locally. It also traded in timber from Lebanon; its craftsmen were skilled in stone, ivory, glass and precious metalwork. Trading needs led the Phoenicians to develop writing, the abacus for counting, and papyrus books. Unfortunately little of their literature and mythology has survived, yet it was probably through their writings that much of the learning of the E reached Greece.

See also SIDON; TYRE; WRITING.

PHOENIX. *Mythological bird:* Thought by the ancients to be born directly from its parent's corpse, it became a frequent symbol in Christian art because of its analogy to resurrection. *Place:* A harbour in Crete which Paul's ship made for (Acts 27:12). The coastline seems to have changed since then, but a disused bay is still called Phinika and the winter winds are N and E as in Acts 27.

PHRYGIA. A tract of land centred on the W watershed of the great Anatolian plateau. Most of Phrygia was incorporated into the Roman province of Asia in 116 BC, its E extremity (Phrygia Galatica) being included in the new province of Galatia in 25 BC. Christian churches in the area at Laodicea, Colossae, Hierapolis and Pisidian Antioch were in Greek, not native, communities. They were probably founded by people converted at Pentecost (Acts 2:10). Paul may have visited the area (Acts 16:6; 18:23), the names usually being taken, however, to mean Phrygia Galatia.

PHYLACTERIES. Standardized by the 2nd cent. AD, they consist of 2 black hollow cubes made from animal skins from 1.25 to 4 cm sq. One is fastened to the forehead, the other to the left hand, by leather straps, by Jewish men during morning prayers. In them are placed 4 OT passages (Ex. 13:1-10; 13:11-16; Dt. 6:4-9; 11:13-21), written by hand on parchment. They are not mentioned in the OT, and were quite unknown among the Samaritans. They were probably a late innovation brought in by the Hasidim (HASIDAEANS); the LXX treats the passages on which they are based as metaphorical (Ex. 13:9, 16; Dt. 6:8; 11:18). Even in NT times they were worn only by a minority of people, although always by the Pharisees (*cf.* Mt. 23:5). They are treated by Jews in a highly spiritual, but not necessarily superstitious, way.

PI-BESETH. Mentioned in Ezk. 30:17, the site of a temple to Ubastet, a lioness or cat goddess. The site is Tell Basta, on the Nile SE of Zagazig.

PIETY. The word is used rarely in modern EVV (*e.g.* Acts 3:12), and the word translated thus in AV is now usually rendered as 'godliness' (*e.g.* 2 Pet. 3:11) or 'religion' (*e.g.* 2 Tim. 3:5). It is a comprehensive term for the practice of personal Christian faith in worship and service of God and in reverent obedience to his laws. It is characterized by its two essential features, faith in Christ and practical love to Christians (1 Jn. 3:22ff.). It includes the practical expression of faith in a life of repentance, resisting temptation and overcoming sin; in habits of prayer, thanksgiving, and reverent observance of the Lord's Supper; in cultivating hope, love, generosity, joy, self-control, patient endurance and contentment; in the quest for honesty, uprightness and the good of others; in respect for divinely constituted authority in church, state, and family. See also GODLINESS.

PIG. The Israelites were not allowed to eat pig meat (Lv. 11:7; Dt. 14:8). There are 2 good hygienic reasons for that. As a scavenger, the pig was likely to pick up and transmit infection from diseased food, and it is host to the tapeworm which causes trichinosis. The pig stood for anything despicable and hated (*cf.* Pr. 11:22; Lk. 15:15), and was considered as of the same order as demons (*cf.* Mt. 8:30ff.).

PIGEON: See DOVE.

PIHAHIROTH. An unidentified place on the border of Egypt (Ex. 14:2ff.; Nu. 33:7f.).

PILATE. Pontius Pilate, the Roman procurator of Judaea who authorized the crucifixion of Jesus, belonged to the equestrian or upper middle class. Little is known of his career before AD 26 when he was appointed by the emperor Tiberius to be the 5th 'prefect' of Judaea, the title 'procurator' (or governor) being used later. He had full control of the province and the occupying army, and the power of enforcing or reprieving the death penalty. He also appointed the high priests and controlled the temple and its funds; he possessed the high priest's vestments and only released them for special festivals.

According to the Jewish historian Josephus he antagonized the Jews from the start by bringing (temporarily) Roman standards bearing the emperor's image into Jerusalem. He diverted temple funds to build an aqueduct, and the subsequent riot may have been connected with the reprisals reported in Lk. 13:1f. He later needlessly slaughtered a number of Samaritans, for which he was recalled to Rome for an enquiry c. AD 37, the outcome of which is unknown. The 1st-cent. writer Philo described him as rigid, harsh and spiteful, who used bribery, violence and brutality. The NT verdict is that he was a weak man ready to serve expediency rather than principle, allowing Jesus to be crucified not out of fear of the Jews but out of fear of imperial displeasure if news of more trouble in Judaea reached the ears of Tiberius; this is clear from his mockery of the Jews in the wording of the inscription on Jesus' cross (Jn. 19:19ff.).

PILGRIMAGE. The concept of pilgrimage as a journey of religious significance to a sacred spot, such as Abraham's visit to Mt Moriah (Gn. 22), is known from earliest times, although the Bible has no technical term for it. Journeys to the main religious feasts ('pilgrimage festivals') in Jerusalem were well established by NT times (*e.g.* Lk. 2:41ff.).

There is another sense, however, in which the term or idea is used in the Bible. Although in modern EVV the word pilgrimage occurs rarely (in Ps. 119:54 it means 'earthly existence'), the concept of dwelling temporarily or 'sojourning' in the world is common. In the NT the idea is expressed by describing God's people as 'exiles' travelling through the world (1 Pet. 1:1, 17; 2:11), living in time and space but having been chosen by God for eternal life and therefore being fundamentally different to non-believers.

For the technical use of 'sojourner', see FOREIGNER.

PILLAR (MONUMENTAL). Stones set up on end are found throughout the ancient world, and are often associated with a temple or shrine. In the OT, pillars were always set up primarily as memorials. Rachel's grave had one (Gn. 35:20); Jacob

435

erected them as memorials of his visions of God (Gn. 28:18ff.; 35:13ff.); the Israelites commemorated significant incidents with them, such as crossing the Jordan (Jos. 4:1ff.) and victory over the Philistines (1 Sa. 7:12). In Canaanite religion pillars were identified with local gods and were venerated, and Israel was commanded to destroy any they found (Ex. 23:24), for which see also ASHERAH. For structural pillars see BUILDING; JACHIN AND BOAZ.

PINNACLE. Part of the temple buildings (Mt. 4:5; 'highest point', NIV) mentioned in connection with Jesus' temptations. It may have been in the SE corner with a fearful drop to the Kidron Valley.

PIRATHON. Home of a judge (Jdg. 12:13ff.) and David's captain Benaiah (2 Sa. 23:30); modern Ferata 9 km WSW of Shechem.

PISGAH, ASHDOTH-PISGAH. Pisgah is a common noun denoting a ridge on a mountain or hill; 'The Pisgah' (*e.g.* Nu. 21:20) thus refers to any ridge on the plateau E of Jordan. Ashdoth-pisgah means 'the slopes of Pisgah' and could refer to the entire edge of the Moabite plateau (*e.g.* Dt. 3:17). From such a headland, probably Ras es Siyaghah, the lower 2nd N ridge of Mt Nebo, Moses viewed the promised land (Dt. 3:27).

PISIDIA. A highland area in Asia Minor at the W end of the Taurus mountains and the home of lawless tribes. The Seleucids founded Pisidian Antioch to control them. Paul's 'danger from robbers...in the wilderness (2 Cor. 11:26) may refer to this area. In the 2nd cent. AD the Roman Peace brought prosperity to Pisidia, with several strong churches.

PIT. A deep hole in the ground, natural or artificial, used for a variety of purposes. Artificial pits (or cisterns) for storing water (Is. 30:14) were often bulbous cavities with a narrow neck about the width of a man. Pits were also used for trapping animals (Is. 24:18). Metaphorically the pit is the underworld or place of the dead (Ps. 28:1), or the dire circumstances from which God rescues his people (Ps. 40:2). The bottomless pit in Rev. 9:1f. is a picture of hell. Ancient Hebrew laws legislated for accidents caused by people carelessly leaving pits uncovered (Ex. 21:33f.). See also ABYSS; CISTERN; HELL; POOL.

PITCH: See BITUMEN.

PITHOM (lit. 'mansion of the god Atum'). An Egyptian city where the Israelites were enslaved as building labourers (Ex. 1:11). It was probably in Wadi Tumilat, at Tell el-Maskhuta or Tell er-Retaba, close to Tjeku which may be the biblical Succoth (Ex. 12:37). Egyptian inscriptions tell of escape attempts by slaves from the area. See also EXODUS.

PLAGUES OF EGYPT. A series of 10 demonstrations of God's miraculous power to the Egyptian pharaoh as

Moses sought the release of the enslaved Israelites. The first 9 demonstrate God's use of the created order to achieve his ends. They have been shown to follow a logical and connected sequence beginning with an abnormally high flooding of the Nile in the usual flood months of July and August, the series of plagues ending the following March. The element of miracle is bound up with the timing, duration and intensity of the plagues; the 10th plague is wholly supernatural.

The first plague turned the Nile blood-red (Ex. 7:14ff.). The higher the Nile, the more earth it carries in suspension, especially fine red earth from the basins of the Blue Nile and Atbara. It could also bring down microcosms and bacteria which would further colour the water and kill the fish, creating a stench. *The second plague* was a sudden and unusual invasion of frogs (Ex. 8:1ff.), fleeing from the polluted banks and backwaters, but dying possibly from internal anthrax. The high water would favour an extra high breeding rate of gnats (mosquitoes) which formed *the third plague* (Ex. 8:16ff.), and which were followed by flies (*stomoxys calcitrans*) in *the fourth plague* (Ex. 8:20ff.).

The fifth plague afflicted cattle in the fields, possibly with the frog-borne anthrax which cattle in stalls would not contract (Ex. 9:1ff.). *The sixth plague* of boils (Ex. 9:8ff.) was probably skin anthrax transmitted through bites from the flies which bred in decaying vegetation; this would strike about December/January, and affected hands and feet especially (v. 11). *The seventh plague* of hailstorms fits the climate of Upper Egypt, but not the (spared) Goshen area, in early February (Ex. 9:13ff.). The high rains in Ethiopia and Sudan which had led to the exceptional flood provided favourable conditions for locust breeding, leading to dense swarms by March, *the eighth plague* (Ex. 10:1ff.). After the waters had subsided the red earth dried into fine dust and was whirled up by a *khamsin* wind to create a thick, dark dust cloud, *the ninth plague* (Ex. 10:21ff.); in the Wadi Tumilat, the Israelites would miss the worst of it. *The final plague* brought evidence of God's supreme control over the world, as the first-born males died. In later centuries, the plague phenomena were still to inspire awe among the Israelites (Ps. 78:43ff.). See also EXODUS.

PLAIN, CITIES OF THE. Chiefly Sodom, Gomorrah, Admah, Zeboiim and Bela or Zoar (Gn. 14:2). Scholars are divided over whether these were N of the Dead Sea, or now lie buried beneath the S tip of the Dead Sea, which once formed the S extension of the 'Circle (or Plain) of the Jordan' (*cf.* Dt. 34:3). It was an attractive area to Lot because of its extensive pasturage (Ex. 13:10), but it was to become desolate. The cities were probably destroyed by an earthquake accompanied by an explosion of gaseous deposits, which was seen as a judgment from God (*cf.* Dt. 29:23). Sodom became a byword for brazen sin (Is. 3:9), which Genesis highlights as sexual perversion (19:4f.; *cf.* Ezk. 16:49ff.). Lot's vicious offer of his daughters (v. 8) shows how far the spirit of the place had demoralized him.

PLANTS. Several problems relate to the identification of biblical plants. One is that botanical knowledge was not so comprehensive in ancient times as it is today. Another is that plants which exist in the area today may not have done so in biblical times. And a third is that translators disagree over the precise rendering of some words. Among the plants named or referred to in the Bible are the following.

Broom was a common shrub 2-4 m high with white pea flowers in spring; Elijah sheltered under one (1 Ki. 19:4f.). Its roots produce good charcoal which was used for incendiary arrows (Ps. 120:4) and for warmth (Jb. 30:4). The *castor-oil* plant may have sheltered Jonah (Jon. 4:6) and it withers quickly, but the *bottle-gourd* fits the description more accurately. Many species of *crocus* flower in winter in Palestine (Is. 35:1); the polyanthus narcissus may in fact be intended because the Hebrew original implies a truly bulbous plant. The present-day *hyssop* was not known in biblical times in Palestine. The plant so rendered (*e.g.* Ps. 51:7) was probably the Syrian marjoram, 20-30 cm high with white flowers and growing in rocky places. The hyssop used at Jesus' crucifixion (Jn. 19:29) was probably a reed or stick.

The *lily* of the Song of Songs is thought to have been the hyacinth; in Ho. 14:5 it is probably the yellow flag iris (the French 'fleur de lis'); and the lilies decorating the temple (1 Ki. 7:19) were probably carvings of water-lilies. The lilies of the field (Mt. 6:28) may have been poppy anemonies, white daisies or crown marguerites. *Mandrake,* a shrub of the nightshade family with mauve flowers in winter and yellow fruits in spring, was reputed to have emetic, purgative, narcotic and aphrodisiac properties (Gn. 30:14). *Mildew* was a common fungus attacking crops and regarded as God's punishment (Am. 4:9). The *mustard* used by Jesus to illustrate his teaching about the kingdom and faith (Mt. 13:31; 17:20) may have been black mustard, since its seeds were used for both culinary purposes and for oil in NT times.

Myrtle is a hillside shrub 2-3 m high with fragrant evergreen leaves and scented white flowers used as perfumes; it is used to symbolize God's generosity (*e.g.* Is. 55:13). *Nettles* in Jb. 30:7 are difficult to identify precisely; true nettles (a different word) are probably referred to in Is. 34:13; Hos. 9:6. The *pods* fed to pigs (Lk. 15:16) were the seed-pods of the carob tree, also called the locust bean. *Reed* is a general term for water-loving plants found in swamps and by river banks. In Ex. 2:3, 5 and Is. 19:6 it is the reed-mace, still common around the Nile (the Red Sea means literally 'the Sea of Reeds'); elsewhere the term is general. Reed stalks if leant on break erratically and can pierce the hand (*cf.* Is. 36:6). Reeds also served as measuring rods and gave their name to a 6 cubit measure (Ezk. 40:3-8).

The true *rose* is uncommon in Palestine, and the 'rose of Sharon' (Song 2:1) is difficult to identify. Anemone, narcissus, tulip and crocus have all been suggested. *Rushes* were woven into rope or used for fuel (Jb. 41:2, 20); the bowing rush of Is. 58:5 is more likely to be the *papyrus* plant which is easily bent by the wind and hangs down (for more detail on this see PAPYRI AND OSTRACA). Over 20 different words are used in the Bible to describe *thistles, thorns* and similar plants, making exact identification difficult. Generally, thorns symbolized fruitlessness (Gn. 3:18; Mt. 7:16) but when kept under control served as effective hedges against wild animals (Mt. 21:33). Thorns provided a popular quick-burning fuel (Ps. 58:9). In the parable of the sower, the 'thorns' (Mt. 13:7) were probably the rapid-growing milk thistle which infests field margins. The crown of thorns given to Jesus (Mt. 27:29) was plaited from some local material, perhaps the long thorny branches of the 'christ thorn' shrub, or the small spiny burnet (see also THORNS, CROWN OF).

The *vine of Sodom* in Dt. 32:32 may be a figurative expression; if not, it is a plant with a powdery substance under an attractive rind, probably the colocynth, a wild gourd which trails on sandy ground near the Dead Sea and has bitter, lightweight fruits (see below). *Weeds* were a scourge of useless, troublesome plants. Those in Jesus' parable (Mt. 13:24ff.) were probably darnel grass which in the leafy stage resembles wheat but if allowed to grow till harvest can be clearly distinguished by its small ear. If wheat grain is contaminated with its seeds, people who eat it can fall ill. The *wild gourds* (colocynth) of 2 Ki. 4:39 look like small melons but are a violent and possibly dangerous purge. Many species of *wormwood* grow in Palestine, all having a strong bitter taste and used in Scripture as a symbol of bitterness, sorrow and calamity (Am. 5:7).

See also CROPS; GRAIN; TREES.

PLASTER. Inner, and sometimes outer, walls were often coated with plaster made from clay (Lv. 14:42f.). A finer surface was obtained with plaster made from crushed limestone or gypsum, which could then be painted or inscribed (Dt. 27:2ff.).

POETRY. *Old Testament.* Poetry, especially in the form of song or hymn, has an important place in Hebrew literature. The Jews loved music, and were famous for it; in 701 BC King Hezekiah apparently included musicians in his tribute-tax to the Assyrian Sennacherib, and the Babylonians repeatedly asked the exiled Jews to sing to them (Ps. 137:3). The Hebrew language is rhythmic, even in passages which are not strictly poetry. Many prophetic oracles were given in poetic form, as modern translations show, as were the contents of the books of Proverbs, Ecclesiastes, Song of Songs and Job. The largest collection of poetry is of course the book of Psalms, although the long period over which the psalms were written and the lack of precise knowledge about early vocalization of the language makes it difficult to create a coherent theory of the Hebrews' poetic principles.

Certainly there was no metre as such, and the rhythm was variable. The best definition is perhaps that coined by Gerard Manley Hopkins: 'sprung rhythm' which 'consists in scanning by accents or stresses alone, without any account of the number of syllables'. So each 'beat' is provided by each unit of stress regardless of the syllables within it. A common feature of poetry was the use of 'parallelism', in which the second line of a couplet restates an idea which has been expressed in the first line. An example of 'synonymous parallelism' is: 'Deliver me from my enemies, O my God, protect me from those who rise up against me' (Ps. 59:1). But there are other kinds, for example 'antithetical parallelism': 'The Lord knows the way of the righteous, but the way of the wicked will perish' (Ps. 1:6).

Hebrew poetry makes use of many literary devices, including alliteration and assonance. But its genius lies chiefly in its imagery. It steals music from the morning stars; it rules the ragings of the sea. It drives on the clouds and rides on the wings of the wind. The bread of its harvest never wastes, its wine is forever new. The strings it touches belong to the harp of God. Its rhythm is that of the soaring spirit, felt only by him who has the music of heaven in his soul. Its great theme is the personal encounter with the living God.

New Testament. There are 4 typically Hebrew hymns in Luke's Gospel, for which see BENEDICTUS, GLORIA IN EXCELCIS, MAGNIFICAT, and NUNC DIMITTIS. There are early Christian hymns, possibly of mixed Hebrew and Greek traditions, in the NT letters, such as Eph. 5:14; 1 Tim. 3:16. The whole of the NT is full of quotations from OT poetry—parts of Hebrews and Romans consist almost entirely of such quotations. Paul quoted from Greek poets. In Acts 17:28 there seems to be a fragment from Aratus of Cilicia (315-240 BC); in Tit. 1:12 a quote from Epimenides of Crete; and in 1 Cor. 15:33 is an iambic trimeter of Menander (342-291 BC).

There is a considerable amount of poetic language in the NT, which may have been quotation or exalted prose. It is sometimes difficult to distinguish poetry and prose in Hebrews and passages such as Rev. 5:12-14, and there are strong parallelisms in passages such as Jn. 3:20f. and Phil. 3:3-10. There are examples of alliteration, as in Mt. 16:18 (Peter, *petros*; rock, *petra*). And the traditional imagery of Hebrew apocalyptic poetry or prophecy is used in Jesus' teaching about the end times (Mt. 24) and also in Revelation where sometimes the imagery is difficult to interpret simply because the original poetic allusion is now obscure.

See also MUSIC AND MUSICAL INSTRUMENTS.

POISON. Poisonous plants, such as hemlock (Ho. 10:4) and gourds (2 Ki.

4:39), existed in Palestine. So did poisonous reptiles, to whose bite the words of the wicked are likened (Ps. 140:3; *cf.* Jas. 3:8).

POLICE. There was no regular police force in ancient times. In Acts 16:35 the 'police' escorted the magistrates; they carried axes and bundles of rods as symbols of his power.

POMEGRANATE: See TREES.

PONTUS. The coastal strip of N Asia Minor, politically a complex of Greek republics, temple estates and Iranian baronies. The Romans were temporarily ejected in the 1st cent. BC but they reconquered it and administered it with Bithynia as a Roman province. The church was established by the time of 1 Pet. 1:1, but its origins are unknown.

POOL. Pools of water collected during winter and spring were an important source of supply in summer. Artificial pools were often dug inside walled cities, sometimes fed via a tunnel from a spring outside. See BETHESDA; CISTERN; SILOAM.

PORCH, PORTICO. In Solomon's palace, perhaps a suite of rooms (1 Ki. 7:6f.); in Jn. 5:2 the pool of Bethesda was surrounded by an arcade supported by pillars to give shelter.

POTIPHAR. A high officer of the Egyptian pharaoh, in whose household Joseph became chief steward (Gn. 39:1ff.).

POTIPHERA. The priest at On (Heliopolis), possibly of the sun-god Re, whose daughter Asenath became Joseph's wife (Gn. 41:45).

POTTER, POTTERY. Pottery first appeared in the ancient Near East *c.* 8000 BC, but the potter's wheel was not invented until *c.* 4000 BC. The potter sat on the edge of a small pit which housed the wheels which were usually two stones, one pivoted upon the other. In some arrangements, the upper stone was the surface on which he worked the clay, but it was sometimes a flywheel which he kicked with his feet to turn the working stone at the top of a short pole. The clay used for fine pots or slips was prepared by treading out coarser clay in water with the feet (Is. 41:25). Pebbles, shells, bone implements and also pottery fragments (shards) were used as tools to smooth, shape and decorate the pottery. The potter's work is described in Je. 18:3f.

The types of pottery found at archaeological sites are a valuable aid in dating the level of occupation being examined. There is an easily traceable the development of pottery through the entire biblical period. The earliest (Neolithic) pots were simple although of varying shapes, made from coarse clay tempered with chopped straw. The kaolin used in the Negeb gave pottery there a distinct cream colour. In the early and middle Bronze Ages (3150-1550 BC) spouted pots appeared, and single-handled pitchers. The oil lamp made its first appearance at this time, too. Jars and pitchers usually had small, rounded bases so that they could stand in indentations on uneven floors. In the late Bronze Age (1550-1200 BC) the combed decorations gave way to red and black geometric and animal decorations. The round 'pilgrim flask' was introduced, and two-handled Mycenaean jars were imported into Palestine. Early Iron Age (1200-1000 BC) pottery in Palestine adopted the 2-handled style for bowls and pots. During the Israelite monarchy (1000-800 BC) the standard and regularity of pottery improved. The finest dishes were very thin and decorated with bands of red slip. In late OT and inter-testamental times, narrow elongated flasks were often put into tombs. Coarse pottery of the Roman (NT) period has a ribbed appearance.

The biblical terms used for pottery items cannot be identified with certainty. Among them are a large spouted oil jar (2 Ki. 4:2); a pottery (or metal) disc for pancakes, and a cooking pot (Lv. 2:5, 7); a wine jar (Je. 48:12); a wash-basin (Jn. 13:5); and a large dish (Mt. 26:23).

See also BOX; CONTAINERS; CUP; FLESHPOTS; WASHBASIN.

POVERTY. Although the OT stresses that God blesses those who keep his commandments (Dt. 28:1ff.) and that the righteous are prospered with material possessions (Ps. 112:1ff.), there were numbers of poor people at every stage of Israel's history. Poverty could be caused by natural disasters, invasions by enemies, and through oppression by powerful neighbours. The wealthy were commanded to support the poor, especially the most vulnerable, orphans, widows, and people who owned no land (Dt. 15:1ff.; Am. 2:6f.). The psalmists sometimes struggled with the problem as to why wealth so often ended up in unworthy hands, concluding that true faith might be materially unprofitable but produced the true riches of knowing God (Ps. 73).

Jesus was born into a poor but not destitute family (Lk. 2:24). Some of his disciples were reasonably well off (Mk. 1:20) and he had some wealthy friends (Jn. 12:3), but he shared a common fund with the 12 (Jn. 12:6), going without many comforts (Lk. 9:58). He taught that riches were dangerous (but not evil in themselves), because it was easier for the poor to have an attitude of complete dependence on God (Lk. 6:20, 24). He encouraged hospitality (Lk. 14:12ff.) and giving charitable aid (Lk. 18:22). Paul raised money for poor Christians in Jerusalem (Gal. 2:10). In his letter, James vehemently condemned those who allowed distinctions between rich and poor in the church (Jas. 2:1ff.). Running the risk of poverty through generosity brings spiritual blessing (2 Cor. 8-9).

See also CHARITY; WEALTH.

POWER. True power, the ability to exercise authority effectively, belongs to God alone (Ps. 62:11), and is shown in creation (Ps. 148:5) and in his sustaining of the world (Ps. 65:5ff.). He delegates some of his authority to people (Gn. 1:26ff.; Ps. 8:5ff.) but also demonstrates his power in human affairs (Ex. 15:6). Jesus was given all authority (Mt. 28:18), and used it to forgive sins (Mt. 9:6) and cast out evil spirits (Mt. 10:1), ministering in the power of the Holy Spirit (Lk. 4:14). That same power was active in the life of the church (Acts 4:7, 33). Paul saw God's power displayed pre-eminently in the resurrection of Jesus (Eph. 1:19f.), a power which is available to strengthen the believer (Eph. 3:16). See also AUTHORITY.

POWER OF THE KEYS. A phrase used to describe the authority Jesus gave to his disciples in Mt. 16:19; 18:18; Jn. 20:22f. It operates in two ways. First, through preaching, the kingdom of God is opened to believers and shut to the impenitent. Secondly, by discipline, serious offenders are excluded from the church until they repent. The symbolism derives from the fact that a key was given to each Jewish scribe at his ordination (*cf.* Mt. 13:52; Lk. 11:52). If the church is truly filled with the Spirit of God, then it gives the actual judgment of God himself. 'Binding and loosing' is then more than an authoritative pronouncement of the conditions of entrance into the kingdom; it determines who have accepted the conditions. This power was given in a special sense to Peter. At Pentecost it was he who opened the door of faith to the Jews, and later to the Gentiles and Samaritans, but Mt. 18:18 and Jn. 20:23 make it clear that the same authority is given to all the apostles

and to men of like faith and spirit ever since. See also BINDING AND LOOSING; PETER.

PRAETORIUM. Originally the Roman army commander's tent, and then the army headquarters, the word came to mean a governor's residence (Mt. 27:27). In Phil. 1:13 Paul may refer to the emperor's residence if writing from Rome, or the detachment of guards stationed in Ephesus if writing from there.

PRAISE. The Bible is punctuated by outbursts of praise rising spontaneously from the joy which is characteristic of the life of God's people. God himself takes delight in his creation (Gn. 1; Ps. 104:31) and all creation expresses its joy in praise (Jb. 38:7). Mankind was created to rejoice in God's works (Ps. 90:14ff.) and in the Lord himself (Phil. 4:4). The coming of God's kingdom or rule is marked by the restoration of joy and praise (Ps. 96:11ff.; Lk. 2:13f.). Praise is the mark of God's people (Eph. 1:3ff.) and the refusal to render it is the mark of the ungodly (Rom. 1:21). It is a duty and is not dependent upon mood, feeling or circumstance (*cf.* Jb. 1:21). Worship in the temple included 'glad shouts and songs' (Ps. 42:4) and dancing (Ps. 149:3) accompanied by a variety of musical instruments (Ps. 150).

New forms of praise expressed the early Christians' faith (*cf.* Mk. 2:22) although they continued to attend the temple (Acts 3:1). People healed or forgiven by Jesus broke out into spontaneous praise (Mk. 2:12). The church used the old Psalms but also new Christian hymns (Col. 3:16); Phil. 2:6-11 may have been a hymn of praise, and the doxologies of Rev. 1:4ff.; 5:9ff.; 15:3f. must have been used in public worship. Praise and sacrifice are closely connected in the OT (e.g. Dt. 26:10f.); in the NT the self-offering of the Christian to God is part of praise (Rom. 12:1; cf. Heb. 13:15), and prayer always includes praise (Phil. 4:6).

PRAYER. Communion with God is the highest activity of which people are capable. The biblical doctrine of prayer, however, emphasizes God's character and the necessity of being in a right covenant relationship with him (Jn. 4:24), and that God does not therefore automatically 'hear' every prayer (Is. 1:15).

Old Testament. In patriarchal times prayer was often described as 'calling on the name of the Lord' (Gn. 12:8). There was a directness and familiarity in prayer (Gn. 15:2ff.), and it was associated with sacrifice (Gn. 26:25). From the time of Moses to the Monarchy, one of the main prayer emphases was on intercession (Moses, Ex. 32:11ff.; Samuel, 1 Sa. 7:5ff.; Solomon, 1 Ki. 8:22ff.; Hezekiah, 2 Ki. 19:14ff.). Throughout the Bible, prayer was often effective (Gn. 19:17ff.), but not always (Ex. 32:30ff.); Jeremiah was even forbidden to pray for the rebellious people (Je. 7:16). Indeed, prayer must have been a vital part of the prophets' ministry. Through prayer they received God's

word (Dn. 9:20ff.; cf. Is. 6:5ff.), sometimes after having had to wait a long time (Hab. 2:1ff.). For Jeremiah at least, it was an agonizing experience (20:7ff.) as well as an intimate communion with God (15:15ff.). Among the Psalms are prayers for forgiveness (51), protection (59), healing (22; 61) and vindication (109).

The centrality of Israel's religion disappeared at the time of the exile, when the temple was destroyed. Prayer became an important religious obligation and remained so when the temple was rebuilt. Ezra and Nehemiah emphasized the spiritual factor in devotion (Ezr. 8:22f.; Ne. 4:4, 9). There do not seem to have been fixed rules concerning the posture for prayer (lifting hands, Ps. 28:2; standing, 1 Sa. 1:26; kneeling, 1 Ki. 8:54; bowing, 1 Ki. 18:42). There were stated hours for prayer (Dn. 6:10) but it was considered effective at any time. Mechanical, repetitious prayers did not become common until shortly before the NT period, when saying them was considered to be one of the acts which merited God's favour.

New Testament. Jesus encouraged persistence in prayer (Lk. 11:5ff.) built on confidence in a generous heavenly Father (Mt. 7:7ff.). Prayer must be humble and penitent (Lk. 18:10ff.), simple (Mt. 6:5f.), forgiving (Mt. 18:21ff.), and expectant (Mk. 11:24). Prayer which is an experiment will achieve little; prayer which is faith surrendering to God's will achieves much (Mk. 9:23). Jesus had little to say about the specific content of prayer (Mt. 6:11, 13), but he did teach two important things about the method of prayer. Prayer is to be offered to him always (as it was when he lived on earth, *cf.* Mt. 8:2; 9:18). It is also to be offered 'in his name' (Jn. 14:13), for through him we have access to the Father. To pray in his name is to pray as he prayed and to pray to the Father as Jesus made him known. Jesus himself prayed secretly (Lk. 5:15f.), and especially at times of spiritual conflict (Jn. 12:20ff.). In his prayers he offered thanks (Lk. 10:21), sought guidance (Lk. 6:12ff.), interceded (Jn. 17:6ff.), and had fellowship with God (Lk. 9:28ff.).

The early church was born in an atmosphere of prayer (Acts 1:4) through which the Holy Spirit was poured out (Acts 2:4; 4:31). Church leaders were clearly people of prayer (Acts 10:9; 16:25). Paul's letters reveal the Holy Spirit as an assistant in prayer (Rom. 8:14, 26) and as a gift from him (1 Cor. 14:14ff.; *cf.* Eph. 6:18). Prayer, Paul wrote, is vital (Rom. 12:12), and part of the Christian's 'armour' against evil (Eph. 6:13ff.). He often broke out into prayer in his letters; *e.g.* Rom. 1:8ff. is full of thanks to God and intercession for his friends. In Eph. 1:15ff. and 3:14ff. he prays that his readers will receive deeper spiritual insight, resulting in greater love for Christ and perfection of character.

See also LORD'S PRAYER.

PRAYER OF MANASSEH: See APOCRYPHA.

PREACHING. In the NT, this is the public proclamation of the Christian gospel to non-Christians, and not what it tends to mean today, the teaching and exhortation of those who already believe. The most common NT word for preaching means 'to proclaim as a herald', and in the ancient world the herald was someone of importance. A second word means 'to bring good news', and from it comes the English 'evangelize'. The teaching of believers is usually described by another word and distinguished from preaching (*e.g.* Mt. 4:23); preaching proclaims what God has done in Christ and teaching draws out the implications for Christian conduct.

A prominent feature of NT preaching is the sense of divine compulsion; through it God himself breaks into human affairs (*e.g.* Acts 4:20; 1 Cor. 9:16). Another feature is its clarity and simplicity, not obscured by eloquent wisdom and high-sounding words (1 Cor. 1:17; 2:2ff.). The radical upheaval in a person's heart and conscience is created by the Spirit of God working through the straightforward presentation of the message. The basic content of Jesus' message was that God's rule or kingdom had now invaded the realm of evil powers and was winning a decisive victory, fulfilling OT predictions (Lk. 4:16ff.). The basic content of the apostles' preaching was Jesus Christ crucified, risen and exalted (1 Cor. 1:23; 15:12; 2 Cor. 4:5). These decisive acts of God, which brought his 'kingdom' into human history, confronted people with the necessity of repentance and offered them forgiveness of sins. Preaching is best understood as the way in which God reveals himself, a timeless link between God's redemptive act and man's acceptance of it.

PREDESTINATION. The Bible conceives of God's purposes for people being expressed both by his commands to them (which they can obey or disobey) and by his direct ordering of their circumstances. The words translated 'destine', 'predestine', 'prepare beforehand', 'foreknow' and similar expressions refer to God's plan of events, and especially to his plans for the circumstances and destinies of people; the wider aspects of his cosmic plans and government are referred to under the general theme of PROVIDENCE.

Old Testament. The OT lacks words for predestination in a general sense but it often speaks of God purposing or planning specific things. God the Creator has unlimited power, so his purposes are certain to be fulfilled (Is. 43:13). He directs everything towards the purpose for which he made it and determines every detail of life (Pr. 16:4, 33). The idea that mankind's organized opposition could in any way thwart his purposes is absurd (Ps. 2:1ff.). Indeed, nothing can prevent the occurrence of events he has predicted (Is. 14:24ff.). On the occasions when God apparently changes his mind (*e.g.* Je. 18:8) the context makes clear that the point is to emphasize God's truly personal nature, and not to throw doubt on his control of human affairs. The OT also makes clear that God governs human history to bring about his own purposes for

human welfare (*e.g.* Gn. 12:3; Is. 9:1ff.; Dn. 7). In this context Israel is chosen by God to be his covenant people and to be a blessing to other nations (Ps. 67), even though they did not merit such choice (Dt. 7:6f.).

New Testament. NT writers take for granted the OT faith that God is the sovereign Lord of events and history. Hence Jesus' ministry fulfilled prophecies made centuries before (*e.g.* Mt. 1:22f.; Gal. 3:8). The idea of God's election or calling of people is applied not to the nation of Israel but to individual Christians (Eph. 1:4); God's saving grace given to people (which includes their knowledge of, response to, and preservation in the gospel) flows from divine election in eternity. In Acts, responses to the apostles' preaching are consistently regarded as the fruits of God's prior grace (*e.g.* 2:47; 11:18). In John's Gospel, Jesus says that he has come to save particular individuals whom the Father has 'given' him (Jn. 6:37ff.), to whom he in turn gives assurance of eternal life (6:39f.; 10:28).

Paul elucidates this most fully. God had a plan from all eternity to save a church (Eph. 3:3ff.), and believers may rejoice that as part of that plan God predestinated them personally to share in it (Rom. 8:28ff.). They were not chosen through their own merit (2 Tim. 1:9); the calling itself elicits the response of faith (Rom. 8:28ff.) and is not given on the basis of God's foresight of a favourable response. The doctrine is used by Paul to reassure believers of their eternal destiny and to emphasize their debt to

God's mercy. Regarding those who do not respond to God, Rom. 9:19ff. seems to imply that their hardening attitude is itself part of the predestinating purpose. However, Paul's stress in the context is more on God's long restraint of his wrath against people who are ripe for it.

See also ELECTION; REPROBATE.

PREPARATION. A day preceding the weekly sabbath and the annual Passover festival (*e.g.* Mt. 27:62), on which people got ready for it physically and spiritually.

PRESBYTER: See ELDER.

PRIDE. The biblical emphasis on pride—and its opposite, humility—is unparalleled in other religious or ethical systems. Rebellious pride which refuses to depend on and submit to God is the root and essence of sin. It was revealed in the devil's attempt to become independent of God (Is. 14:12ff.; Lk. 10:18), and he instilled it into Adam and Eve (Gn. 3:5). Pride remains the devil's chief means for ensnaring people (1 Tim. 3:6). Hence human arrogance is shown to be hateful to God (*e.g.* Pr. 8:13). It was denounced by the prophets (Je. 13:9).

By contrast, Greek teaching at the end of the OT period regarded pride as a virtue and humility as a failing, although insolence was a source of moral evil in Greek tragedies. The NT ethic consciously reverted to the OT emphasis. Jesus himself was filled with humility (Mt. 11:29), and pride was one of the defilements issuing from the human heart (Mk. 7:22). God favours the meek and resists the proud (Jas. 4:6; 1 Pet. 5:5, quoting Pr. 3:34). Arrogance and ostentation are thus to be avoided by Christians (Jas. 4:16; 1 Jn. 2:16). Paul insisted that pride was the chief cause of unbelief among the Jews, for his gospel ruled out self-righteousness; salvation is not of works 'lest any man should boast' (Eph. 2:9; *cf.* Rom. 3:27; 9:30-10:4; 1 Cor. 1:20ff.).

See also HUMILITY.

PRIESTS AND LEVITES (OLD TESTAMENT). The relationship between the priests who are descendants of Aaron, and the Levites who are the other members of the same tribe of Levi, is one of the thorny problems of OT religion.

Biblical data. In the Pentateuch (Gn.-Dt.) the Levites had an important role in constructing the tabernacle (Ex. 38:21) and transporting and erecting it (Nu. 1:47ff.). They were forbidden to serve as priests, for this was reserved only for Aaron's descendants, but they were dedicated to an auxiliary ministry for the priests (Nu. 3:5ff.). They were representatives of, or substituted for, the first-born of all the other tribes to whom God was entitled (Nu. 3:40ff.; *cf.* Ex. 13:13). Each of the 3 Levite families had special responsibilities. The descendants of Kohath carried the tabernacle furniture (Nu. 3:29ff.); those of Gershon looked after the coverings, screens and hangings (Nu. 3:21ff.); and those of Merari carried and erected the tabernacle framework (Nu. 3:35ff.). They were, together, 'gifts' of Israel to serve the priests (Lv. 8:11f.). Their service began at 25 years of age; at 50 years of age they went into semi-retirement (Nu. 8:24ff.). The Levites had no exclusive right to a portion of the promised land but were supported by the tithes of the people (Nu. 18:23f.); the priests then received a tithe of the levitical tithe and parts of the sacrificial offerings (Nu. 18:8ff.). 35 cities throughout the land were set aside for the Levites (Nu. 35:1ff.). In Deuteromony 'Levitical priests' is used (*e.g.* 18:1); while some scholars have suggested that this implies no distinction between priests and Levites, it is quite possible that it means 'priests of the tribe of Levi'; the distinction seems to be maintained in the different portions given to each (Dt. 18:3ff.).

The priests were more prominent than Levites in Jos., having the crucial task of carrying the ark of the covenant. The distinction between them is maintained (*e.g.* Jos. 21:1ff.). In Jdg. Micah's Levite is said to be from Judah, implying either a geographical location or that people of other tribes could become Levites (Jdg. 17-18); the latter may have been the case with Samuel, who was of the tribe of Ephraim (1 Sa. 1:1). There was considerable religious laxity at the time, with numerous shrines paying scant heed to the laws of Moses (*cf.* Jdg. 18:31).

The books of Chronicles amplify the role of the Levites. Their close co-operation with the priests in caring for some of the holy containers and the 'bread of the presence' (1 Ch. 9:28ff.) may indicate that the rigid division suggested earlier had broken down during the times of the kings. David's orders in 1 Ch. 23 show that substantial changes took place because the permanent location of the ark of the covenant in Jerusalem made obsolete the Levites' role as porters, and because the king took on responsibility for official religion.

The role of Levites after the Exile is briefly alluded to by Isaiah, Jeremiah and Ezekiel. The latter forces a sharp cleavage between the levitical priests (sons of Zadok) who kept faithful to God, and the Levites who had gone after idols (44:10ff.). Ezekiel appears to be suggesting a return to the original distinction found in Nu. Many priests but relatively few Levites returned to Jerusalem after the Exile (Ezr. 2:36ff.), perhaps because many Levites had taken on priestly status. Levites played a full part in the restoration of the temple (Ezr. 3:8ff.; 6:16ff.), repairing the city wall (Ne. 3:17) and instructing the people (Ne. 8:7ff.). During Nehemiah's absence from Jerusalem Tobiah the Ammonite took over the storeroom for levitical offerings and the Levites had to flee to the fields in order to get food (Ne. 13:4ff.). The high priesthood remained in the family of Eleazar, Aaron's 3rd son, until the time of Eli, who was descended from Ithamar, Aaron's 4th son. It was restored to Eleazer's family again from Solomon's time when Zadok became high priest until *c.* 174 BC when it became the patronage of the ruling power.

Wellhausen's reconstruction. The development in the 19th cent. of the documentary hypothesis for the formulation of the Pentateuch, and its emphasis on a post-exilic date for the 'priestly code', led to a drastic re-evaluation of the development of the religion of Israel. Wellhausen especially believed that Ezekiel reduced the Levites to temple slaves even though they had previously carried out priestly functions (Ezk. 44:6ff.). Ezekiel exempted the sons of Zadok because they had been faithful and also because they officiated at the central sanctuary at Jerusalem. The Aaronic priesthood was reckoned by Wellhausen to be a fiction to give priesthood a respectable anchor in the days of Moses, and so the priest-Levite distinction was introduced into the 'priestly code' of OT documents to bolster the position of the Jerusalem priests over all others.

However, it has already been seen above that the distinction between priests and Levites is clear in Dt., which is not part of the 'priestly code', and Wellhausen's theories have been strongly challenged on this and other details. Ezekiel's intention was clearly to re-establish old custom, and in any case the priests in the priestly code are sons of Aaron, not as in Ezekiel the sons of Zadok. The Levites could not have developed as a distinct class in the short time Wellhausen allows, especially on foreign soil. W. F. Albright has pointed out that Israel would have been unique among its neighbours if it had not had a leading or high priest and the lack of emphasis

on this office in the monarchy represents a decline from earlier practice. Levites, he suggests, may have been promoted to priests. Therefore while it is hazardous to assume that the legislation of the Pentateuch was fully carried out, it is even more tenuous to argue that because laws were not enforced they did not exist, as Wellhausen suggested. See also PENTATEUCH.

PRIESTS, PRIESTHOOD (NEW TESTAMENT). All NT references to priests assume an historical and religious continuity with the OT. Their functions therefore are not explained (*e.g.* Lk. 1:5; 10:31), and they are accepted as lawful by Jesus (*e.g.* Mt. 8:4). The only exception to this usage is the reference to the pagan priest of Zeus in Acts 14:13.

However, a majority of references to priests, and especially chief (or high) priests, are in a context of conflict. Their opposition to Jesus mounted as his claims and mission became clearer, such as his challenge to sabbath legislation (Mt. 12:1ff.) and also his parables which censured religious leaders (*e.g.* Mt. 21:45f.). The conflict intensified after the Palm Sunday procession and subsequent cleansing of the temple (Mt. 21) and reached its climax in his arrest and trial (Mt. 26-27). The plural 'chief priests' describes members of the high-priestly family and ruling and former high priests. The conflict continued in the early church (Acts 4:1; 5:17), with high-priestly authority behind the persecution organized by Paul before

449

his conversion (Acts 9:1f., 14).

At the root of this conflict lay the Christian conviction and Jewish suspicion that the life, death, resurrection and ascension of Jesus spelt the end of the old priestly structures (*cf.* Mt. 12:6; Mk. 10:45; Jn. 2:19). The author of Hebrews gives this concept its greatest NT expression. Jesus is portrayed as the new and true high priest who alone can take away sin (5:5ff.), his priesthood attaining the perfection the old one failed to reach (ch. 7), and continuing for all eternity (ch. 8). Hence all Christians, not just a priestly order, have full and regular access to God (10:11ff.).

As the body of Christ and the 'new Israel', the church is anointed to a priesthood within the world (Rev. 1:6). It is a mediatorial service which declares the will of God to people, brings their needs before God in prayer, and worships him obediently (1 Pet. 2:5, 9). Ultimately God's people will share Jesus' victory over the world and demonstrate his loving sovereignty in it (Rev. 5:10). But it is a corporate priesthood; no individual leader or minister is called a priest in the NT. The post-apostolic writings quickly moved in that direction, however, and Hippolytus and Tertullian (*c.* AD 200) seem to have pioneered the use of the titles 'priest' and 'high priest' for Christian ministers. See also MINISTRY.

PRINCE. A variety of biblical words are thus translated in EVV, but they usually have a wider meaning than 'member of a royal family'. For example, in Ezk. 37:24f. it refers to the Messiah, in Dn. 10:13, 21 to the guardian angels of countries. See also SATRAP.

PRISON. Several incidents of imprisonment are recorded in the Bible. Joseph was probably held in a fortress (Gn. 39:20ff.). Egyptian prisons served as forced-labour compounds, 'lock-ups' and remand centres. Samson was held in what is literally called 'the house of the prisoners' (Jdg. 16:21, 25). Jeremiah was held in the palace guards' rooms (32:2, 8), and also in a water storage cistern (37:16; 38:6). Hanani the prophet was held in stocks (2 Ch. 16:10). King Jehoiachin of Judah was under house arrest in the Babylonian palace complex according to contemporary documents; Ezekiel portrays him as being transported in a cage (19:9), something not unknown from other sources.

In the NT, John the Baptist was put in prison and according to the Jewish historian Josephus was held at Fort Machaerus E of the Dead Sea, where 2 dungeons have been discovered, one of them still showing traces of fetters. The apostles were held in what is literally 'a public place of watching' (Acts 5:18). Peter was probably held in Fort Antonia in Jerusalem (Acts 12:3ff.), where Paul was also imprisoned later (Acts 21:34; 23:30). At Philippi Paul seems to have been in an inner, perhaps underground chamber containing stocks (Acts 16:24), but in Rome he was under house arrest with a soldier always chained to him (Acts

28:16, 30).

See also CRIME AND PUNISH-MENT.

PROCONSUL. The governor of a Roman province administered by the Senate because it did not require a standing army; *e.g.* Sergius Paulus in Cyprus *c.* AD 47 (Acts 13:7).

PROCURATOR. The title of both a Roman province's financial officer and also of a governor of a Roman province of the third class, such as Judaea which was governed by procurators (or prefects) AD 6-41, 44-66. Among them was Pontius PILATE (AD 26-36, Mt. 27:2). They were generally responsible for military and financial administration but were subject to the imperial legate of Syria.

PROMISE. There is no special term in the OT for promising; where EVV use the word they translate a Hebrew statement that someone spoke a word with some future reference. A promise may be assurance of continuing action ('I will be with you') or the announcement of a future event. What God says, he can and will achieve (Is. 55:10f.), and he commands the future (Is. 41:26). All the OT promises of God are confirmed in Christ (2 Cor. 1:20), and NT writers rejoice that God has kept his promise (*e.g.* Lk. 1:68ff.). Waiting for the promised return of Christ (2 Pet. 3:4ff.) the church sets out on its missionary task with the assurance of his presence (Mt. 28:20) and bearing the news that all who believe in him shall become 'children

of the promise' (Gal. 3; Rom. 4; 9). See also COVENANT; OATHS; PRO-PHECY; WORD.

PROMISED LAND. The term refers to promises to Abraham that his descendants would be God's special people and that they would live in Canaan (Gn. 12:2, 5, 7). All the earth belongs to the Creator God (Ps. 95:4ff.), and he gave a specific part of it to Israel (Dt. 26:5ff.). It was not Israel's to do what she liked with, however; it remained God's and Israel was denounced by prophets for defiling it (*e.g.* Je. 2:7). Jeremiah also saw that Israel's identity and worship did not depend on the land (Je. 29:4ff.). In the NT, the writers recognized that the true or new Israel, the Christian church, is not limited to a specific land for its identity and worship. Today there is growing scholarly interest in the role of the land in biblical prophecy and whether this has any relationship to political Zionism and the restoration of the Jews to Israel. See also ISRAEL; JUDAISM; PALESTINE.

PROPHECY, PROPHETS.

1. Old Testament.

The office of prophet. Moses constituted a standard of comparison for all future prophets (Dt. 18:15ff.). He was specifically and personally called by God (Ex. 3:1-4:17; *cf.* Is. 6; Je. 1:4ff.; Am. 7:14f.). Only the false prophet took the office upon himself (Je. 14:14). The prophet thus stood before people as one who had stood before God (1 Ki. 17:1). Through the prophet,

451

history became revelation because there was added to the situation a man who was prepared beforehand to say what it meant (as Moses did at the Exodus), something the pagan gods could never inspire (cf. Is. 45:20ff.). The prophets were concerned with the whole of life, with social ethics as well as with personal piety. Moses outlined the most philanthropic law code known to the ancient world, concerned for the helpless (Dt. 24:19ff.) and opposed to the oppressor (Lv. 19:9ff.). Like Moses, many prophets played an active statesman's role in national affairs; like him they used symbols (Nu. 21:8) as well as words to convey their message; and like him they found intercessory prayer was a vital ingredient of their ministry (Nu. 27:5).

The titles of prophets. They were frequently called men of God (Dt. 33:1; 1 Sa. 9:6), and God himself sometimes addressed them as his servants (2 Ki. 17:13). The main OT word for prophet means either 'one who is called' or 'one who calls'; the exact meaning is uncertain but both suit the nature of OT prophets. Two other words are sometimes translated 'seer' (1 Ch. 29:29) as well as 'prophet'. The OT usage seems to indicate that the words are synonymous and do not refer to different kinds of prophets.

Foretelling and forthtelling. The prophets were primarily concerned with bringing God's word to the people. They were convinced that the words they spoke were not merely God's opinion but that their proclamation itself radically changed the whole

situation: God had intervened and spoken decisively through them. Almost every prophet appears on the biblical stage first as a foreteller of future events (e.g. Am. 1:2). The vision of the wrath to come is made the basis of a call to repentance, the vision of future bliss is made the basis of a call to continued faithfulness. This made the prophets quite different from the pagan fortune-tellers, whom Israel was warned to avoid like the plague (Dt. 18:9ff.). But some prophets clearly had extraordinary telepathic and clairvoyant gifts. Elisha, for example, knew what was being said at a distance (2 Ki. 6:12). There is no real reason to question their ability to foretell personal names far into the future (1 Ki. 13:2); for all they knew the event might happen the next day, but it was still predictive prophecy.

Inspiration of prophets. In most cases the way in which the prophet received his message from God is described in tantalizingly vague ways: 'the word of the Lord came…'. It is a statement of a direct, personal awareness; in the context of close fellowship God gives the prophet his words (Je. 1:9). Dreams and visions had some place in prophetic inspiration although not every dream (or fanciful hope) was of the Lord (cf. Je. 31:26 with 23:28). But even so, this still tells us nothing about the mechanics involved in the miracle of inspiration. There are 18 OT references to the work of the Holy Spirit in inspiring prophets (e.g. 1 Ch. 12:18; Mi. 3:8), although these are spread unevenly across the OT time-span. This may have been because some prophets such as Jeremiah (who never mentions the Spirit) took this aspect of God's creative work through him as read. Some OT prophets experienced more overpowering 'spirit-possession' (*e.g.* 1 Sa. 10:6, 10, and see also 'prophets and Israel's religion' below).

Methods of communication. Each prophet spoke his message or oracle in a way unique to his own personality, so while the words are God's, they are also those of a particular man. That does not thereby render them less infallible; they certainly believed with absolute conviction that God was speaking through them. On some occasions the word was visual rather than oral, such as the symbolic actions of Elisha (2 Ki. 13:14), Isaiah (Is. 20), Jeremiah (Je. 19), and Ezekiel (Ezk. 12).

The prophetic writings. Each of the prophetic books in the OT must contain only a selection of the prophet's words, and several of them show signs of having been edited. For example, the Judaean references in Hosea may have been added after the fall of Samaria when the prophet's oracles were carried S; in Isaiah chs. 38-39 have been taken out of chronological sequence to provide an introduction to chs. 40-55. The prophets certainly wrote some of their oracles (*e.g.* Je. 29:1ff.), and in Jeremiah's case at least a lengthy statement of his prophecies was made by a secretary (Je. 36). Also a prophet sometimes was associated with a group he presumably taught and who retained his words (Is. 8:16); the book of Isaiah could have been a manual of instruction for the prophet's disciples. Groups (or 'sons') of prophets seem to have worked under the general supervision of a senior prophet (2 Ki. 2:3ff.; 4:38; 9:1ff.). In Am. 7:14, Amos is probably asserting the authenticity of his call against the accusation of lacking official status, rather than casting a slur on prophetic groups to whom we may owe some OT books.

True and false prophets. The distinction was important: the biblical prophets themselves faced challenges from false prophets (*e.g.* Je. 28) and it must have been difficult for observers to judge between them. Some have suggested that prophetic 'ecstasy' was a sign of false prophets, since it was a feature of Baalism, but it was a feature of some true prophets also (1 Sa. 9-10). Similarly, the 'professional' prophets cannot automatically be branded as false, since Samuel was one such, and Nathan was almost certainly a court official. There are 4 OT discussions about the issue. In Dt. 18 there is a negative test; if a prophesied event does not happen, then the prophet is false. (But it is not sufficient to say that fulfilment is proof of authenticity; false prophets can get it right too, Dt. 13:1ff.). In Dt. 13, the standard is a theological one: a prophet must be regarded as false if he leads people to other gods or challenges the law of God given through Moses.

Jeremiah gives a similar answer. In 23:9ff. he can find no external tests such as 'ecstasy', professional status, or techniques employed. Instead, he says the false prophet leads towards immorality and promises peace without requiring obedience, the true one points towards holiness and speaks of God's judgment on sin which must be accounted for before peace is possible. Ultimately Jeremiah knows that he is right only because like Moses he has stood before God (23:18, 21f.; *cf.* Nu. 12:6ff.). Ezekiel (12:21-14:11) also says that false prophets are guided by their own wisdom, not God's, and offer only shallow optimism devoid of moral content.

Prophets and Israel's religion. Some cult officials also acted as prophets. For example, a Levite was inspired by the Spirit of God to bring a prophetic message at a time of national anxiety (2 Ch. 20:14). In some of the Psalms a prophetic voice seems to break out, probably that of the prophet associated with the cult (*e.g.* 60; 75; 82). Possibly the guilds of levitical singers after the Exile were the survivors of groups of cultic prophets attached to the sanctuaries. Prophetic guilds are referred to in, for example, 1 Sa. 10:5; prophets are associated with temple singers in 2 Ch. 29:25; prophets and priests are often coupled together in a way that suggests professional association (*e.g.* 2 Ki. 23:2). However, the existence of an official cult of prophets remains a theory.

On occasions, the prophets were outspoken opponents of Israelite religion. Amos says that God spurns current cultic practice, but makes it clear that the reason is not the practice itself which is abhorrent to God, but the lack of moral concern and holy living on the part of those who bring sacrifices and join in the rituals (Am. 5:21ff.). Isaiah too brings strong condemnation of sacrifices, the sabbath and even prayer (ch. 1), but with the intention of showing that it is all useless in the context of a blatantly sinful life (v. 15). Indeed, Isaiah himself experienced his great vision of God and renewal of life in the context of a cultic setting (Is. 6). In Je. 7:22 the prophet appears to deny that God ever commanded sacrifices ('I did not just give them commands about sacrifices' NIV) but the word translated 'about' is more accurately rendered 'because of' or 'for the sake of'. In other words, sacrifices do not force God to act or speak, nor does he stand in need of them. The cult does not exist in its own right but for the sake of the spiritual needs of the people who are committed to obeying God's moral law. The prophet's task throughout OT times was to call people to obedience; the priest reminded them of the efficacy of blood shed for the forgiveness of their sins. Beginning with Moses who was both prophet and priest, the close unity of the two offices in Israel's religion continued throughout its history. It found its fulfilment in Jesus Christ who like Moses combined in his own person both offices, as Prophet to reveal God's new covenant, and as Priest to make the ultimate sacrifice by which that covenant was established.

2. New Testament.

Continuity with the OT. The OT prophetic line ended with John the Baptist (Mt. 11:13). There were prophetic utterances at the births of both John and Jesus (Lk. 1:46ff., 67-79). Frequently the Gospel writers see the ministry of Jesus as fulfilling the message of the OT prophets (*e.g.* Mt. 1:22f.; 26:56; Lk. 24:25ff.). He himself said he came to fulfil the law and prophets (Mt. 5:17); he pointed back to them as having brought a permanent revelation of God which was itself sufficient to lead people to repentance (Lk. 16:29ff.). He used and accepted the title of prophet for himself (Mt. 13:57; Lk. 13:33), and the apostles ultimately recognized him as the great promised prophet like Moses (Acts 3:22ff.). But he was also a perfect teacher, the Son of God who had sent the prophets (Mt. 23:34, 37), and the Word of God made flesh (Jn. 1:1ff.).

Prophecy in the church. Jesus made clear that among the tasks of the promised Holy Spirit there was prophetic inspiration (Mt. 10:19f.; Jn. 16:12ff.). The first preachers spoke in the power of the Spirit just as the OT prophets had (1 Pet. 1:10ff.). This Spirit makes every Christian a potential prophet, for 'the testimony of Jesus is the Spirit of prophecy' (1 Cor. 14:1, 31; Rev. 19:10). Prophecy is repeatedly included among the gifts of the Spirit (Rom. 12:6; 1 Cor. 12:10; 1 Thes. 5:19f.; 1 Pet. 4:10f.). It is different from teaching in that it is an utterance immediately inspired by direct revelation from the Holy Spirit, although it may of course reiterate scriptural truths.

Paul gives full guidance on the use of the gift in 1 Cor. 14. The gift was open to all, under the sovereign distribution of the Holy Spirit. It was an intelligible word of revelation from God for upbuilding and encouragement. It was not to be abused by people falling into uncontrolled frenzy, nor was it to be exercised without being checked by elders and other prophets, for the existence of false prophets and prophecy was recognized (*cf.* Mt. 7:15; Acts 13:5ff.; 1 Jn. 4:1ff.). False prophets might even work miracles but must not be believed on account of them (Mk. 13:22; *cf.* Mt. 7:22). True prophets will be known by their holiness, conformity to the teachings of Scripture and the apostles (*cf.* 1 Cor. 14:37f.), by bringing glory to Christ (Jn. 16:14), and the consistency of their message with that of other true prophets. Above all, the gift is useless unless it proceeds from a loving heart and is ministered in a loving way (1 Cor. 12:31-13:3).

Some prophets appear to have been set apart for regular ministry, such as Agabus (Acts 11:28; *cf.* Eph. 4:11). Prophetic ministry was exercised when Timothy was set apart for his work (1 Tim. 1:18; 4:14). The prophets predicted as well as proclaimed. They received dreams and visions as well as direct words (Acts 10:9ff.). Agabus used symbols (Acts 21:10f.), and on this occasion his word was accepted as correct but was not taken as a directive.

Prophecy in later ages. Some have argued that there can be no prophecy today, partly because prophets and apostles are closely linked in Eph. 4:11 as founders of the NT church, and partly because the closure of the NT

455

canon excludes any further revelation. But 1 Cor. 13:8ff. sees prophecy passing away only when the 'perfect' comes (in the next life). And while there can be no fresh revelation of doctrine, there seems no good reason why the living God, who both speaks and acts, cannot use the gift of prophecy for local guidance to a nation, church or individual, or to warn by way of prediction or reminders, in accordance with the Scriptures.

PROPHETESS. In both testaments the term is used for women as 'prophet' is for men. Among those mentioned are Moses' sister Miriam (Ex. 15:20), Huldah who brought God's word to king Josiah (2 Ki. 22:14), and Philip's 4 daughters in Caesarea (Acts 21:9). The prophetic gift was exercised by both sexes in the NT (1 Cor. 11:4f.; *cf.* Acts 2:17). See also previous article.

PROPITIATION. It means primarily 'the removal of wrath by offering a gift'. The wrath or strong anger of God at sin is clearly taught in the OT, often being placed firmly alongside his righteous forgiveness of the penitent (*e.g.* Nu. 14:18; Ps. 7:11). Pardon is a gracious gift of God, and although sacrifices were offered even this method of atonement was provided by God himself (Lv. 17:11).

Throughout the NT, God is shown to be utterly against sin, whether or not the term 'wrath' is used (Rom. 1:18). It is against the background of this wrath that Paul sees the work of Jesus Christ. The sentence of God's anger hung over the entire world, but

Christ's saving work includes deliverance from it, and the idea of propitiation is strongly suggested in Rom. 3:21ff. In 1 Jn. 2:2 Jesus is described as our propitiation, having in verse 1 been described as our 'advocate'; someone who needs an advocate is in dire peril and 'propitiation' captures the sense of this. The NT is adamant that God hates sin, and that his wrath is only put away by Jesus' atoning death. See also ATONEMENT; EXPIATION.

PROSELYTE. The Hebrew term originally meant 'resident alien' but it later came to mean a non-Jew who fully participated in Jewish religion. The OT encouraged a warm welcome to foreigners who chose to live among Israelites (Lv. 19:34). They were to be received into religious fellowship on condition of circumcision (Ex. 12:48); they were bound by the same law and treated no differently from those born Israelites (Nu. 15:16, 30). There are visions in the OT of a brotherhood unfettered by racial tradition and prejudice (Is. 19:18ff.; 56:3ff.; Zp. 2:11).

Proselytes, who admired Jewish monotheism and morality, became numerous as Jews were scattered across the Greek and later the Roman empires after the end of the Old Testament period. Some worshipped and studied in the synagogues only, others went through the rites of circumcision and baptism and so were able to offer sacrifices; the former may have been called 'God fearers'. Many rabbis abhorred proselytes, however; the Babylonian Talmud refers to them as sores on Israel's skin. The exceptional comment in Mt. 23:15 may have referred to one particular incident. Exclusiveness has disfigured Judaism throughout history even though the OT rebukes it.

In NT times there was a steady flow of proselytes into Judaism (*cf.* Acts 2:10; 6:5; 13:43). The early church was largely recruited from the ranks of uncircumcised Jewish sympathizers. Had Paul not won the argument against the imposition of full Jewish rites on these Gentile Christians, world history might have been vastly different.

PROSTITUTION. The OT speaks of both common prostitutes and also sacred prostitutes attached to pagan shrines; Tamar is referred to as both (Gn. 38:15, 21 RSV mg). During the Israelite monarchy male cult prostitutes became widespread (1 Ki. 14:24). Rahab the harlot (prostitute) was commended for her faith in hiding Joshua's spies (Heb. 11:31; Jas. 2:25) and became an ancestress of Christ (Mt. 1:5). In the NT, prostitutes were among those who repented at the preaching of John the Baptist (Mt. 21:31f.). Many nude female figurines have been found by archaeologists throughout the ancient Near East depicting goddesses which were venerated in cult prostitution. Aphrodite was the goddess of Corinth and the patroness of prostitutes who were probably in Paul's mind (1 Cor. 6:15f.) when he condemned prostitution as defiling bodies which are 'temples' of the Holy Spirit (vv. 18ff.).

Unrepentant immoral people will be excluded from heaven (Rev. 21:8; 22:15). Spiritual apostasy is often pictured as prostitution in the OT (*e.g.* Is. 57:3ff.; Hos. 1:2).

PROVERB. The biblical use of the word is wider than normal English usage. It may indeed be a pithy saying condensing the wisdom of experience (1 Sa. 24:13) but also a byword (1 Ki. 9:7) or taunt (Is. 14:4). Proverbs, along with parables, were important ingredients in Jesus' ministry (Lk. 4:23). See also next article, and WISDOM; WISDOM LITERATURE.

PROVERBS, BOOK OF. A collection of collections of pithy sayings, Proverbs is a guidebook for successful living. Without overtly stressing the great prophetic themes, it shows how Israel's distinctive faith affected common life. It falls into 8 sections.

The importance of wisdom (1:1-9:18). Each idea is discussed at length in a didactic poem, strongly contrasting the results of seeking wisdom and living foolishly. Several hundred proverbs cover such issues as violent crime (1:10ff.); rash pledges (6:1ff.); duplicity (6:12ff.); and sexual impurity (5:3ff.). The author of this deeply religious section (*cf.* 3:5ff.) is anonymous since 1:1-6 probably refers to the whole book and 10:1 introduces material which is described as Solomon's. Some of its material is parallel to Ugaritic and Phoenician literature.

The proverbs of Solomon (10:1-22:16). This is the oldest section of the book.

Furthermore, scholars are increasingly accepting the accuracy of the tradition of Solomon's wisdom which this section claims to distil (*cf.* 1 Ki. 4:29ff.). About 375 proverbs appear here, in no systematic order, stressing the profits of wisdom.

The words of the wise (22:17-24:22). These are maxims on such topics as care for the poor (22:22); respect for the king (23:1ff.); discipline of children (23:13f.); and chastity (23:26ff.). The relationship of 22:17-23:11 with proverbs of Amenemope of Egypt is now recognized; but whichever was the original, Proverbs belongs consistently to the OT revelation.

Additional sayings of the wise (24:23-34) is separate from, but similar to, the previous section, with a keen sense of social responsibility (vv. 28f.).

Additional proverbs of Solomon (25:1-29:27). The content, although not the style, is similar to 10:1-22:16. The statement of 25:1 led to the Jewish view that Hezekiah and his company wrote the Proverbs, but it refers only to editing of chs. 25-29.

The words of Agur (30:1-33). Agur and others in 30:1 defy identification. An opening note of agnosticism (2-4) is answered by a statement about God's eternal changelessness (5-6) followed by a prayer (7-9), and a series of extended proverbs in which the number 4 is prominent. *The words of Lemuel* (31:1-9) includes warnings against excess and is notably influenced by the Aramaic language. *In praise of a virtuous wife* (31:10-31) is an acrostic poem and probably one of the latest additions to the book.

Date of compilation. It could not have been completed before Hezekiah's time (*c.* 715-686 BC), and chs. 30-31 may have been added during or after the Exile. The final editing was probably in the 5th cent. BC, incorporating much older material.

Influence on the NT. It is quoted several times (*e.g.* 3:11f. = Heb. 12:5f.; 10:12 = Jas. 5:20 and 1 Pet. 4:8). Jesus fulfilled the wisdom writings by revealing the fullness of God's wisdom (Mt. 12:42). As a commentary on the law of love, Proverbs helps pave the way for the incarnation of love in Christ.

PROVIDENCE. There is no single biblical word to express this idea. In Christian theology it usually means the unceasing activity of the Creator in looking after all his creation. He sustains his creatures in ordered existence (Acts 17:28; Col. 1:17; Heb. 1:3), guides and governs all events (*cf.* Ps. 107), and directs everything to its appointed goal for his glory (Eph. 1:9ff.). This view of God caring for the world must be distinguished from pantheism which absorbs the world into God; deism, which cuts it off from him; dualism, which divides control of the world between God and another power; indeterminism, which denies any control at all; determinism, which destroys human responsibility; chance, which denies the controlling power is rational; and fate, which denies it to be benevolent. It is a function of God's sovereignty.

In the natural order, God rules all creatures (Jb. 38-41) and all happenings from storms and plagues (Ps. 29; Ex. 7-11) to the death of a sparrow (Mt. 10:29) or the roll of a dice (Pr. 16:33). Human life and health is his to give and take away (Jb. 1:21). Since the world's regularity depends on God, the Bible finds no difficulty in the occasional miraculous irregularity; nothing is too hard for God in his world (Gn. 18:14). In human history, God has been executing a plan of salvation with its goal the creation of a world-wide church (Eph. 3:3ff.) and through this the reintegration of a disordered cosmos (Rom. 8:19ff.) under the rule of Christ at his second coming (Eph. 1:9ff.). God uses opposition to his plans for his own glory (Ps. 2:1ff.; Acts 4:25ff.).

The doctrine raises questions when applied to the individual. Why do the wicked prosper? The Bible suggests theirs is a temporary prosperity and that God will, after giving them time to repent, bring judgment on them (Ps. 73:17ff.; Rom. 2:3ff.). Or why do the righteous suffer? They will be vindicated, biblical writers assert, when God finally destroys wickedness (Ps. 37); he uses their suffering to purify them (Pr. 3:11f.; Heb. 12:5ff.); besides, the supreme good is knowing God, irrespective of outward circumstances (Hab. 3:17f.). The NT recognizes that fellowship with Christ includes involvement in his sufferings (Mt. 10:24f.; Jn. 15:18ff.; Phil. 3:10ff.; 1 Pet. 4:12ff.). Christians are sustained by God (2 Cor. 1:3ff.; Phil. 4:19) in whom all things work together for his glory (Rom. 8:28). Trusting his providence, they can wait patiently for him (Jas.

5:7ff.; 1 Pet. 5:6f.). The individual's decisions remain his own, and he is morally responsible for them, even though God's control is absolute.

PSALMS, BOOK OF. It would be difficult to overestimate the significance of this book. In it are mirrored the ideals of religious piety and communion with God; of sorrow for sin and the search for perfection; of walking unafraid in darkness by the light of faith; of obedience to God's law, delight in his worship, fellowship with his friends, and reverence for his Word; of humility when chastened, trust when evil strikes, and serenity when life's storms rage. But for all that, the Psalms are primarily songs to be sung; they are not sermons or theological treatises.

Formation of the book. Psalms was undoubtedly the 'hymnbook' of the second temple, but much of its content is earlier than the Exile. This type of poetry is also found elsewhere in the OT (*e.g.* Ex. 15; 1 Sa. 2:1ff.), and in Babylonian and Ugaritic literature. Indeed, it persisted among the Jews for some time into the Christian era.

No fewer than 73 psalms are attributed to David. Other authors named are Asaph (50; 73-83), the sons of Korah (42-49; 84-85; 87-88), Solomon (72; 127), Heman (88), Ethan (89), and Moses (90). Attempts have been made to discredit the claim that David himself wrote the psalms attributed to him, although the prominence of the king in many psalms has convinced recent scholars that the main period of composition was during the Monarchy. David certainly was a musician (1 Sa. 16:14ff.) and a poet (2 Sa. 1:17ff.; 3:33f.), and his reputation lived on centuries after his death (Am. 6:5).

The book as we now have it consists of 5 sections, the division going back to the early beginnings of the LXX (3rd cent. BC). A doxology closes each book. The divisions are: Pss. 1-41; 42-72; 73-89; 90-106; 107-150. Some psalms (or parts of them) occur in more than one section (*e.g.* 14 and 53). Many scholars believe that 3 early collections (Davidic; Korahite, Asaphite and Davidic; anonymous) were divided into 5 to match the books of Moses (the Pentateuch).

Technical terms used. Some of the terms were already obscure in the 3rd-2nd cents. BC, and so any comments must be tentative. Among the headings, *Songs of Ascents* were probably pilgrim or processional songs for festivals. *Maskil* seems to mean 'making wise or skilful' and the psalms so headed describe various chastening experiences; the name may refer, however, to literary style. *Miktam* probably means 'a plea for protection'. Some have *according to* in the heading which may be a liturgical direction or a tune name. The names which follow it (such as 'The Hind of the Dawn', Ps. 22) cannot be fully explained today, although it has been suggested that some relate to cultic ceremonies during which the psalm was sung. For example, Ps. 56 ('The Dove on Far-off Terebinths') may relate to a ritual like that of Lv. 14:5ff. *Selah* occurs 71 times within the body of some psalms, and

is still obscure; it may instruct worshippers or musicians to lift up their voices or instruments in a refrain or interlude. *Higgaion* evidently calls for music.

Liturgical approach. A landmark in modern study of the Psalms came early in the 20th cent. when H. Gunkel distinguished classes of psalms by attending to the worship situation they sprang from rather than the historical event possibly underlying them, and to the common thoughts and recurrent features of style and imagery. Among the classes he isolated are Hymns of Praise, Laments, and Royal Psalms. This approach has been developed by other scholars, relating psalms more closely to rituals and cultic 'drama'. There can be no doubt that many psalms were written and collected specifically for worship, but the historical details in some headings need not be despised or discounted as a result. It should also be noted that the psalmist could speak as a prophet (*cf.* Acts 2:30f.).

Theology of Psalms. At the centre of the psalmists' religious life is the knowledge of God. They sing of his majesty in creation revealing him as ever-present, all-knowing and all-powerful. He is also the God of history, the lawgiver, and the vindicator of the oppressed. Their chief delight is prayer to God, for they believe in his providence, trust in his presence, rejoice in his righteousness, rest in his faithfulness and confide in his nearness. Some psalms, however, are prayers to God for vengeance ('imprecatory psalms'), in which the idea is of the psalmist's hate for those who hate God (Ps. 139:21f.). Behind the calls for judgment and the curses is a recognition of God's moral governance of the world. For those living under the old covenant, it was natural to pray for the destruction of God's enemies in this life; for Christians under the new covenant, it is now natural to pray for their repentance and salvation, while retaining belief in a future judgment for the unrepentant. These imprecatory psalms are not devoid of value now, for they point to the psalmists' zeal for righteousness and their refusal to condone sin.

Some psalms provide a picture of the hoped-for Messiah, who will be a king against whom the nations rebel vainly (Ps. 2). The Messianic age is depicted in Ps. 72, and in Ps. 110 the Messiah is Victor, Priest and King. There is also a hint of the Messiah's suffering in Pss. 22; 69, although such psalms were not considered Messianic until Jesus interpreted them as such (e.g. Lk. 24:44ff.).

Christian approach to Psalms. Psalms was Jesus' prayer book in synagogue services and temple festivals. He used it in his teaching, met temptation with it, quoted it from the cross and died with it on his lips. From earliest times the church modelled its great hymns on Psalms (e.g. Lk. 1:46ff.). It inspired persecuted apostles (Acts 4:25f.) and it set forth their profoundest beliefs about Jesus (Heb. 1:6, 10ff.; 2:6ff.; 5:6; 10:5ff.). In all ages, Christians have found it 'a Bible in miniature' (Luther); illuminated by the gospel it still aids and inspires worship of the eternal God.

See also POETRY.

PSEUDEPIGRAPHA. Jewish writings which were excluded from the OT and which find no place in the Apocrypha. They are valuable for the light which they shed on the Jewish background to the NT. The majority are published under assumed names, hence the collective title; they are generally apocalyptic in content. There are 2 distinct groups.

The Palestinian group. This has 3 literary types. The first is poetry, represented by the anti-Sadducean *Psalms of Solomon* (1st cent. BC). The second is legend, expanding biblical history. The *Testaments of the Twelve Patriarchs* was a Pharisaic production of the late 2nd cent. BC, with later additions, based on Gn. 49. The later additions contain some of the best moral injunctions of pre-Christian Judaism. The *Book of Jubilees* purports to be a revelation to Moses and advocates a 364-day year to ensure Jewish feasts are kept regularly. It was well known at Qumran. Other legendary works include the *Life of Adam and Eve*, an imaginary reconstruction of events after the fall; the *Martyrdom of Isaiah*, which is partly Jewish and partly Christian, telling how Isaiah was sawn in two (cf. Heb. 11:37) with a later interpolation which witnesses the birth, death and resurrection of Jesus.

The most important literary type in this group is apocalypse, the *Book of Enoch* being the chief example. A

461

composite work written during the last 2 cents. BC, it has a vision of judgment, some parables, an astronomical section, visions of the flood and world history down to the Messianic age, and a collection of exhortations. It is cited in the NT letter of Jude. *2 Enoch* tells of Enoch's journey through the seven heavens and contains noble ethical teaching similar to that in the Apocryphal work Ecclesiasticus. The *Assumption of Moses* has an apocalyptic view of world history, and has a marked absence of references to a Messiah. Both the *Apocalypse of Ezra* and *Apocalypse of Baruch* are pessimistic accounts of Israel's sufferings with vague glimmers of hope for a coming golden or Messianic age.

The Jewish-Hellenistic group. This too has 3 main literary types. One is propaganda, such as the *Letter of Aristeas* (*c.* 100 BC), commending Jewish law to Hellenistic (Greek-culture) contemporaries. The *Sibylline Oracles* were produced *c.* 140 BC by an Alexandrian Jew (books 3-5) and later extensively added to by Christian writers; they call on Greeks to cease pagan worship. The second type is philosophical, such as *4 Maccabees* in which a legalistic Jew with stoic leanings discusses the control of the passions by reason. There is also some apocalyptic literature in this group, *e.g.* the *Greek Baruch*.

Relevance. The pseudepigrapha shows the inter-testamental period, in which prophecy had ceased, to be a perplexing time. The literature attempted to reconcile prophetic promises with the current disastrous course of history. Many NT writers may have known the books. There was a strong emphasis on the future age as distinct from the present, although the Messianic hope was not so dominant as it had been earlier. Individualism and universalism were beginning to overshadow nationalism, and Pseudepigraphical literature especially countered Pharisaic legalism despite such views being held in some of its works.

See also next article; APOCALYPTIC; APOCRYPHA; DEAD SEA SCROLLS.

PSEUDONYMITY. The practice of attributing literary works to assumed authors, widely used in the ancient world. Such writings enjoyed considerable popularity among Jews and Christians. They raise in modern times the ethical question of using other people's names to give credibility to a work, for some of the authors were undoubtedly sincere.

Many Greek works were attributed to the authors' teachers; Plato's followers frequently did this. Straight forgery for commercial benefit was also used in the Greek world. For the Jews, however, the reasons were rather different. Prophecy had ceased, so any authoritative message for Jews in the 2 centuries before Christ could only be established, it was thought, by attributing it to a hero of the past. In the case of apocalyptic writing, this device may have been part of the genuine symbolism. It may also have been for self-preservation in a society occupied by a hostile power. Probably, however, the Jews paid more attention to content than authorship and had little interest in literary property.

By the 2nd cent. AD there were pseudonymous Christian Gospels, Acts, Letters and Apocalypses. Most came from heretical sources, seeking support by claiming to reveal secret teaching of established apostles. There is some evidence that the church took a firm stand against the practice. Tertullian, for example, defrocked an Asian presbyter who confessed to writing the *Acts of Paul* out of his love for the apostle. For this reason, the assumption by some scholars that certain NT books are pseudonymous rasies acute psychological and moral problems.

See also NEW TESTAMENT CANON.

PTOLEMAIS. The name given in the late 3rd or early 2nd cent. BC by Ptolemy I or II of Egypt to the seaport of Accho 13 km N of Carmel. It was the only natural harbour S of Phoenicia in OT times, but is mentioned only once (Jdg. 1:31). As Ptolemais it played an important role in the Jews' struggle for freedom in the 2nd cent. BC (1 Macc. 5:15; 12:45ff.). In Paul's day it was a Roman colony (Acts 21:7). Modern Acre, it is now overshadowed by Haifa across the bay.

PTOLEMY. The name borne by the 14 kings of the purely Macedonian Greek dynasty that ruled Egypt *c.* 323-30 BC. Ptolemy, one of Alexander the Great's marshals, had himself appointed as satrap of Egypt in 323 BC after Alexander's death, taking the title king of Egypt in 304 BC when the Greek empire was carved up among the marshals. Egypt was the king's personal estate run on business lines for maximum profit. There was early on a large community of Greek-speaking Jews at Alexandria, the capital, from among whom came the Greek OT, the Septuagint (LXX). Palestine was controlled by the Ptolemies until Antiochus III of the rival Seleucid empire drove Ptolemy V out in the period 202-198 BC.

Some of the Ptolemies feature in the Apocrypha. Among them are Ptolemy VI (1 Macc. 10:51ff.; 11:1ff.), Ptolemy VII (1 Macc. 1:18; 15:16), and 2 nonroyal members of the family: a general of Antiochus Epiphanes (1 Macc. 3:38; 2 Macc. 4:45) and the son-in-law of Simon Maccabaeus who murdered Simon in 135 BC (1 Macc. 16:11ff.). The last of the line was the son of Cleopatra and Julius Caesar, Ptolemy XIV, before Rome took over Egypt in 30 BC.

PUBLIUS. The 'chief man' of Malta (Acts 28:7); the title appears to be correct local usage at the time.

PUDENS. A Roman Christian who greeted Timothy (2 Tim. 4:21), traditionally a senator leading a house church in S Pudentiana.

PURIM. A Jewish festival celebrated during 13-15 Adar. The book of Esther, which describes the festival's origin, is read at it. It celebrates the deliverance of the Jews through Esther and Mordecai from Haman's plot to murder them in the 4th or 5th cent. BC. In 2 Macc. 15:36 the defeat of Nicanor by Judas Maccabaeus is celebrated 'the day before Mordecai's day'. See also ESTHER.

PURITY. In OT times, ceremonial purity was obtained by certain rites during the performance of religious duties. Most Israelite ceremonial purifications had sanitary and ethical significance, and were codified in the law of Moses. The prophets later stressed the ethical need for purity and the NT lifts the meaning of the term into the moral and spiritual realm. Purity means a state of heart completely devoted to God, with no mixed motives or divided loyalties, the result of which is the vision of God (Mt. 5:8; *cf.* Mk. 7:14ff.). While rightly ordered sexual activity is not 'polluting' (Heb. 13:4), chastity or purity outside of marriage is necessary (1 Cor. 6:19f.) as an expression of inner devotion to Jesus.

PUT, PHUT. 1. The 3rd son of Ham (Gn. 10:6). 2. A place whose warriors along with others could not save Thebes (Na. 3:8f.). It is an African locality, but precisely where is disputed.

PUTEOLI. Modern Pozzuoli, near Naples, which became an important arsenal and trading post after its capture by the Romans in 338 BC. Paul disembarked there en route for Rome (Acts 28:13).

QUAIL. Almost the smallest of game birds, it provided meat for the Israelites in the desert (Ex. 16:13). Quail migrate across the Sinai peninsula, and at certain seasons travel in large flocks a metre or two above the ground.

QUARTUS. 'Fourth.' He was a Roman Christian whose greetings are conveyed in Rom. 16:23. Possibly brother of Erastus, even perhaps of Tertius ('third').

QUEEN. The term is usually used in the Bible to describe female monarchs of other nations (*e.g.* 1 Ki. 10:1; Acts 8:27). Athaliah became the only Israelite queen in biblical history (2 Ki. 11:1ff.). The wife of a reigning king was rarely concerned with the affairs of state, exceptions being Bathsheba (1 Ki. 1:15ff.) and Jezebel (1 Ki. 21). The most important woman in Israel's and Judah's royal household was the queen mother, who could sit at the monarch's right hand (1 Ki. 2:19). That this was not a merely honorary position is clear in the case of Maacah who remained queen mother during her grandson's reign (1 Ki. 15).

QUEEN OF HEAVEN. People in Jerusalem made cakes, burned incense and made other offerings to this goddess which may have been Astarte, Ashtaroth or the Canaanite Anat, or 'the stars' (Je. 7:18; 44:17ff., 25).

QUIRINIUS. Publius Sulpicius Quirinius was consul at Rome in 12 BC, became proconsul of Asia in 3 BC, adviser to the heir-apparent Gaius Caesar AD 3-4, and imperial legate of Syria-Cilicia AD 6-9; after that he lived in Rome and died in AD 21. At the beginning of his Syrian governorship he organized a census in Judaea which had just become a Roman province (Acts 5:37).

The census of Lk. 2:1f. must have been at least 9 years earlier, however, to coincide with the birth of Jesus. It is quite possible that Quirinius was governor (or an additional legate) of Syria on an earlier occasion; an inscription, unfortunately mutilated, speaks of a legate of Syria entering the office 'for the second time', and the other details could well be matched with Quirinius. There are also other possibilities. Tertullian in his copy of Lk. 2 apparently had Saturninus, not Quirinius. And the verse could perhaps be rendered: 'This enrolment was earlier than that held when Quirinius...'.

QUMRAN. A wadi, and an ancient ruin nearby, NW of the Dead Sea. It was practically unknown until 1947 when the 'Dead Sea Scrolls' were found hidden in caves there. Excavations at the nearby ruins revealed occupation dating back to the time of the Judaean kings. The most impor-

tant period of the site's history, however, was from the 2nd cent. BC to the 1st century AD. A complex of buildings from this period formed the headquarters of the Jewish religious community to which the Dead Sea Scrolls belonged. It was damaged by an earthquake in 31 BC and lay derelict until being repaired after 4 BC. This phase of occupation appears to have ended violently c. AD 68, perhaps in the Roman mopping-up operation. For more detail, see DEAD SEA SCROLLS; ESSENES.

QUOTATIONS (IN THE NEW TESTAMENT). There are some 250 specific quotations of the OT in the NT, and over 750 more indirect or partial quotations and allusions. For example, Revelation has no quotations but is interlaced with allusions to OT texts. The introductory formulae such as 'the Scripture says' (e.g. Mt. 19:4) point to the essential connection between God's message in the old and new covenants. Most quotations are from the Greek OT (LXX), although variant readings are sometimes chosen deliberately to bring out the fulfilment seen by the NT writer (e.g. 1 Cor. 15:54f.). This merging of commentary with quotation is also known from Qumran and early non-biblical Christian texts.

Some passages are quoted quite out of their original historical context; Hosea's reference to the Exodus, for example, is 'fulfilled' by the baby Jesus' return from Egypt (Mt. 2:15). A passage referring to Solomon is applied both to Jesus (Heb. 1:5) and the church (2 Cor. 6:18). This is because the NT writers see the new age of Christ prefigured typologically in the OT, and they see the church as the 'new Israel'.

There are also quotations from other sources. Eph. 5:14 may be an early Christian hymn; Jude 14 comes from the Jewish *Book of Enoch*; Acts 17:28 is from a pagan writer.

R

RAAMAH (lit. 'trembling'). A son of Cush (Gn. 10:7) whose tribe may have lived N of Marib in Yemen.

RAAMSES, RAMESES. A city of Egypt where the Hebrews were forced labourers (Ex. 1:11; 12:37). It was the famous E-Delta residence of Rameses II (*c.* 1290-1224 BC). Remains of a palace and other buildings at Qantir 30 km S of Tanis are probably the original site. See also EXODUS.

RABBAH. 1. The capital of Ammon, now Amman, capital of Jordan, 35 km E of the R. Jordan. Ammonite power grew simultaneously with Israel, and David and Joab overran it (2 Sa. 10; 12:26ff.). Rebuilt and renamed Philadelphia by Ptolemy Philadelphus (285-246 BC), it became an important city of the Decapolis. See also AMMON, AMMONITES. 2. A town and associated villages in Judah, possibly near Gezer (Jos. 15:60).

RABBI, RABBONI. Rabbi was a reverential form of address which came to be the title of authorized teachers of the Jewish law. In NT times it was still a title of honour rather than office, and was given to John the Baptist and Jesus. In Mt. 23:7f. the disciples are warned against such titles of honour, for God is their teacher and they are all 'brothers'.

RABMAG. The title of the Babylonian court official Nergal-sharezer when Jerusalem was destroyed in 587 BC (Je. 39:3, 13). The exact meaning of the title is unknown.

RABSARIS. The title of a chief official (lit. 'chief of the court eunuchs') of Assyria (2 Ki. 18:17) and Babylon (Je. 39:3, 13). The title is common in Assyrian texts.

RABSHAKEH. The title of a senior Assyrian official who with others demanded the surrender of Jerusalem (2 Ki. 18:17). He was spokesman of the delegation. He ranked below the army commander (see TARTAN).

RACA. In Mt. 5:22 (AV) probably an Aramaic term of abuse.

RACHEL (lit. 'ewe'). An Aramaean woman, the second and favourite wife of Jacob who was her first cousin. A beautiful woman (Gn. 29:17), she was mother of Jacob's two youngest sons, Joseph and Benjamin. She was capable of devious behaviour (Gn. 31:19, 34f.). She was met by Jacob when shepherding her father's flocks and he helped her to water them. Her father Laban welcomed Jacob into his household, and tricked him into working 14 years in lieu of payment in order to marry Rachel, but Jacob's love for her never wavered (Gn. 29:30). Such a custom, and that of giving a slave-girl as part of Rachel's dowry, is known from other contemporary documents.

Rachel was unable to have children for some years; infertility was a well-known problem in the ancient Near East and the husband would often take a second wife or concubine because of it. Again, contemporary documents testify to the practice of the infertile wife 'adopting' children from a secondary marriage as her own. Rachel readily accompanied Jacob back to Palestine after her father had used up the money set aside for her dowry (Gn. 31:15), stealing his household gods perhaps for protection rather than revenge (Gn. 31:19). She died between Bethel and Bethlehem, giving birth to Benjamin. Jacob marked her grave with a monument which was still standing in Saul's day (1 Sa. 10:2).

RAHAB. *Person:* A prostitute who lived in a house built into the town wall of Jericho and who hid Joshua's two spies in return for protection when Israel took the town (Jos. 2). She is commended in the NT for her faith (Heb. 11:31; *cf.* Jas. 2:25) and was almost certainly an ancestress of Jesus (Mt. 1:5).

Symbol: The name for a female monster of chaos, associated with LEVIATHAN. Although in English this name is similar to that of the person, in Hebrew the spelling is different and there is no connection between the two. God is said to smite Rahab (*e.g.* Jb. 26:12); generally it is a symbol for Egypt (clearly so in Ps. 89:10).

RAIN. Rainfall was a vital event in biblical lands. The early rains in Palestine fall mid-September to mid-October accompanied by a brilliance in the sky due to atmospheric change (Jb. 37:21). The main effective rains fall October to March, with light spring rains in April-May. The summers are hot and dry. The climate has not changed substantially within historical times. Occasional and prolonged droughts, with disastrous effects, are recorded in the OT (*e.g.* 1 Ki. 17:7). God is shown to be the rain-giver as opposed to the Baalim which were associated with springs, wells and streams (Je. 14:22), a claim well vindicated in Elijah's challenge to the priests of Baal (1 Ki. 18:17ff.). Rainfall is associated symbolically with God's blessings and gifts (Dt. 33:13; Ps. 72:6f.). See also CLOUD; DEW; PALESTINE; WATER.

RAINBOW. There is no special word for it in Hebrew; the word for a war-bow is used. In Gn. 9:13 what was ordinarily a symbol of war became a symbol of mercy and peace (*cf.* Ezk. 1:28; Rev. 4:3; 10:1).

RAMAH (lit. 'height'). The name of several places, all on elevated sites. Two are especially important. 1.

Ramah of Benjamin, near Bethel, where the Levite and his concubine planned to stay (Jdg. 19:13) and close to Deborah's home (Jdg. 4:5). Asa destroyed a fort there (1 Ki. 15:17ff.). 2. The birthplace and home of Samuel (1 Sa. 1:19; 7:17) where Saul first met him (1 Sa. 9:6ff.). David found refuge there (1 Sa. 19:18). The site is uncertain.

RAMOTH-GILEAD. A walled city in Gad's territory, E of the Jordan. It was a city of refuge (Jos. 20:8) assigned to the Levites (Jos. 21:38), and possibly identical to Mizpah (Jdg. 11:29). Its modern site is uncertain. It changed hands between Israel and Syria several times (*cf.* 1 Ki. 22:3f.; 2 Ki. 8:28f.).

REBECCA, REBEKAH. Isaac's wife, the daughter of Bethuel, Abraham's nephew. The account of how Abraham's servant found her for Isaac strongly emphasizes the guidance and overruling providence of God (Gn. 24). She was infertile for the first 20 years of her marriage but then bore the twins Esau and Jacob (Gn. 25:20ff.). A strong-willed woman, she favoured Jacob while Isaac favoured Esau, which inevitably destroyed the family unity. She planned the deception by which Jacob received his father's blessing in preference to Esau, then sent him away to save his life on the pretext of finding a wife (Gn. 27). In the NT, Paul uses her to illustrate God's election of people by grace (Rom. 9:10).

RECHABITES. Jehonadab (or Jonadab), the son of Rechab, gave his family name its special connotation by his extreme zeal for God (2 Ki. 10:15ff.) which he expressed in a series of regulations including commitment to nomadism (Je. 35:5ff.). His descendants won divine approval for their desire to preserve pure faith (Je. 35:18f.). See also NOMADS.

RECONCILIATION. Four NT passages deal with the work of Christ as reconciliation: Rom. 5:10f.; 2 Cor. 5:18ff.; Eph. 2:11ff.; Col. 1:19ff. Reconciliation means the removal of enmity, bridging over a quarrel in such a way that a good and right relationship is restored. Sinful people are God's enemies (Rom. 5:10); the NT pictures God as a vigorous opponent of all that is evil. The way to reconciliation is to grapple with the root cause of the enmity. So Christ died to put away sin and so open up the way for true reconciliation between man and God. The NT stress is always on man (the guilty party) being reconciled to a holy, loving God, but that does not mean that there is no change in God's attitude, for his 'wrath' is no longer exercised towards us. See also ATONEMENT.

REDEEMER, REDEMPTION. Redemption is the deliverance from some evil or bondage by payment of a price or ransom. In the ancient world prisoners of war or slaves might be released on such a payment. In OT law the owner of a dangerous animal could be executed if the animal gored someone to death, but he could redeem his life by paying a ransom.

This concept was taken up by the early Christians to describe the work of Christ, who gave his life 'as a ransom for many' (Mk. 10:45). Sinful people are in bondage to sin (Jn. 8:34) for which death is the only possible consequence (Rom. 6:23). The cross of Christ is the price paid to release the slaves, to let the condemned prisoners go free. Even in the OT, where God is said to have redeemed his people from Egypt and where there is no actual 'price' paid (Ex. 6:6; Ps. 77:14f.), there is the thought of his effort being the 'price'. The NT word for this costly redemption occurs only 10 times (there is another word which means simply deliverance without a price being paid). The price is Christ's shed blood (Eph. 1:7; *cf.* 1 Cor. 6:19f.). The Christian response to that gracious provision is to live a life of service to Christ which does not submit again to the slavery of sin (Gal. 5:1).

RED SEA. The sea that divides NE Africa from Arabia. It extends 1,900 km from the straits of Bab el-Mandeb near Aden N to the S tip of the Sinai peninsula, then splits for another 300 km N into the Gulfs of Suez and Aqabah. In ancient times the name also included the Arabian and Indian Seas to the NW coast of India. In the OT the term 'sea of reeds' (often translated Red Sea) covers the two following areas.

The Bitter Lakes region in the Egyptian Delta. It is likely that it was in this region that God caused a wind to dry up the shallow water and allow the Israelites to cross safely before the waters returned and the area became treacherously marshy again (Ex. 14-15). This area is known to be affected by strong E winds, and the Shur desert for which the Israelites made is opposite it. *The Gulfs of Suez and Aqabah* are referred to by the same term 'sea of reeds' in the subsequent journeying of the Israelites around the Sinai peninsula (*e.g.* Nu. 14:25; 1 Ki. 9:26, the Gulf of Aqabah). Such narrow and broad use of the same terminology is not unknown in ancient literature. See also EXODUS.

REED: See PLANTS.

REFINER, REFINING. In the ancient world crude metal was remelted to remove impurities and to make metal castings, by being heated in pottery crucibles (Pr. 17:3). The term for refiner is often rendered 'goldsmith' in EVV for the process was especially applied to precious metals. God is said to be like a master refiner purifying people's inner selves (*e.g.* Ps. 66:10; Is. 48:10). Sometimes, however, even the heat of adversity fails to achieve this purpose (Je. 6:27ff.). See also MINING AND METALS.

REGENERATION. A word used to describe the radical and permanent change in a person's whole outlook achieved by the Holy Spirit. The word itself is used only twice in the NT, in Mt. 19:28 ('new world', RSV) to refer to the future restoration of everything, and in Tit. 3:5 to refer to the change in an individual. Other terms which relate to it are 'new birth' (Jn. 3:3, 7; 1 Pet. 1:3, 23), describing the initial act of renewal, and 'being renewed' (Col. 3:10), describing the continuous application and expression of regeneration. It was prefigured in the OT by such passages as Je. 31:31ff., which sees God's law written on human hearts, and Ezk. 37:1ff., Ezekiel's vision of dry bones brought to life by God's breath.

The NT regards the effects of sin to be so serious that without regeneration a person cannot enter the kingdom of God. The initiative is God's, whose decisive act of regenerating someone is once and for all (Jn. 1:13; 3:3ff.). As a result, the individual actively repents, believes in Jesus, and then lives in newness of life (*cf.* 1 Jn. 3:9; 4:7; 5:4). There is no change in the personality itself, but the person is controlled differently; instead of being ruled by the law of sin, he or she is now directed by the Holy Spirit towards God. However, the regenerate person is not yet perfect, but has to grow (1 Pet. 2:2) and be continually filled with the Spirit (Rom. 8:4, 9, 14; Eph. 5:18).

The means by which regeneration is ministered to a person have been disputed. 1 Pet. 1:23 and Jas. 1:18 refer to God's Word as a means of new birth; Tit. 3:5 relates it to baptism. But as John distinguishes between regeneration and the faith that results (Jn. 1:12f.), Peter and James are referring to the whole process, not the means. Also, regeneration is possible before baptism (Acts 10:44f.; 16:14f.).

Therefore regeneration comes to people directly from the Holy Spirit; God's Word brings it to expression in faith and repentance; and baptism bears witness to it.

REHOB. *Person:* The father of Hadadezer (2 Sa. 8:3). *Places:* 1. The northernmost city of Canaan seen by Joshua's spies (Nu. 13:21), probably near the source of the Jordan. 2. A city in Asher given to the Levites (Jos. 19:28; 21:31).

REHOBOAM. The son of Solomon and Naamah, who became the last king of the united Israel and the first king of Judah as a separate kingdom. Solomon's repressive measures to fund his projects led to confrontation between Rehoboam and the 10 N tribes. He increased the repression and the N tribes rebelled and made Jeroboam their king (1 Ki. 12). Pagan practices appeared in Judah during his reign (1 Ki. 14:22ff.) but when Rehoboam was told that an Egyptian invasion was punishment for this, he repented (2 Ch. 12:5ff.). He was an ancestor of Jesus (Mt. 1:7).

REHOBOTH (lit. 'broad places'). 1. A well dug by Isaac near Gerar (Gn. 26:22). 2. A city probably beside Wadi el-Hesa (Gn. 36:37).

REHOBOTH-IR. One of 4 cities built by Asshur (NIMROD) in Assyria (Gn. 10:11f.), but unknown today. It may refer to Assur.

REHUM. A post-exilic name; in Ezr.

4:8 he may be an administrator or 'postmaster'.

REI. In 1 Ki. 1:8 only, an officer of David's guard.

REJECTION. A variety of terms is used to describe God's rejection of unrepentant people after careful consideration. In Je. 6:30 such people are likened to 'refuse silver', permanently tainted. In Rom. 1:28 God gives up those who have refused to consider him to the consequences of their deeds. But Paul writes of his fear of rejection (disqualification, 1 Cor. 9:27), not in the sense of losing his salvation but of losing his 'reward' (*cf.* 3:10ff.).

RELIGION. The word is used occasionally in the NT. In Jas. 1:26f. and Acts 26:5 it refers to the outward expression, not the content, of belief. In 1 Tim. 3:16 and 2 Tim. 3:5 the word 'godliness' would be better. Hesitance over the use of the word today stems from the conviction that Christianity is not simply one among many religions but is distinct from them all.

REPENTANCE. In the OT, the term is used both of God and man. Generally, the Hebrew word meaning 'to change one's mind' is used only of God (*e.g.* 1 Sa. 15:10f.). This does not imply that he behaves arbitrarily, but that his relationship with his people is a changing one. When his people sin, he may 'repent' of his good intentions and allow more evil as a consequence (*e.g.* Je. 18:10), but he remains a faithful God who loves them still and

longs to restore them ('repent of the evil he caused', Je. 42:10). For man's part, the call to repent usually uses a stronger word which means 'to turn back', as in the eloquent plea of Ho. 6:1ff. The classic example of national repentance, when Israel turned back to follow God's law again, was in Josiah's time (2 Ki. 22-23).

In the NT, there is a note of remorse attached to repentance (*e.g.* Lk. 18:13), but it is more than feeling sorry or even than changing one's mind. The concept is that of a complete alteration of the basic motivation and direction of one's life, and is often equivalent to 'conversion'. This explains why John the Baptist called 'righteous' Jews to repent (Mt. 3:2). Jesus repeated the call to repentance (*e.g.* Lk. 15:10), illustrating its radical nature in the parable of the lost son (Lk. 15:11ff.) and its total submission to God's unmerited mercy in the parable of the tax collector (Lk. 18:13). To convert is to become like a child, living in humble dependence on and trust in the Father (Mt. 18:3f.).

The call to repentance figured in the apostles' preaching (*e.g.* Acts 2:38; 8:22), sometimes with the double requirement to turn from sin and to God (*e.g.* 3:19). Christians may need to repent of sin after their initial conversion (*e.g.* 2 Cor. 7:9ff.; 1 Jn. 1:5-2:2). Paul generally seems to have stressed more the concept of faith than that of repentance and forgiveness.

REPHAIM. One of the pre-Israelite peoples inhabiting Palestine, among those defeated by Chedorlaomer (Gn.

14:5). They were formidable people, physically large (Dt. 2:21). In Ps. 88:10 the name is rendered 'the dead', possibly referring to early inhabitants of the land long-since dead. They are also known in the Bible as EMIM (Dt. 2:11), and ZAMZUMMIM (Dt. 2:20f.); see also ANAK.

REPHAN. In Acts 7:43, which quotes the Greek version of Am. 5:26, a god connected with the planet Saturn. The name is substituted for, or possibly corrupted from, the Hebrew KAIWAN.

REPHIDIM. The Israelites' last stopping place before they reached Mt Sinai, where they fought Amalek, and Moses appointed deputy judges (Ex. 17:1-19:2). Possibly Wadi Refayid in SW Sinai.

RESEN. An Assyrian city between Nineveh and Calah (Gn. 10:12), possibly Hamam Ali on the Tigris 13 km S of Nineveh.

REST. Apart from the obvious non-theological sense (as in the sabbath, Gn. 2:2f.; Ex. 31:15), the word also has a theological meaning of peace and well-being. It was promised to Israel as something to be enjoyed in Canaan (Dt. 3:20), but because of unbelief the promise was largely unfulfilled (Ps. 95:8ff.; cf. Heb. 3:7-4:10). Christians already have God's 'rest' (Heb. 12:22ff.; Mt. 11:28ff.) but a greater one awaits them in heaven (Heb. 4:9).

RESTORATION. The OT prophets

looked forward to a day when God would restore his people to their own land in a time of prosperity and bliss (e.g. Je. 27:22). This came to be associated with the Messiah, but Jesus pointed out that it began with John the Baptist (Mt. 17:11). Jesus did not deny there would be such a restoration in the future (Acts 1:6) and Peter looked forward to it at Jesus' return (Acts 3:19ff.).

RESURRECTION. While there are myths of resurrection connected with the cycle of seasons in the beliefs of the ancient world, there is nothing to compare with the astounding claim of the Christian apostles and Scriptures that an individual, Jesus of Nazareth, truly died and overcame death by rising again to live and reign eternally. The NT, full of hope as a result of its stress on Christ's resurrection and its belief that we too shall rise again, stands in marked contrast to the general hopelessness in the face of death which characterized the thought of the time. The Greeks hoped for immortality, free from the shackles of the body; the Jews expected the same body to be raised. But the Christian hope was for a transformed body suited to express individual life in the age to come.

Old Testament. There is little about resurrection in the OT. There are a few cases of individuals being restored to life, however: e.g. 1 Ki. 17:17ff.; 2 Ki. 4:18ff.; 13:21. The plainest statement about it is in Dn. 12:2 which envisages a resurrection to life of righteous people and resurrection to judgment of godless people. Some of the Psalms look for it (*e.g.* Ps. 49:14f.) and there is some thought of it in Jb. 19:25ff. The idea became more prominent in the inter-testamental period, although there was no uniformity of belief and the Sadducees continued to deny resurrection into NT times.

Jesus' resurrection. Three people were raised from the dead by Jesus (Jairus' daughter, the widow of Nain's son, and Lazarus), and they seem to have been restored to their former life. They show Jesus as the master of death, as did his prophecies that he would rise after three days (*e.g.* Mk. 8:31). The Gospels record that on the 3rd day after his crucifixion the tomb in which he had been placed was found to be empty, and they and 1 Cor. 15 record numerous appearances of Jesus for some weeks afterwards.

Some have suggested that the disciples stole his body. They are portrayed, however, not as schemers but as defeated and dispirited people, hiding out of fear for their own lives; besides, the tomb was guarded. It is unlikely that they would have faced the later persecutions knowing their faith was based on a lie. If their foes had removed the body, they needed only to produce it when the apostles began preaching to disprove the resurrection claim for good, but they did not do so.

There are 10 different appearances of Jesus recorded in the NT, and they are not easy to harmonize, showing that the accounts are independent. Some of the incidents involved only individuals, others groups (one of 500 people), and they are very unlike hallucination experiences. As a result the disciples became transformed people, ready to suffer for Jesus, and with his resurrection central to their worship, beliefs and behaviour (Col. 2:12). They believed emphatically that Jesus was truly risen, not that he merely lived on in the continued preaching of his message nor that they could speak figuratively of him being alive because of the new spiritual freedom they experienced.

The resurrection of believers. The NT asserts that Jesus is the first example of what will be true for all believers, based on Jesus' own teaching (Jn. 6:39ff.; 11:25; 1 Cor. 15:21f.). But he also spoke of a resurrection to judgment (Jn. 5:29); all will rise, but only those who have trusted him for his atoning death are assured of eternal life. Paul differentiates the spiritual body from the physical one (1 Cor. 15:42ff.); Jesus had already said that some physical functions will cease in heaven (Mk. 12:25). Jesus' risen body is the model, recognizable at times (Mt. 28:9) yet able to perform differently (Jn. 20:19); Jesus could apparently conform to the limitations of physical life or not as he chose.

Implications. For Paul, the resurrection of Jesus was of cardinal importance (1 Cor. 15:14, 17); the whole of Christian faith hung on it. If Christ did not rise, we have no assurance that our salvation has been accomplished, and no certain hope for the future (*cf.* 1 Cor. 15:32). But because of the resurrection, we have all that plus the incentive and the power to live a new life now (Col. 3:1); the resurrection is on-going.

See also CHRONOLOGY OF THE NEW TESTAMENT; ESCHATOLOGY; JESUS CHRIST, LIFE OF.

RETURN OF JESUS CHRIST: See ESCHATOLOGY.

REUBEN. Jacob's first-born son by Leah, whose admirable characteristics were offset by his incestuous relationship with Bilhah, Jacob's concubine (Gn. 35:22). It was Reuben who advised his brothers not to kill Joseph, who intended to rescue him (Gn. 37:21ff.), and who offered his own sons as a guarantee for Benjamin's safety (Gn. 42:37). His status as first-born was never denied, but his traditional 'double portion' of the family inheritance went ultimately to Joseph's 2 sons who became heirs of land in Canaan (Gn. 49:4). Reuben's tribe occupied land E of Jordan, remaining a pastoral rather than agricultural tribe. It was not mentioned on the Moabite Stone *c.* 830 BC, indicating it had no important battle role, but was not forgotten by Israel as a whole (*cf.* Ezk. 48:7, 31).

REUEL. Several OT people, including Moses' father-in-law who was also called Jethro (Ex. 2:18; 3:1).

REVELATION. *The concept of revelation.* The biblical idea is of something hidden being unveiled so that it may be seen and known for what it is. Hence, God the Creator actively discloses his nature, character and purposes so that people may know him. His disclosures are always made in the context of a demand for trust in, and obedience to, what is revealed. Revelation, in other words, is a mandatory rule of faith and conduct (*cf.* Dt. 29:29). It especially concerns God's purposes, both what he has done and what he requires his people to do (*e.g.* Gn. 12:1ff.; Ex. 3:7ff.; Am. 3:7). In the NT, Jesus told his disciples what the Father had revealed (Jn. 15:15), and God revealed to Paul the mystery of his eternal purposes in Christ (Eph. 1:9ff.; 3:3ff.).

There is also a sense of revelation in which God comes to individuals and makes himself known to them (*e.g.* Ex. 3:2ff.; 6:3; Gal. 1:15f.). God is not only the author of his message, but the messenger as well, so that when people meet his word they are also met by him and he calls them to respond to his word. Older Protestant theologians tended to equate revelation with inspiration, defining the former as God's communication of his truth and the latter as his enabling the writers to record it faithfully. More recent theologians have stressed God's revelation through his direction of history and his making people aware of his presence and claims. In fact, the biblical conception of revelation demands that these two concepts be held together as complementary, not contradictory.

The necessity of revelation. God is so far from mankind that he cannot be seen (Jn. 1:18; 1 Tim. 6:16), and his thoughts cannot be guessed (Is. 55:8ff.). Even Adam, in the perfect setting of Eden, needed God to teach him (Gn. 2:16f.). However, mankind's perception of spiritual matters has become dulled by Satan (2 Cor. 4:4) and sin (*cf.* 1 Cor. 2:14), so that it is beyond our natural ability to know God. Even though his character is constantly presented through creation and conscience (Rom. 1:19ff.; 2:12ff.), he is not recognized or known, and people pervert the glimmers of revelation they do see by turning to idolatry (*cf.* Rom. 1:22ff.). There is therefore a need for revelation of God's forgiveness, and for the spiritual enlightenment to perceive it. The Jews had a revelation of God's mercy in the OT, but there was still a veil which prevented them from fully understanding it (2 Cor. 3:14ff.), and they fell victim to legalistic misinterpretation of it (Rom. 9:31-10:4). This need for divine enlightening is also stressed by Jesus (Mt. 11:25ff.; Jn. 6:44f.; 10:26ff.).

The content of revelation. In the OT, the foundation and framework of Israel's religion was the covenant in which God pledged himself to Abraham's clan as their God, with the consequent obligation that they were to be faithful to him (Gn. 17:1ff.). The character of the covenant was made more explicit in God's revelation of the law to Moses (Ex. 19:3ff.). Once written, that law was regarded as a definitive and permanently valid disclosure of God's will (Dt. 31:9ff.). Israel was promised a succession of prophets who would bring the people God's words (Dt. 18:15ff.; Je. 1:9). One of their roles was to give God's answers to individuals who sought his

particular guidance (1 Sa. 9:6ff.). The chief emphases of the OT revelation of God are upon God's uniqueness as Creator and Ruler, his holiness, and his covenant faithfulness.

In the NT, Christ and the apostles are the agents of a new revelation, fulfilling the OT covenant. God has spoken through his Son (Heb. 1:1ff.) as his final and crowning revelation. Jesus perfectly revealed the Father through his words and works (Jn. 1:18; 14:7ff.). In him the fullness of God dwelt (Col. 1:19), and through him all God's saving purposes were worked out (1 Tim. 2:5; 1 Cor. 1:30). Through Christ God revealed the secret of his purpose to save the church and restore the cosmos (1 Cor. 2:7ff.; Col. 1:19ff.), abolishing ancient divisions (Eph. 2:11-3:6).

See also INSPIRATION; PROPHECY.

REVELATION, BOOK OF. The last book of the NT, abounding in symbolism of a type that is not used today and to which we no longer possess the key. The symbolism was understood at the time it was written, and so the author felt no need to give explanations. Revelation is an example of apocalyptic literature and is the only NT book of its type (although there are other apocalyptic passages, *e.g.* Mt. 24). It is however unique in its restraint and prophetic content (*cf.* 1:1ff.) among other known (and usually anonymous) ancient apocalypses.

Contents. Messages from Jesus to 7 churches in the Roman province of Asia (1-3); visions of God and the

Lamb (4-5); the 7 seals opened (6:1-17; 8:1) and an interlude (7); the 7 trumpets sounded (8:2-9:21; 11:15-19) with another interlude (10:1-11:14); various wonders in heaven (12-14); the 7 plagues unleashed (15-16); judgments pronounced (17-19); visions of the new heavens and earth (20-22). The recurrence of the number 7 implies that some incidents are repeated, being described in different ways.

Author and date. Tradition has identified the internal hints (1:1, 9; 22:9) with John the apostle, the author of the Gospel of John and the three letters of John. The view dates back to Justin Martyr (*c.* AD 140). The main objection to this view is that the original Greek is unlike that of the other Johannine writings, showing scant respect for the rules of the language, and many scholars today deny apostolic authorship. It was clearly written at a time when the church was persecuted. If 17:9f. refers to Roman emperors, then the 5th was Nero and the book thus written shortly after his time; 17:11 may refer to the known myth that Nero had come alive again. It could also date from the persecution under Domitian at the end of the 1st cent. AD, a view stated by some early writers such as Irenaeus and Eusebius, and favoured by most modern scholars. Then the church was more established, and therefore more liable to the degeneration Rev. describes.

Interpretation. There are 4 main ways of looking at the book. The *preterist view* takes Rev. as describing past events, recording the author's conviction that God would judge the Roman empire for its evils. Certainly it is rooted in the author's own time, but it does have futuristic predictions (*e.g.* chs. 21-22). The *historicist view* sees it as a sweeping panorama of history between the first and second comings of Christ. This view was held by the Reformers, but no such interpretations have agreed on the precise episodes the symbols refer to, nor have they accounted for events in the E but concentrate on the W. The *futurist view* maintains that chs. 4-22 all deal with the end time. While taking the predictive elements seriously, this view removes the book entirely from the author's own time, and it would have had little meaning for his original readers. The *idealist or poetic view* suggests that Revelation is to encourage suffering Christians to endure to the end, employing symbolic language for nothing more than imaginative descriptions of God's victory. This can be linked with other views, although it does not take predictive elements seriously. Difficult as it is, it is likely that the book embodies all 4 elements, past, historical, future and poetic. Ultimately it does stress faithfulness under opposition, and assurance that God will triumph.

For some symbols see separate articles such as BEAST; SEA OF GLASS; *etc.*; see also APOCALYPTIC.

REWARD. The rewards given by God to people are seen as blessings and punishments reflecting his justice (Dt.

7:10; Ps. 58:11). It was expected that obedience would bring temporal rewards (Dt. 28), although the false conclusions that righteousness is rewarded automatically and that suffering is a certain sign of sin are rejected (as in Jb.; Pss. 37; 73). Jesus promised rewards to his disciples, always coupled with self-denial and suffering for the gospel's sake (Mk. 9:41; 10:29f.), and discouraged desire for human reward (Mt. 6:1). The ultimate reward of salvation in Christ depends entirely on God's grace (Rom. 6:23), begins in time (2 Cor. 5:5) and is complete in heaven (Rev. 21:3).

REZEPH. An important caravan centre on the Euphrates-Hamath route, destroyed by the Assyrians (2 Ki. 19:12); modern Resafa, 200 km ENE of Hama, Syria.

REZIN. The king of Damascus who with Pekah of Samaria threatened Ahaz of Judah (2 Ki. 15:37). He was killed by the king of Assyria in 732 BC (2 Ki. 16:9).

REZON. He fled from David and occupied Damascus, becoming its ruler (1 Ki. 11:23ff.). He may be identified with Hezion (cf. 1 Ki. 15:18); if so, he founded a dynasty of ARAM.

RHEGIUM. A port on the Italian shore of the Strait of Messina; shipping wanting to navigate the dangerous strait would wait there for favourable winds (Acts 28:13).

RHODA (lit. 'rose'). A slave at John Mark's mother's house (Acts 12:13ff.).

RHODES. The large island between Crete and the SW extremity of Asia Minor, lying across the main sea route between the Aegean and Phoenician ports. Three federated Greek states on it shared a common capital, also called Rhodes. Paul briefly visited it (Acts 21:1), by which time it was merely a leisure and learning resort.

RIBLAH, RIBLATH. A place in the Hamath district of Syria, on the R. Orontes 56 km NE of Baalbek. An easily defended site commanding the main Egypt-Euphrates route, it was chosen by Neco II as Egyptian HQ after he defeated Josiah at Megiddo in 609 BC (see also 2 Ki. 23:29ff.). Nebuchadrezzar of Babylon took it over in 605 BC and from it directed operations against Jerusalem 589-587 BC (2 Ki. 25:6, 20f.).

RIGHTEOUSNESS. The original OT word probably derives from an Arabic root meaning 'straightness', hence an action which conforms to a norm. The biblical understanding includes a basic ingredient of relationship between God and people (Je. 9:24) and between person and person (Je. 22:3). In the latter case, it is action which conforms to the requirements of relationship and promotes well-being and peace; for the later prophets especially it includes helping the poor and needy (Am. 5:12, 24).

In the relationship between God and people, righteousness implies a person's correct relationship to the will of God. God himself is righteous (Ps. 7:9) and thus a righteous judge (Ps. 9:4) and saviour (Is. 45:21). 'The righteous one' was a title of the coming Messiah (Is. 53:11; *cf.* Acts 3:14). The NT uses righteousness in the sense of conformity to the demands and obligations of God's will (Gal. 3:21). Human righteousness falls short of God's requirements (Rom. 3:9ff.), but true righteousness (a true relationship with God) is given to those who trust Jesus Christ and his atoning work (Rom. 3:21ff.). This brings the believer into eternal life under the rule of God (Rom. 6:12ff.) and must be expressed by righteousness of life (Phil. 3:12f.).

RIMMON. *Pagan god:* The title ('Thunderer') of the Damascus storm-god Hadad. Naaman took soil from Israel to Rimmon's temple to worship Israel's God there (2 Ki. 5:17f.). *Person:* The father of Ishbosheth's assassins (2 Sa. 4:2ff.). *Places:* 1. En-Rimmon in the Negeb near Edom (Jos. 19:7), probably Kh. er-Ramamim 16 km NNE of Beersheba. 2. A village in Zebulun (Jos. 19:13), possibly Rummaneh 10 km NNE of Jerusalem. 3. A cliff near Gibeah (Jdg. 20:45), possibly Rammon 8 km E of Bethel.

RIVER. Several OT words are thus translated, not always accurately. For example, the Jabbok in Dt. 2:37 was a wadi, dry in summer but a torrent in winter, a characteristic employed sometimes as a symbol of the power of enemies (Ps. 124:4). See articles under specific river names.

RIZPAH (lit. 'hot stone', 'a live coal'). One of Saul's concubines who was also taken by Abner (2 Sa. 3:7). She bore 2 sons to Saul, Mephibosheth and Armoni, who with the sons of Michal were given by David to the Gibeonites as repayment for Saul's atrocities (2 Sa. 21:1ff.); the other Mephibosheth, Jonathan's son, was spared.

ROCK. In the OT, a symbol of security (Ps. 40:2), often used of God (2 Sa. 22:32). Ps. 118:22, Is. 8:14 and 28:16 are important symbols taken up in the NT to describe Jesus, the rock rejected by the Jews becoming the cornerstone of God's true temple. Paul identified Jesus with the water-bearing rock of Israel's desert journey (1 Cor. 10:1ff.). For Peter as a 'rock', see PETER; POWER OF THE KEYS.

ROD (STAFF). A word with many meanings including a walker's or shepherd's stick (Ps. 23:4; Mk. 6:8); an instrument of punishment (1 Cor. 4:21); a soldier's club (2 Sa. 23:21); a symbol of authority (Ex. 4:20); a magician's wand (Ex. 7:12); a measuring stick (Rev. 11:1).

ROMAN EMPIRE. The geographical and administrative entity around the Mediterranean controlled by the Roman system of government, but which was far less rigid than the modern usage of 'empire' implies. The word *imperium* primarily signified the sovereign authority entrusted by the Roman people to the elected magistrates, embracing every form of executive power including the religious, military and judicial. When a Roman province was created, generally speaking its existing government was not suspended nor was it added to the Roman state. The Roman-appointed governor (whose title varied with the locality) worked in association with friendly powers in the area to preserve Rome's military security; in peacetime he was more of a diplomat than a monarchical ruler. The empire was held together more by Roman military might than by direct centralized administration. It embraced hundreds of satellite states which each enjoyed its individually negotiated rights and privileges. Piecemeal individual and community entitlements to Roman citizenship sometimes bought the loyalty of local people. It was not until AD 212, when citizenship was extended to all free residents, that the provinces became imperial territories in the modern sense.

This art of 'diplomatic imperialism' was developed during Rome's early dealings with its Italian neighbours. Rome acquired the leadership of the league of Latin cities, and gradually built up treaty relations with all the Italian states S of the Po valley. Sicily became the first country to be made a province, in 241 BC, and Sardinia followed in 235 BC. The province of Africa was formed after the destruction of Carthage in 146 BC. The area in S Gaul between the Alps and the Cevannes became known as 'The Province' in 121 BC, its inhabitants being called *provinciales* (hence Pro-

vence today). The province of Syria in which the Gospel and early Acts narratives are set was created by Pompey in 66 BC; most of Greece and Asia Minor—the regions of Acts and the NT letters—had been absorbed into Roman provinces in the 2nd cent. BC.

Until the 1st cent. BC the provincial governors were Roman magistrates in power usually only for a year and competition for the positions did nothing for stable government. After Caesar Augustus came to power a professional class of administrators appointed by the emperor was created. Three of the governor's main responsibilities are well illustrated in the NT. One was the maintenance of military security and public order. Fear of Roman military intervention led to Jesus' betrayal (Jn. 11:48ff.) and the threat of civil riot led to Paul's arrest (Acts 21:31ff.). The second was the collection of taxes, which the Caesars had put on an equitable census basis (Lk. 2:1); both Jesus and Paul defended Rome's right to collect money this way (Lk. 20:22ff.; Rom. 13:6f.). The third was jurisdiction; both by reference from the local authorities (Acts 19:38) and by appeal against them (Acts 25:9f.), legal proceedings were concentrated around Roman tribunals. Christians like Paul were happy to praise and use Roman justice (Acts 24:10).

The NT is bathed in the atmosphere of the Roman empire. Caesar's decree summoned Joseph to Bethlehem (Lk. 2:4) where Jesus was born, and Caesar's possible displeasure sealed Jesus' death warrant (Jn. 19:12). He is to be obeyed (1 Pet. 2:13), yet in the end he overreaches his authority and attacks the saints, to be finally punished by God (Rev. 17:5f., 14).

See also CAESAR; COLONY; ROME.

ROMANS, LETTER TO THE. *Contents.* Introduction and reasons for writing (1:1-15); doctrinal exposition (1:16-8:39), including the equal guilt before God of Jews and Gentiles (1:18-3:20), God's provision of justification through faith, and Abraham's example (3:21-5:21), and the union of the believer with Christ and its effects on his life (6:1-8:39); the problem of Israel (9:1-11:36), including the rightness of God's decisions (9:1-29), Israel's many opportunities to repent (9:30-10:21), and hope for Israel through the Gentiles (11:1-36); practical exhortations (12:1-15:13) relating to personal character (12), neighbourliness (13), and the need for tolerance among Christians over certain scruples (14:1-15:13); conclusion, warnings, and greetings (15:14-16:27).

The church at Rome. Little is known about its origins. It may have been founded by converts from the Day of Pentecost who returned home, but travel to Rome was relatively easy from the provinces and many Christians must have been among the travellers. By the time Paul, aware of Rome's strategic significance, wrote this letter, the church was large and well-established. A few years later the Christian community was significant enough for the emperor Nero to make it a scapegoat for the fire of Rome.

Claims that Peter founded the church can be dismissed for he was still in Jerusalem when the emperor Claudius expelled the Jews from Rome (possibly the Christians too) and the church had begun before that. And Paul would surely have mentioned Peter if he was head of the church. However, there is a strong early tradition that both Peter and Paul were martyred in Rome. The church was mostly Gentile but with a number of Jews; at times Paul addresses Jews (*e.g.* 4:1), at others Gentiles (*e.g.* 11:13). There is no evidence of Jewish-Gentile tension as in the letter to the Galatians.

Date and place of writing. In 15:25 Paul says he is on his way to Jerusalem with famine relief, and in 15:24, 28 he is looking no longer E but to the W and Spain. This fits well into the end of his 3rd missionary journey (Acts 20). There are indications in ch. 16 that he sent it from Corinth (Phoebe was a deaconess at Cenchreae, near Corinth, for example). A date between AD 57 and 59 would fit the known data about Paul's travels.

Purpose. Paul wants the Roman church to support him on his mission to Spain (15:24), and realizes too that he may have some spiritual gift to impart to them on the way (1:11f.). He may have heard of practical difficulties there which he addressed (especially ch. 14), and there is an allusion to false teachers in 16:17ff. But these are incidental purposes, and do not account for the treatise-like nature of Romans. It may well be that he wanted to deposit with this strategically important church a statement of his doctrinal position, although it is not a full statement of all his beliefs because it omits any proper treatment of the last things and the nature of the church.

Integrity. Few scholars doubt that Romans is an authentic letter of Paul. But more have questioned the authenticity of ch. 16 not because it is not Pauline but because it does not seem to belong to this letter. He seems to know too many people in a church he has never visited, for example. But because many people travelled to Rome, it is not surprising that some of his friends were among them. His commendation of Phoebe, unusual if he was unknown in Rome, fits in with the fact that people there did know him from previous places. There are indications that copies of the letter circulated without chs. 15 and 16, but this is most likely explained by it having been shortened by the heretical Marcion, with whom some of the textual variations are associated.

Leading themes. Five stand out. *The righteousness of God* is introduced at the beginning (1:17), and has 4 aspects: God's promises must be fulfilled in accordance with his character (3:3f.); his abhorrence of sin expressed by his wrath (2:5); the manifestation of righteousness in Christ's death (3:25f.); and the link between righteousness and faith (3:22). God's righteousness thus declares as righteous those who by nature are at enmity with God (5:10). *The goodness of God* is revealed not only by his righteous salvation of people (5:8) but also by his kindness and patience

(2:4). God's love is so enduring that nothing can separate the believer from it (8:35ff.). Even in his rejection of Israel, God demonstrates his mercy (10:21; 11:22). God's will is perfectly good for each person (12:2). *The sovereignty of God* is stressed especially in chs. 9-11 in relation to Israel's destiny. God's sovereign purposes are shown not only in the inclusion of Gentiles into his kingdom, but also in his promised restoration of Israel. Whatever the problems, Paul asserts, God's ways must always be right (11:33ff.).

Two related themes are especially highlighted in Romans. *The grace of God* is seen in the context of human sinfulness (the sinful nature, 'flesh' in some EVV) which Paul sees almost as a personal enemy attempting to destroy the soul (ch. 7). It reduces mankind to a wretchedness from which only Christ can deliver us. To achieve that deliverance, God took the initiative; Christ's death on the cross is God's provision for mankind so that sin may be forgiven (ch. 6). Alongside this is Paul's high regard for *the law of God* which is good (7:12) but completely ineffective as a means of salvation. However, the law consists of more than the mere letter of the laws given through Moses. Paul writes of the law of the Spirit (8:2) which produces in the believer a new way of looking at (but not disobeying) the requirements of a Father with whom he has an entirely new relationship. Christian life is not a matter of submitting to a legal code but is a Spirit-controlled life involving the qualities of righteousness, peace and love (5:3ff.; 14:17; 15:13, 30).

ROME. Founded traditionally in 753 BC on its 7 hills, Rome was a meeting-place rather than the home of a pre-existing people, attracting people from all over the Mediterranean. In NT times it was flourishing. Multi-storey tenement buildings housed a population of over a million. The aristocracy lived in suburban villas and country estates. The Caesars had furnished the heart of the city with an array of public buildings perhaps never equalled in any capital. It was an economic, trading, literary, artistic and administrative centre. In the book of Revelation it became the symbol of corrupt power and material lust, which persecuted the saints (ch. 17).

The origins of the church are obscure, perhaps because it was not closely connected with Paul. It is possible that Jews from Rome were converted on the Day of Pentecost, or Christian travellers took the gospel to the capital. Paul's first link with it was through Priscilla and Aquila who had fled from Rome to Corinth when Claudius expelled the Jews (Acts 18:2). He later decided he must visit Rome (Acts 19:21), planning to do so on the way to Spain (Rom. 15:24). The people he wrote to in Rom. 16 were friends he had met elsewhere on his travels, and who acknowledged him as an absent leader. Several of the references are to household units (16:5, 10f., 14f.). He finally reached Rome as a prisoner and a veil falls over his story (Acts 28:30f.). The Christian community was clearly large because the emperor Nero could direct his atrocities towards it c. AD 64.

In the late 2nd cent. AD the tradition appeared that Peter had worked and died as a martyr in Rome; in the 4th cent. AD it was claimed that he was the first bishop of Rome. The 2nd-cent. *First Letter of Clement* implies that both Peter and Paul died as martyrs there. Tombs alleged to be those of the apostles were found in the 4th cent. The possibility that Peter died there must be allowed, but that he founded the church or led it for any considerable time is much more doubtful.

See also ROMAN EMPIRE.

ROPE: See CORD.

ROSH. Benjamin's seventh son (Gn. 46:21).

RUFUS (lit. 'red'). Probably the same man in Mk. 15:21 (Simon of Cyrene's son, presumably known in Rome when Mk. was published there) and Rom. 16:13, whose mother had also cared for Paul.

RUHAMAH (lit. 'pitied'). A symbolic name for Israel in Ho. 2:1 (AV).

RULING SPIRITS: See ELEMENTS, ELEMENTAL SPIRITS.

RUMAH. In 2 Ki. 23:36 only; possibly Kh. al-Rumah 35 km inland from Mt Carmel.

RUNNER. Urgent messages were sent in ancient times by a swift runner (2 Sa. 15:1), the term later coming to mean a letter-carrier (Je. 51:31) often on horseback (Est. 8:10, 14).

RUTH. A Moabite woman who lived in the time of the Judges, and the heroine of the biblical book bearing her name. She had married the Israelite Mahlon who had moved to Moab with his father Elimelech, his mother Naomi and brother Chilion. The brothers died leaving no sons; Naomi decided to return to Israel and Ruth went with her. She claimed the protection of Naomi's relative Boaz who agreed to act as her kinsman-redeemer and married her. Their son Obed was the grandfather of David. See also next article.

RUTH, BOOK OF. *Contents.* The widowed Naomi returns from Moab to Bethlehem with her Moabite daughter-in-law Ruth (1); Ruth gleans in Boaz's field and appeals to him to become her kinsman-redeemer (2-3); Ruth and Boaz are married, Obed is born (4).

Authorship, date and purpose. It contains no clue as to its author; tradition ascribes it to Samuel. The setting is the period of the Judges (1:1) but the writing is later (former customs are explained in 4:1ff.). Estimates of the book's value have varied wildly. Among the suggestions are that it was David's family tree; a tract to counter the later exclusivism of Ezra and Nehemiah; or a humanitarian plea on behalf of the childless widow. Perhaps there was no motive, other than it was a story to be told.

See also previous article.

SABAEANS: See SHEBA.

SABBATH, LORD'S DAY. The Bible lays down the principle that 1 day in 7, 'the sabbath', is to be observed as a day holy to God. The commandment (Ex. 20:8ff.) is based on the fact that God himself rested (literally 'ceased') from his creative labour on the 7th 'day' of creation (Gn. 2:2); the principle still applies even if the 'day' of creation was not a literal 24-hour period. Although some have suggested the sabbath derived from Babylonian practice, the Babylonians had a 5-day week and their 'sabbaths' were not days of cessation of labour.

The day was a gift from God (*cf.* Ex. 16:29) for remembrance of him, and it also had a humanitarian purpose in which slaves were shown mercy by being allowed a regular rest (Dt. 5:14ff.). Sabbath legislation was integral to the OT law (*cf.* Lv. 19:3, 30), and on one occasion the importance of it was demonstrated by the death sentence being pronounced on a man who broke it (Nu. 15:32ff.). The prophets called for right observance of sabbaths (*e.g.* Is. 56:2ff.; 58:13) and condemned their abuse (Ho. 2:11); they stressed that God's day must be observed in God's appointed way. Nehemiah, after the Exile, reinforced the ban on sabbath trading (Ne. 10:31; 13:15ff.; *cf.* Am. 8:5). In the period between the Testaments the Jews developed minute details of how the sabbath was to be properly observed, and it was this legalism which Jesus so roundly condemned, identifying himself as Lord of the sabbath (Mk. 2:23ff.). He regularly attended synagogue worship on the sabbath (Lk. 4:16), but showed it was not wrong to do good or to prepare food on the sabbath (Lk. 6:1-11).

On the 1st day of the week—the day after the Jewish sabbath—Jesus rose from the dead, and this quickly became 'the Lord's day' on which Christians met for worship and used as their 'sabbath' (Rev. 1:10; *cf.* Acts 20:7). Paul perhaps assumes this in 1 Cor. 16:2 where he commands Christians to set aside their gifts on that day, although he does not make specific reference to a meeting. Before the Christian era, the 1st day of the month in Asia Minor and Egypt was called 'Emperor's Day' and so it would have been natural for Christians to adopt the idea and call their sabbath 'the Lord's day' in commemoration of the resurrection which pointed to Jesus' Lordship (*cf.* Rom. 1:4).

SABBATICAL YEAR. In the OT, after 6 years of crop production the land was to be left fallow for the 7th year (Lv. 25:2ff.). The poor could glean whatever grew; what they left was for the wild animals (Ex. 23:11). God promised that the 6th year would yield enough food to cover the period before the next possible harvest (Lv. 25:20f.). The sabbatical year was observed at times (Ne. 10:31; 1 Macc. 6:49, 53) and its avoidance was condemned (2 Ch. 36:21). Each 50th year was a jubilee in which the sabbath year sanctions were also enforced and land reverted to its original owners. The law reminded Israel that God owned the land, and that the sabbath principle must be carefully observed in all aspects of life.

SABTA, SABTAH. The 3rd son of Cush (Gn. 10:7) and probably a tribe in S Arabia.

SABTECA. The 5th son of Cush (Gn. 10:7), otherwise unknown, and probably a tribe in S Arabia.

SACKCLOTH. A coarse cloth usually made of goats' hair, and black in colour (Rev. 6:12). Sackcloth was worn as a sign of mourning (2 Sa. 3:31), penitence for sins (1 Ki. 21:27), or special prayer for deliverance (2 Ki. 19:1f.). It was usually worn next to the skin (2 Ki. 6:30). Palestinian shepherds wore it normally, because it was cheap and durable. Prophets sometimes wore it when they preached as a symbol of repentance (Is. 20:2). It is used symbolically for darkness in Is. 50:3.

SACRAMENTS. In general usage in the church after the NT period, the term was applied to rites such as baptism and the Lord's Supper. In everyday usage the term applied to a pledge or security deposited by the parties in a lawsuit and forfeited for a sacred purpose, and to the oath of loyalty to the emperor taken by a Roman soldier. These ideas combined to produce the concept of a sacred rite which was a pledge or token, the receipt of which involved an oath of loyalty.

The usual definition accepted by Reformed and Roman Churches is that a sacrament is an outward and visible sign, ordained by Christ, setting forth and pledging an inward and spiritual blessing; in Augustine's terms it is 'the visible word'. The obligation to continue NT rites depends on 3 factors: their institution by Jesus, his express command for their continuance, and their essential use as symbols of divine acts integral to the gospel revelation. Only baptism and the Lord's Supper fulfill all these requirements, and both are said in the NT to be necessary until the return of Christ (Mt. 28:19f.; 1 Cor. 11:26). Some churches, however, also regard as sacraments the rites of confirmation, orders, marriage, penance and extreme unction.

The elements of the sacraments have no power of themselves; their efficacy depends on Christ's command and their proper use by faithful people. Through them people are brought into communion with Christ in his death and resurrection (Rom. 6:3f.; 1 Cor. 10:16). It is the gospel word or covenant promise accompanying the signs which give them their meaning and efficacy (cf. Acts 2:38ff.). Rightly received, the sacraments convey blessings to the believer, but these blessings are not confined to the sacraments. The sacraments recall us to the death and resurrection of Christ and remind us of our obligation voluntarily to live a holy life.

See also BAPTISM; LORD'S SUPPER.

SACRIFICE AND OFFERING.

1. Old Testament.
Historical development. Many nations besides Israel practised sacrifices (*e.g.* Jdg. 16:23). The records of ancient Ugarit (*c.* 1400 BC) clearly indicate a developed ritual of sacrifices bearing similar names to those of the OT. Such parallels have led some scholars to conclude that Israelite sacrifices owe their origins to Babylonian, Canaanite or ancient nomadic rituals and fellowship meals. However, throughout its history, Israelite practice had many distinctive features of its own.

The earliest sacrifices mentioned in the OT are gift-offerings (Gn. 4:3f.) and a burnt offering (Gn. 8:20). Abraham probably offered burnt sacrifices regularly (*cf.* Gn. 22), and Jacob held a sacrificial meal to seal a covenant (Gn. 31:54). Noah's burnt offering had an atonement aspect, while most other early sacrifices seem to have been to honour God and to thank him for his goodness. After the Exodus the chief sacrifices were those associated with the 3 great festivals (see below). Other sacrifices for individual and national needs were for dedication (1 Sa. 6:14) and celebration (1 Sa. 1:3). When the temple was built by Solomon worship and sacrifice became more centralized. The prophets reacted against abuses and pagan elements brought into the cult (*e.g.* Is. 1:11ff.; Am. 4:4f.) but Ezekiel looked forward to a purified, centralized worship in the future (Ezk. 40-48). After the Exile, the temple and cult were reinstated and were valued (Hg. 1-2) when they were vehicles of sincere worship (Mal. 1:6ff.).

Sacrificial materials. An animal or bird offering had to be from the 'clean' (edible) creatures and could be a bullock, sheep, goat, dove or pigeon but not a camel or an ass (Ex. 13:13). Wild animals were not to be sacrificed because in a sense they already 'belonged' to God while domestic animals had become man's by his labours (*cf.* Ps. 50:9ff.; 2 Sa. 24:24). The main principle was that the best were to be given to God; the refrain 'without blemish' occurs regularly (*e.g.* Lv. 1:3). Human sacrifices are reported in the OT (Jdg. 11:29ff.; 2 Ki. 21:6) but they were prompted by non-Israelite practices and were everywhere condemned (Lv. 20:4f.; Je. 7:31ff.). Wine offerings were referred to in the basic laws (Nu. 28:7), and oil offerings were also made (Gn. 35:14). Incense was an offering made on its own (Ex. 30:7) and with a cooked cereal offering (Lv. 2).

Sacrificial occasions. The first public sacrifices which are well-attested were at the seasonal festivals, the Feasts of Unleavened Bread (connected with the Passover, Jos. 5:10ff.), Firstfruits or Weeks, and Ingathering or Booths or Tabernacles (Ex. 23:14ff.; 34:18ff.; Dt. 16). A twice-daily burnt offering began to be made at some point in Israel's history. The Passover was a family occasion (Ex. 12). Among other prescribed sacrifices were those for cleansing of lepers (Lv. 14), purification after childbirth (Lv. 12), and consecration of a priest (Lv. 8-9). First-born animals and first fruits of the crops were regular seasonal offerings (Ex. 13; 23:19), probably to deconsecrate the herd or crop; all was God's until the offering of part in lieu of the whole was made, then man was allowed to consume it.

Sacrificial rituals. The major animal sacrifices of Lv. 1-5 are described in a framework of a stereotyped ritual which has 6 acts, 3 belonging to the priest and 3 to the worshipper. (1) The worshipper brings the offering to the place of sacrifice. (2) He lays one or both hands on it, possibly confessing his sin and thus transferring his sin to the animal, or to identify himself with the offering. (3) He slaughters the animal (except in the case of national offerings, when the priest kills the animal). (4) The priest collects the blood and spatters it against all four corners of the altar. (5) He burns the blood and fat, especially the fat of the kidneys, liver and intestines; in some sacrifices the skin was burnt as well. (6) The remaining portions of the sacrifice are eaten in a sacrificial meal either by the priest and worshippers together (as in the peace offering), by the priests and their families, or by the priests alone. The sacrificial meal associated with the peace offering was the popular accompaniment of local worship in early times (1 Sa. 9). It became less important with the centralization of worship, but Ezk.

46:21ff. still made provision for it.

Types of sacrifice. There are 4 major types in the OT. The *burnt offering* was possibly the earliest and most typically Hebrew sacrifice. It was a regular rite (1 Ki. 9:25), was always offered on great occasions (1 Ki. 3:4), and remained dominant throughout the OT period (Ezr. 3:2ff.). It was originally made to atone for sin (Lv. 1:4), but later also may have had in it an element of homage and thanksgiving. The *cereal offering* (meal offering) often accompanied burnt offerings (Nu. 15:1ff.), although it could be made independently. According to Lv. 2 it could be of flour, baked cakes, or raw grain, together with salt, oil and frankincense. A memorial portion was burnt, the remainder eaten by the priests; it too was part of the Israelite's offering for forgiveness of sins. Likewise the *peace offerings* and *thank offerings* (*e.g.* 1 Sa. 13:9) were associated with atonement, but often followed by a joyous fellowship meal celebrating forgiveness (Lv. 3; 7). The priests had a specified portion of the sacrifice (Lv. 7:32ff.). This class of offering also included 'vow offerings', offered on fulfilment of some kind of promise made to God, and the 'freewill offering' (Lv. 22:18ff.).

The 4th type of sacrifice included the *guilt and sin offerings*. These were more concerned with ceremonial defilement than moral offence, although the moral aspect was not entirely absent. There were sin offerings for lepers (Lv. 14; *cf.* Mk. 1:44) and for women after childbirth (Lv. 12; *cf.* Lk. 2:24). They are not mentioned in Dt. and scarcely figure in the OT historical narratives, probably because they were of a personal and individual nature. The distinction between these offerings is unclear; the guilt offering seems to be rather more concerned with sins against other people and the sin offering with sins against God. Different animals were used according to a person's circumstances or status. A bull was offered for the high priest and the community, a male goat for a ruler, a female goat or lamb for an ordinary person, turtle-doves or pigeons for the poor, and flour for the very poor (Lv. 4; 5). The sin offerings for the high priest (Lv. 4:1ff.) and the whole community (Lv. 4:13ff.) followed more solemn ritual in which the blood of the animal was sprinkled in front of the curtain of the sanctuary and the meat was burnt outside the camp, not eaten (Lv. 6:30; *cf.* Heb. 13:11). On the Day of Atonement, the blood was sprinkled on the ark of the covenant.

The meaning of the sacrifices. Often the purpose is said to be to atone (*e.g.* Lv. 1:4), which may be understood as 'to cover', 'to wipe away' or 'to ransom by substitute'. The 2nd tends to be favoured by modern scholars, but the 3rd element is clearly present (*cf.* Lv. 17:11). All aspects of the sacrifice were important for achieving atonement, including the victim's death, the presentation of its blood, and its disposal, and none should be emphasized above the others. The substitutionary theory retains the emphasis on personal relationships, whereas the other views tend to descend to sub-personal or even magical levels. The fact that some sin offerings were eaten by the priests does not negate the substitutionary theory, because it may have been thought that the priests by their superior ceremonial holiness 'absorbed' the sin which had been transferred to the victim, or that the death of the victim 'neutralized' the sin placed on it.

The sacrificial system was something given by God (Lv. 17:11). Sacrifices were not human remedies but God's provision within the terms of the covenant. But the system was not perfect. There were no specific sacrifices for breach of the covenant itself (*cf.* Ex. 32:30ff.) and the system was open to abuse when the moral requirements behind it were ignored. In Is. 53 the highest point of OT religion is reached, as all that is valuable in the cult is taken up into a person, the Servant of the Lord, who makes sacrificial atonement and calls for love and personal allegiance.

2. New Testament.

The OT sacrifices were still being offered in NT times. Sacrifices were offered by or for Jesus according to custom at his 'presentation' in the temple (Lk. 2:42); he celebrated the Passover with its sacrificial lamb; and he assumed people would continue making sacrifices as his teaching stressed the moral obligations which lay behind them (*e.g.* Mt. 5:23f.). Even after the resurrection the apostles still attended the temple and Paul on at least one occasion offered sacrifices for the interruption of vows (Acts 21:20ff.;

cf. Nu. 6:10ff.). But in principle these sacrifices were made unnecessary because the old covenant was being swept away (Heb. 8:13).

The sacrifice of Jesus. The letter to the Hebrews stresses the superiority of Jesus' atoning sacrifice of himself once for all (10:1-18). That sacrifice is one of the chief themes of the whole NT. Jesus is the sacrificial lamb of God who takes away sin (Jn. 1:29, 36; 1 Pet. 1:18f.), the true Passover lamb (1 Cor. 5:6ff.); he is a sin offering (Rom. 8:3), and he is the guilt-offering Suffering Servant of Is. 53 (*cf.* 1 Jn. 1:7ff.). Some commentators have argued from Jesus' continual heavenly priestly ministry (Heb. 8:1ff.; 9:11, 24) that his death was not the main ingredient and that his 'sacrifice' goes on for ever. But this is denied elsewhere in Hebrews (*e.g.* 1:3; 7:27). The costly part of the sacrifice, the victim's death, is over; his presentation before God is something which has everlasting (and hence continual) effect, and he thus continues to intercede for his people (7:24f.) without repeating his sacrifice.

Sacrifice and the Lord's Supper. These are indissolubly connected by being complementary to each other. The NT words 'do' and 'remembrance' (1 Cor. 11:24f.) cannot carry a technical sacrificial meaning, as if the eucharist was a fresh sacrifice. But the argument of 1 Cor. 10:14ff. demands the view that the eucharist is a feast upon Christ's sacrifice and corresponds to Jewish fellowship meals. The meaning of the meal was not so much the appropriation of atonement as celebration of the fellowship with God which atonement effected, symbolized by a feast with God. On the basis of Jn. 6, there seems no doubt that what happens when Jesus' words are heard and applied also happens when the bread and the wine are received, in an equally spiritual way.

Spiritual sacrifices. These are frequently mentioned in the NT (*e.g.* Rom. 12:1; 1 Pet. 2:5). The OT writers had also referred to them occasionally (*e.g.* Ps. 51:16f.). They may be material and even involve death in the sense of sacrificing oneself for the Lord's sake (*e.g.* Phil. 2:17), but they never have a prescribed ritual, and are never referred to in the context of atonement. It appears that every act of a Spirit-filled person can be reckoned as a spiritual sacrifice; it becomes a 'sacrifice' in the sense that it is devoted to God and is acceptable to him because of the effects of the sacrifice of Christ (Heb. 13:15; 1 Pet. 2:5).

See also ATONEMENT; CLEAN AND UNCLEAN; FEASTS; LORD'S SUPPER.

SADDUCEES. Information about the Sadducees has survived only in sources generally hostile towards them, including the NT. Their name may be derived from Zadok, either Solomon's contemporary (*cf.* Ezk. 44:15f.) or a hypothetical early leader of the party, but even this is far from certain. Their origins are disputed; a political party, a religious party, a rural aristocratic body, and state officials have all been suggested. They were boorish, as rude to their peers as they were to aliens, counting disputes with

their teachers as a virtue. They had no following among ordinary people. Many Sadducees were priests, and almost all priests appear to have been Sadducees. Under the Herods and Romans they dominated the Sanhedrin, but died out after the temple was destroyed in AD 70. Their religion was conservative, accepting the permanent validity only of the written laws of the Pentateuch. They rejected doctrines of resurrection, angels and demons, and believed prosperity and adversity were solely the outcome of a person's course of action.

SAINTS: See HOLINESS.

SAKKUTH. In Am. 5:26 (RSV, GNB), the Assyrian god of war, sun and light, or Saturn. Other EVV such as NEB, NIV regard this astral interpretation as improbable and see in the word a reference to a tent-shrine.

SALAMIS. A port on the E coast of Cyprus, rivalling and eventually superseding the Roman capital Paphos in importance. Its harbour is now silted up. In NT times it had a large Jewish community (Acts 13:5).

SALECAH, SALCAH. A place in the extreme E of Bashan occupied by Gad (1 Ch. 5:11); possibly modern Salhad.

SALEM. The district ruled by Melchizedek (Gn. 14:18), usually identified with Jerusalem, although some link it with Salim, further E. The name means 'safe, at peace'. See

JERUSALEM; SALIM.

SALIM. A place near Aenon on the R. Jordan where John baptized (Jn. 3:23), probably the Salim (Salumias) or Tell Abu Sus 12 km S of Beisan. The Samaritans identify a Salim in Samaria with the Salem of Gn. 14:18.

SALMON, SALMA. 1. The father of Boaz, Ruth's husband (Ru. 4:20). 2. A son of Caleb (not the Caleb associated with Joshua), father of groups associated with the Kenites (1 Ch. 2:51ff.).

SALMONE. A promontory at the E end of Crete now called Cape Sidero (Acts 27:7).

SALOME. 1. One of the women who saw Jesus' crucifixion and went to the tomb on Easter morning (Mk. 15:40; 16:1). She was probably the mother of the sons of Zebedee (*cf.* their unnamed mother in Mt. 27:56), and the sister of Jesus' mother (the unnamed sister of Jn. 19:25). This would make James and John cousins of Jesus. 2. Herodias' daughter by her 1st husband Herod Philip, usually identified as the dancing girl of Mk. 6:22; she married her father's half-brother Philip the tetrarch.

SALT. The Hebrews had access to unlimited supplies of salt on the shores of the Dead Sea (Zp. 2:9) and the nearby hill of Salt. It was rock or fossil salt, the outer layer of which was flavourless and discarded (Mt. 5:13). Salt was used for preserving and seasoning food (Mt. 5:13; Mk. 9:50; Col. 4:6). It was often used to ratify agreements and thus became a symbol of faithfulness. See also HERBS AND SPICES.

SALT, CITY OF. In Jos. 15:62, a frontier post of Judah 'in the wilderness', identified with an Iron Age settlement at QUMRAN.

SALT, VALLEY OF. Saline encrustations in steppe and desert land are common, so certain identification of the place so named (*e.g.* 2 Sa. 8:13) is impossible. Traditionally it is a plain SSW of the Dead Sea overlooked by a salt range and passing into salt marshes, but there are other possibilities.

SALVATION. *Old Testament.* The main OT word for salvation has the basic meaning of 'bring into a spacious environment ('wide place', Ps. 18:36), with the metaphorical sense of being freed from limitation. It can refer to deliverance from disease (Is. 38:20, *cf.* v. 9), trouble (Je. 30:7) or enemies (Ps. 44:7). God alone can save his people (Is. 43:11), as he saved Israel from Egypt (Ps. 106:7ff.) and from Babylon (Je. 30:10). The Exodus was the great example of God's saving deliverance which moulded all subsequent understanding of salvation. Israel's experience of God's past salvation projected its faith forward in anticipation of God's full and final rescue in the future (Is. 43:11ff.; Ezk. 36:22f.). In the later periods of OT history this hope is expressed in terms of 'the day of the Lord' which would combine judgment with deliverance (Joel 2:1f.; Am. 5:18). This hope was seen as a new exodus to be fulfilled in the return from Exile (Is. 43:14ff.) but its disappointing and limited results projected the hope further forward to a new age (Is. 65:17f.). God's saving activity implies an agent, and while he employs human 'saviours' (*e.g.* Jdg. 3:9), he alone is the people's saviour (Ho. 13:4). The 'Servant songs' of Isaiah embody in the Servant God's moral salvation, although the term saviour is not actually given to him (*e.g.* Is. 49:1ff.).

New Testament. Non-religious usage of the term is almost entirely confined to a few references to people's lives being saved from acute danger (*e.g.* Acts 27:20, 31). Otherwise it refers to moral and spiritual deliverance. The word salvation is mentioned only once in the Synoptic Gospels (Lk. 19:9) but Jesus used 'save' and similar terms to describe what he came to do (*e.g.* Mt. 20:28) and to indicate what is demanded of people (Mk. 8:35). The references suggest that salvation was present in the person and ministry of Jesus, and especially in his death, and this is underlined in John's Gospel. People become God's children by trusting Christ, and especially his death, entering his kingdom through a new birth into eternal life (1:12f.; 3:5, 14ff.). This concept of salvation is illustrated by such metaphors of Jesus as bread (6:33ff.) and light (8:12). Eternal life is experienced now in a continuing relationship with Christ (15:5). In Acts, the apostolic proclamation is the call to repentance and the promise of forgiveness of sins for those who desire to be saved from a corrupt world (Acts 2:38ff.; 16:30ff.).

For Paul, there can be no salvation by means of keeping the Jewish law because it only serves to illustrate mankind's sin, and cannot remove it (Rom. 3:19f.). Instead, salvation is God's free gift to those who trust in the righteousness of Christ who has redeemed them by his death and justified them by his resurrection (Rom. 3:21ff.). The Holy Spirit then gives the believer the power to live a new life, ultimately to be conformed to Christ himself (Rom. 8:29). The letter to the Hebrews shows how the OT rituals provided only a superficial salvation, and that these have been replaced by the one sacrifice of Christ who was both priest and offering (Heb. 9:26; 10:12).

For James salvation cannot be by intellectual acknowledgment of God's existence without a corresponding change of heart resulting in works of righteousness (Jas. 2:14ff.). In 1 Pet. 1:5; 2:24f. salvation is both a present reality and a future promise. The book of Revelation and 1 John both see salvation in terms of cleansing from sin by virtue of Jesus' shed blood (1 Jn. 2:1f.; Rev. 1:5f.); admission to the heavenly city of salvation is open only to those who have trusted 'the lamb's' sacrificial death (Rev. 20:15; 21:27).

Relationship to non-biblical views. There are some parallels between the NT concept of salvation and passages in the Dead Sea Scrolls; one especially is close to the NT doctrine of salvation as acquittal through utter reliance on

491

God's mercy and grace. But the documents lack the NT's universal offer of salvation. The seeds of Gnostic teaching were clearly present in NT times; the Gnostics claimed salvation by special personal knowledge of God, which was intellectual rather than moral. Gnosticism divided soul and body, teaching that salvation was the soul's escape from the domination of physical passions and astrological forces. In the 2nd and 3rd cents. AD these ideas were wedded to Christian themes to produce Gnostic sects which the church had to counter.

The NT writers also had to distinguish their doctrine of salvation from current ideas held by the mystery religions. Those claimed to offer salvation from fate, which was achieved by the meticulous performance of cultic rituals. Their language parallels the NT (in such concepts as 'new birth' and titles such as 'Lord and Saviour') but the differences between the religions and the NT are stark. Their salvation was essentially non-moral, and there were no great saving acts. The cult of emperor worship perpetuated the age-long mirage of salvation through political power and organization. The Emperor Augustus after 31 BC was commonly called 'Saviour of the world', although this did not necessarily imply full divine powers. Later emperors such as Caligula, Nero and Domitian did take their divine 'status' seriously.

Biblical summary. The biblical concept of salvation has 3 essential aspects. It is historical in that it is effected through God's intervention in human affairs, and not through moral merit or religious practice; the emphasis is on salvation through Jesus' death (*e.g.* Eph. 1:7). It is moral and spiritual, in that it relates to deliverance from sin and moral guilt (Rom. 5:1), but not necessarily to deliverance from suffering in this life (*e.g.* 2 Cor. 11:23ff.). And finally it is eschatological, that is it relates to the establishment of God's kingdom, with the gift of God's riches in this life (Eph. 1:3) and the promise of future blessedness when salvation is completed at the return of Christ (*e.g.* Phil. 3:20).

See also ATONEMENT; FORGIVENESS; JUSTIFICATION; RECONCILIATION; REDEMPTION.

SAMARIA. The name of the N Israel capital and the territory surrounding it. It was built on a hill 11 km NW of Shechem by king Omri of Israel, who named it after the original landowner (1 Ki. 16:24). It had a temple for Baal of Sidon (Melqart), and other pagan shrines, which were eventually removed by King Jehu (2 Ki. 10:19ff.). Samaria was long considered by the prophets to be a centre of idolatry (*e.g.* Je. 23:13). It was besieged by the Syrian army on two occasions but miraculously delivered (2 Ki. 6:8ff., 24ff.; 7:3ff.).

Shalmaneser V of Assyria besieged and captured it 725-722 BC; his successor Sargon II deported many people from the area and the existence of N Israel was effectively ended (2 Ki. 17:18). The inhabitants were replaced by colonists from other parts of the

Assyrian empire (2 Ki. 17:24f.).

It was initially favourable to Alexander the Great who captured it in 331 BC, but when his prefect there was murdered he destroyed the city. Pompey began to rebuild it but Herod embellished it and named it Sebaste (Augusta) in honour of the emperor. Despite the antagonism between Judah and Samaria, Jesus travelled through it (Lk. 17:11; Jn. 4:4); Philip preached the gospel in the area (Acts 8:5).

Among the ruins uncovered by archaeologists was a palace from Ahab's time with a wide court in which lay a reservoir or pool (*cf.* 1 Ki. 22:38). A nearby storeroom contained over 200 plaques or fragments of ivories, possibly inlays from Ahab's furniture (*cf.* 1 Ki. 22:39). The remains of the city in Alexander's time are well preserved, including a round tower, a fortress and part of the city wall. The Roman city is notable for its great temple to Augustus built over the Israelite palaces.

See also next article.

SAMARITANS. In the OT they are only mentioned once, as the people imported to Samaria by Sargon king of Assyria (2 Ki. 17:29). There is little reason to believe that these people were the ancestors of the Samaritans often referred to in the NT, despite the assertion of the Jewish historian Josephus that they were. The earliest references to the later Samaritans indicate that they lived at Shechem (*e.g.* Ecclus. 50:26; 2 Macc. 5:22f., 'Gerizim'; *cf.* Jn. 4:5f.). And nothing that is known of later Samaritan religion suggests the pagan influence of 2 Ki. 17 and Ezr. 4.

The NT Samaritans as a distinctive group probably originated in the late 4th cent. BC when Shechem was rebuilt. As not all the N Israelites were exiled in 721 BC (2 Ch. 30) it is not surprising that there were still people adhering to the Israelite faith (Ezr. 4:2). A temple was built on Mt Gerizim and this led to a hardening of attitude between Jerusalem Jews and the Samaritans. This rival temple was destroyed by the Maccabaean warrior John Hyrcanus *c.* 128 BC, but the friction continued. During a Passover between AD 6 and 9, some Samaritans desecrated the Jerusalem temple by scattering bones in it. The main Samaritan theological writings now available date only from the 4th cent. AD and later, so it is not possible to reconstruct their beliefs in NT times in detail. They regarded only the Pentateuch (Gn.-Dt.) as authoritative, and looked forward to the return of Moses. The NT is mostly favourable towards them (*e.g.* Lk. 10:30ff.; 17:16ff.).

SAMGAR-NEBO. In Je. 39:3, one of Nebuchadrezzar's officers, possibly a title (*i.e.* 'Nergal-sharezer the Simmagir').

SAMOS. An island in the Aegean Sea off the Asia Minor coast SW of Ephesus, made a free state by Augustus in 17 BC; Paul sailed by it (Acts 20:15).

SAMOTHRACE. A small mountainous island in the N Aegean with a town of the same name (modern Samothraki). It was a centre of the mystery cult of the Kabeiroi fertility gods. Paul called there (Acts 16:11).

SAMSON. One of Israel's judges. His name derives from the Hebrew for 'sun' and it has been suggested that his stories are connected with sun mythology, but the essential historicity of the biblical record can hardly be doubted, and it is not unlikely that Israelites used a common Canaanite name. The Philistines had infiltrated Israelite territory and were dominating Judah (Jdg. 15:11). Samson waged a one-man campaign against them. He may be dated *c.* 1070 BC.

His birth was announced by an angel (Jdg. 13:3), and he was dedicated as a Nazirite although he seems to have taken seriously only one of the vows, that concerning his hair. He married a Philistine, killed 30 Philistines in revenge for their trickery (Jdg. 14:11ff.) and when his wife was given to someone else destroyed Philistine crops (Jdg. 15:2ff.). His abnormal strength later enabled him to escape arrest and kill more Philistines (Jdg. 15:9ff.). His uncontrolled sex urge proved his downfall. He became infatuated with Delilah who collaborated with the Philistines and eventually extracted from Samson the secret of his great strength. In one final act, he demolished the probably over-stressed Philistine temple to which he was chained, killing himself along with more Philistines (Jdg. 16).

Despite his sensuality, irresponsibility and lack of true religious concern, he is included in the NT heroes' gallery (Heb. 11:32). In OT times, a charismatic anointing did not necessarily produce holiness of life, but in the dark ages of the Judges period the sovereign God was able to use such a person. The Samson narratives are conspicuously devoid of the religious comment elsewhere in the book, as if the editor allows the stories to testify openly to the prevailing low conditions.

SAMUEL. The prophet who was contemporary with Saul and David, whose name is given to the 2 biblical books of Samuel. In Acts 3:24 he is regarded as the first of the prophets, in Acts 13:20 as the last of the judges. His mother Hannah had been unable to have children for some while, and when she conceived Samuel she dedicated him to God as a Nazirite. He was brought up in the temple at Shiloh by Eli, where he experienced a prophetic call (1 Sa. 1-3). After the Philistines captured the ark of the covenant, Samuel led Israel to victory at Mizpah (1 Sa. 4) and then became a circuit judge (1 Sa. 7). In his old age the Israelites demanded a king, and Samuel received divine guidance to anoint Saul (1 Sa. 8-12). After Saul exceeded his powers and offered sacrifices, Samuel had no more to do with him (1 Sa. 13-15), and privately anointed David as Saul's successor (1 Sa. 16). His combination of prophet, judge, war leader, national leader and perhaps priest has caused some scholars to doubt the historicity of the narratives. However, the judges combined judicial, national and military roles, and some prophets embraced priestly functions. At a period of crisis and transition, Samuel was called upon to fill an exceptional role. See also next article.

SAMUEL, BOOKS OF. The 2 books were originally one; the division goes back to the LXX but in the Hebrew Bible they were never divided until the 15th cent. AD. The LXX also linked them to Kings, and the Latin Bible (Vulgate) called all four 1-4 Kings (retained as subtitles in the AV). Many scholars believe that Samuel-Kings was once an entity, although editorial structures and formulae are very different.

Contents. The books cover the period *c.* 1050-950 BC. Samuel's early years (1 Sa. 1:1-7:14); Samuel and Saul (1 Sa. 7:15-15:35); Saul and David (1 Sa. 16-31); the early years of David's reign (2 Sa. 1-8); King David and his court (2 Sa. 9-20); appendix (2 Sa. 21-24).

Sources and composition. The title is not fully appropriate because Samuel's death is recorded in 1 Sa. 25:1 and he could not have been the author of the whole work. No one lived right through the eras of the 3 principal characters, Samuel, Saul and David, and there is no doubt that the author used earlier documents. Statements such as 'to this day' (*e.g.* 1 Sa. 27:6) suggest a further time lapse between the events and the composition of the book. At present, scholars tend to regard Samuel as an amalgam of individual narratives brought together in stages. In 1904, A. Kennedy suggested 5 basic documents were involved, and his scheme has been followed with modifications by others: a history of Samuel's early years; a history of the ark of the covenant; a favourable history of the monarchy; a hostile history of the monarchy; and a court history of David. But the exact number and nature of sources is still a cause of debate. It is generally agreed that the editor was very discreet in adding his own touches to the documents he selected.

Purpose. There is clearly a tension in the books, combining both positive and negative views of the monarchy. Rather than simply amalgamating documents with opposing views, Samuel's final author was typically prophetic, seeing the monarchy as an institution ordained by God but taking a detached view of each king. Apart from his biographical concern, the author was also very interested in election and rejection.

SANBALLAT (lit. 'Sin (the moon-god) has given life').An opponent of Nehemiah. According to papyri found at Elephantine, he was governor of Samaria in 407 BC. If he was, or hoped to become, governor when Nehemiah returned to Jerusalem in 445 BC, he probably wanted control of Judaea as well, hence his opposition to Nehemiah. He may have been an Israelite; his religion was probably syncretistic (*cf.* 2 Ki. 17:33).

SANCTIFICATION, SANCTIFY.

Old Testament. The Hebrew root word has 2 basic meanings. It can mean 'set apart for exclusive use', 'separated', 'regarded as sacred in contrast to the profane', or it can mean 'brightness', an idea related to purification. God is depicted as holy and majestic, and his people are called to recognize his holiness and his sovereign claims over them (Is. 6:3ff.; 8:13). Both objects (such as the tabernacle, Ex. 29:44; garments, Lv. 8:30; fields, Lv. 27:17) and people (Ex. 19:14; 28:41) could be sanctified (or consecrated) in the sense of being set apart for God's use. This sanctification could be simply external and ritual and was not always accompanied by the deeper inner reality. God required a moral response from his people reflecting his righteousness (Dt. 4:6ff.); the prophets disparaged external rituals which were not accompanied by holy living (*e.g.* Is. 1:4, 11).

New Testament. The emphasis is on inward transformation leading to purity of thought and deed expressed in lives of goodness and godliness. There is an occasional use of the idea in its OT sense of consecration (*e.g.* Mt. 23:17ff.; Jn. 17:17ff.), and the letter to the Hebrews acts as a bridge between this and the sense of moral and spiritual change. Jesus, by his sacrifice, not only set his people apart but also equipped them inwardly to worship and serve God (Heb. 10:10). Paul sometimes regards sanctification as a status conferred on believers (*e.g.* 1 Cor. 1:2). But he also sees it as a moral and spiritual transformation of the person who has been justified before God by faith in Christ. God's will is our sanctification (1 Thes. 4:3); to be sanctified wholly is to be conformed to Christ's image (Col. 3:10). As justification implies rescue from the penalty of sin, so sanctification implies rescue from the pollution of sin.

The extent of sanctification in Christian experience has been disputed. Some see it either as a crisis experience subsequent to conversion in which the root of sin in our lives is pulled up or the principle of sin is rubbed out. Others regard it as a process of growth, but even they are divided. Some maintain that perfection at least of loving motives (*cf.* Mt. 5:48), if not of conduct, is possible in this life. Others suggest that God requires conformity to his law only to the extent that our abilities allow, and hence that 'perfection' is possible (although this cannot really be maintained in the light of the normal interpretation of Dt. 6:5). Many suggest however that full perfection is not possible until Christ returns (1 Jn. 3:2f.). The NT lays equal stress on both God's part and ours in sanctification. There is an intense struggle against sin to be fought (Rom. 7-8; Gal. 5) and God does not transform a person without their active co-operation in the battle against sin. The Holy Spirit works through the believer's faithful dependance upon him to produce increasing spiritual maturity.

See also HOLINESS; SPIRIT, HOLY.

SANCTUARY. A place set apart for religious worship. The term is used in the Bible almost exclusively for places where Israel's God was worshipped. Archaeologists have uncovered many pagan sanctuaries. Israel's first sanctuary was the mobile tabernacle (Ex. 25-31; 36-40). When the people settled in Canaan, David planned and Solomon built a permanent temple (1 Ch. 22:19). It was defiled by later kings who allowed pagan practices in it (*e.g.* Ezk. 5:11). See also TABERNACLE; TEMPLE.

SAND. Found extensively along the Mediterranean shores of Palestine and Egypt, and in deserts, it is a striking symbol of countless crowds (*e.g.* Rev. 20:8). It also conveys the idea of instability (Mt. 7:26).

SANHEDRIN. The highest tribunal of the Jews which met in Jerusalem, and also the name for lesser tribunals, often translated 'council' in EVV. According to tradition it originated with the 70 elders who helped Moses (Nu. 11:16ff.), and Ezra is supposed to have reorganized this group after the Exile (*cf.* the elders of Ezr. 5:5; 6:14, and the officials of Ne. 2:16; 4:14). Later the Greeks allowed a Jewish 'senate' of elders representing the nation (1 Macc. 12:6; 2 Macc. 4:44), apparently presided over by the high priest. Under the Romans it had wide powers. Julius Caesar extended its powers over all Judaea; these were curtailed during the reign of Herod the Great (37-4 BC) and extended again AD 6-66 when the internal government of the country was in the Sanhedrin's hands. But during Jesus' lifetime those

powers were restricted to Judaea; the Sanhedrin had no authority over him when he was in Galilee. After AD 70 it was abolished, the replacement Court of Judgment having only moral and religious authority.

The Sanhedrin was originally composed of the predominantly Sadducean priestly aristocracy, but Pharisees and scribes were included from the days of Queen Alexandra (76-67 BC). In NT times it consisted of the acting and former high priests, their families, elders and scribes presided over by the acting high priest (*cf.* Mt. 26:3f., 57ff.). The local councils (*e.g.* Mt. 5:22; 10:17) were courts of at least 7 elders, in large towns up to 23 elders.

At the time of Jesus the Sanhedrin had civil jurisdiction according to Jewish law and some criminal jurisdiction as well. It could order arrests by its officers (Mt. 26:47; Acts 5:17ff.), and could judge cases not involving capital punishment; those required Roman confirmation (Jn. 18:31). It was the Sanhedrin which charged Jesus with blasphemy (Mt. 26:57ff.), Peter and John with false teaching (Acts 4), and Paul with breaking the law of Moses (Acts 22-24). The Romans reserved the right to interfere at any point, as in Acts 23. The Jerusalem Sanhedrin had definite (but now unknown) meeting times; local councils met on the 2nd and 5th days of the week. They sat in a semicircle and had 2 clerks of court. For acquittal a simple majority was required; for condemnation a two-thirds majority. The benefit always lay with the accused, and there are elements about the trial of Jesus which point to a miscarriage of normal justice.

SAPPHIRA. Wife of Ananias, Christians who lied about their gifts to the church (Acts 5:1ff.).

SARAH, SARAI (lit. 'princess'). The principal wife of Abraham who was also his half-sister (Gn. 20:12). She twice posed as his sister to avoid Abraham being murdered by rival suitors (Gn. 12; 20). She was unable to have children and gave her maid Hagar to Abraham as a surrogate mother for their heir. But in her old age she was promised a son; she laughed at the idea but Isaac was duly born, at which Sarah asked for Hagar and her son Ishmael to be thrown out (Gn. 18; 21). She died aged 127 (Gn. 23:1ff.) and is named as an example of faith (Is. 51:2; Heb. 11:11). Paul writes of Sarah as the mother of the people of God's promise (Rom. 9:9).

SARDIS. A city in the Roman province of Asia, in the W of what is now Asiatic Turkey. It was the capital of the ancient kingdom of Lydia and a byword for wealth. Despite its clifftop location it was captured by both Cyrus (546 BC) and Antiochus the Great (214 BC). In Rev. 3:1ff. the church there seems to have been imbued with the spirit of the place, relying on past reputation without any present achievement, and failing to be vigilant. The 'white garments' relate to its luxury clothing trade.

SARGON. The ruler of Assyria 722-705 BC. He is named only once in the OT (Is. 20:1) but his campaigns in Syria and Palestine lie behind Isaiah's prophecies. He completed the defeat of Samaria (2 Ki. 17:5f.) c. 722 BC, indecisively attacked Babylon, and then defeated Syria and its allies at Qarqar in 720 BC. At this time Isaiah warned Judah not to trust Egypt to help it against the Assyrian threat (Is. 10:5ff.). In 716 Sargon sent armies against the Arabs in Sinai, receiving tribute-tax from them and from Egypt. He crushed a rebellion at Ashdod in 712 BC (Is. 20:1), Judah narrowly escaping invasion. Sargon was succeeded by his son Sennacherib in 705 BC, having been killed in action. See also ASSYRIA.

SARID. In Jos. 19:10, 12, a S border town of Zebulun; its location is not known.

SARSECHIM. A Babylonian official in Jerusalem after its capture in 587 BC (Je. 39:3).

SATAN. The name of the prince of evil, meaning 'adversary'. OT references are few. He incites David to number Israel (1 Ch. 21:1), makes an accusation against the high priest Joshua (Zc. 3:1f.) and brings havoc to Job (Jb. 1-2). Most information about this being who sinned from the beginning (1 Jn. 3:8) comes from the NT, where among his names are the devil (Mt. 4:1ff.), Beelzebul (Mt. 12:24ff.), the ruler of this world (Jn. 14:30), and the prince of the power of the air (Eph. 2:2). He is depicted as hostile to God.

Jesus came into the world to destroy all his works (1 Jn. 3:8) and confronted massive temptation in his ultimately successful mission (Mt. 4:1ff.; Heb. 4:15). The NT writers depict the ongoing conflict in severe terms. The devil prowls like a lion for prey (1 Pet. 5:8), but also cunningly disguises himself as a friend (2 Cor. 11:14).

Christians are never free from spiritual warfare, for which God has provided them with 'armour' (Eph. 6:11ff.). So clad, they can successfully resist Satan (Jas. 4:7; *cf.* 1 Pet. 5:9), but must give him no opportunity to strike (Eph. 4:27) and must look for the escape route God provides for tempted Christians (1 Cor. 10:12f.). He worked through Jesus' followers (Mt. 16:23) as well as through his enemies (Jn. 8:44), and inspired Judas to betray Jesus (Jn. 13:2). People may so give themselves over to him that in effect they belong to him (1 Jn. 3:8ff.). He hinders mission (1 Thes. 2:18; *cf.* Mk. 4:15) and may have physical effects on people (Lk. 13:16). But he can act only within the limits God imposes (Jb. 1:12), and will be totally destroyed by Jesus at the end (Rev. 20:10); his defeat has already been achieved through Jesus' death (Jn. 12:31; 16:11).

See also ANTICHRIST; DEMONS; EVIL SPIRITS.

SATRAP. A provincial governor in the Persian empire (*e.g.* Ezr. 8:36; Est. 3:12). There were 20 satrapies; Syria-Palestine was part of the satrapy 'Beyond the River' (Ne. 3:7), *i.e.* W of the Euphrates.

SATYR. 'Hairy one', 'he-goat'. Possibly gods appearing like goats ('goat idols', NIV); referred to occasionally in OT (*e.g.* Lv. 17:7; Is. 13:21).

SAUL. The first king of Israel, whose pathetic story is covered in 1 Sa. 9-31. He was a man of great physique and courage. He was anointed by Samuel, who had first warned the Israelites what they were letting themselves in for (1 Sa. 8; 10). Saul soon won a great victory, and was magnanimous in it (1 Sa. 11). Three times, however, he disqualified himself from his role. Through his impatience he exceeded his powers by offering sacrifices (1 Sa. 13:7ff.), for which Samuel prophesied the rejection of Saul's kingship. Then he disobeyed God by sparing some of the Amalekites (1 Sa. 15), and thirdly he resorted to a medium in order to obtain an interview with the deceased Samuel. However one interprets the result of this attempt to communicate with the dead, Saul's doom was made clear (1 Sa. 28). His later years were spent in bitter conflict with his eventual successor David, for details of which see DAVID. He was particularly susceptible to moodiness and inner uncertainty, but his disobedience is presented by the biblical authors as inexcusable.

For Saul of Tarsus in the NT, see PAUL.

SAVOUR. Used in AV to mean a fragrant aroma (2 Cor. 2:15f.), savoury taste (Mt. 5:13), or 'to favour' in Mt. 16:23.

SCAPEGOAT. In Lv. 16:8, 10, a goat is chosen 'for Azazel' and released into the desert bearing Israel's sins, symbolically taking them away to the region of death.

SCEPTRE. An often ornate staff or rod carried as a symbol of personal authority, usually by kings but also by others (cf. Ps. 23:4; Ezk. 19:11). Ps. 45:6 is applied to Jesus (Heb. 1:8) whose sceptre is one of righteousness.

SCEVA. The father of the 7 magicians who used a spell for exorcism incorporating the name of Jesus. They were repudiated by the demons and attacked by the demon-possessed man (Acts 19:13ff.). The incident demonstrated that the name of Jesus was not an automatically effective formula. The description 'Jewish high priest' may have been self-adopted for advertisement.

SCHOOL: See EDUCATION.

SCORPION. There are 12 species in Palestine, the largest up to 15 cm but most are much smaller and none has a normally fatal sting. They are mentioned proverbially in 1 Ki. 12:11 (possibly referring to a studded whip) and elsewhere. Jesus' parallel to an egg (Lk. 11:12) recalled the egg-shaped fatty main segment of many scorpions.

SCOURGE, SCOURGING. The scourging with a multi-tailed whip studded with bone or lead (Mt. 27:26) was a preliminary stage in carrying out

a crucifixion; that proposed in Lk. 23:16 may have been intended as a substitute punishment.

SCRIBES. *Old Testament.* They were important professional writers in ancient Israel, employed by the public to transcribe contracts, write letters and keep accounts and records (Je. 32:12; 36:26ff.). Others worked in public administration ('recorder', 1 Ki. 4:3), and the Chief Scribe was a royal adviser (1 Ch. 27:32). Some had religious roles (2 Ki. 12:10), but until the Exile the scribal profession was separate from the priesthood. After the Exile they assumed the role of copyists, preservers and interpreters of the religious law (Ezr. 7:6). Ezra was both priest and scribe (Ezr. 7:11) and possibly acted as adviser on Jewish affairs at the Babylonian court. By the 2nd century BC most scribes were priests. They wore fine clothes with a pen-case or inkhorn hanging from a girdle (Ezk. 9:2); they used reed pens and sometimes styli for writing cuneiform script. See also WRITING.

New Testament. The scribes were experts in religious law (cf. Ecclus. 38:24) and had become a distinct political party as a result of the repressive measures of Antiochus Epiphanes against the Jews in the 2nd century BC. They originated the synagogue services. They claimed their oral traditions (legal decisions) to be more important than the written law (Mk. 7:5ff.), which easily led to religious formalism. They gathered pupils around them and lectured in the temple (Lk. 2:46). They also administered the law as unpaid judges in the Sanhedrin, hence their title 'lawyers' (*e.g.* Mt. 22:35). They were distinct from, yet mostly belonged to, the Pharisees' party. They clashed with Christ (*cf.* Mt. 7:28f.), persecuted the apostles (Acts 4:5ff., but some sided with Paul against the Sadducees, Acts 23:9), and some believed in Jesus (see Mt. 8:19). See also EDUCATION.

SCRIPTURE. Whenever the NT refers to 'the Scriptures', the original readers would have understood the implication that the term included the whole OT, in which the gospel was rooted and which Christ fulfilled (Lk. 24:44; 2 Tim. 3:15ff.). In referring to the Scriptures in 1 Cor. 15:3 Paul relates the resurrection of Jesus (not the 'third day' itself) to prophecy. The question as to when Christian writings came to be regarded as Scripture is uncertain. In 2 Pet. 3:16 there may be an early reference to Paul's writings as Scripture, although it can be translated 'they twist the Scriptures *as well*'. In 1 Tim. 5:18 Paul quotes perhaps from a collection of early Christian sayings and from the OT and gives both the status of Scripture. He also uses the scriptural designation 'it is written' in 1 Cor. 2:9 for an otherwise unknown quotation, which occurs in other (non-biblical) Christian writings. See also BIBLE; NEW TESTAMENT CANON.

SCYTHIANS. A tribe of horse-riding nomads and warriors from W Siberia inhabiting the Black Sea–Caspian area from *c.* 2000 BC. They assisted Assyria against the Medes, relieving Nineveh *c.* 630 BC, and later attacked Palestine. They established their capital at Neapolis in the Crimea in 110 BC. Paul refers to them in Col. 3:11.

SEA. The sea most referred to in the Bible is of course the Mediterranean (the 'Great Sea', *e.g.* Jos. 1:4). The Hebrews had little enthusiasm for the sea, however, their fear perhaps stemming from the ancient Semitic belief that the sea personified the power that fought against God. But their God was the sea's Creator (Gn. 1:9f.) and Controller (Ps. 104:6ff.). Some of the manifestations of his power were against the sea (Ex. 14-15; *cf.* Mt. 14:25ff.). In the world to come, the sea will disappear (Rev. 21:1). See also SHIPS AND BOATS.

SEA OF GLASS. Seen by John in his vision of heaven (Rev. 4:6; 15:2). The crystal-like appearance contrasts with the opacity of ancient glass and symbolizes purity; the fire in it suggests God's wrath. The victory song beside it recalls that of the Iserlites beside the Red Sea (Ex. 15).

SEAL, SEALING. *Old Testament.* Engraved seals were common in ancient times. They were used as a mark of authority (Est. 8:8ff.); to witness documents (Ne. 9:38); to secure a document (Is. 29:11) or a door (Dn. 6:17); and as a symbol of what is securely held, such as someone's sins before God (Jb. 14:17). The commonest form was the cylinder seal which was rolled over clay. Stamp or

501

scarab seals were also used on clay or wax lumps. They were worn on a cord round the neck (Gn. 38:18); scarab seals or seal stones were also set into signet rings (Est. 3:12). Hard semi-precious stones were engraved by specialists to make seals, but poor people could buy roughly-engraved seals made of terracotta, limestone or wood.

Before the monarchy cylinder seals had patterns, well-filled designs, or rows of men. Later Palestinian seals, usually oval, had images of lions, winged human-headed lions or sphinxes (cherubim), griffins or the winged uraeus-snake; Egyptian motifs including the lotus flower and the ankh symbol were also common. After the 7th cent. BC, most seals had only a 2-line inscription. Many seals bear the owner's name and perhaps his title; one jasper seal found at Megiddo is inscribed 'Of Shema, servant of Jeroboam' (*i.e.* Jeroboam II). The impression of a seal found at Lachish is inscribed 'Of Gedaliah who is over the household' and may have belonged to the governor of Judah (2 Ki. 25:22ff.). Such seals reveal a range of Hebrew names wider than that of the OT, and the titles they bear widen our knowledge of the administration of the times. Jar handles were also stamped either with the place of manufacture or the owner's name, and many of these have been recovered.

New Testament. The literal sense is occasionally mentioned, as in the sealing of Jesus' tomb (Mt. 27:66) and the apocalyptic scroll (Rev. 5:1f.).

Figuratively, it is used by Paul in the sense of a seal of approval in Rom. 15:28 (RSV mg.); of the Corinthians being a vindication of his apostleship (1 Cor. 9:2); and of circumcision as a confirming seal of the faith which existed before the rite took place (Rom. 4:11; *cf.* Rev. 7:2ff.).

Paul's most important use of the term is 'sealing with the Spirit'. In Eph. 1:13 the idea is of possessing now a guarantee of what is to come (*cf.* Eph. 4:30; 2 Cor. 1:21f.). Although this has sometimes been linked to baptism, it clearly relates primarily to the gift of the Holy Spirit as such, whether or not this gift is associated with baptism. So a person is sealed at the point of commitment, which may or may not be related to the baptism which expresses that commitment. The point of Paul's use of the term is to stress the fact that the Christian is authenticated by the Holy Spirit; the Spirit is the stamp of the person's new 'owner', and thus guarantees his eternal security, and confirms God's covenant with him.

SEBA. The son of Cush (Gn. 10:7), and a land and people in S Arabia. The wealth of Seba is mentioned figuratively as part of Israel's ransom (Is. 43:3); the tall Sabaeans were to acknowledge Israel's God (Is. 45:14). Possibly an older name for SHEBA.

SECACAH. A settlement in NE Judah (Jos. 15:61), possibly Kh. es-Samrah, a fortified site controlling irrigation works.

SECRET: See MYSTERY.

SECU. A place visited by Saul when searching for David (1 Sa. 19:22); possibly Kh. Shuweikeh 5 km N of el-Ram (Ramah).

SECUNDUS. A Thessalonian Christian who accompanied Paul with a gift to Jerusalem (Acts 20:4). The Latin name is attested in Thessalonian inscriptions.

SEED. The fertilized and mature ovule of a flowering plant which enables the species to perpetuate itself. The offspring of people are also called 'seed' (*e.g.* Gn. 3:15). In his parables, Jesus used seed symbolically to represent God's word sown in people's hearts (Mk. 4:3ff.), his people scattered through the world (Mt. 13:24ff.), and the small beginnings of the kingdom (Mt. 13:31f.). In 1 Cor. 15:35ff. Paul describes the relationship of the resurrection body to the physical body in terms of that between a full-grown plant and its seed.

SEIR. A mountain (Gn. 14:6), a land where Esau went to live (Gn. 32:3), and a people (Ezk. 25:8), all in the general area of Edom.

SELA. Meaning 'rock' or 'cliff', it may be used of any rocky place, and occurs several times in the OT. The main site so named is a fortress city of Moab captured by Amaziah of Judah and renamed Joktheel (2 Ki. 14:7), and may be referred to also in Is. 42:11; Ob. 3. It is traditionally identified as a rocky outcrop behind Petra and remains of a 7th-cent. BC settlement have been found there. But es-Sela 4 km NW of Bozra suits the evidence better.

SELAH. An isolated word occurring 71 times in Psalms and 3 times in Habakkuk, assumed to be a musical or liturgical sign although its meaning is unknown. It may be an instruction to choristers or musicians to lift up their voices or instruments, or to worshippers to lift up their hands or voices in prayer. It has also been seen as a cry like 'Amen'.

SELEUCIA. The former port of Antioch in Syria (1 Macc. 11:8) 8 km N of the Orontes R. and 25 km from Antioch itself. Founded by Seleucus Nicator in 301 BC, it lay at the foot of Mt Rhosus in the NE corner of a fertile plain still noted for its beauty. Antiochus the Great captured it in 219 BC and beautified it. The Romans made it a free city in 64 BC; it began to decay early in the Christian era. It is referred to in Acts 13:4, and is possibly inferred in Acts 14:26; 15:30, 39.

SELEUCUS. One of Alexander the Great's generals who founded the Seleucid empire which covered most of Asia Minor before the Roman conquest. The Maccabaean revolt, and the rise of the main religious sects of Jesus' time, resulted from the Seleucid attempt to secure Palestine.

SELF-CONTROL. The last of the 9 fruits of the Spirit in Gal. 5:22f., where it seems to be opposed to drunkenness and carousing in the corresponding list of vices (vv. 19ff.). In 2 Pet. 1:6

503

it appears as the midpoint in a believer's moral progress which begins with faith and culminates in love. In 1 Cor. 7:9 Paul uses the word in the sense of chastity but he was not thereby advocating universal celibacy (*cf.* 1 Tim. 4:2f.). A second NT word with a similar meaning is often rendered 'temperate' (*e.g.* 1 Tim. 3:2) which makes a specific reference to drunkenness but it can also have a wider meaning of self-control as in 1 Tim. 3:11. Rather than being under the influence of drink, believers are told to be 'drunk' with righteous zeal for the Christian warfare inspired by the Holy Spirit (Eph. 5:18).

SENAAH. Exiles belonging here returned from Babylon (Ezr. 2:35); it may have been near Jericho.

SENATE. In Acts 5:21, the SANHEDRIN.

SENIR. A peak in the Hermon range with fir trees growing on its slopes (Ezk. 27:5).

SENNACHERIB. The ruler of Assyria 705-681 BC. He marched on Babylon and in 702 BC defeated its ruler Merodach-baladan (who had sent envoys to Judah seeking support, 2 Ki. 20:12ff.). Hezekiah of Judah led an anti-Assyrian coalition and had called for help from Egypt (Is. 30:1ff.), and Sennacherib campaigned against the coalition in 701 BC. The kings of Sidon, Arvad, Byblos, Beth-ammon, Moab and Edom submitted to him; towns like Ashkelon which did not were

despoiled. He destroyed 46 walled towns and many villages in Judah from which he took 200,150 captives. From Lachish he sent officers to demand the surrender of Jerusalem (2 Ch. 32:9). His own account speaks of having Hezekiah shut up 'like a caged bird' in Jerusalem (*cf.* 2 Ki. 18:13ff.) but does not mention any conclusion of the siege or the plague which destroyed his army (2 Ki. 19:32ff.).

A further campaign against Babylon was concluded with the sack of the city in 689 BC. At home he reconstructed Nineveh, building a splendid palace and an aqueduct to irrigate parks and large tracts of land. The king was assassinated by two of his sons while worshipping, and another, Esarhaddon, took over the throne (2 Ki. 19:37). The apparent lack of time-gap between his Palestinian campaign and death in the biblical record does not of itself imply he had a second, later Palestinian campaign of which no other records exist as some scholars have suggested.

SEPHAR. A mountain or promontory in S Arabia defining the border of Joktan's territory (Gn. 10:30); the town Zafar has been suggested.

SEPHARAD. The place where captives from Jerusalem were exiled (Ob. 20). It is unidentified but could have been Sardis in Asia Minor.

SEPHARVAIM. A city captured by Assyria (2 Ki. 17:24, 31). It was probably in Syria and may be the same as the later Sibraim near Damascus

(Ezk. 47:16).

SERAIAH (lit. 'Yahweh has prevailed'). Several OT people are so named, including David's scribe (2 Sa. 8:17) also called SHAVSHA (1 Ch. 18:16), and the chief priest at the time of Zedekiah who was killed by the Babylonians (2 Ki. 25:18ff.).

SERAPHIM. These heavenly beings are mentioned only in Is. 6. They were human in form but had 6 wings, 2 for flying, 2 for shielding their faces and 2 for shielding their feet. They were stationed above God's throne and apparently led the worship. One touched Isaiah's lips with a burning ember in an act of purification and announced that Isaiah's sin had been removed. They appear to have been distinct moral creatures and not projections of the imagination, and exercised an atoning ministry as well as extolling God's character.

SERMON ON THE MOUNT. The title commonly given to the teachings of Jesus recorded in Mt. 5-7. It is a character-sketch of those who have already entered the kingdom of God and a description of the ethical life which is now expected of them.

Contents. The blessedness of the kingdom (5:3-16); the relationship of Jesus' message to the old order (5:17-48); practical instructions for Christian conduct including charitable giving, prayer, fasting and living in love (6:1-7:12); challenge to dedicated living (7:13-29).

Composition. It was once taken for granted that the Sermon was a single discourse, and it is presented as such by Matthew; the people sat down and Jesus taught them (5:1f.), and afterwards they were astonished (7:28). However, most scholars now agree that it is a compilation of Jesus' sayings because of its condensed nature, its wide range of topics, the often abrupt switch from topic to topic, and the fact that 34 of its verses occur in other Gospels in more suitable contexts (*e.g.* the Lord's Prayer is given in response to a question about prayer in Lk. 11:1). There are also other apparent collections of sayings inserted into Matthew's narrative (*e.g.* 9:35-10:42; 13; 18; 24-25). However, it is more likely that Matthew took an existing sermon source and expounded it by adding relevant material, rather than that he drew together a collection of sayings in an arbitrary manner. Certainly it has a real unity marked by the logical development of its basic theme presented in the Beatitudes, of the quality and conduct of life in the kingdom.

Circumstances. Both Matthew and Luke (in the shorter version often called the Sermon on the Plain, Lk. 6:20-49) place it in the 1st year of Jesus' public ministry. It was given before the religious leaders could muster their opposition but after Jesus' fame had spread. It is natural to assume that the teaching was given on one of the foothills which surrounded the N plain in Galilee. It is primarily addressed to Jesus' disciples (Mt. 5:1f.), but it is clear that others were present too (Mt. 7:28f.), presumably listening in as Jesus taught his already-committed followers.

Language and interpretation. There are clear elements of poetry in the Sermon. For example, Mt. 7:6 is a clear illustration of 'synonymous parallelism', and the Lord's Prayer is made up of 2 stanzas both having 3 lines of 4 beats each (see POETRY). Hence some of the Sermon is not meant to be taken with the same kind of inflexible literalism as prose might be. The apparent encouragement to pluck out one's eye to avoid lust is meant to illustrate an attitude and does not constitute a command (Mt. 5:29). Likewise, the command to be perfect (Mt. 5:48) is not a new law but a broad principle, a prophetic injunction, an ethic for a new age designed for those who have received new power. But it still demands a high quality of conduct. Rather than providing detailed instructions the Sermon gives general principles and shows how they affect Christians' lives. 'It would be a great point gained,' wrote James Denney, 'if people would only consider that it was a Sermon, and was *preached*, not an *act* which was passed.' So it is not a programme for world-improvement but principles for those who have denied the world in order to enter the kingdom. It is not idealistic, but neither will it be fully accomplished until the kingdom is fully established.

SERPENT: See SNAKE.

SERPENT, BRONZE. On the borders of Edom, the rebellious Israelites were punished by deadly snakebites. Moses was commanded by God to make a bronze replica of a serpent so that whoever looked at it might live (Nu. 21:4ff.). It later became an idol (serpents were significant in paganism), and was destroyed by Hezekiah (2 Ki. 18:4). The bronze serpent enforced the lesson that deliverance of any kind came only through dependence on God, which Jesus reiterated (Jn. 3:14).

SERPENT'S STONE. The scene of the slaughter of animals by Adonijah near En-rogel, SE of Jerusalem (1 Ki. 1:9).

SERVANT, MINISTER. Servants are found in the OT as personal assistants (*e.g.* Ex. 24:13) and domestic servants (1 Ki. 10:5). In the NT, Jesus appears as 'one who serves' (Lk. 22:27), and following his example Christians are to serve one another (Mk. 10:43). So the apostles called themselves servants of God (2 Cor. 6:4), of the gospel (Eph. 3:7), and of the church (Col. 1:25). As well as the general term for service (from which came the word 'deacon', *cf.* Acts 6:2ff.), the NT also uses the word 'slave' to denote Christian service, although this is often translated servant in RSV (*e.g.* Col. 4:12). Also, a term used originally for public service is taken over by the NT to denote angels ('ministering spirits', Heb. 1:14) and again the service of one Christian to another (Phil. 2:25). The idea is always that of loving service to God or man, although it should be noted that secular powers sometimes can be described as servants of God (Rom. 13:4, 6). See also DEACON; MINISTRY; SLAVE.

SERVANT OF THE LORD. *Old Testament.* Four passages in Isaiah were identified by B. Duhm in 1892, and have been regarded since, as 'servant songs': 42:1-4; 49:1-6; 50:4-9; 52:13-53:12. The term 'servant' is used elsewhere in Isaiah to refer to Israel as a nation (*e.g.* 41:8), and elsewhere in the OT to refer to individuals with a close relationship with God (*e.g.* 2 Sa. 7:5). However in the Servant Songs it includes a distinctive reference to a 'Servant figure' whose obedient, undeserved suffering leads to death as the means of taking away the people's sin.

Three lines of interpretation have been suggested. The Servant could be collective, that is the prophet's ideal for either the whole nation of Israel or more probably a faithful remnant within it. Secondly, the Servant could be an individual. Indeed, the language used is strongly individualistic, describing the birth, suffering, death and eventual triumph of a person rather than a group. Traditionally he has been seen as the Messiah, in later Palestinian Judaism as well as in Christianity. The 3rd possibility combines the other two, into 'corporate personality', because the texts seem to combine both. Hence the Servant is Israel, summing it up in all he represents (49:3), yet is *also* a person with a mission to Israel (49:5f.). The vicarious nature of his suffering as the people's substitute is possible only because he is Israel, its representative head.

New Testament. There are relatively few formal quotations from the Servant passages, but the idea that the Messiah must suffer is constantly repeated, and the Servant passages are the main OT source for such a concept. Among the direct quotes are Is. 53:12 in Lk. 22:37, and allusions to Is. 53:10-12 in Mk. 10:45; 14:24. Jesus' mission was outlined in Mk. 1:11 in terms of Is. 42:1. Peter gave Jesus the title Servant in his sermons in Acts 3:13, 26 (*cf.* the prayer of Acts 4:27, 30), and the influence of the figure is clear in 1 Pet. 2:21ff.; 3:18. Paul's writings also contain allusions which indicate that he saw Jesus' atoning work foreshadowed in Is. 53 (*e.g.* Phil. 2:6ff.). There are NT passages which draw on the Servant Songs to describe other aspects of Jesus' mission (*e.g.* Mt. 12:18ff.) which show that the early church believed the Servant figure was God's pattern for the Messiah.

See also MESSIAH.

SETH. The 3rd son of Adam and Eve, born after the murder of Abel (Gn. 4:25). The genealogy of Noah passed through him.

SEVEN WORDS, THE. The title given to Jesus' utterances from the cross. The 1st was a prayer for forgiveness for his executors, revealing an unexpected and undeserved love (Lk. 23:34). The 2nd was spoken to the penitent bandit, assuring him of a place in Paradise (Lk. 23:43). The 3rd combines sympathetic assurance to his mother with caring instructions to the beloved disciple (Jn. 19:25-27), despite his own agony at the time. These 3 words were probably spoken before noon. The 4th, the cry of desolation, was uttered during the mysterious darkness (Mt. 27:45f.; Mk. 15:33f.), and the 5th soon followed it when Jesus complained of thirst (Jn. 19:28). The 6th word was the triumphant cry, 'It is finished' (Jn. 19:30), referring to his atoning mission, and the 7th was a quote from Ps. 31:5, the pious Jew's evening prayer (Lk. 23:46).

SHAALBIM. An Amorite village near Mt Heres and Aijalon, brought into subjection by the tribe of Joseph (Jdg. 1:35). Possibly modern Selbit, 5 km NW of Aijalon.

SHAARIM. A place between Azekah and the fork to Gath and Ekron (1 Sa. 17:52; cf. Jos. 15:36).

SHADOW. The image cast by a solid body between the sun or light and another body. Its constant variation and final disappearance is a picture of transient human life (1 Ch. 29:15); its gloominess is like death (Ps. 23:4). The welcome relief of shade is like the protection of God (Ps. 91:1); God himself, unlike shadows, never changes (Jas. 1:17). Ancient ceremonies were like a shadow of the reality to come in Christ (Heb. 10:1).

SHALISHAH. A district visited by Saul when searching for his donkeys (1 Sa. 9:4), which had its own god or shrine (2 Ki. 4:42); its location is unknown.

SHALLUM. Several OT people are named thus, including the 16th king of (N) Israel c. 745 BC (2 Ki. 15:10, 13ff.); the 18th king of Judah c. 609 BC, also called JEHOAHAZ (2 Ki. 23:30ff.); the 'keeper of the wardrobe' and husband of the prophetess Huldah (2 Ki. 22:14).

SHALMAN. The destroyer of Beth-arbel (Ho. 10:14). He could be the Assyrian Shalmaneser V or Salamanu, king of Moab.

SHALMANESER (lit. 'the god Sulman is my chief'). The name of several kings of Assyria. The one to whom Hoshea of Israel became subject (2 Ki. 17:3) was Shalmaneser V (727-722 BC), son of Tiglath-pileser III, who probably defeated Samaria (2 Ki. 17:6) although his son Sargon II claimed its final overthrow in 722/1. Although not named in the Bible, Shalmaneser III fought an Israel-Syria coalition at Qarqar in 853 BC and claims to have defeated Hazael of Damascus (cf. 1 Ki. 19:15).

SHAME. A number of biblical words are thus translated. Most frequently it relates to the idea of contempt, derision and humiliation. It is the result of disregarding God's law (Ho. 4:6f.), is sent on God's enemies (Ps. 132:18), and may be a punishment (Ps. 44:15). Less frequent is the sense of shyness or bashfulness (Gn. 2:25), sometimes related to physical nakedness. The basic biblical concept is that of a mental state of humiliation due to sin.

References to sexual matters are illustrative or figurative, and do not indicate any more basic connection of shame with sex than with any other function which causes embarrassment when misused.

SHAMGAR. A man who brought Israel relief from the Philistines by killing 600 with a sharp metal-tipped ox-goad (Jdg. 3:31; 5:6). He was not a judge as such, and lived before the battle of Kishon *c.* 1125 BC.

SHAMMAH. Several OT people including David's brother (1 Sa. 16:9); one of David's heroes (2 Sa. 23:11); another of David's warriors (2 Sa. 23:25).

SHAPHAN. The state secretary who reported to King Josiah the discovery of the book of the law and read it to him (2 Ki. 22:3ff.). All 3 of his sons assisted Jeremiah in some way (Ahikam, Je. 26:24; Elasah, Je. 29:3; Gemariah, Je. 36:10ff.); his grandson Gedaliah was governor of Judah and also helped Jeremiah (Je. 39:14).

SHAPHIR. A town in the Philistine plain which Micah prophesied against (Mi. 1:11); its location is uncertain.

SHAREZER. 1. A son of the Assyrian Sennacherib who with his brother Adrammelech murdered their father in 681 BC (2 Ki. 19:37). 2. A contemporary of Zechariah (Zc. 7:2); the text, however, is difficult and perhaps should be read as the common name Belshazzar or the place Bethelsharezer.

SHARING: See FELLOWSHIP.

SHARON. The largest of the coastal plains of N Palestine, between the marshes of the lower Crocodile R. (Nahr ez-Zerka) and the valley of Aijalon. It runs 80 km N–S and is 15 km wide. Today it is one of Israel's richest agricultural regions, planted with citrus groves. In biblical times it was thickly forested (*cf.* Is. 35:2), not colonized by the Israelites although used for pasturage (1 Ch. 5:16). The 'rose of Sharon' (Song 2:1ff.) suggests flowers of the dense undergrowth.

SHARUHEN. A Simeonite settlement (Jos. 19:6), either Tell el-Fara 24 km S of Gaza or Tell el-Huweilfeh just N of Kh. Rammamein. Also mentioned in Egyptian texts as a Hyksos fortress around 1550 BC.

SHAUL (lit. 'asked for', in Hebrew the same name as Saul). Among those mentioned is a king of Edom (1 Ch. 1:48f.).

SHAVEH, VALLEY OF. Near Salem, also called the King's Valley (Gn. 14:17f.; 2 Sa. 18:18), possibly the top of Jerusalem's Hinnom Valley.

SHAVSHA. David's secretary of state (1 Ch. 18:16), also called Seraiah (2 Sa. 8:17), Shisha (1 Ki. 4:3), and Shera (2 Sa. 20:25). The name indicates that he may have been an Egyptian.

SHEAR-JASHUB. A symbolic name given to one of Isaiah's sons to indicate that 'a remnant shall return' (Is. 7:3).

SHEBA. Several people have this name in the OT, but its most important uses are for places. *City:* A place allotted to Simeon in S Palestine near Beersheba (Jos. 19:2), possibly the older part of Beersheba. *Land:* The homeland of the queen who visited Solomon (1 Ki. 10:1ff.), probably the territory of the Sabaeans in SW Arabia. Originally camel nomads, they had probably settled by Solomon's time in the E of what is now Yemen. They are most frequently referred to in the OT as traders or raiders (Jb. 1:15; 6:19). They traded in gold, spices, jewels and frankincense (1 Ki. 10:2; Is. 60:6), and from Joel 3:8 it would seem they were slave traders at times, too. They founded colonies at oases in N Arabia which served as caravan bases. Sheba was ruled by priest-kings and its people worshipped the sun, moon and stars. See also next article and SEBA.

SHEBA, QUEEN OF. An unnamed Sabaean monarch who travelled from Sheba to Jerusalem to test Solomon's wisdom (1 Ki. 10:1ff.). She may also have visited him to negotiate a trade agreement, because Solomon's control of trade routes jeopardized the traditional Sabaean income from caravans which crossed their territory. Assyrian and S Arabian texts testify to the existence of female monarchs in the 8th cent. BC. Her willingness to make the 2,000 km trip by camel is contrasted to Jewish complacency by Jesus in Mt. 12:42. See also previous article.

SHEBARIM. In Jos. 7:5 it is better understood as quarries (as most modern EVV). Limestone was quarried all through biblical times; see STONE, STONEMASON.

SHEBNA. A state official under Hezekiah who was rebuked by Isaiah for preparing his own conspicuous monumental tomb (Is. 22:15ff.). The inscribed lintel of such an 8th-cent. BC tomb, belonging to a royal official, has been recovered.

SHECHEM. An important town in central Palestine, in the hill country of Ephraim near Mt Gerizim; the site is Tell Balata 50 km N of Jerusalem and 9 km SE of Samaria. It is the first Palestinian site mentioned in Genesis; Abraham camped there (Gn. 12:6f.), as did Jacob (Gn. 33:18f.) who buried his foreign idols there (Gn. 35:4). After the Israelite conquest, Joshua renewed the nation's covenant with God (Jos. 8:30ff.) and also gave his parting speech there (Jos. 24). But it was still a centre of Canaanite worship in the time of the judges and was destroyed by Gideon's son Abimelech (Jdg. 9). After Solomon's death it was at Shechem that the 10 N tribes rejected Rehoboam as king and anointed Jeroboam as their king. He restored the city and made it his capital for a time (1 Ki. 12). Later the Assyrians destroyed it 724-721 BC. Around 300 BC Shechem became the chief city of the Samaritans who built a temple on Mt Gerizim. John Hyrcanus destroyed the temple in 128 BC and the town in 108 BC, after which it was rebuilt and named Flavia Neapolis after the Roman emperor Flavius Vespasianus. It has been suggested that it is the same as Sychar (Jn. 4:5), but this has not been proved.

SHEEP. The importance of sheep in biblical times is indicated by the fact that they are mentioned over 400 times in the OT, and 70 in the NT. They were first domesticated for their meat and fat. By careful breeding, wool was developed and provided the most useful and easily available fibre for clothes (*cf.* 2 Ki. 3:4). Their milk was consumed mostly in the form of curds, and as a basic food was more important than the meat which was usually eaten only as part of sacrificial meals. In NT times sheep were often kept under cover in winter and fed chaff and barley. They were in various colours and patterns (Gn. 30:32) and probably few were just white.

They are used extensively in the Bible as symbols or pictures. Often they are seen as picture of mankind, helpless, easily led astray and lost (Is. 53:6), but also happily restored (Ps. 23; *cf.* Jn. 10). Jesus is regarded as the ultimate sacrificial 'lamb' (Jn. 1:29). Sheep were often kept with goats in mixed flocks, and the two animals may look very alike (*cf.* Mt. 25:32).

See also SHEPHERD.

SHEERAH. The name means 'a female relative'. A daughter of Ephraim (1 Ch. 7:24), she is the only biblical example of a woman town-builder.

SHEKINAH. The radiance, glory or presence of God dwelling among his people, and the nearest Jewish equivalent to the Holy Spirit. The term is later than the Bible but the concept underlies the teaching that God dwells among his people (Ex. 29:45f.). The glory of God is seen in such things as the lightning and cloud on Mt Sinai (Ex. 19:16) and the bright cloud which descended on the tent of meeting and led Israel through the desert (Ex. 40:34ff.). God's glory is also present in a special way in the heavenly temple and city (Rev. 15:8; 21:23). It was seen at Jesus' transfiguration (Lk. 9:32), and will be seen when Jesus returns to earth (Mk. 8:38). See also GLORY.

SHELAH. Several OT people including Judah's younger son by Shua (Gn. 38). Also in Ne. 3:15 the pool better known as SILOAM.

SHEM. Noah's eldest son, one of the 8 people to survive the flood (Gn. 7:13). Through him the line of descent of Abraham and hence of the Messiah is traced (Lk. 3:36). Among his descendants named in Gn. 10:21ff. there are a number known to have spoken related languages in ancient times, and the convenience term 'Semitic' has been applied to them. Shem lived 600 years (Gn. 11:10f.).

SHEMUEL. A leader of the tribe of Simeon who assisted in the division of Canaan (Nu. 34:20).

SHEOL, HADES. The place of the dead. Its OT meaning moves between ideas of the grave, the underworld, and the state of death. Throughout the ancient Near East, the dead were pictured as existing in a realm below the earth (Ezk. 31:15, 17). It was a place of darkness (Jb. 10:21f.), silence (Ps. 94:17) and forgetfulness (Ps. 88:12). Occasionally it is associated with judgment (*e.g.* Ps. 49:13f.), but God is present there (Ps. 139:8) and able to rescue people from it (Ps. 16:10). OT words such as Abaddon (Ps. 88:11) and the Pit (Ps. 30:3) are probably synonyms for Sheol.

Later Jewish literature divided Sheol between the wicked and righteous, which may underlie the imagery of Jesus' parable of the rich man and Lazarus (see Lk. 16:19ff.). The NT equivalent word is Hades (Acts 2:27, quoting Ps. 16:10). Its gates (symbols of its power) cannot prevail against the church (Mt. 16:18). Jesus holds the key to Hades and to death itself (Rev. 1:18); their power is broken (Rev. 6:8) and both are to be banished for ever (Rev. 20:13f.).

See also DEATH.

SHEPHELAH. The low hill tract between the coastal plain of Palestine and the high central ranges (*e.g.* 1 Ki. 10:27; Je. 17:26).

SHEPHERD. Used in the Bible both of people who look after sheep and also for those who have political or spiritual responsibility for other people. The literal shepherd had to find grass and water in a dry and stony land (Ps. 23:2), protect his animals from weather and predators (*cf.* Am.

3:12), and retrieve those which strayed (Mt. 18:12). He might use dogs to help him (Jb. 30:1).

God is often portrayed as his people's shepherd (*e.g.* Pss. 23:1; 80:1), caring for (Is. 40:11) and retrieving those he scatters in his anger (Je. 31:10). Unfaithful shepherds of the people are to be judged (Je. 25:32ff.; Ezk. 34) because they have fed themselves and have neglected their charges. Jesus' mission was to be the chief shepherd (Jn. 10; 1 Pet. 2:25). His sheep respond to his voice, just as flocks respond to the distinctive call of their shepherd in the East today.

See also SHEEP.

SHESHACH. In Je. 25:26; 51:41 (AV, NIV) an artificial word-play on 'Babylon'.

SHESHBAZZAR. The person made governor (literally 'prince') of Judah by the Persian king Cyrus (Ezr. 1:8), to whom the temple treasures were entrusted (Ezr. 5:14f.).

SHIBAH. The name of a well dug by Isaac's servants (Gn. 26:33). It means 'seven' or 'oath', thus reviving the old name of Abraham's well (Beersheba, Gn. 21:22-34).

SHIBBOLETH. A test word by which the Gileadites detected the escaping Ephraimites (Jdg. 12:5f.). In the local Ephraim dialect *sh* became *s*; the word means 'a stream in flood'. Used today, often disparagingly, for the catchword of a party.

SHIELD: See ARMOUR.

SHIHOR: See EGYPT, RIVER OF.

SHIHOR-LIBNATH. A small river forming part of the S boundary of Asher's territory (Jos. 19:26), probably Nahr ez-Zerqa S of Mt Carmel.

SHILOH. The place where the tent of meeting was set up in the early days of Israel's conquest of Canaan (Jos. 18:1), and the principal Israelite sanctuary during the time of the judges (Jdg. 18:31). By the time of Eli and his sons the sanctuary had become a well-established structure for centralized worship, and Joshua's tent had been replaced by a more permanent temple (1 Sa. 1:9). The priesthood was later transferred to Nob (1 Sa. 22:11) and Shiloh ceased to be a religious centre. The site is modern Seilun, on a hill 14 km N of Bethel. It was occupied *c.* 2100-1600 BC and again *c.* 1200-1050 BC. No sign of an early Israelite temple has been found. In Gn. 49:10 the AV reference to Shiloh is probably to be translated with RSV 'until he comes to whom it belongs'.

SHIMEATH. The Ammonite mother of one of Joash's murderers (2 Ki. 12:21).

SHIMEI. The OT mentions 19 people with this name. One was a grandson of Levi; his family, the Shimeites, were partly responsible for maintaining the tent of meeting (Nu. 3:21ff.). The best-known was a relative of Saul who cursed David (2 Sa. 16:5ff.).

David accepted the rebuke meekly but he later concluded that Shimei had sown dissention wilfully (1 Ki. 2:8f.). Solomon had him killed on a false charge after first showing kindness to him (1 Ki. 2:36ff.).

SHIMRON-MERON. A Canaanite city allied to Hazor and captured by Joshua (Jos. 12:20); possibly Tell es-Semuniyeh 5 km SSE of Bethlehem.

SHINAR. A name for Babylonia (Gn. 10:10; Is. 11:11), known also from non-biblical texts.

SHIPS AND BOATS. Both Egypt and Mesopotamia were divided by rivers and canals, making water transport essential. Rafts made from reeds appear in pictographs *c.* 3500 BC, and round coracles modelled in clay *c.* 3500 BC and depicted on Assyrian reliefs *c.* 870 BC remain in use on the Euphrates today made from wood and hide. Official transport in Sumer was in vessels with high stems and sterns and propelled by paddles or poles; a model of one found in a tomb dates to *c.* 3000 BC. An actual Egyptian boat *c.* 2600 BC was found by the pyramid of Cheops at Giza; it was 43.4 m long. Ships powered by sail and oar were used on the Red Sea.

Old Testament. The ship remained a source of wonder to the non-seafaring Hebrews (*cf.* Pr. 31:14). Assyrian sculptures *c.* 700 BC show long-range merchant ships, possibly Phoenician, with round bows and double banks of oars. Egyptian tomb paintings show that Phoenician ships had a keel (unlike the Egyptian ships) and a fence-like structure along the deck. Some larger vessels carried a cargo of 450 tonnes and were sail-powered. Short-range Phoenician ships were paddled, and had high stem and stern posts. The OT reference to 'ships of Tarshish' (such as in 1 Ki. 22:48f.) is to Phoenician merchant vessels. A warship is referred to in Is. 33:21; it had a streamlined hull and a ram at the front, powered by double-banked oarsmen (*cf.* Ezk. 27:8). The Greeks were particularly skilful at fighting in such ships.

New Testament. The boats on the Sea of Galilee were used for fishing (Mt. 4:21f.) and communications (Mt. 8:23ff.). They were not large and were powered by both sail and oar (*cf.* Mk. 6:48). On the Mediterranean, war 'long ships' (their length 8–10 times their width) kept close to the shore; merchant 'round ships' (their length 3–4 times their width) crossed the open sea when weather conditions were favourable. Most seagoing ships were 70–300 tonnes but the Roman governor Pliny mentions one of 1,300 tonnes. Most of Paul's journeys were probably undertaken in small coastal vessels, although his journey to Rome was in two large grain ships with 276 crew and passengers (Acts 27:37); about the same time the historian Josephus sailed in one carrying 600 people.

Descriptions and ancient wrecks which have been discovered show that these large ships had a central mast with long yard-arms carrying a large square mainsail and possibly a small topsail, and a small foremast sloping forward almost like a bowsprit; the foresail would be used to help steerage (*cf.* Acts 27:40). The bows were swept up to a carved or painted figure (Acts 28:11); the raised stern also had a statue of the patron god of the home port. Two large oars at the stern acted as rudders. Three or more anchors were carried, with a wooden stock and lead or stone arms, and with marker-buoys attached. A dinghy was towed astern, hoisted on board in storms (Acts 27:16f.), and used in harbour rather than as a lifeboat; in shipwrecks, sailors clung to debris. The risks were great (Paul survived 3 shipwrecks before his journey to Rome, 2 Cor. 11:25) but so were the financial rewards (see also Rev. 18:19). Passengers mostly camped on deck or in the holds. Ships rarely ventured out in the winter months (*cf.* Acts 27:9), because the cloudy skies made navigation by the sun and stars impossible.

See also ARK; TWIN BROTHERS.

SHISHAK. A Libyan prince who founded Egypt's 22nd Dynasty as Pharaoh Sheshonq I and reigned *c.* 945-924 BC. He harboured Jeroboam who had fled from Solomon (1 Ki. 11:40). He later invaded Palestine and subdued Judah (1 Ki. 14:25f.).

SHITTIM. 1. The final campsite, opposite Jericho, of the Israelites before they crossed the Jordan (Jos. 2:1; 3:1); possibly Tell el-Hammam or Tell el-Kefrein. 2. A valley mentioned in Joel 3:18 W of the Jordan, either Judaean wadis generally or the lower part of the Kidron valley. For shittim wood, see TREES (acacia).

SHOA. In Ezk. 23:23, possibly the Sutu of Akkadian documents, Semitic nomads who migrated from the Syrian desert to E of Baghdad.

SHOBACH. The Aramaean commander in charge of Hadadezer's forces (2 Sa. 10:16); he was killed in battle against David (1 Ch. 16:18).

SHOBAL. 1. The father of a clan, and a Horite leader (Gn. 36:23, 29) probably related to: 2. Caleb's son who founded Kireath-jearim (1 Ch. 2:50).

SHOBI. An Ammonite prince of Rabbah who like his father Nahash showed kindness to David (2 Sa. 17:27ff.).

SHOVEL. Bronze shovels were used to clear the ashes from the altar of burnt offering (Ex. 27:3; 1 Ki. 7:40, 45).

SHOWBREAD: See BREAD OF THE PRESENCE.

SHUA. Several OT people including Hebor's daughter (1 Ch. 7:32) and one of Abraham's sons by Keturah (Gn. 25:2).

SHUAL, LAND OF. A district in Benjamin, probably near Michmash (1 Sa. 13:17).

SHULAMMITE. A term applied to the heroine in Song 6:13, which is now not understood.

SHUNEM, SHUNAMMITE. A town in Issachar's territory, probably modern Solem. It was the scene of Elijah's resurrection miracle (2 Ki. 4:8ff.; cf. 2 Ki. 8:1ff.), and the home town of Abishag (1 Ki. 1:3, 15).

SHUR. A desert area in the NW of the Sinai isthmus between the Wadi el-Arish on the E and the present Suez canal on the W. It lay on the direct route from Egypt to S Palestine (1 Sa. 27:8).

SIBMAH. A town taken from the Amorites for Reuben (Jos. 13:19), later reverting to the Moabites (Is. 16:8f.), famous for its vines. Possibly Kh. Qurn el-Qibsh, 5 km WSW of Heshbon.

SIDDIM, VALLEY OF. Probably a fertile region S of the Lisan peninsula, later submerged by the S extension of the Dead Sea through earthquake activity (Gn. 14:3).

SIDON. A major walled city and port in ancient Phoenicia, now located on the coast of Lebanon. It was a principal Canaanite fortification (see Gn. 10:19) which resisted Israel (Jdg. 10:12). Ashurnasirpal II c. 880 BC claimed it as a vassal; Shalmaneser III exacted tribute-tax from it in 841 BC; Sennacherib captured it (cf. Is. 23:2ff.). It recovered its independence but was captured by the Babylonians c. 587 BC (cf. Je. 27:3ff.). It later provided the bulk of the Persian shipping fleet, but it was destroyed after a rebellion c. 350 BC. The Romans granted it local autonomy. Its chief god had always been Eshman, the god of healing; it is thus significant that Jesus healed a girl in the area (Mk. 7:24ff.). Many Sidonians heard Jesus (Mk. 3:8); Paul visited it en route for Rome (Acts 27:3).

SIGN. It can mean a visible mark intended to convey a message (*cf.* Gn. 4:15), a reminder (Gn. 9:12) or a prophetic omen (1 Sa. 2:34). The return of Jesus would be indicated by signs in the heavens (Mt. 24:30). But the most important biblical meaning is 'a work of God'. The plagues in Egypt were signs of God's active presence among his people (Ex. 4:28), and Israel was assured that when God revealed himself again it would be with signs ('portents', Joel 2:30). Signs and wonders demonstrated God's activity in the missionary work of the early church (Rom. 15:19), and are recorded in Acts (*e.g.* 2:43; 4:30). Jesus, however, refused to provide signs on demand (Mk. 8:11f.), and warned that false teachers could also do them (Mk. 13:22; *cf.* Rev. 13:13f.). The term is used most frequently in John's Gospel which is anxious to demonstrate the relationship between faith and signs. Faith in Jesus merely because of the signs is shallow (Jn. 4:48; 6:2); the sign points forward to Jesus' death and resurrection and the new life of the Spirit (12:37ff.). See also MIRACLE; POWER; SYMBOL; WONDER.

SIHON. An Amorite king who conquered the Moabites shortly before Israel's arrival in Transjordan (Nu. 21:26). He was killed by Israel after he had not allowed them to pass through his territory (Nu. 21:21ff.); the victory was a landmark in Israelite history (*cf.* Ps. 135:10f.).

SILAS. A leading member of the Jerusalem church who also had prophetic gifts (Acts 15:32), almost certainly identical to Silvanus (*e.g.* 2 Cor. 1:19) which is probably the Latinized form of 'Silas'. He was sent from Jerusalem to welcome into fellowship the Gentiles converted at Antioch (Acts 15:22ff.), and later became Paul's travelling companion (Acts 15:36ff.). He was a Roman citizen (Acts 16:37ff.). He is associated with Paul in 1 Thes. 1:1; 2 Thes. 1:1, and was also Peter's amanuensis (1 Pet. 5:12), which may account for some of the resemblances in wording in the 3 letters and the decree of Acts 15.

SILK. True silk is obtained from the cocoon of a Chinese moth fed on the leaves of white mulberry, but another species of silk moth is indigenous to the E Mediterranean, feeding on oak and cypress leaves. Production of transparent silk in Cos and Sidon may be intended in Ezk. 16:10, 13; Rev. 18:12 also mentions it.

SILOAM. One of Jerusalem's principal water supplies was the intermittent pool of Gihon below the Fountain Gate (Ne. 3:15) and ESE of the city. It fed water along an open canal to the Lower or Old Pool, which was probably the Pool of Siloam mentioned in Jn. 9:7ff., with the 'Tower of Siloam' sited on the Ophel ridge above it (Lk. 13:4). Traces of a Herodian bath and open reservoir have been found, but these cannot be positively identified with the NT Siloam. King Hezekiah, threatened with invasion by Assyria, diverted the upper Gihon waters through a tunnel into an upper pool in W Jerusalem (2 Ki. 20:20). An inscription found in the tunnel tells how the 2 teams of tunnellers met at mid-point, a remarkable engineering feat as the 540 m tunnel twists through and around various rock strata. Hezekiah's tunnel begins from an earlier one built by the Jebusites and possibly mentioned in 2 Sa. 5:8.

SILVER: See ART; MINING AND METALS; MONEY.

SIMEON. 1. The 2nd son of Jacob and Leah, who remained in Egypt as a hostage of his (unrecognized) brother Joseph (Gn. 42:24), and who was rebuked by his father Jacob for his violent nature (Gn. 49:5ff.). 2. The tribe of Simeon had a portion in S Palestine, but was not named in Moses' final blessing (Dt. 33). It was usually inferior to its neighbour Judah, and is not mentioned after the Exile. 3. A righteous man in Jerusalem longing for the Messiah to come, who had received the revelation that he would see Messiah before he died. On seeing Jesus he uttered the hymn now called Nunc Dimittis, telling of the role of Christ, and also predicting Mary's suffering (Lk. 2:25ff.). 4. A disciple at Antioch with prophetic and teaching gifts, probably an African (Acts 13:1f.).

SIMON. A number of NT people are so named, including Jesus' apostle, also called Peter; another apostle, the 'Cananaean' or 'Zealot' (Mt. 10:4; Lk. 6:15); a brother of Jesus (Mt. 6:3); a Pharisee in whose home Jesus was anointed (Lk. 7:40); a tanner in Joppa with whom Peter lodged (Acts 9:43). See also next article; PETER.

SIMON MAGUS. In Acts 8:9ff. a pagan wonder-worker who had amazed the local Samaritans. He claimed to be a manifestation of God (v. 10). Simon professed conversion to Christ and was baptized, no doubt sincerely (v. 13). However, when he saw Philip's signs and wonders, and the Holy Spirit given when Peter and John laid hands on the converts, he offered cash in return for the gift (vv. 17ff.). Peter's crushing rebuke terrified him (v. 24); he was obsessed with the idea of power.

The NT has nothing more to say about Simon, but a tangle of traditions survives in early Christian writings. Irenaeus and Hippolytus describe doctrines of his cult. He apparently claimed to have appeared to the Samaritans as the Father, to Jews as the Son, and to the world at large as the Holy Spirit. He preached salvation by faith in himself and his consort Helen, but allowed unrestrained moral liberty. Hippolytus says he was buried alive, promising to reappear in 3 days.

SIN. *Definitions.* Essentially, sin is directed against God; it is a violation of what his glory demands (Rom. 8:7). Several shades of meaning are implied by the use of different original Hebrew (OT) and Greek (NT) words. For example the most common OT word has the idea of 'missing the mark' or 'deviating from the goal' (used in a graphic non-moral sense in Jdg. 20:16; in the moral sense in Ex. 20:20). Another means 'rebellion' (morally, 1 Ki. 8:50; politically, 1 Ki. 12:19); another means perversion or 'twisting' ('done wickedly', 2 Sa. 24:17; literally, Is. 24:1); and another 'going astray' ('erred', 1 Sa. 26:21). The NT has its equivalent to 'missing the target' or 'deviating from the road' which is the general NT term for sin (as in Jn. 8:46). There is also a word for a measuring mistake or blunder ('trespasses' in Mt. 6:14f.; Eph. 2:1). Other NT words for sin include 'ungodliness' (Rom. 1:18); 'lawlessness' ('iniquity' in 2 Cor. 6:14); and 'evil', making use of a word which means moral and spiritual depravity which links sin with Satan (1 Jn. 3:12).

Origins. Sin was present in the universe before Adam and Eve sinned (*cf.* Jn. 8:44; 2 Pet. 2:4), but the Bible does not deal directly with how it originated. Rather, it is concerned with the origin of sin in human life (*cf.* Jas. 1:13f.). The demonic temptation in Gn. 3 is a subtle suggestion that mankind should aspire to equality with God and an enticement to rebellion against him. By asserting their independence from God, mankind called into question the very nature of their existence, and withheld the worship and love which is the proper response to God's majesty and grace. Hence the origin of sin is not so much in an outward deed but in an inward aspiration which was then expressed outwardly.

Consequences. There were 5 consequences of Adam and Eve's action. Mankind's attitude to God was now one of shame and fear (Gn. 3:7ff.; Jn. 3:20). God's wrath against sin was revealed (Gn. 3:24). The whole race became infected with sin (see next paragraph). The physical earth was affected by the curse on mankind (Gn. 3:17; Rom. 8:20). And death was introduced to humanity as the penalty of sin (Gn. 2:17; 3:19), in which the elements of mankind's nature are separated and mankind itself is separated from God.

Imputation to others. Adam's sin had a profound effect on the whole human race, which Paul emphasizes in Rom. 5:12ff. He explains that 'all sinned in Adam', that is there is racial solidarity in Adam because he was a representative head of the human race. It is not simply that all sin and therefore are guilty; nor that there is a kind of hereditary affliction which makes us sinful. Just as Christians are 'saved' through the representative headship of Christ who sacrificed himself for them, says Paul, so all humans are sinful through their early representative, Adam. Everyone's subsequent moral experience is indeed that of sinning, so in actual practice all do fall short of God's standard (Rom. 3:23). The principle which accomplishes our salvation and makes us heirs of eternal life is the same kind of principle by which we became sinners and heirs of death (*cf.* 1 Cor. 15:22).

Depravity. The Bible makes it clear that sinful acts stem from a sinful heart (Mk. 7:20ff.). We never exist apart from the sin of Adam reckoned as ours (Ps. 51:5); from whatever angle mankind is viewed, there is an absence of that which is well-pleasing to God. All have become corrupted and have 'the mind of the flesh' (Rom. 8:5ff.). In other words, there is no aspect of human life which is not affected by our fallenness, and hence no aspect which might serve as a possible justification of ourselves before God and his law. Of course, people differ in the extent to which this is expressed. Some are downright evil (Rom. 1:24ff.), but conscience and the operation of God's law can still bring about civil righteousness (Rom. 2:14f.). Such actions are not sufficient to please God in the sense of earning eternal salvation, however (Rom. 8:7f.).

An unchangeable nature. The sinful nature cannot be changed by human effort. We cannot of ourselves obey God's law (Rom. 7) nor even discern his truth (1 Cor. 2:14). In Jesus' words, corrupt trees cannot produce good fruit (Mt. 7:18). The only possibility of change lies in God drawing us to himself (Jn. 3:3ff.; 6:44f.). It is a psychological, moral and spiritual impossibility for natural man to receive the things of God's Spirit; hence the stress on God's grace in the NT.

God's reaction to sin. Since sin is an act against God, he cannot remain indifferent towards it; his reaction is usually termed his 'wrath'. There is an intensity of indignation, displeasure and vengeance expressed often in the OT (*e.g.* Is. 10:1ff.), and this is continued in the NT (*e.g.* Rom. 1:18; 2:5ff.). This is not a fitful loss of temper but resolute disapproval; because it stems from God's holiness it is not malicious but righteous detestation. The torments of conscience occasionally reflect his displeasure in our awareness.

The conquest of sin. Despite its stress on sin and its consequences, the Bible never loses sight of hope, for it testifies to God's continuous provision for the forgiveness and ultimate destruction of sin, through the life, death and resurrection of Jesus Christ (Mk. 10:45). In Christ, God has conquered sin. Those who trust him are already released from the guilt and judgment of sin, and already experience to some extent conquest of its power in their human lives. The process will be completed in the new creation (Rev. 21:22-22:5).

See also DEATH; EVIL; FALL; REDEMPTION; SALVATION; WRATH.

SIN, DESERT (WILDERNESS) OF. An area the Israelites travelled through between Elim and Mt Sinai (Ex. 16:1), possibly Debbet er-Ramleh, a sandy area in the SW Sinai peninsula.

SINAI, MOUNT. The location of this mountain is uncertain, and several possible places have been suggested. The most likely, and with a tradition of 1,500 years behind it, is Jebel Musa at the S end of a short granite ridge in the Sinai Peninsula. Sinai is also called Mt Horeb in the OT. The Israelites reached it in the 3rd month after their Exodus from Egypt and camped on a plain from which Sinai's peak was visible (Ex. 19). On it, God revealed his commandments to Moses, and made the covenant with Israel which was to bind the nation together and to him. It was also the place where Elijah received his recommissioning (1 Ki. 19:8ff.). In the NT, Sinai is used to signify bondage to the law of Moses (Gal. 4:21ff.); although not named it is clearly in mind in Heb. 12:18ff. as the old covenant is contrasted with the new one of 'Mt Zion'.

SINEW. Seen in Jb. 10:11; Ezk. 37:6 as that which binds the bones together. The custom of Gn. 32:32 may stem from a belief that the thigh was the seat of life.

SION. In Dt. 4:48 (AV), Mt Hermon (Sirion).

SIRAH. A place where Abner hid; probably Ain Sarah, 2.5 km NW of Hebron (2 Sa. 3:26).

SIRION. The Canaanite name for Mt HERMON.

SISERA. The commander of Jabin's army who was treacherously killed by Jael (Jdg. 4:15ff.; 5:24ff.); he was perhaps also the petty king of Harosheth-hagoiim, possibly Tell el-Amr 19 km NW of Megiddo.

SITNAH (lit. 'hatred', 'contention'). The name given to a well dug by Isaac's servants (Gn. 26:21) in GERAR.

SKULL, THE. The name of the place where Jesus was crucified, sometimes called Calvary or Golgotha (Mt. 27:33). It was a conspicuous site outside Jerusalem, and a garden with a tomb was located nearby, but the exact location is uncertain. A possible site is that of the church of the Holy Sepulchre, which lay outside the city wall in Christ's time, and tradition from the 4th cent. AD supports the identification. Another is the Garden Tomb, which looks more like the Gospel descriptions but has no long tradition to support it.

SLANDER. Speaking falsely against someone or defaming them. Forbidden in the OT law (Lv. 19:16), it springs from an evil heart (Mk. 7:22) and is to be banished from the Christian community (2 Cor. 12:20; Eph. 4:31; Col. 3:8; 1 Pet. 2:1).

SLAVE, SLAVERY. *Old Testament.* Slaves are known to have existed in the ancient Near East from earliest times, although they were not always the personal 'property' of their owners to be used in any way desired. They could acquire legal rights, which included ownership of other slaves and the power to conduct their own business. Slaves were acquired in a variety of ways. They might be taken as prisoners of war (*e.g.* 1 Sa. 4:9; 2 Ki. 5:2), or born to slave parents (Gn.

17:12f.). They were bought and sold like merchandise (Gn. 17:12f.; 37:26, 36). People facing insolvency might be forced to sell themselves or their children into slavery to pay debts (Lv. 25:39ff.; 2 Ki. 4:1). Abduction into slavery was, however, a capital offence in Israel's law (Ex. 21:16) and in the laws of surrounding nations, hence the dismay of Joseph's brothers when they discovered him alive (Gn. 45:3; 50:15). The price of slaves varied like that of other commodities; Joseph's price of 20 shekels of silver (Gn. 37:28) is known to be precisely the current price during the patriarchal age (*c.* 1700 BC) in the Near East. By Assyrian times (8th cent. BC) it had risen to 50 shekels (*cf.* 2 Ki. 15:20).

The Israelite law sought to prevent the wholesale drift of the population into slavery and serfdom. Therefore, a Hebrew who was forced into slavery through debt was required to give a maximum 6 years' service and then was released and given sufficient assets to make a new start, although if he had married while a slave his wife and children had to stay in slavery, or he could voluntarily stay in service permanently (Ex. 21:2ff.; Dt. 15:12ff.). Release was in any case to be granted in the Jubilee (every 50th) year (Lv. 25:39ff.). Female slaves were subject to further laws. A woman's chief slave might become a surrogate mother for her master's children (*cf.* Gn. 16). A female slave could marry her master or one of his sons, or become a properly maintained concubine.

The treatment of slaves varied. Some were trusted (*cf.* Gn. 24), others were treated harshly although to kill a slave was a punishable offence (Ex. 21:20f.). In patriarchal times a childless master could adopt his slave as his heir (Gn. 15:3). Many ancient documents reveal that large numbers of slaves ran away. Sometimes extradition treaties returned them to their own land if they fled across the border (this may have been the case in 1 Ki. 2:39ff.), although slaves who returned to their homeland often were not extradicted but given their freedom (*cf.* Dt. 23:15f.).

State slavery was restricted in Israel. David used captured foreigners for forced labour (2 Sa. 12:29ff.), and Solomon conscripted descendants of the Canaanites rather than true Israelites (1 Ki. 9:15, 20ff.). People were also conscripted into the more menial religious duties at the sanctuary: Moses put warriors to work with the Levites (Nu. 31:28ff.), and David had dedicated foreigners (Nethinim) assisting the Levites (*cf.* Ezr. 8:20). It should be noted that the economy of the nations in the ancient Near East was never substantially based on slave labour, unlike Greek and Roman society. And the Israelite slave laws breathed a degree of humanity and care into the slavery which did exist.

New Testament. the law which gave Jewish slaves freedom in the 7th year seems to have been continued, and the Jews felt a strong obligation to ransom their family members who were enslaved to Gentiles. There was therefore no fundamental division of Jewish society into slaves and freemen. By contrast, Greek slavery was justified by the classical theory that a natural class of slaves existed; since only the citizen class were, strictly speaking, human, slaves were merely chattels. Slavery was therefore taken largely for granted, even if the extremes of bad treatment were rare. The heroic slave revolts in the centuries before Christ were the result of rapid Roman conquests and a consequent glut of prisoners of war who were forced into slavery.

In NT times there was little warfare, and outside of Italy there were few slave ranches. Domestic slaves were an index of the owner's wealth, and where only one or two were owned they worked at the owner's own trade; in Athens the fact that slaves and owners were indistinguishable, and on familiar terms, was a stock theme of comedy. In Rome, slaves fulfilled many public duties, and medical and educational professions were commonly filled by slaves. Up to one-third of Rome's population may have been slaves. Freedom could be readily arranged if the owner wished, and conditions were steadily improving, if for no other reason than better conditions were conducive to better work. Cruelty was generally condemned.

None of Jesus' 12 disciples appear to have been slaves or owners, but the institution often featured in Jesus' parables (*e.g.* Mt. 21:34ff.), because its setting afforded a suitable analogy for the kingdom of God. Jesus stressed the disciples' relationship to him both as servant (Mt. 10:24; Jn. 13:13ff.) and friend (Jn. 15:15); on one occasion he became their servant (Jn. 13:4ff.). Church membership outside Palestine often included both slaves and owners, but the division had become meaningless in the community of Christ (Gal. 3:28). There was some desire for emancipation, which Paul did not oppose if the opportunity was offered, although he put no overt pressure on owners (1 Cor. 7:20ff.; *cf.* Phm. 8, 14). The fraternal bond of Christian owner and slave should lead to good service (1 Tim. 6:1f.), and this contained within it the implication that slavery belonged to the old order which was passing away.

SLEEP. Apart from the literal sense, 'sleep' is also used figuratively in both Testaments. It can signify laziness (Pr. 24:33f.) or the spiritual torpor (Eph. 5:14) which makes people unprepared for Jesus' coming (Mt. 25:5). Christians are to stay awake, *i.e.* keep vigilant (1 Thes. 5:4ff.). Sleep also signifies physical death (Jn. 11:11ff.; 1 Cor. 15:18). Visions sometimes came in sleep (1 Sa. 3:2ff.), see DREAM.

SLING. This was used by shepherds to ward off wild animals (1 Sa. 17:34ff., 40). The Egyptians, Assyrians and Babylonians employed it as a war weapon, as did the Benjaminites of Israel (1 Ch. 12:2). It was a patch of leather (for the stone) with two cords; it was whirled above the head and one cord was suddenly released and the stone flew out.

SMYRNA. A city in the Aegean coast

of the Roman province of Asia (modern Izmir, in Asiatic Turkey). It was refounded on an ancient site in the 3rd cent. BC and became one of Asia Minor's most prosperous cities. It was a natural port in a fertile area, famous for its beauty and magnificent buildings. The church was probably founded by preachers from Ephesus (Acts 19:10). It encountered Jewish opposition and was promised a true crown for faithfulness (Rev. 2:9f.), an image which alluded to the city's richness and historical reputation.

SNAKE, SERPENT. A reptile with a head and body but no limbs, sliding along the ground so that with its flickering tongue it is said to lick the dust (Gn. 3:14). There is a wide range of species in Palestine of which only about 6 are potentially lethal, and only a small percentage of their bites prove fatal. EVV differ on their translation of biblical names; in Is. 11:8 the asp (now obsolete) is the *cobra*, which lives in holes and is very poisonous. The snakes ('fiery serpents' AV) which plagued Israel in the desert (Nu. 21; *cf.* Jn. 3:14) were probably *carpet vipers*, notorious for striking without provocation (unusual for snakes); their bite can cause death in a few days. They can become numerous over limited areas in Asia and Africa. The adder which cannot be charmed (Je. 8:17) was probably the *desert viper*. Palestine's largest *common viper* cannot be certainly identified with any biblical reference but it could well be that to which Jesus and John the Baptist likened the Pharisees (Mt. 3:7; 12:34);

such vipers bear their live young in batches, which fits the image. This could also be the snake which bit Paul (Acts 28:3), although it is no longer found on Malta. Protection against snakes is one of Jesus' promises of supernatural aid to the 70 evangelists (Lk. 10:19).

Snakes and their characteristics are often used symbolically in the Bible. Jeremiah sees Egypt like a hissing snake slithering down its hole to escape its enemies (Je. 46:22); the Psalmist likens the wicked to a venomous snake (Ps. 58:4). The devil is represented by a snake in the Garden of Eden (Gn. 3), and called 'that old serpent' in Rev. 12:9ff.; 20:2. The snake is therefore a biblical symbol of deceit (Mt. 23:33), although its wisdom is something Christians should match (Mt. 10:16). Occasionally the serpent is a mystical creature symbolizing opposition to God, as in Is. 27:1 where it is parallel to Leviathan. The prophet is announcing judgment on Assyria (land of the swift or fleeing Tigris), Babylonia (land of the twisting Euphrates), and Egypt the 'dragon monster' (*cf.* Ezk. 29:3). The fleeing serpent of Jb. 26:12f. is less clear; perhaps these verses refer to God's victory over chaos at creation. Snake gods were recognized in other cultures, as symbols of protection, evil and fertility.

For Israel's experience in the desert, see SERPENT, BRONZE.

SNARE: See HUNTING.

SNOW. Snowfalls are rare S of

Hebron and unknown along the Mediterranean coast and Jordan valley; they are more frequent in the central hills and 2 are recorded in the Bible and Apocrypha (2 Sa. 23:20 = 1 Ch. 11:22; 1 Macc. 13:22). The snow of the Lebanon mountains was proverbial, however (Je. 18:14). It is a wonder of God's power (Ps. 147:16), and symbolizes purity (Rev. 1:14) and God's cleansing of a repentant sinner (Is. 1:18).

SNUFFERS. Instruments to trim the lamp wicks in the tabernacle and temple; in 1 Ki. 7:50, perhaps some form of scissors, in Nu. 4:9 more like tongs.

SO. In 2 Ki. 17:4, the Egyptian king with whom Hoshea king of Israel conspired c. 726/5 BC and thus brought Assyrian retribution on Israel. It has not proved possible to identify him, but So could have been an abbreviation of Pharaoh Osorkon IV (c. 727-716 BC), or possibly the name of a lesser kinglet acting as an army commander under him.

SOAP. In Je. 2:22 the word 'soap' probably means 'lye' (also used for another OT word in Is. 1:25; Jb. 9:30), a solution of potash (potassium carbonate) and soda (sodium carbonate) which acts as a simple detergent. It was obtained by filtering water through vegetable ash. The word 'lye' in Je. 2:22 (AV 'nitre') is saltpetre; mixed with oil it formed a kind of soap.

SOCOH, SOCO. 1. A town SE of

Azekah near where David killed Goliath (1 Sa. 17); it was probably an important administrative centre. 2. A place in the highlands near Debir (Jos. 15:48; v. 35 refers to 1.). 3. A town in the Hepher area (1 Ki. 4:10), probably Tell er-Ras 24 km NW of Shechem.

SODOM AND GOMORRAH: See PLAIN, CITIES OF THE.

SOJOURNERS: See FOREIGNER; PILGRIMAGE.

SOLOMON. The 3rd king of Israel, c. 971-931 BC, the son of David and Bathsheba. David confirmed him as his successor after Adonijah, David's oldest surviving son, had already claimed the throne and held a coronation feast (1 Ki. 1). Solomon had Adonijah executed for his rash request for David's maid Abishag. Of Adonijah's chief supporters, Abiathar the priest was banished and Joab the army commander was murdered (1 Ki. 2:24ff.). Solomon then reigned unchallenged. He took office as Israel's first dynastic ruler, on the grounds of succession rather than divine call, but he received God's *charisma* when he asked God for the gift of wisdom with which to execute his responsibility (1 Ki. 3:3ff.). He exceeded his contemporaries in wisdom and collected and composed thousands of proverbs and songs (1 Ki. 4:29ff.). Two collections of biblical proverbs bear his name (Pr. 10:1-22:16; 25:1-29:27), the entire book crediting him as the chief collector (Pr. 1:1). Canticles (Song of Solomon) and

Ecclesiastes traditionally have been ascribed to him. Jewish, Arabian and Ethiopian folklore abounds with tales about his wisdom and magical powers.

He replaced Israel's tribal boundaries by 12 (or 13) administrative districts each of which was obliged to provide support for the court for one month per year (1 Ki. 4:7ff.); his food requirements would have made this an onerous task (1 Ki. 4:22f.). He recruited Israelites for forced labour although probably not as full slaves (1 Ki. 5:13ff.; 9:15ff.). This caused considerable resentment; the labour superintendent Adoram (Adoniram) was finally assassinated (1 Ki. 12:18). He was an enterprising trader and controlled the N–S caravan routes; his links with Hiram of Tyre gave him sea power too. His chief port was Eziongeber (Elath) on the Gulf of Aqabah. 1 Ki. 9:26ff.; 10:11ff. list the goods carried in his Phoenician-manned ships. He became the chief agent in the horse and chariot trade; Hittites and Aramaeans bought Egyptian stock through him (1 Ki. 10:28f.). The famous visit of the Queen of Sheba (1 Ki. 10:1-13) was probably connected with trade agreements.

He apparently conducted no major military campaigns. He made the most of numerous foreign alliances, not least that with Hiram of Tyre who provided architectural skill and wood for Solomon's palace and temple (1 Ki. 5:1ff.). He had a ring of strategic cities round the border manned by charioteers (1 Ki. 9:15ff.). However, Hadad the Edomite apparently harassed the S flank and Rezon captured Damascus and set up an independent kingdom in what had been David's N HQ. These events are seen by the author of 1 Kings as divine judgments (1 Ki. 11:14ff., 23ff.).

Solomon had one fatal flaw. Many of his international treaties were sealed by marriages to foreign princesses. They brought with them foreign religions in which he sometimes participated to placate his wives (1 Ki. 11). The seed sown was to produce bitter fruit in later generations.

For his temple, see TEMPLE.

SONG OF SOLOMON, SONG OF SONGS (CANTICLES). This OT book was not accepted into the canon as authoritative Scripture without dispute, probably because of its erotic nature. The objections, however were outweighed by its traditional Solomonic authorship and allegorical interpretation which lifted it above the sensual level.

Authorship and date. The traditional ascription to Solomon is based on references to him in the book (1:1, 5; 3:7, 9, 11; 8:11). He was famed for his song-writing (1 Ki. 4:32; *cf.* Pss. 72, 127). Numerous words and phrases akin to Aramaic imply that the final editing of the book took place after his time, although occasional apparently Greek loan-words do not require it to be dated as late as the Greek period because trade links existed with the area from Solomon's time onwards.

Literary qualities. The intensely personal speeches take 2 forms: dialogue (*e.g.* 1:9ff.) and soliloquy (*e.g.* 2:8-3:5). It is not easy to identify the participants in the conversation apart from the 2 lovers; daughters of Jerusalem are mentioned and respond (*e.g.* 1:5, 8), and statements have been attributed to citizens of Jerusalem (3:6-11) and Shulem (8:5). The lovers may be reconstructing the responses of others, however (*e.g.* the Shulammite seems to quote her brothers in 8:8f.). The power of the poetry lies in the intensity of love and devotion it expresses. The intimacy may be too detailed, and the imagery strange (*e.g.* 4:2ff.), for Western taste and appreciation, but it must be remembered that the Song is a product of a distant time and place.

Theories of interpretation. There is little agreement about the Song's origin, meaning and purpose. The vivid and erotic lyrics, the virtual absence of overt religious themes, and the vagueness of its plot challenge scholarship and tempt imagination. Five main approaches have been taken. The early rabbis and church Fathers saw it as *an allegory*, a picture of God's loving dealings with his people, or Christ's love for the church, sometimes straining detail of meaning from specific images. Closely related is the *typical* interpretation, preserving the literal sense but seeing in it a higher spiritual meaning; this stresses the themes of love and devotion without pressing details. But these views do not find much support in the text itself. The *dramatic* interpretation sees the Shulammite desperately trying to stay faithful to her shepherd lover despite the strong advances of Solomon, but there is scarcely any evidence of such a Hebrew dramatic tradition. *Nuptial songs* and *liturgical rites* have been suggested, although more popular today is the view that the Song is a collection of *love poems* not restricted to one occasion. What can be asserted is that it illustrates the rich wonders of human love, providing a wholesome balance between the extremes of sexual excess and an ascetic denial of the essential goodness of physical love; as such it then reminds us of a love which is purer still.

SONS OF GOD: See CHILDREN OF GOD.

SOPATER, SOSIPATER. Sopater was a Macedonian Christian who accompanied Paul from Troas to Asia (Acts 20:4); Sosipater is called Paul's kinsman (perhaps convert) in Rom. 16:21. Some consider them to be the same person.

SOREK, VALLEY OF. Delilah's home (Jdg. 16:4), the Wadi al-Sarar, a valley between Jerusalem and the Mediterranean offering a convenient inland route.

SOSTHENES. The chief ruler of the Corinth synagogue, possibly the successor or colleague of the converted Crispus. He was assaulted in court after Gallio disallowed a Jewish prosecution of Paul, perhaps out of spite for his weakness (Acts 18:17); possibly he was later the co-sender of 1

Corinthians (1:1).

SOUL. The usual Hebrew word occurs 755 times in the OT and has the primary meaning of 'possessing life' (Gn. 2:7), and so is used of animals (Gn. 1:20, 'creatures') as well as people. In many cases, especially in Psalms, it stands for the life principle. It also refers to various states of consciousness, including the seat of appetite (Jb. 33:20, 'life'), the source of emotion (Ps. 86:4), and is associated with the will (Ps. 24:4). It also denotes a (whole) person (Gn. 2:7; Ezk. 18:4). Although seen as departing at death (Gn. 35:18), it is never used for the spirit of the dead. In the NT it has similar meanings, although its sense of 'life' is more than physical (Mk. 8:35). Paul uses it for life (Rom. 16:4) and desire (Eph. 6:6, 'heart'). Other NT writers say it (*i.e.* the person) can be saved (*e.g.* Jas. 5:20). See also HEART; LIFE; SPIRIT.

SPAIN. From the 3rd cent. BC it was the scene of a struggle between Carthage and Rome; Rome's ultimate conquest of all Spanish tribes was not complete until just before Christ's birth. Paul planned to visit it (Rom. 15:24, 28), but whether he did is uncertain. See also TARSHISH.

SPARROW. The house sparrow is very common in Palestine and almost identical to the W European bird. It may be referred to in Mt. 10:29, although the original word implies other assorted small birds which were (and are) killed and sold.

SPEAR. The spear, with a wooden shaft and metallic head, was a basic weapon of infantry (*cf.* 1 Sa. 13:19), favoured by the Sumerians from 3000 BC. Lighter javelins were used by charioteers. It seems also to have been a symbol of authority (1 Sa. 22:6).

SPECK. In Mt. 7:3ff.; Lk. 6:41f., a small twig, straw or piece of wool small enough to enter the eye, used by Jesus to symbolize a minor fault.

SPICE: See HERBS AND SPICES.

SPINNING AND WEAVING. Two implements were used for spinning flax, wool, and goat hair: the distaff (held in the left hand) on which were wound the raw fibres, and the spindle worked by the right hand to twist the short natural fibres into yarn (Pr. 31:19). The spindle had a wooden shank 23-30 cm long, with a piece of stone or clay to give it momentum. Spinning was done by women, weaving by men and women; a weavers' guild is implied in 1 Ch. 4:21. Whether horizontal or vertical looms were usual is uncertain; horizontal ones were used in Egypt, and to bind Samson (Jdg. 16:13). The weaver's beam of 1 Sa. 17:7 was the means of raising and lowering the warp threads to allow the shuttle carrying the transverse woof thread to pass between them.

SPIRIT, HOLY SPIRIT. The Hebrew word translated 'spirit' has various meanings in the OT. It can mean wind (Ex. 10:13; 1 Ki. 19:11); breath or 'spirit' in the sense of the life and vitality of living creatures (Gn. 6:17; Ps. 31:5); and divine power (Jdg. 3:10; 1 Sa. 10:6). The different senses tend to merge in with one another; *e.g.* Ps. 78:39 (wind and breath), Ezk. 3:12, 14 (wind and divine power), Ezk. 37:9f. (wind, breath and divine power). At the heart of the term is the experience of a mysterious, awesome power, viewed as a manifestation of divine energy.

In later and NT times, the meanings of human spirit, angelic or demonic spirit, and divine Spirit predominate, and are more distinct. In the NT it is used nearly 40 times to denote the dimension of the human personality whereby relationship with God is possible (*e.g.* Rom. 8:16). Slightly more frequent is the sense of demonic spirits which afflict people (Mk. 1:23). There are occasional references to good heavenly spirits (Heb. 1:14) and the spirits of the dead (1 Pet. 3:19). But most frequent is the sense of God's Spirit, the Holy Spirit, used over 250 times. However the range of meaning is still reflected in some ambiguous passages (Lk. 1:80; 1 Cor. 14:14, 32).

Old Testament characteristics. In the earliest passages there is little distinction between natural and supernatural; the wind could be (poetically) a blast from God (Ps. 18:15). It was conceived more in terms of supernatural power than moral quality, too; the Spirit of God was not yet conceived as the *Holy* Spirit (Jdg. 14:19). In later passages spirit more clearly distinguishes the divine from the human (*e.g.* Is. 31:3; *cf.* Jn. 4:24), and denotes the Godward dimension of

human existence (Ps. 51:12). The prophets before the Exile were reluctant to attribute their inspiration to the Spirit of God; Mi. 3:8 is an exception. Instead, they spoke of God's word (Am. 3:8) or hand (Is. 8:11), perhaps reacting against cult professionalism and abuse (Je. 5:13; 6:13).

During and after the Exile the work of the Spirit received more emphasis. The Spirit's role as inspirer of prophecy was asserted (Is. 59:21; Ezk. 3:1, 24). The tradition which saw artistic skill as an activity of the Spirit (Ex. 31:2ff.; *cf.* his work at creation, Gn. 1:2), together with the idea of the Spirit being the Spirit of a holy God, forged a link between the Spirit and more aesthetic and moral qualities, although he is called Holy Spirit only 3 times (Ps. 51:11; Is. 63:10f.). The future participation of the Spirit in establishing the new age is stressed (Is. 44:3f.); then people would be re-created by the Spirit to enjoy a more vital and immediate relationship with God (Ezk. 36:26f.).

In the period between the Testaments the role attributed to God's Spirit again diminished and Wisdom is credited with the inspiration of prophecy (Ecclus. 24:1, 33). The rabbis restricted the Spirit to prophecy which they believed had ended with Haggai, Zechariah and Malachi; so they concluded that the Spirit had been withdrawn. The Spirit had inspired the law which was now the supreme authority.

The Spirit in the Synoptic Gospels. In the context in which the Spirit had been subordinated to Wisdom and the law, John the Baptist created some excitement because he was widely recognized as a prophet (Mt. 11:9f.). He proclaimed that the outpouring of the Spirit was imminent, which would be an experience of the fire of judgment and purification (Mt. 3:11f.). Jesus caused an even bigger stir by claiming that the new age was already effective through his ministry (Lk. 17:20f.). This presupposed that the Spirit was working through him in a unique way, releasing Satan's prisoners (Mt. 12:24ff.) and proclaiming good news to the poor (Mt. 11:5; cf. Is. 61:1f.). This special working of the Spirit began at Jesus' conception (Lk. 1:35) and he was anointed by the Spirit at his baptism (Mt. 3:16f.). Jesus promised the aid of the Spirit to his disciples in their suffering (Mk. 13:11) and the Spirit's blessing to all who seek him (Lk. 11:13).

The Spirit and entry into the Christian life. In Acts, the gift of the Spirit, the hallmark of the new age, is the starting-point of the disciples' fully Christian faith (11:17). In pioneer situations it was the manifestation of the Spirit which revealed the converts' acceptance by God (10:44f.). For Paul, too, the gift of the Spirit is the beginning of the new Christian life (Gal. 3:2f.); a person can only become and be a Christian by the work of the Spirit (Rom. 8:9ff.). For John, the Spirit likewise effects the new birth (Jn. 3:3ff.), and also gives (God's) life which flows through the believer like a river (Jn. 6:63; 7:37ff.).

For the first Christians the Spirit was thought of in terms of divine power clearly manifest by its effects in the recipient's life; the impact of the Spirit left little doubt that a significant change had been worked by God. Among the experiences were joy (1 Thes. 1:6); illumination (2 Cor. 3:14ff.); liberation (Rom. 8:2); moral transformation (1 Cor. 6:9ff.); and the receipt of various gifts (1 Cor. 1:4ff.). Therefore, many of Paul's allusions to baptism could be understood as an abbreviation of a fuller allusion to the experience of being baptized by the Spirit into Christ (1 Cor. 12:13). Birth by the Spirit, rather than the symbol of water baptism, is clearly uppermost in Jn. 3 and in Acts (*e.g.* Acts 8:12ff.; 11:15ff.). In Acts 8, the implication is that the Samaritans' experience was short of full conversion (they had believed *Philip*, v.12), and their subsequent experience of the Spirit was their initiation into Christ.

The Spirit as the power of the new life. The gift of the Spirit is the first instalment of a lifelong process of transformation into the likeness of Christ (Eph. 1:13f.), the firstfruits of the harvest of righteousness (Gal. 5:16ff.). Life is therefore qualitatively different after conversion, becoming a daily response to the Spirit's claims through his power in a personal relationship with God (Rom. 8). But the process is not complete until Christ returns, and hence there is conflict in this life between the claims of the Spirit and the longings of the old nature (Rom. 7:14ff.).

The Spirit of community. The common participation in the Spirit makes a group of diverse individuals one body in Christ (1 Cor. 12:13). The body can only grow in maturity as each member lets the Spirit be expressed through them in word and deed ((Eph. 4:3ff.). The Spirit reveals God's new truth in continuity with the old (Jn. 14:26; 16:12f.). Through the Spirit Jesus is present to the believer (Jn. 14:16ff.); hence the mark of the Spirit is to recognize Jesus' status (1 Cor. 12:3; 1 Jn. 5:6ff.), and to reproduce his character in daily life (2 Cor. 3:18).

See also BAPTISM; BODY OF CHRIST; CONVERSION; COUNS-ELLOR;EVIL SPIRITS; GUIDANCE; INSPIRATION; LIFE; POWER; PRO-PHECY; SPIRITUAL GIFTS; TRINITY; WIND.

SPIRITS IN PRISON: See DESCENT INTO HADES.

SPIRITUAL GIFTS. The term translates the Greek plural noun *charismata*, and has the idea of God's grace visibly expressed in word or deed. The singular form is used of God's gift of salvation through Christ (Rom. 5:15f.; 6:23) and of any special grace or mercy (1 Cor. 7:7; 2 Cor. 1:11, 'blessing'). The plural form is used chiefly to denote the gifts of the Holy Spirit given to Christians for special service. These were promised in the OT (Joel 2:28), and by Christ (Mk. 13:11; Jn. 14:12). The promises were fulfilled on the day of Pentecost (Acts 2). The primary purpose of the gifts is the edification of the whole church (1 Cor. 12:4ff.); they also have the func-

tion of convicting unbelievers and leading them to conversion (1 Cor. 14:21ff.). The once-popular view that they were for the founding of the church and were withdrawn by the 4th cent. AD is contrary to historical and biblical evidence. Paul envisages the gifts continuing to the return of Christ (1 Cor. 13:8ff.), and their inter-mittent appearance in the past may have been affected by the fluctuating faith and spirituality of the church, and by the sovereign purposes of God (1 Cor. 12:11).

The 4 main lists of gifts differ from one another and each is clearly incomplete (Rom. 12:6-8; 1 Cor. 12:4-11, 28-30; Eph. 4:7-12; *cf.* 1 Pet. 4:10f.). The gifts fall into 2 main categories: those which equip believers for the ministry of the word, and those which equip them for prac-tical service. Some were exercised in regular ministry, and others were manifest occasionally; some enhanced natural ability and others were clearly special endowments. Among the gifts involving speaking are *apostles*, a title originally used of the 12 (Mt. 10:2) but claimed by Paul (*e.g.* Rom. 1:1) and applied to others (*e.g.* Barnabas, Acts 14:4; Andronicus and Junia, Rom. 16:7). Their special function was to proclaim the gospel (Gal. 2:7ff.). *Pro-phets* conveyed divine revelations of temporary significance with a message of edification, exhortation and consolation (1 Cor. 14:3f.; *cf.* Acts 11:28; 13:1f.). *Distinguishing spirits* was complementary to prophecy (1 Cor. 14:29). *Teachers* did not utter fresh revelation but expounded and applied

Christian truth. Related to this gift was the *message of knowledge*, although the *message of wisdom* was insight probably related to apostles, evangelists or prophets. *Speaking with tongues* and *interpretation* are discussed in this context in relation to their use in public worship rather than in private devotion.

Of the practical service gifts, *faith* by which special deeds are accomplished (*cf.* Mt. 18:19f.) is related to *gifts of healings* and *working of miracles* and can be termed 'gifts of power'. Several 'gifts of sympathy' are listed, including *helping* (the weak), *almsgiving, works of mercy*, and *service* (probably the work of the 'deacons'). Finally, there is *administration*, which has the sense of guiding the church, and *leadership* which is similar.

See also APOSTLE; DEACON; PROPHECY; TONGUES, GIFT OF.

SPITTING. The Oriental custom of spitting on a person conveyed deep enmity (Nu. 12:14; Mt. 26:67). Jesus spat and used saliva in healing miracles (Mk. 7:33; 8:23; Jn. 9:6), a technique common to both Jews and Greeks.

SPOKESMAN. In Acts 24:1, Tertullus, a speech-writer, accepted a barrister's brief for himself. His fine speech was matched by Paul's who elsewhere disdained the rhetorician's professional skill (1 Cor. 2:4). See also TERTULLUS.

SPORT: See GAMES.

STACHYS. A friend of Paul (Rom.

16:9); the name is uncommon.

STAFF: See ROD.

STANDARD: See BANNER.

STARS. The term is used of any luminous body seen in the sky, except the sun and moon, and is not a subject of scientific curiosity to Bible writers. The huge number of stars reflects God's great generosity (Heb. 11:12), and provides a majestic revelation of his power (Ps. 8:3f.). Israelites were constantly tempted to worship gods associated with stars and planets, but the stars are insignificant compared with God himself (Am. 5:26; Acts 7:43). The biblical view of the universe is much closer to the modern rational approach to its vast majestic space than to pagan myths about it (*cf.* Ps. 104). God's acts of redemption and judgment are foreshadowed by astronomical signs (Is. 13:9f.; Joel 2:10; Mt. 24:29f.; Rev. 8:10ff.). The word 'star' is also used symbolically for dignity (*e.g.* Rev. 1:16).

Some constellations are mentioned in the Bible. The Bear (Ursa Major) with its 'children' (the 7 main stars in the group) is mentioned in Jb. 9:9; 38:32. Orion, 'the Hunter', (the range of colour and brightness among its stars illustrating 1 Cor. 15:41) and the Pleiades are both mentioned in Jb. 9:9; 38:31; Am. 5:8. The phrases 'binding the chains' and 'loosing the cords' in Jb. 38:31 may refer to the supposed heralding of spring by Pleiades and autumn by Orion. Mazzaroth in Jb. 38:32 is obscure; it may refer to the signs of the Zodiac. Also obscure is 'the chambers of the south' (Jb. 9:9); possibly it means the stars on the S horizon.

The star of Bethlehem in Mt. 2 has been explained in 4 ways. Halley's Comet is one suggestion (11 BC) or another comet in 4 BC, but it is doubtful if either would have been seen long enough or would fit the chronology of Jesus' birth. Secondly, it could have been a planetary conjunction; Jupiter, Saturn and Venus were in conjunction in 7 BC but could hardly be called 'a star'. Thirdly it may have been a supernova, a faint star becoming suddenly bright. They are rare in our galaxy but are entirely unpredictable; Chinese astronomers did record one about the time of Mt. 2. It is not unfitting that light a billion times the light of the sun should be poured out to herald the birth of the saviour of the world. This points to the fourth possible explanation of the star, that it was an entirely supernatural phenomenon, inexplicable by natural standards.

See also CREATION.

STEPHANAS. A Corinthian Christian, one of few people baptized by Paul personally (1 Cor. 1:16), commended for his voluntary service (1 Cor. 16:15ff.); he probably carried the Corinthian correspondence with Fortunatus and Achaicus.

STEPHEN. 'Crown.' One of the 7 men ('deacons') chosen to look after the distribution of welfare to widows, recorded as being outstanding among them (Acts 6:1ff.). Probably a Hellenistic (Greek-culture) Jew, he fell foul of the Jews and was charged with blasphemy. With angelic face, he accused the Jews of killing the Messiah, and he faced his martyrdom with the same spirit as Jesus (Acts 7; *cf.* Lk. 23:34, 46). The persecution of the church which followed led to more widespread preaching of the gospel (Acts 8:4; 11:19), and Stephen's death was undoubtedly a factor in the conversion of Saul of Tarsus (Paul; *cf.* Acts 7:58; 8:1, 3; 22:20). Above all, Stephen's review of OT history clearly stated the church's universal mission for the first time. His thesis that the Christian church was the true nation of God which OT ritual foreshadowed is developed in the letter to the Hebrews. Having the true temple, altar and sacrifice, they lived the truly pilgrim life and were rejected, as were the prophets and Jesus, by the Jews.

STEPS. The shadow apparently going backwards across 10 steps of the king's palace was a sign that king Hezekiah would recover from his illness (2 Ki. 20:8ff.; Is. 38:8).

STEWARD. The word is used in both Testaments to describe someone like a manager, with delegated responsibility (*e.g.* Is. 22:15; Lk. 16:1ff.). Christians are called to be stewards of Jesus' mission and government in the world (Eph. 3:2).

STOCKS. Two large pieces of wood between which a prisoner's feet, and possibly his neck and hands, were wedged (Je. 20:2f.; Acts 16:24); see also PRISON.

STOICS. The Stoic School of philosophy derived its name from the Stoa Poikile, the portico in Athens where Zeno (335-263 BC) first taught. The teaching had been modified by the time Paul encountered Stoics (Acts 17:18). They sought salvation by aligning their will with the inherent Reason (or God) of the universe, the Logos. This fitting into the natural order was not for pleasure but was to be a wholly disinterested virtue. Hence our use of 'stoic' to indicate suppression of emotion and indifference to pain or pleasure. Some Stoics, such as the emperor Marcus Aurelius, set high standards of personal conduct.

STONE, STONEMASON. *Materials.* Flint occurs abundantly in chalk and chalk-derived gravel. It is a close-grained hard rock which can produce a sharp cutting edge. Man's earliest cutting tools and weapons were made from it (*cf.* Ex. 4:25). Away from the alluvial plains of Mesopotamia stone was plentiful. In Palestine limestone was used for building and for water pots; sandstone and basalt were also available for building. Marble, a close-grained white or cream crystalline limestone, came from Minoa and also parts of Greece and Assyria; large quantities were incorporated into the temple (see 1 Ch. 29:2). Apart from building purposes, stones were a convenient weapon (1 Sa. 17:40) or means of execution (Acts 7:58f.). They closed tombs (Mt. 27:60) and acted as landmarks (2 Sa. 20:8).

Stonemasons used similar tools to carpenters, sawing blocks of limestone and trimming them with mallets and chisels. Metal forge-hammers were used to shape hard stone (*cf.* Je. 23:29). Large blocks of stone were quarried by driving wooden wedges into them and soaking the wedges until the expansion caused the stone to crack. Masons also quarried tombs out of natural caves or solid limestone (fine examples dated 1st cent. BC–2nd cent. AD have been found in Jerusalem), and dug water storage cisterns (some required the removal by hand of 400,000 cu m of limestone). By the 1st cent. BC large building blocks used in Herod's projects were so well dressed that they could be aligned without mortar, and it is still impossible to insert a knife into the joints of the remains. Masons cut inscriptions on tombs, too.

Symbolic uses. Jesus is described as a stone in the NT (Mk. 12:1ff., applying Ps. 118:22), using the image of the carefully chosen and perfectly made coping stone which completes a building. He has been exalted to the headship of the new Israel despite being rejected by the original 'builders' of Israel (Acts 4:11). The cornerstone of 1 Pet. 2:6 (*cf.* Is. 28:16) is part of the foundation; the author sees Christians as building stones incorporated into the 'temple' which Christ supports and heads (vv. 4f.).

STONING. The usual Hebrew form of execution (*e.g.* Lv. 20:27; Acts 7:58). The law required two prosecution witnesses who had to throw the first stone (Dt. 13:9f.; Jn. 8:7).

STORE-CITIES. Towns where provisions, often revenue paid in kind, and weapons were kept by the central government as reserve supplies and to maintain frontier and defence forces. The Hebrews built Egypt's store-cities Pithom and Raamses (Ex. 1:11); Israelite store-cities are referred to in 2 Ch. 8:4ff.; 32:28 and elsewhere.

STORK, CRANE. The white stork migrates N along the Jordan valley in March–April; the crane is a bird of similar build and also a migrant (Je. 8:7).

STORM. Violent rainstorms generally occur at the start of the rainy season in Palestine, or at the start of new spells of rain during the cooler months. Thunderstorms are most frequent in November–December in the Jordan valley, sometimes with hail. Windstorms can sweep down on the Sea of Galilee (Mk. 4:37f.). Storms can devastate growing crops (Is. 28:2). See also PALESTINE; RAIN; THUNDER; WHIRLWIND; WIND.

STRANGLED (THINGS). Animals killed without draining their blood. This method was repugnant to Jews (Dt. 12:23; Acts 15:20ff.).

STUMBLING BLOCK. Any barrier which causes a person to fall; used symbolically of idols (Ezk. 14:3f.) and, for a different reason, of Jesus (1 Pet. 2:8). In 1 Cor. 1:23 the word originally meant the trigger-stick of a trap.

SUBURB. In AV it generally means uncultivated pasture land.

SUCCOTH. 1. The first stop on the Exodus route (Ex. 12:37), possibly in the E part of Wadi Tumilat, the normal way out from Egypt for displaced persons. 2. A city in the Jordan valley (Jdg. 8:5, 16); modern Tell Akhsas or Tell Deir Allah.

SUCCOTH-BENOTH. An object made by the Babylonians exiled in Samaria c. 722 BC and named among pagan gods; possibly shrines of female goddesses (2 Ki. 17:30).

SUFFERING. The Bible regards suffering as an intrusion into a world which God created good (Gn. 1:31). When sin entered it, so did suffering in the form of conflict, pain, decay, drudgery and death (Gn. 3:15ff.). The work of Christ is to release people from suffering, death and sin (Mt. 1:21; Rom. 8:21; 1 Cor. 15:26). Though Satan has the power to make people suffer (Jb. 1:12; 2:6; 2 Cor. 12:7), he operates only under the control of God who will finally abolish suffering in the new heaven and earth (Rev. 21:4).

The burden of suffering has always been felt keenly by God's people and hence has had to be related to the facts of God's love and righteousness. True faith can wait in the dark without understanding God's purposes in suffering (Hab. 2:2ff.), and can find in God's presence and goodness a more decisive factor than even the bitterness of pain (Ps. 73). The book of Job shows one person battling with the problem to reach a certainty in which he can triumph over his troubles yet without being able to explain the reason for them.

Suffering can be the direct result of sin (Gal. 6:8), God's punishment (Jdg. 2:22-3:6) or a means by which people are tested and purified (1 Pet. 1:7). The Servant of God was prefigured in Is. 53 as suffering on behalf of God's people, and the NT writers see Christian suffering as sharing in Christ's suffering (2 Cor. 1:5ff.), and accept it as part of their calling to serve (Phil. 1:29; 1 Pet. 4:1f.).

See also HEALTH AND HEALING.

SUKKIIM. Libyan auxiliaries in the Egyptian army (2 Ch. 12:3).

SUMER, SUMERIANS. The lower part of ancient Mesopotamia or S Iraq between modern Baghdad and the Persian Gulf was known as Akkad (ACCAD), a flat area crossed by the R. Tigris and R. Euphrates. It was settled *c.* 4500 BC by Sumerians, who were eventually absorbed by the Semites of the area *c.* 1750 BC. The origins of the Sumerians are not known, but their civilization may lie behind Gn. 1-11. One of their chief cities was Ur (*cf.* Gn. 11:28), which became the capital in the latter period of Sumerian history (*c.* 2100-1960 BC). After the Sumerians disappeared, their language remained that of religion, science, business and law for many centuries.

The Sumerians are credited with the invention of writing; their cuneiform script and literary styles were adopted and developed by many nations. They are perhaps best known for their myths of the creation of the world and of civilization, of a heroic age of perfection and of mankind's failure, and of the flood. Their society seems to have grouped villages around larger cities to form city-states controlled by a council of senators and soldiers under the leadership of a chief man, later a king who was regarded as the vice-regent of the city's chief god. The Sumerians bequeathed to later generations concepts of law and government; their astronomy and mathematics subdivided time and area into degrees from which we derive our hours, minutes and linear measurements; and they developed the wheel both for transport and pottery.

See also ACCAD; CREATION; ERECH; FLOOD; WRITING.

SUN. Many references relate to the time of day. The Bible also mentions such effects of the sun as causing crops to grow (Dt. 33:14) or wither (Mt. 13:6), and causing physical injury by its heat (Ps. 121:6). It is a symbol of constancy (Ps. 72:5), and of God's glory (Rev. 1:16) which outlasts the sun (Rev. 21:23). The Messiah is seen as a healing sun (Mal. 4:2). On the day of the Lord, the sun will be eclipsed (Joel 2:10; 3:15; Rev. 6:12; 8:12). Sun worship was forbidden in Israel (Dt. 4:19) but was practised at times (2 Ki. 23:11).

SUPH, SUPHA. In Dt. 1:1, an uncertain location which AV takes plausibly as the Gulf of Aqabah. In Nu. 21:14, a probably different and equally uncertain place.

SURETY: See GUARANTEE.

SUSA. A royal city of Persia (Dn. 8:2; Ne. 1:1) whose ruins now lie near the R. Karun. It was sacked by Ashurbanipal of Assyria in 645 BC who exiled its people to Samaria (Ezr. 4:9), but it later flourished and the palace built there by Darius I figures prominently in ESTHER.

SUSANNA, BOOK OF: See APOCRYPHA.

SWINE: See PIG.

SWORD. The most frequently mentioned weapon in the Bible. The earliest swords were usually straight, double-edged and more like daggers. Sickle-shaped swords appeared *c.* 2500 BC, and the long straight sword became common a century later. Swords were usually housed in sheaths suspended from a belt (2 Sa. 20:8). In both Testaments it is a synonym for war or a symbol of God's word (Eph. 6:17). See also WAR.

SYCHAR. A Samaritan town (Jn. 4:5), probably Askar, 1 km N of Jacob's well, on Mt Ebal.

SYCOMORE: See TREES.

SYENE (SEVENEH). A place (modern Aswan) on the 1st cataract of the Nile marking the boundary between Egypt and Nubia. It was close to the island community of Elephantine where some Jews sought refuge after the fall of Jerusalem in 587 BC. It was a terminus for river traffic and a source of red granite (syenite) for buildings. It is mentioned in Ezk. 29:10; 30:6; and also as a place from which refugees shall return to Israel (Is. 49:12).

SYMBOL. The word is not found in the Bible but objects are often used to represent or recall some greater reality; the distinction between the object and the reality symbolized is always maintained.

Three kinds of symbols are employed in the OT. *Personal symbols* occur where one man represents or symbolizes a group (*cf.* 2 Sa. 18:3) or stands in the place of God as a symbol of God's presence (Ex. 7:1ff.), and in the frequent phrase 'man of God'. *Objective symbols* represent God's presence. The rainbow is a reminder that his wrath has passed and that he will keep his covenant (Gn. 9:13), the bronze serpent symbolizes his healing power (Nu. 21:9), the altar symbolizes the meeting-place between God and man, the ark of the covenant symbolizes God's continuing presence, and the temple represents his universal power. All the objects and vestments in Israel's worship were appropriate symbols of greater reality. *Acted symbols* demonstrate or introduce new circumstances, such as when a slave's ear was pierced to signify his membership of a household (Ex. 21:6). Circumcision may represent the dedication of reproductive powers to divine guidance and the incorporation of the child into the community. The prophets used symbolic actions to convey their messages. Isaiah went about naked as a symbol of Egypt's impending defeat and captivity (Is. 20:2ff.); Ezekiel built a model to demonstrate God's planned siege and destruction of Jerusalem (Ezk. 4:1ff.).

The situation is different in the NT: there are no symbolic persons for Jesus Christ is God (Jn. 10:30), and the disciples were servants, not representatives. However, Jesus performed symbolic actions, his healings for example demonstrating the approach of God's kingdom. He gave the disciples a memorial meal by which they could symbolize his eternal presence within the church, and in baptism sin is symbolically washed away; the sacraments of eucharist and baptism become not only illustrations but also channels of divine grace. The cross is used symbolically, too, to represent historical fact and to summarize some essential features of Christian faith.

The church has never forbidden the use of symbols, because they are rooted in human nature and experience, however it has never encouraged them lest in stressing the symbols people lose sight of the Lord they represent and point towards.

See also SACRAMENT; SIGN.

SYNAGOGUE. The name for a Jewish meeting place in NT times. More than any other institution, it gave character to the Jewish faith. It was where people and leaders kept in touch with one another and where the law was taught. As well as a place of worship and prayer, it also provided a focus for community life. It is still the centre of Jewish religious life today.

The synagogue seems to have arisen as a place for instruction and prayer during the Exile when temple worship at Jerusalem was impossible; a basis for its origin may be reflected in Ezk. 20:1. The history of the synagogue's growth is unknown, but by the 1st cent. AD one existed wherever Jews lived; a minimum of 10 adult males was required for worship. Large cities possessed numerous synagogues; one legend says there were 394 in Jerusalem when it was destroyed in AD 70. They are mentioned in the Gospels as places where Jesus ministered (*e.g.* Lk. 4:16) and the apostles used them as starting-places for their evangelism (*e.g.* Acts 13:5, 14). The buildings were probably modelled on the Jerusalem temple. An ark containing the scrolls of the Law and Prophets was at one end facing the entrance; in front of it and also facing the entrance and the congregation were the 'best' (or chief) seats (Mt. 23:6) for religious leaders. Men and women sat in different sections.

Synagogues were governed by elders who had power to discipline and punish members. The chief officer (*cf.* Mk. 5:22) supervised the service; the attendant fetched the scrolls (Lk. 4:20) and executed the punishment of scourging. An interpreter then paraphrased the readings into the vernacular Aramaic. Any suitably qualified person could speak (Lk. 4:16; Acts 13:15). The sabbath service had 5 parts: (1) the Shema was read (Dt. 6:4-9; 11:13-21; Nu. 15:37-41); (2) prayers were recited including the 18 petitions and benedictions; (3) a section of the Law was read, originally in a 3-year cycle; (4) then a section of the Prophets was read, the reader making his own choice (Lk. 4:16ff.); (5) the Scripture was expounded and the service concluded with a benediction.

SYNZYGUS. In Phil. 4:3 (AV) probably not a name but an affectionate term 'yoke fellow' for Luke.

SYRACUSE. A city with a large harbour on the coast of E Sicily and the seat of the island's government. Paul stayed there for 3 days (Acts 28:12).

SYRIA, SYRIANS. In the English OT this term denotes the ARAMAEANS. Syria existed as a political unit during the Hellenistic period from 312 BC. It was annexed by Rome in 64 BC. The Roman province of Syria covered the area of the Gospels and early Acts. See also ANTIOCH (Syrian); DAMASCUS.

SYROPHOENICIAN. An inhabitant of Phoenicia around Tyre and Sidon which in NT times was part of the Roman province of Cilicia and Syria; also called 'Canaanite' (Mk. 7:26; *cf.* Mt. 15:22)

SYRTIS. In Acts 27:17, quicksands W of Cyrene on the N African coast; now called the Gulf of Sidra.

T

TAANACH. A city (modern Tell Taannek) on the S edge of the valley of Jezreel, guarding a pass across Mt Carmel following the Wadi Abdullah. The Israelites defeated its king (Jos. 12:21) but could not possess it for some time (Jos. 17:11f.). The site bears the marks of destruction in the Late Bronze Age (1550-1200 BC), perhaps associated with Jdg. 5:19.

TABERNACLE. The portable sanctuary which symbolized the presence of God among the Israelites in the desert and later in Canaan. It consisted of a set of 10 violet-blue, purple and scarlet linen curtains with woven figures of cherubim, draped over a wooden framework, and covered externally with goats'-hair curtains and rams skins. The acacia-wood framework was probably made from 48 ladder-like sections which would be lighter and more easily transported than solid planks; it was overlaid with gold. The roof appears to have been flat, and it would have needed wooden struts across the roof to prevent the curtains from sagging and thus causing the sides to collapse inwards. Construction details are given in Ex. 26.

The interior was divided into 2 compartments by a veil (Ex. 26:31ff.). The first compartment was 'the holy place', the second 'the holy of holies'. In the latter stood the ark of the covenant (Ex. 25:10ff.); this had a slab (the 'mercy seat') made of pure gold and with a cherub at each end, resting on top, on which the propitiatory blood of sacrifices was sprinkled. The holy place contained the altar of incense (Ex. 30:1ff.) made from acacia wood and overlaid with pure gold. It had horns projecting at the corners. On the N side stood a table for the BREAD OF THE PRESENCE (Showbread, Ex. 25:23ff.), and on the S side a 7-branched lampstand in the form of a stylized tree (Ex. 25:31ff.).

The tabernacle stood in the W half of a courtyard, with its door facing E (Ex. 27:9ff.). The yard was bounded by linen curtains, and a gate was set in the E wall. In the E half of the courtyard was the altar of burnt offering (Ex. 27:1ff.). It was a hollow framework of acacia wood overlaid with copper. From the ground to a ledge halfway up was a copper grating possibly providing a draught for the fire in the centre. Between the altar and the gate was the laver (Ex. 30:17ff.), a copper basin which held water for the priests' ablutions. When Israel camped in the desert, the tents nearest the tabernacle were those of the priests and Levites (Nu. 2).

Arguments against the historicity of the descriptions of the tabernacle have been considerably modified as theories about OT sources have been revised and as portable pavilions employing practically the same construction techniques as those given for the tabernacle have been discovered.

A number of practical details are clearly omitted from the biblical description (making reconstruction difficult) because the purpose of the record is to point out the main (and symbolic) features and not to provide a working drawing.

Theologically, the tabernacle signifying God's dwelling place on earth is of immense importance. It began the series of God's 'residences' which passed through the temple to the person of Christ and then the 'body of Christ', the church. Its symbols conveyed spiritual meanings to the Israelites (cf. Heb. 8:5) which were often stated quite clearly (e.g. the ark and mercy seat, Ex. 25:16, 22; Lv. 16:15f.). The author of Hebrews builds on some of the symbolism to show that Christ has entered into the real holy place of God's presence with a perfect sacrifice for sins (Heb. 6:19f.). He implies that he could have expounded all the tabernacle symbolism in a similar way (Heb. 9:5), although later extravagant attempts to do just that have brought some disrepute to the subject.

See also ALTAR; ARK OF THE COVENANT.

TABERNACLES, FEAST OF. Also known as the feast of booths or ingathering, it was one of the 3 great pilgrimage festivals of the Jewish year, kept from 15th to 22nd of the 7th month, when all the crops had been harvested. Every Israelite male was required to appear at it, and during it everyone born an Israelite was required to live in temporary booths made from tree and palm branches. Sacrifices were made each day. It reminded the Jews of their desert wanderings and that all their life rested on God's redemption. The feast is prescribed in Ex. 23:14ff.; Lv. 23:39ff.; Dt. 16:13ff.; the water-pouring custom in Jn. 7:37f. was a later addition.

TABLE. The table in the desert (Pss. 23:5; 78:19) was a prepared area or skin laid on the ground. Elsewhere, it was a common article of furniture made from wood or metal; to eat at a king's table (2 Sa. 9:7) was an honour.

TABOR. 1. A steep-sided mountain rising from the Plain of Jezreel 588 m above sea-level. There was an idolatrous shrine on it in Hosea's time (Ho. 5:1), and a town was built there later. Traditionally it was the scene of the transfiguration of Christ, but this is unlikely. 2. Possibly a town on or near the mountain in Jos. 19:22; Jdg. 8:18; 1 Ch. 6:77. 3. A quite different town (in Benjamin) in 1 Sa. 10:3.

TADMOR. In 2 Ch. 8:4, usually identified with modern Tudmor, 'Palmyra' 200 km NE of Damascus, mentioned in Assyrian texts *c.* 1100 BC.

TAHPANHES. An important Egyptian settlement in the E Delta to which some Jews fled *c.* 586 BC taking Jeremiah with them (Je. 43). It is located at Tell Defneh, 43 km SSW of Port Said. 'Pharaoh's palace' (Je. 43:9) may be the fortress of Psammetichus I which has been excavated.

TAHPENES. An Egyptian queen whose sister the pharaoh married off to Hadad of Edom (1 Ki. 11:19f.).

TAHTIM-HODSHI. In 2 Sa. 24:6 (AV), probably Kadesh of the Hittites.

TALITHA CUMI ('Little girl, arise'). Jesus' words in a Galilean Aramaic dialect spoken to Jairus' daughter; Talitha is an affectionate term like 'little lamb' (Mk. 5:41).

TALMAI. 1. A Canaanite descendant of Anak (Jos. 15:14). 2. The ruler of Geshur whose daughter Maacah married David and bore Absalom (2 Sa. 3:3; 13:37); the name is also known from non-biblical texts.

TALMUD AND MIDRASH.

1. Talmud.

This is the source from which Jewish law is derived, and is binding on orthodox Jews. It is composed of the *Mishnah*, the oral law which was in existence by the end of the 2nd cent. AD, and the *Gemara* which is comments on the Mishnah by Rabbis from AD 200 to 500. It contains *Halakhah*, legal enactments and precepts, and *Haggadah*, non-legal interpretations. Liberal Jews do not consider it authoritative. It is important for our knowledge of how the Jews interpreted the OT and it throws light on the NT.

The *Mishnah* has 6 main divisions, or orders: Seeds (agricultural laws and duties); Feasts; Women (including marriage and divorce rules); Fines (including civil legislation and commercial deals); Sacred Things (including sacrifices, clean and unclean animals); and Purifications (cleanness and uncleanness of objects and persons). It is marked by brevity, clarity and comprehensiveness, and was used as a textbook in rabbinical academies. Most of the discussions in the Talmud are in dialogue form, with lengthy digressions into the Haggadah.

See also TARGUM.

2. Midrash.
Jewish expositions of or commentaries upon scriptural passages (cf. 'the Commentary on the Book of the Kings', 2 Ch. 24:27, which probably emphasized some religious truth). Sometimes the term indicates a branch of rabbinic learning to do with the rules of traditional (written) law, used in contrast to Mishnah. Exposition and commentary became especially necessary after the Exile in Babylon, and Midrashic activity ended soon after the completion of the Babylonian Talmud (5th cent. AD).

TAMAR. *People:* Three OT women. 1. Judah's daughter-in-law, whose story illustrates ancient marriage customs (Gn. 38). 2. David's daughter violated by Amnon (2 Sa. 13). 3. A daughter of Absalom (2 Sa. 14:27). *Place:* A city near the Dead Sea (Ezk. 47:19).

TAMBOURINE: See MUSIC AND MUSICAL INSTRUMENTS.

TAMMUZ. A pagan god whose cult was characterized by ritual offerings and laments (Ezk. 8:14). Tammuz was said to be a Sumerian shepherd before the flood who married the goddess Ishtar. It is unlikely that he rose from the dead in the original story, as was once thought.

TANNER. Leather, the treated skins of sheep and goats, was used for some items of clothing (Nu. 31:20). Skins sewn together provided cheap containers for water or wine (Mt. 9:17), and also shields and helmets for soldiers. Sandals of seal or porpoise skin (RSV 'leather', Ezk. 16:10) were a sign of luxury; this was also used for the upper covering of the tabernacle (Ex. 25:5, RSV 'goatskins'). Tanning took place outside towns. Animal fat was scraped from the skin, and the hair removed by scraping, soaking in urine or rubbing with lime. Then the skin was dressed by smoking or rubbing with oil, or tanned with suitable bark, wood or leaves.

TAPPUAH. 1. A village in the Shephelah, possibly Beit Netif 18 km W of Bethlehem (Jos. 15:34). 2. A town in Ephraim, possibly Sheikh Abu Zarad 12 km S of Shechem (Jos. 12:17).

TAR: See BITUMEN.

TARGUM. An Aramaic translation or paraphrase of some part of the OT. Targums exist for all OT books except Ezra, Nehemiah and Daniel. They came into being as the synagogue evolved after the Exile, when Aramaic began to replace Hebrew as the Jews' language. It therefore became customary for a reading of the Hebrew Scriptures in the synagogue service to be followed by an oral rendering into Aramaic. As time passed, these renderings became more fixed and traditional, and were committed to writing probably from the 2nd cent. BC.

Even the most literal targums brought place-names up to date, smoothed over textual difficulties and clarified obscure passages. Some of the paraphrase targums expand the text considerably, substantially altering the text and inserting additional material ('midrash'). Their value today is that they offer major evidence for the vernacular speech of ancient Palestine, and hence for the study of NT language and background. They also offer an important witness to the OT text.

See also TALMUD AND MIDRASH; TEXTS AND VERSIONS.

TARSHISH. A grandson of Noah, and the name also refers both to his descendants and their territory. Several OT references suggest that Tarshish bordered on the sea (*e.g.* Jon. 1:3). It was rich in metals exported to places such as Joppa and Tyre (Je. 10:9; Ezk. 27:12). This would point to a mineral-rich area in the W Mediterranean, and Tartessus in Spain has been favoured by many scholars; certainly the Phoenicians were attracted by the mineral wealth and founded colonies there. However, some references (*e.g.* 1 Ki. 10:22; 22:48) refer to Tarshish ships sailing in the Red Sea, perhaps pointing to a land in Africa, though the word may have come to describe a type of ship rather than its destination. These ships symbolize wealth and the day of judgment was pictured in terms of their destruction (Is. 2:16); in popular imagination Tarshish became a distant paradise.

TARSUS. A city on the Cilician plain 16 km inland from the coast. Its remains suggest that in Roman times it housed a population of 500,000. On the navigable R. Cydnus, it had a skilfully engineered port and a highway led through the Taurus mountains 50 km away. Nothing is known of its origin, but it appears sporadically in history; it is mentioned on Shalmaneser's obelisk as having been overrun by the Assyrians in the 9th cent. BC. It was granted some degree of independence after the Romans defeated Antiochus the Great in 189 BC (*cf.* the growth of independence by 171 BC revealed in 2 Macc. 4:30ff.). Cilicia was made a Roman province in 65/64 BC by Pompey, and the Roman citizenship of some of its Jews probably dates from this settlement. Among their descendants was the apostle Paul (Acts 21:39; 22:25ff.).

TARTAK. A pagan god worshipped by people of Avva who were deported to Samaria (2 Ki. 17:31). Its identity is uncertain.

TARTAN. The highest official in Assyria after the king, and titular head of the province where Harran was capital (*cf.* 2 Ki. 18:17).

TASSEL: See DRESS; FRINGE.

TATTENAI. The Persian governor of the Samaria district (Ezr. 5:3ff.); he is mentioned in a cuneiform inscription in Babylon dated 5 June 502 BC.

TAVERNS, THREE. A place 50 km SE from Rome on the Via Appia (Acts 28:15).

TAX COLLECTOR. Someone employed by a tax farmer or contractor to collect tax or customs duties on behalf of the Romans. A class of men who undertook state contracts of various kinds, including tax collection, existed by 212 BC. The system was open to abuse and from the beginning the collectors seem to have been prone to extortion and malpractice. The main contractors were often (but not always) foreign to the provinces they worked in; their subcontractors and collectors were often natives. Zacchaeus was probably the contractor for Jericho and had collectors under him (Lk. 19:2). They were hated and despised by Jews not only for extortion, but also because continual contact with Gentiles made such people ceremonially unclean (*cf.* 'tax collectors and sinners' in Mt. 9:10f.).

TAXES. Regular payments extracted from a state and its provinces by its own rulers. In Israel's early days the only taxes were for the maintenance of the tabernacle and its ministers (Dt. 18:1ff.), but with the monarchy came heavier demands (1 Sa. 8:15ff.). In NT times, Roman provinces paid regular poll-taxes to Caesar in Roman coinage (Mt. 22:17) and Herodian rulers collected dues in their realms (Mt. 17:24ff.). See also previous article and CENSUS; TRIBUTE-TAX.

TEKOA. A town in Judah (modern Kh. Taqua) 10 km S of Bethlehem, the home of Amos (Am. 1:1), and of a wise woman who sought to reconcile David and Absalom (2 Sa. 14:1f.). It was reinhabited after the Exile (Ne. 3:5).

TELAIM. The place where Saul gathered his army before attacking the Amalekites and sinned by offering sacrifices (1 Sa. 15); possibly Telem (Jos. 15:24) in the Negeb.

TELASSAR. A place inhabited by 'the people of Eden' (2 Ki. 19:12; Is. 37:12), probably between the R. Euphrates and R. Balih where Assyrian texts locate Beth-Eden. No Telassar is known there; a Til-Assur, known from Assyrian texts, appears to lie near the Assyrian-Elam border.

TEMA. The son and descendants of Ishmael and the area they inhabited. A desert oasis (Is. 21:14), probably Taima 400 km NW of Medina in NW Arabia.

TEMAN. Esau's grandson, who may have given his name to a district, town or tribe in N Edom (Je. 49:20; Ezk. 25:13). Its inhabitants were renowned for wisdom (Je. 49:7); Eliphaz, who came to Job, was a Temanite (Jb. 2:11). Habakkuk speaks of God coming from Teman (Hab. 3:3). Possibly Tawilan, a large Edomite town in 8th-6th cents. BC.

TEMPERANCE: See SELF-CONTROL; see also WINE AND STRONG DRINK.

TEMPLE. Some of mankind's earliest structures were shrines or temples where a god could be worshipped in his 'house'; the tower of Babel (Gn. 11:4) is the first religious structure to be mentioned in the Bible. In Mesopotamia, which Abraham left, each city had a temple for its patron god. The nomadic Patriarchs had no use for a permanent shrine, although they did commemorate God's appearances by means of altars or monumental pillars (*e.g.* Gn. 28:22). When Israel moved from Egypt to settle in Canaan their shrine was a mobile tabernacle or tent of meeting; the nations around them had temples (*e.g.* 1 Sa. 5:5), the remains of some of them having been unearthed by archaeologists. King David began collecting material for a permanent temple in Jerusalem, his capital, and his son Solomon constructed it.

Solomon's temple. It was built on the E side of what is now known as the Old City of Jerusalem, in the Haram esh-Sharif area, although the precise location is uncertain. The highest part of the rock, now covered by 'the Dome of the Rock', may have been the innermost sanctuary and part of Araunah's threshing floor which David bought as the site (2 Sa. 24:18ff.).

The building is described in 1 Ki. 6-7 and 2 Ch. 3-4. It was rectangular, orientated E–W; it probably stood on a platform, and probably had 2 courtyards. The bronze altar for burnt offerings stood in the inner courtyard and between the altar and the temple porch was a huge bronze laver (basin) for ritual washings. The porch was flanked by 2 pillars called Jachin and Boaz which were not essential parts of the physical structure. Just inside the porch was the holy place where ordinary rituals were performed. It was lit by latticed windows near the ceiling, and contained the golden incense-altar, 5 pairs of lampstands, the table for sacred bread, and the instruments of sacrifice. Further in, and closed off by cypress doors, was the 'holy of holies', a perfect cube and probably only entered annually by the high priest for the atonement ceremony. Each room was panelled with cedar wood, and the walls and doors were decorated with flowers, trees and cherubim. On upper floors were rooms for stores, offerings and probably accommodation.

Solomon hired a Tyrian to oversee the work and Phoenician craftsmen to execute it (1 Ki. 5:10, 18; 7:13f.) and it is therefore not surprising to find some parallels to Canaanite and Phoenician handiwork in the temple. The ground plan is very similar to a small shrine of the 9th cent. BC excavated at Tell Tainat on the R. Orontes, and a Late Bronze Age shrine at Hazor also provides some parallels to the temple's plan and construction technique.

Later, invaders raided the treasures Solomon had collected in the temple (1 Ki. 14:26) and Judaean kings used them to buy political power or peace (1 Ki. 15:18; 2 Ki. 16:8). Three centuries after it was built, Josiah (*c.* 640 BC) needed to undertake extensive repairs to the structure (2 Ki. 22:4ff.). Then in 587 BC it was looted and destroyed by the Babylonian invader Nebuchadrezzar (2 Ki. 25:9ff.).

Ezekiel's temple. Ezekiel had a vision of a new temple *c.* 571 BC (Ezk. 40-43), although it was never built. It was placed in a square walled courtyard pierced by 3 fortified gates, and containing outbuildings for storage and accommodation. Otherwise the basic pattern of the temple was similar to Solomon's.

The Second temple. This was built by the exiles who returned to Jerusalem bringing quantities of the looted implements with them (Ezr. 1; 3:1ff.). It was smaller than Solomon's, but few details have been preserved. The ark of the covenant had disappeared and was never replaced, and only a single 7-branched lamp stood in the holy place (*cf.* 1 Macc. 1:21ff.; 4:49ff.). The Maccabees cleansed the temple in 164 BC after it had been desecrated by Antiochus Epiphanes, and fortified the enclosure so well that it resisted Pompey's siege for 3 months in 63 BC. This temple lasted for 500 years.

Herod's temple. This was a major redevelopment of the second temple, begun in 19 BC; the main structure was completed in 10 years but work continued until AD 64. An area 450 m N-S and 300 m E-W was levelled and enclosed by a wall built from massive blocks 1 m high and 5 m long (*cf.* Mk. 13:1), parts of which still stand today. At the SE corner overlooking the Kidron ravine, the inner courtyard was 45 m above the rock, perhaps the site of the 'pinnacle' (Mt. 4:5). At the NW corner the fortress of Antonia dominated the enclosure; it housed a Roman garrison. The outer court had a portico inside the walls (Jn. 10:23; Acts 3:11), where scribes held their schools and debates (Lk. 2:46; 19:47) and money-changers had their stalls (Lk. 19:45f.). Notices in Greek and Latin warned that no responsibility could be taken for the death of any Gentile who ventured beyond this outer court.

The next court (Women's Court) contained the chests for gifts (Mk. 12:41ff.). Then, a little higher, was the Court of Israel, where Jewish men could go; they could also go into the Priest's Court at the Feast of Tabernacles to walk round the altar. The enclosed shrine followed Solomon's pattern, a curtain dividing the holy of holies from the holy place (*cf.* Mk. 15:38). The magnificent cream stone and gold building was barely finished before it was destroyed by the Romans in AD 70, and its treasures carried in a triumphal procession to Rome as depicted on the Arch of Titus.

Temple in the NT. Jesus greatly respected the Jerusalem temple (the house of God, Mt. 12:4; 23:17, 21). He cleansed it (Jn. 2:17) and the thought of its destruction made him weep (Lk. 19:41ff.). But he also saw himself as greater than the temple (Mt. 12:6); it had become a cover for Israel's spiritual barrenness (Mk. 11:12ff.), and would finally have to be destroyed (Mk. 13:2). This statement, linked misleadingly with his prophecy that his body ('temple') would be destroyed but raised on the 3rd day (Mk. 9:31) formed the testimony of the false witnesses at his trial (Mk. 14:57f.). His death and resurrection caused a new temple, the congregation of his people, to replace the old (cf. Mt. 18:20).

Time elapsed before the full ramifications of this became apparent, and the first Christians continued to worship at the temple (cf. Acts 2:46; 3:1ff.). Stephen's defence at his trial attacked Jewish attitudes to the temple (Acts 7), and the Council of Jerusalem points towards the doctrine found in the NT letters, that the church is God's new temple (Acts 15:14ff.). This doctrine is most clearly expounded by Paul (e.g. 1 Cor. 3:16f.; Eph. 2:19ff.). The practical implication is that holiness and unity are required in Christian living; schism profanes the 'temple' (1 Cor. 3:5ff.). The concept of the church as a sanctuary leads 1 Pet. 2:4ff. to regard Christians as 'priests'.

In Heb. and Rev. comes the concept of a heavenly temple. It was an image common among the Semites and helped to sustain Jewish hope in the period between the Testaments when it looked as if the temple of Jerusalem would never become the expected metropolis of the world. Hebrews says that the heavenly temple is the original, the earthly one a mere copy (8:5; 9:24), and it is the assembly of the church triumphant (12:23). In Rev., the celestial temple is part of the author's grand scheme of spiritualization, and again is essentially the company of God's faithful people (14:1). The new Jerusalem has no temple because the presence of God has taken its place (21:3, 22ff.; 22:3f.).

See also ALTAR; BREAD OF THE PRESENCE; JACHIN AND BOAZ; JERUSALEM; PRIESTS AND LEVITES; PRIESTS (NT); SACRIFICE; TABERNACLE.

TEMPLE SERVANTS. Called Nethinim (AV, RSV mg.), these are mentioned only in Ezr. and Ne. (except for 1 Ch. 9:2 = Ne. 11:3). The name means 'those who are given'; Ezr. 8:20 says David and the princes had given them for the service of the Levites. They were possibly descendants of Canaanite or foreign prisoners, like the Gibeonites of Jos. 9:27; the foreign names in Ezr. 2:43ff. would support this.

TEMPTATION. The biblical idea of temptation is not primarily one of seduction, but of putting someone to the test. This may be done for a benevolent purpose, of proving or improving the person's quality, or with the malicious aim of showing up the person's weakness or trapping him or her into wrong action. So the Pharisees 'tested' Jesus (the word is the same as for 'tempt') in the sense of trying him out, to see if he would prove his Messiahship in their terms (Mk. 8:11). Christians should test ('examine') themselves regularly to ensure their faith is truly up to the mark (2 Cor. 13:5). People may test God by behaviour which is a defiant challenge to him to prove the truth of his words and the justice of his ways (Ps. 78:18).

God tests his people by putting them in situations which reveal the quality of their faith and devotion (Gn. 22:1; Jdg. 2:22). He thus purifies them as metal is refined (Ps. 66:10), leading them to enlarged assurance of his love for them (Rom. 5:3ff.). Satan tests God's people by manipulating circumstances within the limits God allows (Jb. 1:12; 2:6; 1 Cor. 10:13), in an attempt to make them desert God's will. He is called the tempter (Mt. 4:3), who is always trying to make Christians fall (1 Pet. 5:9). God allows temptations to occur (Mt. 4:1), but he does not prompt his people to do wrong (Jas. 1:12ff.). Christians are to pray not to be exposed to temptation (Mt. 6:13), and to be watchful so they do not yield to its pressure (Mt. 26:41).

TEN COMMANDMENTS. These were originally uttered by God to Moses on Mt Sinai in the hearing of all Israel, and twice written by God on 2 stone tablets (Ex. 19:16-20:17; 31:18; 32:15f.; 34:1, 28). Moses later published them in a slightly modified form (Dt. 5:6-21). They contained the essence of the covenant made between God and his people at Sinai, which in turn reflected the nature of ancient treaties between a king and his vassals. The basic principles were elaborated in the book of the covenant (Ex. 20:22-23:33) which served as the legal instrument in the ratification of the covenant (Ex. 24:1-8). Ancient treaties began with a preamble identifying the covenant lord (*cf.* Ex. 20:2a) and a historical prologue (v. 2b). Then followed the obligations, the foremost of which was the requirement of loyalty to the covenant lord or the outlawing of all alien alliances (vv. 3-17). Another section enunciated sanctions on offenders or blessings on the obedient, sometimes interspersed among the stipulations (*cf.* vv. 5b, 6, 7b, 12b).

God disclosed himself in terms of the law. This fact points to the need for personal devotion to God as his people truly fulfil that law; the biblical ethic is rooted in biblical religion. The law is not condemnation of human sin so much as a summons to godliness which is the goal of restored covenant relationship. In applying the commandments today, which are indeed normative for God's people in all times, we must take into account the fact that they reflect the OT perspective on God's historical purposes (*e.g.* the commandment about the sabbath relates to the promise of Israel's residence in Canaan, Dt. 5:33, as does the whole law, Dt. 6:1ff.), and that our perspective on those purposes since Christ is different.

TENT. A collapsible structure of cloth or skins supported on poles and held firm by ropes staked into the ground. Tents were among mankind's earliest manufactured habitations (*cf.* Gn. 4:20). The Hebrew Patriarchs lived in tents (Gn. 18:1), as did Israel after the

Exodus (Ex. 33:8). The Rechabite sect continued the practice as an ideal (Je. 35:7). 'Tent' came to be used for any kind of dwelling; in 1 Ki. 8:66 'homes' is literally 'tents'. For Israel's tent of meeting, see TABERNACLE.

TERAH. Abraham's father who emigrated from Ur to Haran, identified as an idolater in Jos. 24:2; his name is usually connected with the moon god.

TERAPHIM. These objects are mentioned in every OT period, and in Israelite contexts are almost always condemned (*e.g.* 2 Ki. 23:24). They were associated with divination and spiritism (Jdg. 17:5; 2 Ki. 23:24), but the OT nowhere describes what they looked like or how they were used. They are associated with the home in Gn. 31:30ff. ('household gods') where they appear to be fairly small and were stolen for protection on the journey, and in 1 Sa. 19:13ff. ('images') where the implication is of something life-size. They were probably associated with a type of spirit, sometimes evil, sometimes good, known to the Hittites as *tarpish*. See also DIVINATION.

TERTIUS. The amanuensis who wrote Romans at Paul's dictation (Rom. 16:22). He adds his own greetings which suggests he also had Roman connections; the name is Latin.

TERTULLUS. A fairly common Roman name, in the NT the accuser of Paul before Felix (Acts 24:1ff.). His speech indicates he was a Jew, having (like Paul) Roman citizenship and a Roman name. His flattery is typical of the rhetoric of the period. See also SPOKESMAN.

TETRARCH. A title originally used in classical Greek to denote the ruler of a quarter of a region, given by the Romans to any ruler of an oriental province. In the NT the noun is used solely of Herod Antipas, although in Lk. 3:1 the verb is applied to others.

TEXTS AND VERSIONS. We have no original MSS for any biblical books but texts and versions provide the raw material for what is known as textual criticism; the aim is to provide a text as near as possible to the original. Generally the older the text the greater is its authority, although the history of the document itself must be examined before a verdict can be reached about its variant readings. Common scribal errors can be unmasked by careful comparison of different texts and versions. Among such errors are failure to repeat a letter or word; repeating what occurs only once; false recollection of a similar passage or MS; omitting a passage between identical words; omitting a line; confusing similar letters; inserting marginal notes into the body of the text. The groups of texts and versions may be divided as follows.

1. OT: Hebrew.
The Semitic alphabet existed long before Moses' time; Moses himself would have been familiar with Egypt-

ian literary methods (*cf.* Nu. 33:2). Peoples from the same cultural background as the Hebrews were literate from 3000 BC onwards, and from 2000 BC onwards people were being trained as expert copyists. The Hebrews were probably as advanced in writing as their contemporaries, employing the same methods to ensure the accurate transmission of their texts as were developed by the Egyptians and Babylonians. After the Exile, the scribes were probably the chief preservers of the text of Scripture, being trained as accurate copyists.

The Massoretes succeeded the scribes as custodians of the text and were active *c.* AD 500-1000. They introduced a system of 'pointing' or vocalizing (*i.e.* adding vowel signs to) the Hebrew text; while Hebrew remained a spoken language it was written in consonants only, with a few vowel letters in cases where a word might be ambiguous. They stressed the importance of preserving even the smallest letter (*cf.* Mt. 5:18), and left the consonantal text unchanged; any corrections they felt necessary or variations they found were put in the margin. They placed textual notes at the top or bottom of pages, and even counted the number of letters in a book. The text they used was clearly a single type, which was recognized as authoritative after the fall of Jerusalem in AD 70. The edition produced by Jacob ben Chayyim for the second rabbinic Bible published in Venice in 1524-5 came to be accepted as practically a standard text.

The Dead Sea Scrolls revolutionized OT study by going back 800 years before the Massoretic textual apparatus. They provided the first examples of a biblical Hebrew text from the pre-Christian era, about 1,000 years older than the MSS known previously. The scroll of Isaiah has many instances of common scribal errors, but none the less constitutes an important witness to the reliability of the now-accepted text. As the Qumran community is unlikely to have collaborated with Jerusalem officials in adhering to any one reading, the scrolls take us back beyond the different revisions towards the common textual ancestor of both the temple and Dead Sea versions.

The Hebrew Pentateuch of the Samaritans is unquestionably derived from an ancient text, for the split between Jerusalem Jews and the Samaritans which began in the 5th cent. BC was complete by the 2nd cent. BC, to which this text is assigned. The text was probably based on a much earlier one. The oldest existing MS of part of it probably dates from the 13th cent. AD. There are many differences between the Samaritan and the Massoretic texts, some of them deliberate changes (for example, to show that God had specially chosen Mt Gerizim, not Ebal, in Dt. 27:2ff.) and others due to misunderstanding, dialect, and the attempt to remove all anthropomorphic expressions. Variant readings among the Samaritan MSS indicate that the Samaritans had no trained scribes and did not properly collate MSS. Despite some recent attempts to assert the superiority of the Samaritan text, the Massoretic text is without doubt the best text available to us.

2. OT: Greek.

The oldest and most important Greek translations of the OT are in the Septuagint (LXX). The original translations were later radically revised, and the LXX MSS now present mixtures of revised and unrevised translations; they also contain many apocryphal books. Different parts appear to have been translated at different times and at different places; it was not collected into a single volume until after the 2nd cent. AD.

The Alexandrian Jewish philosopher Aristobulus (*c.* 170 BC) said that a translation of the Law (Gn.-Dt.) was made during the reign of Ptolemy II Philadelphus (285-247 BC), and there is no reason to doubt this. From Aristeas, who wrote *c.* 170-100 BC, comes the claim that 72 Jewish experts from Jerusalem worked on this translation of the Law (from which comes the title Septuagint, from 'Seventy', which later generations applied to the whole Greek OT). Both writers claimed there had been earlier translations; this cannot be proved. The whole OT was in Greek by the end of the 2nd cent. BC according to the prologue of Ecclus.

Among the revisions were one made by Origen *c.* AD 245, arranged in 6 parallel columns (hence called the *Hexapla*), containing the Hebrew text, a Greek transliteration, 3 other Greek translations, and Origen's own translation. The *Lucianic recension* made by Lucian the martyr near the end of the 3rd cent. AD presents readings which seem to be based on a Hebrew text better than the Massoretic, although they probably already existed in the Greek he worked from, rather than being supplied by him. Some translations follow the Hebrew so closely that the result would have been unintelligible to a Greek who knew no Hebrew. Some are more idiomatic. But all translators depart at times from the Hebrew, sometimes out of reverence (Ex. 24:10 is modified to 'they saw *the place where* the God of Israel stood'), sometimes to incorporate interpretations.

There is uncertainty about the status given to the Greek translations. The Jewish historian Philo claimed that the translators were directly inspired by God and wrote 'as though dictated to by an invisible prompter'. Aristeas did not make such a direct claim, but his invented stories about the translation process, including the reading of the completed text to the assembled Jewish community who pronounced curses on anyone who should subsequently alter it, suggest that he wished to assert its canonicity. The apocryphal books included in the Greek translations would never have been regarded as inspired even by Alexandrian Jews. There is evidence that efforts were made in Palestine in the 2 centuries before Christ to bring the Greek into closer line with the Hebrew. The NT writers quoted from both Greek and Hebrew OT texts.

Later Christians produced their own Greek OT translations, and some of the early church fathers who knew no Hebrew tended to regard the Greek versions as equally inspired. Eventually, Jerome made a new *Latin* translation direct from the Hebrew, not the Greek, which is now known as the Vulgate.

The Greek translations are valuable for 4 main reasons. They witness to the influence of Hellenism on Judaism; they form a bridge between the theological language of the OT and NT; they were the OT translations used by the early church fathers when they were building their formal theologies; and they are an important part of the evidence for the reconstruction of the history of the Hebrew OT text. However, even where the Massoretic text makes no sense and the LXX offers a plausible understanding, the Greek text still must be examined closely because the LXX may only be a conjecture and not a translation of a now lost and better Hebrew text.

3. OT: Syriac version.

Syriac is the name usually given to Christian Aramaic, an E Aramaic dialect. The Syriac version, which after the LXX is the oldest and most important translation of the Hebrew OT, has traces of W Aramaic language in it, however, which indicates that the translator(s) had contact with Jerusalem. It was probably a literal translation made by Jewish scholars for a Jewish community in Adiabene, the ruling house of which had been converted to Judaism *c.* AD 40. It was then taken over by the Syriac church and improved in style, and this text was accepted as standard by the 5th cent. AD. The Syriac church had taken root in Arbela, the capital of Adiabene, in the 1st cent. AD. In the 4th cent. AD the Syriac version was revised to bring it into closer harmony with the LXX. The original version has been known since the 9th cent. AD as the *Peshitta*, or 'simple' translation.

There is no uniformity of rendering Hebrew words in the various books of the Syriac version, which implies that it was made by a variety of authors. Sometimes it agrees with the *Lucianic* LXX where both differ from the Massoretic text. The translation of Psalms is free and shows considerable influence of the LXX; Proverbs and Ezekiel closely resemble the Jewish Targums; Chronicles is a paraphrase and was possibly translated later, in Edessa in the 3rd cent. AD. A schism in the Syriac church in the 5th cent. AD led to Nestorius being expelled for heresy from the bishopric of Constantinople in 431, and he took the Peshitta Bible with him. The Eastern church which originated with this schism remained more isolated than others, with the result that its texts have undergone fewer revisions based on Hebrew and Greek versions. Other Syriac versions were made in the 6th and 7th cents. AD. The oldest surviving dated version of the Peshitta is dated AD 464 containing the Pentateuch minus Leviticus. The writings of Syriac fathers quote from the OT and thus provide readings from this version from an early date; Aphraat's *Letters* (337-345) contain quotes, for example.

4. NT manuscripts and versions.

Before the original text can be determined, scholars need to study the relationships between documents, sometimes establishing a 'family tree' which charts the stages of transmission. Sometimes they have to make informed choices between different texts, and suggest emendations where difficulties or textual corruptions cannot be resolved. There are many thousands of Greek MSS of part or the whole of the NT. Some 88 are written on *papyrus*; others on *parchment* are sometimes works of great beauty. Most are in the form of fragments or codices (*i.e.* like bound books rather than scrolls). Some parchments were re-used with the original text rubbed out; these are called *palimpsests*.

The parchments are divided into 3 types: continuous texts, subdivided into uncials (written in capital letters) and miniscules (in lower case letters); and texts arranged according to lectionaries for reading at daily services or festivals. Among the important uncials are Codex Sinaiticus, a 4th-cent. text of OT and NT with corrections made in the 6th cent., and Codex Vaticanus which lacks the NT after Heb. 9:14; both probably originated in Egypt. Codex Alexandrinus is a 5th-cent. text of OT and NT, probably from Constantinople, and Codex Bezae is from the 4th or 5th cent. giving both Latin and Greek incomplete text of the Gospels and Acts.

Miniscules are generally later in date, but may be faithful copies of earlier MSS; for example, one numbered 579 is closely allied to Codex Vaticanus and may present an even older text.

By the mid-3rd cent. at least some parts of the NT had been translated from the Greek original into Latin, Syriac and Coptic. Later, these versions themselves became the basis for others, and were occasionally revised according to the Greek text available. They are therefore an important secondary source for textual criticism, and the detective story becomes more complex because the history of the version has to be investigated before its clues to the original Greek can be assessed. Problems arise, however, because no language can reproduce perfectly another language, for there may be no exact equivalents of certain linguistic forms.

There are some 30 fragments of pre-Vulgate (4th-cent.) Latin versions, and they show a bewildering richness of variant readings. The Syriac church was first introduced to the Gospels in the form of the *Diatessaron*, a harmony of the 4 Gospels made by Tatian *c.* AD 180, but this was gradually replaced by the separated Gospels retaining much of Tatian's language. In the 4th cent. a revision was made of the whole Syriac NT to a Greek standard akin to Codex Vaticanus; this Peshitta NT became the 'authorized version' of the Syriac churches, and was probably composed by several people. Bible remains are found in several Coptic dialects, but their history has not yet been traced in any detail. The earliest ones date from the 3rd cent. AD.

5. NT: Analysis and history of manuscripts.

It is not possible to relate all the branches of NT texts to one stem, as it were, and thus to arrive conclusively at the archetypal text. Westcott and Hort in the 19th cent. whittled the texts down to 2 main types, those attested by Codex Sinaiticus and Codex Vaticanus, and those attested by Codex Bezae (Latin). They were able to reject the latter as generally inferior, although at times on partly subjective grounds. The analysis has not been universally approved, and objective criteria have to be carefully established in order to choose between variant readings. Enough remains of NT documents about which there is no doubt to enable studies to be made of the characteristic style and linguistic usage of individual writers, against which disputed readings can be compared. Studies on NT economic and cultural background may provide information to base decisions on, and church history reveals what issues were debated at certain times and which may have influenced certain translations. It is important to notice, however, that the text is nowhere so insecure as to necessitate the alteration of the basic gospel; those who love the Bible as God's Word will desire the greatest accuracy possible in the minutest details.

During the period when the NT canon was being established, there were tendencies to emend the Greek text according to prevailing fashion, in the case of the Gospels even attempting to gain close verbal identity between them. Sometimes traditions were added or words omitted. No known text is without corruption, although some very good ones exist. Some have suggested that there was an attempt in the 3rd or 4th cents. to get back to the early text, but there is little direct evidence for this, and recent discoveries have shown that the text type of Codex Vaticanus existed much earlier, in the 2nd cent. Christian scholars in the 3rd and 4th cents. did not create new texts so much as select from the variety which existed. The task of NT textual criticism is vast and unfinished. Many advances have been made since the material began to be collected and analysed rationally in the 17th cent. The work of post-war scholars should bring us nearer to the true words of the apostles, but even they cannot but build on the foundations laid long ago.

See also BIBLE; BIBLICAL CRITICISM; NEW TESTAMENT CANON; OLD TESTAMENT CANON; PAPYRI; TALMUD AND MIDRASH; TARGUM.

THADDAEUS. The name occurs only in the list of the 12 apostles (Mt. 10:3; Mk. 3:18). In Lk. 6:16; Acts 1:13 the equivalent person is Judas the son of James, and there is little doubt they are the same. The name suggests warmth of character and devotedness.

THEATRE. Greek theatres were usually cut into a naturally concave hillside and there was thus no limit to size so long as the acoustics were adequate. The seats were arranged around a dancing space in front of a raised stage. Theatres were cultural centres and might also be used for official assemblies (Acts 19:29).

THEBES. ('No', AV.) Once Egypt's most magnificent capital, it was sited on both banks of the Nile 530 km upstream from Cairo. On the E side were 2 vast temple precincts now known as Karnak and Luxor, and on the W side a row of royal funerary temples and a vast necropolis of rock-cut tombs. During the 18th-20th Dynasties (c. 1550-1070 BC) great treasures of Asia and Africa poured into Thebes, and were plundered by the Assyrians in 663 BC. Its fate made a lurid comparison for the prophecy about the fall of Assyria's mighty Nineveh (Na. 3:8ff.). Jeremiah (46:25) and Ezekiel (30:14ff.) later spoke against Thebes.

THEBEZ. A fortified city on Mt Ephraim where Abimelech was killed by a millstone thrown from a window (Jdg. 9:50ff.); modern Tubas, 16 km N of Nablus.

THEOPHILUS (lit. 'friend of God'). The person to whom Luke and Acts are dedicated (Lk. 1:3; Acts 1:1). Some have considered it equivalent to 'dear reader', but more probably he was a real person, possibly belonging to the equestrian order and in some official position (cf. the title 'most excellent', Lk. 1:3).

THESSALONIANS, LETTERS TO THE. *Contents (1 Thes.):* Greeting (1:1); thanksgiving for their faith (1:2-10); Paul's explanation of his recent conduct (2:1-16); narrative of events since he left Thessalonica (2:17-3:10); prayer for early reunion with them (3:11-13); encouragement to holy living (4:1-12); teaching about Jesus' second coming (4:13-5:11); exhortations and final greetings (5:12-28). *Contents (2 Thes.):* Greetings (1:1-2); thanksgiving and encouragement (1:3-12); events which must precede Jesus' second coming (2:1-12); more thanksgiving and encouragement (2:13-3:5); the need for discipline (3:6-15); prayer and final greetings (3:16-18).

Authorship. Both letters are sent by Paul, Silvanus (Silas) and Timothy (1 Thes. 1:1; 2 Thes. 1:1) but the author is clearly Paul. In 1 Thes. he speaks in the first person (2:18), refers to Timothy in the third person (3:2, 6) and in 2 Thes. 3:17 he adds his personal signature which relates to the 'I' of 2:5. His authorship of 1 Thes. has been little disputed, but more doubt has been expressed about 2 Thes. Its style is said to be more formal, and the teaching in 1 Thes. about the unexpectedness of Jesus' return seems to be contradicted by the outline in 2 Thes. of events which must happen before Jesus' return, which is contained in a passage of apocalyptic teaching unparalleled in any of Paul's other writings. However, it is unlikely to have been forged (cf. 2:2), and both letters were included in the earliest known collected edition of Paul's letters. The solution is probably to be found in the occasion and relation of the 2 letters.

Occasion. Paul and his colleagues had to leave Thessalonica hastily in the summer of AD 50 after planting a church there (Acts 17:1ff.). Their converts had not received all the teaching Paul wished to give them, and they were exposed to persecution. He sent Timothy there (*cf.* Acts 18:5), who reported that they were zealous but troubled by ethical problems and questions about Jesus' return. Paul wrote 1 Thes. immediately, teaching chastity and that people who died before Jesus' return would not be at a disadvantage. After a while he received further news that some people believed Jesus' coming was so imminent that there was no point in working, so he wrote 2 Thes. to explain that certain things must happen before the return of Jesus, and to encourage honest work and discourage spongers.

Teaching. Apart from Gal., 1 and 2 Thes. are Paul's earliest surviving writings, and give an illuminating insight into Christian faith and life 20 years after Jesus' death and resurrection. Jesus' equality with the Father is assumed (1 Thes. 1:1; 3:11; 2 Thes. 1:1; 2:16). God is holy and expects holiness in his people, especially in sexual relations (1 Thes. 4:3) and honest work (1 Thes. 4:11f.; 2 Thes. 3:10ff.). Both letters reflect the early interest in Jesus' return and the unhealthy excesses which arose. Paul stresses that although he hopes to be alive then, he does not know if he will be; his task is to be faithful in his mission so that on

that day he will be unashamed.

THESSALONICA. Situated at the junction of important international land-routes, it became the principal city of Macedonia, and has remained a major city to the present day. It was the first place where Paul's preaching achieved a numerous and socially-prominent following. His opponents resorted to mob violence and the authorities took the minimum action to move him on without causing him hardship (Acts 17:1ff.). Despite its problems, the church flourished and remained a crown to his efforts (1 Thes. 1:8ff.). See also previous article.

THEUDAS. In Acts 5:36, an imposter (possibly posing as the Messiah) who some time before AD 6 gathered a band of 400 men, which was dispersed after he was killed. His was probably one of several disorders which broke out after Herod's death in 4 BC.

THIGH. Sometimes it denotes the locality of sexual organs, and hence one's offspring. To swear an oath by placing the hand under another's thigh perhaps invoked the support of a person's descendants to enforce the oath (Gn. 24:2f.). Hitting the thigh is a sign of anguish (Je. 31:19). See also SINEW.

THISTLES AND THORNS: See PLANTS.

THOMAS. One of the 12 apostles whose name comes from an Aramaic word meaning twin, for which John gives the Greek equivalent Didymus (*e.g.* 11:16). Willing to go S to possible death with Jesus (Jn. 11:16), he is best known as the 'doubter' who disbelieved the accounts of Jesus' resurrection until Jesus personally appeared to him, after which Thomas confessed him as Lord and God (Jn. 20:24ff.).

THORNS, CROWN OF. Made by the Roman soldiers and placed on Jesus' head before the crucifixion, it mocked his claim to be 'king of the Jews'. A number of plants in Palestine have sharp spines. Thorns are sometimes used to symbolize sin (Mt. 13:7). See also PLANTS.

THRESHOLD. The stone slab at a doorway (usually of a sacred building) which may have contained the sockets in which the door-posts swivelled (*e.g.* Is. 6:4).

THRONE. Used of a seat of special importance (1 Ki. 2:19), and as a symbol of dignity and authority (2 Sa. 3:10). God's 'throne' is transcendent (Is. 66:1), but his presence was 'enthroned' on the ark of the covenant (1 Sa. 4:4). Jesus received David's throne or rule (Lk. 1:32); he will judge mankind from his heavenly 'throne' of authority (Mt. 25:31ff.), with the disciples enthroned to assist him (Mt. 19:28)

THUMB. Putting sacrificial blood on a priest's thumb, big toe and ear symbolized the dedication of the means of doing, walking and hearing (Ex.

29:20). Cutting off a defeated enemy's thumbs symbolized his powerlessness (Jdg. 1:6f.).

THUNDER. It is most frequent in Palestine during the winter. Desert thunderstorms with dramatic results are recorded in 1 Sa. 7:10 and 2 Ki. 3:4ff. Thunder is associated with God's creative voice (Ps. 104:7) and law-giving (Ex. 19:16), with the voice which answered Jesus (Jn. 12:28f.) and voices in heaven (*e.g.* Rev. 14:2).

THYATIRA. A city in the Roman province of Asia, in the W of what is now Asiatic Turkey (modern Akhisar). In a low-lying corridor, it was a frontier garrison and a centre for dyeing, clothes-making, pottery and brass-working. Lydia (Acts 16:14) was probably the overseas agent of a Thyatiran manufacturer; the purple dye was made from the madder root into the 20th cent. The letter in Rev. 2:18-29 alludes to this city's circumstances; 'Jezebel' is probably a symbolic name of a teacher in the church who compromised with pagan practices, perhaps connected with trade guilds.

TIBERIAS. A city on the W shore of the Sea of Galilee which subsequently gave its name to the lake. It was founded by Herod Antipas *c.* AD 20 and named after the emperor Tiberius. The site of its beautiful buildings included a former graveyard, making it unclean to orthodox Jews. It was a thoroughly Gentile city and there is no record of Jesus ever visiting it (*cf.* Jn.

6:1, 23).

TIBERIUS. The 'Caesar' of the Gospels (named in Lk. 3:1). He was 56 when he succeeded his stepfather Augustus in AD 14. He loyally and unimaginatively continued Augustus' policies for 23 years, but spent his latter years of rule in disgruntled semi-retirement on Capri.

TIBHATH. In 1 Ch. 18:8, a town in the Aramaean kingdom of ZOBAH.

TIDAL. One of 4 kings who subdued 5 others in Abraham's time (Gn. 14:1ff.). His name derives from an Anatolian name in turn based on that of a sacred mountain, but he cannot yet be identified from other sources. 'Goiim' in his title means 'nations, groups'. Alliances of kings are attested in ancient Mesopotamian and Anatolian records.

TIGLATH-PILESER, TILGATH-PILNESER. The 3rd king of Assyria to be so called, also known in the OT and Assyrian records as Pul (*e.g.* 2 Ki. 15:19); he ruled 745-727 BC. In 743 BC he marched against N Syrian states, and among those he subdued and exacted tribute-tax from were Tyre, Damascus and Samaria (*cf.* 2 Ki. 15:19f.). In response to opposition Tiglath-pileser attacked the W again in 734 BC. He plundered the Phoenician sea ports, and exacted tribute-tax from Ahaz of Judah (2 Ch. 28:19ff.). When Rezin of Damascus and Pekah of Israel besieged Jerusalem, Ahaz appealed to the Assyrian king for help (2 Ki. 16:7).

Tiglath-pileser took Damascus in 732 BC, and despoiled Israel at the same time, taking many people captive. Ahaz paid for Assyrian help by becoming its vassal, which involved religious compromise (2 Ki. 16:10f.). See also ASSYRIA.

TIGRIS. A river rising in the Armenian Mountains, running 1,900 km SE through Mesopotamia to join the Euphrates 64 km N of the Persian gulf. It was one of the rivers which bordered Eden (Gn. 2:14).

TILE. So far as is known, roof tiles were not used in Palestine in OT and NT times; in Lk. 5:19 it should be translated 'roofing'.

TIME. *Time measurement.* By NT times the Jews divided daylight into 12 hours (*cf.* Jn. 11:9) which obviously varied in length according to the time of year, and in any case the absence of accurate clocks meant that the time of day was indicated more generally than it is today. The times most frequently mentioned are the 3rd, 6th and 9th hours (*e.g.* Mt. 20:3ff.). Both Jews and Romans counted their hours from sunrise, although Jews reckoned the civil day to begin at sunset and the Romans reckoned it to begin at midnight.

Times and seasons. Quite often 'hour' is used very unspecifically as 'a point of time', and this is especially clear in the death of Jesus which is described as 'his hour' (Mk. 14:41; Jn. 7:30). This concern with the right time or God's appointed time is seen in both

Testaments; Ec. 3:1ff. is the classic exposition of it. Hence the Bible does not stress the abstract continuity of time so much as the God-given content of certain moments of history. God's purposes are working towards a goal, hence the Hebrew concept of time was of a progressive line; by contrast many ancient nations saw time as a recurring cycle. God is sovereign in appointing the time (or events) by which he advances his purposes in the world (Ps. 31:15; Mk. 13:32).

Time and eternity. God is not limited by time (Pss. 90:2; 145:13), and phrases such as 'for ever and ever' (Gal. 1:5) point to that which has always existed and will always exist. The relationship between this timelessness and time as we experience it has been much debated, not least because 'timelessness' seems to imply something quite detached from the world. But the Bible does not delve into such philosophical issues; it stresses simply that God is 'king of (all) ages' (1 Tim. 1:17).

The two ages. Jesus began his ministry by announcing that 'the time is fulfilled' (Mk. 1:15). His coming has brought 'the last times' or the 'new age' into existence (1 Pet. 1:20). There is also, however, a future point of transition between this age and the age to come (Eph. 1:21), but the gift of the Holy Spirit brings a foretaste of what is to be (Eph. 1:14). Christians possess eternal life now and will enter into it more fully by resurrection (Jn. 11:23ff.). Meanwhile, they must make the most of the timely opportunities God provides for his service and

honour (2 Cor. 6:2; Eph. 5:16).
See also CALENDAR.

TIMNA. A male and female name appearing in the OT, *e.g.* Gn. 36:12; 1 Ch. 1:51.

TIMNAH. 1. A town on Judah's N border which often changed hands betwen Israelites and Philistines (Jdg. 14:1); possibly Batashi 9 km S of Gezer. 2. A copper-mining site S of Hebron (Jos. 15:57).

TIMNATH-SERAH, TIMNATH-HERES. Joshua's personal inheritance and burial-place (Jos. 19:50; 24:30). Possibly Kh. Tibneh, 27 km from Shechem and Jerusalem on a deep ravine, close to the traditional site of Joshua's tomb.

TIMOTHY. The son of a Jewish mother and Greek father, and a native of Lystra (Acts 16:1; 2 Tim. 1:5). He probably became a Christian on Paul's 1st missionary journey which took in Lystra (*cf.* 2 Tim. 3:11). His mother also became a Christian, but when is unclear. Paul included Timothy in his travelling group, a decision which appears to have been endorsed by others (*cf.* 1 Tim. 1:18; 4:14), circumcising him first to avoid needlessly offending local Jews. He was sent alone to Thessalonica to encourage the church (1 Thes. 3:1f.); he was present with Paul at Corinth (2 Cor. 1:19), and went with him to Jerusalem (Acts 20:4f.), finally being left at Ephesus (1 Tim. 1:3). He was evidently timid by nature and Paul urged the Corinthians not to despise him (1 Cor. 16:10f.; *cf.* 2 Tim. 1:6ff.). Occasionally admonished by Paul (2 Tim. 1:8; 2:22), he is commended more warmly than any other for his loyalty (*e.g.* Phil. 2:19ff.). He became a prisoner himself (Heb. 13:23) but of his last years nothing is known.

TIMOTHY AND TITUS, LETTERS TO.

The two Letters to Timothy and the Letter to Titus are commonly grouped together as the Pastoral Letters. They belong to the period close to the end of Paul's life and are addressed to 2 of his closest associates. They contain gems of spiritual encouragement and theological insight which have enriched the devotional life of the church.

Contents. 1 Timothy: Paul and Timothy (1:1-20); worship and order in the church (2:1-4:16); discipline within the church (5); miscellaneous injunctions (6). 2 Timothy: Paul's regard for Timothy (1:1-14); Paul and his associates (1:15-18); special directions to Timothy (2); predictions about the last days (3:1-9); more advice to Timothy (3:10-17); Paul's farewell message (4). Titus: Greetings (1:1-4); the kind of people to be appointed as elders or bishops (1:5-9); the Cretan false teachers (1:10-16); Christian behaviour (2:1-10); teaching about God's grace and Christian living in a pagan world (2:11-3:7); closing admonitions (3:8-15).

Historical background. There is no independent evidence of the events of Paul's life at the time of writing, but some facts can be gleaned from the letters. He was not in prison when he wrote 1 Tim. and Tit., but he was when he wrote 2 Tim. (1:8; 2:9). Paul had recently been in the Ephesus area (1 Tim. 1:3) and had recently visited Crete (Tit. 1:5). He calls Titus to join him at Nicopolis (3:12). In 2 Tim. Paul refers to Onesiphorous seeking him in Rome (1:16f.) and the implication is that Paul is still imprisoned there. In 4:13, 20 he seems to have visited Troas and Miletus recently, and possibly Corinth. This data cannot be fitted into the narrative of Acts. The natural explanation is that Paul was released from the imprisonment mentioned at the end of Acts, had a further period of activity in the E, and was then re-arrested, tried and finally executed in Rome.

Purpose. All 3 letters give the associates of Paul exhortations and encouragements about their responsibilities. 2 Tim. is clearly the apostle's final charge to his timid colleague. There are warnings about ungodly people who will trouble the church, and instructions about church leadership. The purpose of the other 2 letters is less clear because Paul has apparently only just left the recipients. Much of the instruction probably had been given orally, and the letters were to strengthen the recipients' hands; Timothy seems to have trouble commanding respect (1 Tim. 4:12f.), and Titus had a particularly difficult constituency (Tit. 1:10f.). There was no need for Paul to dwell on the great doctrines; he wanted to remind his friends to steer the church clear of false teachers.

Authenticity. Paul's authorship of these letters has been challenged in modern times. However, such objections have to be set against the fact that the Pastoral Letters have some of the strongest and earliest attestation of all the NT documents; and they were widely used from the time of Polycarp (early 2nd cent. AD). The objections relate to 4 issues. The historical problem mentioned above is one, but the addition of fictitious personal notes into an anonymous letter is improbable, and an unnecessary suggestion if the possibility of Paul being temporarily released from Rome is allowed. Secondly, the church structures in the letters are said to reflect later 2nd-cent. conditions, but they are in fact still more 'primitive' than those known in the 2nd cent. Thirdly, the absence of Paul's doctrinal emphases and the presence of stereotyped phrases such as 'the faith' has troubled some scholars, but as noted above these letters are essentially personal notes to close colleagues in which doctrinal teaching was unnecessary. Finally, the letters do contain an unusually large number of words not found elsewhere in the NT or in Paul's writings. But the letters are short, with a limited vocabulary, and one man could use different styles; some suggest he used a different amanuensis to take down his dictation. It can still be maintained that these letters are genuine writings of Paul.

TIPHSAH. In 1 Ki. 4:24, probably Thapsacus, an important crossing on the W bank of the Middle Euphrates.

TIRAS. A son of Japheth (Gn. 10:2), usually identified with the Tursha, N invaders mentioned by Merenptah of Egypt in the 13th cent. BC.

TIRHAKAH. Egypt's Ethiopian pharaoh who reigned *c.* 690-664 BC, who appears from 2 Ki. 19:9 to have been the army commander leading the Egyptian forces defeated by Sennacherib in 701 BC.

TIRSHATHA. In AV (*e.g.* Ezr. 2:63) probably a Persian title like 'His Excellency' (RSV 'governor')

TIRZAH. A Canaanite town noted for its beauty (Song 6:4), lying in the N part of Mt Ephraim at the head of the Wadi Farah along which lay a major land route. It was the capital of (N) Israel for a while (1 Ki. 15:21; 16:6). The large mound of Tell el-Farah, 11 km NE of Nablus, has been excavated and the poor houses and extensive administrative buildings found there confirm the picture drawn by the prophets (Is. 9:8ff.; Am. 5:11).

TISHBITE, THE. A title given to Elijah (*e.g.* 1 Ki. 17:1) referring to his place of origin, the town Tishbe in Gilead, traditionally located at al-Istib 12 km N of the Jabbok.

TITHES. The custom of giving one-tenth of income or produce for religious purposes. It was known before the law of Moses (*e.g.* Gn. 14:17ff.) and was practised in many ancient nations. The law of Moses later stipulated that every 10th animal and one-tenth of agricultural produce was to be given to God; produce (but not livestock) could be redeemed by giving instead the cash value plus an extra one-fifth of that value (Lv. 27:30ff.). The tithes were given to the Levites (Nu. 18:21ff.) because they had no means of income for their religious service; they were instructed to give a tithe of the tithe themselves to the priests (Nu. 18:26ff.). Tithes were normally to be taken to Jerusalem (Dt. 12:5ff.; *cf.* 14:22ff.). These simple rules were later turned by Israelite teachers into a grievous burden which separated religious duty from the moral law, a tendency which Jesus condemned (Mt. 23:23f.).

TITUS. Although not mentioned in Acts, he was one of Paul's trusted Gentile companions. He accompanied Paul and Barnabas to Jerusalem during the Gentile controversy (Gal. 2:1ff.). Titus was evidently Paul's representative at Corinth (2 Cor. 8:6, 16f.) who had the delicate task of smoothing out the tension between Paul and the church. From 2 Cor. 2 and 7 it seems he probably carried an additional now lost letter to Corinth. The letter addressed to him suggests he accompanied Paul to Crete and consolidated the work there. He was a stronger character than Timothy (*cf.* 2 Cor. 7:15), full of integrity (2 Cor. 12:18). It has been speculated that he was Luke's brother, hence his omission from Acts. See also TIMOTHY AND TITUS, LETTERS TO.

TOB. An Aramaean city-state N of Gilead; the city was probably al-Taiyiba 20 km ENE of Ramoth-gilead (Jdg. 11:3).

TOBIAH. One of Nehemiah's principal opponents, described as 'servant', possibly an honourable title for a high-ranking Persian official, and an Ammonite, possibly referring to his ancestry; he appears to have been at least half Jewish for his name means 'Yahweh is good' (Ne. 2:10). He was probably deputy to Sanballat, governor of Samaria. A clan by the same name was unable to prove its Israelite ancestry (Ezr. 2:60; Ne. 7:62).

TOBIT: See APOCRYPHA.

TOGARMAH. The 3rd son of Gomer (Gn. 10:3). The city named after him supplied horses to Tyre (Ezk. 27:14); possibly Gurun, 120 km W of Malatya.

TOLA. One of the minor judges, he ruled Israel for 23 years after Abimelech (Jdg. 10:1).

TONGUE. Used both of the physical organ and of human language. Dumbness was apparently believed to be caused by some paralysis of the tongue (Ps. 137:6; Mk. 7:35). It is used parallel to or in place of lip or mouth. It can be sharp (Ps. 64:3; Rev. 1:16) and a tremendous influence for good or ill (Jas. 3:5f.). In Ps. 55:9 'tongue' refers to the confusion of languages created at Babel (Gn. 11:1ff.), and in Rev. 5:9 it describes nations with different languages. See also next article.

TONGUES, GIFT OF. Speaking in tongues, or 'glossolalia', is mentioned as a spiritual gift in the NT (*e.g.* Acts 2:1ff.; 1 Cor. 12-14). On the Day of Pentecost the disciples broke into praise in tongues which seemed like drunken babbling to the crowd which gathered but which some visitors could understand as their own language (Acts 2:8, 13). Mentioned in Mk. 16:17 (not part of the original Gospel) as a sign following faith in Christ, it accompanied the outpouring of the Holy Spirit on several occasions (Acts 10:44ff.; 19:6), incidents seen as repetitions of the giving of the Spirit at Pentecost to signify God's acceptance of new classes of believers into the cautious Jewish-Christian church (*cf.* Acts 11:15ff.).

In Corinth, not all Christians spoke in tongues (1 Cor. 12:10, 30), and there it seems to have been a continuing gift rather than an initial experience. Tongues are seen as meaningful utterances inspired by the Holy Spirit, employed primarily for personal worship (1 Cor. 14:2, 14ff.), under the control of the speaker (1 Cor. 14:27f.). In public worship they are to be accompanied by an intelligible interpretation (1 Cor. 14:5, 13, 27). Tongues were not foreign languages at Corinth (Paul uses another word for such in 1 Cor. 14:10f.) but neither were they meaningless ecstatic sounds. A definite linguistic form is suggested by the word 'interpret', used elsewhere to mean 'translate'; Paul probably regarded them as heavenly languages. The Corinthians so overrated them, however, that Paul imposed restrictions on their public use and emphasized the greater value of prophecy.

See also SPIRITUAL GIFTS.

TOPHEL. In Dt. 1:1 only, perhaps a stopping place during the Israelites' journey; the location is uncertain.

TOPHETH. A 'high place' in the valley of Hinnom outside Jerusalem where pagan child sacrifices were offered (2 Ki. 23:10).

TORCH. A long pole with oil-soaked rags wrapped around the top (Jn. 18:3); it is probably intended in Mt. 25:1-8.

TOWN CLERK. In Acts 19:35, the president of the assembly in Ephesus; his manner indicates he was a Roman aristocrat.

TRACHONITIS. The district around Trachon, modern al-Laja, a pear-shaped area of volcanic rock E of Galilee and S of Damascus, generally infertile (Lk. 3:1).

TRADE AND COMMERCE. *Old Testament.* Being a natural bridge between Europe and Asia in the N and Africa in the S, Palestine has always been enriched by trade; Ezk. 27:12-25 presents a cross-section of world commerce which passed through it. Palestine itself exported grain, oil and wine to Phoenicia to the N, and iron, oil and wine to Egypt in the S. Solomon developed trade with Arabian and African states from whom he imported spices and gold. Asphalt from the Dead Sea was so important as to influence international politics in the period between OT and NT times. Wool was also exported from Palestine. Manufacturing began to be developed in Palestine from about the 8th cent. BC, and the prophets showed their concern about the social crises caused by a shift from a largely agricultural economy to a mixed agricultural and industrial economy. Goods were made to standardized forms with assembly-line techniques, although they were mostly for the home market and not for export. Coined money was not used until towards the end of the OT period.

For overland travel, the ass was the main beast of burden until David's time, when the camel became more popular. Some of Palestine's wealth came from caravan traders who bought supplies as they passed through the land, and goods entering the country were taxed. At the local market place people absorbed foreign news. The main trade routes N–S ran either side of the Judaean uplands; the one just E of the Jordan valley was known as the King's Highway. The E–W routes were less profitable except for the southernmost one bringing Arabian trade into Palestine. Sea trade was important for Palestine only during the time of Solomon and Jehoshaphat; Philistines, then later the Phoenicians and Greeks, generally ran the sea trade.

New Testament. By NT times, major international trade was in the hands of the Romans, and state interference in it was already visible. The legal machinery by which a mark on hand or head could prevent a non-conformist from trading was in place (*cf.* Rev. 13:16f.). Rome, with a 1st-cent. AD population of about one million, was one vast market. The satiric Rev. 18 speaks of its wealth and volume of trade and forecasts the economic disruption which would follow the loss of such a market. Ostia, Rome's port, was full of warehouses.

Romans traded far and wide (*cf.* the 'far country' of Mt. 25:14 AV). Germany, the Baltic countries, India and possibly even China were on their itinerary, made possible by the widespread peace which was policed by Rome and by the lack of political frontiers over wide stretches of the world. No cargo lists survive, however, so it is difficult to be certain what goods were traded. Oysters and probably tin went from Britain to Rome; Gaul exported textiles. Nor is there much information about the business organization behind the trading. Some localities clearly specialized in certain products and specialist traders like Lydia (Acts 16:14) created and operated their own markets. The imagery of Rev. 3:14-18 is partly drawn from the commercial specialities of Laodicea which included black woollen garments and eye salve probably made from kaolin found at the nearby Hierapolis thermal springs. At Ephesus the silver traders, specializing in images of the goddess Artemis, created a powerful lobby (see Acts 19). The Gospels sometimes draw on trading imagery, such as the parables of the merchant and of the talents (Mt. 13:45f.; 25:14ff.), and Paul travelled on merchant ships.

See also next article; MONEY; SHIPS AND BOATS; TRAVEL.

TRADE GUILDS. Skilled workers often lived in specialist quarters of the larger towns and cities, and organized themselves into craft or trade guilds or 'families' (cf. 1 Ch. 4:21). By NT times they were powerful political groups often working under imperial licence (cf. Acts 19:24ff., where Christianity threatened traders' vested interests). A guild of butchers stirred unsuccessful action against the church in Bithynia just after NT times, because of loss of sales of sacrificial meat. Christians could not work easily if they did not belong to guilds, but as most guilds had pagan gods as patrons such membership was fraught with spiritual problems.

TRADITION. Teaching which is handed down to others, particularly from a teacher to his disciples. The concept is often present without the word being mentioned. Between the OT and NT periods, the rabbis added to the OT teaching which became regarded as authoritative as Scripture by Jesus' time. He condemned the tradition which rejected or made God's Word 'void' (Mt. 15; Mk. 7). Jesus himself placed his own teaching alongside Scripture as an authoritative commentary (e.g. Mt. 5:21f., 27f.). He could do so as the Spirit-anointed Messiah; his personal authority is stressed in contrast to other tradition (e.g. Col. 2:8).

Christian tradition in the NT has 3 elements: the facts of Christ (1 Cor. 15:3); the theological interpretation of those facts (e.g. the argument of 1 Cor. 15); and the manner of life which flows from them (1 Cor. 11:2). In 1 Tim. 5:18; 2 Pet. 3:16 apostolic tradition is placed alongside Scripture and described as such because of the unique combination of eyewitness testimony and Spirit-guided witness which lay behind it (cf. Jn. 15:26f.; 16:13). The environment in which the Gospels were written was deeply concerned with correct handing-on of tradition and not so interested in supplementing fact with imagined improvement as some scholars have suggested, hence the tradition contained in them can on this and other grounds be regarded as historically accurate.

See also NEW TESTAMENT CANON.

TRANCE. The overriding of normal consciousness and perception, the state in which some NT visions were received (Acts 10:10; 11:5; 22:17)

TRANSFIGURATION. A specific manifestation of Jesus' heavenly glory on a mountain (probably Hermon) to Peter, James and John. Jesus was transformed and his clothes shone with brightness. Moses and Elijah appeared and talked to him. When Peter suggested making shelters for them, a voice from a cloud declared Jesus' Sonship and authority, and the vision ended (see Mk. 9:2-8). The glory denotes the royal presence, the kingdom of God among his people. Moses and Elijah represented the OT Law and Prophets witnessing to, and being superseded by, the Messiah. Their conversation about his 'departure' (literally 'exodus', Lk. 9:31) probably concerned not only his death but his death and resurrection as the means of redemption for God's people, and hence how Jesus was to fulfil the OT.

TRAVAIL. A word connected with childbirth pains occasionally used metaphorically as in Rom. 8:22.

TRAVEL. *Old Testament times.* Individuals tended to remain in their home areas so as not to lose their status as citizens, and trade caravans and military forces were the main groups on the move. There is evidence of group migration during the Middle Bronze Age (2200-1550 BC), however. Properly constructed roads were unknown before the Roman period. Roads were either paths used regularly by animals and people, although in a few cases limited clearance, levelling and bridge-building was done on roads between provincial centres (*cf.* Is. 40:3). Even the royal roads of the Persians, including the 2,600 km major link between Sardis and Susa, were probably not paved except in city areas. Major international N–S highways, such as the coastal 'way of the sea' (Is. 9:1) and the King's Highway E of the Jordan (Nu. 20:17), were crossed by less important E–W roads. Travellers nor-

mally walked, although the donkey and camel were used both for riding and carrying goods. Ox wagons carried heavy loads and probably people too (*cf.* Gn. 46:5); horses and chariots were mostly for military purposes. Travellers probably had to provide and fend for themselves on journeys prior to Roman times. Sea travel did not normally feature in Israelite life.

New Testament times. The Roman peace made travel relatively safe; the Gospels and Acts record without comment long and short journeys within the Roman empire, and non-biblical sources confirm the NT picture. People travelled on foot to Jerusalem for festivals (*e.g.* Lk. 2:41ff.). Christianity first spread along the great roads which led to Rome, and the Roman support for shipping and the extermination of sea pirates and many land brigands by Caesar Augustus made long journeys like Paul's relatively easy.

Roman roads followed a generally straight course, those over 6–8 m wide were paved and minor roads were surfaced with sand or gravel and cambered to ditches 3 or 6 m apart. Milestones were set every 1,000 paces (1,480 m) to record the distance to the nearest road-head or city. Maps, and lists of resting places, were available. The royal courier service carried communications and provided transport for officials. Resting places with horses were placed every 25 miles for official business. Ordinary travellers had to make their own arrangements. Inns were available. They were however generally of a low standard and some were little more than brothels. Normal distances covered would be 16 Roman miles a day on foot, 25 by horse and carriage, although couriers could cover 100 miles a day. Most people walked, but light carriages were used (*cf.* Acts 8:29).

See also SHIPS AND BOATS; TRADE AND COMMERCE.

TRAYS. Gold vessels used for removing lamp trimmings from the tabernacle or temple (*e.g.* Ex. 25:38).

TREASURE, TREASURY. 'Treasure' usually refers to valuables such as silver or gold; in Mt. 2:11 it means a box containing valuables. 'Treasury' and 'treasure house' are used to signify a store for valuables, generally attached to a religious sanctuary (*e.g.* 1 Ki. 7:51); in Mk. 12:41; Lk. 21:1 it refers to the 13 trumpet-shaped offertory boxes in the Court of the Women (or their near vicinity, Jn. 8:20). Metaphorically, wisdom is to be treasured (Pr. 2:1); the sky is God's treasury of life-giving rain (Dt. 28:12). Wholehearted service, which will be recorded by God in the next life, is like laying up treasure in heaven; the heart stores our treasure, *i.e.* that which we value most and which determines our interests (Mt. 6:19ff.).

TREES. Trees and timber are frequently mentioned in the Bible. Palestine was never thickly forested although woodlands did exist in areas now devoid of trees. Timber was an important raw material for buildings, ships, farm implements and home furnishings and utensils. It is not always possible to identify accurately the trees mentioned in the Bible, because present-day standards of botanical accuracy were not followed by ancient writers; their terminology was not so comprehensive as ours and translators sometimes disagree over the precise identification of some biblical tree names. The main species in RSV are listed below.

Acacia (shittim, AV) occur in desert wadis; these thorny trees were among the few in Sinai likely to provide wood of sufficient size for the tabernacle (Ex. 25:5, 10, 23). *Algum* (2 Ch. 9:10f.) was probably the Cilician fir, or possibly a juniper or cypress. *Almond* blooms in Palestine as early as January with pink-flushed white blossoms; its beauty was copied in ornamental work (Ex. 25:33f.) and its nuts provided food and oil. *Almug* (1 Ki. 10:11f.) is traditionally identified with red sandalwood, but this is uncertain. *Apple* grows in parts of Palestine today, and is probably an accurate translation (*e.g.* Song 2:3); some have suggested the apricot but it may not have been grown there so early. For *balsam*, see poplar.

Cedar provided highly esteemed timber and grew abundantly on Mt Lebanon although it is now only a scattered and protected tree; used in great buildings (1 Ki. 5:6ff.), its great size was a symbol of grandeur (Ps. 92:12). *Cypress* (Is. 41:19) provides excellent timber and thick foliage, although the term may include other conifers. *Ebony* from Africa was used extensively for furniture in Egypt (*cf.*

Ezk. 27:15). *Fir* (*e.g.* Ezk. 27:5) refers to conifers generally. *Holm* (Is. 44:14) was probably a native oak (some have suggested plane). Holm-oak is not native to Palestine, but 3 species of *oak* do grow there. It was a favourite tree for shade (1 Ki. 13:14), but its hard timber is referred to only rarely (*cf.* Ezk. 27:6, which mentions Bashan where the Tabor oak grows well today). Crimson or scarlet dye (Ex. 25:4) was obtained from a scale insect which covered branchlets of the kermes oak.

Palm refers to the date-palm, a tall unbranched tree with a tuft of leaves at the crown. It flourishes in groves in the Jordan valley but in biblical times appears to have been planted singly (*cf.* Jdg. 4:5). It typified grace and uprightness (Ps. 92:12) and provided a woman's name, Tamar (*e.g.* 2 Sa. 13:1). *Plane* grows in rocky streambeds (Ezk. 31:8). *Pomegranate* is a small tree or bush with spreading branches, bright red flowers and apple-shaped fruit. A refreshing drink is made from the fruit juice, and ornamental pomegranates were used for decoration (Ex. 28:33; 1 Ki. 7:20). *Poplar* was used by Jacob (Gn. 30:37) and is called balsam in RSV (*e.g.* 2 Sa. 5:23f.); it grows near water-courses.

The *sycamine* of Lk. 17:6 is also known as black mulberry, with blood-red edible fruits. The *sycomore* is the sycomore-fig, a sturdy tree with spreading branches. Its timber was used for coffins and other objects in Egypt; the fruits are edible and cultivated (Am. 7:14). It was the tree Zacchaeus climbed (Lk. 19:4). *Tamarisk* is a soft-wooded tree of desert wadis

(*e.g.* 1 Sa. 22:6). *Terebinth*, the small turpentine tree (Is. 6:13), occurs frequently in the hills; the larger Atlantic terebinth grows in hotter, drier places and resembles the oak. *Willow* is commonly found beside perennial streams (Is. 44:4) and forms thickets. The willows of Babylon (Ps. 137:2) are now thought to have been poplars.

See also GOPHER WOOD.

TRIBES OF ISRAEL. The Israelites entered Canaan as 12 tribes, descended from the 12 sons of Jacob who heard their father's death-bed prophecies concerning them (Gn. 49). Before they entered Canaan, Moses had already appointed land E of the Jordan to Reuben, Gad and the half-tribe of Manasseh; the rest of the tribes were to settle in the W (Nu. 32:33f.; 34:1-35:8). Only Levi possessed no inheritance; instead each tribe was to set aside towns for the Levites. After Solomon, the nation was split into two N and S, the 10 N tribes represented in some biblical texts by Ephraim and usually called Israel, the 2 S tribes represented by, and called, Judah. The N tribes were taken captive into Assyria in the 8th cent. BC and lost their identity; the S tribes were exiled to Babylon early in the 6th cent. BC and returned about 50 years later. After this Exile the tribal distinctions practically disappeared. See also ISRAEL; JUDAH.

TRIBULATION. A word sometimes employed in EVV to denote affliction, anguish or distress (*e.g.* Dt. 4:30). It is inevitable for, and is to be expected by,

Christians (Mt. 13:21; Jn. 16:33). In some sense this is a participation in the sufferings of Jesus (Col. 1:24), and it is seen as instrumental in promoting a person's moral transformation into the likeness of Christ (Rom. 5:3f.). Such tribulations belong to the 'last days', the kingdom of the end time, and therefore witness to the presence of God's kingdom (Mt. 24:9ff.; Rev. 7:14); and they will intensify before Jesus' return (Mt. 24:21). See also SUFFERING.

TRIBUTE-TAX. An imposed levy forced on one country by another as a mark of subjugation was a common feature of international relationships in the biblical world. Its purpose was to weaken a hostile state and to increase the conqueror's wealth. It was simple to collect because the subject state was responsible for delivering it; if it failed to arrive the state was deemed to be in rebellion and would be dealt with severely. It assumed its greatest importance in the history of Assyria. Jehu of Israel had to pay tribute to Shalmaneser III (858-824 BC), whose Black Obelisk portrays Jehu bowing down to the Assyrian king. Thereafter tribute was paid to a succession of Assyrian kings by several kings of Israel and Judah.

Tribute-tax paid to Israel is rarely mentioned in the OT, however (*e.g.* Ps. 72:10), probably because Israel was not often powerful enough to exact it; 2 Sa. 8:6 is a rare exception. Incidents such as 2 Ki. 20:12 refer to gifts, not taxes.

See also TAX.

TRINITY. The word is not found in the Bible. Though first used by Tertullian at the end of the 2nd cent. AD, it did not find a formal place in Christian theology until the 4th cent. It is, however, the distinctive and all-comprehensive doctrine of the Christian faith. It makes 3 affirmations: that there is only one God; that the Father, Son and Holy Spirit is each God; and that each is a distinct Person.

Biblical basis. The doctrine underlies the revelation of God in both Testaments. In OT times, God's revealed truth had to hold its own in a pagan environment, so nothing that would imperil the oneness of God could be given away. So the OT stresses that God is one, but there are passages in which God, Word and Spirit are brought together as 'co-causers of effects' (*e.g.* in creation, Gn. 1:2f.; in dealing with Israel, Is. 63:8-10). At times in the unfolding of God's redemption, the 'angel of the Lord' appears to be a divine being (*e.g.* Gn. 16:2-13). The Messiah has deity ascribed to him even when he is seen as a person separate from God (Is. 7:14; 9:6). The Spirit equips the Messiah for his work (Is. 61:1) and his people for their response (Joel 2:28).

In the NT, the coming of John the Baptist re-awakened some people's awareness of the Holy Spirit (*cf.* Mt. 3:11). The birth and baptism of Jesus were both associated with heavenly revelation of the Trinity (Lk. 1:35; 3:22). Jesus' teaching was trinitarian throughout. He spoke of the Father who sent him, of himself who revealed the Father, and of the Holy

Spirit by whom he and the Father work; their interrelations are especially stressed in Jn. 14:7-10. He thus both distinguished between, and also made an identity with, all 3 Persons. His final commission to the disciples was a Trinitarian formula (Mt. 28:19).

The rest of the NT indicates that Jesus had instructed his disciples more clearly about this subject than the Gospels record. Peter represented the phenomenon of Pentecost as the activity of the Trinity (Acts 2:32f.). Paul writes of the gifts of the Spirit in Trinitarian terms (1 Cor. 12:4ff.), and sums up the apostolic doctrine in a Trinitarian benediction (2 Cor. 13:14). This confession of God as One in Three took place without struggle or controversy by a people indoctrinated for centuries in the faith of one God and who were not conscious of any break with their ancient faith in regard to the nature of God.

Formulation. For the first Christians the Trinity was a fact of experience which was only later formulated into a doctrine. Under Athanasius it was proclaimed as the faith of the church at the Council of Nicea in AD 325; a century later Augustine gave the formulation enshrined in the so-called Athanasian Creed, accepted by all Trinitarian churches to this day. Three truths are recognized in the relationship between the Persons. First, there is unity in diversity; there are 3 forms in which the divine essence exists. 'Person' is an inadequate term because the doctrine does not imply *individuals*; God is one in essence, personality and will but is manifest in diverse Persons, characteristics and operations. Secondly, the 3 Persons are equal in dignity, nature and honour (*cf.* Jn. 5:18; 1 Cor. 2:10f.). Thirdly, the Persons operate in diverse ways: the Father works through the Son by the Spirit, hence the subordination of relationship (not of nature) implied in Jn. 14:28; 16:14.

Implications. The doctrine of the Trinity means that God is revealable and communicable; there was self-revelation and communication within the Trinity long before creation. It means the Trinity is the basis of true fellowship in the world, for God is a fellowship within himself. And it means there is variety in the universe which reflects the diversity of God's nature.

TROAS. The principal seaport of NW Asia Minor, 20 km SSW of the site of Troy (Ilium). Its artificial harbours provided necessary shelter from prevailing N winds, and it was the port for crossing to Neapolis in Macedonia for the land-route to Rome, and was thus a strategic place in Roman communications. Paul found an 'open door' for mission there (2 Cor. 2:12; *cf.* Acts 16:8ff.; 20:5ff.).

TROGYLLIUM. In Acts 20:15 (RSV mg.), a promontory close to Samos.

TROPHIMUS. An Ephesian Christian who accompanied Paul to Europe and later returned to Troas and waited to go with Paul to Jerusalem (Acts 20:1ff.). Jews falsely assumed he had been taken beyond the court of the Gentiles at the temple and began a riot (Acts 21:27ff.). In 2 Tim. 4:20, Paul reports that he left Trophimus sick at Miletus; which journey this relates to is unclear.

TRUMPET: See MUSIC AND MUSICAL INSTRUMENTS.

TRUMPETS, FEAST OF. The 1st day of the 7th month, the start of the civil year, was to be a solemn rest day. It was signalled by blowing rams' horns, but the significance of this is unknown (Lv. 23:24; Nu. 29:1).

TRUTH. Like knowledge, the term is used in both Testaments to mean intellectual facts which can be discovered to be true or false (1 Ki. 10:6) or, more commonly, to indicate the moral attribute of truth in a person (Gn. 42:16). Truth is an attribute of God (Je. 10:10), who is utterly reliable. Therefore he judges in truth (Ps. 96:13), and demands a truthful response to him by outward obedience to the law (Ps. 119:151), and by true motives (Ps. 51:6). The NT has 3 overlapping senses of truth. It can mean the dependability of God (Rom. 3:7) and people (Eph. 5:9). It can mean that which is really true as opposed to that which is false (Eph. 4:25); the Christian faith especially is 'the truth' (Eph. 1:13). The Holy Spirit leads people into truth (Jn. 16:13) and disciples know it and live in it (Jn. 8:32, 44). It can also mean that which is real as opposed to that which is a copy (Heb. 8:2ff.).

TRYPHAENA AND TRYPHOSA. Two women, probably sisters and possibly twins, greeted in Rom. 16:12 and noted for their service. The names ('delicate' and 'dainty') were quite common.

TUBAL-CAIN. The son of Lamech who was a metalsmith and the discoverer of cold-forging of native copper and meteoric iron (Gn. 4:22).

TURBAN. A head garment of the high priest (Ex. 28:4, 36ff.), which carried a plate engraved 'holy to the Lord'. Its removal signified judgment (Ezk. 21:26); its restoration signified God's acceptance (Zc. 3:5).

TWIN BROTHERS, TWIN GODS. The sign of the Greek ship in which Paul sailed from Malta to Puteoli (Acts 28:11). Castor and Pollux were sons of Leda in Greek mythology; their images were probably fixed either side of the bow.

TYCHICUS. An Asian who accompanied Paul to Jerusalem (Acts 20:4) and who was also Paul's personal envoy to several churches, probably taking letters with him (Eph. 6:21f.; Col. 4:7ff.; 2 Tim. 4:12; Tit. 3:12).

TYPOLOGY. A way of describing the biblical history of salvation so that some of its early phases are seen as anticipations ('types') of its later phases, or its later phases are seen as fulfilments ('antitypes') of earlier ones. Two OT events are repeatedly presented in this way: the creation and the Exodus of Israel from Egypt. The Exodus is itself seen as a new creation; the God who restrained the sea at creation did so at the Exodus (Gn. 1:9f.; Ex. 14:21ff.). The Creator's overthrow of the symbol of chaos, Rahab and the dragon (Jb. 26:12), is applied to his victory over Egypt at the Exodus (Ps. 89:8ff.; *cf.* Is. 30:7). The restoration of Israel in Babylon is seen as both a new creation and a new exodus (Is. 43; 51:9).

The typological relation between OT and NT was described by Augustine: 'In the OT the NT lies hidden; in the NT the OT stands revealed.' Christian salvation is treated as a new creation, exodus and restoration. John's Gospel echoes the creation narrative (Jn. 1:1ff.); Paul describes Christians as a 'new creation' (2 Cor. 5:17); Rev. (22:1ff.) looks forward to a whole new order of existence. Jesus' parents escaped to and from Egypt, recalling Israel's early experience of the Exodus (Mt. 2:15); Jesus is seen as the antitypical Passover lamb (1 Cor. 5:7f.). The good news ('gospel') of new restoration has strong precedents in Is. 40-66. The NT also views Adam as a 'type' of Jesus, for each is a representative head of humanity (Rom. 5:14), and the details of the ancient forms of worship are seen as fulfilled by Jesus' death and ascension (Heb. 9:6ff.).

From the early 2nd cent. AD, some Christian writers began to take typological interpretations of the OT to extremes, reducing the OT to a book of anticipatory pictures of the person and work of Christ.

TYRANNUS. Either the founder or owner of a lecture hall used by Paul in Ephesus (Acts 19:9); nothing more is known of him.

TYRE. The principal seaport on the Phoenician coast, 40 km S of Sidon and 45 km N of Akko. It had 2 harbours, one on an offshore island and another on the mainland. It is known from Egyptian texts *c.* 1850 BC, and took an early part in the sea trade in luxuries with Egypt which led to Egyptian campaigns to control the Phoenician coast. With the decline of Egypt Tyre remained independent; its King Hiram (*c.* 979-945 BC) was on friendly terms with David and Solomon (1 Ki. 5:1ff.), and he built a causeway linking the 2 harbours. This period is known as the golden age of Tyre, and its people later became the merchant princes of the E Mediterranean (Is. 23:8). Their primary trade was in their own glass and scarlet-purple dye made from the murex mollusc. Jezebel, the daughter of Ethbaal, king of Tyre, married Israel's Ahab to confirm the alliance between the two nations; she imported pagan ways and worship with her.

Tyre paid tribute-tax to the Assyrian Adad Nirari in 803 BC, and later to Tiglath-pileser III, but by peaceful submission to the world-dominating Assyrians it retained considerable autonomy. It eventually fell to Sargon II in 722 BC, as did Samaria. In collusion with Egypt the Tyrians made several unsuccessful attempts to rebel. The Babylonians took over Assyrian domination (*cf.* the prophecies in Je.

27:1ff.; Ezk. 26:1ff.). Tyre was captured by Alexander the Great in 332 BC. Herod I rebuilt the main temple which would have been standing when Jesus visited the district (Mt. 15:21ff.). Tyrians heard Jesus speak (Mk. 3:8; cf. Mt. 11:21f.). There were Christians active there in the 1st cent. AD (Acts 21:3ff.).

U

ULAI. The canal or river flowing E of Susa in SW Persia where Daniel had a vision (Dn. 8:16). It is illustrated in earlier Assyrian reliefs, but its course is now unrecognizable.

UNBELIEF. This is seen in the NT as disobedience, not doubt, and as such is the prime sin that the Spirit convicts the world of (Jn. 16:9): it is an affront to God (1 Jn. 5:10). See FAITH.

UNCLEAN (THINGS): See CLEAN AND UNCLEAN.

UNKNOWN GOD. An altar was dedicated to the unknown god in Athens (Acts 17:23). Non-biblical writers also testify to 'anonymous altars' there; Diogenes Laertius said several were once erected to avert a plague.

UNLEAVENED BREAD: See FEASTS; PASSOVER.

UPHAZ. An unidentified source of fine gold (Je. 10:9). It may mean simply 'refined gold' (as in 1 Ki. 10:18), or be a mis-copy of the similar Hebrew name OPHIR.

UR OF THE CHALDEES. The city which Abraham left to go to Haran (Gn. 11:28ff.). It is generally believed to be modern Tell el-Muqayyar 14 km W of Nasiriyeh on the R. Euphrates in S Iraq. Spectacular discoveries include a temple-tower (ziggurat) built by Ur-Nammu (c. 2150-2050 BC). The history and economy of the city is known from many inscribed tablets and buildings. Its principal god Nannar (Sin) was also worshipped at Haran. See also BABEL; CHALDEA.

URBANUS. A common name for a Roman imperial slave (Rom. 16:9).

URIAH, URIJAH (lit. 'Yahweh is my light'). 1. A Hittite in David's army; David committed adultery with Uriah's wife Bathsheba and had Uriah killed in battle (2 Sa. 11). 2. A corrupt priest (2 Ki. 16:10ff.; Is. 8:2). 3. A prophet who supported Jeremiah (Je. 26:20ff.).

URIEL (lit. 'God is my light'). A Kohathite chief who helped bring the ark of the covenant to Obed-edom's house (1 Ch. 15:5, 11).

URIM AND THUMMIM. Means provided by God for the guidance of his people, especially leaders (Dt. 33:8). Virtually nothing is known about them and they seem to have disappeared between the early monarchy and the Exile (Ezr. 2:63). On the occasions when Urim and Thummin are consulted, no negative answers are recorded. They seem to relate to the high priest's garments (Ex. 28:30; *cf.* 1 Sa. 14:3, 41f.). It has been suggested that they were flat objects taken or tossed out of a pouch to give replies to prayerful questions.

UTENSILS (HOUSEHOLD): See CONTAINERS; FLESHPOTS.

UZ. *People:* Among others, son of Aram and grandson of Shem (Gn. 10:23). *Place:* The homeland of Job (Jb. 1:1). The location is uncertain; traditionally it has been identified with Hauran S of Damascus. Some scholars however prefer a more S location in the area between Edom and N Arabia, because Job's friends appear to come from that region.

UZAL. *Person:* An Arabian descendant of Joktan (Gn. 10:27). *Place:* In Ezk. 27:19, possibly Izalla in NE Syria from which Nebuchadrezzar procured wine.

UZZA. Several OT people, the best-known of whom sought to steady the ark of the covenant in transit and was struck dead (2 Sa. 6:3ff.).

UZZI. Among others, a priest descended from Eleazar (Ezr. 7:4).

UZZIAH (lit. 'Yahweh is my strength'). An alternative form is Azariah. He was made the 10th king of Judah after his father's assassination *c.* 767 BC, probably having been co-regent since *c.* 791 BC when his father was imprisoned, a fact required by the chronology of his stated 52-year reign (2 Ki. 14:13ff.; 15:2). Uzziah extended Judah's borders, successfully campaigned against neighbouring states, fortified Jerusalem, and maintained godliness although for a cultic misdemeanour became a leper (2 Ch. 26).

UZZIEL. The founder of a levitical family subdivision (Nu. 3:19, 30); its members helped bring the ark of the covenant to Jerusalem (1 Ch. 23:12, 20).

V

VAGABOND. In Pr. 6:11 (RSV only), NIV 'bandit'; he and the lazy person will become poor.

VALLEY. The landscape of Palestine is cut by many narrow valleys and intermittent streams (wadis). Perennial rivers flow through broader valleys. For details, see articles under valley names.

VANITY, VAIN. Three OT words are thus translated, with shades of meaning attached to each. The main one, which is used in the exposition on the vanity or futility of much of human life in Ecclesiastes, means literally a breath or vapour, and thus that which is insubstantial or worthless, especially idol worship. A vain offering (Is. 1:13) is ritual without righteousness. The second word has the idea of that which is foul, evil or unseemly, as in speech ('empty words', Ps. 41:6); the third means a waste ('emptiness', Is. 40:17). In the NT non-Christian living is in vain ('futile', Eph. 4:17), and pagan gods are vain things (*i.e.* devoid of purpose, Acts 14:15). The false piety of the Pharisees was empty (Mt. 6:7); complacent Christian service can become vain (2 Cor. 6:1).

VASHTI, QUEEN: See ESTHER.

VEGETABLES. Vegetables were grown in gardens (*e.g.* 1 Ki. 21:2), and wild plants were gathered for use as vegetables. Several are named in the Bible. For *beans*, see lentils below. *Cucumber* was probably the snake cucumber in Nu. 11:5, well-known in ancient Egypt. *Garlic* was also known in Egypt, as was the salad *leek* (Nu. 11:5). *Lentils*, from the pea family, were carried on long journeys or used as emergency food (Ezk. 4:9) and formed the 'pottage' associated with Esau (Gn. 25:29ff.). Beans were also used as a substitute for grain meal (2 Sa. 17:28). *Water melons* were known in Egypt, as were *onions* (Nu. 11:5). See also FOOD; HERBS AND SPICES.

VESTMENTS, VESTURE. An archaic word, usually simply denoting dress (Gn. 49:11). In 2 Ki. 10:22, vestments were sacred garments of pagan priests; See also DRESS.

VIAL. A flask (1 Sa. 10:1) or bowl (Rev. 5:8).

VICTORY. The primary biblical assertion is that victory belongs to God (1 Sa. 17:47; 1 Cor. 15:54ff.). Sometimes his victory is the defeat of his people, however (*e.g.* Jdg. 2:14); to preserve his moral righteousness he must do 'strange deeds' (Is. 28:21) against them. Ultimately his holy government of world history will result in the great victory of the Day of the Lord when all creation will be renewed (Ezk. 38-39; Rev. 19). Meanwhile, his people can experience God's victory by the obedience of faith (Ps. 20; Eph. 6:16; 1 Jn. 5:4f.), because they have been set free by his son (Jn. 8:31ff.). The OT associates PEACE; RIGHTEOUS-NESS; and SALVATION with victory.

VILLAGE. Usually a small unwalled group of dwellings, as opposed to a walled 'city' which might not be much larger. The distinction between towns and villages is not always maintained: Bethlehem is called both (Lk. 2:4; Jn. 7:42). Villages were often grouped as 'daughters' near a walled city to which people would retreat in wartime. A village might have its own local government of elders (Ru. 4:2).

VINE, VINEYARD. The common grape-vine is a slender plant which trails on the ground or climbs supports. It was cultivated in Palestine before the Hebrew invasion (Gn. 14:18; Nu. 13:20ff.), and remained an important part of Israel's social and economic life (1 Ki. 4:25; Ezk. 27:18). Vineyards were prepared by terracing hillsides and building stone retaining walls. A boxthorn hedge or a wall topped with dead spiny burnet surrounded the yard to deter thieves and wild animals, and a shelter for guards and labourers was placed in it (Is. 5:1ff.; Mk. 12:1ff.). Vines were planted in rows about 2.5 m apart and pruned each spring (Jn. 15:2). When the grapes matured, they were gathered in baskets and trodden out in wine presses—a happy time of singing (cf. Is. 16:10). When a vineyard became unproductive it was abandoned and the dry vines used for fuel and making charcoal (Ezk. 15:4; Jn. 15:6).

Apart from their use in winemaking, grapes were an important part of people's diet, supplying iron and other essential minerals. Grapes were laid out (often on housetops) to dry in the sun to form raisins, which provided an easily-carried source of energy (Nu. 6:3; 1 Sa. 25:18; 30:12). The vine was the emblem of peace and prosperity. It also symbolized the people of God, his 'vine' planted in the promised land (Ps. 80:8ff.; Is. 5:1ff.). Five of Jesus' parables use vinegrowing images, and he described himself as the true vine with whom all true believers have an organic relationship.

See also AGRICULTURE; FOOD; WINE AND STRONG DRINK.

VINEGAR. A sour liquid resulting from fermentation in wine or other strong drink. It was drunk by farm labourers (the 'wine' in Ru. 2:14) and was offered to Jesus as refreshment (Mk. 15:36, different from the anodyne in v. 23).

VIPER: See SNAKE.

VIRGIN. Literally a woman who has never had sexual intercourse, the term is also used symbolically for nations (Je. 18:13). A similar term means a woman who has not yet had children although she may be married, and is usually translated 'young woman'. It is this word which is used in Is. 7:14, translated in the LXX by the Greek word for virgin and related in Mt. 1:23 to Jesus' virgin birth. Isaiah's sign to Ahaz primarily meant that a woman (perhaps already pregnant) would shortly have a child, and within that short time the political tide would have so changed that the child could be called Immanuel, 'God with us'. See also next article; IMMANUEL.

VIRGIN BIRTH. By this term Protestant Christians usually mean virginal conception—that Mary conceived Jesus without normal sexual relations. Roman Catholics believe this but also maintain that Jesus passed out of Mary's body in such a way as to leave her medically still a virgin. Mary's perpetual virginity after Jesus' birth is also partly maintained by the claim that she never had sexual relations with Joseph, but this is unlikely in view of the 'until' in Mt. 1:25.

There are two independent NT accounts of Jesus' virginal conception (Mt. 1:18ff.; Lk. 1:26ff.). Some supporting evidence includes apparent rumours about his legitimacy (Jn.

8:41), and Paul's use of a general term for Jesus' coming and not the usual term which tends to associate the husband (Rom. 1:3; Phil. 2:7); in Gal. 4:4 he states explicitly and unusually that Jesus was 'born of a woman'. There is evidence from soon after AD 100 that the virgin birth was also accepted by Christian writers. If a child had been conceived through the act of Joseph and Mary, God could not have *become* this man, he could only have attached himself in some way to him (as the Nestorian heresy claimed) or have filled the man spiritually as the Holy Spirit filled the ancient prophets. Neither of these concepts fits the biblical testimony of the incarnation of God in human flesh; it is possible to consider the Creator fashioning in Mary the additional genes and chromosomes necessary fully to unite human and divine natures in one person.

VIRTUE. Used occasionally in EVV to denote moral worth (2 Pet. 1:5).

VISION. It is virtually impossible to draw clear distinctions between dreams, trances and visions. The emphasis in visions seems to be on the unusual nature of the experience and on its character as revelation; it points to a special awareness of God (Je. 1:11). It may come by day (Acts 9:7; 10:3ff.) or night (Gn. 46:2). The outstanding OT examples are the experiences of Ezekiel (*e.g.* 12:27) and Daniel (*e.g.* 10:7); the supreme set of NT visions is found in Rev. See also DREAM; PROPHECY.

VOW. Vows are always used with reference to God, to perform (Gn. 28:20ff.) or abstain from (Ps. 132:2ff.) something in return for God's favour (Nu. 21:1ff.), or as an expression of devotion to him (Ps. 22:25). Once made, they were regarded as binding (Dt. 23:21ff.). What already belongs to the Lord cannot be vowed or consecrated (Lv. 27:26). A vow has no virtue in itself (Ps. 51:16ff.). Paul's vow was a temporary Nazirite vow (Acts 18:18). See also NAZIRITE; OATHS.

VULTURE: See EAGLE, VULTURE.

WAFER. Thin, homemade BREAD (Ex. 29:2).

WAGES. The payment for services rendered. In OT society hired labourers were not common. The family worked the farm and the wages of slaves and family members would be paid in produce. The OT legislated against unscrupulous employers who were not to take advantage of people's economic weakness (Dt. 24:14f.). In the NT preachers who do not have other employment are to receive fair pay (1 Cor. 9:14; 1 Tim. 5:18) but none are to preach for monetary reward (Tit. 1:7). Paul used the image to describe the unearned grace of God and the just payment of punishment for sin (Rom. 4:4f.; 6:23).

WALK. Most biblical occurrences of this word refer to the literal sense of moving on foot. Sometimes it is used for one's way of life (Lv. 26:23f.). In the NT the word is that used for setting plants in a row or for soldiers walking in line, and refers to a person's way of life (Rom. 6:4).

WAR. Palestine was strategically sited on the main trade route between Mesopotamia and Egypt where there was conflict; Palestine could not therefore avoid becoming a frequent theatre of—and prize for—war. In addition, the people of Israel secured their land only by conquest of, and then continued defence against, other settlers.

Generally in the ancient Near East, war was a sacred undertaking with the honour of the national god at stake. The difference for Israel was that their transcendent God did not rise and fall with the fortunes of his people. But he was very much involved in his people's struggles as 'the God of the armies of Israel' (1 Sa. 17:45). After victorious battle, Israel often set apart for God (usually by total destruction) all the people and possessions of the place they had taken and failure to observe this 'ban' was punished (Jos. 7). Later in Israel's history God set himself to fight against the nation for its sin (Je. 21:5ff.). In the days before Israel had a standing army fighting men were summoned by trumpet (Jdg. 3:27) or messenger (1 Sa. 11:7).

In the NT, Jesus made it clear that his kingdom was not to be extended by military methods (Jn. 18:36; *cf.* Mt.

26:52). However the NT recognizes that secular powers have some policing role (Rom. 13:4) and soldiers who were baptized by John were not encouraged to desert (Lk. 3:14; *cf.* Acts 10:1f.). In the early church military service was generally frowned upon, although Tertullian for example made allowances for those who were already soldiers before their conversion. The idea of warfare is applied to the Chritian life; the Christian is called to fight, and is equipped for, a spiritual battle (Eph. 6:10ff.). Consequently military language is used to describe the personal discipline this battle requires (*e.g.* 1 Pet. 2:11). The ultimate victory in this battle will come when Jesus returns (2 Thes. 1:7ff.), depicted in Rev. 16; 19; 20. Before that time there will be many wars (Mt. 24:6) but the peace Jesus eventually brings will never end (*cf.* Is. 9:7).

See also ARMOUR; ARMY; BOW AND ARROW: FORTIFICATION; SLING; SPEAR; SWORD.

WARS OF THE LORD, BOOK OF THE. A document mentioned in Nu. 21:14f., although parts of vv. 17f. and 27-30 come from the same source. It was a collection of songs commemorating Israel's battles, probably compiled after David's time.

WASHBASIN. In Pss. 60:8; 108:9, probably a wide shallow bowl for washing the feet used as a picture of Moab's inferiority.

WATCH. A threefold (Jdg. 7:19) or fourfold (Mk. 6:48) division of night;

see also TIME.

WATCHMAN, WATCHTOWER.
Watchtowers were built to defend livestock and crops (2 Ch. 26:10; Is. 5:2). More complex towers were built into city fortifications. At Tell en-Nasbeh, for example, towers about 30 m apart have been unearthed. Early Israelite towers were square but round ones later became usual. Herod the Great built 3 massive towers in Jerusalem. Watchmen in towers looked out for attacks or for strangers approaching the city gate (2 Sa. 18:24ff.). See also FORTIFICATION.

WATER. Water figures prominently in the Bible because many of its events are set in an area where water is generally in short supply. Drought was serious (1 Ki. 17:1ff.); rain or water was a sign of God's blessing (Ps. 23:2). Invading armies often cut off a city's water supply (2 Ki. 3:19, 25); Hezekiah averted potential disaster when under siege by building a tunnel (which still exists) from a spring outside the city to the pool of Siloam (2 Ch. 32:30).

Symbolically, thirst describes spiritual longing or need (Ps. 42:1); God is the source of 'living water' (Je. 2:13; Jn. 7:38). The cleansing property of water is also used symbolically in rituals as a sign of spiritual purification (Nu. 19:1ff.). A developed form of ritual washing practised by Jewish sects before and during NT times provided the background to John's baptism of repentance and the imagery of Christian baptism. But water could also kill; the Israelites had a general fear of the deep sea (Ps. 32:6).

WAY. Used symbolically of God's purposes (Ps. 67:2) or man's conduct (Ps. 1:1). In the NT Jesus contrasted the two ways a person could go in life (Mt. 7:13f.). The Christian church's oldest title appears to have been 'the Way' (Acts 9:2; 19:9). In Jn. 14:6 Jesus claimed to be the only way to relationship with God.

WAYMARK. In Je. 31:21, a heap of stones to mark a track.

WEALTH. The Bible often views wealth as a blessing from God (Ps. 112:1ff.) and a consequence of God's generosity (1 Tim. 6:17). However, possession of wealth brings with it the responsibility to give liberally to the poor (1 Tim. 6:18f.), following Jesus' own example (2 Cor. 8; 9). It also brings the dangers of failing to acknowledge God as its source (Ho. 2:8), of trusting in riches (Ps. 52:7) so much that true submission to God proves impossible (Mk. 10:23ff.; Lk. 12:21; Rev. 3:17). The Bible warns against covetousness, the desire to be rich, saying that the love of money is the root of all evil; Christians are to learn contentment with what they have (1 Tim. 6:7ff.). The rich who fall into these dangers are frequently denounced (*e.g.* Jas. 5). See also CHARITY; MAMMON; POVERTY.

WEAPONS: See BOW AND ARROW; SLING; SPEAR; SWORD.

WEAVING: See SPINNING AND WEAVING.

WEEKS, FEAST OF: See FEASTS; PASSOVER.

WEIGHTS AND MEASURES.

1. Old Testament.
Standards varied from place to place and there is no evidence that even Israel as a single nation ever used an integrated system. David did pronounce certain standards ('king's weight', 2 Sa. 14:26) but the rabbinic tradition that standard measures were deposited in the temple is unverified (*cf.* 1 Ch. 23:29). The law did insist that Hebrews kept to honest weights and measures (Lv. 19:35f.; *cf.* Ezk. 45:10ff.), and the prophets denounced merchants who did not (Mi. 6:11f.). Weights in any case had a margin of error up to 6% and so all modern equivalents can only be approximate; the main weights and measures are set out in the illustrated section.

Weights were stones carved in shapes, usually with a flat base and often inscribed with their weight and the standard they followed. They were carried in a pouch or bag (Dt. 25:13; Pr. 16:11); a purchaser could then check his weights with those of merchants anywhere (*cf.* Gn. 23:16). The talent was the largest unit used to weigh metals and large quantities; a 'light' talent weighed about 30 kg, a 'heavy' or 'double' talent about 60 kg. The talent was divided into 60 minas of 50 shekels each (or possibly 50 minas of 60 shekels each); hence there

were 3000 shekels, the basic weight, to a talent. The shekels varied from about 10 g to 13 g, depending on whether they were 'royal', 'common' or 'temple' shekels. The shekel was further divided into 2 bekahs of 10 gerahs each. The peres (plural parsin) of Dn. 5:25ff. was possibly a half-shekel, and the writing on the wall thus read superficially 'Mina, mina, shekel, half-shekel'.

Linear measures. These were based on easily applied 'natural' units. The common cubit was the distance from elbow to finger tip, or 6 palms; the standard Hebrew cubit for more precise measurement was 44-45 cm; the royal cubit was a handbreadth longer than the standard. The span, the outstretched hand from little finger to thumb, was half a cubit, the palm or handbreadth was the width of the hand at the base of the four fingers. A reed was 6 cubits. Distance before the Exile was reckoned very approximately by such things as a bowshot (Gn. 21:16), a ploughed furrow (1 Sa. 14:14) or a day's journey (1 Ki. 19:4). In Maccabaean times Greek measures were introduced into Jewish reckoning.

Area was often described by the linear dimensions or circumference (*e.g.* 1 Ki. 7:23). An acre of farmland (1 Sa. 14:14) was reckoned as the area a pair of yoked animals could plough in a day. In Babylonia this was 1,618 sq m, in Roman times 2,529 sq m.

Dry capacity measures derived originally from the containers which held an agreed amount. Hence a homer was a donkey-load, and was equal to the later kor. The ephah was a container large enough to hold a person (Zc. 5:7) and used for cereals, and was equal to the liquid measure of a bath. An omer was a bowl, a tenth of an ephah.

Liquid capacity was based on the bath which seems to have varied between 21 and 46 litres; the common bath is reckoned at 22 litres. A hin ('a pot') was about one-sixth of a bath.

2. New Testament.

Weights. Only two are mentioned, the pound of Jn. 12:3; 19:39, which was the Roman libra (327.45 g), and the 'hundredweight' or talent of Rev. 16:21, which has been variously estimated between 20 and 41 kg.

Linear measures still related to parts of the body. The Romans had two different cubits, the one in use in Palestine probably being the Philetarian cubit of 52.5 cm. The fathom of Acts 27:28 was the length of outstretched arms (about 1.8 m). The Roman stadion was 185 m, from which comes the English word stadium as the race-course at Olympia was exactly a stade long. The mile was 8 stades, 1,478.5 m (Mt. 5:41). No *measures of area* are used in the NT.

Dry capacity. The quart of Rev. 6:6 was just over a litre; it was the daily ration of grain per man in Xerxes' army. The 'measures' of Mt. 13:33; Lk. 13:21 would be 12.3 litres each, but the measures of Lk. 16:7 were the kor, rated at about 395 litres. The bushel of Mt. 5:15 was a grain measuring container holding about 8.75 litres.

Liquid capacity. The pot of Mk. 7:4 was a measure of about 500 cc. The measure of oil in Lk. 16:6 was equivalent to the OT bath, of about 39.5 litres. The stone water-pots at Cana in Jn. 2 held between 80 and 120 litres each.

WELL. An artificial shaft sunk to reach underground water, percolating or collected, or to reach a natural underground spring. The word might also mean a water-storage cistern (probably in 1 Ch. 11:17f.) which could be used as a dungeon (Je. 38:6). Water was precious in the Near East and wells could be (and remain) subjects of fierce disputes (Gn. 21:25). See also CISTERN; WATER.

WHEEL. Early wheels were made of wooden planks pegged together, with leather tyres. By *c.* 1500 BC lighter spoked wheels were in use. Daniel and Ezekiel saw wheels in their visions of heaven (Ezk. 1; 10; Dn. 7:9).

WHIRLWIND. In the OT this may refer to any violent storm and not only a rotary movement of air (Jb. 37:9; Je. 23:19). It may symbolize a sudden attack (Je. 4:13) or God's wrath (Ho. 8:7). See also WIND.

WICKED. The term may be used simply to mean wrong (Ps. 18:21), but more often it refers to active evil or mischief. It denotes perversity of mind (Rom. 1:29) which is seated in the heart (Je. 17:9; Mk. 7:21ff.) and inspired by Satan (Mt. 13:19; 1 Jn. 3:12). The Psalms grapple with the question, and provide a partial answer, as to why the wicked prosper and the righteous suffer (*e.g.* Ps. 37:35f.). The certainty of eventual punishment for the wicked is maintained throughout Scripture (Ps. 9:17; Mt. 13:49).

WIDOW. The Hebrew law made special provision for widows and also for orphans at a time when there was no organized social welfare or casual employment for women (*e.g.* Ex. 22:22ff.; Dt. 14:29). Widows were often overlooked by men, so God had a special concern for them (Ps. 68:5); kindness to them was a mark of true religion (Is. 1:17; *cf.* Mal. 3:5). The Christian church inherited from Judaism this concern to provide for widows (Jas. 1:27), and one of the earliest examples of church charitable work was the daily distribution of money to needy widows (Acts 6:1ff.). Paul laid down detailed instructions about this, suggesting that younger widows should be encouraged to remarry (1 Cor. 7:8ff.; 1 Tim. 5:9f.). See also CHARITY.

WILDERNESS. In the Bible this term covers not only the barren deserts of sand dunes or rock but also the steppe-lands which were suitable for grazing livestock (as in Ex. 3:1). Sometimes the Hebrew word for relatively bare wildernesses in Judaea is often rendered as a proper name, Jeshimon (*e.g.* 1 Sa. 23:19). The Arabah, specifically an area S of the Dead Sea, is also a common name for steppe or scrubland (as in Je. 17:6). For Israel's wilderness wanderings, see EXODUS.

WIND. The Hebrews conceived of climate being affected by the 4 winds (Je. 49:36; Rev. 7:1). The vast power of the wind suggested that it was the breath of God (Is. 40:7) or the Holy Spirit (Jn. 3:8), and was controlled by him (Mk. 4:41). Specific winds are mentioned in the Bible although the 4 cardinal points used in the names may not be especially accurate, because compound names are impossible in Hebrew. Among them are the S or E wind, which sometimes implies the hot sirocco, burning up vegetation (Ps. 103:16). The W wind is sometimes seen as the bringer of rain (1 Ki. 18:44f.). The 'northeaster' which shipwrecked Paul (Acts 27:14) was a typhonic winter storm associated with low pressure over Libya or the Gulf of Gabes. Symbolically wind may stand for nothingness (Is. 41:29) or the passing nature of human life (Ps. 78:39). See also PALESTINE; WHIRLWIND.

WINE AND STRONG DRINK. *Old Testament.* 'New wine' was not unfermented grape juice (for fermentation sets in very quickly) but wine made from the first drippings of juice before the winepress was trodden; as such it would be particularly potent (*cf.* Acts 2:13). Indeed, the term wine is never applied on the rare occasions when juice is squeezed from grapes straight into a cup (Gn. 40:11), and therefore always had some alcohol content. Wine, together with grain, stands for the good gifts of life from God (Gn. 27:28), although as a discipline it is sometimes to be abstained from for some religious rituals (Lv. 10:9; Nu. 6:3). The abstinence of the Rechabites was more to preserve a nomadic style of living (Je. 35:7). Alongside the blessing of wine is also its curse through misuse, which is often warned against (*cf.* Ps. 104:15 with Is. 28:7; Ec. 10:19 with Is. 5:11).

New Testament. The references are fewer but the good and bad effects are again alongside each other. John the Baptist abstained in view of his special commission (Lk. 1:15), but Jesus' first recorded miracle in John's Gospel was to turn a large quantity of water into wine (Jn. 2) and he won a reputation for 'eating and drinking' with social outcasts. On the cross he refused the spiced wine which would have acted as a mild anaesthetic and clouded his mind (Mk. 15:23) but not the 'vinegar' or common wine of labourers (v. 36). He used common knowledge about wine to illustrate the profound effect of his kingdom on the old system (Mk. 2:22). The people of this world are intoxicated with greed and violence (Rev. 17:2ff.). By contrast, Christians are to be filled with the Spirit—under his control—rather than to allow themselves to be controlled by alcohol (Eph. 5:18); Paul clearly recognized certain similarities between the two conditions. Timothy was encouraged to drink wine for his health (1 Tim. 5:23), but the same letter warns against excess (1 Tim. 3:8). Paul suggests that abstinence may be necessary for the sake of weaker people (Rom. 14:21).

WINNOWING: See AGRICULTURE; FORK; GRAIN CROPS.

WISDOM. *Old Testament.* In the OT wisdom is intensely practical, the art of being successful and of forming the correct plan to gain the desired results. Leaders were in special need of it and some were granted it (*e.g.* Joshua, Dt. 34:9; David, 2 Sa. 14:20; Solomon, 1 Ki. 3:9ff.). It was an attribute of the promised Messiah (Is. 11:2). A special class of wise men seems to have developed during the time of Israel's kings (*cf.* Je. 18:18). However, wisdom in its fullest sense belongs to God (Dn. 2:20ff.), and it includes complete knowledge (Pr. 15:3) and control of natural (Is. 28:23ff.) and historical (Is. 31:2) processes. From wisdom he both created (Ps. 104:24) and judges people righteously (Ps. 73). True human wisdom thus stems from the Lord (Pr. 1:7) and is applied to daily living; this combination of insight and obedience was related by the prophets to the knowledge of God (Ho. 4:1, 6). When God was squeezed out of wisdom, it became practical atheism drawing prophetic rebuke (Is. 5:21). In Pr. 8 wisdom is personified. This may be using 'Wisdom' to describe God himself, or it may be due to the fact that the Hebrews resisted abstraction and so dealt with objects or ideas as if they had personality, rather than to the idea that wisdom had some independent or divine existence. See also WISDOM LITERATURE.

New Testament. Wisdom has the same practical nature as in the OT, and is usually God-given or God-opposing. Divorced from God, it becomes impoverished (1 Cor. 2:4f.) or devilish (Jas. 3:14ff.). Jesus promised his wisdom for when his followers were under trial (Lk. 21:15). It was necessary not only for leaders (Acts 6:3) but for all believers (Col. 1:9; Jas. 1:5). God's wisdom is especially demonstrated in the life and death of Christ (Rom. 11:33) and manifested in the church (Eph. 3:10). Jesus claimed to have wisdom (Mt. 12:42) and astonished the crowds with it (Mt. 13:54). Paul calls Jesus God's wisdom (1 Cor. 1:24, 30), perhaps seeing in his new revelation a reflection of the relationship between the old law and wisdom (Dt. 4:6). Jesus is worshipped in heaven for his complete wisdom (Rev. 5:12; cf. Col. 2:3).

WISDOM LITERATURE. A type of literature common in the ancient Near East in which instructions for successful living are given or the complexities of human existence are discussed. There are 2 major types: proverbial wisdom, with short pithy sayings (as the book of Proverbs), and speculation wisdom in the form of monologues (e.g. Ecclesiastes) or dialogues (e.g. Job). Even the speculative wisdom is practical and earthy, not theoretical. Throughout the Near East there grew up a class of scribes or wise men whose task was to create or collect pithy wise sayings. By the 7th cent. BC they were sufficiently important in Judah to be classed alongside priests and prophets (Je. 8:8f.; 18:18), but there is some doubt as to whether they were professionals or simply wise citizens.

They employed several literary devices as aids to memory. These included poetic parallelism (Pr. 18:10) and comparisons (Pr. 17:1). Riddles (Jdg. 9:7ff.; 1 Ki. 10:1), parables (2 Sa. 12:1ff.), and allegories (Is. 5:1ff.) were also part of their repertoire, and Jesus' wisdom was expressed in like manner. Some psalms have also been classified as 'wisdom poetry' (e.g. Pss. 127; 133). Although wisdom was an international phenomenon (cf. 1 Ki. 4:31), biblical wisdom literature has its own stamp, claiming that true wisdom comes from God (cf. Jb. 28:20ff.). See also previous article.

WISDOM OF SOLOMON: See APOCRYPHA.

WISE MEN: See MAGI.

WITCH: See MAGIC AND SORCERY.

WITNESS. The term is not used in the Bible in the common English verbal sense of 'to see', and is mostly used as a noun of people or things bearing witness (e.g. Gn. 31:48; Jos. 22:34; Is. 44:8; Acts 22:20). The associated term 'testimony' is used as a technical religious concept in the OT, meaning a sign or reminder (e.g. Ex. 16:34).

WOE. The literal rendering of a Greek word meaning 'alas for'. So when Jesus says 'Woe to...' (e.g. Lk. 6:24ff.) he is not so much pronouncing judgment as deploring the miserable condition of people who are spiritually blind. In Mt. 11:21f. his pronounce ment is followed by a prophecy of consequent doom. In Rev. 9:12 three 'woes' are various disasters.

WOLF. Up to NT times it was common enough to be a menace to livestock, although not to people. It is only mentioned metaphorically in the Bible, often for people misusing their authority (*e.g.* Zp. 3:3; Mt. 7:15).

WOMAN. Woman, like man, was made in God's image (Gn. 1:27). In Hebrew laws the mother was to be honoured (Ex. 20:12) and obeyed (Dt. 21:18ff.); she was exempt from sabbath labour (Ex. 20:10), and could become a landowner in her own right if there were no male heirs. There are many examples of biblical women such as Miriam and Deborah playing an important part in national life, and of the great influence wielded against true religion by women such as Jezebel. Later, because of rabbinical teaching, women tended to be given an inferior role.

In the NT, Jesus had a number of encounters with women. His own mother was 'blessed' by God (Lk. 1:28, 42) and Jesus commended her into John's keeping at the cross (Jn. 19:26f.). Jesus forgave, taught and healed women just as he did men, and they in turn served him and provided for his needs; he thus put them on an equal footing with men, demanding from them the same standards and offering them the same salvation as men. After the resurrection women received the Holy Spirit (Acts 2:1ff., 18); a woman's house became the

church centre for Jerusalem (Acts 12:12); Paul's first convert in Europe was a woman (Acts 16:14); and in the early church women exercised important ministries (*e.g.* Acts 21:9). Paul, in laying down the principle of equality of the sexes before God (Gal. 3:28), dealt with local situations by requiring that the conventions of the time should be observed.

WOMB. The formation of the baby in the womb is regarded by biblical writers as a mystery of God's action (Ec. 11:5). Barrenness is said to be 'a closed womb' (1 Sa. 1:5). It is used to symbolize life's beginnings (Is. 49:1).

WOOL. Wool was the basic fabric for clothing and was therefore highly valued, being part of the 'firstfruits' offered to priests (Dt. 18:4) and included in tribute-tax (2 Ki. 3:4). The reason for the Hebrew ban on mixed fabric is unclear (Dt. 22:11), although the creation of static electricity in it would make it uncomfortable. Washed wool is a picture of purity (Is. 1:18). See also SHEEP.

WORD. In the OT, 'the word of God' is a phrase used 394 times of a divine communication in one of several forms. It is an extension of God's personality and hence is to be heeded by all (Ps. 103:20). It stands for ever (Is. 40:8) and once uttered cannot return unfulfilled (Is. 55:11). It is used as a synonym for the law in Ps. 119. In the NT it is used for the Christian message (Mk. 2:2; Gal. 6:6), although in the synoptic gospels Jesus himself always used the plural, 'my words' (*e.g.* Mk. 8:38).

In John's Gospel and Letters, and in Revelation, the term is sometimes used in a technical sense. It occurs most explicitly in Jn. 1:1, where the significance of Christ as 'the Word' (*Logos*) is employed theologically. This has been linked unsatisfactorily to the law of God and to the personification of wisdom in Pr. 8. The most likely reason for its use is that the author is drawing on Greek philosophical imagery to explain the truth to his readers in terms familiar to them. The Jewish philosopher Philo had frequently used the term Logos. He derived the term from Stoic (Greek) sources, identifying the Logos with God's plan and God's power of creation, and also with the OT Angel of the Lord and the Name of God. He used many terms to describe the Logos, including Advocate (Paraclete) and Son of God. He termed it both a second God and the Ideal Man, giving it both unity with and distinction from God. The stress of the NT is to show how Jesus exhausts all preparatory imagery and thought, and gives fresh meaning to terminology which had been used for lesser mysteries.

See also ORACLE.

WORK. Work was part of God's purposes for mankind from the beginning (Gn. 2:15) and is seen in the OT as a provision of divine wisdom (Ps. 104:19ff.; Is. 28:23ff.). The entrance of sin changed work from a joy to a toil (Gn. 3:16ff.); although not bad in itself, it has lost its true value. When it

becomes an end in itself it results in idolatry (*cf.* Ec. 2:4ff.) and some have used it to exploit or oppress others (Ex. 1:11ff.; Jas. 5:4). But through the redemption of Christ, work has been transformed again into a means of blessing. Idleness, even with religious motives, was condemned in the NT (1 Thes. 4:11; 2 Thes. 3:10). Jesus working as a carpenter (Mk. 6:3) sanctified ordinary work. Paul set an example of honest labour in order not to become a financial burden to the church he served (Acts 18:3), but he also advocated a fair remuneration for church leaders (1 Tim. 5:17); *cf.* Lk. 10:7). Ordinary tasks become for the Christian a service for God and are thus to be done to his honour (Col. 3:23f.) and in the service of one's neighbour (Mt. 25:40).

The term 'work' is also used to describe God's acts of creation and providence (*e.g.* Pss. 92:5; 111:2). In John's Gospel it is also applied to the work of salvation committed by the Father to the Son (*e.g.* Jn. 4:34; 15:24). Salvation therefore comes by God's grace, not human works. See also next article; HIRELING; WAGES.

WORKS. Apart from the general sense of God's activity and human labour (see previous article), the term 'works' is used in the NT in two special ways. First, it refers to the works of Jesus which reveal that he was both Messiah and Son of God (*e.g.* Mt. 11:2ff.; Jn. 10:37f.). Secondly, it refers to the demonstration of God's activity through the life of a believer (Mt. 5:16; Jn. 14:12). The NT calls for behaviour which is appropriate to the new life even though entry into that life is by God's grace, not human effort (Eph. 2:8ff.; Jas. 2:14ff.; *cf.* Rom. 8:7f.; 1 Cor. 3:8ff.).

WORLD. The world, in the sense of the physical universe, was something good made by God (Jn. 1:10; *cf.* Gn. 1:31). In the NT the word is often used in a more specific sense for the 'world' of human beings (Jn. 16:21), the kingdoms of which were offered to Jesus during his desert temptations (Mt. 4:8f.), and which God loved enough to send his Son into (Jn. 3:16). As a result of sin (Rom. 5:12) this world has now become disordered and is in the grip of Satan (1 Jn. 5:19). Its dominant characteristics are pride and covetousness (1 Jn. 2:16).

It is pervaded by a spirit of its own which must be removed by God's Spirit if it is not to exercise control over human reason and understanding (1 Cor. 2:12; Col. 2:20). Such a change and the ability to overcome this world is a product of the new birth (1 Jn. 5:4ff.), made possible because Jesus has freed those who trust him from the grip of evil (Jn. 12:31f.; 14:30f.). The Christian can therefore no longer set his or her affection on this world because it contains within itself the seeds of its own decay (1 Jn. 2:15ff.); to befriend the world is to become God's enemy (Jas. 4:2). Before his death, Jesus prayed that his followers would be kept safe from the evil influences of the world (Jn. 17:9ff.). But he also sent them right into it (Mt. 28:19) to be its light (Mt. 5:14), for one day he will set it free from its bondage (Rom. 8:21; *cf.* Rev. 11:15).

WORSHIP. The basic biblical concept is that of service; the main biblical words for worship originally signified the labour of hired servants. In order to worship God, his people must exhibit reverence and wonder. The OT emphasis is largely on congregational worship (*e.g.* Ps. 42:4), in which ritual was prominent, though the prophets in particular were anxious to point out that worship involved lifestyle as well as attending gatherings. Although the rituals of sacrifices and incense-burning might become mechanical, many people could still express love and gratitude to God through public praise and prayer (*e.g.* Pss. 79; 93). When the temple in Jerusalem was destroyed and many Jews were exiled to Babylon, this congregational need was met by the synagogue services which continued even after the temple was rebuilt.

Jesus participated in both temple and synagogue worship but taught that true worship was the love of the heart towards God and which was also offered to God in terms of personal care for others (Lk. 10:25ff.; Jn. 4:20ff.; Jas. 1:27). The early Christians worshipped on the first day of the week (Acts 20:7), in believers' homes, with praise, prayer, Scripture readings, and the love feast (1 Cor. 11:23ff.; Eph. 5:19; Col. 3:16).

WRATH. A word which describes the permanent attitude of a holy and just God when confronted by sin and evil

(Rom. 1:18-32). It is a personal quality of God without which he would cease to be fully righteous and his love would degenerate into sentimentality. It is consistent, not fitful or spasmodic like human anger, but until the final day of judgment (Rom. 2:5) it is always tempered with mercy (*cf.* Ho. 11:8ff.). Human rebellion against God is so persistent that in their unredeemed state people are inevitably objects of God's wrath (Eph. 2:3), and obedience to the law of Moses cannot of itself rescue them (Rom. 4:15). But through the death and resurrection of Jesus, God has graciously provided for those who will trust in him deliverance from wrath and its consequent punishment and death (Rom. 5:9; 1 Thes. 1:10). See also GOD; JUDGMENT.

WRITING. Writing was a hallmark of civilization and progress in the ancient Near East from at least 3100 BC onwards. The commonest words for writing occur over 450 times in the OT and NT.

Biblical references. Moses is said to have written down God's words and laws (*e.g.* Ex. 17:14; 24:4; Dt. 31:19, 22). Joshua wrote a copy of the renewed covenant (Jos. 24:26). Samuel wrote a charter for kingship (1 Sa. 10:25), and the kings themselves wrote instructions and letters (2 Sa. 11:14). Scribes were employed at all periods to keep records (*e.g.* 1 Ch. 24:6). Some of the prophets wrote down their messages or dictated them to scribes (*e.g.* Is. 8:1; 30:8; Je. 36:27f.). After the Exile, Ezra was himself a scribe and the book bearing his name mentions letters and records (*e.g.* 4:4ff.; 8:34). Jesus could read and write (Lk. 4:16ff.; Jn. 7:14; 8:6). Luke wrote up the records of Jesus' life and the history of the early church (Lk. 1:3; Acts 1:1), and Paul, often using an amanuensis (secretary), wrote numerous letters (*e.g.* Rom. 15:15; 16:22).

Writing materials and implements. Inscriptions were carved on stone or rock surfaces throughout the OT period. Stone tablets were the earliest medium; apparently no larger than 45 by 30 cm, they were used for royal and religious texts (*cf.* Ex. 32:16). The tablets used by Isaiah (30:8) and Habakkuk (2:2) were most probably wooden boards coated with wax; the earliest known was found at Nimrud, Assyria with a composition of 6,000 lines and is dated *c.* 705 BC. Similar boards were used in NT times (Lk. 1:63). Clay tablets or flat tiles were inscribed or written on (Ezk. 4:1), and broken pottery (potsherds) was used for short memoranda written in ink. Papyrus is not mentioned in the OT but was in use from the 11th cent. BC, and is probably meant in 2 Jn. 12. Parchment made from animal skins was used at least from the Persian period (5th cent. BC) and its use for copies of biblical texts at Qumran by NT times probably reflects earlier Jewish practice.

Stone and clay were inscribed with chisels and gravers. The scribe's pen of Je. 8:8 was a reed split or cut to act as a brush for ink; in Egypt they were 15-40 cm long with the end cut to a chisel shape which could write thick or thin strokes. By Greek and Roman times (3rd cent. BC onwards) reeds were cut to a point and then split like a quill-pen, and were used in NT times (3 Jn. 13). Ink was usually black carbon (charcoal) mixed with gum or oil for use on parchment or with a metallic substance for use on papyrus; it was kept as a dried cake onto which the scribe dipped his moistened pen. The Romans also used the juice of the cuttle-fish and like most inks this could be washed out easily and the writing material re-used (*cf.* Nu. 5:23). The 'writing case' of Ezk. 9:2f. may have been a palette, a narrow rectangular board with a groove for the pens and hollows for the cakes of red and black ink.

Types of documents. Tablets have been mentioned already; larger historical records were sometimes written on clay prisms or barrel-shaped cylinders. The usual form of a 'book' in Bible times was a scroll or roll of papyrus, leather or parchment written inside (recto) and when necessary on the outside (verso) also (*cf.* Ezk. 2:10). It was inscribed in as many columns, and was therefore as long as required (*cf.* Je. 36:23). In NT times 'the books' came to be a term for the collected Scriptures (2 Tim. 4:13). About the 2nd cent. AD the roll began to be replaced by the codex, a collection of sheets of writing material folded and fastened together at one edge, an important step towards the development of the modern book. It was adopted as the norm for Christian OT and NT Scriptures by the end of the

2nd cent., and was generally accepted outside Christian circles by the 4th cent. AD.

Scripts. Three kinds were used in ancient times. *Hieroglyphs* were pictorial signs, originally pictures to represent objects, later used to signify sounds. In Egypt, phonetic signs were usually added in front of the picture sign to determine its precise meaning or sound. This original hieroglyphic system was later modified by the Egyptians into a hieratic script which was a cursive form of the hieroglyphic (a flowing script as opposed to carefully printed letters). An even more rapid form of writing, the demotic, appeared in the 7th cent. BC, and like the other two remained in use until about the 5th cent. AD. They became forgotten forms until the early 19th cent. when scholars rediscovered how to decipher them.

The second form of script was *cuneiform*, a system of wedge-shaped incisions in clay or stone used because curves could not be engraved very easily. This script developed word-signs (ideograms) to represent similar sounds with different meanings (*e.g.* meat, meet). It was fully developed in Babylonia and was used elsewhere by *c.* 2800 BC and had at least 500 different signs. In the 15th-13th cents. Akkadian cuneiform was the international medium for diplomacy and commerce. Several other languages used cuneiform script. At Ras Shamra cuneiform was used to transcribe an alphabet; 29 signs were developed for consonants and 3 for vowels, and the order of this alphabet prefigured the later Hebrew order. It was easier to learn than the Akkadian cuneiform but was not widely used. The Persians used a modified cuneiform alongside the later Aramaic linear script.

The third form, *linear* script, was developed shortly after 2000 BC when a scribe in Syro-Palestine, perhaps at Byblos, realized that his language could be represented by far fewer signs than were used in the existing writing systems—one sign for each consonant. Vowels were not to be represented separately until the Greeks took over the alphabet. This invention placed literacy within reach of everyone and broke the monopoly of the professional scribes for the first time. Examples of this ancestor of all alphabets have been found in Palestine dating from shortly before 1500 BC. During the next 500 years the signs were further simplified and lost their original semi-pictorial form. From 1000 BC onwards the direction of writing—right to left—was standardized. It provided a readily available tool for the Israelites to record God's laws and works, and many examples from later centuries show how the alphabet became more cursive. The Aramaeans adopted the Canaanite alphabet as they settled in Syria after 1000 BC and as their language spread so their script began to supersede cuneiform script in Assyria and Babylonia. The more formal squarer and angular Hebrew style developed in the Hasmonaean period (c. 150-30 BC) from earlier formal and cursive scripts. The Greeks, perhaps in the 9th century BC, created the first true alphabet with vowel signs as well as consonants by using Phoenician symbols for sounds the Greeks did not possess to represent the vowels they required.

Literacy and literary methods. Evidence for the extent of literacy among ordinary people in biblical times is meagre. Gideon captured a young man who could write (Jdg. 8:14), and the teaching of writing to children (cf. Is. 10:19) was carried out by schools attached to shrines and by the invention of the alphabet (cf. Is. 10:19). Most higher state officials were probably literate, but scribes remained the professional writers and recorders for many centuries; there were 6 scribes to a population of 2,000 at Alalah in Syria c. 1800-1500 BC, and this is probably indicative of the general level of literacy in important towns. Documents were stored in boxes or jars (Je. 32:14), laid up in temples (1 Sa. 10:25) or in special archives (Ezr. 6:1). Assyrian kings such as Ashurbanipal (c. 650 BC) at Nineveh collected copies of texts for their libraries. When copying texts, scribes often quoted the source and stated its condition and whether the text had been checked with the original document. Authorship was frequently, although not invariably, anonymous.

See also EDUCATION; PAPYRUS; SCRIBE; TEXTS AND VERSIONS.

XERXES: See AHASUERUS.

Y

YAHWEH: See GOD, NAMES OF.

YARN. Goat and camel hair, cotton, linen and silk are the yarns mentioned in the Bible (*e.g.* Est. 1:6; Rev. 18:12). See also LINEN; SILK; WOOL.

YEAST: See LEAVEN.

YOKE. A wooden frame joining two animals (usually oxen) together (*e.g.* 1 Sa. 11:7). Also used to symbolize one person's subjection to another (Je. 27:12). For the 'yokefellow' of Phil. 4:13 see SYNZYGUS.

Z

ZAANAN. In Mi. 1:11, possibly the Zenan in Judah (Jos. 15:37).

ZAANANNIM, ZAANAIM. A place near Kedesh where Heber camped

(Jdg. 4:11), possibly Khan et-Tuggar 4 km NE of Tabor.

ZABAD. Several OT people including one of David's heroes (1 Ch. 11:41); and a conspirator against Joash (2 Ch. 24:26) whose correct name was JOZACHAR.

ZABBAI. 1. Someone forced to put away his foreign wife (Ezr. 10:28). 2. The father of a Baruch contemporary with Nehemiah, possibly the same as 1 (Ne. 3:20).

ZABDI. Several OT people including Achan's grandfather who shared in the loot from Ai (Jos. 7:1, 17f.).

ZACCHAEUS. A chief tax collector at Jericho, who climbed a tree to see Jesus and subsequently became a disciple, showing his repentance by giving away half his fortune and making fourfold compensation to those he had defrauded (Lk. 19:1ff.). See also TAX COLLECTOR.

ZADOK. Several OT people, chief of whom was a descendant of Aaron and priest with Abiathar at David's court, in charge of the ark of the covenant (2 Sa. 15:24f.). His descendants discharged chief-priestly duties until the temple was destroyed in 587 BC, and after its restoration until 171 BC (*cf.* Ezk. 44:15ff.). The Qumran community remained loyal to the Zadok priesthood and looked forward to its restoration again.

ZAIR. In 2 Ki. 8:21, a place on the

border of Edom, possibly identical with ZIOR.

ZALMON. *Person:* One of David's heroes (2 Sa. 23:28). *Places:* A mountain near Shechem (Jdg. 9:48) but its identification is uncertain. In Ps. 68:14 the mountain is probably Jebel Hauran E of the Jordan.

ZAMZUMMIM. An Ammonite name for the REPHAIM (Dt. 2:20).

ZANOAH. 1. A town in the Shephelah (Jos. 15:34), modern Khirbet Zanu 3 km S of Beth-shemesh. 2. A town in the hills near Juttah (Jos. 15:56), possibly Kh. Beit Amra, Kh. Zanuta or Kh. Yaqin.

ZAPHENATH-PANEAH. An Egyptian name given to Joseph at his investiture by the Pharaoh; the original meaning may be 'Joseph who is called Ipankh', the latter being a common name at that time (Gn. 41:45).

ZAPHON. A town in Gadite territory in the Jordan valley (Jos. 13:27; Jdg. 12:1); the location is uncertain.

ZAREPHATH (lit. 'smelting place'). A small Phoenician town originally belonging to Sidon and 13 km S of it. Elijah lodged with a widow there and raised her son from death (1 Ki. 17:8ff.; Lk. 4:25f.).

ZARETHAN (ZEREDAH). A place near a ford of the Jordan, on the W side, possibly Tell al-Saidiya (Zeredah in 2 Ch. 4:17).

ZEAL. In modern English zeal is fervour in advancing a cause or in giving service. Biblically the original can also have a bad sense (*e.g.* 'envious' in Ps. 37:1; 'jealousy', Acts 5:17) as well as good (2 Sa. 21:2; 2 Cor. 7:7). God's zeal means his jealous concern for his own people and their welfare (*e.g.* Is. 9:7). Paul described himself as zealous in his pre-conversion Jewish life (Gal. 1:14) and describes Christians as zealous for good deeds (Tit. 2:14), something Peter encourages (1 Pet. 3:13). In the NT the associated adjective and verb are variously translated as 'eager' (Eph. 4:3); 'do your best' (2 Tim. 2:15); and 'strive' (Heb. 4:11).

ZEALOT. One of Jesus' disciples was surnamed Zealot (Lk. 6:15), either because of his zealous temperament or because he was formerly associated with the party of Zealots. The party was founded by Judas the Galilean who led a revolt against Rome in AD 6, calling payment of taxes to Rome treason to God. Their name recalled the zeal for God of the Maccabees (1 Macc. 2:24ff.). The revolt was crushed but the Zealots remained active even beyond the fall of their last stronghold, Masada, in AD 74.

ZEBAH. One of 2 Midian kings captured and killed by Gideon who was then asked to become Israel's king. He refused (Jdg. 8).

ZEBEDEE (lit. 'the gift of Yahweh'). The father of James and John, husband of Salome; a Galilean fisherman living near Bethsaida (Mt. 27:56; Mk. 1:19f.; 15:40).

ZEBOIIM, ZEBOYIM. A city destroyed with Sodom and Gomorrah (Dt. 29:23) near ADMAH.

ZEBOIM. 1. A valley near Michmash (1 Sa. 13:18), modern Wadi Abu Daba. 2. A town near Lydda (Ne. 11:34).

ZEBUL. The ruler of Shechem who rescued Abimelech from Gaal's revolt (Jdg. 9:26ff.).

ZEBULUN. The 10th son of Jacob, his 6th by Leah. The tribe of his descendants was able to possess more of its allotted land than most of the tribes of Israel because its broad wedge in S Galilee was comprised largely of virgin country with no great cities (Jos. 19:10ff.). It shared a strategic commercial position with Issachar (*cf.* Dt. 33:18), and supplied considerable military and economic support to David (1 Ch. 12:33, 40). Many of its inhabitants were deported to Assyria by Tiglath-pileser (2 Ki. 15:29). It was the home area of the prophet Jonah (2 Ki. 14:25) and of Jesus (Mt 4:13ff.).

ZECHARIAH, ZACHARIAH, ZACHARIAS. Some 28 men bear this name in the Bible. 1. The best known is the prophet who with Haggai (Ezr. 5:1; 6:14) encouraged the rebuilding of the temple in 520 BC. He was probably a young man when he began prophesying but the latter part of the book bearing his name may belong to his old age (see next article). 2. The father of John the Baptist (Lk. 1:5).

ZECHARIAH, BOOK OF. *Contents.* Prophecies dated 520-518 BC during the reconstruction of the temple: Introduction and first vision (1:1-17); second vision (1:18-21); third vision (2); fourth vision (3); fifth vision (4); sixth vision (5:1-4); seventh vision (5:5-11); eighth vision (6:1-8); Joshua is crowned as a symbol of the Messiah (6:9-15); questions of observing fasts (7:1-8:23). Undated prophecies possibly from a later period in Zechariah's ministry: Judgment of Israel's enemies (9); evil shepherds give place to God's leader (10); the Good Shepherd rejected by the people (11); Jerusalem repents (12); Jewish prophecy ceases when the Good Shepherd is killed (13); blessings and judgments of God's kingdom (14).

Authorship and unity. Throughout chs.1-8 Zechariah is named as the author and the period is that of Ezr. 5-6; the identification with the prophet of Ezr. 5:1; 6:14 is generally accepted. Chs. 9-14 are more problematic and some scholars deny that they come from Zechariah and even that they form a unity in themselves. There are 3 main reasons for this. First, chs. 1-8 are full of hope, while chs. 9-14 show bad leadership and have no reference to the rebuilt temple. However, some prophets did have long ministries (Jeremiah's was over 40 years) and if these prophecies were uttered in Zechariah's old age they could belong to a time when first enthusiasm had died down. Secondly, there is a reference to Greece as the dominant power in 9:13; it was Persia in the time of chs. 1-8. However, Zechariah may have seen the growth of Greek influence and the Greek defeat of a Persian invasion in 480 BC; other prophets also name Greece (Javan, Is. 66:19; Ezk. 27:13); and the criticism assumes predictive prophecy cannot occur. Thirdly, there is a derogatory reference to prophecy in ch. 13 and the apocalyptic pictures in ch. 14 are said to come from a later period. But the prophet is saying that true prophecy will cease rather than belittling it, and there is no objective reason why apocalyptic imagery could not be used before the inter-testamental period. Positively, there are definite links between the two sections (*e.g.* the return of the nation, 2:6, 10; 10:6ff.). The unity of the book cannot be proved, but it does not need to be abandoned too readily.

ZEDAD. A site on the N border of the promised land (Nu. 34:8; *cf.* Ezk. 47:15), probably Sadad, 110 km ENE of Byblos.

ZEDEKIAH. Several OT people, chief of whom was the 21st and last king of Judah *c.* 597-587 BC. He was placed on the throne by Babylon's King Nebuchadrezzar. The leading citizens had been deported (2 Ki. 24:16ff.), and Zedekiah was unable to resist the bad advice given by people who remained. He revolted (2 Ki. 24:20) and so brought about the final siege and consequent destruction of Jerusalem. He was captured, blinded

and deported (2 Ki. 25). Jeremiah had warned him not to revolt but to submit to Babylon (Je. 27-29).

ZELOPHEHAD. A grandson of Gilead who died leaving 5 daughters but no male heir; his case established the law of inheritance for daughters when there was no male heir (Nu. 27). The custom is also attested in other nations.

ZELZAH. In 1 Sa. 10:2, possibly the village Beit Jala between Bethel and Bethlehem.

ZEMARAIM. A town (Jos. 18:22) and a mountain (2 Ch. 13:4) near Bethel.

ZEMARITES. A Canaanite tribe (Gn. 10:18) based at modern Sumra on the coast N of Tripoli.

ZENAS. A lawyer accompanying Apollos to an unknown destination (Tit. 3:13); he was probably expert in Roman rather than Jewish law.

ZEPHANIAH (lit. 'Yahweh has hidden'). The only biographical reference to this prophet is in the book bearing his name (1:1), where he appears to be a descendant of King Hezekiah. He prophesied during the early reign of Josiah (Hezekiah's great-grandson) and was contemporary with Nahum and Jeremiah. See also next article.

ZEPHANIAH, BOOK OF. *Contents.* Warning of the impending Day of the Lord (1:1-2:3); judgment on foreign nations (2:4-15); judgment on

Jerusalem and subsequent blessing (3).

Historical background. Judah's religious condition had deteriorated since Hezekiah's death to external ritual and even idolatry. Josiah was able to carry out his reforms (2 Ki. 22-23, 621 BC) because the Assyrians who dominated the Near East were fending off Scythian invaders, the ferocity of whom provided the background for Zephaniah's picture of God's wrath.

Message. He denounced idolatry and declared that God's judgment on Judah and its neighbours was imminent. Beyond the doom he saw a better day; God must bring his people through the fire to prepare them for their work. Some of the abuses he denounced were removed by Josiah.

ZEPHATHAH. In 2 Ch. 14:10, one of several valleys near Mareshah.

ZER. A fortified city in Naphtali's territory (Jos. 19:35).

ZERAH. Several OT people including: 1. A son of Judah by Tamar and twin of Perez (Gn. 38:27ff.). 2. An Ethiopian who invaded Judah (2 Ch. 14:9ff.; 16:8). He was routed at Mareshah by Asa *c.* 897 BC, and was probably an Ethiopian army commander leading Egyptian troops on behalf of Pharaoh Osorkon I.

ZERED. A wadi crossed by the Israelites (Nu. 21:12; Dt. 2:13f.), probably Wadi el-Hesa running into the Dead Sea from the SE.

ZERUBBABEL. A descendant of the Judaean royal family who returned with Jewish exiles from Babylon in 537 BC and laid the foundations of the temple (Ezr. 3). With Joshua he was again in the lead when the rebuilding work was resumed in 520 BC (Ezr. 5-6; Hg. 1-2). He was encouraged by the visions of Zechariah; Zc. 4:6ff. promises that his work would be completed. In Hg. 1:1; 2:2 he is called 'governor'; he was the son of Shealtiel and hence grandson of the exiled King Jehoiachin.

ZERUIAH. David's sister (1 Ch. 2:16; possibly step-sister, 2 Sa. 17:25), and mother of his 3 officers Abishai, Joab and Asahel (2 Sa. 2:18).

ZEUS. One of the two Greek gods (Hermes, the other, was Zeus' messenger) whom the people of Lystra thought they recognized in Barnabas and Paul (Acts 14:12f.). In his speech, Paul took up the familiar picture of Zeus as god of the weather and used it to display the principles of the gospel.

ZIBA. Saul's servant who introduced Jonathan's son Mephibosheth to David and who was appointed steward of Mephibosheth's estate (2 Sa. 9). He became treacherous in an attempt to get all the land (2 Sa. 16:1ff.), later receiving half of it under David's settlement (2 Sa. 19).

ZIKLAG. A place near the Edomite border (Jos. 15:31) captured from the Philistines by David; possibly Tell Sera

25 km SE of Gaza.

ZILPAH. Leah's maid who became mother of Gad and Asher (Gn. 29:24; 30:9ff.).

ZIMRAN. A son of Abraham by his concubine Keturah (Gn. 25:2).

ZIMRI. 1. A Simeonite prince executed by Phinehas for bringing a Midianite wife into the Israelite camp (Nu. 25:6ff.). 2. King of (N) Israel for a week *c.* 876 BC before he burned his palace over his own head when public opinion sided with Omri (1 Ki. 16:9ff.).

ZIN. An extensive wilderness area, within the broader region termed the 'Negeb', traversed by the Israelites after the Exodus, between Kadesh-barnea and the border between Judah and Edom.

ZIOR. In Jos. 15:54, possibly the same place as ZAIR.

ZIPH. 1. A town in S Judah (Jos. 15:24), possibly al-Zaifa. 2. A town in the hill country of Judah (Jos. 15:55) which became a major administrative centre in Hezekiah's reign; modern Tell Zif 7 km SE of Hebron.

ZIPPOR. Father of the Moabite king Balak who cursed Israel (Nu. 22:2).

ZIPPORAH. Daughter of Jethro, a Midianite priest, and wife of Moses (Ex. 2:16ff.).

ZIZ. In 2 Ch. 20:16, probably Wadi Hasasa just N of Engedi.

ZOAN. The effective capital of Egypt *c.* 1100-660 BC, hence its prominence as the seat of pharaoh's counsellors (Is. 19:11, 13). It was called Tanis by the Greeks; the site is San el-Hagar near the S shore of Lake Menzaleh in NE Delta.

ZOPHAR. The 3rd of Job's friends; his brutal commonsense is given in chs. 11; 20.

ZOPHIM. In Nu. 23:14, a high part of the Pisgah Mts from which Balaam could see the Israelites at Shittim.

ZORAH. A town closely connected with Samson (Jdg. 13:2); modern Sara on the N side of the Wadi al-Sarar, the biblical valley of Sorek.

ZUZIM. A people conquered by Chedorlaomer (Gn. 14:5), their chief village being modern Ham NE of the Gilboa Mts in N Jordan. Some equate them with the ZAMZUMMIM.